Stanley

Col

Channel Islands and Isle of Man Stamps

26th Combined edition

STANLEY GIBBONS LTD
London and Ringwood

By Appointment to Her Majesty The Queen
Stanley Gibbons Ltd, London
Philatelists

Published by Stanley Gibbons Ltd
Editorial, Publications Sales Offices
and Distribution Centre:
7 Parkside, Christchurch Road, Ringwood,
Hants BH24 3SH

26th COMBINED EDITION

British Library Cataloguing in Publication Data.
A catalogue record for this book is available from the British Library.

Errors and omissions excepted
the colour reproduction of stamps is only as accurate as the printing process will allow.

ISBN-13: 978-0-85259-767-5
ISBN-10: 0-85259-767-3

Item No. R2855-10

Printed by Latimer

Contents

Introductory Notes

Scope. The listing of **stamps** for Guernsey and Jersey comprises German Occupation issues, the 1958–69 Regionals and the issues of the Independent Postal Administrations from their inception in 1969. Isle of Man sections cover the 1958–71 Regionals and the issues of the Independent Postal Administration from 1973 onwards.

Information is given on:

- Designers and printers
- The different printings for definitives and postage dues
- Distinctive papers
- Such varieties as imperforates and missing colours
- Phosphors
- Cylinder and plate numbers
- Sheet sizes and imprints
- Quantities sold
- Withdrawal and invalidation dates

The 'Notes' on page 1 may be found helpful in further explanation.

The checklist also covers:

- Miniature sheets
- First-day covers
- Presentation packs and Yearbooks
- Gutter pairs
- Stamp booklets
- Stamp sachets (listed, but unpriced)
- Postal stationery commemorative cards and covers

Items outside the scope and therefore omitted are: cylinder and plate varieties; non-postage stamps, such as revenues; and other classes of postal stationery.

Layout. Stamps are set out chronologically by date of issue. In the catalogue lists the first numeral is the Stanley Gibbons catalogue number; the black (boldface) numeral alongside is the type number referring to the respective illustration. The denomination and colour of the stamp are then shown. Before February 1971 British currency was:
£1=20s One Pound = twenty shillings and
1s=12d One shilling = twelve pence.

Upon decimalisation this became:

£1=100p One pound = one hundred (new) pence

The catalogue list then shows two price columns. The left-hand is for unused stamps and the right-hand for used.

Our method of indicating prices is:

Numerals for pence, e.g. 5 denotes 5p (5 pence). Numerals for pounds and pence, e.g. 4.25 denotes £4.25 (4 pounds and 25 pence). For £100 and above, prices are in whole pounds and so include the £ sign and omit the zeros for pence.

Size of illustrations. To comply with Post Office regulations illustrations of stamps and booklets are three-quarters linear size. Where illustrations are further reduced (miniature sheets and some booklet covers) actual sizes are given. Illustrations of watermarks are actual size.

Prices. Prices quoted in this catalogue are our selling prices at the time the book went to press. They are for stamps in fine condition; in issues where condition varies we may ask more for the superb and less for the sub-standard. With unused stamps prices are for unmounted mint (though where not available unmounted, mounted mint stamps are often supplied at a lower price). Used prices are normally for stamps postally used but may be for stamps cancelled-to-order where this practice exists. All prices are subject to change without prior notice and we give no guarantee to supply all stamps priced, since it is not possible to keep every catalogue item perpetually in stock. Commemoratives may, at times, only be available in complete sets. Individual low value stamps sold at 399, Strand are liable to an additional handling charge.

The minimum price quoted is 10 pence. For individual stamps prices between 10 pence and 95 pence are provided as a guide for catalogue users. The lowest price charged for individual stamps or sets purchased from Stanley Gibbons Ltd is £1.

Perforations. The 'perforation' is the number of holes in a length of 2 cm, as measured by the Gibbons Instanta gauge. The stamp is viewed against a dark background with the transparent gauge put on top of it. Perforations are quoted to the nearest half. Stamps without perforation are termed 'imperforate'.

***Se-tenant* combinations.** *Se-tenant* means 'joined together'. Some sets include stamps of different design arranged se-tenant as blocks or strips and, in mint condition, these are usually collected unsevered as issued. Where such combinations exist, the individual stamps are priced normally as mint and used singles. The set prices refer to the unsevered combination plus singles of any other values in the set.

First Day Covers. Prices for first day covers are for complete sets used on special covers, the stamps of which bear an official postmark for first day of issue. Where the stamps in a set were issued on different days, prices are for a cover from each day.

Catalogue numbers used. The checklist uses the same catalogue numbers as the Stanley Gibbons Stamps of the World catalogue, 2010 edition.

Latest stamps recorded in this edition appeared in early June 2010.

Specialist Philatelic Society. Channel Islands Specialists Society. Membership Secretary:
Moira Edwards, 86 Hall Lane, Sandon, Chelmsford, Essex CM2 7RQ.

Amendments to the 2010 edition

A number of additions, amendments and corrections have been made to this edition and we would particularly like to thank Ray Dixon for his assistance. Help and information have also been provided by David Gurney and David Aggersberg.

NOTES ON THE CATALOGUE LISTINGS

Printings

For definitives and postage due stamps released by the independent Postal Administration we give the dates of the printings as announced, and relate them in the listings to the actual stamps involved. Users will therefore be able to see at a glance how many printings have been made of any particular item.

Cylinder and Plate Numbers

Following the listing of each issue we give the printers' cylinder or plate numbers known to us.

Sheet size

In describing the sheet arrangement we always give the number of stamps across the sheet first. For example, '50 (5310)' indicates a sheet of fifty stamps in ten horizontal rows of five stamps each.

Paper

Only distinctive types are mentioned. Granite paper can be easily distinguished by the coloured lines in its texture. Chalky or chalk-surfaced applies to paper which shows a black line when touched with silver.

Perforations

Perforations are normaly given to the nearest half and the Instanta gauge is our standard. In this checklist we state if a perforation is by a line (L) or a comb (C) machine. A line machine only perforates one line at a time and consequently it requires two operations to do the horizontal and vertical perforations and where these intersect an irregular-shaped hole often results. A comb machine perforates three sides at a time and therefore produces a single hole at all corner inter-sections. The differences are easily seen in blocks of four.

The various perforations in this checklist are expressed as follows:

Perf 14: Perforated alike on all sides.
Perf 14×15: Compound perforation. The first figure refers to top and bottom, the second to left and right sides.

Abbreviations

des = designer, designed
eng = engraver, engraved
litho = lithographed
mm = millimetres
MS = miniature sheet
No. = number
perf = perforated
photo = photogravure
recess = recess-printed
typo = typographed
wmk(d) = watermark(ed)

Channel Islands

C **1** Gathering Vraic

C **2** Islanders gathering Vraic

Broken Wheel (R.20/5)

Third Anniversary of Liberation

(Des J. R. R. Stobie (1d.), or from drawing by E. Blampied (2½d.). Photo Harrison and Sons)

1948 (10 May). Wmk Mult G VI R. Perf 15×14 (C).

C1	C **1**	1d. scarlet	25	30
C2	C **2**	2½d. ultramarine	25	30
		a. Broken wheel	15·00	
First Day Cover			35·00	

These stamps were primarily intended for use in the Channel Islands although they were also available at eight head post offices in Great Britain.

Cylinder Nos.: 1d. 2; 2½d. 4.
Sheets: 120 (6×20).
Quantities sold: 1d. 5,934,000; 2½d. 5,398,000.

Guernsey

THE GERMAN OCCUPATION 1940–1945

The first German soldiers to arrive in Guernsey set foot on the island on 30 June 1940 and an official notice appeared in the local newspaper the following day announcing the occupation.

The first evidence of the occupation, philatelically, came towards the end of the year when supplies of Great Britain 1d. stamps then in use began to dry up. It was decided that the bisecting of 2d. stamps for use as 1d.'s be allowed and this commenced on 27 December. The decision to print 1d. stamps locally had been taken in October, but these were not ready and were eventually issued on 18 February 1941. In the meantime the two currently available 2d. stamps, the 1937 definitive and the 1940 Postal Centenary, were bisected and used, as were 2d. stamps of the reign of George V which were in collectors' hands. Other values are also known to have been bisected and used, and were allowed to pass through the post in most instances without a postage due charge being made.

The Swastika overprints, previously listed as Nos. SW1 and SW2 are now considered to be bogus.

As previously mentioned, the locally printed 1d. stamps were issued on 18 February 1941. The ½d. stamp was released on 7 April 1941 and the 2½d. on 12 April 1944. This last stamp was issued in an effort to economise on the use of paper as it was found that sealed letters were franked with two 1d. stamps and one ½d. or a larger number of ½d.'s, a gross waste in times of shortage. Many printings of these stamps were made, the most notable being on the French bank-note paper in 1942.

Shades of these issues abound, the more outstanding ones being the bluish green (4th) and olive-green (8th) printings of the ½d., and the pale vermilion (11th) printing of the 1d. During the occupation Guernsey stamps were only valid on mail within the Channel Islands. Letters sent overseas were despatched via the German Feldpost system. The stamps continued to be used after the liberation in 1945 until 13 April 1946.

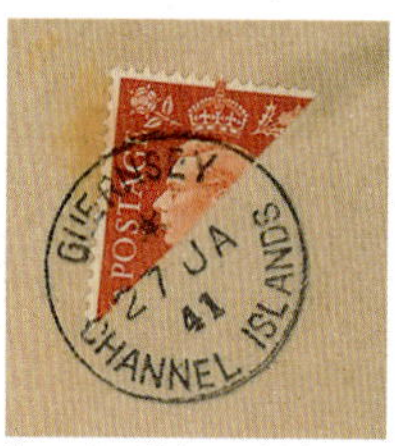

Example of bisected 2d.
King George VI definitive (B55)

The Bisects

1940 (27 Dec).

(a) Stamps of King George V

Cat. No.		*Price on Cover*
BS1	1912–22 2d. orange	£300
BS2	1924–26 2d. orange	£300
BS3	1934–36 2d. orange	£325
	(b) Stamps of King George VI	
BS4	1937 1d. scarlet	£700
BS5	1938 2d. orange	45·00
BS6	1940 Stamp Centenary 1d. scarlet	£700
BS7	1940 Stamp Centenary 2d. orange	35·00
BS8	1940 Stamp Centenary 2½d. ultramarine	£1500
BS9	1940 Stamp Centenary 3d. violet	

Forged postmarks on fake bisects are known from Guernsey Head Post Office ('2 JA 41'), Market Place ('19 FE 41' or '7 AP 41'), St. Sampson ('27 DE 40') and The Vale ('18 FE 41').

The bisects are priced on philatelic cover. Those which were used commercially are worth more, particularly Nos. BS5 and BS7.

Invalidated: 22.2.41 (last postings were postmarked 24.2.41.)

1 Arms of Guernsey

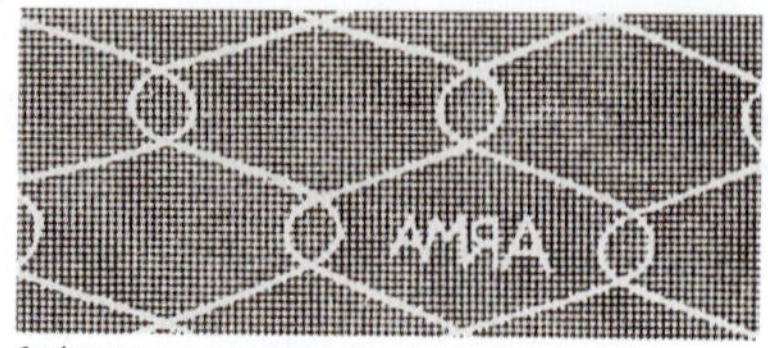

1a Loops

Stamps issued during the German Occupation

(Des E. W. Vaudin. Typo Guernsey Press Co Ltd)

1941–44. Rouletted.

(a) White paper. No wmk.

Cat. No.	*Type No.*		*Unused*	*Used*
1	**1**	½d. light green (7.4.41)	6·00	3·50
		a. Emerald-green (6.41)	6·00	2·00
		b. *Bluish green* (11.41)	32·00	13·00
		c. Bright green (2.42)	22·00	10·00
		d. *Dull green* (9.42)	4·00	2·00
		e. Olive-green (2.43)	45·00	25·00
		f. *Pale yellowish green* (7.43 and later) (shades)	4·00	3·00
		g. Imperf (pair)	£225	
		h. Imperf between (horizontal pair)	£750	
		i. Imperf between (vertical pair)	£875	
2		1d. scarlet (18.2.41)	3·25	2·00
		a. *Pale vermilion* (7.43) (etc)	5·00	2·00
		b. Carmine (1943)	3·50	2·00
		c. Imperf (pair)	£175	90·00
		d. Imperf between (horizontal pair)	£750	
		da. Imperf vert (centre stamp of horizontal strip of 3)		
		e. Imperf between (vertical pair)	£875	
		f. Ptd double (scarlet shade)	£110	
3		2½d. ultramarine (12.4.44)	13·00	12·00
		a. *Pale ultramarine* (7.44)	10·00	7·00
		b. Imperf (pair)	£550	
		c. Imperf between (horizontal pair)	£1100	
1 *First Day Cover*				10·00
2 *First Day Cover*				15·00
3 *First Day Cover*				20·00
		(b) Bluish French bank-note paper. Wmk **1a** (sideways)		
4	**1**	½d. bright green (11.3.42)	30·00	22·00
5		1d. scarlet (9.4.42)	16·00	22·00
4 *First Day Cover*				£300
5 *First Day Cover*				£100

The dates for the shades of Nos. 1/3 are the months in which they were printed as indicated on the printer's imprints (see below). Others are issue dates.

Printings and imprint: The various printings can be identified from the sheet imprints as follows:

½d. 1st Printing 240M/341
2nd Printing 2×120M/6/41
3rd Printing 3×120M/6/41
4th Printing 4×120M/11/41
5th Printing 5×120M/2/42
6th Printing 6×240M/2/42
7th Printing 7×120M/9/42
8th Printing 8×120M/2/43
9th Printing 9×120M/7/43
10th Printing 10×120M/10/43
11th Printing Guernsey Press Co., (stop and comma)
12th Printing Guernsey Press Co. (stop only, margin at bottom 23 to 27 mm)
13th Printing Guernsey Press Co. (stop only, margin at bottom 15 mm)

1d. 1st Printing 120M/41
2nd Printing 2×120M/2/41
3rd Printing 3×120M/6/41
4th Printing 4×120M/6/41
5th Printing 5×120M/9/41
6th Printing 6×240M/11/41
7th Printing 7×120M/2/42
8th Printing 8×240M/4/42
9th Printing 9×240M/9/42
10th Printing 10×240M/1/43
11th Printing 11×240M/7/43
12th Printing Guernsey Press Co.
13th Printing PRESS TYP.
14th Printing 'PRESS' (inverted commas unlevel)
15th Printing 'PRESS' (inverted commas level, margin at bottom 28 mm)
16th Printing 'PRESS' (inverted commas level, margin at bottom 12 mm)

2½d. 1st Printing Guernsey Press Co.
2nd Printing 'PRESS' (inverted commas unlevel)
3rd Printing 'PRESS' (inverted commas level, margin at bottom 22 mm)

4th Printing 'PRESS' (inverted commas level, margin at bottom 15 mm)

The numbered imprints occur in the left-hand corner, bottom margin on the 1st printing of the 1d., and central, bottom margin on all other printings of all three values.

In the numbered imprints, for example, 2×120M/6/41, the '2' indicates the number of the printing; '120M' denotes the number of stamps printed in thousands, in this case 120,000; and '6/41' denotes the date of the printing, June 1941.

In the first ten printings of the ½d. and the first eleven printings of the 1d. the printing details are prefixed by the name of the printer, 'Guernsey Press Co.'

Sheets: 60 (6×10).
Quantities printed: ½d. 1,772,160; 1d. 2,478,000; 2½d. 416,640.
Withdrawn and invalidated: 13.4.46.

REGIONAL ISSUES

Although specifically issued for regional use, these issues were initially valid for use throughout Great Britain. However, they ceased to be valid in Guernsey and Jersey from 1 October 1969 when these islands each established their own independent postal administration and introduced their own stamps.

DATES OF ISSUE. Conflicting dates of issue have been announced for some of the regional issues, partly explained by the stamps being released on different dates by the Philatelic Bureau in Edinburgh or the Philatelic Counter in London and in the regions. We have adopted the practice of giving the earliest known dates, since once released the stamps could have been used anywhere in the U.K.

INVALIDATION. The regional issues of Guernsey were invalidated for use in Guernsey and Jersey on 1 November 1969. The stamps continued to be valid for use in the rest of the United Kingdom until 29 February 1972. Those still current remained on sale at philatelic sales counters until 30 September 1970.

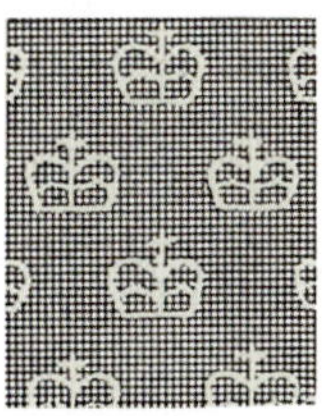

1b Multiple Crowns

2

3

(Des E. A. Piprell. Portrait by Dorothy Wilding Ltd. Photo Harrison and Sons)

1958–67. Wmk Type **1b**. Perf 15×14 (C).

6	**2**	2½d. rose-red (8.6.64)	35	40
7	**3**	3d. deep lilac (18.8.58)	30	30
		p. One centre phosphor band (24.5.67)	15	20
8		4d. ultramarine (7.2.66)	25	30
		p. Two phosphor bands (24.10.67)	15	20
6/8p *Set of 3*			70	80
6 *First Day Cover*				30·00
7 *First Day Cover*				20·00
8 *First Day Cover*				10·00

Cylinder Nos.: 2½d. 1, 3; 3d. (ord) 4, 5; 3d. (phos) 5; 4d. (ord) 1; 4d. (phos) 1
Sheets: 240 (12×20).
Quantities sold (ordinary only): 2½d. 3,485,760; 3d. 25,812,360; 4d. 4,415,040.
Withdrawn: 31.8.66 2½d.
Sold out: 6.3.68 3d. and 4d. (ordinary); 10.68 4d. (phosphor); 11.68 3d. (phosphor).

1968–69. No wmk. Chalk-surfaced paper. One centre phosphor band (Nos. 10/11) or two phosphor bands (others). Perf 15×14 (C).

9	**3**	4d. pale ultramarine (16.4.68)	10	20
		Ey. Phosphor omitted	45·00	
10		4d. olive-sepia (4.9.68)	10	15
		Ey. Phosphor omitted	45·00	
11		4d. bright vermilion (26.2.69)	20	25
12		5d. royal blue (4.9.68)	20	30
9/12 *Set of 4*			50	1·00
10, 12*First Day Cover*				3·00

No. 9 was not issued in Guernsey until 22 April.
Cylinder Nos. 4d. (pale ultramarine) 1; 4d. (olive-sepia) 1; 4d. (brightvermilion) 1; 5d. 1.
Sold out; 3.69 4d. ultramarine.
Withdrawn: 30.9.69 (locally), 30.9.70 (British Philatelic Counters) 4d.olive-sepia, 4d. bright vermilion and 5d.

INDEPENDENT POSTAL ADMINISTRATION

Guernsey established their own independent postal administration on 1 October 1969 and introduced their own stamps.

NO WATERMARK. All the following issues are on unwatermarked paper.

4 Castle Cornet and Edward the Confessor

5 Map and William I

6 Martello Tower and Henry II

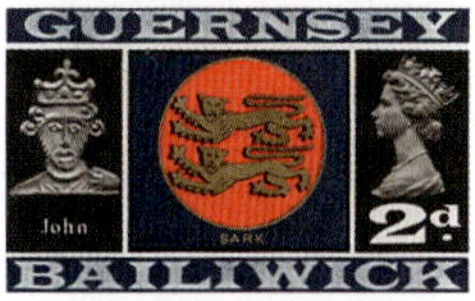

7 Arms of Sark and King John

8 Arms of Alderney and Edward III

9 Guernsey Lily and Henry V

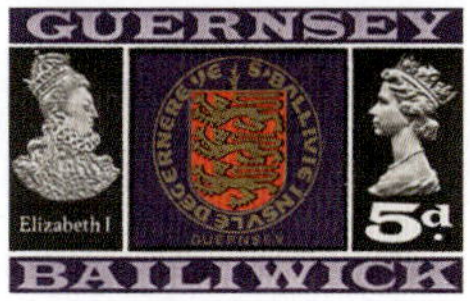

10 Arms of Guernsey and Elizabeth I

11 Arms of Alderney and Charles II

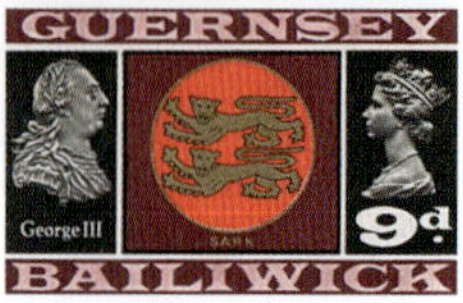

12 Arms of Sark and George III

13 Arms of Guernsey and Queen Victoria

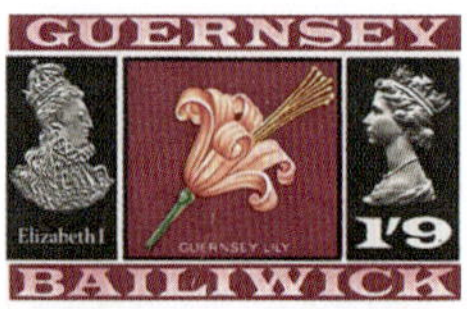

14 Guernsey Lily and Elizabeth I

15 Martello Tower and King John

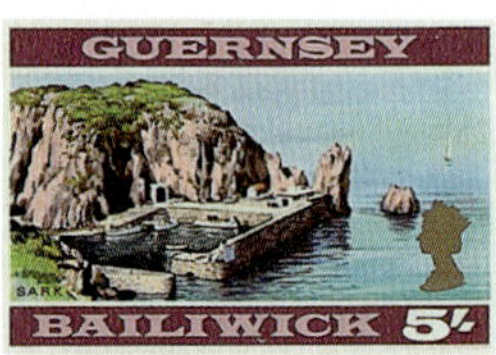

16 View of Sark

17 View of Alderney

18 View of Guernsey

Two types of 1d. and 1s.6d.

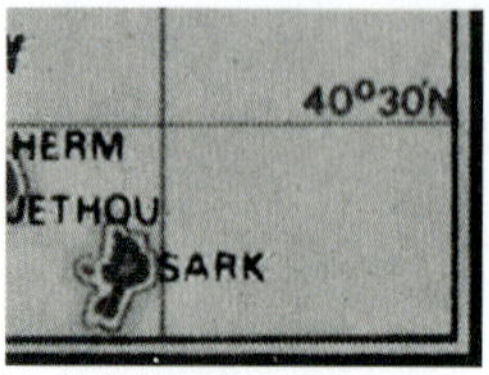

I Latitude inscr '40° 30' N'

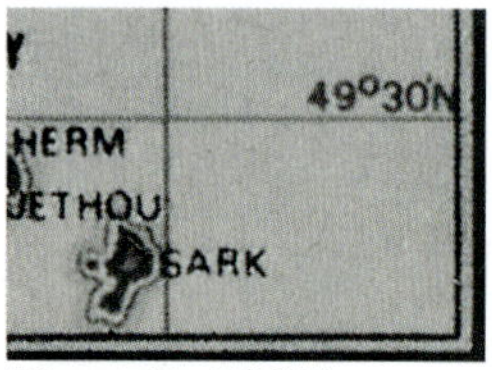

II Corrected to '49° 0' N'

(Des R. Granger Barrett. Photo Harrison (½d. to 2s.6d.), Delrieu (others))

1969 (1 Oct)–**70**. Perf 14 (½d. to 2s.6d.) or 12½ (others), all comb.

13	**4**	½d. deep magenta and black (a)	10	10
		a. Thin paper	60	60
14	**5**	1d. bright blue and black (I) (a)	10	10
		a. Thin paper (b)	50	50
14*b*		1d. bright blue and black (thin paper) (II) (eg)	30	30
		c. Booklet stamp with margins (thick paper) (C)	40	40
15	**6**	1½d. yellow-brown and black (a)	10	10
16	**7**	2d. gold, brt red, dp blue & blk (a)	10	10
		a. Thin paper (g)	40	40
17	**8**	3d. gold, pale greenish yellow, orange-red and black (a)	15	15
		a. Error. Wmk Block CA	£1350	
		ai. Wmk inverted	£1200	
		b. Thin paper (g)	50	50
18	**9**	4d. multicoloured (a)	20	25
		a. Booklet stamp with margins (C)	40	45
		ab. Yellow omitted	£750	
		ac. Emerald (stem) omitted	£750	
19	**10**	5d. gold, bright vermilion, bluish violet and black (a)	20	20
		a. Booklet stamp with margins (C)	50	50
		b. *gold* (inscription etc.) omitted (booklets)	£1350	
20	**11**	6d. gold, pale greenish yellow, light bronze-green & black (a)	20	30
		a. Thin paper (g)	45	45
21	**12**	9d. gold, brt red, crimson & blk (a)	30	30
		a. Thin paper (g)	3·00	1·70
22	**13**	1s. gold, brt verm, bistre & blk (a)	30	30
		a. Thin paper (g)	1·00	75
23	**5**	1s.6d. turquoise-grn & blk (I) (a)	25	30
		a. Thin paper (d)	1·70	3·25
23*b*		1s.6d. turquoise-green and black (thin paper) (II) (eg)	2·00	1·70
24	**14**	1s.9d. multicoloured (a)	80	80
		a. *Emerald* (stem) omitted	£850	
		b. Thin paper (g)	2·20	1·90
25	**15**	2s.6d. brt reddish violet & black (a)	3·50	3·00
		a. Thin paper (g)	5·50	4·50
26	**16**	5s. multicoloured (a)	2·50	2·50
27	**17**	10s. multicoloured (a)	16·00	18·00
		a. Perf 13½×13 (f)	35·00	36·00
28	**18**	£1 multicoloured (a)	2·20	2·20
		a. Perf 13½×13 (fh)	2·20	2·20
13/28a *Set of 16*			24·00	26·00
13/28 *First Day Cover*				28·00
13/28 *Presentation Packs (incl. both* 1d. *and* 1s.6d.) (3) (9.70)			40·00	
13/25 *Set of 13 Gutter Pairs*				

Thinner paper – see note after Jersey No. 29.

There was no postal need for the ½d. and 1½d. values as the ½d. coin had been withdrawn prior to their issue in anticipation of decimalisation. These values were only on sale at the Philatelic Bureau and at the Crown Agents as well as in the U.S.A.

Type **18** was re-issued as a booklet pane in 2001. See No. 927.

Printings: (a) 1.10.69; (b) 24.11.69; (c). 12.12.69; (d) 1.70; (e) 4.2.70; (f) 4.3.70; (g) 18.5.70; (h) 7.71.

Cylinder Nos.: ½d., 1½d., 2s.6d. 1A–1A, 1B–1B; 1d. (I) 1A–1A (a); 2A–2A, 2B–2B (b); 1d. (II) 2A–2A, 2B–2B (e); 3A–3A, 3B–3B (g) 2d.,3d/, 5d., 6d., 9d., 1s. 1A, 1B (each ×4); 4d., 1s.9d. 1A, 1B (each ×5); 1s.6d. (I) 1A–1A, 1B–1B (a); 1A–2A, 1B–2B (d); 1s6d. (II) 1B–1B, 1A–2A, 1B–2B (e); 2A–3A, 2B–3B (g) 2B–3B; 5s to £1 None.
Sheets: 60 (2 panes (5×6) most sheets of the 5s., 10s. and £1 weredivided into two panes before issue.
Imprint: Central, bottom margin (½d. to 2s.6d.).
Quantities sold ½d. 2,480,000; 1d. (Nos. 14/14b) 1,560,971; 1½d. 980,000; 2d. 574,610; 3d. 487,199; 4d. 2,782,490; 5d. 1,393,193; 6d. 456,275; 9d. 374,975; 1s 435,773; 1s.6d. (Nos. 23/23b) 627,003; 1s.9d. 255,111; 2s.6d. 225,732; 5s. 165,047; 10s (No. 27) 114,000; 10s. (No. 27*a*) 55,200; £1 (No. 28) 120,000; £1 (No. 28a) 141,802.
Sold out: 8.71 10s. (No. 27a).
Withdrawn: 6.10.69, ½d., 1½d.; 4.2.70, 1d. (No. 14), 1s.6d. (No. 23); others 14.2.72 (except for No. 28a which remained on sale with Decimal definitives until 31.3.76).

Although officially withdrawn the ½d., 1d. (No. 14), 1½d. and 1s.6d. (No. 23) were subsequently included in*Presentation Packs*, whilst the ½d. and 1½d. remained on sale at the Philatelic Bureau until 14 February 1972.

Invalidated: 14.2.72 (except £1).

19 Isaac Brock as Colonel

20 Sir Isaac Brock as major-General

21 Isaac Brock as Ensign

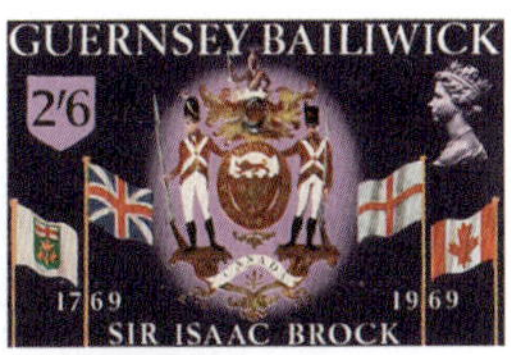

22 Arms and Flags

Birth Bicentenary of Sir Isaac Brock

(Litho Format)

1969 (1 Dec). Perf 13½×14 (2s.6d.) or 14×13½ (others), all comb.

29	**19**	4d. multicoloured	20	20
30	**20**	5d. multicoloured	20	20
31	**21**	1s.9d. multicoloured	90	75
32	**22**	2s.6d. multicoloured	90	75
29/32 *Set of 4*			2·00	1·70
First Day Cover				3·25
Presentation Pack			3·75	
Set of 4 Gutter Pairs			£130	

Plate Nos. 4d., 2s.6d. 1A, 1B, 1C, 1D. (each ×6); 5d. 1A, 1B, 1C, 1D. (each ×7); 1s.9d. 1A, 1B, 1C, 1D. (each ×5).
Sheets: 60 (2 panes 5×6) 2s.6d.; (2 panes 6×5) others.
Imprint: Right-hand corner, bottom margin.
Quantities sold: 4d. 940,956; 5d. 732,658; 1s.9d. 224,157; 2s.6d. 218,955.
Withdrawn: 30.11.70.
Invalidated: 14.2.72.

23 H.M.S. *L103* (landing craft) entering St. Peter's Harbour

24 H.M.S. *Bulldog* and H.M.S. *Beagle* (destroyers) entering St. Peter Port

25 Brigadier Snow reading the Proclamation

25th Anniversary of Liberation

(Des and photo Courvoisier)

1970 (9 May). Granite paper. Perf 11½ (C).

33	**23**	4d. blue and pale blue	20	20
34	**24**	5d. brown-lake and pale grey	40	20
35	**25**	1s.6d. bistre-brown and buff	1·20	90
33/5 *Set of 3*			1·50	1·10
First Day Cover				2·40
Presentation Pack			4·00	

Cylinder Nos.: A1–1, B1–1 (all values).
Sheets: 25 (5×5).
Imprint: Left-hand corner, top margin (4d., 5d.); bottom corner, left-hand margin (1s.6d.).
Quantities sold: 4d. 968,873; 5d. 817,958; 1s.6d. 248,532.
Withdrawn: 8.5.71.
Invalidated: 14.2.72.

26 Guernsey 'Toms'

27 Guernsey Cow

28 Guernsey Bull

29 Freesias

Agriculture and Horticulture

(Des and Photo Courvoisier)

1970 (12 Aug). Granite paper. Perf 11½ (C).

36	**26**	4d. multicoloured	55	20
37	**27**	5d. multicoloured	70	20
38	**28**	9d. multicoloured	2·50	1·30
39	**29**	1s.6d. multicoloured	2·75	2·40
36/9 *Set of 4*			5·00	4·00
First Day Cover				5·00
Presentation Pack			18·00	

Cylinder Nos.: A1–1–1–1, B1–1–1–1, C1–1–1–1, D1–1–1–1 (all values).
Sheets: 25 (5×5).
Imprint: Central, bottom margin.
Quantities sold: 4d. 1,082.608; 5d. 1,000,000; 9d. 237,685; 1s.6d. 241,816.
Withdrawn: 11.8.71.
Invalidated: 14.2.72.

30 St. Anne's Church, Alderney

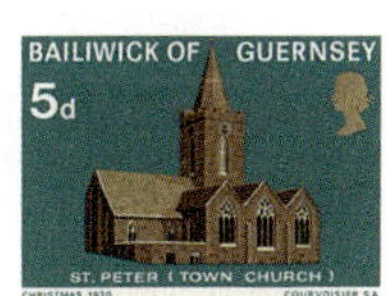

31 St. Peter's Church, Guernsey

32 St. Peters Church, Sark

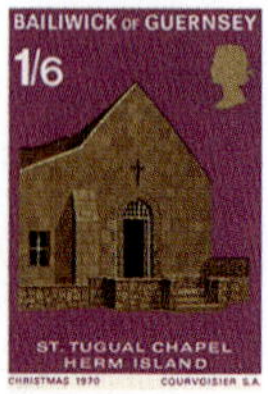

33 St. Tugual Chapel, Herm

Christmas. Guernsey Churches (1st series)

(Des and photo Courvoisier)

1970 (11 Nov). Granite paper. Perf 11½ (C).

40	**30**	4d. multicoloured	20	10
41	**31**	5d. multicoloured	20	10
42	**32**	9d. multicoloured	1·20	1·00
43	**33**	1s.6d. multicoloured	1·50	1·20
40/3 *Set of 4*			2·50	2·00
First Day Cover				2·10
Presentation Pack			5·00	

See also Nos. 63/6.

Cylinder Nos.: A1–1–1–1 or B1–1–1–1 (all values).
Sheets: 50 (5×10) 4d., 5d.; (10×5) others.
Quantities sold: 4d. 815,737; 5d. 668.886; 9d. 236,833; 1s.6d. 223,907.
Withdrawn: 10.11.71.
Invalidated: 14.2.72.

34 Martello Tower and King John

Decimal Currency

(Photo Harrison (½p. to 10p.), Delrieu (others))

1971 (6 Jan)–**73**. Designs as Type **4** etc., but values inscribed in decimal currency as in Type **34**. Chalk-surfaced paper. Perf 14 (½p. to 10p.) or (13½×13) (others), all comb.

44	**4**	½p. deep magenta and black (b)	10	15
		a. Booklet stamp with .margins. Glazed, ordinary paper	15	20
		ab. Ditto. Chalk-surfaced paper (f)	15	20
45	**5**	1p. bright blue and black (II) (b)	10	10
46	**6**	1½p. yellow-brown and black (b)	15	15
47	**9**	2p. multicoloured (b)	15	15
		a. Booklet stamp with margins. Glazed, ordinary paper	20	20
		ab. Ditto. Chalk-surfaced paper (f)	20	20
		ac. Emerald (stem) omitted	£1500	
		b. Glazed, ordinary paper (b)	20	20
48	**10**	2½p. gold, bright vermilion, bluish violet and black (bf)	15	10
		a. Bright vermilion omitted	£1400	
		b. Booklet stamp with margins. Glazed, ordinary paper	20	20
		ba. Ditto. Chalk-surfaced paper (f)	20	20
49	**8**	3p. gold, pale greenish yellow, orange-red and black (bf)	20	20
50	**14**	3½p. mult (glazed, ordinary paper) (b)	20	20
51	**7**	4p. multicoloured (b)	20	20
52	**5**	5p. turquoise-green & black (II) (b)	20	20
53	**11**	6p. gold, pale greenish yellow, lt bronze-green and black (b)	20	20
54	**13**	7½p. gold, brt verm, bistre & blk (b)	30	35
55	**12**	9p. gold, brt red, crimson & blk (b)	65	65
56	**34**	10p. bright reddish violet & blk (a)	1·70	1·70
		a. Ordinary paper. Bright reddish violet and deep black (d)	1·20	1·20
57	**16**	20p. mult (glazed, ordinary paper) (ag)	70	70
		a. Shade* (e)	70	70
58	**17**	50p. mult (glazed, ordinary paper) (aeh)	1·20	1·20
44/58 *Set of 15*			5·00	5·25
First Day Covers (2)				9·00
44/58, 28a *Presentation Packs* (3)			12·00	
44/56 *Set of 13 Gutter Pairs*			18·00	

*No. 57 has the sky in a pale turquoise-blue; on No. 57a it is pale turquoise-green.

Printings: (a) 6.1.71; (b) 15.2.71; (c). 3.72; (d) 1.9.72; (e) 25.1.73; (f) 2.4.73; (g) 10.74; (h) 7.75.

Cylinder Nos.: ½p., 1p., 1½p., 5p., 10p. 1A–1A, 1B–1B; 2p., 3½p. 1A, 1B (each ×5); 2½p., 3p., 4p., 6p., 7½p., 9p. 1A, 1B (each ×4); 20p none; 50p. 21–22–23–24. Sheets from ptg (g) have an additional S99 (reversed).
On the 3½p. only four '1A' Nos. are shown in the margin, the black '1A' being omitted in error.
Sheets: 50 (2 panes 5×5) ½p to 10p.; 30 (5×6) others.
Imprint: Central, bottom margin (½p. to 10p.).
Quantities sold: ½p. 980,959; 1p. 568,509; 1½p. 559,576; 2p.2,512,903; 2½p. 4,469,578; 3p. 2,245,564; 3½p. 317,523; 4p. 527,696; 5p. 511,742; 6p. 346,255; 7½p. 322,905; 9p. 349,211; 10p. 538,153;20p 630,888; 50p 258,150.

In addition to the 10p.–£1 pack, a 10p.–50p. Presentation pack also exists.

Withdrawn: 1.4.75 ½p. to 10p. (½p., 9p. 10p. and *Presentation Packs* sold out by 5.74); 31.3.76 20p., 50p.

35 Hong Kong 2c. of 1862

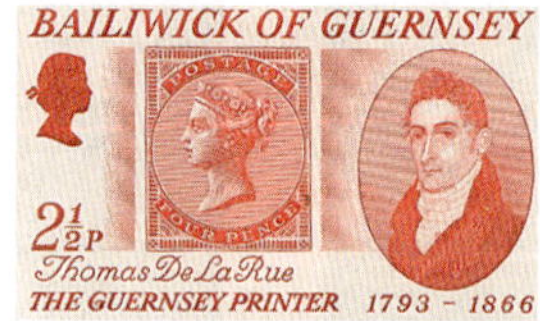

36 Great Britain 4d. of 1855–7

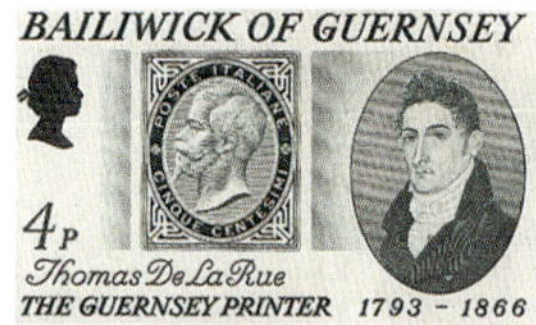

37 Italy 5c. of 1862

38 Confederate States 5c. of 1862

Thomas De La Rue Commemoration

(Des and recess De La Rue)

1971 (2 June). Perf 14×13½ (C).

59	**35**	2p. dull purple to brown-purple*	35	15
60	**36**	2½p. carmine-red	35	15
61	**37**	4p. deep bluish green	1·10	1·00
62	**38**	7½p. deep blue	1·40	1·20
59/62 *Set of 4*			2·75	2·20
First Day Cover				4·00
Presentation Pack			4·00	

*These colours represent the extreme range of shades of this value. The majority of the printing, however, is an intermediate shade.

Plate Nos.: 1A, 1B each.
Sheets: 25 (5×5).
Imprint: Central, bottom margin.
Quantities sold: 2p. 897,742; 2½p. 1,404,085; 4p. 210,691; 7½p. 199,424.
Withdrawn: 1.6.72.

39 Ebenezer Church, St. Peter Port

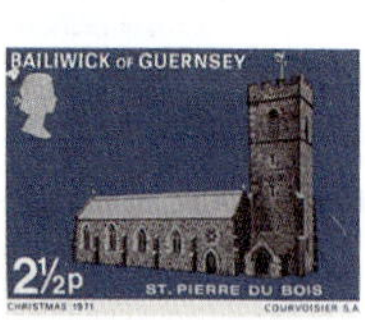

40 Church of St. Pierre du Bois

41 St. Joseph's Church, St. Peter Port

42 Church of St. Phillipe de Toteval

Christmas. Guernsey Churches (2nd series)

(Des and photo Courvoisier)

1971 (27 Oct). Granite paper. Perf 11½ (C).

63	**39**	2p. multicoloured	10	10
64	**40**	2½p. multicoloured	10	10
65	**41**	5p. multicoloured	1·00	1·00
66	**42**	7½p. multicoloured	1·00	1·00
63/6 *Set of 4*			2·00	2·00
First Day Cover				3·00
Presentation Pack			4·00	
Set of 4 Gutter Pairs			16·00	

Cylinder Nos: A1–1–1–1, B1–1–1–1, C1–1–1–1, D1–1–1–1 (all values).
Sheets: 50 (2 panes 5×5).
Imprint: central, bottom margin (2p., 2½p.) or left-hand corner, bottom margin (5p., 7½p.).
Quantities sold: 2p. 991,155; 2½p. 916,004; 5p. 223,412; 7½p. 215,768.
Withdrawn: 26.10.72.

43 *Earl of Chesterfield* (1794)

44 *Dasher* (1827)

45 *Ibex* (1891)

46 *Alberta* (1900)

Mail Packet Boats (1st series)

(Des and photo Courvoisier)

1972 (10 Feb). Granite paper. Perf 11 (C).

67	**43**	2p. multicoloured	15	10
68	**44**	2½p. multicoloured	15	10
69	**45**	7½p. multicoloured	40	35
70	**46**	9p. multicoloured	60	50
67/70 *Set of 4*			1·00	95
First Day Cover				3·00
Presentation Pack			3·00	

See also Nos. 80/3.
Cylinder Nos.: A1–1–1–1 or B1–1–1–1 (all values).
Sheets: 25 (5×5).
Imprint: Central, bottom margin.

Quantities sold: 2p. 973,503; 2½p. 954,263; 7½p. 288,929; 9p. 289,340.
Withdrawn: 9.2.73.

47 Guernsey Bull

World Conference of Guernsey Breeders, Guernsey

(Photo Courvoisier)

1972 (22 May). Granite paper. Perf 11½ (C).

71	**47**	5p. multicoloured	30	30
*First Day Cover**				2·50
Gutter Pair			4·50	

*Prepared by the Royal Guernsey Agricultural and Horticultural Society.
Cylinder Nos.: A1–1–1–1, B1–1–1–1.
Sheets: 50 (2 panes 5×5).

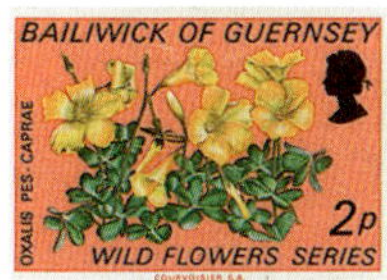

48 Bermuda Buttercup

49 Heath Spotted Orchid

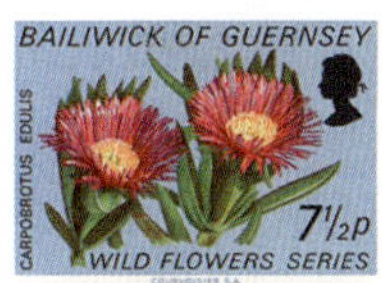

50 Kaffir Fig

51 Scarlet Pimpernel

Wild Flowers

(Des and photo Courvoisier)

1972 (24 May). Granite paper. Perf 11½ (C).

72	**48**	2p. multicoloured	10	10
73	**49**	2½p. multicoloured	10	10
74	**50**	7½p. multicoloured	50	50
75	**51**	9p. multicoloured	60	60
72/5 *Set of 4*			1·00	1·00
First Day Cover				2·50
Presentation Pack			3·25	
Set of 4 Gutter Pairs			4·00	

Cylinder Nos.: A1–1–1–1, B1–1–1–1, C1–1–1–1, D1–1–1–1 (all values).
Sheets: 50 (2 panes 5×5).
Imprint: 2p., 7½p. Central, bottom margin, others left-hand corner, bottom margin.
Quantities sold: 2p. 1,006,041; 2½p. 1,028,826; 7½p. 249,471; 9p. 244,839.
Withdrawn: 23.5.73.

52 Angels adoring Christ

53 The Epiphany

54 The Virgin Mary

55 Christ

Royal Silver Wedding and Christmas

(Des and photo Courvoisier)

1972 (20 Nov). Designs show stained glass windows from Guernsey Churches. Granite paper. Perf 11½ (C).

76	**52**	2p. multicoloured	10	10
77	**53**	2½p. multicoloured	15	10
78	**54**	7½p. multicoloured	30	25
79	**55**	9p. multicoloured	35	35
76/9		*Set of 4*	80	70
		First Day Cover		1·10
		Presentation Pack	1·90	
		Set of 4 Gutter Pairs	2·50	

Cylinder Nos.: A1–1–1–1, B1–1–1–1 each.
Sheets: 50 (2 panes 5×5).
Imprint: Central, bottom margin of each pane.
Quantities sold: 2p. 878.893; 2½p. 1,037,387; 7½p. 314,972; 9p 313,367.
Sold out: By 31.3.73.

56 *St. Julien* (1925)

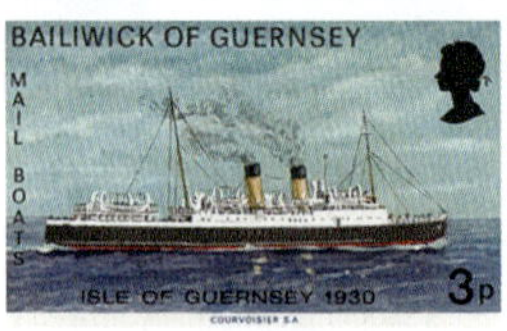

57 *Isle of Guernsey* (1930)

58 *St. Patrick* (1947)

59 *Sarnia* (1961)

Mail Packet Boats (2nd series)

(Des and photo Courvoisier)

1973 (9 Mar). Granite paper. Perf 11½ (C).

80	**56**	2½p. multicoloured	10	10
81	**57**	3p. multicoloured	20	20
82	**58**	7½p. multicoloured	40	40
83	**59**	9p. multicoloured	45	45
80/3		*Set of 4*	1·10	1·00
		First Day Cover		1·40
		Presentation Pack	2·00	
		Set of 4 Gutter Pairs	5·00	

Cylinder Nos.: All values A1–1–1–1, B1–1–1–1, C1–1–1–1, D1–1–1–1.
Sheets: 50 (2 panes 5×5).
Imprint: Central, bottom margin of each pane.
Quantities sold: 2½p. 947,888; 3p. 1,274,699; 7½p. 278,998; 9p 263,569.
Withdrawn: 8.3.74. (3p. and *Presentation Pack* sold out earlier).

60 Supermarine Sea Eagle

61 Westland Wessex Trimotor

62 De Havilland D.H.89 Dragon Rapide

63 Douglas DC-3

64 Vickers Viscount 800 *Anne Marie*

50th Anniversary of Air Service

(Des and photo Courvoisier)

1973 (4 July). Granite paper. Perf 11½ (C).

84	**60**	2½p. multicoloured	10	10
85	**61**	3p. multicoloured	10	10
86	**62**	5p. multicoloured	25	25
87	**63**	7½p. multicoloured	35	30
88	**64**	9p. multicoloured	45	40
84/8		*Set of 5*	1·10	1·00
		First Day Cover		1·50
		Presentation Pack	2·00	
		Set of 5 Gutter Pairs	4·00	

Cylinder Nos.: A1-1-1-1, B1-1-1-1 each.
Sheets: 50 (2 panes (5×5).
Imprint: Central, bottom margin of each pane.
Quantities sold: 2½p. 918,953; 3p. 1,285,890; 5p. 313,882; 7½p. 294,369; 9p. 288,225.
Withdrawn: 3.7.74. (5p. and *Presentation Pack* sold out earlier).

65 'The Good Shepherd'

66 Christ at the Well of Samaria

67 St. Dominic

68 Mary and the Child Jesus

Christmas

(Des and photo Courvoisier)

1973 (24 Oct). Designs show stained glass windows from Guernsey Churches. Granite paper. Perf 11½ (C).

89	**65**	2½p. multicoloured	10	10
90	**66**	3p. multicoloured	10	10
91	**67**	7½p. multicoloured	30	30
92	**68**	20p. multicoloured	40	40
89/92 *Set of 4*			75	75
First Day Cover				90
Presentation Pack			1·50	
Set of 4 Gutter Pairs			2·50	

Cylinder Nos.: A1–1–1–1, B1–1–1–1 each.
Sheets: 50 (2 panes 5×5).
Imprint: Central, bottom margin of each pane.
Quantities sold: 2½p. 1,284,342; 3p. 1,285,851; 7½p. 367,714; 20p. 367,625.
Withdrawn: 23.10.74.

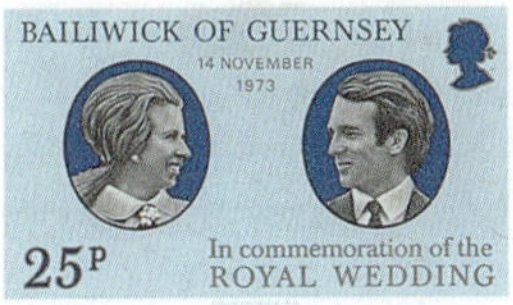

69 Princess Anne and Capt. Mark Phillips

Royal Wedding

(Des G. Anderson. Photo Courvoisier)

1973 (14 Nov). Granite paper. Perf 11½ (C).

93	**69**	25p. multicoloured	45	45
First Day Cover				75
Presentation Pack			90	
Gutter Pair			1·50	

Cylinder Nos.: A1–1–1–1, B1–1–1–1.
Sheets: 50 (2 panes 5×5).
Imprint: Central, bottom margin of each pane.
Quantity sold: 392,767.
Withdrawn: 13.11.74.

70 *John Lockett*, 1875

71 *Arthur Lionel*, 1912

72 *Euphrosyne Kendal*, 1954

73 *Arun*, 1972

150th Anniversary of Royal National Life-boat Institution

(Des and photo Courvoisier)

1974 (15 Jan). Granite paper. Perf 11½ (C).

94	**70**	2½p. multicoloured	10	10
95	**71**	3p. multicoloured	10	10
96	**72**	8p. multicoloured	30	20
97	**73**	10p. multicoloured	35	25
94/7 *Set of 4*			70	60
First Day Cover				1·00
Presentation Pack			1·60	
Set of 4 Gutter Pairs			1·50	

Cylinder Nos.: A1–1–1–1, B1–1–1–1 each.
Sheets: 50 (2 panes 5×5).
Imprint: Central, bottom margin of each pane.
Quantities sold: 2½p. 1,016,058; 3p. 1,162,020; 8p. 393,660; 10p. 393,668.
Withdrawn: 14.1.75 (8p., 10p. and *Presentation Pack* sold out earlier).

74 Private, East Regt., 1815

75 Officer, 2nd North Regt., 1825

76 Gunner, Guernsey Artillery, 1787

77 Gunner, Guernsey Artillery, 1815

78 Corporal, Royal Guernsey Artillery, 1868

79 Field Officer, Royal Guernsey Artillery, 1895

80 Sergeant, 3rd Regt., 1867

81 Officer, East Regt., 1822

82 Field Officer, Royal Guernsey Artillery, 1896

83 Colour-Sergeant of Grenadiers, 1833

84 Officer, North Regt., 1832

85 Officer, East Regt., 1822

86 Field Officer, Rifle Company, 1868

87 Private, 4th West Regt., 1785

88 Field Officer, 4th West Regt., 1824

89 Driver, Field Battery,Royal Guernsey Artillery, 1848

90 Officer, Field Battery, Royal Guernsey Artillery, 1868

91 Cavalry Trooper, Light Dragoons, 1814

Guernsey Militia

(Photo Courvoisier (½p to 10p.), Delrieu (others))

1974 (2 Apr)–**78**. Granite paper (½p. to 10p.). Perf 11½ (½p. to 10p.), 13×13½ (20, 50p.) or 13½×13 (£1), all comb.

98	**74**	½p. multicoloured (ak)	10	10
		a. Booklet strip of 8 (98×5 and 102×3) †	35	
		b. Booklet pane of 16 (98×4, 102×6 and 103×6) †	75	
99	**75**	1p. multicoloured (acj)	10	10
		a. Booklet strip of 8 (99×4, 103, 105×2 and 105a) (8.2.77) †	55	
		b. Booklet strip of 4 (99, 101×2, and 105a) (7.2.78) †	35	
100	**76**	1½p. multicoloured (a)	10	10
101	**77**	2p. multicoloured (al)	10	10
102	**78**	2½p. multicoloured (a)	10	10
103	**79**	3p. multicoloured (a)	10	10
104	**80**	3½p. multicoloured (a)	10	10
105	**81**	4p. multicoloured (abc)	10	10
105*a*	**82**	5p. multicoloured (f)	15	15
106	**83**	5½p. multicoloured (a)	10	10
107	**84**	6p. multicoloured (ae)	10	10
107*a*	**85**	7p. multicoloured (f)	25	25
108	**86**	8p. multicoloured (ah)	15	10
109	**87**	9p. multicoloured (am)	15	10
110	**88**	10p. multicoloured (ai)	15	10
111	**89**	20p. multicoloured (d)	75	40
112	**90**	50p. multicoloured (d)	2·00	1·00
113	**91**	£1 multicoloured (d)	2·50	1·75
98/113 *Set of 18*			5·50	4·25
First Day Covers (3)				5·75
Presentation Packs (3)			5·50	
Set of 15 Gutter Pairs (Nos. 98/110)			3·50	

†Nos. 98a/b come from a special booklet sheet of 88 (8×11), and Nos. 99a/b from booklet sheets of 80 (two panes 8×5). These sheets were put on sale in addition to the normal sheets. The strips and panes have the left-hand selvedge stuck into booklet covers, except for No. 99b which had the strip loose, and then folded and supplied in plastic wallets.

Printings: (a) 2.4.74; (b) 10.74; (c). 12.74; (d) 1.4.75; (e) 12.75; (f) 29.5.76; (g) 6.76; (h) 7.76; (i) 11.76; (j) 8.2.77; (k) 7.77; (l) 12.77; (m) 8.12.78.

Plate Nos.: 20p to £1 none; A1–1–1–1, B1–1–1–1 1½p., 2p., 6p.; A1–1–1–1, B1–1–1–1 others.

Sheets: 20p to £1, 25 (5×5); others, 100 (2 panes 10×5).

Imprint: Central, bottom margin of each page.

Quantities sold: ½p. 1,173,560; 1p. 1,367,828; 1½p. 525,248; 2p. 1,098,053; 2½p. 1,124,091; 3p. 1,953,796; 3½p. 1,891,493; 4p. 3,435, 614; 5p. 2, 920,246; 5½p. 634,870; 6p. 2,006,983; 7p. 3,103, 925; 8p. 811, 418; 9p. 717,815; 10p. 1,133, 141; 20p. 788, 840; 50p 570,505; £1 464,428.

Withdrawn: 12.2.80 ½p. to 20p; 4.2.81 50p., £1.

92 Badge of Guernsey and U.P.U. Emblem

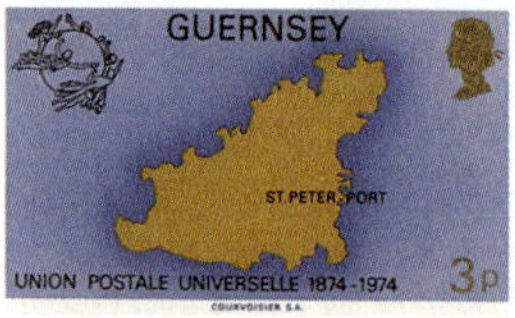

93 Map of Guernsey

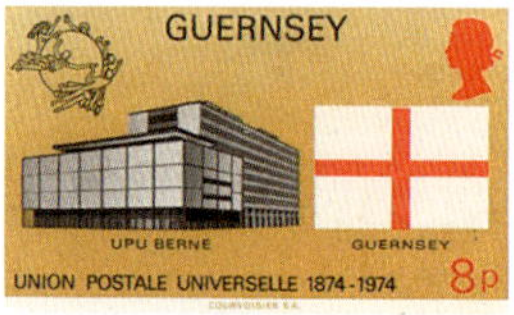

94 U.P.U. Building, Berne, and Guernsey Flag

95 'Salles des Etats'

Centenary of Universal Postal Union

(Photo Courvoisier)

1974 (7 June). Granite paper. Perf 11½ (C).

114	**92**	2½p. multicoloured	10	10
115	**93**	3p. multicoloured	10	10
116	**94**	8p. multicoloured	20	20
117	**95**	10p. multicoloured	20	20
114/17 *Set of 4*			50	50
First Day Cover				75
Presentation Pack			90	
Set of 4 Gutter Pairs			1·50	

Cylinder Nos.: 2½p., 8p. A1–1–1, B1–1–1; 3p. A1–1–1–1, B1–1–1–1; 10p. A1–1–1–1–1, B1–1–1–1–1.

Sheets: 50 (2 panes 5×5).

Imprint: Central, bottom margin.

Quantities sold: 2½p. 1,231,657; 3p. 1,839,674; 8p. 345,271; 10p. 356,501.

Withdrawn: 6.6.75.

96 'Cradle Rock'

97 'La Baie de Moulin Huet'

98 'Au Bord de la Mer'

99 Self-portriat

Renoir Paintings

(Des and photo Delrieu)

1974 (21 Sept). Perf 13 (C).

118	**96**	3p. multicoloured	10	10
119	**97**	5½p. multicoloured	10	10
120	**98**	8p. multicoloured	25	25
121	**99**	10p. multicoloured	25	25
118/21 *Set of 4*			60	60
First Day Cover				90
Presentation Pack			1·40	

Sheets: 25 (5×5).
Imprint: Right-hand corner, top margin (3p. and 5½p.), and bottom corner, right-hand margin (others).
Quantities sold: 3p. 670,648; 5p. 422,677; 8p. 377,615; 10p. 391,095.
Withdrawn: 20.9.75.

100 Guernsey Spleenwort

101 Guernsey Quillwort

102 Guernsey Fern

103 Least Adder's Tongue

Guernsey Ferns

(Des and photo Courvoisier)

1975 (7 Jan). Granite paper. Perf 11½ (C).

122	**100**	3½p. multicoloured	10	10
123	**101**	4p. multicoloured	10	10
124	**102**	8p. multicoloured	25	25
125	**103**	10p. multicoloured	25	25
122/5 *Set of 4*			60	60
First Day Cover				90
Presentation Pack			1·40	
Set of 4 Gutter Pairs			1·40	

Cylinder Nos.: 3½p., 4p., 8p. each A1-1-1-1, B1-1-1-1, C1-1-1-1, D1-1-1-1; 10p. A1-1-1-1-1, B1-1-1-1-1, C1-1-1-1-1, D1-1-1-1-1.
Sheets: 50 (2 panes 5×5).
Imprint: Central, bottom margin.
Quantities sold: 3½p. 1,089,142; 4p. 1,370,743; 8p. 430,672; 10p. 443,636.
Withdrawn: 6.1.76.

104 Victor Hugo House

105 Candie Gardens

106 United Europe Oak, Hauteville

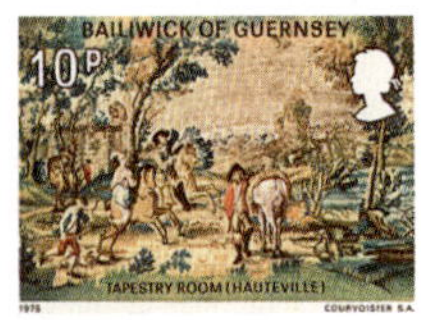

107 Tapestry Room, Hauteville

Victor Hugo's Exile in Guernsey

(Des and photo Courvoisier)

1975 (6 June). Granite paper. Perf 11½ (C).

126	**104**	3½p. multicoloured	10	10
127	**105**	4p. multicoloured	10	10
128	**106**	8p. multicoloured	25	25
129	**107**	10p. multicoloured	25	25
126/9 *Set of 4*			60	60
First Day Cover				80
Presentation Pack			1·90	
MS130 114×143 mm Nos. 126/9			65	90
First Day Cover				6·50

Cylinder Nos.: A1-1-1-1, B1-1-1-1 each.
Sheets: 50 (5×10) 3½p., 10p.; (10×5) others.
Imprint: Central, left-hand margin (3½p., 10p.) or central, bottom margin (4p., 8p.).
Quantities sold: 3½p. 810,327; 4p. 1,346,628; 8p. 377,637; 10p. 369,282; miniature sheet 269,217.
Withdrawn: 5.6.76.

108 Globe and Seal of Bailiwick

109 Globe and Guernsey Flag

110 Globe, Guernsey Flag and Alderney Shield

111 Globe, Guernsey Flag and Sark Shield

Christmas

(Des and photo Delrieu)

1975 (7 Oct). Perf 13 (C).

131	**108**	4p. multicoloured	10	10
132	**109**	6p. multicoloured	10	10
133	**110**	10p. multicoloured	25	25
134	**111**	12p. multicoloured	25	25
131/4 *Set of 4*			60	60
First Day Cover				90
Presentation Pack			1·00	

Sheets: 25 (5×5).
Imprint: Central, left-hand margin (4p., 6p.); central, bottom margin (10p., 12p.).
Quantities sold: 4p., 678,619; 6p. 667,413; 10p. 392,529; 12p. 361,548.
Withdrawn: 6.10.76.

112 Les Hanois

113 Les Casquets

114 Quesnard

115 Point Robert

Lighthouses

(Des and photo Courvoisier)

1976 (10 Feb). Granite paper. Perf 11½ (C).

135	**112**	4p. multicoloured	10	10
136	**113**	6p. multicoloured	10	10
137	**114**	11p. multicoloured	20	20
138	**115**	13p. multicoloured	25	25
135/8 *Set of 4*			60	60
First Day Cover				80
Presentation Pack			1·00	
Set of 4 Gutter Pairs			1·50	

Cylinder Nos.: A1–1–1–1, B1–1–1–1 each.
Sheets: 50 (2 panes 5×5).
Quantities sold: 4p. 846,362; 6p. 900,899; 11p. 366,468; 13p. 348,358.
Withdrawn: 9.2.77.

116 Milk Can

117 Christening Cup

Europa. Handicrafts

(Des and photo Courvoisier)

1976 (29 May). Granite paper. Perf 11½ (C).

139	**116**	10p. brown and green	20	20
140	**117**	25p. grey and blue	40	35
139/40 *Set of 2*			60	55
First Day Cover				75
Presentation Pack			1·20	

Sheets: 9 (3×3).
Quantities sold: 1,185,014 of each.
Sold out: 4.6.76.

118 Pine Forest, Guernsey

119 Herm and Jethou

120 Grand Greve Bay, Sark

121 Trois Vaux Bay, Alderney

Views

(Des and photo Courvoisier)

1976 (3 Aug). Granite paper. Perf 11½ (C).

141	**118**	5p. multicoloured	10	10
142	**119**	7p. multicoloured	10	10
143	**120**	11p. multicoloured	25	25
144	**121**	13p. multicoloured	25	25
141/4 *Set of 4*			60	60
First Day Cover				80
Presentation Pack			1·00	
Set of 4 Gutter Pairs			1·50	

Cylinder Nos.: A1–1–1–1, B1–1–1–1 each.
Sheets: 50 (2 panes 5×5).
Quantities sold: 5p. 661,771; 7p. 1,016,350; 11p. 349,773; 13p. 336,027.
Withdrawn: 2.8.77.

122 Royal Court House, Guernsey

123 Elizabeth College, Guernsey

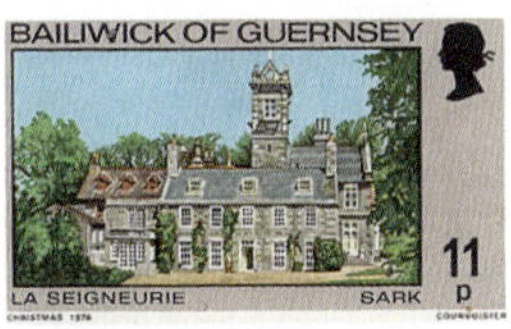

124 La Seigneurie, Sark

125 Island Hall, Alderney

Christmas. Buildings

(Des and photo Courvoisier)

1976 (14 Oct). Granite paper. Perf 11½ (C).

145	**122**	5p. multicoloured	10	10
146	**123**	7p. multicoloured	10	10
147	**124**	11p. multicoloured	25	25
148	**125**	13p. multicoloured	25	25
145/8 *Set of 4*			60	60
First Day Cover				85
Presentation Pack			1·00	
Set of 4 Gutter Pairs			1·50	

Cylinder Nos.: A1–1–1–1–1, B1–1–1–1–1 each.
Sheets: 50 (2 panes 5×5).
Imprint: Central, bottom margin.
Quantities sold: 5p. 1,097,445; 7p. 1,051,184; 11p. 371,155; 13p. 352,347.
Withdrawn: 13.10.77.

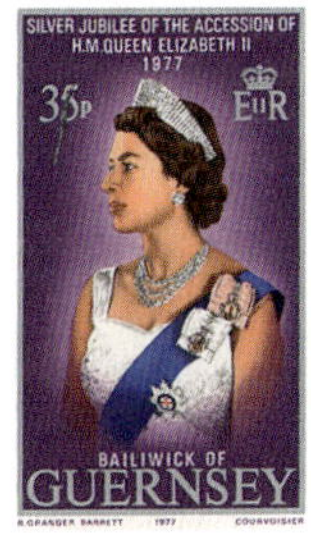

126 Queen Elizabeth II **127**

Silver Jubilee

(Des R. Granger Barrett. Photo Courvoisier)

1977 (8 Feb). Granite Paper. Perf 11½ (C).

149	**126**	7p. multicoloured	20	15
150	**127**	35p. multicoloured	55	40
149/50 *Set of 2*			65	55
First Day Cover				70
Presentation Pack			90	

Cylinder Nos.: 7p. A1–1–1–1–1, B1–1–1–1–1; 35p. A1–1–1–1–1–1.
Sheets:25 (5×5).
Imprint: Central, bottom margin.
Quantities sold: 7p. 1,004,250; 35p. 536,971.
Withdrawn: 7.2.78.

128 Woodland, Talbot's Valley

129 Pastureland, Talbot's Valley

Europa. Landscapes

(Des and photo Courvoisier)

1977 (17 May). Granite paper. Perf 11½ (C).

151	**128**	7p. multicoloured	15	15
152	**129**	25p. multicoloured	45	45
151/2 *Set of 2*			60	60
First Day Cover				70
Presentation Pack			90	
Set of 2 Gutter Pairs			1·40	

Cylinder Nos.: A1–1–1–1–1, B1–1–1–1–1 each.
Sheets: 50 (2 panes 5×5).
Imprint: Right-hand corner, bottom margin.
Quantities sold: 7p. 1,371,463; 25p. 598,453.
Withdrawn: 16.5.78.

130 Statue-menhir, Castel

131 Megalithic Tomb, St. Saviour

132 Cist, Tourgis

133 Statue-menhir, St. Martin

Prehistoric Monuments

(Des and photo Courvoisier)

1977 (2 Aug). Granite paper. Perf 11½ (C).

153	**130**	5p. multicoloured	10	10
154	**131**	7p. multicoloured	10	10
155	**132**	11p. multicoloured	25	25
156	**133**	13p. multicoloured	25	25
153/6 *Set of 4*			60	60
First Day Cover				75
Presentation Pack			90	
Set of 4 Gutter Pairs			1·40	

Cylinder Nos.: A1–1–1–1, B1–1–1–1 each.
Sheets: 50 (2 panes 5×5).
Imprint: Central, right-hand margin (5p. and 13p.); Central, bottom margin (others).
Quantities sold: 5p. 747,236; 7p. 1,077,714; 11p. 390,927; 13p. 373,063.
Withdrawn: 1.8.78.

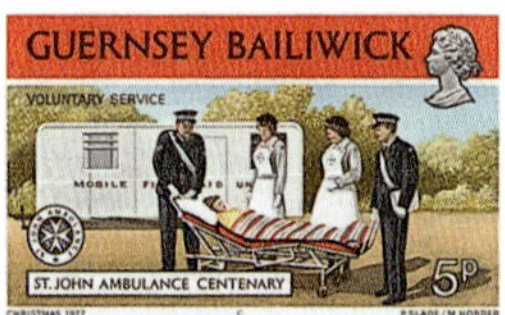

134 Mobile First Aid Unit

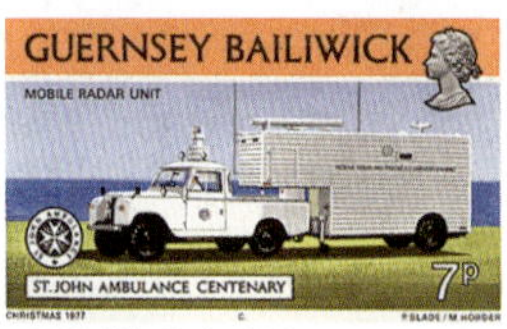

135 Mobile Radar Unit

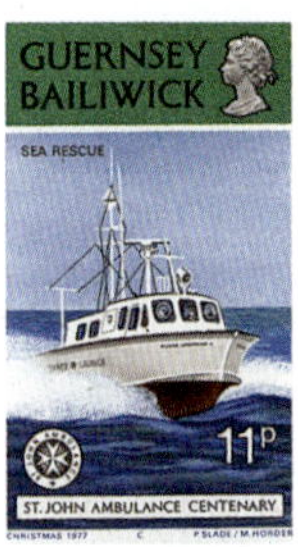

136 Marine Ambulance *Flying Christine II*

137 Cliff Rescue

Christmas. St. John Ambulance Centenary

(Des P. Slade and M. Horder. Photo Courvoisier)

1977 (25 Oct). Granite paper. Perf 11½ (C).

157	**134**	5p. multicoloured	10	10
158	**135**	7p. multicoloured	10	10
159	**136**	11p. multicoloured	25	25
160	**137**	13p. multicoloured	25	25
157/60 *Set of 4*			60	60
First Day Cover				75
Presentation Pack			90	
Set of 4 Gutter Pairs			1·40	

Cylinder Nos.: 5p. A1–1–1–1–1, B1–1–1–1–1; others A1–1–1–1, B1–1–1–1.
Sheets: 50 (2 panes 5×5).
Imprint: Right-hand corner, bottom margin (7p. and 11p.); top, right-hand margin (others).
Quantities sold: 5p. 1,218,293; 7p. 1,155,448; 11p. 406,244; 13p. 383,489.
Withdrawn: 24.10.78.

138 View from Clifton, c 1830

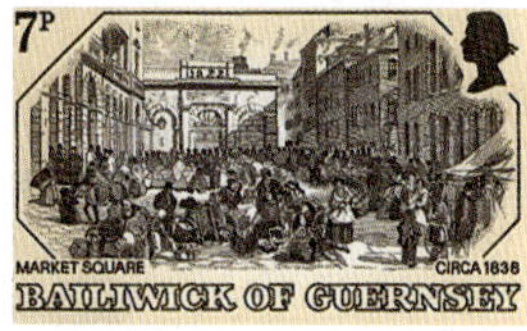

139 Market Square, St. Peter Port, c. 1838

140 Petit-Bo Bay, c 1839

141 The Quay, St. Peter Port, c. 1830

Old Guernsey Prints (1st series)

(Des, recess and litho De La Rue)

1978 (7 Feb). Perf 14×13½ (C).

161	**138**	5p. black and light stone	10	10
162	**139**	7p. black and cream	10	10
163	**140**	11p. black and light pink	25	25
164	**141**	13p. black and light azure	25	25
161/4 *Set of 4*			60	60
First Day Cover				75
Presentation Pack			90	
Set of 4 Gutter Pairs			1·40	

See also Nos. 249/52.
Plate Nos.: All values 1A–1A, 1B–1B, 1C–1C, 1D.–1D.
Sheets: 50 (2 panes 5×5).
Imprint: Left-hand corner, bottom margin.
Quantities sold: 5p. 858,816; 7p. 930,955; 11p. 442,009; 13p. 338,163.
Withdrawn: 6.2.79.

142 Prosperity Memorial

143 Victoria Monument

Europa. Monuments

(Des R. Granger Barrett. Litho Questa)

1978 (2 May). Perf 14½ (C).

165	**142**	5p. multicoloured	10	10
		a. Imperf between stamp and right margin		
166	**143**	7p. multicoloured	25	25
165/6		*Set of 2*	30	30
First Day Cover				45
Presentation Pack			55	

Sheets: 20 (5p. 5×4; 7p. 4×5).
Quantities sold: 5p. 2,581,345; 7p. 2,370,766.
Withdrawn: 1.5.79.

144 Queen Elizabeth

145 Queen Elizabeth

25th Anniversary of Coronation

(Des R. Granger Barrett from bust by Arnold Machin. Photo Courvoisier)

1978 (2 May). Granite paper. Perf 11½ (C).

167	**144**	20p. black, grey and bright blue	45	45
First Day Cover				60
Presentation Pack			60	
Gutter Pair			90	

Cylinder Nos.: A1–1–1, B1–1–1.
Sheets: 50 (2 panes 5×5).
Imprint: Right-hand corner, bottom margin.
Quantity sold: 488,466.
Withdrawn: 1.5.79.

Royal Visit.

(Des R. Granger Barrett from bust by Arnold Machin. Photo Courvoisier)

1978 (28 June). Granite paper. Perf 11½ (C).

168	**145**	7p. black, grey and bright green	20	20
First Day Cover				45
Presentation Pack			50	
Gutter Pair			40	

Cylinder Nos.: A1–1–1, B1–1–1.
Sheets: 50 (2 panes 5×5).
Imprint: Top corner, right-hand margin.
Quantity sold: 1,149,768.
Withdrawn: 27.6.79.

146 Northern Gannet

147 Firecrest

148 Dartford Warbler

149 Spotted Redshank

Birds

(Des John Waddington Ltd. Photo Courvoisier)

1978 (29 Aug). Granite paper. Perf 11½ (C).

169	**146**	5p. multicoloured	10	10
170	**147**	7p. multicoloured	20	15
171	**148**	11p. multicoloured	30	20
172	**149**	13p. multicoloured	40	30
169/72		*Set of 4*	85	70
First Day Cover				75
Presentation Pack			1·20	
Set of 4 Gutter Pairs			1·50	

Cylinder Nos.: All values A1–1–1–1, B1–1–1–1, C1–1–1–1, D1–1–1–1.
Sheets: 50 (2 panes 5×5).
Imprint: Right-hand corner, bottom margin.
Quantities sold: 5p. 750,011; 7p. 924,627; 11p. 442,395; 13p. 432,106.
Withdrawn: 28.8.79.

150 Solanum

151 Christmas Rose

152 Holly

153 Mistletoe

Christmas

(Des and photo Courvoisier)

1978 (31 Oct). Granite paper. Perf 11½ (C).

173	**150**	5p. multicoloured	10	10
174	**151**	7p. multicoloured	10	10
175	**152**	11p. multicoloured	20	20
176	**153**	13p. deep blue-green, grey and greenish yellow	25	25
173/6		*Set of 4*	60	60
First Day Cover				90
Presentation Pack			95	
Set of 4 Gutter pairs			1·50	

Cylinder Nos.: 13p. A1–1–1, B1–1–1; others A1–1–1–1, B1–1–1–1.
Sheets: 50 (2 panes 5×5).
Imprint: 5, 7p. central, bottom margin; others central, right-hand margin.
Quantities sold: 5p. 1,222,140; 7p. 1,246,260; 11p. 409,168; 13p. 372,991.
Withdrawn: 30.10.79.

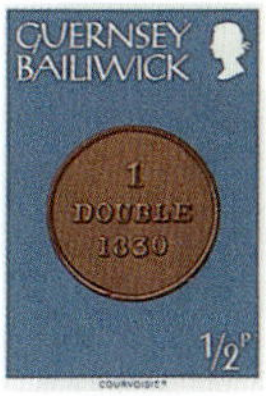

154 One Double, 1830

155 Two Doubles, 1899

156 Four Doubles, 1902

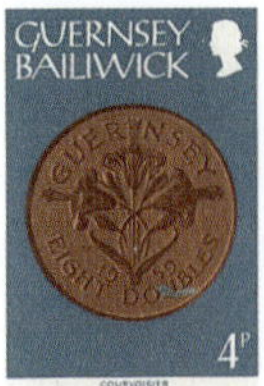

157 Eight Doubles, 1959

158 Three Pence, 1956

159 Five New pence, 1968

160 Fifty New pence, 1969

161 Ten New pence, 1970

162 Half New Penny, 1974

163 One New Penny, 1971

164 Two New Pence, 1971

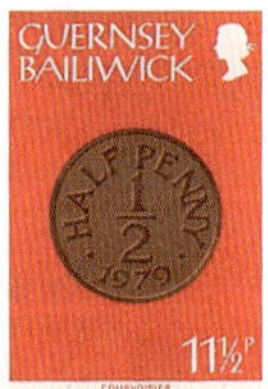

165 Half Penny, 1979

166 One Penny, 1977

167 Two Pence, 1977

168 Five Pence, 1977

169 Ten pence, 1977

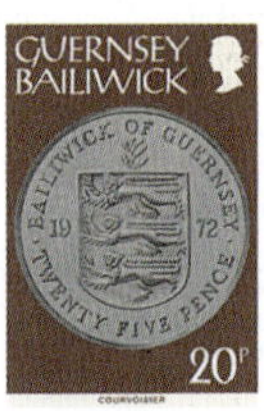

170 Twenty-five Pence, 1972

171 Ten Shillings Wiliam I Commem, 1966

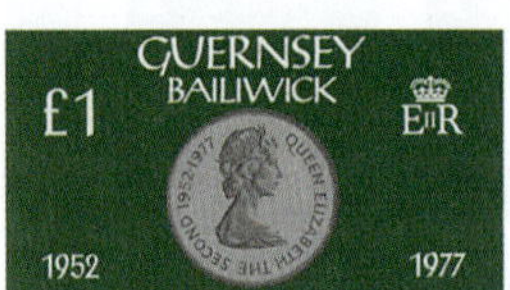

172 Silver Jubilee Commemorative Crown, 1977

173 Royal Silver Wedding Commemorative Crown, 1972

174 Seal of the Bailiwick

Coins

(Des R. Reed and Courvoisier (£5). Photo Courvoisier)

1979 (13 Feb)–**83**. Granite paper. Perf 11½ (C).

177	**154**	½p. multicoloured (a)	10	10
		a. Booklet pane. Nos. 177×2, 178×3, 179×2, 181, 183 and 187 (C)	70	
		b. Booklet pane. Nos. 177×2, 178, 179×2, and 187×3 (C)	90	
178	**155**	1p. multicoloured (al)	10	10
		a. Booklet strip of 4. Nos. 178×2, 179 and 182	40	
179	**156**	2p. multicoloured (a)	10	10
		a. Booklet strip of 5. Nos. 179, 182×2 and 184×2	90	
180	**157**	4p. multicoloured (a)	10	10
		a. Booklet pane of 10. Nos. 180 and 184, each ×5 (d)	1·20	
		b. Booklet pane of 15. Nos. 180, 184 and 190, each ×5(d)	2·50	
		c. Booklet pane of 10. Nos. 180×2, 185×3 and 191×5 (k)	1·90	
		d. Booklet pane of 15. Nos. 180, 185 and 191, each ×5 (k)	2·20	
181	**158**	5p. grey-black, silver and chestnut (a)	10	10
		a. *Grey-black, silver and yellowish brown* (f)	30	40
		b. Booklet pane of 10. Nos. 181a×5, 184×4 and 191 (f)	1·70	
		c. Booklet pane of 15. Nos. 181a, 184 and 191, each ×5 (f)	2·20	
182	**159**	6p. grey-black, silver and brown-red (a)	15	10
183	**160**	7p. grey-black, silver & grn (a)	15	15
184	**161**	8p. grey-blk, silver & brn (agij)	15	15
185	**162**	9p. multicoloured (a)	15	15
186	**163**	10p. mult (green background) (a)	30	25
187		10p. mult (orge background (b)	20	15
188	**164**	11p. multicoloured (a)	20	15
189	**165**	11½p. multicoloured (b)	20	15
190	**166**	12p. multicoloured (a)	20	15
191	**167**	13p. multicoloured (ah)	25	20
192	**168**	14p. grey-blk, silver & dull bl (a)	25	20
193	**169**	15p. grey-blk, silver & bistre (a)	25	25
194	**170**	20p. grey-black, silver and dull brown (a)	30	30
195	**171**	50p. grey-black, orange-red and silver (b)	85	60
196	**172**	£1 grey-black, yellowish green and silver (b)	1·70	1·10
197	**173**	£2 grey-black, new blue and silver (b)	3·75	2·00
198	**174**	£5 multicoloured (e)	8·00	8·00
177/98 Set of 22			15·00	12·00
First Day Covers (4)				14·00
Presentation Packs (4)			18·00	
Set of 22 Gutter Pairs			30·00	

Nos. 177a/b, 178a, 179a, 180a/d and 181b/c come from special booklet sheets of 40 (8×5) (Nos. 177a and 178a), 30 (6×5) (Nos. 177b, 180a/b, 180d and 181b/c), 25 (5×5) (No. 179a) or 20 (4×5) (No. 180c). These were put on sale as complete sheets or separated into strips, folded and either affixed by the selvedge to booklet covers or supplied loose in plastic wallets.

The booklet sheets containing Nos. 177a/b show either four (No. 177a) or three (No. 177b) different arrangements of the same stamps.

Printings: (a) 13.2.79; (b) 5.2.80; (c). 6.5.80; (d) 24.2.81; (e) 22.5.81; (f) 2.2.82; (g) 4.82; (h) 5.82; (i) 7.82; (j) 11.82; (k) 14.3.83; (l) 6.83.
Cylinder Nos.: 5, 6, 7, 8, 14, 15, 20, 50p., £1, £2 A1–1–1, B1–1–1; others A1–1–1–1, B1–1–1–1.
Sheets: ½ to 20p. 100 (2 panes 10×5); 50p. to £5 50 (2 panes 5×5).
Imprint: 50p. top corner, left-hand margin; £1, £2 right-hand corner, bottom margin; £5 bottom corner, right-hand margin; others central margin.

Quantities sold: ½p. 1,285,162; 1p. 1,888,850; 2p. 1,249,506; 4p. 650,195; 5p. 1,110,783; 6p. 1,678,775; 7p. 1,683,430; 8p. 3,059,366; 9p. 1,952,892; 10p. (No. 186) 484,956; 10p. (No. 187) 1,751,126; 11p. 711,268; 11½p. 351,422; 12p. 957,197; 13p. 1,459,086; 14p. 595,744; 15p. 677,289; 20p. 960,124; 50p. 863,760; £1 537,871; £2 375,786.
Withdrawn: 4.2.81 10p. (No. 186); 22.7.85 (all other values except £5); 31.12.98 £5.

175 Pillar Box and Postmark, 1853, Mail Van and Postmark, 1979

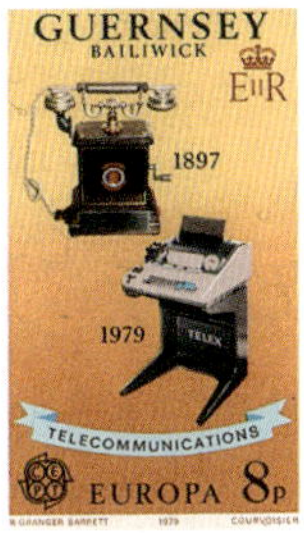

176 Telephone, 1897 and Telex Machine, 1979

Europa. Communications

(Des R. Granger Barrett. Photo Courvoisier)

1979 (8 May). Granite paper. Perf 11½ (C).

201	**175**	6p. multicoloured	10	10
202	**176**	8p. multicoloured	20	20
201/2 *Set of 2*			30	30
First Day Cover				45
Presentation Pack			55	

Cylinder Nos.: Both values A1–1–1–1, B1–1–1–1.
Sheets: 20 (5×4).
Quantities sold: 6p. 1,863,564; 8p. 2,293,379.
Withdrawn: 7.5.80.

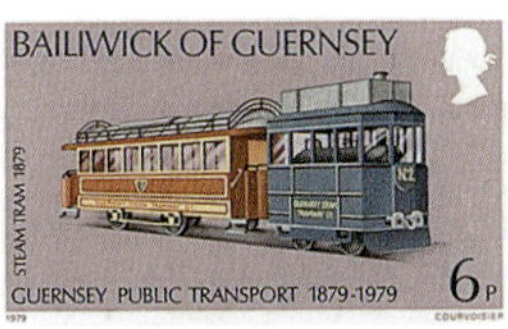

177 Steam Tram, 1879

178 Electric Tram, 1896

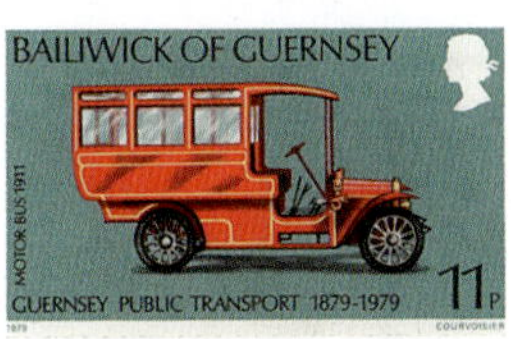

179 Motor Bus, 1911

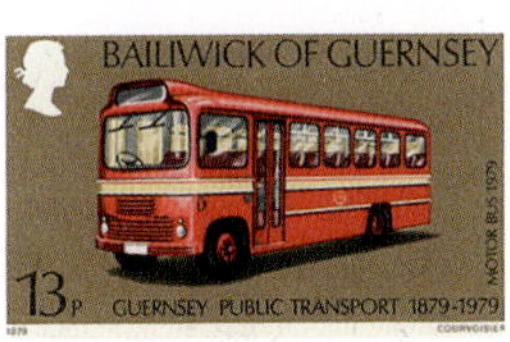

180 Motor Bus, 1979

History of Public Transport

(Photo Courvoisier)

1979 (7 Aug). Granite paper. Perf 11½ (C).

203	**177**	6p. multicoloured	10	10
204	**178**	8p. multicoloured	15	10
205	**179**	11p. multicoloured	20	15
206	**180**	13p. multicoloured	20	25
203/6 *Set of 4*			60	55
First Day Cover				70
Presentation Pack			1·20	
Set of 4 Gutter Pairs			1·40	

Cylinder Nos.: 6p. A1–1–1–1–1, B1–1–1–1–1; others A1–1–1–1, B1–1–1–1.
Sheets: 50 (2 panes 5×5).
Imprint: Central, bottom margin.
Quantities sold: 6p. 676,046; 8p. 981,431; 11p. 384,701; 13p. 371,882.
Withdrawn: 6.8.80.

181 Bureau and Postal Headquarters

182 'Mails and Telegrams'

183 'Parcels'

184 'Philately'

10th Anniversary of Guernsey Postal Administration

(Des R. Granger Barrett. Photo Courvoisier)

1979 (1 Oct). Granite paper. Perf 11½ (C).

207	**181**	6p. multicoloured	10	10
208	**182**	8p. multicoloured	15	10
209	**183**	13p. multicoloured	20	15
210	**184**	15p. multicoloured	25	25
207/10 *Set of 4*			65	55
First Day Cover				80
Presentation Pack			1·10	
Set of 4 Gutter Pairs			1·40	
MS211 120×80 mm. Nos. 207/10			80	80
First Day Cover				1·20

One copy of a pre-release sample as No. 210, but with a face value of 11p., is known. Such stamps were not sold for postal purposes.
Cylinder Nos.: All values A1–1–1–1, B1–1–1–1.
Sheets: 50 (2 panes 5×5).
Imprint: Central, bottom margin.
Quantities sold: 6p. 1,254,914; 8p. 1,376,682; 13p. 389,524; 15p. 386,234; miniature sheet 398,443.
Withdrawn: 30.9.80.

185 Major-General Le Marchant

186 Admiral Lord de Saumarez

Europa. Personalities

(Des and photo Courvoisier)

1980 (6 May). Granite paper. Perf 11½ (C).

212	**185**	10p. multicoloured	15	15
213	**186**	13½p. multicoloured	30	25
212/13 *Set of 2*			45	0·40
First Day Cover				70
Presentation Pack			80	

Cylinder Nos.: Both values A1–1–1–1–1, B1–1–1–1–1, C1–1–1–1–1, D1–1–1–1–1.
Sheets: 20 (5×4).
Quantities sold: 10p. 2,794,871; 13½p. 1,715,880.
Withdrawn: 5.5.81.

187 Policewoman with Lost Child

188 Police Motorcyclist escorting Lorry

189 Police Dog-handler

60th Anniversary of Guernsey Police Force

(Litho John Waddington Ltd)

1980 (6 May). Perf 13½×14 (C).

214	**187**	7p. multicoloured	15	15
215	**188**	15p. multicoloured	25	25
216	**189**	17½p. multicoloured	30	25
214/16 *Set of 3*			65	60
First Day Cover				85
Presentation Pack			1·00	
Set of 3 Gutter Pairs			1·40	

Plate Nos: All values 1A, 1B, 1C, 1D. (each ×4).
Sheets: 50 (2 panes 5×5).
Imprint: Central, bottom margin.
Quantities sold: 7p. 907,714; 15p. 352,802; 17½p. 337,551.
Withdrawn: 5.5.81.

190

191

192

193

T **190/3** show Golden Guernsey Goats.

Golden Guernsey Goats

(Des P. Lambert. Photo Delrieu)

1980 (5 Aug). Perf 13 (C).

217	**190**	7p. multicoloured	10	10
218	**191**	10p. multicoloured	20	15
219	**192**	15p. multicoloured	25	20
220	**193**	17½p. multicoloured	40	35
217/20 *Set of 4*			85	80
First Day Cover				95
Presentation Pack			1·20	
Set of 4 Gutter Pairs			1·70	

Cylinder Nos.: 7p. 598–599–600–601–602–603; 10p. 578–580–581–583; 15p. 605–606–607–608–609–610; 17½p. 621–622–623–624–625–626.
Sheets: 50 (2 panes 5×5).
Imprint: Bottom margin.
Quantities sold: 7p. 779,424; 10p. 931,214; 15p. 364,917; 17½p. 329,133.
Withdrawn: 4.4.81.

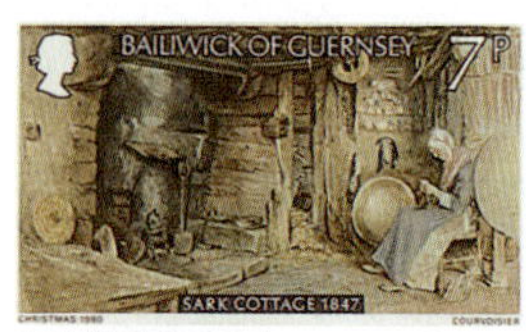

194 'Sark Cottage'

195 'Moulin Huet'

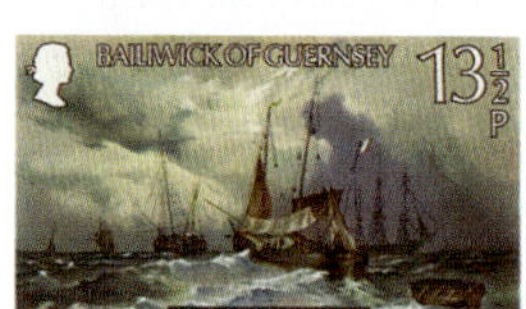

196 'Boats at Sea'

197 'Cow Lane'

198 'Peter Le Lievre'

Christmas. Peter le Lievre Paintings

(Photo Courvoisier)

1980 (15 Nov). Granite paper. Perf 11½ (C).

221	**194**	7p. multicoloured	15	10
222	**195**	10p. multicoloured	20	15
223	**196**	13½p. multicoloured	25	20
224	**197**	15p. multicoloured	25	25
225	**198**	17½p. multicoloured	40	35
221/5 *Set of 5*			1·10	95
First Day Cover				1·40
Presentation Pack			1·50	
Stamp-cards (set of 5)			2·00	4·00
Set of 5 Gutter Pairs			2·50	

Cylinder Nos.: All values A1–1–1–1, B1–1–1–1.
Sheets: 50 (2 panes 5×5).
Imprint: 15, 17½p. top corner, right-hand margin; others right-hand corner, bottom margin.
Quantities sold: 7p. 1,199,280; 10p. 1,159,622; 13½p. 397,812; 15p. 432,182; 17½p. 359,116.
Withdrawn: 14.11.81.

199 *Polyommatus icarus*

200 *Vanessa atalanta*

201 *Aglais urticae*

202 *Lasiommata megera*

Butterflies

(Photo Harrison)

1981 (24 Feb). Perf 14 (C).

226	**199**	8p. multicoloured	15	15
227	**200**	12p. multicoloured	20	20
228	**201**	22p. multicoloured	35	35
229	**202**	25p. multicoloured	40	40
226/9 *Set of 4*			1·00	1·00
First Day Cover				2·20
Presentation Pack			1·70	
Set of 4 Gutter Pairs			2·20	

Cylinder Nos.: All values 1A, 1B (each ×5).
Sheets: 50 (2 panes 5×5).
Imprint: Right-hand corner, bottom margin.
Quantities sold: 8p. 986,229; 12p. 971,801; 22p. 438,478; 25p. 438,575.
Withdrawn: 23.2.82.

203 Sailors paying respect to 'Le Petit Bonhomme Andriou' (rock resembling head of a man)

204 Fairies and Guernsey Lily

Europa. Folklore

(Des C. Abbott. Litho Questa)

1981 (22 May). Perf 14½ (C).

230	**203**	12p. gold, red-brown & cinnamon	25	15
231	**204**	18p. gold, indigo and azure	30	35
230/1 *Set of 2*			55	50
First Day Cover				65
Presentation Pack			80	
Set of 2 Gutter Pairs			1·10	

Plate Nos.: 12p. 1B, 1F, 1G, 1H (each ×3); 18p. 1B, 1D., 1F, 1G, 1H (each ×3).
Sheets: 20 (2 panes 5×2).
Imprint: Central, left-hand margin.
Quantities sold: 12p. 2,516,514; 18p. 1,937,023.
Withdrawn: 21.5.82.

205 Prince Charles

206 Prince Charles and Lady Diana Spencer

207 Lady Diana

208 Royal Family

Royal Wedding

(Des C. Abbott. Litho Questa)

1981 (29 July). Perf 14½ (C).

232	**205**	8p. multicoloured	15	10
		a. Strip of 3. Nos. 232/4	75	75
233	**206**	8p. multicoloured	15	10
234	**207**	8p. multicoloured	15	10
235	**205**	12p. multicoloured	25	25
		a. Strip of 3. Nos. 235/7	1·10	1·10
236	**206**	12p. multicoloured	25	25
237	**207**	12p. multicoloured	25	25
238	**208**	25p. multicoloured	65	60
232/8 *Set of 7*			2·00	1·60
First Day Cover				3·25
Presentation Pack			3·25	
Stamp-cards (set of 7)			2·00	7·00
MS239 104×127 mm. Nos. 232/8. P 14 (C)			2·50	2·50
First Day Cover				4·00

Plate Nos.: 8p. 1A, 1C (each ×6); 12p. 1B (×6); 25p. 1A (×6).
Sheets: 8p., 12p. 60 (6×10) each value in strips of 3 across sheet, 25p. 30 (3×10).
Imprint: Bottom corner, right-hand side margin.
Quantities sold: 8p. 2,115,103; 12p. 2,235,005; 25p. 510,608; miniature sheet 432,743.
Withdrawn: 28.7.82.

209 Sark Launch

210 Britten Norman 'short nose' Trislander Airplane

211 Hydrofoil

212 Herm Catamaran

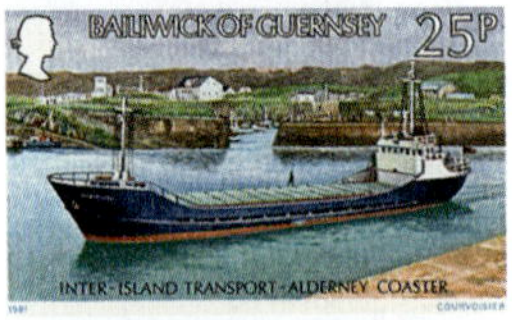

213 *Sea Trent* (coaster)

Inter-island Transport

(Des and photo Courvoisier)

1981 (25 Aug). Granite paper. Perf 11½ (C).

240	**209**	8p. multicoloured	15	15
241	**210**	12p. multicoloured	25	20
242	**211**	18p. multicoloured	30	35
243	**212**	22p. multicoloured	45	65
244	**213**	25p. multicoloured	55	75
240/4 *Set of 5*			1·50	2·00
First Day Cover				2·00
Presentation Pack			2·00	
Set of 5 Gutter Pairs			3·00	

Cylinder Nos.: All values A1–1–1–1, B1–1–1–1.
Sheets: 50 (2 panes 5×5).
Imprint: Right-hand corner, bottom margin.
Quantities sold: 8p. 790,215; 12p. 785,488; 18p. 457,763; 22p. 469,315; 25p. 466,112.
Withdrawn: 24.8.82.

214 Rifle Shooting

215 Riding

216 Swimming

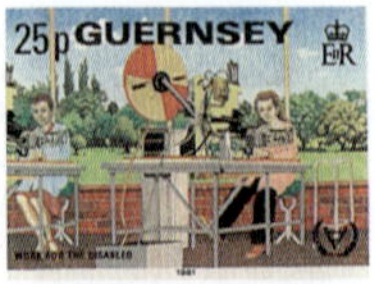

217 Circuit Construction

International Year for Disabled Persons

(Des P. le Vasseur. Litho Questa)

1981 (17 Nov). Perf 14½ (C).

245	**214**	8p. multicoloured	15	10
246	**215**	12p. multicoloured	25	20
247	**216**	22p. multicoloured	45	35
248	**217**	25p. multicoloured	55	55
245/8 *Set of 4*			1·20	1·10
First Day Cover				1·10
Presentation Pack			1·60	
Set of 4 Gutter Pairs			2·40	

Plate Nos.: All values 1A, 1B, 1C, 1D., 1E, 1F, 1G, 1H (each ×4).
Sheets: 50 (2 panes 5×5).
Imprint: Foot of right-hand margin on each pane.
Quantities sold: 8p. 912,908; 12p. 910,614; 22p. 280,882; 25p. 287,725.
Withdrawn: 16.11.82.

218 Jethou

219 Fermain Bay

220 The Terres

221 St. Peter Port

Old Guernsey Prints (2nd series). Sketches by T. Compton

(Des, recess and litho De La Rue)

1982 (2 Feb). Perf 14×13½ (C).

249	**218**	8p. black and pale blue	15	15
250	**219**	12p. black & pale turquoise-grn	25	20
251	**220**	22p. black and pale yellow-brown	40	40
252	**221**	25p. black and pale rose-lilac	50	50
249/52 *Set of 4*			1·10	1·10
First Day Cover				1·40
Presentation Pack			1·60	
Set of 4 Gutter Pairs			2·20	

Plate Nos.: All values 1A–1A, 1B–1B, 1C–1C, 1D.–1D.
Sheets: 50 (2 panes 5×5).
Imprint: Left-hand corner, bottom margin.
Quantities sold: 8p. 350,198; 12p. 346,515; 22p. 346,661; 25p. 244,669.
Withdrawn: 1.2.83.

222 Sir Edgar MacCulloch (founder-president) and Guille-Allés Library, St. Peter Port

223 Norman Invasion Fleet crossing English Channel, 1066 ('history')

224 H.M.S. *Crescent*, 1793 ('history')

225 Dragonfly ('entomology')

226 Common Snipe caught for Ringing ('ornithology')

227 Samian Bowl 160-200 A.D. ('archaeology')

Centenary of La Société Guernesiaise

(Des G. Drummond. Photo Courvoisier)

1982 (28 Apr). Granite paper. Perf 11½ (C).

253	**222**	8p. multicoloured	15	15
254	**223**	13p. multicoloured	30	15
255	**224**	20p. multicoloured	40	25
256	**225**	24p. multicoloured	50	40
257	**226**	26p. multicoloured	60	50
258	**227**	29p. multicoloured	65	55
253/8 *Set of 6*			2·30	1·70
First Day Cover				2·00
First Day Cover (Nos. 254/5)				2·00
Presentation Pack			2·50	
Presentation Pack (Nos. 254/5)			1·70	
Stamp-cards (*set of 6*)			2·00	4·00

The 13p. and 20p. (Nos. 254/5) also include the Europa C.E.P.T. emblem in the designs.

Cylinder Nos.: 24p. A1–1–1–1, B1–1–1–1, C1–1–1–1, D1–1–1–1; others A1–1–1–1–1, B1–1–1–1–1, C1–1–1–1–1, D1–1–1–1–1.
Sheets: 20 (5×4).
Quantities sold: 8p. 921,095; 13p. 2,820,311; 20p. 1,491,351; 24p. 315,735; 26p. 309,919; 29p. 298,761.
Withdrawn: 27.4.83.

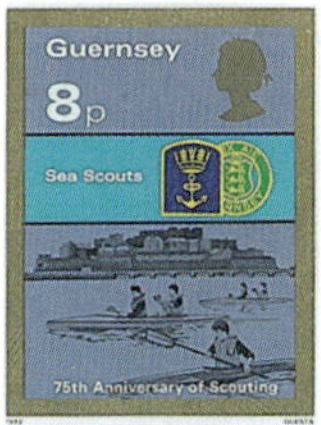

228 Sea Scouts

229 Scouts

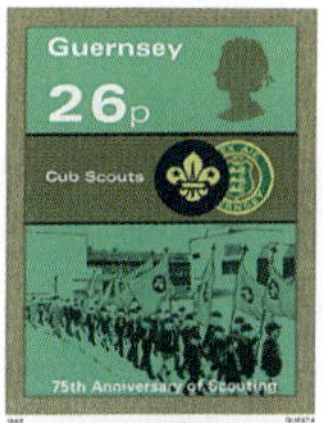

230 Cub Scouts

231 Air Scouts

75th Anniversary of Boy Scout Movement

(Des W.L.G. Creative Services Ltd. Litho Questa)

1982 (13 July). Perf 14½×14 (C).

259	**228**	8p. multicoloured	15	25
260	**229**	13p. multicoloured	30	25
261	**230**	26p. multicoloured	55	50
262	**231**	29p. multicoloured	65	1·10
259/62 *Set of 4*			1·50	2·10
First Day Cover				2·20
Presentation Pack			2·00	
Set of 4 Gutter Pairs			3·00	

Plate Nos.: 8p. 1A, 1B, 1C, 1D. (each ×6); others 1A, 1B, 1C, 1D. (each ×7).
Sheets: 50 (2 panes 5×5).
Imprint: Bottom corner, right-hand margin.
Quantities sold: 8p. 796,018; 13p. 930,924; 26p. 237,958; 29p. 233,204.
Withdrawn: 12.7.83.

232 Midnight Mass

233 Exchanging Gifts

234 Christmas Meal

235 Exchanging Cards

236 Queens Christmas Message

Christmas

(Des Lynette Hammant. Photo Harrison)

1982 (12 Oct). Perf 14½ (C).

263	**232**	8p. multicoloured	15	15
		a. Black (Queen's head, value and inscr) omitted	£2750	
264	**233**	13p. multicoloured	25	15
265	**234**	24p. multicoloured	50	45
266	**235**	26p. multicoloured	55	50
267	**236**	29p. multicoloured	65	55
263/7 *Set of 5*			1·90	1·60
First Day Cover				2·00
Presentation Pack			2·40	
Set of 5 Gutter Pairs			3·75	

Cylinder Nos.: All values 1A, 1B (each ×5).
Sheets: 50 (2 panes 5×5).
Imprint: Right-hand corner, bottom margin.
Quantities sold: 8p. 944,560; 13p. 927,844; 24p. 227,145; 26p. 249,110; 29p. 232,323.
Withdrawn: 11.10.83.

237 Flute Player and Boats

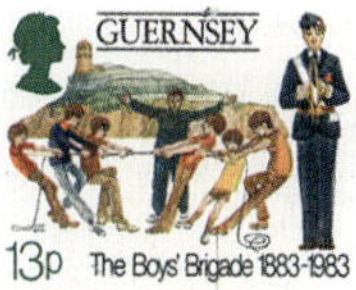

238 Cymbal Player and Tug 'o' war

239 Trumpet Player and Bible Class

240 Drummer and Cadets marching

241 Boys Brigade Band

Centenary of Boys– Brigade

(Des Sally Stiff. Photo Harrison)

1983 (18 Jan). Perf 14 (C).

268	**237**	8p. multicoloured	15	10
269	**238**	13p. multicoloured	25	20
270	**239**	24p. multicoloured	40	40
271	**240**	26p. multicoloured	55	50
272	**241**	29p. multicoloured	65	55
268/72 *Set of 5*			1·70	1·60
First Day Cover				1·90
Presentation Pack			2·00	
Set of 5 Gutter Pairs			3·50	

Cylinder Nos.: All values 1A, 1B (each ×5).
Sheets: 50 (2 panes 5×5).
Imprint: Bottom margin, right-hand corner.
Quantities sold: 8p. 671,921; 13p. 538,257; 24p. 223,069; 26p. 234,482; 29p. 214,723.
Withdrawn: 17.1.84.

242 Building Albert Pier Extension, 1850s

243 St. Peter Port Harbour, 1983

244 St. Peter Port, 1680

245 Artists Impression of Future Development Scheme

Europa. Great Works of Human Genius. Development of St. Peter Port Harbour

(Des J. Larrivière. Artwork C. Abbott. Photo Courvoisier)

1983 (14 Mar). Granite paper. Perf 11½ (C).

273	**242**	13p. multicoloured	20	15
		a. Horiz pair. Nos. 273/4	75	70
274	**243**	13p. multicoloured	20	15
275	**244**	20p. multicoloured	30	30
		a. Horiz pair. Nos. 275/6	1·00	1·00
276	**245**	20p. multicoloured	30	30
273/6 *Set of 4*			1·60	1·50
First Day Cover				1·60
Presentation Pack			2·20	

Cylinder Nos.: Both values A1–1–1–1–1, B1–1–1–1–1.
Sheets: 20 (4×5). The two designs of each value were printed together, *se-tenant*, in horizontal pairs throughout.
Quantities sold: 13p. 1,884,714; 20p. 1,676,250.
Withdrawn: 13.3.84.

246 'View at Guernsey'

247 'Children on the Seashore'

248 'Marine, Guernsey'

249 'La Baie du Moulin Huet à travers les Arbres'

250 'Brouillard à Guernesey'

Centenary of Renoir's visit to Guernsey

(Des and photo Courvoisier)

1983 (6 Sept). Granite paper. Perf 11×11½ (13p.) or 11½ (others), all comb.

277	**246**	9p. multicoloured	20	15
278	**247**	13p. multicoloured	25	25
279	**248**	26p. multicoloured	55	50
280	**249**	28p. multicoloured	85	80
281	**250**	31p. multicoloured	1·00	90
277/81 *Set of 5*			2·50	2·40
First Day Cover				3·00
Presentation Pack			3·25	
Stamp-cards (set of 5)			1·50	4·00
Set of 5 Gutter Pairs			5·00	

Cylinder Nos.: 13p. A1–1–1–1–1, B1–1–1–1–1, C1–1–1–1–1, D1–1–1–1–1; others A1–1–1–1–1, B1–1–1–1–1.
Sheets: 40 (2 panes 4×5).
Quantities sold: 9p. 547,148; 13p. 757,838; 26p. 185,045; 28p. 219,830; 31p. 305,219.
Withdrawn: 5.9.84.

251 Launching *Star of the West*, 1869, and Capt. J. Lenfestey

252 Leaving St. Peter Port

253 Off Rio Grande Bar

254 Off St. Lucia

255 Map of 1879–80 Voyage

Guernsey Shipping (1st series). *Star of the West* (brigantine)

(Des R. Granger Barrett. Litho Questa)

1983 (15 Nov). Perf 14 (C).

282	**251**	9p. multicoloured	20	20
283	**252**	13p. multicoloured	25	15
284	**253**	26p. multicoloured	50	50
285	**254**	28p. multicoloured	85	75
286	**255**	31p. multicoloured	95	80
282/6 *Set of 5*			2·50	2·10
First Day Cover				2·40
Presentation Pack			3·25	
Set of 5 Gutter Pairs			4·75	

See also Nos. 415/19.
Plate Nos.: 26p., 31p. 1C, 1D. (each ×5); others 1A, 1B (each ×5).
Sheets: 50 (2 panes 5×5).
Imprint: Bottom corner, right-hand margin.
Quantities sold: 9p. 706,809; 13p. 974,736; 26p. 236,974; 28p. 216,279; 31p. 218,647.
Withdrawn: 14.11.84.

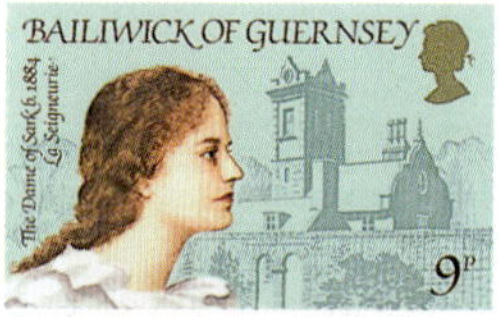

256 Dame of Sark as Young Woman

257 German Occupation, 1940–45

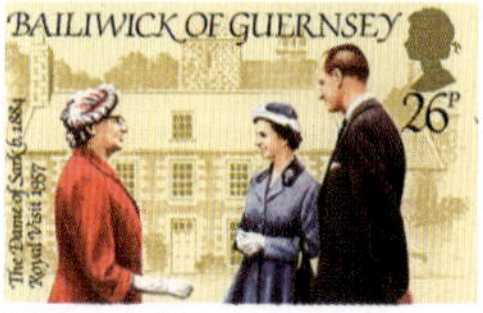

258 Royal Visit, 1957

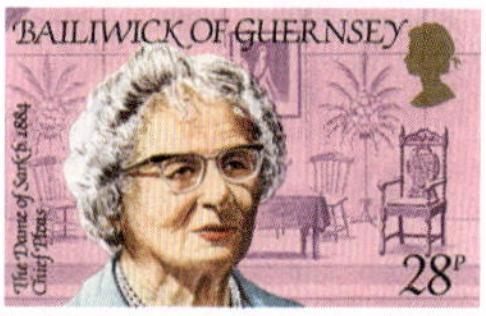

259 Chief Pleas

260 'Dame of Sark' Rose

Birth Centenary of Sibyl Hathaway, Dame of Sark

(Des Jennifer Toombs. Litho Questa)

1984 (7 Feb). Perf 14½ (C).

287	**256**	9p. multicoloured	20	20
288	**257**	13p. multicoloured	30	15
289	**258**	26p. multicoloured	70	55
290	**259**	28p. multicoloured	75	70
291	**260**	31p. multicoloured	80	75
287/91 *Set of 5*			2·50	2·10
First Day Cover				2·50
Presentation Pack			3·00	
Set of 5 Gutter Pairs			5·00	

Plate Nos.: 13p. 1A, 1B, 1C, 1D. (each ×5); others 1A, 1B, 1C, 1D., (each ×7).
Sheets: 50 (2 panes 5×5).
Imprint: Bottom corner, right-hand margin.
Quantities sold: 9p. 637,566; 13p. 836,270; 26p. 315,561; 28p. 293,716; 31p. 270,742.
Withdrawn: 6.2.85.

261 C.E.P.T. 25th Anniversary Logo

Europa

(Des J. Larrivière. Litho Questa)

1984 (10 Apr). Perf 15×14½ (C).

292	**261**	13p. cobalt, dull ultramarine & blk	25	15
293		20½p. emerald, deep dull grn & blk	55	50
292/3 *Set of 2*			75	60
First Day Cover				1·20
Presentation Pack			1·50	

Plate Nos.: Both values 1A, 1B (each ×3).
Sheets: 20 (4×5).
Imprint: Bottom corner, right-hand margin.
Quantities sold: 13p. 1,680,033; 20½p. 903,972.
Withdrawn: 9.4.85.

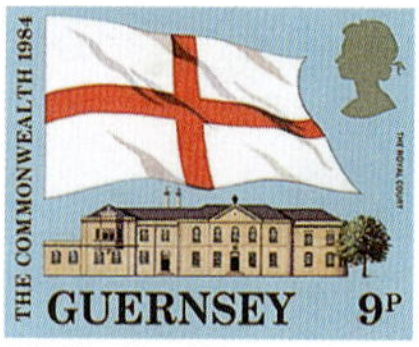

262 The Royal Court and St. George's Flag

263 Castle Cornet and Union Flag

Links with the Commonwealth

(Des C. Abbott. Litho Questa)

1984 (10 Apr). Perf 14×14½ (C).

294	**262**	9p. multicoloured	20	15
295	**263**	31p. multicoloured	85	85
294/5 *Set of 2*			1·00	95
First Day Cover				1·20
Presentation Pack			1·50	

Plate Nos.: Both values 1A, 1B, 1C, 1D. (each ×6).
Sheets: 20 (4×5).
Imprint: Bottom corner, right-hand margin.
Quantities sold: 9p. 1,419,845, 31p. 285,099.
Withdrawn: 9.4.85.

264 Little Chapel

265 Fort Grey

266 Chapel St. Apolline

267 Petit Port

268 Little Russel

269 The Harbour, Herm

270 Saints

271 St. Saviour

272 New Jetty (inscr 'Cambridge Berth')

273 Belvoir, Herm

274 La Seigneurie, Sark

276 St. Saviour's Reservoir

275 Petit Bot

277 St. Peter Port

278 Havelet

279 Hostel of St. John

280 Le Variouf

281 La Coupee, Sark

282 King's Mills

283 Town Church

284 Grandes Rocques

285 Torteval Church

286 Bordeaux

287 Albecq

288 L'Ancresse

Bailiwick Views

(Des C. Abbott. Litho Questa)

1984 (18 Sept)–**91**. Perf 14½ (C).

296	**264**	1p. multicoloured (c)	10	10
297	**265**	2p. multicoloured (c)	10	10
		a. Booklet pane. Nos. 297×2, 299×4, 300×2 and 305×2 (d)	1·60	
298	**266**	3p. multicoloured (a)	10	10
		a. Booklet pane. Nos. 298, 299×2, 306×4 and 309×3 (f)	2·00	
299	**267**	4p. multicoloured (a)	10	10
		a. Booklet pane. Nos. 299×2, 304×3 and 307×5	2·50	
		b. Booklet pane. Nos. 299, 304 and 307, each ×5	2·50	
		c. Booklet pane. Nos. 299×4, 306 b×3 and 309c×3 (g)	2·75	
		d. Booklet pane. Nos. 299,301, 306 b×3 and 309 d×3 (h)	3·25	
		e. Black ptg double	£500	
300	**268**	5p. multicoloured (c)	15	10
		a. Booklet pane. Nos. 300×2, 301×2, 309×3 and 310b×3 (j)	3·75	
301	**269**	6p. multicoloured (c)	15	15
		a. Booklet pane. Nos. 301×4, 308×4 and 310×2 (i)	3·25	
		b. Uncoated paper		
		c. Black ptg double		
302	**270**	7p. multicoloured (c)	15	15
303	**271**	8p. multicoloured (c)	20	15
304	**272**	9p. multicoloured (a)	20	10
		a. Booklet pane. Nos. 304×4 and 308×6 (b)	2·50	
		b. Booklet pane. Nos. 304×2 and 308×8 (b)	2·50	
		c. Black ptg double		
305	**273**	10p. multicoloured (a)	25	15
		a. Booklet pane. Nos. 305 and 308, each ×5 (e)	3·00	
306	**274**	11p. multicoloured (c)	25	15
		a. Booklet pane. Nos. 306 and 309, each ×5 (f)	3·25	
306*b*	**275**	12p. multicoloured (g)	35	15
		ba. Booklet pane. Nos. 306b and 309c, each ×5	3·00	
		bb. Booklet pane. Nos. 306b and 309d, each ×4 (h)	3·50	
		bc. Black ptg double	£500	
307	**276**	13p. multicoloured (a)	25	25
308	**277**	14p. multicoloured (a)	25	20
		a. Booklet pane. Nos. 308 and 310, each ×5 (i)	3·75	
		b. Uncoated paper	£650	
309	**278**	15p. multicoloured (C)	30	30
		a. Booklet pane. Nos. 309 and 310b, each ×5 (j)	5·50	
		b. Imperf at sides and foot (horiz pair)		
309*c*	**279**	16p. multicoloured (g)	30	20
		ca. Black and red ptgs double		
309*d*	**280**	18p. multicoloured (h)	30	20
		da. Black ptg double	£500	
310	**281**	20p. multicoloured (a)	45	25
		a. Uncoated paper	£850	
310*b*	**282**	21p. multicoloured (j)	45	30
310*c*	**283**	26p. multicoloured (j)	70	50
		ca. Imperf at sides and foot (horiz pair)	£1250	

311	**284**	30p. multicoloured (c)	65	60
312	**285**	40p. multicoloured (a)	70	70
313	**286**	50p. multicoloured (a)	80	75
314	**287**	£1 multicoloured (a)	1·90	1·50
315	**288**	£2 multicoloured (c)	3·75	3·50
296/315 *Set of 25*			12·00	10·00
First Day Covers (5)				15·00
Presentation Packs (3)			15·00	
Stamp-cards (set of 25)			7·00	22·00
Set of 25 Gutter Pairs			24·00	

For 11p, 12p., 15p. and 16p. stamps in a smaller size see Nos. 398/9*a*.

Booklet panes Nos. 297a, 298a, 299a/c, 304a/b, 305a, 306a and 306ba have margins all round and were issued, folded and loose, within the booklet covers. Booklet panes Nos. 299d, 300a, 306bb, 308a and 309a have the outer edges imperforate on three sides and were also issued loose within the booklet covers.

Nos. 299e, 301c, 306bc and 309da come from an example of booklet pane No. 299d.

Nos. 301b, 308b and 310a come from examples of booklet panes Nos. 301a and 308a.

Unfolded booklet panes (with and without margins) were also available from the Philatelic Bureau and Head Post Office.

In addition to the presentation packs listed, there was a Tourists Definitive Pack containing the original set of 20, selling price £5.50.

Printings: (a) 18.9.84; (b) 19.3.85; (c). 23.7.85; (d) 2.12.85; (e) 1.4.86; (f) 30.3.87; (g) 28.3.88; (h) 28.2.89; (i) 27.12.89; (j) 2.4.91.
Plate Nos.:All values 1A, 1B, 1C, 1D. (each ×5).
Sheets: 1p., 3p., 8p., 12p., 14p., 15p., 18p., 26p., 40p., 100 (2 panes 10×5); others 100 (2 panes 5×10).
Imprint: Bottom, right-hand margin of each pane.
Quantities sold: 1p. 1,397,906; 2p. 1,240,037; 3p. 460,949; 4p. 478,679; 5p. 690,128; 6p. 560,950; 7p. 302,367; 8p. 425,421; 9p. 1,959,119; 10p. 1,692,125; 11p 1,510,077; 12p. 2,837,219; 13p. 730,405; 14p. 3,925,313; 15p. 2,631,599; 16p. 1,322,353; 18p. 1,398,065; 20p. 2,149,053; 21p. 1,675,329; 26p. 210,575; 30p. 790,261; 40p. 604,514; 50p 765,831; £1 647,055; £2 666,177.
Withdrawn: 21.5.93.

289 'A Partridge in a Pear Tree'

290 'Two Turtle Doves'

291 'Three French Hens'

292 'Four Colly Birds'

293 'Five Gold Rings'

294 'Six Geese a-laying'

295 'Seven Swns a-swimming'

296 'Eight Maids a-milking'

297 'Nine Drummers drumming'

298 'Ten Pipers piping'

299 'Eleven Ladies dancing'

300 'Twelve Lords a-leaping'

Christmas. 'The Twelve Days of Christmas'

(Des R. Downer. Litho Questa)

1984 (20 Nov). Perf 14½ (C).

316	**289**	5p. multicoloured	15	15
		a. Sheetlet of 12. Nos. 316/27	2·00	2·00
317	**290**	5p. multicoloured	15	15
318	**291**	5p. multicoloured	15	15
319	**292**	5p. multicoloured	15	15
320	**293**	5p. multicoloured	15	15
321	**294**	5p. multicoloured	15	15
322	**295**	5p. multicoloured	15	15
323	**296**	5p. multicoloured	15	15
324	**297**	5p. multicoloured	15	15
325	**298**	5p. multicoloured	15	15
326	**299**	5p. multicoloured	15	15
327	**300**	5p. multicoloured	15	15
316/27 *Set of 12*			2·00	1·70
First Day Cover				2·00
Presentation Pack			2·50	

Sheets: 12 (4×3) containing Nos. 316/27 *se-tenant*.
Imprint: Bottom, left-hand margin.
Quantity sold: 271,168 sheetlets.
Withdrawn: 19.11.85.

301 Sir John Doyle and Coat of Arms

302 Battle of Germantown, 1777

303 Reclaiming Braye du Valle, 1806

304 Mail for Alderney, 1812

150th Death Anniversary of Lieutenant-General Sir John Doyle

(Des E. Stemp. Photo Courvoisier)

1984 (20 Nov). Granite paper. Perf 11½ (C).

328	**301**	13p. multicoloured	30	25
329	**302**	29p. multicoloured	65	60
330	**303**	31p. multicoloured	75	70
331	**304**	34p. multicoloured	90	85
328/31 *Set of 4*			2·40	2·10
First Day Cover				2·50
Presentation Pack			3·25	
Set of 4 Gutter Pairs			4·75	

Cylinder Nos.: All values A1–1–1–1–1–1, B1–1–1–1–1–1, C1–1–1–1–1–1, D1–1–1–1–1–1.
Sheets: 50 (2 panes 5×5).
Quantities sold: 13p. 642,178; 29p. 460,535; 31p. 450,051; 34p. 465,982.
Withdrawn: 19.11.85.

Yearbook 1984

1984 (1 Dec). Comprises Nos. 287/95, 298/9, 304/5, 307/8, 310, 312/14, 316/31 and A13/17.

Yearbook	35·00

Withdrawn: 29.3.86.

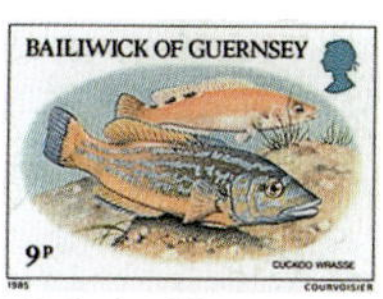
305 Cuckoo Wrasse

306 Red Gurnard

307 Red Mullet

308 Mackerel

309 Oceanic Sunfish

Fish

(Des P. Barrett. Photo Courvoisier)

1985 (22 Jan). Granite paper. Perf 11½ (C).

332	**305**	9p. multicoloured	30	25
333	**306**	13p. multicoloured	40	25
334	**307**	29p. multicoloured	90	90
335	**308**	31p. multicoloured	90	90
336	**309**	34p. multicoloured	90	90
332/6		*Set of 5*	3·00	3·00
First Day Cover				3·00
Presentation Pack			3·50	
Set of 5 Gutter Pairs			7·00	

Cylinder Nos.: 13p., 29p. A1–1–1–1–1, B1–1–1–1–1, C1–1–1–1–1, D1–1–1–1–1; others A1–1–1–1, B1–1–1–1, C1–1–1–1, D1–1–1–1.
Sheets: 50 (2 panes 5×5).
Quantities sold: 9p. 465,322; 13p. 724,941; 29p. 221,392; 31p. 174,948; 34p. 157,422.
Withdrawn: 21.1.86.

310 Dove

40th Anniversary of Peace in Europe

(Des C. Abbott. Litho Questa)

1985 (9 May). Perf 14×14½ (C).

337	**310**	22p. multicoloured	60	60
First Day Cover				90
Presentation Pack			1·20	
Gutter Pair			1·50	

Plate Nos.: 1A, 1B, 1C, 1D. (each ×4).
Sheets: 50 (2 panes 5×5).
Imprint: Bottom, right-hand margin of each pane.
Quantity sold: 246,024.
Withdrawn: 8.5.86.

311 I.Y.Y. Emblem and Young People of Different Races

312 Girl Guides cooking over Campfire

International Youth Year

(Des Suzanne Brehaut (9p.), Mary Harrison (31p.). Litho Questa)

1985 (14 May). Perf 14 (C).

338	**311**	9p. multicoloured	25	15
339	**312**	31p. multicoloured	75	70
338/9		*Set of 2*	1·00	1·00
First Day Cover				1·20
Presentation Pack (with No.342)			3·00	

Plate Nos.: Both values 1A, 1B, 1C, 1D., 1E, 1F (each ×6).
Sheets: 20 (5×4).
Imprint: Bottom, right-hand margin.
Quantities sold: 9p. 1,246,421; 31p. 264,938.
Withdrawn: 13.5.86.

313 Stave of Music enclosing Flags

314 Stave of Music and Musical Instruments

Europa. European Music Year

(Des Fiona Sloan (14p.), Katie Lillington (22p.). Litho Questa)

1985 (14 May). Perf 14×14½ (C).

340	**313**	14p. multicoloured	30	25
341	**314**	22p. multicoloured	60	55
340/1		*Set of 2*	90	80
First Day Cover				1·00
Presentation Pack			1·00	

Plate Nos.: Both values 1A, 1B, 1C, 1D., 1E, 1F (each ×6).
Sheets: 20 (4×5).
Imprint: Bottom, right-hand margin.
Quantities sold: 14p. 1,742,651; 22p. 879,421.
Withdrawn: 13.5.86.

315 Guide Leader, Girl Guide and Brownie

75th Anniversary of Girl Guide Movement

(Des Karon Mahy. Litho Questa)

1985 (14 May). Perf 14 (C).

342	**315**	34p. multicoloured	1·00	90
First Day Cover				1·00

Plate Nos.: 1A, 1B, 1C, 1D. (each ×6).
Sheets: 20 (5×4).
Imprint: Bottom, right-hand margin.
Quantity sold: 182,426.
Withdrawn: 13.5.86.

316 Santa Claus

317 Lussibruden (Sweden)

318 King Balthazar

319 Saint Nicholas (Netherlands)

320 La Befana (Italy)

321 Julenisse (Denmark)

322 Christkind (Germany)

323 King Wenceslas (Czechoslovakia)

324 Shepherd of Les Baux (France)

325 King Caspar

326 Baboushka (Russia)

327 King Melchior

Christmas. Gift-bearers

(Des C. Abbott. Photo Courvoisier)

1985 (19 Nov). Granite paper. Perf 12½ (C).

343	**316**	5p. multicoloured	25	15
		a. Sheetlet of 12. Nos. 343/54	3·00	3·00
344	**317**	5p. multicoloured	25	15
345	**318**	5p. multicoloured	25	15
346	**319**	5p. multicoloured	25	15
347	**320**	5p. multicoloured	25	15
348	**321**	5p. multicoloured	25	15
349	**322**	5p. multicoloured	25	15
350	**323**	5p. multicoloured	25	15
351	**324**	5p. multicoloured	25	15
352	**325**	5p. multicoloured	25	15
353	**326**	5p. multicoloured	25	15
354	**327**	5p. multicoloured	25	15
343/54 *Set of 12*			3·00	3·00
First Day Cover				3·50
Presentation Pack			3·75	

Sheets: 12 (4×3) containing Nos. 343/54 *se-tenant*.
Imprint: Central, bottom margin.
Quantity sold: 236,937 sheetlets.
Withdrawn: 18.11.86.

328 ' Vraicing'

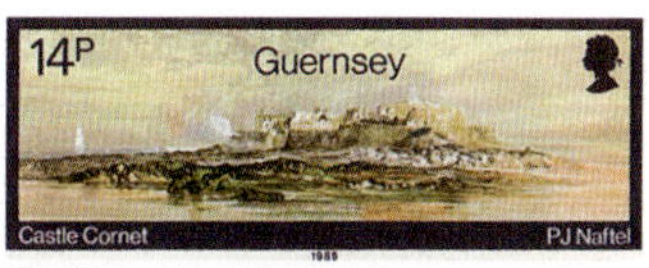

329 'Castle Cornet'

330 'Rocquaine Bay'

331 'Little Russel'

332 'Seaweed-gatherers'

Paintings by Paul Jacob Naftel

(Des and photo Harrison)

1985 (19 Nov). Perf 15×14 (C).

355	**328**	9p. multicoloured	20	20
356	**329**	14p. multicoloured	25	25
357	**330**	22p. multicoloured	65	65
358	**331**	31p. multicoloured	1·00	1·00
359	**332**	34p. multicoloured	1·20	1·20
355/9 *Set of 5*			2·75	2·75
First Day Cover				3·00
Presentation Pack			3·50	
Set of 5 Gutter Pairs			5·50	

Cylinder Nos.: All values 1A, 1B (each ×5).
Sheets: 50 (2 panes 5×5).
Imprint: Left-hand margin of each pane.
Quantities sold: 9p. 398,472; 14p. 452,728; 22p. 164,922; 31p. 197,422; 34p. 173,428.
Withdrawn: 18.11.86.

Yearbook 1985

1985 (Dec). Comprises Nos. 296/7, 300/3, 306, 309, 311, 315, 332/59 and A18/27.

Yearbook .... 55·00

Withdrawn: 31.12.86.

333 Squadron off Nargue Island, 1809

334 Battle of the Nile, 1798

335 Battle of St. Vincent, 1797

336 H.M.S. *Crescent* off Cherbourg, 1793

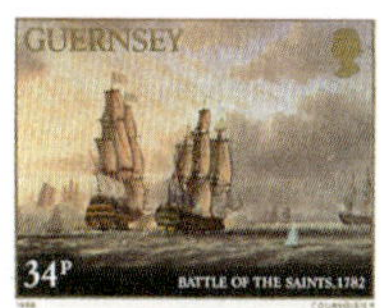

337 Battle of the Saints, 1782

150th Death Anniversary of Admiral Lord De Saumarez

(Des T. Thompson. Photo Courvoisier)

1986 (4 Feb). Granite paper. Perf 11½ (C).

360	**333**	9p. multicoloured	30	25
361	**334**	14p. multicoloured	40	30
362	**335**	29p. multicoloured	75	70
363	**336**	31p. multicoloured	1·10	95
364	**337**	34p. multicoloured	1·20	1·00
360/4 *Set of 5*			3·00	3·00
First Day Cover				3·25
Presentation Pack			3·25	
Set of 5 Gutter Pairs			7·00	

Cylinder Nos.: All values A1-1-1-1-1, B1-1-1-1-1.
Sheets: 40 (2 panes 5×4).
Quantities sold: 9p. 456,518; 14p. 706,727; 29p. 157,693; 31p. 163,612; 34p. 160,724.
Withdrawn: 3.2.87.

338 Profile of Queen Elizabeth II (after R. Maklouf)

60th Birthday of Queen Elizabeth II

(Des C. Abbott. Litho Questa)

1986 (21 Apr). Perf 14 (C).

365	**338**	60p. multicoloured	1·20	1·20
First Day Cover				1·50
Presentation Pack			2·50	
Gutter Pair			3·00	

Plate Nos.: 1A, 1B, 1C, 1D. (each ×4).
Sheets: 40 (2 panes 5×4).
Imprint: Bottom, right-hand margin of each pane.
Quantity sold: 169,661.
Withdrawn: 20.4.87.

339 Northern Gannet and Nylon Net (Operation Gannet')

340 Whitsun Orchid

341 Guernsey Elm

Europa. Nature and Environmental Protection

(Des P. Newcombe. Photo Courvoisier)

1986 (22 May). Granite paper. Perf 11½ (C).

366	**339**	10p. multicoloured	30	30
367	**340**	14p. multicoloured	40	40
368	**341**	22p. multicoloured	70	70
366/8 *Set of 3*			1·20	1·20
First Day Cover				1·90
Presentation Pack			1·90	

Cylinder Nos.: All values A1–1–1–1–1–1, B1–1–1–1–1–1, C1–1–1–1–1–1, D1–1–1–1–1–1.
Sheets: 20 (4×5).
Quantities sold: 10p. 977,212; 14p. 995,123; 22p. 662,565.
Withdrawn: 21.5.87.

342 Prince Andrew and Miss Sarah Ferguson **343**

Royal Wedding

(Des C. Abbott. Litho Questa)

1986 (23 July). Perf 14 (14p.) or 13½×14 (34p.), both comb.

369	**342**	14p. multicoloured	60	50
370	**343**	34p. multicoloured	1·00	90
369/70 *Set of 2*			1·20	1·20
First Day Cover				2·00
Presentation Pack			2·00	
Set of 2 Gutter Pairs			3·25	

Plate Nos.: Both values 1A, 1B, 1C, 1D., 1E, 1F (each ×5).
Sheets: 50 (2 panes 5×5).
Imprint: Bottom, right-hand margin of each pane.
Quantities sold: 14p. 292,018; 34p. 199,297.
Withdrawn: 22.7.87.

344 Bowls

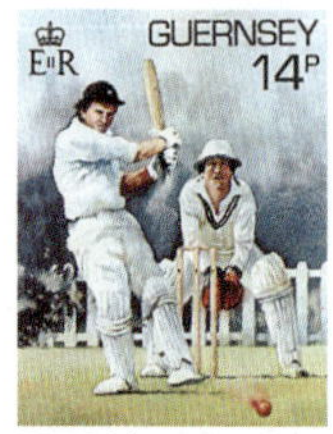

345 Cricket

346 Squash

347 Hockey

348 Swimming

349 Shooting

Sport in Guernsey

(Des R. Goldsmith. Litho Questa)

1986 (24 July). Perf 14½ (C).

371	**344**	10p. multicoloured	25	20
372	**345**	14p. multicoloured	35	20
		a. Black (face value, inscr etc.) printed treble	£275	
373	**346**	22p. multicoloured	50	45
		a. Black (face value, inscr etc.) printed treble		
374	**347**	29p. multicoloured	90	80
375	**348**	31p. multicoloured	90	80
376	**349**	34p. multicoloured	1·00	90
371/6 *Set of 6*			3·50	3·00
First Day Cover				3·25
Presentation Pack			4·00	
Set of 4 Gutter Pairs			7·00	

Plate Nos.: All values 1A, 1B, 1C, 1D. (each×4).
Sheets: 50 (2 panes 5×5).
Imprint: Bottom, right-hand margin of each pane.
Quantities sold: 10p. 399,897; 14p. 985,699; 22p. 212,203; 29p. 141,882; 31p 157,751; 34p. 156,164.
Withdrawn: 23.7.87.

350 Guernsey Museum and Art Gallery, Candie Gardens

351 Fort Grey Maritime Museum

352 Castle Cornet

353 National Trust of Guernsey Folk Museum

Centenary of Guernsey Museums

(Des Sir Hugh Casson. Litho Questa)

1986 (18 Nov). Perf 14 (C).

377	**350**	14p. multicoloured	30	15
378	**351**	29p. multicoloured	85	80
379	**352**	31p. multicoloured	85	80
380	**353**	34p. multicoloured	1·00	90
377/80 *Set of 4*			2·75	2·40
First Day Cover				3·00
Presentation Pack			3·00	
Set of 4 Gutter Pairs			5·50	

Plate Nos.: All values 1A, 1B, 1C, 1D. (each ×5).
Sheets: 50 (2 panes 5×5).
Imprint: Bottom, right-hand margin of each pane.
Quantities sold: 14p. 796,879; 29p. 141,974; 31p. 159,326; 34p. 144,074.
Withdrawn: 17.11.87.

354 'While Shepherds watched their Flocks by Night'

355 'In the Bleak Mid-Winter'

356 'O Little Town of Bethlehem'

357 'The Holly and the Ivy'

358 'O Little Christmas Tree'

359 'Away in a Manger'

360 'Good King Wenceslas'

361 'We Three Kings of Orient Are'

362 'Hark the Herald Angels Sing'

363 'I saw Three Ships'

364 'Little Donkey'

365 'Jingle Bells'

Christmas. Carols

(Des Wendy Bramall. Photo Courvoisier)

1986 (18 Nov). Granite paper. Perf 12½ (C).

381	**354**	6p. multicoloured	20	10
		a. Sheetlet of 12. Nos. 381/92	2·50	2·50
382	**355**	6p. multicoloured	20	10
383	**356**	6p. multicoloured	20	10
384	**357**	6p. multicoloured	20	10
385	**358**	6p. multicoloured	20	10
386	**359**	6p. multicoloured	20	10
387	**360**	6p. multicoloured	20	10
388	**361**	6p. multicoloured	20	10
389	**362**	6p. multicoloured	20	10
390	**363**	6p. multicoloured	20	10
391	**364**	6p. multicoloured	20	10
392	**365**	6p. multicoloured	20	10
381/92 *Set of 12*			2·50	2·50
First Day Cover				2·75
Presentation Pack			3·00	

Sheets: 12 (4×3) containing Nos. 381/92 *se-tenant*.
Imprint: Central, bottom margin.
Quantity sold: 226,119 sheetlets.
Withdrawn: 17.11.87.

Yearbook 1986

1986 (Dec). Comprises Nos. 360/92 and A28/31.

Yearbook	36·00	

Withdrawn: 31.12.87

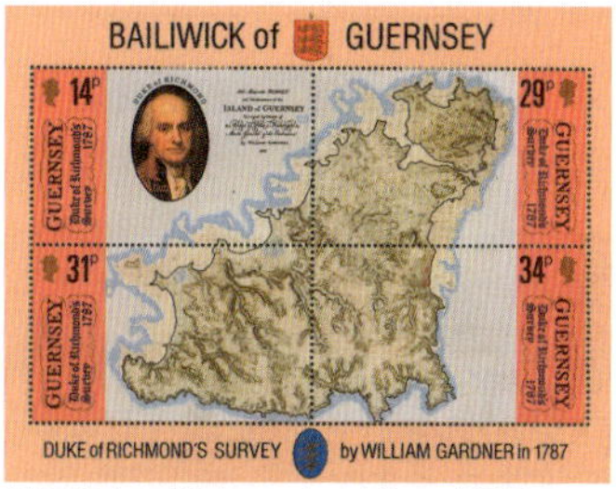

366a Duke of Richmond and Map of 1787
(Illustration reduced size. Actual size 134×103 mm)

Bicentenary of Duke of Richmond's Survey of Guernsey

(Des J. Cooter. Litho Questa)

1987 (10 Feb). Perf 14½×14 (C).

First Day Cover		4·50
Presentation Pack	3·75	
MS393 134×103 mm **366a** 14p., 29p., 31p., 34p. multicoloured	2·50	2·75

Quantity sold: 176,655.
Withdrawn: 9.2.88.

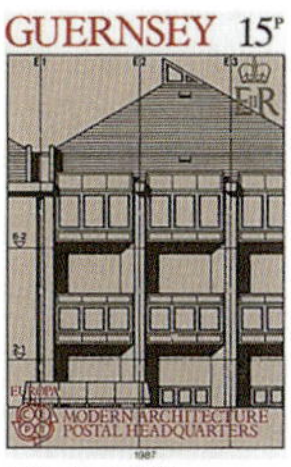

367 Post Office Headquarters

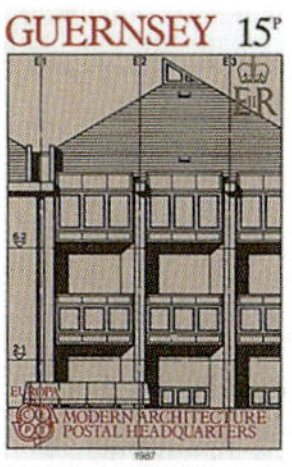

368 Architect's Elevation of Post Office Headquarters

369 Guernsey Grammar School

370 Architect's Elevation of Grammar School

Europa. Modern Architecture

(Des R. Reed. Litho Cartor)

1987 (5 May). Perf 13×13½ (C).

394	**367**	15p. multicoloured	25	20
		a. Horiz pair. Nos. 394/5	75	75
395	**368**	15p. multicoloured	25	20
396	**369**	22p. multicoloured	30	35
		a. Horiz pair. Nos. 396/7	1·20	1·20
397	**370**	22p. multicoloured	30	35
394/7 *Set of 4*			1·70	1·70
First Day Cover				2·20
Presentation Pack			2·50	

Plate Nos.: Both values 1A, 1B, 1C, 1D. (each ×4).
Sheets: 20 (4×5), the two designs for each value printed together, *se-tenant*, in horizontal pairs throughout the sheets.
Quantities sold: 15p. 595,661 pairs; 22p. 434,886 pairs.
Withdrawn: 4.5.88.

Coil Stamps

(Photo Harrison)

1987 (15 May)–**88**. As Nos. 306, 306*b*, 309 and 309*c*, but smaller., 22×18 mm (11p., 16p.) or 18×22 mm (12p., 15p.). Perf 14×14½ (11p., 16p.) or 14½×14 (12p., 15p.), all comb.

398	**274**	11p. multicoloured (a)	50	50
398*a*	**275**	12p. multicoloured (b)	40	40
399	**278**	15p. multicoloured (a)	60	60
399*a*	**279**	16p. multicoloured (b)	50	50
398/9*a* *Set of 4*			1·70	1·70
First Day Covers (2)				12·00

Printings: (a) 15.5.87; (b) 28.3.88.
Coils: Rolls of 1000 (a) or 500 (b).
Withdrawn: 26.12.89 11p., 15p.; 22.5.92 12p., 16p.

371 Sir Edmund Andros and La Plaiderie, Guernsey

372 Governor's Palace, Virginia

373 Governor Andros in Boston

374 Map of New Amsterdam (New York), 1661

350th Birth Anniversary of Sir Edmund Andros (colonial administrator)

(Des B. Sanders. Photo Courvoisier)

1987 (7 July). Granite paper. Perf 12 (C).

400	**371**	15p. multicoloured	30	15
401	**372**	29p. multicoloured	80	60
402	**373**	31p. multicoloured	85	75
403	**374**	34p. multicoloured	1·10	1·00
400/3 *Set of 4*			2·50	2·20
First Day Cover				3·00
Presentation Pack			3·25	
Set of 4 Gutter Pairs			5·00	

Cylinder Nos.: All values A1–1–1–1–1–1, B1–1–1–1–1–1.
Sheets: 40 (2 panes 5×4).
Quantites sold: 15p. 707,843; 29p. 129,462; 31p. 136,308; 34p. 129,527.
Withdrawn: 6.7.88.

375 The Jester's warning to Young William

376 Hastings Battlefield

377 Norman Soldier with Pennant

378 William the Conqueror

379 Queen Matilda and Abbaye aux Dames, Caen

380 William's Coronation Regaila and Halley's Comet

900th Death Anniversary of William the Conqueror

(Des P. le Vasseur. Litho Cartor)

1987 (9 Sept). Perf 13½×14 (C).

404	**375**	11p. multicoloured	20	15
405	**376**	15p. multicoloured	30	25
		a. Horiz pair. Nos. 405/6	60	60
406	**377**	15p. multicoloured	30	25
407	**378**	22p. multicoloured	60	60
		a. Horiz pair. Nos. 407/8	1·20	1·20
408	**379**	22p. multicoloured	60	60
409	**380**	34p. multicoloured	1·00	1·10
404/9 *Set of 6*			2·75	2·75
First Day Cover				3·00
Presentation Pack			3·75	
Set of 4 Gutter Pairs			5·50	

Plate Nos.: All values 1A, 1B, 1C, 1D. (each ×4).
Sheets: 40 (2 panes 4×5), the two designs for the 15p. and 22p. values were printed together,*se-tenant*, in horizontal pairs throughout the sheets.
Imprint: Bottom, left-hand margin.
Quantities sold: 11p. 639,904; 15p. 241,572 pairs; 22p. 142,718 pairs; 34p. 131,655.
Withdrawn: 8.9.88.

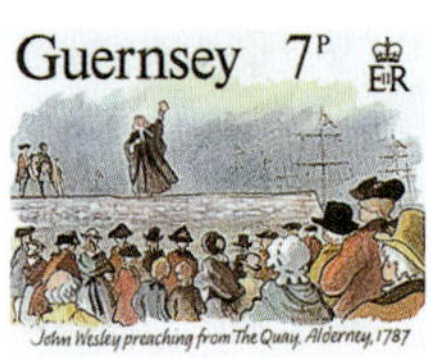

381 John Wesley preaching on the Quay, Alderney

382 Preaching at Mon Plaisir, St. Peter Port

383 Preaching at Assembly Rooms

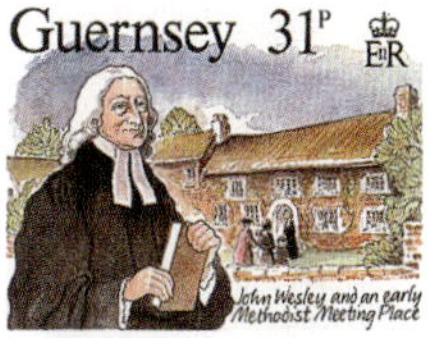

384 Wesley and La Ville Baudu (early Methodist meeting place)

385 Wesley and first Methodist Chapel, St. Peter Port

Bicentenary of John Wesley's Visit to Guernsey

(Des R. Geary. Litho Questa)

1987 (17 Nov). Perf 14½ (C).

410	**381**	7p. multicoloured	20	15
411	**382**	15p. multicoloured	25	25
412	**383**	29p. multicoloured	80	75
413	**384**	31p. multicoloured	90	85
414	**385**	34p. multicoloured	90	85
410/14 *Set of 5*			2·75	2·50
First Day Cover				3·00
Presentation Pack			3·75	
Set of 5 Gutter Pairs			5·50	

Plate Nos.: All values 1A, 1B, 1C, 1D. (each ×4).
Sheets: 50 (2 panes 5×5).
Imprint: Bottom, right-hand margin of each pane.
Quantities sold: 7p. 762,772; 15p. 887,797; 29p. 122,322; 31p. 126,591; 34p. 125,863.
Withdrawn: 16.11.88.

Yearbook 1987

1987 (Dec). Comprises Nos. **MS**393/7, 400/14 and A32/6.

Yearbook	37·00

Withdrawn: 31.12.88.

386 *Golden Spur* off St. Sampson's Harbour

387 Entering Hong Kong Harbour

388 Anchored off Macao

389 In China Tea Race

390 *Golden Spur* and Map showing Voyage of 1872–74

Guernsey Shipping (2nd series). *Golden Spur* (full-rigged ship)

(Des R. Granger Barrett. Litho B.D.T.)

1988 (9 Feb). Perf 13½ (C).

415	**386**	11p. multicoloured	25	25
416	**387**	15p. multicoloured	35	35
417	**388**	29p. multicoloured	1·00	1·00
418	**389**	31p. multicoloured	1·00	1·00
419	**390**	34p. multicoloured	1·20	1·20
415/19 *Set of 5*			3·00	3·00
First Day Cover				3·00
Presentation Pack			3·50	
Set of 5 Gutter Pairs			6·50	

Plate Nos.: All values 1A, 1B, 1C, 1D. (each ×4).
Sheets: 50 (2 panes 5×5).
Imprint: Central, side margins of each pane.
Quantities sold: 11p. 213,291; 15p. 214,048; 29p. 136,246; 31p. 143,815; 34p. 141,177.
Withdrawn: 8.2.89.

391 Rowing Boat and Bedford 'Rascal' Mail Van

392 Rowing Boat and Vickers Viscount 800 Mail Plane

393 Postman on Bicycle and Horse-drawn Carriages, Sark

394 Postmen on Bicycles and Carriage

Europa. Transport and Communications

(Des C. Abbott. Litho Questa)

1988 (10 May). Perf 14½ (C).

420	**391**	16p. multicoloured	35	35
		a. Horiz pair. Nos. 420/1	80	70
421	**392**	16p. multicoloured	35	35
422	**393**	22p. multicoloured	70	70
		a. Horiz pair. Nos. 422/3	1·40	1·40
423	**394**	22p. multicoloured	70	70
420/3 *Set of 4*			2·00	1·90
First Day Cover				2·20
Presentation Pack			2·50	

Plate Nos.: Both values 1A, 1B, 1C, 1D. (each ×5).
Sheets: 20 (4×5), the two designs for each value printed together, *se-tenant*, in horizontal pairs throughout the sheets.
Imprint: Top, right-hand margin.
Quantities sold: 16p. 387,699 pairs: 22p. 359,634 pairs.
Withdrawn: 9.5.89.

395 Frederick Corbin Lukis and Lukis House, St. Peter Port

396 Natural History Books and Reconstructed Pot

397 Lukis directing Excavation of Le Creux ès Faies and Prehistoric Beaker

398 Lukis House Observatory and Garden

399 Prehistoric Artifacts

Birth Bicentenary of Frederick Corbin Lukis (archaeologist)

(Des Wendy Bramall, Photo Courvoisier)

1988 (12 July). Granite paper. Perf 12½ (C).

424	**395**	12p. multicoloured	25	25
425	**396**	16p. multicoloured	30	25
426	**397**	29p. multicoloured	90	85
427	**398**	31p. multicoloured	90	85
428	**399**	34p. multicoloured	90	90
424/8 *Set of 5*			2·50	2·50
First Day Cover				3·00
Presentation Pack			3·50	
Set of 5 Gutter Pairs			5·00	

Cylinder Nos.: 29p., 34p. A1–1–1–1, B1–1–1–1, C1–1–1–1, D1–1–1–1; others A1–1–1–1–1, B1–1–1–1–1, C1–1–1–1–1, D1–1–1–1–1.
Sheets: 40 (2 panes 5×4).
Quantities sold: 12p. 634,056; 16p. 510,713; 29p. 120,538; 31p. 114,192; 34p. 134,358.
Withdrawn: 11.7.89.

400 *Cougar* , *Rocky* and *Annabella* (power-boats) and Westland Wessex Rescue Helicopter off Jethou

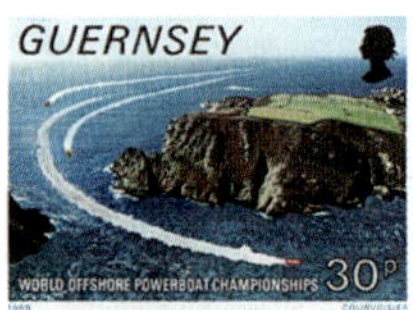

401 *Paul Picot* and other Powerboats in Gouliot Passage

402 Start of Race at St. Peter Port

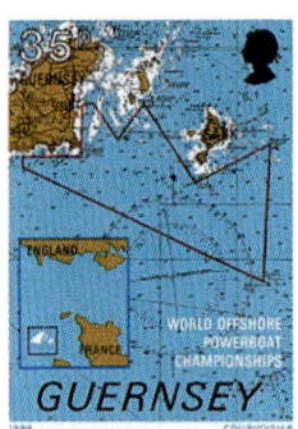

403 Admiralty Chart showing Course

World Offshore Powerboat Championships

(Des and photo Courvoisier)

1988 (6 Sept). Granite paper. Perf 12 (C).

429	**400**	16p. multicoloured	35	25
430	**401**	30p. multicoloured	85	85
431	**402**	32p. multicoloured	1·00	90
432	**403**	35p. multicoloured	1·10	1·00
429/32 *Set of 4*			2·50	2·50
First Day Cover				3·00
Presentation Pack			3·00	
Set of 4 Gutter Pairs			5·00	

Cylinder Nos.: 16p., 32p. A1–1–1–1, B1–1–1–1; 30p., 35p. C1–1–1–1, D1–1–1–1.
Sheets: 40 (2 panes 5×4) 16p., 30p. or (2 panes 4×5) others.
Quantities sold: 16p. 582,190; 30p. 127,183; 32p. 166,804; 35p. 128,552.
Withdrawn: 5.9.89.

404 Joshua Gosselin and Herbarium

405 Hares-tail Grass

406 Dried Hares-tail Grass

407 Variegated Catchfly

408 Dried Variegated Catchfly

409 Rock Sea Lavender

Bicentenary of Joshua Gosselin's *Flora Sarniensis*

(Des M. Oxenham. Litho Cartor)

1988 (15 Nov). Perf 13½×14 (C).

433	**404**	12p. multicoloured	25	25
434	**405**	16p. multicoloured	40	35
		a. Horiz pair. Nos. 434/5	80	70
435	**406**	16p. multicoloured	40	35
436	**407**	23p. multicoloured	55	50
		a. Horiz pair. Nos. 436/7	1·10	1·00
437	**408**	23p. multicoloured	55	50
438	**409**	35p. multicoloured	1·00	1·00
433/8 *Set of 6*			2·50	2·50
First Day Cover				3·00
Presentation Pack			3·00	
Set of 4 Gutter Pairs			6·00	

Plate Nos.: All values 1A, 1B, 1C, 1D. (each ×4).
Sheets: 40 (2 panes 4×5), the two designs for the 16p. and 23p values printed together, *se-tenant*, in horizontal pairs throughout the sheets.
Imprint: Bottom, left-hand margin.
Quantities sold: 12p. 562,702; 16p. 378,679 pairs; 23p. 141,152 pairs; 35p. 133,205.
Withdrawn: 14.11.89.

410 Coutances Cathedral, France

411 Interior of Notre Dame du Rosaire Church, Guernsey

412 Stained Glass, St. Sampson's Church, Guernsey

413 Dol-de-Bretagne Cathedral, France

414 Bishops Throne, Town Church, Guernsey

415 Winchester Cathedral

416 St. John's Cathedral, Portsmouth

417 High Altar St. Joseph's Church, Guernsey

418 Mont Saint–Michel, France

419 Chancel, Vale Church, Guernsey

420 Lychgate, Forest Church, Guernsey

421 Marmoutier Abbey, France

Christmas. Ecclesiastical Links

(Des R. Downer. Litho Questa)

1988 (15 Nov). Perf 14½ (C).

439	**410**	8p. multicoloured	20	10
		a. Sheetlet of 12. Nos. 439/50	2·20	2·20
440	**411**	8p. multicoloured	20	10
441	**412**	8p. multicoloured	20	10
442	**413**	8p. multicoloured	20	10
443	**414**	8p. multicoloured	20	10
444	**415**	8p. multicoloured	20	10
445	**416**	8p. multicoloured	20	10
446	**417**	8p. multicoloured	20	10
447	**418**	8p. multicoloured	20	10
448	**419**	8p. multicoloured	20	10
449	**420**	8p. multicoloured	20	10
450	**421**	8p. multicoloured	20	10
439/50 *Set of 12*			2·20	2·20
First Day Cover				2·75
Presentation Pack			3·00	

Sheets : 12 (4×3) containing Nos. 439/50 *se-tenant*.
Imprint: Bottom, left-hand margin.
Quantity sold: 185,939 sheetlets.
Withdrawn: 14.11.89.

1988 (Dec). Comprises Nos. 306*b*, 309*c* and 415/50.

Yearbook	37·00

Withdrawn: 31.12.89.

Yearbook 1988

422 Lé (Tip Cat)

423 Girl with Cobo Alice Doll

424 Lé Colimachaön (hopscotch)

Europa. Children's Toys and Games

(Des P. le Vasseur. Litho Cartor)

1989 (28 Feb). Perf 13½ (C).

451	**422**	12p. multicoloured	25	20
452	**423**	16p. multicoloured	40	40
453	**424**	23p. multicoloured	80	85
451/3 *Set of 3*			1·20	1·20
First Day Cover				1·60
Presentation Pack			1·90	

Plate Nos.: All values 1A, 1B, 1C (each ×4).
Sheets: 20 (4×5).
Imprint: Top, right-hand margin.
Quantities sold: 12p. 839,111; 16p. 829,156; 23p. 448,761.
Withdrawn: 27.2.90.

425 Outline Map of Guernsey

Coil Stamps

(Photo Harrison)

1989 (3 Apr–27 Dec). No value expressed. Perf 14½×14 (C).

454	**425**	14p. ultramarine (b)	60	60
455		18p. emerald (a)	65	70
454/5 *Set of 2*			1·20	1·20
First Day Covers (2)				18·00

No. 454 is inscribed 'MINIMUM BAILIWICK POSTAGE PAID' and No. 455 'MINIMUM FIRST CLASS POSTAGE TO UK PAID'. They were originally sold at 14p. and 18p., but this was changed in line with postage rate rises.

Printings: (a) 3.4.89; (b) 27.12.89.
Coils: Rolls of 500, numbered on the reverse of every fifth stamp.
Withdrawn: 30.6.96.

426 Guernsey Airways De Havilland D.H.86 Dragon Express and Mail Van

427 Supermarine Southampton II Flying Boat at Mooring

428 B.E.A. De Havilland D.H.89 Dragon Rapide

429 Short S.25 Sunderland Mk V Flying Boat taking off

430 Air U.K. British Aerospace BAe 146

431 Avro Shackleton M.R.3

50th Anniversaries of Guernsey Airport (Nos. 456, 458 and 460) and 201 Squadron's Affiliation with Guernsey (Nos. 457, 459 and 461)

(Des N. Foggo. Litho B.D.T.)

1989 (5 May). Perf 13½ (C).

456	**426**	12p. multicoloured	35	30
		a. Booklet pane. No. 456×6	2·00	
457	**427**	12p. multicoloured	35	30
458	**428**	18p. multicoloured	50	50
		a. Booklet pane. No. 458×6	3·00	
459	**429**	18p. multicoloured	50	50
460	**430**	35p. multicoloured	1·00	90
		a. Booklet pane. No. 460×6	6·00	
461	**431**	35p. multicoloured	1·00	1·00
456/61 *Set of 6*			3·25	3·25
First Day Cover				4·75
Presentation Pack			4·50	
Set of 4 Gutter Pairs			6·50	

Each booklet pane has margins all round with text printed at the foot.

Plate Nos.: All values 1A, 1B (each ×4).
Sheets: 50 (2 panes 5×5).
Imprint: Central, side margins of each pane.
Quantities sold: No. 456, 461,080; No. 457, 362,154; No. 458, 436,134; No. 459, 388,274; No. 460, 172,574; No. 461, 149,134.
Withdrawn: 4.5.90.

432 Queen Elizabeth II (June Mendoza)

Royal Visit

(Des A. Theobald. Lithio B.D.T.)

1989 (23 May). Perf 15×14.

462	**432**	30p. multicoloured	75	80
First Day Cover				1·70
Presentation Pack			2·00	

Plate Nos.: 1A (×5).
Sheets: 20 (5×4).
Imprint: Top, right-hand margin.
Quantity sold: 180,900.
Withdrawn: 22.5.90.

433 *Ibex* at G.W.R. Terminal, St. Peter Port

434 *Great Western* (paddle-steamer) in Little Russel

435 *St. Julien* passing Casquets Light

436 Roebuck off Portland

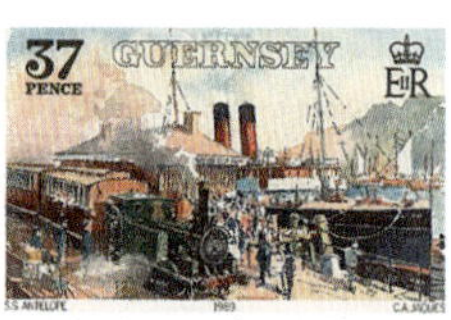

437 Antelope and Boat Train on Weymouth Quay

Centenary of Great Western Railway Steamer Service to Channel Islands

(Des C. Jaques. Litho B.D.T.)

1989 (5 Sept). Perf 13½ (C).

463	**433**	12p. multicoloured	20	20
464	**434**	18p. multicoloured	45	45
465	**435**	29p. multicoloured	70	75
466	**436**	34p. multicoloured	1·00	95
467	**437**	37p. multicoloured	1·20	1·10
463/7 *Set of 5*			3·25	3·00
First Day Cover				4·00
Presentation Pack			5·00	
Set of 5 Gutter Pairs			6·00	
MS468 115×117 mm. Nos. 463/7			3·00	3·25
First Day Cover				7·00

Plate Nos.: All values 1A, 1B (each ×4).
Sheets: 50 (2 panes (5×5).
Imprint: Central, side margins of each pane.
Quantities sold: 12p. 741,870; 18p. 666,520; 29p. 223,570; 34p. 202,570; 37p. 209,020; miniature sheet 74,127.
Withdrawn 4.9.90.

438 Two-toed Sloth

439 Capuchin Monkey

440 White-lipped Tamarin

441 Common Squirrel-Monkey

442 Common Gibbon

10th Anniversary of Guernsey Zoological Trust. Animals of the Rainforest

(Des Anne Farncombe. Litho Cartor)

1989 (17 Nov). Perf 13½×14) (C).

469	**438**	18p. multicoloured	70	70
		a. Strip of 5. Nos. 469/73	3·50	3·50
470	**439**	29p. multicoloured	70	70
471	**440**	32p. multicoloured	70	70
472	**441**	34p. multicoloured	70	70
473	**442**	37p. multicoloured	70	70
469/73 *Set of 5*			3·50	3·50
First Day Cover				3·75
Presentation Pack			4·25	
Stamp-cards (Set of 5)			2·00	7·00

Plate Nos.: 1B (×4).
Sheets: 20 (5×4). Nos. 469/73 were printed in *se-tenant* strips of 5 across the sheet.
Imprint: Top, right-hand margin.
Quantities sold: 148,505 of each value.
Withdrawn: 16.11.90.

443 Star

444 Fairy

445 Candles

446 Bird

447 Present

448 Carol-singer

449 Christmas Cracker

450 Bauble

451 Christmas Stocking

452 Bell

453 Fawn

454 Church

Christmas. Christmas Tree Decorations

(Des Wendy Bramall. Litho B.D.T.)

1989 (17 Nov). Perf 13 (C).

474	**443**	10p. multicoloured	25	15
		a. Sheetlet of 12. Nos. 474/85	2·50	2·50
475	**444**	10p. multicoloured	25	15
476	**445**	10p. multicoloured	25	15
477	**446**	10p. multicoloured	25	15
478	**447**	10p. multicoloured	25	15
479	**448**	10p. multicoloured	25	15
480	**449**	10p. multicoloured	25	15
481	**450**	10p. multicoloured	25	15
482	**451**	10p. multicoloured	25	15
483	**452**	10p. multicoloured	25	15
484	**453**	10p. multicoloured	25	15
485	**454**	10p. multicoloured	25	15
474/85 *Set of 12*			2·50	2·50
First Day Cover				3·00
Presentation Pack			3·50	

Sheets: 12 (3×4) containing Nos. 474/85 *se-tenant*.
Imprint: Central, left-hand margin.
Quantity sold: 229,000 sheetlets.
Withdrawn: 16.11.90.

Yearbook 1989

1989 (17 Nov). Comprises Nos. 309*d*, 451/3, 456/62. **MS**468/85 and A37/41.

Yearbook .... 35·00

Withdrawn: 31.12.90.

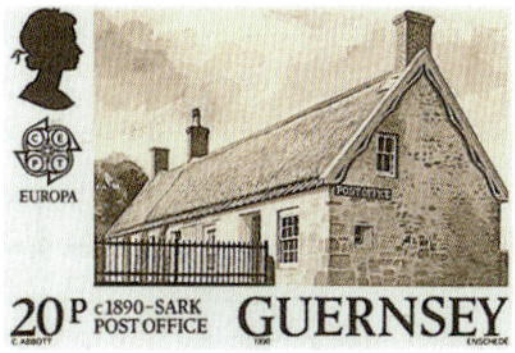

455 Sark Post Office, c 1890

456 Sark Post Office, 1990

457 Arcade Post Office Counter, St. Peter Port, c 1840

458 Arcade Post Office Counter, St. Peter Port, 1990

Europa. Post Office Buildings

(Des C. Abbott. Litho Enschedé)

1990 (27 Feb). Perf 13½×14 (C).

486	**455**	20p. blackish brown, sepia and pale cinnamon	45	45
487	**456**	20p. multicoloured	45	45
488	**457**	24p. blackish brown, sepia and pale cinnamon	60	65
489	**458**	24p. multicoloured	60	65
486/9 *Set of 4*			1·90	2·00
First Day Cover				2·40
Presentation Pack			2·40	

Plate Nos.: Nos. 486 and 488 1A, 1B (each ×3); Nos. 487 and 489 1A, 1B (each ×4).
Sheets: 20 (4×5).
Imprint: Central, side margins.
Quantities sold: No. 486, 498,819; No. 487, 398,759; 488, 495,039; No. 489, 397,759.
Withdrawn: 26.2.91.

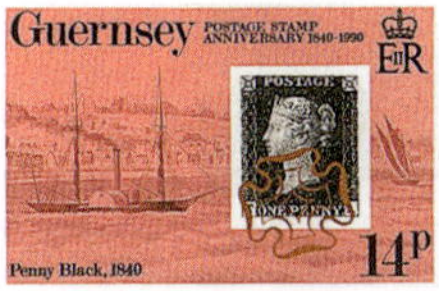

459 Penny Black and Mail Steamer off St. Peter Port, 1840

460 Penny Red, 1841, and Pillar Box of 1853

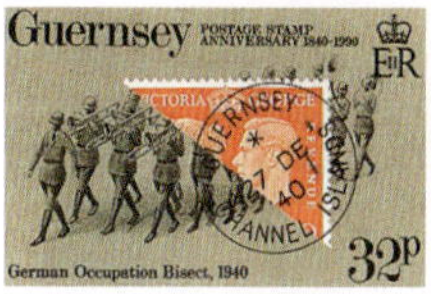

461 Bisected 2d., 1940, and German Army Band

462 Regional 3d., 1958, and Guernsey Emblems

463 Independent Postal Administration 1½d., 1969, and Queue at Main Post Office

150th Anniversary of the Penny Black

(Des Jennifer Toombs. Litho Questa)

1990 (3 May). Perf 14 (C).

490	**459**	14p. multicoloured	35	35
491	**460**	20p. multicoloured	45	45
492	**461**	32p. multicoloured	80	80
493	**462**	34p. multicoloured	1·00	1·00
494	**463**	37p. multicoloured	1·00	1·00
490/4 *Set of 5*			3·25	3·25

First Day Cover		4·00
Presentation Pack	5·50	
Set of 5 Gutter Pairs	6·50	
MS495 151×116 mm. Nos. 490/4	3·25	3·50
First Day Cover		15·00

No. **MS**495 also commemorates 'Stamp World London 90' International Stamp Exhibition. It was reissued on 24 August 1990 overprinted for 'NEW ZEALAND 1990' and sold at this international stamp exhibition in Auckland. (*Price £9 unused, £9·00 used, £20 on first day cover*).

Plate Nos.: 14p., 32p. 1A, 1B (each ×4); 20p., 34p. 1C, 1D. (each ×4); 37p. 1A, 1B, 1C, 1D. (each ×4).
Sheets: 50 (2 panes 5×5).
Imprint: Bottom corner, right-hand margin of each pane.
Quantities sold: 14p. 687,850; 20p. 662,800; 32p. 155,960; 34p. 143,850; 37p. 174,830; miniature sheet 92,701.
Withdrawn: 2.5.91.

464 Lt. Philip Saumarez writing Log Book

465 Anson's Squadron leaving Portsmouth, 1740

466 Ships at St. Catherine's Island, Brazil

467 H.M.S. *Tryal* (sloop) dismasted, Cape Horn, 1741

468 Crew of H.M.S. *Centurion* on Juan Fernandez

250th Anniversary of Anson's Circumnavigation

(Des R. Granger Barrett. Litho Enschedé)

1990 (26 July). Perf 13½×14 (C).

496	**464**	14p. multicoloured	30	30
497	**465**	20p. multicoloured	40	40
498	**466**	29p. multicoloured	80	80
499	**467**	34p. multicoloured	1·00	90
500	**468**	37p. multicoloured	1·10	95
496/500 *Set of 5*			3·25	3·00
First Day Cover				3·75
Presentation Pack			3·75	
Stamp-cards (Set of 5)			2·00	6·00
Set of 5 Gutter Pairs			6·50	

Plate Nos.: 14p., 20p., 29p. 1A, 1B, 1C, 1D. (each x4); 34p., 37p. 1A, 1B (each ×4).
Sheets: 50 (2 panes 5×5).
Imprint: Central, side margins of each pane.
Quantities sold: 14p. 985,850; 20p. 481,400; 29p. 162,800; 34p. 143,500; 37p. 138,450.
Withdrawn: 25.7.91.

469 Grey Seal and Pup

470 Bottle-nosed Dolphin

471 Basking Shark

472 Common Porpoise

Marine Life

(Des Jennifer Toombs. Litho Questa)

1990 (16 Oct). Perf 14½ (C).

501	**469**	20p. multicoloured	45	45
502	**470**	26p. multicoloured	95	95
503	**471**	31p. multicoloured	1·00	1·00
504	**472**	37p. multicoloured	1·20	1·20
501/4 *Set of 4*			3·25	3·25
First Day Cover				4·25
Presentation Pack			3·50	
Set of 4 Gutter Pairs			6·50	

Plate Nos.: 20p., 31p. 1A, 1B (each ×4); 26p., 37p. 1C, 1D. (each ×4).
Sheets: 50 (2 panes 5×5).
Imprint: Top, right-hand margin of each pane.
Quantities sold: 20p. 973,900; 26p. 478,200; 31p. 328,650; 37p. 303,600.
Withdrawn: 15.10.91.

473 Blue Tit and Great Tit

474 Snow Bunting

475 Common Kestrel

476 Common Starling

477 Western Greenfinch

478 European Robin

479 Winter Wren

480 Barn Owl

481 Mistle Thrush

482 Grey Heron

483 Chaffinch

484 Common Kingfisher

Christmas. Winter Birds

(Des Wendy Bramall. Litho B.D.T.)

1990 (16 Oct). Perf 13 (C).

505	**473**	10p. multicoloured	35	15
		a. Sheetlet of 12. Nos. 505/16	3·50	3·25
506	**474**	10p. multicoloured	35	15
507	**475**	10p. multicoloured	35	15
508	**476**	10p. multicoloured	35	15
509	**477**	10p. multicoloured	35	15
510	**478**	10p. multicoloured	35	15
511	**479**	10p. multicoloured	35	15
512	**480**	10p. multicoloured	35	15
513	**481**	10p. multicoloured	35	15
514	**482**	10p. multicoloured	35	15
515	**483**	10p. multicoloured	35	15
516	**484**	10p. multicoloured	35	15
505/16 *Set of 12*			3·50	3·25
First Day Cover				3·50
Presentation Pack			3·75	

Sheets: 12 (3×4) containing Nos. 505/16 *se-tenant*.
Imprint: Central, left-hand margin.
Quantity sold: 237,602 sheetlets.
Withdrawn: 15.10.91.

Yearbook 1990

1990 (1 Nov). Comprises Nos. 486/9, **MS**495, 496/516, A12*a* and A42/6.

Yearbook	35·00

Withdrawn: 31.12.91.

485 Air Raid and 1941 ½d. Stamp

486 1941 1d. Stamp

487 1944 2½d. Stamp

50th Anniversary of First Guernsey Stamps

(Des C. Abbott. Litho B.D.T.)

1991 (18 Feb). Perf 13½ (C).

517	**485**	37p. multicoloured	1·00	1·10
		a. Booklet pane. Nos. 517/19	4·00	
518	**486**	53p. multicoloured	1·30	1·50
519	**487**	57p. multicoloured	1·30	1·50
517/19 *Set of 3*			3·25	3·75
First Day Cover				4·00
Presentation Pack			4·25	
Set of 3 Gutter Pairs			6·50	

Booklet pane No. 517a exists in three versions, which differ in the order of the stamps from left to right and in the information printed on the pane margins.

Plate Nos.: 37p., 53p. 1A, 1B (each ×4); 57p. 1A, 1B, 1C, 1D. (each ×4).

Sheets: 40 (2 panes 5×4).
Imprint: Central, side margins.
Quantities sold: 37p. 260,015; 53p. 250,536; 57p. 250,219.
Withdrawn: 17.2.92.

488 Visit of Queen Victoria to Guernsey, and Discovery of Neptune, 1846

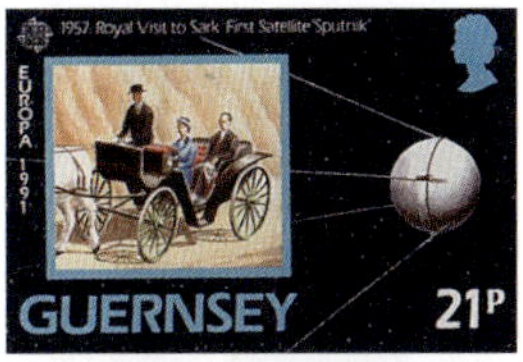

489 Visit of Queen Elizabeth II and Prince Philip to Sark, and Flight of 'Sputnik' (1st artificial satellite, 1957)

490 Maiden Voyage of *Sarnia* (ferry), and 'Vostok 1' (first manned space flight), 1961

491 Cancelling Guernsey Stamps, and First Manned Landing on Moon, 1969

Europa. Europe in Space

(Des Jennifer Toombs. Litho Enschedé)

1991 (30 Apr). Perf 13½×14 (C).

520	**488**	21p. multicoloured	55	50
521	**489**	21p. multicoloured	55	50
522	**490**	26p. multicoloured	65	60
523	**491**	26p. multicoloured	65	60
520/3 *Set of 4*			1·90	1·90
First Day Cover				2·20
Presentation Pack			2·75	

Plate Nos.: Both values 1A, 1B (each ×5).
Sheets: 20 (4×5).
Imprint: Central, side margins.
Quantities sold: No. 520, 390,924; No. 521, 390,834; No. 522, 369,404; No. 523, 370,244.
Withdrawn: 29.4.92.

492 Children in Guernsey Sailing Trust 'GP14' Dinghy

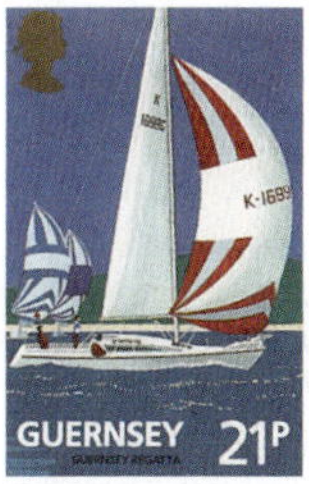

493 Guernsey Regatta

494 Lombard Channel Islands' Challenge Race

495 Rolex Swan Regatta

496 Old Gaffers' Association Gaff-rigged Yacht

Centenary of Guernsey Yacht Club

(Des C. Abbott. Litho B.D.T.)

1991 (2 July). Perf 14 (C).

524	**492**	15p. multicoloured	45	15
525	**493**	21p. multicoloured	70	25
526	**494**	26p. multicoloured	80	80
527	**495**	31p. multicoloured	90	1·10
528	**496**	37p. multicoloured	1·00	1·40
524/8 *Set of 5*			3·50	3·25
First Day Cover				3·75
Presentation Pack			5·00	
Set 5 Gutter Pairs			7·00	
MS529 163×75 mm. Nos. 524/8			3·50	4·00
First Day Cover				10·00

Stamps from No. **MS**529 show 'GUERNSEY' and the face value in yellow.

Plate Nos.: 37p. 1C, 1D. (each ×5); others 1A, 1B (each ×5).
Sheets: 50 (2 panes 5×5).
Imprint: Top corner, right-hand margin of each pane.
Quantities sold: 15p. 711,043; 21p. 708,743; 26p. 188,894; 31p. 158,938; 37p. 138.543; miniature sheet 81,012.
Withdrawn: 1.7.92.

497 Pair of Oystercatchers

498 Three Ruddy Turnstones

499 Dunlins and Ruddy Turnstones

500 Curlew and Ruddy Turnstones

501 Ringed Plover with Chicks

502 Black-headed Gull, Sea Campion and Sea Radish

503 Yellow Horned Poppy

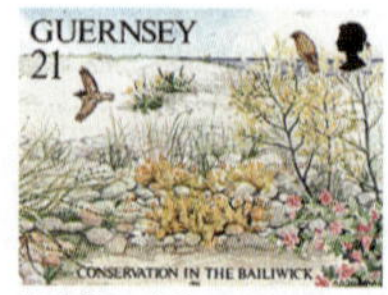

504 Pair of Common Stonechats, Hare's Foot Clover and Fennel

505 Hare's Foot Clover, Fennel and Slender Oat

506 Ruddy Turnstone and Sea Kale on Shore

Nature Conservation. L'Eree Shingle Bank Reserve

(Des Wendy Bramall. Litho Questa)

1991 (15 Oct). Perf 14½ (C).

530	**497**	15p. multicoloured	35	20
		a. Horiz strip of 5. Nos. 530/4	2·75	2·50
531	**498**	15p. multicoloured	35	20
532	**499**	15p. multicoloured	35	20
533	**500**	15p. multicoloured	35	20
534	**501**	15p. multicoloured	35	20
535	**502**	21p. multicoloured	35	20
		a. Horiz strip of 5. Nos. 535/9	2·75	2·50
536	**503**	21p. multicoloured	35	20
537	**504**	21p. multicoloured	35	20
538	**505**	21p. multicoloured	35	20
539	**506**	21p. multicoloured	35	20
530/9 *Set of 10*			4·50	4·00
First Day Cover				5·00
Presentation Pack			5·00	
Stamp-cards (Set of 10)			4·00	10·00

Plate Nos.: Both values 1A, 1B, 1C, 1D. (each ×4).
Sheets: 20 (5×4), the five designs for each value printed together, *se-tenant*, in horizontal strips throughout the sheets.
Imprint: Bottom, left-hand margin.
Quantities sold: 15p. 270,830 strips; 21p. 272,198 strips.
Withdrawn: 14.10.92.

507 'Rudolph the Red-nosed Reindeer' (Melanie Sharpe)

508 'Christmas Pudding' (James Quinn)

509 'Snowman' (Lisa Guille)

510 'Snowman in Top Hat' (Jessica Ede-Golightly)

511 'Robins and Christmas Tree' (Sharon Le Page)

512 'Shepherds and Angels' (Anna Coquelin)

513 'Nativity' (Claudine Lithou)

514 'Three Wise Men' (Johnathan Le Noury)

515 'Star of Bethlehem and Angels' (Marcia Mahy)

516 'Christmas Tree' (Laurel Garfield)

517 'Santa Claus' (Rebecca Driscoll)

518 'Snowman and Star' (Ian Lowe)

Christmas. Children's Paintings

(Litho B.D.T.)

1991 (15 Oct). Perf 13½×13 (C).

540	**507**	12p. multicoloured	30	15
		a. Sheetlet of 12. Nos. 540/51	3·25	3·25
541	**508**	12p. multicoloured	30	15
542	**509**	12p. multicoloured	30	15
543	**510**	12p. multicoloured	30	15
544	**511**	12p. multicoloured	30	15
545	**512**	12p. multicoloured	30	15
546	**513**	12p. multicoloured	30	15
547	**514**	12p. multicoloured	30	15
548	**515**	12p. multicoloured	30	15
549	**516**	12p. multicoloured	30	15
550	**517**	12p. multicoloured	30	15
551	**518**	12p. multicoloured	30	15
540/51 *Set of 12*			3·25	3·25
First Day Cover				3·50
Presentation Pack			3·75	

Sheets: 12 (3×4) containing Nos. 540/51 *se-tenant*.
Imprint: Central, left-hand margin.
Quantity sold: 192,203 sheetlets.
Withdrawn: 14.10.92.

Yearbook 1991

1991 (1 Nov). Comprises Nos. 310*b/c*, 517/51, A12*b* and A47/51.

Yearbook	35·00

Withdrawn: 31.12.92.

519 Queen Elizabeth II, in 1952

520 In 1977

521 In 1986

522 In 1991

40th Anniversary of Accession

(Des C. Abbott. Litho Questa)

1992 (6 Feb). Perf 14 (C).

552	**519**	23p. multicoloured	50	50
553	**520**	28p. multicoloured	65	65
554	**521**	33p. multicoloured	90	90
555	**522**	39p. multicoloured	1·10	1·10
552/5 *Set of 4*			2·75	2·75
First Day Cover				3·25
Presentation Pack			3·25	
Set of 4 Gutter Pairs			5·50	

Plate Nos.: All values 1A, 1B (each ×6).
Sheets: 50 (2 panes 5×5).
Quantities sold: 23p. 773,200; 28p. 479,095; 33p. 212,446; 39p. 219,900.
Withdrawn: 5.2.93.

523 Christopher Columbus

524 Examples of Columbus's Signature

525 *Santa Maria*

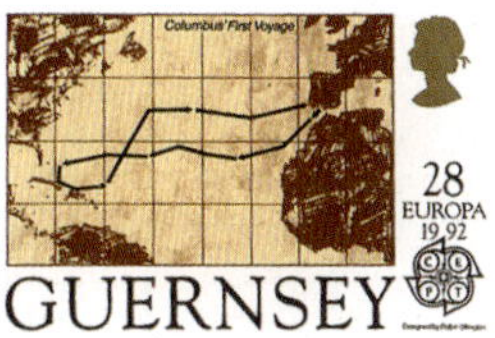

526 Map of First Voyage

Europa. 500th Anniversary of Discovery of America by Columbus

(Des R. Ollington. Litho Walsall)

1992 (6 Feb). Perf 13½×14 (C).

556	**523**	23p. multicoloured	65	60
557	**524**	23p. multicoloured	65	60
558	**525**	28p. multicoloured	1·20	1·20
559	**526**	28p. multicoloured	1·20	1·20
556/9 *Set of 4*			3·25	3·25
First Day Cover				3·75
Presentation Pack			3·75	
MS560 157×77 mm. Nos. 556/9			4·50	5·00
First Day Cover				7·00

No. **MS**560 was reissued on 22 May 1992 overprinted for 'WORLD COLUMBIAN STAMP EXPO 92' and sold at this international stamp exhibition in Chicago. (*Price* 5·00 *unused*, 6·00 used, 9·00 *on first day cover*).

Plate Nos.: All values 1A, 1B, 1C (each ×4).
Sheets: 20 (4×5).
Imprint: Bottom, right-hand margin.
Quantities sold: No. 556, 543,672; No. 557, 575,663; No. 558, 363,124; No. 559, 364,684; miniature sheet 157,166.
Withdrawn: 5.2.93.

527a Guernsey Calves

150th Anniversary of Royal Guernsey Agricultural and Horticultural Society

(Des R. Goldsmith. Litho Questa)

1992 (22 May). Sheet 93×71 mm. Perf 14 (C).

MS561 **527a** multicoloured	2·10	2·00
First Day Cover		3·25
Presentation Pack	2·75	

Quantity sold: 142,549.
Withdrawn: 21.5.93.

528 *Stephanotis floribunda*

529 Potted Hydrangea

530 Stock

531 Anemones

532 Gladiolus

533 *Asparagus plumosus, Gypsophilia Paniculata*

534 Guernsey Lily

535 Enchantment Lily

536 Clematis 'Freckles'

537 Alstromeria

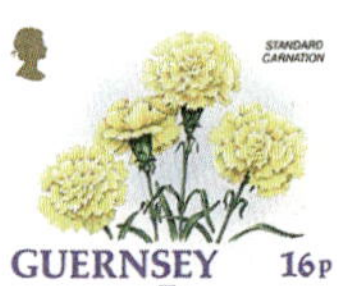

538 Standard Carnation

539 Standard Rose

540 Spray Rose

541 Mixed Freesia

542 Standard Rose

543 Iris 'Ideal'

544 Freesia 'Pink Glow'

545 Lisianthus

546 Spray Chrysanthemum

547 Spray Carnation

548 Single Freesia

549 Floral Arrangement

550 Chelsea Flower Show Exhibit

551 'Floral Fantasia' (exhibit)

Guernsey Flowers

(Des R. Gorringe. Litho Walsall (Nos. 572a, 572ba, 574a, 575a, 576*b* and 577a), Questa (No. 576a), Cartor (No. 582*a*) or B.D.T. (others))

1992 (22 May)–**97**. Perf 14 (£1, £2) or 13 (others), all comb.

562	**528**	1p. multicoloured (b)	10	10
563	**529**	2p. multicoloured (b)	10	10
564	**530**	3p. multicoloured (a)	10	10
565	**531**	4p. multicoloured (a)	15	15
566	**532**	5p. multicoloured (a)	15	15
567	**533**	6p. multicoloured (b)	15	15
568	**534**	7p. multicoloured (b)	20	20
569	**535**	8p. multicoloured (b)	20	20
570	**536**	9p. multicoloured (b)	20	25
571	**537**	10p. multicoloured (a)	25	25
572	**538**	16p. multicoloured (a)	50	35
		a. Perf 14 (ab)	60	50
		ab. Lavender ptg double	£500	
		ac. Booklet pane. Nos. 572a×5 and 574a×3 (a)	4·00	
		ad. Booklet pane of 8 (b)	3·25	
572*b*	**539**	18p. multicoloured (e)	55	45
		ba. Perf 14	55	45
		bb. Booklet pane of 8	4·00	
573	**540**	20p. multicoloured (a)	60	50
574	**541**	23p. multicoloured (a)	60	55
		a. Perf 14	80	60
		ab. Brownish grey ptg double	£500	
		ac. Booklet pane of 8	6·00	
575	**542**	24p. multicoloured (b)	70	60
		a. Perf 14	80	60
		ab. Booklet pane of 8	6·00	
576	**543**	25p. multicoloured (c)	70	60
		a. Perf 14½×15	80	60
		ab. Booklet pane of 4	3·75	
576*b*	**544**	26p. multicoloured (e)	70	60
		ba. Perf 14	80	60
		bb. Booklet pane of 4	3·75	
577	**545**	28p. multicoloured (b)	80	65
		a. Perf 14	1·10	65

		ab. Booklet pane of 4	3·50	
578	**546**	30p. multicoloured (b)	80	70
579	**547**	40p. multicoloured (a)	1·00	75
580	**548**	50p. multicoloured (a)	1·20	90
581	**549**	£1 multicoloured (a)	2·00	1·50
582	**550**	£2 multicoloured (b)	4·00	3·00
582*a*	**551**	£3 multicoloured (d)	6·00	5·00
562/82*a* *Set of 24*			18·00	16·00
First Day Covers (5)				25·00
Presentation Packs(3)			25·00	
*Pack Stamp-cards (Set of*24)			5·00	27·00
Set of 24 Gutter Pairs			40·00	

Nos. 572a, 572ba, 574a, 575a, 576a, 576ba and 577a were only issued in booklets with the upper and lower edges of the panes imperforate and in unfolded booklet panes, available from the Philatelic Bureau and Head Post Office.

For No. 581 in miniature sheets see Nos. **MS**644 (with imprint date '1994') and **MS**681 (with imprint date '1995').

Printings: (a) 22.5.92; (b) 2.3.93; (c). 18.2.94; (d) 24.1.96; (e) 2.1.97, each with appropriate imprint date.

Plate Nos.: £1 1A, 1B (each ×8); £3 1A, 1B, 1C, 1D. (each ×5); others 1A, 1B, 1C, 1D. (each ×6).

Sheets: 1p., 2p., 3p., 4p., 5p., 6p., 7p., 8p., 9p., 10p., 18p., 20p., 40p. 100 (2 panes 10×5); 16p., 23p., 24p., 25p., 26p., 28p., 30p., 50p. (2 panes 5×10); £1, £2, £3 50 (2 panes 5×5).

Imprints: 1p., 2p., 3p., 4p., 5p., 6p., 7p., 8p., 9p., 10p., 18p., 20p., 40p., £1, £2 left-hand corner, top and bottom margin; £3 central, side margins; others top of side margin.

Withdrawn: 31.8.99 1p to £2; 31.8.2003 £3.

552 Building the Ship

553 Loading the Cargo

554 Ship at Sea

555 Ship under Attack

556 Crew swimming Ashore

'Operation Asterix' (excavation of Roman ship)

(Des Studio Legrain. Litho Cartor)

1992 (18 Sept). Perf 13 (C).

583	**552**	16p. multicoloured	45	35
		a. Booklet pane. Nos. 583/7 plus label	3·50	
584	**553**	23p. multicoloured	60	45
585	**554**	28p. multicoloured	80	70
586	**555**	33p. multicoloured	95	90
587	**556**	39p. multicoloured	1·10	1·00
583/7 *Set of 5*			3·50	3·00
First Day Cover				4·25
Presentation Pack			4·25	
Set of 5 Gutter Pairs			7·00	

Booklet pane No. 583a has margins all round and exists with marginal inscriptions in either English, French, Italian or German.

Plate Nos.: All values 1A, 1B, 1C, 1D. (each ×4).

Sheets: 50 (2 panes 5×5).

Imprint: Central, side margins.

Quantities sold: 16p. 904,428; 23p. 743,228; 28p. 308,091; 33p. 281,941; 39p. 291,841.

Withdrawn: 17.9.93.

557 Tram No. 10 decorated for Battle of Flowers

558 Tram No. 10 passing Hougue a la Perre

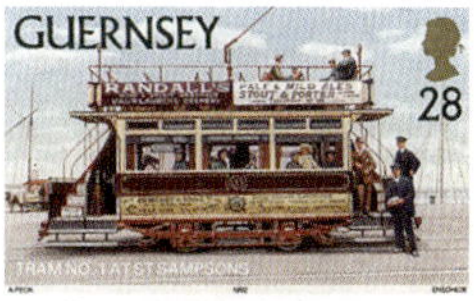

559 Tram No. 1 at St. Sampsons

560 First Steam Tram at St. Peter Port, 1879

561 Last Electric Tram, 1934

Guernsey Trams

(Des A. Peck. Litho Enschedé)

1992 (17 Nov). Perf 13½ (C).

588	**557**	16p. multicoloured	45	30
589	**558**	23p. multicoloured	60	35
590	**559**	28p. multicoloured	75	80
591	**560**	33p. multicoloured	90	1·00
592	**561**	39p. multicoloured	1·10	1·10
588/92 *Set of 5*			3·50	3·25
First Day Cover				4·25
Presentation Pack			4·75	
Set of 5 Gutter Pairs			7·50	

Plate Nos.: 39p., 1A, 1B, 1C, 1D. (each ×6); others 1A, 1B (each ×6).

Sheets: 50 (2 panes 5×5).

Imprint: Central, side margins of each pane.

Quantities sold: 16p. 366,400; 23p. 282,520; 28p. 181,670; 33p 130,920; 39p. 156,170.

Withdrawn: 16.11.93.

562 Man in Party Hat

563 Girl and Christmas Tree

564 Woman and Balloons

565 Mince Pies and Champagne

566 Roast Turkey

567 Christmas Pudding

568 Christmas Cake

569 Fancy Cakes

570 Cheese

571 Nuts

572 Ham

573 Chocolate Log

Christmas. Seasonal Fayre

(Des Wendy Bramall. Litho B.D.T.)

1992 (17 Nov). Perf 13 (C).

593	**562**	13p. multicoloured	30	15
		a. Sheetlet of 12. Nos. 593/604	3·50	3·25
		ab. Gold ptg double		
594	**563**	13p. multicoloured	30	15
595	**564**	13p. multicoloured	30	15
596	**565**	13p. multicoloured	30	15
597	**566**	13p. multicoloured	30	15
598	**567**	13p. multicoloured	30	15
599	**568**	13p. multicoloured	30	15
600	**569**	13p. multicoloured	30	15
601	**570**	13p. multicoloured	30	15
602	**571**	13p. multicoloured	30	15
603	**572**	13p. multicoloured	30	15
604	**573**	13p. multicoloured	30	15
593/604 *Set of* 12			3·50	3·25
First Day Cover				4·00
Presentation Pack			4·50	

Sheets: 12 (3×4) containing Nos. 593/604 *se-tenant*, forming a composite design showing family during Christmas meal.
Imprint: Central, left-hand margin.
Quantity sold: 183,550 sheetlets.
Withdrawn: 16.11.93.

Yearbook 1992

1992 (18 Nov). Comprises Nos. 552/61, 564/6, 571/4, 579/81, 583/604, A12c and A52/5.

Yearbook	35·00	

Withdrawn: 31.12.93.

574 Rupert Bear, Bingo and Dog

574a Rupert and Friends (*Illustration reduced. Actual size*116×97 mm)

Rupert Bear and Friends (cartoon characters created by Mary and Herbert Tourtel)

(Des J. Harold. Litho Walsall)

1993 (2 Feb). Perf 13½×13 (C).

605	**574**	24p. multicoloured	50	75
First Day Cover				2·00
Gutter Pair			1·50	
MS606		116×97 mm. **574a** 16p. Airplane and castle; 16p. Professor's servant and Autumn Elf; 16p. Algy Pug; 16p. Baby Badger on sledge; 24p. Bill Badger, Willie Mouse, Reggie Rabbit and Podgy playing in snow; 24p. Type **574**; 24p. The Balloonist avoiding Gregory on toboggan; 24p. Tiger Lily and Edward Trunk	4·50	4·00
		a. *Black ptg double*		
First Day Cover				4·50
Presentation Pack			6·00	

The 24p. values in No. **MS**606 are as Type **574**; the 16p. designs are smaller, each 25½×26 mm.
Plate Nos.: 24p 1A, 1B (each ×4).
Sheets: 50 (2 panes 5×5).
Imprint: Top left-hand margin of each pane.
Quantities sold: 24p. 523,690; miniature sheet 107,258.
Withdrawn: 1.2.94.

575 Tapestry by Kelly Fletcher

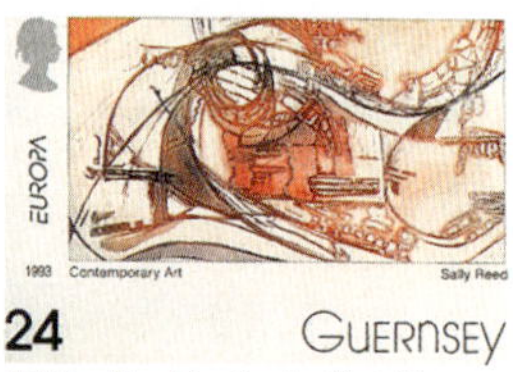

576 'Le Marchi a Passion' (etching and aquatint, Sally Reed)

577 'Red Abstract' (painting, Molly Harris)

578 'Dress Shop, King's Road, (painting, Damon Bell)

Europa. Contemporary Art

(Des B. Bell. Litho Enschedé)

1993 (7 May). Perf 13½×14 (C).

607	**575**	24p. multicoloured	70	70
608	**576**	24p. multicoloured	70	70
609	**577**	28p. multicoloured	80	80
610	**578**	28p. multicoloured	80	80
607/10 *Set of* 4			2·75	2·75
First Day Cover				3·00
Presentation Pack			3·00	

Plate Nos.: 24p. (No. 607) 1A, 1B, 1C, 1D. (each ×5); others 1A, 1B (each ×5).

Sheets: 20 (4×5).
Imprint: Central, side margins.
Quantities sold: No. 607, 289,838; No. 608, 292,450; No. 609, 283,627; No. 610, 280,150.
Withdrawn: 6.5.94.

579 Arrest of Guernsey Parliamentarians, Fermain Bay

580 Parliamentary Ships attacking Castle Cornet

581 Parliamentary Captives escaping

582 Castle Cannon firing at St. Peter Port

583 Surrender of Castle Cornet, 19 December 1651

350th Anniversary of Siege of Castle Cornet

(Des C. Abbott. Litho Questa)

1993 (7 May). Perf 14½×14 (C).

611	**579**	16p. multicoloured	35	35
612	**580**	24p. multicoloured	60	60
613	**581**	28p. multicoloured	75	75
614	**582**	33p. multicoloured	85	85
615	**583**	39p. multicoloured	90	90
611/15 *Set of 5*			3·00	3·00
First Day Cover				3·75
Presentation Pack			3·75	
Set of 5 Gutter Pairs			6·00	
MS616 203×75 mm. Nos. 611/15			3·25	4·00
First Day Cover				10·00

Plate Nos.: All values 1A, 1B (each ×5).
Sheets: 40 (2 panes 4×5).
Imprint: Central, right-hand margin.
Quantities sold: 16p. 253,310; 24p. 289,408; 28p. 125,877; 33p 124,981; 39p. 125,761; miniature sheet 184,308.
Withdrawn: 6.5.94.

584 Playing Cards

585 Fountain Pens

586 Envelope-folding Machine

587 Great Britain 1855 4d. Stamp

588 Thomas de la Rue and Mauritius £1 Banknote

Birth Bicentenary of Thomas de la Rue (printer)

(Des J. Stephenson. Litho (16, 24, 28p.) or recess (33, 39p.) Enschedé)

1993 (27 July). Perf 13½ (C).

617	**584**	16p. multicoloured	40	45
		a. Booklet pane of 4 with margins all round	1·50	
618	**585**	24p. multicoloured	65	65
		a. Booklet pane of 4 with margins all round	2·20	
619	**586**	28p. multicoloured	80	80
		a. Booklet pane of 4 with margins all round	3·00	
620	**587**	33p. carmine-lake	95	95
		a. Booklet pane of 4 with margins all round	3·25	
621	**588**	39p. blackish green	1·10	1·10
		a. Booklet pane of 4 with margins all round	3·75	
617/21 *Set of 5*			3·50	3·50
First Day Cover				3·75
Presentation Pack			4·00	
Set of 5 Gutter Pairs			7·25	

Plate Nos.: 16p., 24p. 1A×4; 28p. 1A, 1B (each ×4); 33p., 39p. 1A.
Sheets: 50 (2 panes 5×5).
Imprint: Central, side margins of each pane.
Quantities sold: 16p. 465,736; 24p. 452,982; 28p. 111,030; 33p. 113,299; 39p. 119,548.
Withdrawn: 26.7.94.

589 'The Twelve Pearls'

590 'Healing Rays'

591 'Hand of God over the Holy City'

592 'Wing and Seabirds' (facing left)

593 'Christ the Healer'

594 'Wing and Seabirds' (facing right)

595 'The Young Jesus in the Temple'

596 'The Raising of Jarius' 'Daughter'

597 'Suffer Little Children to come unto Me'

598 'Pilgrim's Progress'

599 'The Light of the World'

600 'Raphael, Archangel of Healing, with Tobias'

Christmas. Stained Glass Windows by Mary-Eily de Putron from Chapel of Christ the Healer

(Des Jennifer Toombs. Litho B.D.T.)

1993 (2 Nov). Perf 13 (C).

622	**589**	13p. multicoloured	30	15
		a. Sheetlet. Nos. 622/33	3·50	3·25
623	**590**	13p. multicoloured	30	15
624	**591**	13p. multicoloured	30	15
625	**592**	13p. multicoloured	30	15
626	**593**	13p. multicoloured	30	15
627	**594**	13p. multicoloured	30	15
628	**595**	13p. multicoloured	30	15
629	**596**	13p. multicoloured	30	15
630	**597**	13p. multicoloured	30	15
631	**598**	13p. multicoloured	30	15
632	**599**	13p. multicoloured	30	15
633	**600**	13p. multicoloured	30	15
622/33 *Set of 12*			3·50	3·25
First Day Cover				4·00
Presentation Pack			4·00	

Sheets: 12 (3×4) containing Nos. 622/33 *se-tenant*.
Imprint: Central, left-hand margin.
Quantity sold: 150,594 sheetlets.
Withdrawn: 1.11.94.

Yearbook 1993

1993 (2 Nov). Comprises Nos. 562/3, 567/70, 575, 577/8, 582, 605/33, A12d/e and A56/9.

Yearbook	35·00

Withdrawn: 30.12.94.

601 Les Fouaillages (ancient burial ground)

602 Mounted Celtic Warrior

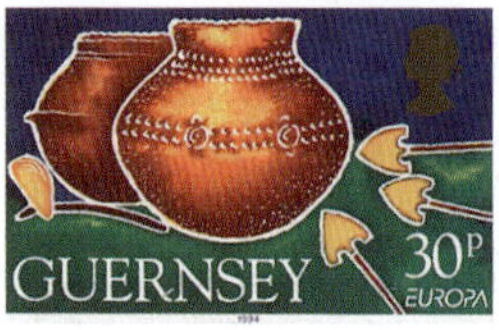

603 Jars, Arrow Heads and Stone Axe from Les Fouaillages

604 Sword, Spear Head and Torque from King's Road Burial

Europa. Archaeological Discoveries

(Des Miranda Schofield. Litho Cartor)

1994 (18 Feb). Perf 13½ (C).

634	**601**	24p. multicoloured	55	55
635	**602**	24p. multicoloured	55	55
636	**603**	30p. multicoloured	80	75
637	**604**	30p. multicoloured	80	75
634/7 *Set of 4*			2·40	2·20
First Day Cover				2·75
Presentation Pack			2·75	

Some sheets of No. 635 were overprinted with the 'Hong Kong '94' emblem on the left margin for sale at this philatelic exhibition.
Plate Nos.: All values 1A.
Sheets: 10 (2×5) with large inscribed margin at left.
Quantities sold: No. 634, 241,910; No. 635, 241,943; No. 636, 237,126; No. 637, 232,797; 'Hong Kong '94' margin opt 31,124 sheets.
Withdrawn: 17.2.95.

605a Canadian Supermarine Spitfires Mk V over Normandy Beaches (*Illustration reduced. Actual size 93×71 mm*)

50th Anniversary of D-Day

(Des N. Trudgian. Litho B.D.T.)

1994 (6 June). Sheet 93×71 mm. Perf 14 (C).

MS638 **605a** £2 multicoloured	4·00	4·25
First Day Cover		6·50
Presentation Pack	5·00	

Quantity sold: 156,793.
Withdrawn: 5.6.95.

606 Peugeot 'Type 3', 1984

607 Mercedes 'Simplex', 1903

608 Humber Tourer, 1906

609 Bentley Sports Tourer, 1936

610 MG TC Midget, 1948

Centenary of First Car in Guernsey

(Des R. Ollington. Litho B.D.T.)

1994 (19 July). Perf 14½×14 (C).

639	**606**	16p. multicoloured	40	40
		a. Booklet pane of 4 with margins all round	1·70	
640	**607**	24p. multicoloured	60	45
		a. Booklet pane of 4 with margins all round	2·75	
641	**608**	35p. multicoloured	90	1·00
		a. Booklet pane of 4 with margins all round	4·00	
642	**609**	41p. multicoloured	1·00	1·00
		a. Booklet pane of 4 with margins all round	4·25	
643	**610**	60p. multicoloured	1·50	1·40
		a. Booklet pane of 4 with margins all round	6·50	
639/43 *Set of 5*			4·00	3·75
First Day Cover				4·25
Presentation Pack			4·75	
Set of 5 Gutter Pairs			8·50	

Plate Nos.: 60p. 1A, 1B, 1C, 1D. (each ×5); others 1A, 1B (each ×5).
Sheets: 50 (2 panes 5×5).
Imprint: Central, side margins of each pane.
Quantities sold: 16p. 279,325; 24p. 238,478; 35p. 114,668; 41p. 116,567; 60p. 117,435.
Withdrawn: 18.7.95.

610a Floral Arrangement (*Illustration reduced. Actual size 110×90 mm*)

'Philakorea '94' International Stamp Exhibition, Seoul

(Des R. Gorringe and M. Whyte. Litho Cartor)

1994 (16 Aug). Sheet 110×90 mm containing stamp as No. 581 with changed imprint date. Perf 13 (C).

MS644 **610a** £1 multicoloured	3·25	3·00
First Day Cover		5·50
Presentation Pack	4·50	

Quantity sold: 78,679.
Withdrawn: 15.8.95.

611 *Trident* (Herm Ferry)

612 Handley Page HPR-7 Super Dart Herald of Channel Express

613 Britten Norman Trislander G-JOEY Aurigny Air Services

614 Bon Marin de Serk (Sark Ferry)

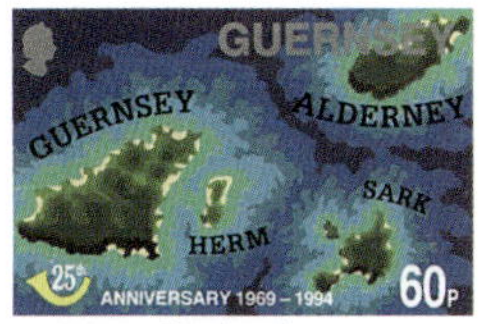

615 Map of Bailiwick

25th Anniversary of Guernsey Postal Administration

(Des A. Copp. Litho Questa)

1994 (1 Oct). Perf 14 (C).

645	**611**	16p. multicoloured	35	30
646	**612**	24p. multicoloured	55	50
647	**613**	35p. multicoloured	85	75
648	**614**	41p. multicoloured	1·00	85
649	**615**	60p. multicoloured	1·40	1·20
645/9 *Set of 5*			3·75	3·25
First Day Cover				3·75
Presentation Pack			4·50	
Stamp-cards (set of 5)			1·60	5·50
MS650 150×100 mm. Nos. 645/9			4·00	4·25
First Day Cover				5·50

Plate Nos.: All values 1A (×5).
Sheets: 20 (5×4).
Imprint: Central, left-hand margin.
Quantities sold: 16p. 218,779; 24p. 188,946; 35p. 129,318; 41p. 139,622; 60p. 140,855; miniature sheet 63,283.
Withdrawn: 30.9.95.

616 Dolls' House

617 Doll

618 Teddy in Bassinette

619 Sweets in Pilar Box and Playing Cards

620 Spinning Top

621 Building Blocks

622 Rocking Horse

623 Teddy Bear

624 Tricycle

625 Wooden Duck

626 Hornby Toy Locomotive

627 Ludo Game

Christmas. Bygone Toys

(Des A. Peck. Litho B.D.T.)

1994 (1 Oct). Perf 13 (C).

651	**616**	13p. multicoloured	40	15
		a. Sheetlet. Nos. 651/6	2·00	2·20
652	**617**	13p. multicoloured	40	15
653	**618**	13p. multicoloured	40	15
654	**619**	13p. multicoloured	40	15
655	**620**	13p. multicoloured	40	15
656	**621**	13p. multicoloured	40	15
657	**622**	24p. multicoloured	75	30
		a. Sheetlet. Nos. 657/62	3·50	4·00
658	**623**	24p. multicoloured	75	30

659	**624**	24p. multicoloured	75	30
660	**625**	24p. multicoloured	75	30
661	**626**	24p. multicoloured	75	30
662	**627**	24p. multicoloured	75	30
651/62 *Set of* 12			5·00	5·50
First Day Covers (2)				6·50
Presentation Pack			5·75	

Sheets: 6 (3×2) containing Nos. 650/5 or 656/61 *se-tenant*.
Imprint: Bottom, left-hand margin.
Quantities sold: 13p. 192,937 sheetlets; 24p 133,416 sheetlets.
Withdrawn: 30.9.95. Comprises Nos. 576, 634/62 and A60/76.

Yearbook 1994

1994 (1 Oct).

Yearbook (softback)	40·00
Yearbook (hardback)	65·00

Withdrawn: 29.12.95.

628 Seafood 'Face'

629 Buckets and Spade 'Face'

630 Flowers 'Face'

631 Fruit and Vegetables 'Face'

632 Sea Shells and Seaweed 'Face'

633 Anchor and Life Belts 'Face'

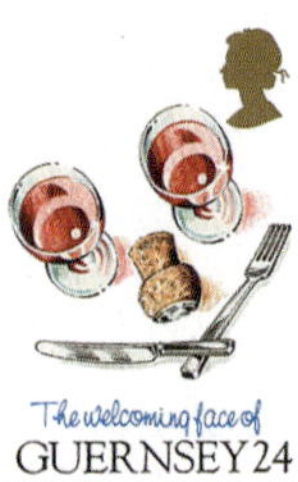

634 Glasses, Cork and Cutlery 'Face'

635 Butterflies and Caterpillars 'Face'

Greetings Stamps. 'The Welcoming Face of Guernsey'

(Des R. Ollington. Litho Questa)

1995 (28 Feb). Perf 14 (C).

663	**628**	24p. multicoloured	60	55
664	**629**	24p. multicoloured	60	55
665	**630**	24p. multicoloured	60	55
666	**631**	24p. multicoloured	60	55
667	**632**	24p. multicoloured	60	55
668	**633**	24p. multicoloured	60	55
669	**634**	24p. multicoloured	60	55
670	**635**	24p. multicoloured	60	55
663/70 *Set of* 8			4·25	4·00
First Day Cover				5·00
Presentation Pack			5·00	
Stamp-cards (set of 8)			1·70	6·00
Set of 8 Gutter Pairs			8·50	
MS671 137×109 mm. Nos. 663/70			4·25	4·25
First Day Cover				8·00

MS671 was used for the make up of stamp booklet SB54.
Plate Nos.: All values 1A, 1B (each x5).
Sheets: 50 (2 panes 5×5).
Imprint: Central, left-hand margin.
Quantities sold: No. 663, 138,328; No. 664, 113,568; No. 665, 138,555; No. 666, 138,474; No. 667, 113,520; No. 668, 113,568; No. 669, 113,573; No. 670, 113,580; miniature sheet 128,702.
Withdrawn: 27.2.96.

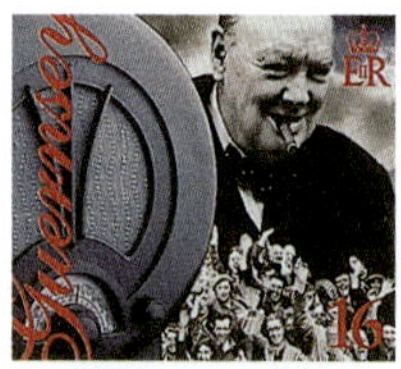

636 Winston Churchill and Wireless

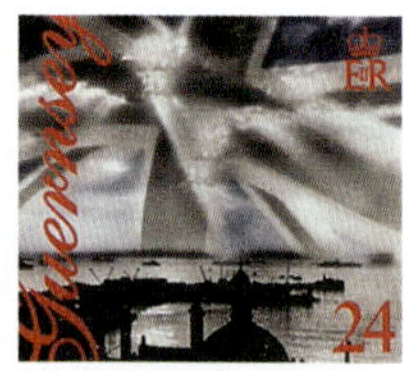

637 Union Jack and Royal Navy Ships off St. Peter Port

638 Royal Arms and Military Band

639 *Vega* (Red Cross supply ship)

640 Rejoicing Crowd

50th Anniversary of Liberation

(Des M. Whyte. Litho Enschedé)

1995 (9 May). Perf 13½×14 (C).

672	**636**	16p. multicoloured	45	30
673	**637**	24p. multicoloured	60	50
674	**638**	35p. multicoloured	90	90
675	**639**	41p. multicoloured	90	90
676	**640**	60p. multicoloured	1·50	1·20
672/6 *Set of* 5			4·00	3·50
First Day Cover				4·50
Presentation Pack			5·50	
Set of 5 Gutter Pairs			8·00	
MS677 189×75 mm. Nos. 672/6			4·50	4·75
First Day Cover				6·00

Plate Nos.: 60p. 1A, 1B, 1C, 1D. (each ×4); others 1A, 1B (each ×4).
Sheets: 50 (2 panes 5×5).
Imprint: Central, side margins.
Quantities sold: 16p. 558,373; 24p. 410,244; 35p 130,472; 41p. 158,351; 60p. 159,394; miniature sheet 86,502.
Withdrawn: 8.5.96.

641 Silhouette of Doves on Ground

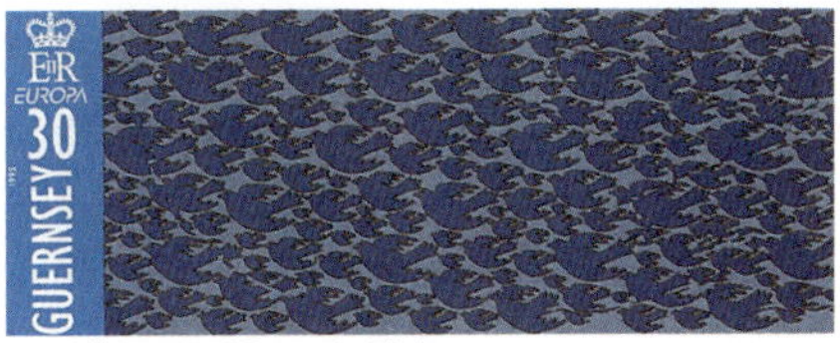

642 Silhouette of Doves in Flight

Europa. Peace and Freedom

(Des K. Bassford. Litho Walsall)

1995 (9 May). Perf 14 (C).

678	**641**	25p. multicoloured	55	65
679	**642**	30p. multicoloured	75	85
678/9 *Set of 2*			1·20	1·50
First Day Cover				2·00
Presentation Pack			2·10	

The designs of Nos. 678/9 each provide a stereogram or hidden three-dimensional image of a single dove designed by D. Burder.

Plate Nos.: Both values 1A, 1B, 1C (each ×4).
Sheets: 10 (2×5).
Imprint: Central, bottom margin.
Quantities sold: 25p. 219,750; 30p. 171,902.
Withdrawn: 8.5.96.

643 Prince Charles, Castle Cornet and Bailiwick Arms

Royal Visit

(Des C. Abbott. Litho Questa)

1995 (9 May). Perf 14 (C).

680	**643**	£1.50 multicoloured	3·00	3·25
First Day Cover				4·00
Presentation Pack			4·00	
Gutter Pair			7·00	

Plate Nos.: 1A, 1B, 1C, 1D. (each ×5).
Sheets: 40 (2 panes 5×4).
Imprint: Central, left-hand margin.
Quantity sold: 140,954.
Withdrawn: 8.5.96.

643a (*Illustration reduced. Actual size* 110×90 mm)

'Singapore '95' International Stamp Exhibition

(Des R. Gorringe and M. Whyte. Litho Cartor)

1995 (1 Sept). Sheet 110×90 mm containing stamp as No. 581 with changed imprint date. Perf 13 (C).

MS681 **643a** £1 multicoloured		3·00	2·75
First Day Cover			4·50
Presentation Pack		3·75	

Quantity sold: 64,768.
Withdrawn: 31.8.96.

644

645

646

647

50th Anniversary of United Nations

(Des K. Bassford. Litho and embossed Enschedé)

1995 (24 Oct). Perf 14×13½ (C).

682	**644**	50p. pale new blue and gold	1·10	1·10
		a. Block of 4. Nos. 682/5	4·25	4·25
683	**645**	50p. pale new blue and gold	1·10	1·10
684	**646**	50p. pale new blue and gold	1·10	1·10
685	**647**	50p. pale new blue and gold	1·10	1·10
682/5 *Set of 4*			4·00	4·25
First Day Cover				5·00
Presentation Pack			5·00	

Plate Nos.: 1A–1A.
Sheets: 36 (6×6). Nos. 682/5 were printed together, *se-tenant*, throughout the sheet with each block of 4 showing the complete United Nations emblem.
Imprint: Central, side margins.
Quantity sold: 448,348.
Withdrawn: 23.10.96.

648 'Christmas Trees for Sale in Bern' (Cornelia Nussbrum-Weibel) **649**

650 'Evening Snowfall' (Katerina Mertikas) **651**

652 'It came upon a Midnight Clear' (Georgia Guback) **653**

654 'Children of the World' **655**

Christmas. 50th Anniversary of U.N.I.C.E.F.

(Adapted M. Whyte from U.N.I.C.E.F. Christmas Cards. Litho B.D.T.)

1995 (16 Nov). Perf 13 (C).

686	**648**	13p. multicoloured	40	15
		a. Horiz pair. Nos. 686/7	80	70
687	**649**	13p. multicoloured	40	15
688	**650**	13p. +1p. multicoloured	40	20
		a. Horiz pair. Nos. 688/9	80	90
689	**651**	13p. +1p. multicoloured	40	20
690	**652**	24p. multicoloured	70	30
		a. Horiz pair. Nos. 690/1	1·40	1·40
691	**653**	24p. multicoloured	70	30
692	**654**	24p. +2p. multicoloured	70	30
		a. Horiz pair. Nos. 692/3	1·40	1·40
693	**655**	24p. +2p. multicoloured	70	30
686/93 *Set of 8*			4·00	4·00
First Day Cover				5·00
Presentation Pack			5·00	

Sheets: 12 (4×3), the two designs for each value printed together, *se-tenant*, in horizontal pairs throughout the sheets, each pair forming a composite design.
Quantities sold: Nos. 686/7, 540,858; Nos. 688/9, 352,684; Nos. 690/1, 365,098; Nos. 692/3, 365,740.
Withdrawn: 15.11.96.

Yearbook 1995

1995 (1 Dec). Comprises Nos. 663/93 and A77/84.

Yearbook	50·00

Withdrawn: 31.12.97.

656 Princess Anne (President, Save the Children Fund) and Children **657** Queen Elizabeth II and people of the Commonwealth

Europa. Famous Women

(Des D. Miller. Litho B.D.T.)

1996 (21 Apr). Perf 14 (C).

694	**656**	25p. multicoloured	55	50
695	**657**	30p. multicoloured	70	75
694/5 *Set of 2*			1·20	1·20
First Day Cover				2·00
Presentation Pack			2·00	

The background designs of Nos. 694/5 continue on to the vertical sheet margins.
Plate Nos.: Both values 1A, 1B (each ×4).
Sheets: 10 (2×5).
Quantities sold: 25p. 224,821; 30p. 268,410.
Withdrawn: 20.4.97.

658 England v U.S.S.R., 1968 **659**

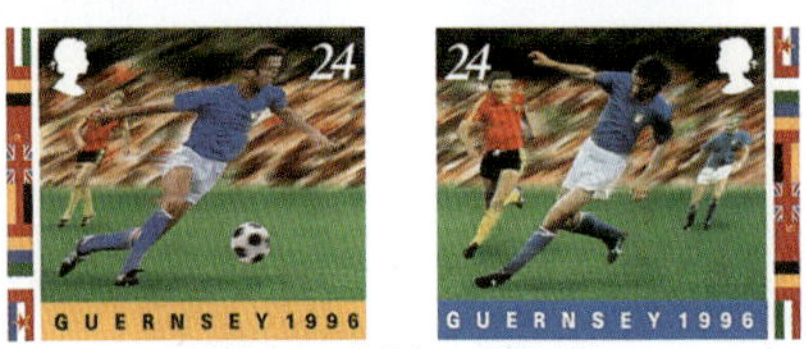

660 Italy v Belgium, 1972 **661**

662 Ireland v Netherlands, 1988 **663**

664 Denmark v Germany, 1992 Final **665**

Final European Football Championship, England

(Des M. Whyte. Litho Questa)

1996 (25 Apr). Perf 14½×14 (C).

696	**658**	16p. multicoloured	55	20
		a. Horiz pair. Nos. 696/7	1·20	1·10
697	**659**	16p. multicoloured	55	20
698	**660**	24p. multicoloured	75	25
		a. Horiz pair. Nos. 698/9	1·50	1·50
699	**661**	24p. multicoloured	75	25
700	**662**	35p. multicoloured	80	40
		a. Horiz pair. Nos. 700/1	1·60	1·60
701	**663**	35p. multicoloured	80	40
702	**664**	41p. multicoloured	95	45
		a. Horiz pair. Nos. 702/3	2·00	1·90
703	**665**	41p. multicoloured	95	45
696/703 *Set of 8*			6·00	5·50
First Day Cover				6·00
Presentation Pack			6·00	
Souvenir Folder (complete sheets)			24·00	

Plate Nos.: All values 1A (×4).
Sheets: 8 (2×4), the two designs for each value printed together, *se-tenant*, in horizontal pairs throughout sheets with illustrated margins, each pair forming a composite design.
Quantities sold: 16p. 386,746; 24p. 369,805; 35p 360,860; 41p. 364,757.
Withdrawn: 24.4.97.

666a Maj-Gen. Brock meeting Tecumseh (Indian Chief) (24p.); Maj-Gen. Isaac Brock on Horseback, 1812 (£1) (*Illustration reduced. Actual size* 110×90 mm)

'CAPEX '96' International Stamp Exhibition, Toronto

(Des A. Peck. Litho Enschedé)

1996 (8 June). Sheet 110×90 mm. Perf 13½ (C).

MS704 **666a** 24p. £1 multicoloured	3·00	2·75
First Day Cover		4·00
Presentation Pack	3·75	

Quantity sold: 93,054.
Withdrawn: 7.6.97.

667 Runner

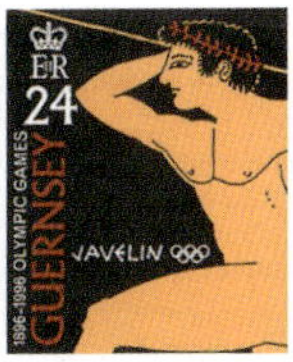

668 Throwing the Javelin

669 Throwing the Discus

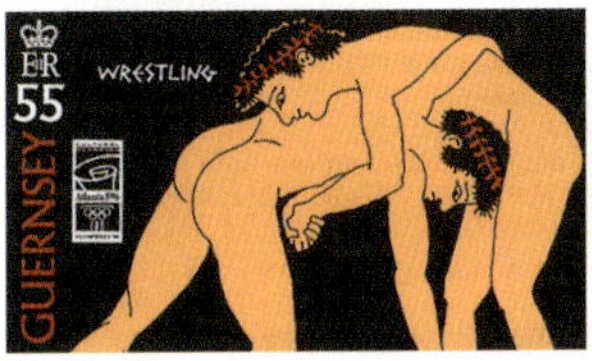

670 Wrestling

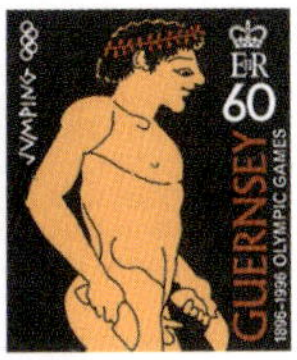

671 Jumping

Centenary of Modern Olympic Games. Ancient Greek Athletes

(Des K. Bassford. Litho Questa)

1996 (19 July). Perf 14 (C).

705	**667**	16p. black, orange-yellow & orge	50	40
706	**668**	24p. black, orange-yellow & orge	95	90
707	**669**	41p. black, orange-yellow & orge	1·10	1·20
708	**670**	55p. black, orange-yellow & orge	1·40	1·50
709	**671**	60p. black, orange-yellow & orge	1·60	1·70
705/9 *Set of 5*			4·50	4·75
First Day Cover				5·00
Presentation Pack			5·00	
Set of 5 Gutter Pairs			9·00	
MS710 192×75 mm. Nos. 705/9			4·50	4·75
First Day Cover				5·75

No. 708 also includes the 'OLYMPHILEX '96' International Stamp Exhibition, Atlanta, logo.

Plate Nos.: All values 1A, 1B (each ×3).
Sheets: 55p 50 (2 panes 5×5); others 100 (2 panes 1035).
Imprint: Central, right-hand margin of top pane.
Quantities sold: 16p. 337,288; 24p. 305,309; 41p. 132,730; 55p. 122,263; 60p. 141,372; miniature sheet 87,045.
Withdrawn: 18.7.97.

672 Humphrey Bogart as Philip Marlowe

673 Peter Sellers as Inspector Clouseau

674 Basil Rathbone as Sherlock Holmes

675 Margaret Rutherford as Miss Marple

676 Warner Oland as Charlie Chan

Centenary of Cinema. Screen Detectives

(Des R. Ollington. Litho Enschedé)

1996 (6 Nov). Perf 15×14 (C).

711	**672**	16p. multicoloured	40	40
		a. Booklet pane. No. 711×3 with margins all round	1·40	
		b. Booklet pane. Nos. 711/15 with margins all round	4·50	
712	**673**	24p. multicoloured	60	60
		a. Booklet pane. No. 712×3 with margins all round	2·30	
713	**674**	35p. multicoloured	85	85
		a. Booklet pane. No. 713×3 with margins all round	2·75	
714	**675**	41p. multicoloured	90	90
		a. Booklet pane. No. 714×3 with margins all round	3·00	
715	**676**	60p. multicoloured	1·40	1·40
		a. Booklet pane. No. 715×3 with margins all round	4·50	
711/15 *Set of 5*			3·75	3·75
First Day Cover				4·75
Presentation Pack			4·75	
Set of 5 Gutter Pairs			7·50	

Plate Nos.: All values 1A, 1B (each ×4).
Sheets: 50 (2 panes 5×5).
Imprint: Central, side margins.
Quantities sold: 16p. 140,740; 24p. 141,567; 35p. 141,953; 41p. 139,648; 60p. 138,363.
Withdrawn: 5.11.97.

677 The Annunciation

678 Journey to Bethlehem

679 Arrival at the Inn

680 Angel and Shepherds

681 Mary, Joseph and Jesus in Stable

682 Shepherds worshipping Jesus

683 Three Kings following Star

684 Three Kings with Gifts

685 The Presentation in the Temple

686 Mary and Jesus

687 Joseph warned by Angel

688 The Flight into Egypt

689 Mary cradling Jesus

690 The Nativity

Christmas

(Des P. le Vasseur. Litho B.D.T.)

1996 (6 Nov). Perf 13 (C).

716	**677**	13p. multicoloured	30	15
		a. Sheetlet. Nos. 716/27	3·50	4·50
717	**678**	13p. multicoloured	30	15
718	**679**	13p. multicoloured	30	15
719	**680**	13p. multicoloured	30	15
720	**681**	13p. multicoloured	30	15
721	**682**	13p. multicoloured	30	15
722	**683**	13p. multicoloured	30	15
723	**684**	13p. multicoloured	30	15
724	**685**	13p. multicoloured	30	15
725	**686**	13p. multicoloured	30	15
726	**687**	13p. multicoloured	30	15
727	**688**	13p. multicoloured	30	15
728	**689**	24p. multicoloured	30	15
729	**690**	25p. multicoloured	30	15
716/29 Set of 14			4·25	4·50
First Day Cover				5·00
Presentation Pack			5·00	
Set of 2 Gutter Pairs (24, 25p)			2·40	

Plate Nos.: 24p, 25p 1A, 1B (each ×4).
Sheets: 13p. 12 (4×3) containing Nos. 716/27 *se-tenant*; 24p., 25p. 100 (2 panes 5×10).
Imprint: 13p. bottom, left-hand margin; 24p., 25p. central, side margins.
Quantities sold: 13p. 1,212,144 sheetlets; 24p. 416,811; 25p. 121,820.
Withdrawn: 5.11.97.

Yearbook 1996

1996 (1 Dec). Comprises Nos. 582*a*, 694/729 and A85/95.
Yearbook .... 60·00
Sold out: 6.99.

691 Holly Blue (*Celastrina argiolus*)

692 Hummingbird Hawk-moth (*Macroglossum stellatarum*)

693 Emperor Moth (*Saturnia pavonia*)

694 Brimstone (*Gonepteryx rhamni*)

695a Painted Lady (*Cynthia cardui*)

Endangered Species. Butterflies and Moths

(Des A. Peck. Litho B.D.T.)

1997 (12 Feb). Perf 14 (C).

730	**691**	18p. multicoloured	55	50
731	**692**	25p. multicoloured	65	60
732	**693**	26p. multicoloured	85	85
733	**694**	37p. multicoloured	1·10	1·10
730/3 Set of 4			2·75	2·75
First Day Cover				3·25
Presentation Pack			3·25	
Souvenir Folder (complete sheets)			25·00	
MS734 92×68 mm. **695a** £1 multicoloured. Perf 13½ (c)			3·00	2·50
First Day Cover				3.75
Presentation Pack			3·50	

No. **MS**734 includes the 'HONG KONG '97' International Stamp Exhibition logo on the sheet margin.
Plate Nos.: All values 1A, 1B (each ×4).
Sheets: 10 (2×5) with designs extending into side margins.
Quantities sold: 18p. 244,917; 25p. 244,899; 26p. 168,917; 37p. 169,909; miniature sheet 147,990.
Withdrawn: 11.2.98.

696 Gilliatt fighting Octopus

697 Gilliatt grieving on Rock

Europa. Tales and Legends. Scenes from *Les Travailleurs de la Mer* by Victor Hugo

(Des M. Wilkinson. Litho Cartor)

1997 (24 Apr). Perf 13½ (C).

735	**696**	26p. multicoloured	55	60
736	**697**	31p. multicoloured	75	65
735/6 Set of 2			1·20	1·20
First Day Cover				2·10
Presentation Pack			2·10	

Plate Nos.: Both values 1A, 1B (each ×4).
Sheets: 10 (2×5) with enlarged inscribed margins at left.
Quantities sold: 26p. 246,098; 31p. 246,080.
Withdrawn: 23.4.98.

698 Shell Beach, Herm

699 La Seigneurie, Sark

700 Castle Cornet, Guernsey

Guernsey Scenes (1st series)

(Litho B.D.T.)

1997 (24 Apr). Self-adhesive. Perf 9½ (diecut).

737	**698**	18p. multicoloured	60	30
		a. Booklet pane of 8	5·00	
738	**699**	25p. multicoloured	70	60
		a. Booklet pane of 8	6·00	

739	**700**	26p. multicoloured	80	75
		a. Booklet pane of 4	4·75	
737/9 *Set of 3*			1·90	1·50
First Day Cover				3·00
Presentation Pack			3·00	

Nos. 737/9 were issued in stamp booklets or as rolls of 100 (18p. and 25p.).

See also Nos. 770/3.

Quantities sold: 18p. 2,789,925; 25p. 2,788,039; 26p. 415,882.

Withdrawn: 31.3.98.

701a 19th-century Shipyard, St. Peter Port (30p.); *Costa Rica Packet* (barque) (£1) (*Illustration reduced. Actual size* 110×90 mm)

'PACIFIC '97' World Philatelic Exhibition, San Francisco

(Des C. Abbott. Litho Questa)

1997 (29 May). Sheet 110×90 mm. Perf 14 (C).

MS740 **701a** 30p. brn-olive & gold; £1 mult	4·00	4·00
First Day Cover		4·50
Presentation Pack	4·50	

Quantity sold: 86,711.

Withdrawn: 28.5.98.

702 Transistor Radio, Microphone and Radio Logos

703 Television, Video Camera and Satellite Dish

704 Fax Machine, Telephones and Mobile Phone

705 Printing Press, Newspaper and Type

706 Stamp, Coding Machine and Postbox

707 C.D., Computer and Disk

Methods of Communication

(Des Miranda Schofield. Litho Cartor)

1997 (21 Aug). Perf 13½×13 (C).

741	**702**	18p. multicoloured	40	40
742	**703**	25p. multicoloured	60	60
743	**704**	26p. multicoloured	60	60
744	**705**	37p. multicoloured	90	85
745	**706**	43p. multicoloured	1·20	1·20
746	**707**	63p. multicoloured	1·50	1·70
741/6 *Set of 6*			4·50	5·00
First Day Cover				5·50
Presentation Pack			5·25	
Set of 6 Gutter Pairs			9·00	

Plate Nos.: All values 1A, 1B (each ×4).

Sheets: 50 (2 panes 5×5).

Imprint: Central, side margins.

Quantities sold: 18p 193,539; 25p. 144,558; 26p. 143,542; 37p. 140,565; 43p. 143,565; 63p. 193,524.

Withdrawn: 20.8.98.

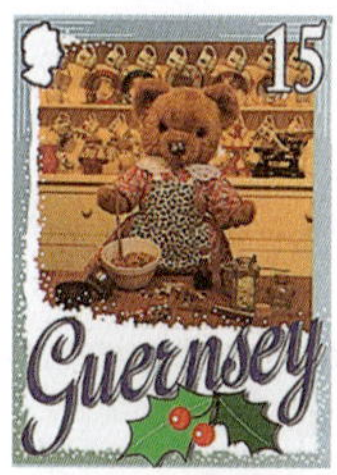

708 Teddy Bear making Cake

709 Teddy Bears decorating Christmas Tree

710 Two Teddy Bears in Armchair

711 Teddy Bear as Father Christmas

712 Teddy Bears unwrapping Presents

713 Teddy Bears eating Christmas Dinner

Christmas. Teddy Bears

(Des Sally Diamond. Litho Walsall)

1997 (6 Nov). Perf 14½×14 (C).

747	**708**	15p. multicoloured	45	45
748	**709**	25p. multicoloured	70	70
749	**710**	26p. multicoloured	70	70
750	**711**	37p. multicoloured	1·00	1·00
751	**712**	43p. multicoloured	1·10	1·10
752	**713**	63p. multicoloured	1·60	1·60
747/52 *Set of 6*			5·00	5·00
First Day Cover				5·50
Presentation Pack			5·25	
Set of 6 Gutter Pairs			10·00	
MS753 123×107 mm. Nos. 747/52			6·00	6·00
First Day Cover				5·75

Plate Nos.: All values 1A, 1B (each ×4).
Sheets: 50 (2 panes 5×5).
Imprint: Central, right-hand margin.
Quantities sold: 15p. 1,793,893; 25p. 443,027; 26p. 143,322; 37p. 118,980; 43p. 119,090; 63p. 118,894; miniature sheet 86,125.
Withdrawn: 5.11.98.

714 Visiting Guernsey, 1957

715 Coronation Day, 1953 (inscr '1947')

716 Royal Family, 1957

717 On Royal Yacht, 1972

718 Queen Elizabeth and Prince Philip at Trooping the Colour, 1987

719 Queen Elizabeth and Prince Philip, 1997

Golden Wedding of Queen Elizabeth and Prince Philip

(Des M. Whyte. Litho Questa)

1997 (20 Nov). Perf 14½ (C).

754	**714**	18p. multicoloured	40	40
		a. Booklet pane. Nos. 754/5, each ×3	3·25	
		b. Booklet pane. Nos. 754/9	5·50	
755	**715**	25p. multicoloured	60	60
756	**716**	26p. multicoloured	60	60
		a. Booklet pane. Nos. 756/7, each ×3	5·00	
757	**717**	37p. multicoloured	90	90
758	**718**	43p. multicoloured	1·00	1·00
		a. Booklet pane. Nos. 758/9, each ×3	8·75	
759	**719**	63p. multicoloured	1·40	1·40
754/9 *Set of 6*			4·50	4·50
First Day Cover				5·50
Presentation Pack			5·25	
Set of 6 Gutter Pairs			9·00	

Plate Nos.: All values 1A, 1B (each ×6).
Sheets: 50 (2 panes 5×5).
Imprint: Central, right-hand margin.
Quantities sold: 18p. 220,866; 25p. 218,707; 26p. 218,240; 37p. 216,772; 43p. 217,837; 63p. 216,874.
Withdrawn: 19.11.98.

Yearbook 1997

1997 (1 Dec). Comprises Nos. 572*b*, 576*b*, 730/59, A70*b*, A72*b*/*c* and A96/109.

Yearbook 55·00

Sold out: 9.99.

720 11th-century (St. Martin)

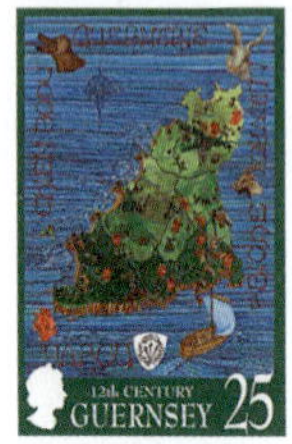

721 12th-century (St. Saviour)

722 13th-century (Vale)

723 14th-century (St. Sampson)

724 15th-century (Torteval)

725 16th-century (Castel)

726 17th-century (St. Andrew)

727 18th-century (Forest)

728 19th-century (St. Pierre du Bois)

729 20th-century (St. Peter Port)

The Millennium Tapestries Project

(Des Sally Diamond. Litho Questa)

1998 (10 Feb). Perf 15×14½ (C).

760	**720**	25p. multicoloured	60	30
		a. Horiz strip of 10 or two strips of 5. Nos. 760/9	5·50	5·50
		b. Booklet pane. Nos. 760/1, each ×2, and 762/3 with margins all round	3·50	
		c. Booklet pane. Nos. 760/1 and 768/9, each ×2 with margins all round	3·50	
761	**721**	25p. multicoloured	60	30
762	**722**	25p. multicoloured	60	30
		a. Booklet pane. Nos. 762/3, each ×2, and 764/5 with margins all round	3·50	
763	**723**	25p. multicoloured	60	30
764	**724**	25p. multicoloured	60	30
		a. Booklet pane. Nos. 764/5, each ×2, and 766/7 with margins all round	3·50	
765	**725**	25p. multicoloured	60	30
766	**726**	25p. multicoloured	60	30
		a. Booklet pane. Nos. 766/7, each ×2, and 768/9 with margins all round	3·50	
767	**727**	25p. multicoloured	60	30
768	**728**	25p. multicoloured	60	30
769	**729**	25p. multicoloured	60	30
760/9 Set of 10			5·50	5·50
First Day Cover				6·25
Presentation Pack			6·00	

Plate Nos.: 1A, 1B (each ×4).
Sheets: 50 (10×5); the ten designs printed together, *se-tenant*, in horizontal strips throughout the sheet.
Imprint: Central, side margins.
Withdrawn: 9.2.99.

730 Fort Grey

731 Grand Havre

732 Little Chapel

733 Guernsey Cow

Guernsey Scenes (2nd series)

(Des Joanna Brehaut. Litho B.D.T.)

1998 (25 Mar). Self-adhesive. Perf 9½ (diecut).

770	**730**	(20p.) multicoloured	45	55
		a. Horiz pair. Nos. 770/1	90	1·10
		b. Booklet pane. Nos. 770/1, each ×4 with margins all round	6·00	
771	**731**	(20p.) multicoloured	45	55
772	**732**	(25p.) multicoloured	50	65
		a. Horiz pair. Nos. 772/3	1·20	1·20
		b. Booklet pane. Nos. 772/3, each ×4 with margins all round	6·00	
773	**733**	(25p.) multicoloured	55	65
770/3 Set of 4			2·00	2·10
First Day Cover				3·00
Presentation Pack			3·00	

Nos. 770/1 are inscribed 'Bailiwick Minimum Postage Paid' and were initially sold at 20p. Nos. 772/3 are inscribed 'UK Minimum Postage Paid' and were initially sold at 25p.

Nos. 770/3 were issued in stamp booklets or as rolls of 100, each roll containing two designs.

Sold out: 6.2001.

734 Fairey IIIC, Balloon, Sopwith Camel and Avro 504

735 Fairey Swordfish, Tiger Moth, Supermarine Walrus and Gloster Gladiator

736 Hawker Hurricane, Supermarine Spitfire, Vickers Wellington, Short Sunderland (flying boat), Westland Lysander and Bristol Blenheim

737 De Havilland Mosquito, Avro Lancaster, Auster III, Gloster Meteor and Horsa Glider

738 Canberra, Hawker Sea Fury, Bristol Sycamore, Hawker Hunter, Handley Page Victor and BAe Lightning

739 Panavia Tornado GR1, BAe Hawk, BAe Sea Harrier, Westland Lynx (helicopter) and Hawker Siddeley Nimrod

80th Anniversary of the Royal Air Force

(Des C. Abbott. Litho Cartor)

1998 (7 May). Perf 13½×13 (C).

774	**734**	20p. multicoloured	50	50
775	**735**	25p. multicoloured	60	60
776	**736**	30p. multicoloured	70	70
777	**737**	37p. multicoloured	90	85
778	**738**	43p. multicoloured	1·00	1·20
779	**739**	63p. multicoloured	1·40	1·50
774/9 Set of 6			5·00	5·00
First Day Cover				5·75
Presentation Pack			5·25	

Plate Nos.: All values 1A (×5).
Sheets: 50 (5×10).
Imprint: Central, side margins.
Withdrawn: 6.5.99.

740a Jules Rimet (first President of FIFA) (30p.); Bobby Moore and Queen Elizabeth II, 1966 (£1.75) (*Illustration reduced. Actual size* 110×90 mm)

150th Anniversary of the Cambridge Rules for Football

(Des A. Peck. Litho Enschedé)

1998 (7 May). Sheet 110×90 mm. Perf 13½×14 (C).

MS780	**740a** 30p., £1.75 multicoloured	4·00	4·00
First Day Cover			5·50
Presentation Pack		5·25	

Withdrawn: 6.5.99.

741 Girls in Traditional Costume watching Sheep Display, West Show

742 Marching Band and 'Battle of Flowers' Exhibit, North Show

743 Prince Charles, Monument and Tank, Liberation Day

744 Goat, Dahlias and Show-jumping, South Show

Europa. National Festivals

(Des Sally Diamond. Litho Enschedé)

1998 (11 Aug). Perf 13½ (C).

781	**741**	20p. multicoloured	45	45
782	**742**	25p. multicoloured	55	55
783	**743**	30p. multicoloured	65	65
784	**744**	37p. multicoloured	85	85
781/4 *Set of 4*			2·20	2·20
First Day Cover				3·75
Presentation Pack			3·50	

Plate Nos.: All values 1A, 1B, 1C (each ×4).
Sheets: 10 (2×5) with enlarged inscribed margin at left.
Imprint: Central, right-hand margin.
Withdrawn: 10.8.99.

745 Outboard Motorboat

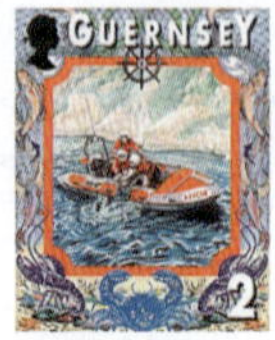

746 St. John Ambulance Inshore Rescue Dinghy

747 Pilot Boat, St. Peter Port

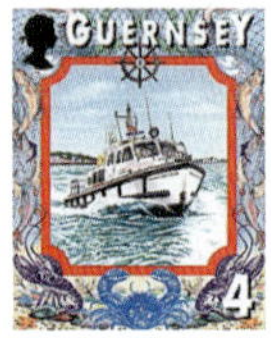

748 *Flying Christine III* (St. John Ambulance launch)

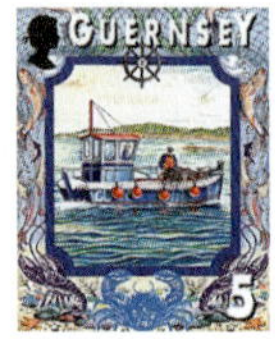

749 Crab-fishing Boat

750 Herm Island Ferry

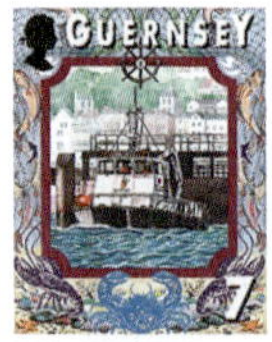

751 *Sarnia* (St. Peter Port Harbour Authority launch)

752 *Leopardess* (States' fisheries protection launch)

753 Trawler

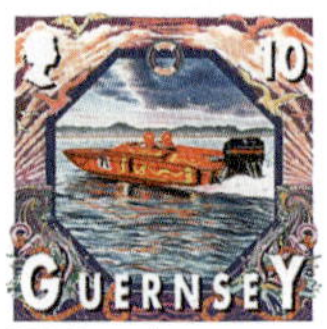

754 Powerboat

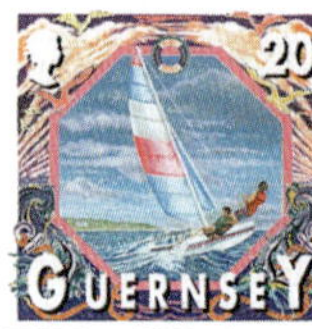

755 Dart 18 Racing Catamaran

756 30ft Bermuda-rigged Sloop

757 Motor Cruiser

758 Ocean-going Sailing Yacht

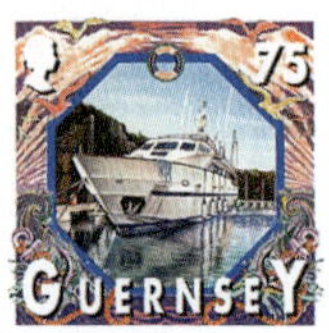

759 Motor Yacht, Beaucette Marina

760 *Queen Elizabeth 2* (liner)

761 *Oriana* (liner)

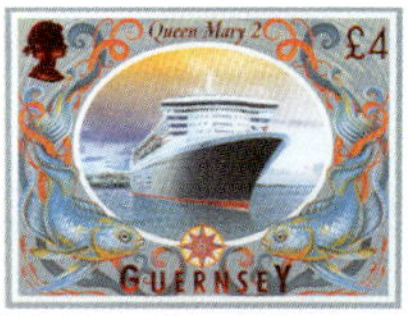

762 Queen Mary 2 (liner)

763 Royal Yacht *Britannia*

Maritime Heritage

(Des M. Wilkinson. Litho Walsall (1p to 75p), litho and embossed Walsall (£1, £3) BDT (£4) or Questa (£5))

1998 (11 Aug)–**2005**. Perf 14 (1p. to 9p.), 14½×14 (10p. to 75p.), 14×14½ (£1, £3), 13½ (£4) or 15×14½ (£5), all comb.

785	**745**	1p. multicoloured (b)	10	10
786	**746**	2p. multicoloured (b)	10	10
787	**747**	3p. multicoloured (b)	10	10
788	**748**	4p. multicoloured (b)	10	10
789	**749**	5p. multicoloured (b)	10	10
790	**750**	6p. multicoloured (b)	10	10
791	**751**	7p. multicoloured (b)	15	20
792	**752**	8p. multicoloured (b)	15	20
793	**753**	9p. multicoloured (b)	20	25
794	**754**	10p. multicoloured (b)	20	25
795	**755**	20p. multicoloured (c)	40	45
796	**756**	30p. multicoloured (c)	60	65
797	**757**	40p. multicoloured (b)	80	85
798	**758**	50p. multicoloured (b)	1·00	1·10
799	**759**	75p. multicoloured (b)	1·50	1·30
800	**760**	£1 multicoloured (b)	2·00	1·80
801	**761**	£3 multicoloured (c)	6·00	5·50
802	**762**	£4 multicoloured (d)	9·00	9·00
803	**763**	£5 multicoloured (a)	13·00	10·00
785/803 *Set of 19*			31·00	28·00
First Day Covers (4)				35·00
Presentation Packs (4)			34·00	
Set of 17 Gutter Pairs (1p. to £3)			25·00	

Printings: (a) 11.8.98; (b) 27.7.99; (c). 4.8.2000; (d) 9.5.2005.
Plate Nos.: £5 1A, 1B, 1C, 1d. (each ×5); £4 1A (×4); others 1A, 1B (each ×4).
Sheets: 1p. to £3.50 (2 panes 5×5); £4 10 (2×5); £5 10 (5×2).
Imprint: Side margins (£5) or centre, left-hand margin (others).
Sold out: 11.2002 (£5).
Withdrawn: 8.2007 (except 20p., 30p., £3 and £4).

Nos. 804/9, T**764/8** are vacant.

769 Modern Tree, Teletubby Po and Playstation

770 1960s Tinsel Tree, Toy Bus and Doll

771 1930s Gold Foil Tree, Panda and Toy Tank

772 1920s Tree, Model of *Bluebird* and Doll

773 1900s Tree, Teddy Bear and Toy Train

774 1950s Tree, Wooden Doll and Spinning Top

150th Anniversary of the Introduction of the Christmas Tree

(Des R. Ollington. Litho B.D.T.)

1998 (10 Nov). Perf 13½ (C).

810	**769**	17p. multicoloured	40	40
811	**770**	25p. multicoloured	60	60
812	**771**	30p. multicoloured	70	70
813	**772**	37p. multicoloured	90	90
814	**773**	43p. multicoloured	90	90
815	**774**	63p. multicoloured	1·50	1·50
810/15 *Set of 6*			4·50	4·50
First Day Cover				5·50
Presentation Pack			5·50	
MS816 160×94 mm. Nos. 810/15			6·00	6·00
First Day Cover				6·00

Plate Nos.: 17p., 25p. 1A, 1B (each ×4); others 1A (×4).
Sheets: 50 (5×10).
Imprint: Central, side margins.
Withdrawn: 9.11.99.

Yearbook 1998

1998 (1 Dec). Comprises Nos. 760/84, 802, 810/16 and A110/23.
Yearbook .... 55·00
Sold out: 4.2001.

775 Elizabeth Bowes-Lyon, 1907

776 On Wedding Day, 1923

777 Holding Princess Elizabeth, 1926

778 At Coronation, 1937

779 Visiting Bombed Areas of London, 1940

780 Fishing near Auckland, New Zealand, 1966

781 At Guernsey Function, 1963

782 Receiving Flowers on Birthday, 1992

783 Presenting Trophy, Sandown Park Races, 1989

784 Opening Royal Norfolk Regimental Museum, Norwich, 1990

Life and Times of Queen Elizabeth the Queen Mother

(Des R. Ollington. Litho Cartor)

1999 (4 Feb). Perf 13 (C).

817	**775**	25p. multicoloured	70	30
		a. Horiz strip of 10 or two strips of 5. Nos. 817/26	6·50	6·50
		b. Booklet pane. Nos. 817/18, each ×2, and 819/20, with margins all round	4·00	
		c. Booklet pane. Nos. 817/18 and 825/6, each ×2, with margins all round	4·00	
818	**776**	25p. multicoloured	70	30
819	**777**	25p. multicoloured	70	30
		b. Booklet pane. Nos. 819/20, each ×2, and 821/2, with margins all round	4·00	
820	**778**	25p. multicoloured	70	30
821	**779**	25p. multicoloured	70	30
		b. Booklet pane. Nos. 821/2, each ×2, and 823/4, with margins all round	4·00	
822	**780**	25p. multicoloured	70	30
823	**781**	25p. multicoloured	70	30
		b. Booklet pane. Nos. 823/4, each ×2, and 825/6, with margins all round	4·00	
824	**782**	25p. multicoloured	70	30
825	**783**	25p. multicoloured	70	30
826	**784**	25p. multicoloured	70	30
817/26 *Set of 10*			6·50	6·50
First Day Cover				6·75
Presentation Pack			6·75	

Plate Nos.: 1A, 1B (each ×5).

Sheets: 50 (10×5), the ten designs printed together, *se-tenant*, as horizontal strips throughout the sheets.

Imprint: Central, side margins.

Withdrawn: 3.2.2000.

785 *Spirit of Guernsey*, 1995

786 *Sir William Arnold*, 1973

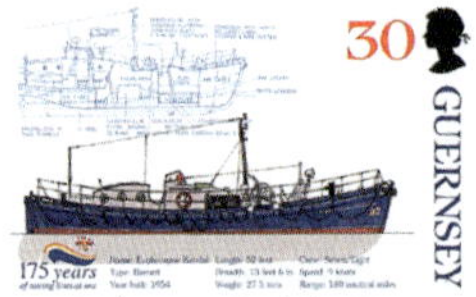

787 *Euphrosyne Kendal*, 1954

788 *Queen Victoria*, 1929

789 *Arthur Lionel*, 1912

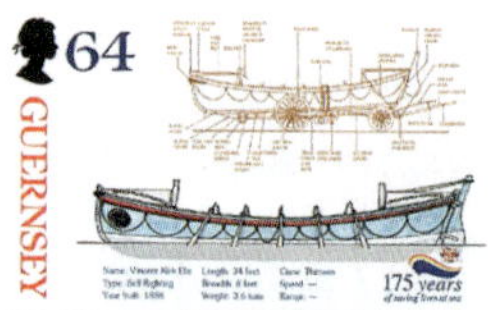

790 *Vincent Kirk Ella*, 1888

175th Anniversary of Royal National Lifeboat Institution

(Des K. Wisdom. Litho Cartor)

1999 (27 Apr). Perf 13½×13 (C).

827	**785**	20p. multicoloured	50	50
828	**786**	25p. multicoloured	60	60
829	**787**	30p. multicoloured	70	70
830	**788**	38p. multicoloured	90	90
831	**789**	44p. multicoloured	1·10	1·10
832	**790**	64p. multicoloured	1·50	1·50
827/32 *Set of 6*			5·00	4·75
First Day Cover				6·00
Presentation Pack			5·75	

Plate Nos.: All values 1A (×5).
Sheets: 50 (5×10).
Imprint: Central, side margins.
Withdrawn: 26.4.2000.

791 Burnet Rose and Local Carriage Label

792 Atlantic Puffin

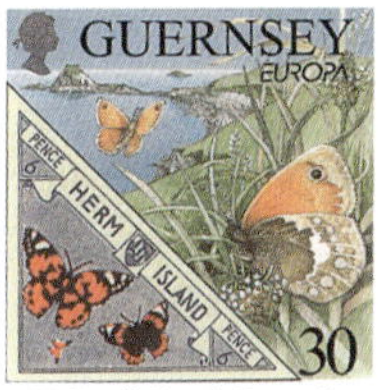

793 Small Heath Butterfly

794 Shells on Shell Beach

Europa. Parks and Gardens. Herm Island

(Des Colleen Corlett. Litho Walsall)

1999 (27 Apr). Perf 13½×13 (C).

833	**791**	20p. multicoloured	50	45
834	**792**	25p. multicoloured	60	75
835	**793**	30p. multicoloured	70	80
836	**794**	38p. multicoloured	90	1·20
833/6 *Set of 4*			2·50	3·00
First Day Cover				4·00
Presentation Pack			3·50	

Plate Nos.: All values 1A, 1B (each ×4).
Sheets: 10 (2×5) with enlarged illustrated margin at left (20, 30p.) or right (25, 38p).
Imprint: Central right (20, 30p.) or left (25, 38p.) margin.
Withdrawn: 26.4.2000.

795 Prince Edward and Miss Sophie Rhys-Jones (*illustraion reduced. Actual size* 93×70 mm)

Royal Wedding

(Des Sally Diamond. Litho B.D.T.)

1999 (19 June). Sheet 93×70 mm. Perf 13 (C).

MS837 **795** £1 multicoloured		2·50	3·00
First Day Cover			4·00
Presentation Pack		3·50	

Withdrawn: 18.6.2000.

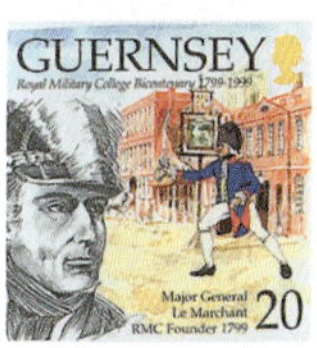

796 Major-General Le Marchant (founder) and Cadet at Sword Drill

797 Duke of York (official sponsor) and Cadet on Horseback

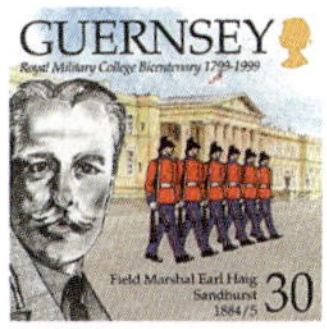

798 Field-Marshal Earl Haig and Cadets on Parade

799 Field-Marshal Viscount Montgomery and Bridging Exercise

800 David Niven (actor) and Rifle Practice

801 Sir Winston Churchill and Tank

Bicentenary of The Royal Military Academy, Sandhurst

(Des R. Ollington. Litho B.D.T.)

1999 (27 July). Perf 14 (C).

838	**796**	20p. multicoloured	50	45
839	**797**	25p. multicoloured	60	55
840	**798**	30p. multicoloured	75	70
841	**799**	38p. multicoloured	90	95
842	**800**	44p. multicoloured	1·10	1·20
843	**801**	64p. multicoloured	1·50	1·75
838/43 *Set of 6*			4·75	5·00
First Day Cover				5·50
Presentation Pack			6·00	

Plate Nos.: All values 1A (×4).
Sheets: 50 (5×10).
Imprint: Lower side margins.
Withdrawn: 26.7.2000.

802 The Nativity

803 Virgin Mary and Child

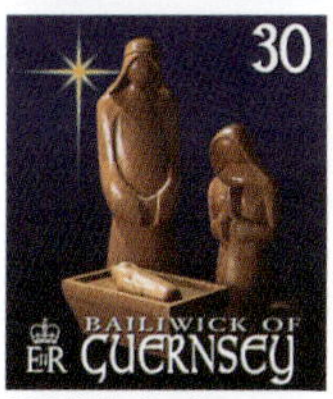

804 Holy Family

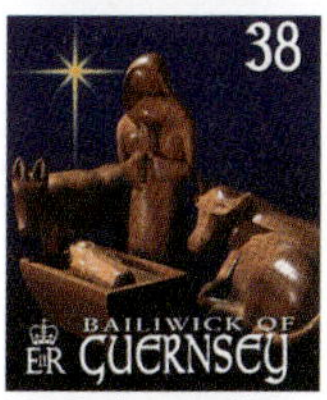

805 Cattle around Manger

806 Adoration of the Shepherds

807 Adoration of the Magi

Christmas. Wood Carvings by Denis Brehaut from Notre Dame Church

(Des Sally Diamond. Litho Questa)

1999 (19 Oct). Perf 14×14½ (C).

844	**802**	17p. multicoloured	45	40
845	**803**	25p. multicoloured	60	55
846	**804**	30p. multicoloured	75	70

847	**805**	38p. multicoloured	90	85
848	**806**	44p. multicoloured	1·10	1·20
849	**807**	64p. multicoloured	1·50	1·70
844/9 *Set of 6*			4·75	5·00
First Day Cover				6·00
Presentation Pack			5·75	
MS850 159×86 mm. Nos. 844/9			5·50	5·50
First Day Cover				6·00

Plate Nos.: All values 1A, 1B, 1C (each ×4).
Sheets: 50 (5×10.).
Imprint: Bottom, right-hand margin.
Withdrawn: 18.10.2000.

Yearbook 1999

1999 (1 Dec). Comprises Nos. 785/94, 797/800, 817/50 and **MS**A124/39.

Yearbook	55·00

Sold out: By 12.2002.

808 'Space Bus' (Fallon Ephgrave)

809 'Children holding Hands' (Abigail Downing)

810 'No Captivity' (Laura Martin)

811 'Post Office of the Future' (Sarah Haddow)

812 'Solar-powered Car' (Sophie Medland)

813 'Woman flying' (Danielle McIver)

New Millennium. 'Stampin' the Future' (children's stamp design competition)

(Litho Questa)

2000 (1 Jan). Perf 14×14½ (C).

851	**808**	20p. multicoloured	60	45
852	**809**	25p. multicoloured	60	55
853	**810**	30p. multicoloured	70	65
854	**811**	38p. multicoloured	90	80
855	**812**	44p. multicoloured	1·20	1·50
856	**813**	64p. multicoloured	1·50	1·75
851/6 *Set of 6*			5·00	5·00
First Day Cover				5·50
Presentation Pack			5·50	

Plate Nos.: All values 1A, 1B (each ×5).
Sheets: 50 (5×10).
Imprint: Lower right-hand margin.
Withdrawn: 31.12.2000.

814 Bristol Blenheim

815 Hawker Hurricane

816 Boulton Paul Defiant II

817 Gloster Gladiator

818 Bristol Beaufighter IF

819 Supermarine Spitfire IIc

60th Anniversary of Battle of Britain. R.A.F. Aircraft

(Des R. Ollington. Litho Cartor)

2000 (28 Apr). Perf 13½×13 (C).

857	**814**	21p. multicoloured	50	50
		a. Booklet pane. Nos. 857 and 859/61	3·50	
		b. Booklet pane. Nos. 857/8, 860 and 862	3·50	
		c. Booklet pane. Nos. 857/9 and 861	3·00	
858	**815**	26p. multicoloured	60	55
		a. Booklet pane. Nos. 858/61	3·50	
859	**816**	36p. multicoloured	95	85
860	**817**	40p. multicoloured	1·00	95
861	**818**	45p. multicoloured	1·10	1·20
862	**819**	65p. multicoloured	1·50	1·50
		a. Booklet pane. No. 862×2	3·00	
857/62 *Set of 6*			5·50	5·50
First Day Cover				5·50
Presentation Pack			5·75	

Plate Nos.: All values 1A (×5).
Sheets: 50 (5×10).
Imprint: Central, side margins.
Withdrawn: 27.4.2001.

820 Guernsey Flag on Kite and '2000'

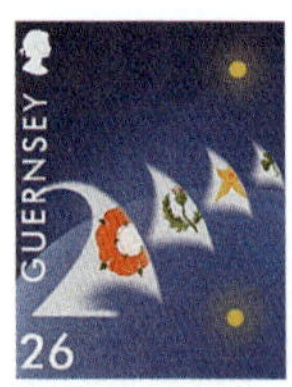

821 Stylized Sails bearing National Flowers

822 'Building Europe'

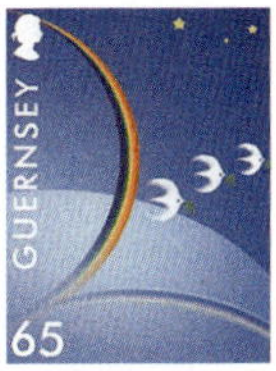

823 Rainbow and Three Doves

Europa

(Des J.-P. Cousin (36p.), KWL (others). Litho B.D.T.)

2000 (9 May). Perf 13 (C).

863	**820**	21p. multicoloured	50	45
864	**821**	26p. multicoloured	60	55
865	**822**	36p. multicoloured	1·00	1·00
866	**823**	65p. multicoloured	1·60	1·75
863/6 *Set of 4*			3·50	3·50
First Day Cover				4·00
Presentation Pack			4·00	

Plate Nos.: All values 1A (×4).
Sheets: 10 (2×5) with enlarged inscribed margin at left.
Imprint: Centre, right-hand margin.
Withdrawn: 8.5.2001.

824 *Iris Stylosa*

825 *Watsonia*

826 *Richardia maculata*

827 *Narcissus bulbocodium*

828 *Triteleia laxa*

829 *Tigridia pavonia*

830 *Agapanthus umbellatus*

831 *Sparaxis*

832 *Pancratium maritimum*

833 *Nerine sarniensis*

'A Botanist's Sketchbook'. Restoration of Candie Gardens, St. Peter Port

(Des Petula Stone. Litho Enschedé)

2000 (4 Aug). Perf 13½×13 (C).

867	**824**	26p. multicoloured	45	30
		a. Horiz strip of 10 or two strips of 5. Nos. 867/76	5·50	6·00
868	**825**	26p. multicoloured	45	30
869	**826**	26p. multicoloured	45	30
870	**827**	26p. multicoloured	45	30
871	**828**	26p. multicoloured	45	30
872	**829**	26p. multicoloured	45	30
873	**830**	26p. multicoloured	45	30
874	**831**	26p. multicoloured	45	30
875	**832**	26p. multicoloured	45	30
876	**833**	26p. multicoloured	45	30
867/76 *Set of 10*			5·50	6·00
First Day Cover				6·25
Presentation Pack			6·50	

Plate Nos.: All values 1A, 1B (each ×5).
Sheets: 50 (10×5). Nos. 867/76 were printed together, *se-tenant*, in horizontal strips of 10 throughout the sheet.
Imprint: Upper side margins.
Withdrawn: 3.8.2001.

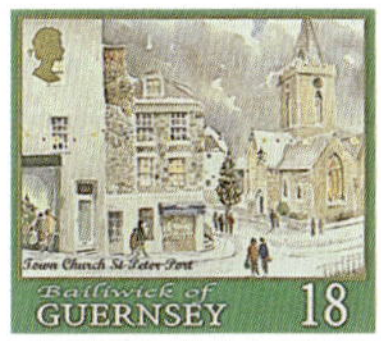

834 Town Church, St. Peter Port

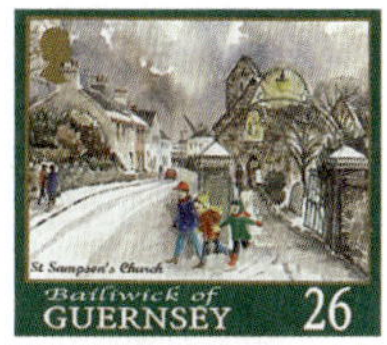

835 Children leaving St. Sampson's Church

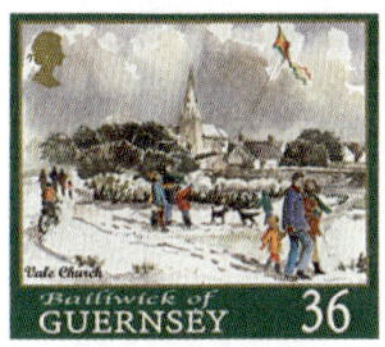

836 Flying Kite by Vale Church

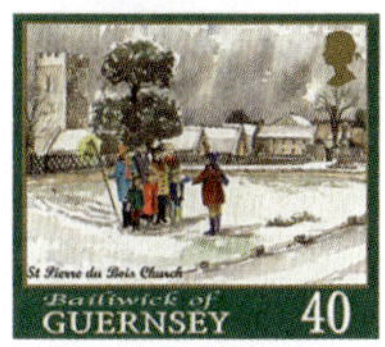

837 Carol singing outside St. Pierre du Bois Church

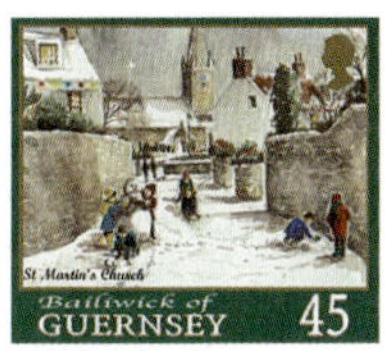

838 Building Snowman near St. Martin's Church

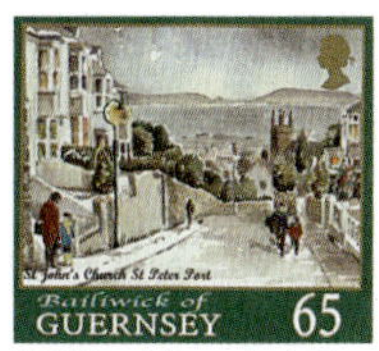

839 Street Scene including St. John's Church, St. Peter Port

Christmas. Guernsey Churches

(Des Gill Brown. Litho Questa)

2000 (19 Oct). Perf 14½×14 (C).

877	**834**	18p. multicoloured	40	40
878	**835**	26p. multicoloured	60	55
879	**836**	36p. multicoloured	90	85
880	**837**	40p. multicoloured	95	1·00
881	**838**	45p. multicoloured	1·10	1·40
882	**839**	65p. multicoloured	1·50	1·75
877/82 *Set of 6*			5·00	5·00
First Day Cover				7·00
Presentation Pack			6·00	
MS883 160×86 mm. Nos. 877/82			6·00	6·00
First Day Cover				8·00

Plate Nos.: All values 1A (×5).
Sheets: 50 (5×10).
Imprint: Bottom, right-hand margin.
Withdrawn: 18.10.2001.

Yearbook 2000

2000 (1 Dec). Comprises Nos. 795/6, 801, 851/83 and A140/61.

Yearbook	65·00

Sold out: By 12.2002.

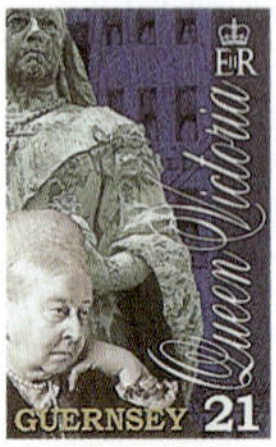

840 Queen Victoria and Diamond Jubilee Statue

841 Letter of Thanks to Guernsey, 1846

842 Statues of Queen Victoria and Prince Albert

843 Stone commemorating 1846 Visit

844 Statue of Prince Albert

845 Victoria Tower, 1848

Death Centenary of Queen Victoria

(Des A. Fothergill. Litho Questa)

2001 (22 Jan). Perf 15×14½ (C).

884	**840**	21p. multicoloured	50	50
885	**841**	26p. multicoloured	60	55
886	**842**	36p. multicoloured	90	85
887	**843**	40p. multicoloured	95	95
888	**844**	45p. multicoloured	1·10	1·10
889	**845**	65p. multicoloured	1·50	1·50
884/9 *Set of 6*			5·00	5·00
First Day Cover				6·00
Presentation Pack			6·00	
MS890 165×80 mm. Nos. 884/9. Perf 14½ (C)			6·00	7·00
a. Imperf			£750	
First Day Cover				7·50

No. **MS**890 includes the logo of the 'Hong Kong 2001' Stamp Exhibition on the sheet margin.

Plate Nos.: All values 1A (×4).
Sheets: 50 (10×5).
Imprint: Central, left-hand margin.
Withdrawn: 21.1.2002.

846 River Kingfisher

847 Garganey

848 Little Egret

849 Little Ringed Plover

Europa. Water, a Natural Treasure. Water Birds

(Des Wendy Bramall. Litho B.D.T.)

2001 (1 Feb). Perf 14×15 (C).

891	**846**	21p. multicoloured	60	40
892	**847**	26p. multicoloured	90	75
893	**848**	36p. multicoloured	1·20	1·50
894	**849**	65p. multicoloured	1·70	1·90
891/4 *Set of 4*			4·00	4·00
First Day Cover				4·50
Presentation Pack			5·00	

Plate Nos.: All values 1A (×4).
Sheets: 10 (2×5) with enlarged inscribed margins at left.
Imprint: Central, right-hand margin.
Withdrawn: 31.1.2002.

850 Cavalier King Charles Spaniel

851 Miniature Schnauzer

852 German Shepherd Dog

853 Cocker Spaniel

854 West Highland White Terrier

855 Dachshund

Centenary of Guernsey Dog Club

(Des A. Peck. Litho B.D.T.)

2001 (26 Apr). Perf 13 (C).

895	**850**	22p. multicoloured	55	50
896	**851**	27p. multicoloured	65	60
897	**852**	36p. multicoloured	90	85
898	**853**	40p. multicoloured	95	95
899	**854**	45p. multicoloured	1·10	1·10
900	**855**	65p. multicoloured	1·50	1·50
895/900 *Set of 6*			5·00	5·00
First Day Cover				6·00
Presentation Pack			6·00	

Plate Nos.: All values 1A (×4).
Sheets: 50 (10×5).
Imprint: Upper right-hand margin.
Withdrawn: 25.4.2002.

856 La Corbiere Sunset

857 Rue des Hougues

858 St. Saviour's Reservoir

859 Shell Beach, Herm

860 Telegraph Bay, Alderney

861 Alderney Railway

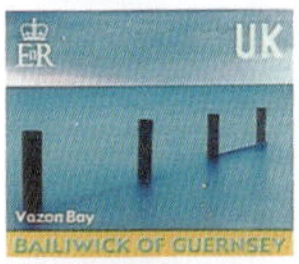

862 Vazon Bay

863 La Coupeé, Sark

864 Les Hanois Lighthouse

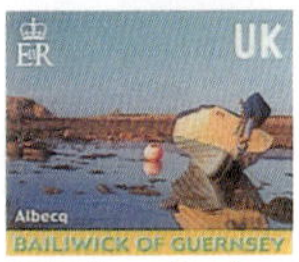

865 Albecq Beach

Island Scenes

(Des Sally Diamond)

2001 (26 Apr). Self-adhesive. Perf 14 (die-cut).

(a) Litho Enschedé (from sheetlets of 10 and booklets)

901	**856**	(22p.) multicoloured	45	50
		a. Sheetlet of 10. Nos. 901/10	8·00	8·50
		b. Booklet pane. Nos. 901/5, each ×2	4·50	
902	**857**	(22p.) multicoloured	45	50
903	**858**	(22p.) multicoloured	45	50
904	**859**	(22p.) multicoloured	45	50
905	**860**	(22p.) multicoloured	45	50
906	**861**	(27p.) multicoloured	55	60
		b. Booklet pane. Nos. 906/10, each ×2	5·50	
907	**862**	(27p.) multicoloured	55	60
908	**863**	(27p.) multicoloured	55	60
909	**864**	(27p.) multicoloured	55	60
910	**865**	(27p.) multicoloured	55	60
901/10 *Set of 10*			8·00	8·80
First Day Cover				8·50
Presentation Pack			9·00	

(b) Photo Enschedé (from rolls of 100)

911	**856**	(22p.) multicoloured	45	50
		a. Strip of 5. Nos. 911/15	7·00	7·50
912	**857**	(22p.) multicoloured	45	50
913	**858**	(22p.) multicoloured	45	50
914	**859**	(22p.) multicoloured	45	50
915	**860**	(22p.) multicoloured	45	50
916	**861**	(27p.) multicoloured	55	60
		a. Strip of 5. Nos. 916/20	7·00	7·50
917	**862**	(27p.) multicoloured	55	60
918	**863**	(27p.) multicoloured	55	60
919	**864**	(27p.) multicoloured	55	60
920	**865**	(27p.) multicoloured	55	60
911/20 *Set of 10*			14·00	15·00

Nos. 901/5 and 911/15 were intended for postage within the Bailiwick and are inscribed 'GY'. They were each initially sold at 22p. Nos. 906/10 and 916/20 were intended for postage to Great Britain and are inscribed 'UK'. They were each initially sold at 27p.

Sheets: Nos. 901/10 were printed in sheetlets of 10 (2×5) or in booklets with the surplus self-adhesive paper around each stamp retained. Nos. 911/20 were printed in rolls of 100, one for each rate, and have the surplus self-adhesive paper removed. The photogravure printing can be identified by the lack of outlines around the inscriptions.

Sold out: By 7.2004 booklets and rolls of 100; by 5.2007 sheetlets.

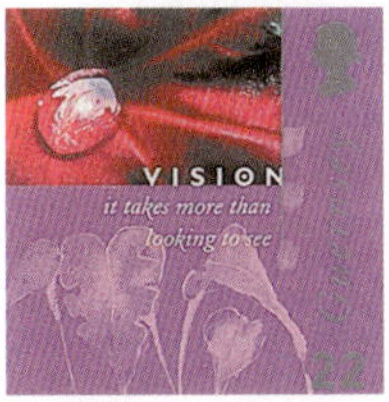

866 Droplets of Water on Leaf ('Vision')

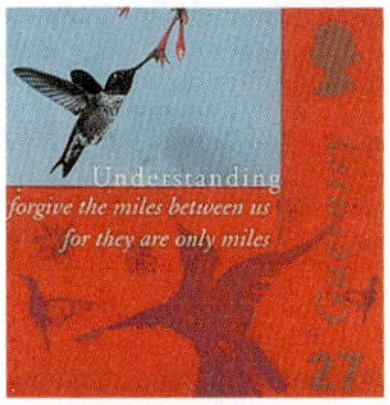

867 Ruby-throated Hummingbird ('Understanding')

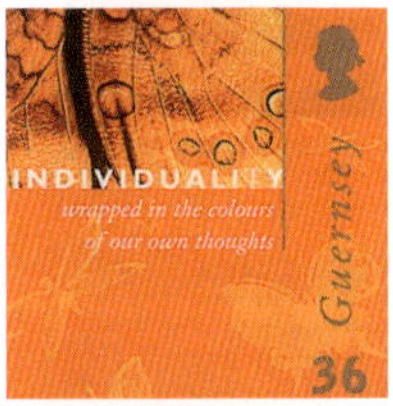

868 Butterfly's Wing ('Individuality')

869 Sea Shell ('Strength')

870 Honeycomb ('Community')

871 Dandelion ('Maturity')

Incorporation of Guernsey Post Ltd

(Des Charlotte Barnes. Litho Walsall)

2001 (1 Aug).

(a) Perf 13½×13 (C)

921	**866**	22p. multicoloured	45	50
		a. Booklet pane of 3	1·20	
922	**867**	27p. multicoloured	55	60
		a. Booklet pane of 3	1·60	
923	**868**	36p. multicoloured	70	75
		a. Booklet pane of 3	2·10	
924	**869**	40p. multicoloured	80	85
		a. Booklet pane of 3	2·40	
925	**870**	45p. multicoloured	90	95
		a. Booklet pane of 3	2·50	
926	**871**	65p. multicoloured	1·20	1·40
		a. Booklet pane of 3	3·75	
921/6 *Set of 6*			4·50	5·00
First Day Cover				5·75
Presentation Pack			5·75	

(b) Design as No. 28 (1969 £1), but redrawn and printed in litho. Perf 14×14½ (C)

927	**18**	£1 multicoloured	5·00	5·50
		a. Booklet pane of 1	5·00	

No. 927 was only sold as part of a £8.05 stamp booklet but loose panes (without stitch holes) were provided free to regular Guernsey Philatelic Bureau customers. In addition to the change of printing process, No. 927 differs from the original 1969 stamp by showing the Queen's portrait without a tiara and by having 'GUERNSEY BAILIWICK' in white instead of grey.

Plate Nos.: All values 1A (×4).
Sheets: 50 (5×10).
Imprint: Upper right-hand margin.
Withdrawn: 31.7.2002.

872 'Tree of Joy', St. Peter Port

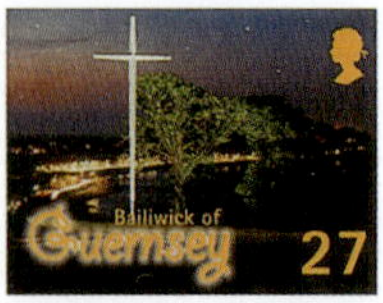

873 Cross, Les Cotils Christian Centre

874 Les Ruettes Cottage, St. Saviour's

875 Farmhouse, Le Preel, Castel

876 Sark Post Office

877 High Street, St. Peter Port

Christmas. Festive Lights

(Des Sally Diamond. Litho Questa)

2001 (16 Oct). Perf 14×14½ (C).

928	**872**	19p. multicoloured	40	45
929	**873**	27p. multicoloured	55	60
930	**874**	36p. multicoloured	75	80
931	**875**	40p. multicoloured	1·00	1·10
932	**876**	45p. multicoloured	1·10	1·20
933	**877**	65p. multicoloured	1·50	1·60
928/33 *Set of 6*			5·00	5·50
First Day Cover				5·75
Presentation Pack			5·75	
MS934 150×100 mm. Nos. 928/33			6·00	6·50
First Day Cover				5·75

No. **MS**934 includes the 'Hafnia 01' International Stamp Exhibition logo on the sheet margin.

Plate Nos.: 19p., 27p. 1A, 1B, 1C, 1D. (each ×4); others 1A (×4).
Sheets: 50 (5×10).
Imprint: Upper right-hand margin.
Withdrawn: 15.10.2002.

Yearbook 2001

2001 (1 Dec). Comprises Nos. 884/910, 921/6, 928/34 and A162/83.

Yearbook ... 65·00

Sold out: By 4.2003.

878 Victor Hugo and St. Peter Port

879 Cosette

880 Valjean

881 Inspector Javert

882 Cosette and Marius

883 Novel and Score for *Les Misérables* (musical by Alain Boublil and Claude-Michel Schönberg)

Birth Bicentenary of Victor Hugo (French author). *Les Misérables* (novel)

(Des R. Ollington. Litho Cartor)

2002 (6 Feb). Perf 13½×13 (C).

935	**878**	22p. multicoloured	45	50
936	**879**	27p. multicoloured	55	60
937	**880**	36p. multicoloured	75	80
938	**881**	40p. multicoloured	90	95
939	**882**	45p. multicoloured	1·10	1·10
940	**883**	65p. multicoloured	1·50	1·60
935/40 *Set of 6*			5·00	5·25
First Day Cover				5·75
Presentation Pack			5·75	
MS941 150×100 mm. Nos. 935/40			5·50	6·00
First Day Cover				7·00

The 27p value reproduces the main image from promotional material for Cameron Mackintosh's musical production.

Plate Nos.: All values 1A (×4).
Sheets: 50 (5×10).
Imprint: Central, side margins.
Withdrawn: 5.2.2003.

884 Juggling

885 Clowns

886 Trapeze Artists

887 Knife Thrower

888 Acrobat

889 High-wire Cyclist

Europa. The Circus

(Des R. Carter. Litho Questa)

2002 (6 Feb). Perf 14½ (C).

942	**884**	22p. multicoloured	45	50
943	**885**	27p. multicoloured	55	60
944	**886**	36p. multicoloured	70	75
945	**887**	40p. multicoloured	80	90
946	**888**	45p. multicoloured	90	95
947	**889**	65p. multicoloured	1·20	1·40
942/7 *Set of 6*			4·50	5·00
First Day Cover				6·50
Presentation Pack			5·75	

Plate Nos.: All values 1A (×4).
Sheets: 10 (2×5) with enlarged illustrated margins at right.
Imprint: Central, left-hand margin.
Withdrawn 5.2.2003.

890 Queen Elizabeth and Crowd

891 Queen Elizabeth at St. Peter Port

892 Queen Elizabeth and Prince Philip at St. Anne's School, Alderney

893 Queen Elizabeth and La Seigneurie, Sark

894 At Millennium Stone, L'Ancresse

895 In Evening Dress, and Floodlit Castle Cornet

Golden Jubilee

(Des Sarah Thomas. Litho B.D.T.)

2002 (30 Apr). Perf 13½ (C).

948	**890**	22p. multicoloured	45	50
		a. Booklet pane. Nos. 948 and 951/3 with margins all round	4·50	
		b. Booklet pane. Nos. 948/50 and 953 with margins all round	3·00	
		c. Booklet pane. Nos. 948/53 with margins all round	4·50	
949	**891**	27p. multicoloured	55	60
		a. Booklet pane. Nos. 949/52 with margins all round	3·00	
950	**892**	36p. multicoloured	70	75
951	**893**	40p. multicoloured	80	85
952	**894**	45p. multicoloured	90	95
953	**895**	65p. multicoloured	1·20	1·40
948/53 *Set of 6*			4·50	5·00
First Day Cover				5·75
Presentation Pack			5·75	

Plate Nos.: All values 1A (×4).
Sheets: 50 (10×5).
Imprint: Upper right-hand margin.
Withdrawn: 29.4.2003.

896a Original Pillar Box, Union Street

150th Anniversary of First Pillar Box

(Des Sally Diamond. Litho Questa)

2002 (30 Apr). Sheet 55×90 mm. Perf 14½×14 (C).

MS954 **896a** £1.75 multicoloured	4·00	4·50
First Day Cover		6·00
Presentation Pack	5·00	

Withdrawn: 29.4.2003.

897 Family and Ferry, La Maseline

898 Passenger Tractors

899 Campsite

900 Cyclists at La Coupée

901 Swimming in Venus Pool

902 La Seigneurie Gardens

903 Posting Cards

904 Carriage Ride

905 Tea at a Café

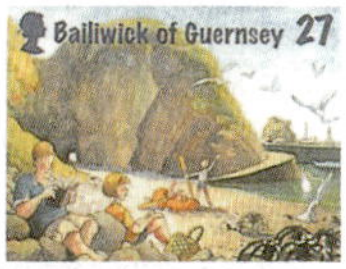

906 On the Beach at Creux Harbour

Holidays on Sark

(Des M. Remphry. Litho B.D.T.)

2002 (30 July). Perf 13 (C).

955	**897**	27p. multicoloured	45	30
		a. Block of 10 of two horiz strips of 5. Nos. 955/64	6·00	6·00
956	**898**	27p. multicoloured	45	30
957	**899**	27p. multicoloured	45	30
958	**900**	27p. multicoloured	45	30
959	**901**	27p. multicoloured	45	30
960	**902**	27p. multicoloured	45	30
961	**903**	27p. multicoloured	45	30
962	**904**	27p. multicoloured	45	30
963	**905**	27p. multicoloured	45	30
964	**906**	27p. multicoloured	45	30
955/64 *Set of 10*			6·00	6·00
First Day Cover				6·50
Presentation Pack			6·50	

Plate Nos.: 1A (×4).
Sheets: 50 (5×10). Nos. 955/64 were printed together, *se-tenant*, in blocks of 10 throughout the sheet.
Imprint: Upper side margins.
Withdrawn: 29.7.2003.

907 Elizabeth College and Cadet Corps Parade, 1934

908 Captain Le Patourel in Action, Tunisia, 1942, and V.C.

909 Captain Le Patourel and Nurse, 1943

910 Award Ceremony, Cairo, 1943

911 Major Le Patourel welcomed Home to Guernsey, 1948

912 Herbert Le Patourel carrying the King's Colour, 1968

60th Anniversary of Herbert Le Patourel's Victoria Cross

(Des A. Theobald. Litho Cartor)

2002 (30 July). Perf 13½×13 (C).

965	**907**	22p. multicoloured	45	50
966	**908**	27p. multicoloured	55	60
967	**909**	36p. multicoloured	70	75
968	**910**	40p. multicoloured	80	85
969	**911**	45p. multicoloured	90	95
970	**912**	65p. multicoloured	1·20	1·40
965/70 *Set of 6*			4·50	5·00
First Day Cover				5·75
Presentation Pack			5·75	

Plate Nos.: All values 1A (×4).
Sheets: 50 (5×10).
Imprint: Central, side margins.
Withdrawn: 29.7.2003.

913a Queen Elizabeth the Queen Mother and Bouquet (*Illustration reduced. Actual size* 140×98 mm)

Queen Elizabeth the Queen Mother Commemoration

(Des M. Whyte. Litho and die-stamped Enschedé)

2002 (4 Aug). Sheet 140×98 mm. Perf 13½ (C).

MS971 **913a** £2 multicoloured	4·50	4·25
First Day Cover		5·00
Presentation Pack	5·00	

Withdrawn: 3.8.2003.

914 Mary and Jesus

915 Mary, Joseph and Jesus in the Stable

916 Angel appearing to Shepherds

917 Shepherds with Mary and Jesus

918 Three Wise Men

919 Stable with Star Overhead

Christmas

(Des Petula Stone. Litho Cartor)

2002 (17 Oct). Perf 13 (C).

972	**914**	22p. multicoloured	45	50
973	**915**	27p. multicoloured	55	60
974	**916**	36p. multicoloured	70	75
975	**917**	40p. multicoloured	80	85
976	**918**	45p. multicoloured	1·00	95
977	**919**	65p. multicoloured	1·50	1·40
972/7 *Set of 6*			4·50	4·50
First Day Cover				5·75
Presentation Pack			6·00	
MS978 130×102 mm. Nos. 972/7			5·00	5·00
First Day Cover				5·75

Plate Nos.: All values 1A (×5).
Sheets: 50 (5×10).
Imprint: Central, side margins.
Withdrawn: 16.10.2003.

Yearbook 2002

2002 (1 Dec). Comprises Nos. 935/78 and **MS**A184/202.

Yearbook	65·00

Sold out: 6.2005.

920 Lancaster Bomber and Crew

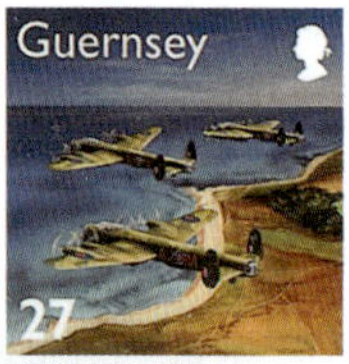

921 Flight of Lancaster bombers crossing English cast

922 Lancaster bombers in enemy searchlights

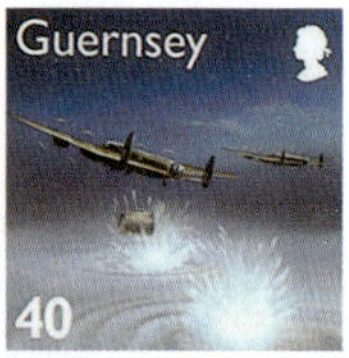

923 Dropping bouncing bombs

924 H.M.S. *Charybdis* (cruiser) and H.M.S. *Limbourne* (destroyer)

Memories of the Second World War (1st issue). 60th Anniversary of Operation Tunnel (£1.50) and Dambusters Raid (others).

(Des N. Watton. Litho Questa)

2003 (30 Jan). Perf 14½ (£1.50) or 14 (others) (both comb).

979	**920**	22p. multicoloured	45	50
980	**921**	27p. multicoloured	55	60
981	**922**	36p. multicoloured	70	75

982	**923**	40p. multicoloured	80	85
983	**924**	£1.50 multicoloured	3·00	3·25
979/83 *Set of 5*			5·50	5·75
First Day Cover				6·50
Presentation Pack			6·50	

See also Nos. 1027/31.
Plate Nos.: All values 1A (×5).
Sheets: 50 (5×10).
Imprint: Upper right-hand margin.
Withdrawn: 29.1.2004.

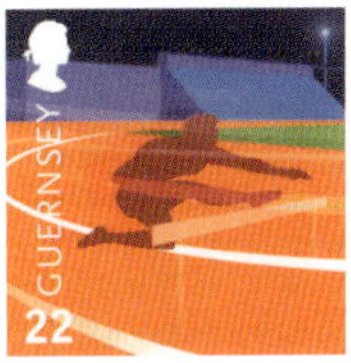

925 Hurdling

926 Cycling

927 Gymnastics

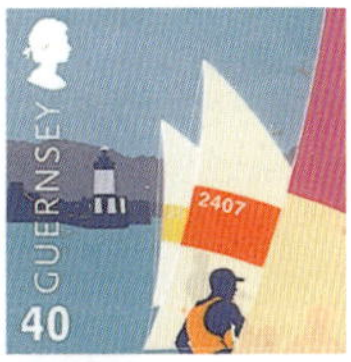

928 Sailing

929 Golf

930 Running

Island Games, Guernsey

(Des Charlotte Barnes. Litho Cartor)

2003 (30 Jan). Perf 12½ (C).

984	**925**	22p. multicoloured	45	50
985	**926**	27p. multicoloured	55	60
986	**927**	36p. multicoloured	75	80
987	**928**	40p. multicoloured	80	85
988	**929**	45p. multicoloured	90	95
989	**930**	65p. multicoloured	1·20	1·40
984/9 *Set of 6*			4·50	5·00
First Day Cover				5·75
Presentation Pack			5·75	
MS990 140×75 mm. Nos. 984/9			5·00	5·00
First Day Cover				5·75

Plate Nos.: All values 1A (×4).
Sheets: 50 (5×10).
Imprint: Central, side margins.
Withdrawn: 29.1.2004.

931 St. Peter Port Harbour ('Naturally Guernsey', 2003)

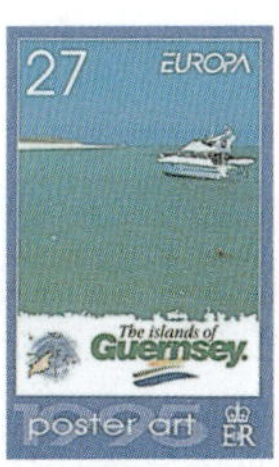

932 Motor-cruiser off Guernsey ('The islands of Guernsey', 1995)

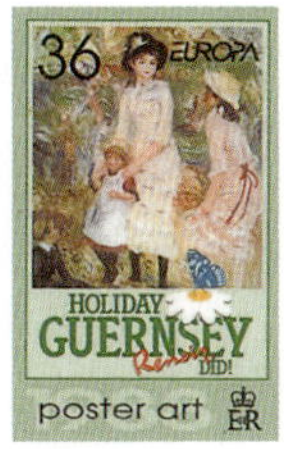

933 'Children on the Seashore' (Renoir) ('Holiday Guernsey', 1988)

934 St. Peter Port Harbour ('Bailiwick of Guernsey', 1978)

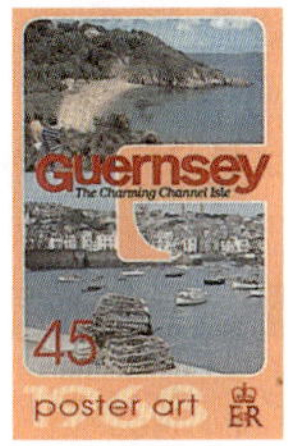

935 St. Peter Port and Cliffs ('Guernsey - The Charming Channel Island', 1968)

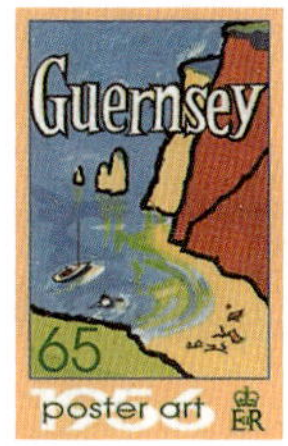

936 Secluded Bay ('Guernsey', 1956)

Europa. Poster Art

(Des M. Quéru. Litho De La Rue)

2003 (10 Apr). Perf 14½ (C).

991	**931**	22p. multicoloured	45	50
992	**932**	27p. multicoloured	55	60
993	**933**	36p. multicoloured	75	80
994	**934**	40p. multicoloured	80	85
995	**935**	45p. multicoloured	90	95
996	**936**	65p. multicoloured	1·20	1·40
991/6 *Set of 6*			5·00	5·00
First Day Cover				5·75
Presentation Pack			5·75	

Sheets: 10 (2×5) with enlarged illustrated margin at right.
Imprint: Central, left-hand margin.
Withdrawn: 9.4.2004.

937a H.M.S. *Guernsey* (*Illustration reduced. Actual size* 117×84 mm)

Decommissioning of H.M.S. *Guernsey* (fishery protection patrol vessel)

(Des K. Taylor. Litho De La Rue)

2003 (10 Apr). Sheet 117×84 mm. Perf 13½×14 (C).

MS997 **937a** £1.50 multicoloured	4·50	4·00
First Day Cover		4·50
Presentation Pack	4·75	

Withdrawn: 9.4.2004.

938 Princess Diana and Baby Prince William

939 Prince William aged 3, with Prince Charles and Prince Harry at Kensington Palace

940 Aged 4, in Parachute Regiment Uniform

941 Aged 7, with Prince Harry on his First Day at Wetherby School

942 Aged 8, with Prince Charles at Guards Polo

943 Aged 9, on Ski Slopes with Princess Diana

944 On First Day at Eton, 1995

945 With Prince Charles and Prince Harry at Balmoral, 1997

946 Wearing Hard Hat during Community Project in Chile, 2000

947 Playing Polo, 2002

21st Birthday of Prince William of Wales

(Des Sally Diamond. Litho Enschedé)

2003 (21 June). Perf 13½×13 (C).

998	**938**	27p. multicoloured	55	30
		a. Horiz strip of 10. Nos. 998/1007	6·50	7·00
		b. Perf 13½×14	55	30
		ba. Booklet pane. Nos. 998b, 1000b, 1003b/4b and 1006b/7b with margins all round	3·25	
		bb. Booklet pane. Nos. 998b, 1001b, 1003b/5b and 1007b with margins all round	3·25	
		bc. Booklet pane. Nos. 998b/1000b, 1002b, 1005b and 1007b with margins all round	3·25	
999	**939**	27p. multicoloured	55	30
		b. Perf 13½×14	55	30
		ba. Booklet pane. Nos. 999b/1002b and 1005b/6b with margins all round	3·25	
		bb. Booklet pane. Nos. 999b, 1001b/1004b and 1006b with margins all round	3·25	
1000	**940**	27p. multicoloured	55	30
		b. Perf 13½×14	55	30
1001	**941**	27p. multicoloured	55	30
		b. Perf 13½×14	55	30
1002	**942**	27p. multicoloured	55	30
		b. Perf 13½×14	55	30
1003	**943**	27p. multicoloured	55	30
		b. Perf 13½×14	55	30
1004	**944**	27p. multicoloured	55	30
		b. Perf 13½×14	55	30
1005	**945**	27p. multicoloured	55	30
		b. Perf 13½×14	55	30
1006	**946**	27p. multicoloured	55	30
		b. Perf 13½×14	55	30
1007	**947**	27p. multicoloured	55	30
		b. Perf 13½×14	55	30
998/1007 *Set of 10*			6·50	7·00
First Day Cover				6·50
Presentation Pack			6·50	

Nos. 998b/1007b were only issued in £8.10 booklets, No. SB72.

Plate Nos.: 1A (×4).

Sheets: 50 (10×5). Nos. 998/1007 were printed together, *se-tenant*, in horizontal strips of ten throughout the sheet.

Imprint: Upper side margins.

Withdrawn: 20.6.2004.

948 Letters of Alphabet

(Des A. Fothergill. Litho and die-stamped Enschedé)

2003 (3 July). Perf 13½ (C).

1008	**948**	£5 pale orange, royal blue and silver	10·00	150
First Day Cover				11·00
Presentation Pack			11·00	

The alphabet letters are printed in thermochromic ink which fades from pale orange to white when exposed to heat.

No. 1008 was retained in use as a definitive stamp.

Sheets: 4 (4×1).

949 Sleeping Boy and Christmas Tree

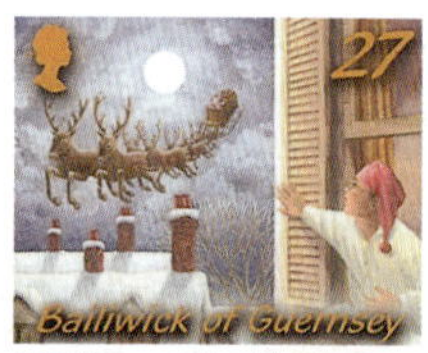

950 Boy opening Shutter to see Santa's Sleigh

951 Santa on Roof with Reindeer

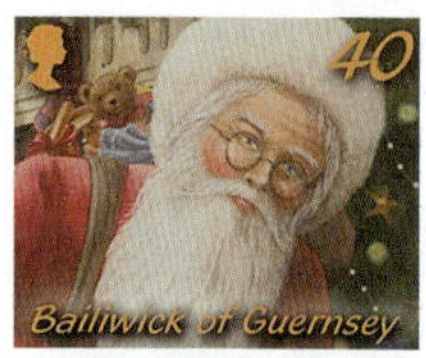

952 Santa with Presents

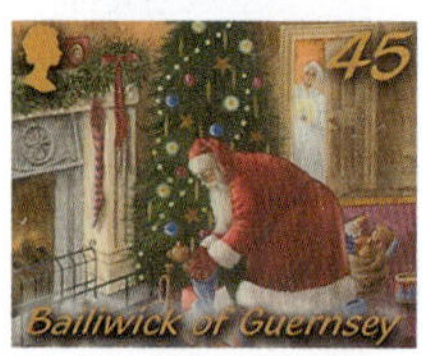

953 Santa leaving Presents under Christmas Tree

954 Santa in Sleigh

Christmas. Scenes from Poem 'Twas the Night before Christmas' by Clement Clarke Moore

(Des Petula Stone. Litho DLR)

2003 (16 Oct). Perf 14×14½ (C).

1009	**949**	10p. multicoloured	20	25
1010	**950**	27p. multicoloured	55	60
1011	**951**	36p. multicoloured	70	75
1012	**952**	40p. multicoloured	80	85
1013	**953**	45p. multicoloured	1·20	1·30
1014	**954**	65p. multicoloured	1·50	1·70
1009/14 *Set of 6*			4·75	5·00
First Day Cover				5·75
Presentation Pack			5·75	
MS1015 130×104 mm. Nos. 1009/14			4·75	4·75
First Day Cover				5·75

Plate Nos.: All values 1A (×4).
Sheets: 50 (5×10).
Imprint: Upper right-hand margin.
Withdrawn: 15.10.2004.

Yearbook 2003

2003 (1 Dec). Comprises Nos. 979/**MS**1015 and **MS**A203/22.

Yearbook	70·00

Sold out: By 3.2007.

955a Golden Snub-nosed Monkey (*Illustration reduced. Actual size 120×85 mm*)

Endangered Species (1st series). Golden Snub-nosed Monkey

(Des J. Kirk. Litho De La Rue)

2004 (29 Jan). Sheet 120×85 mm. Perf 14 (C).

MS1016 **955a** £2 multicoloured	6·50	6·50
First Day Cover		8·50
Presentation Pack	8·50	

Withdrawn: 28.1.2005.

956 'Rosemoor'

957 'Arctic Queen'

958 'Harlow Carr'

959 'Guernsey Cream'

960 'Josephine'

961 ' Blue Moon'

962 'Wisley'

963 'Liberation'

964 'Royal Velvet'

965 'Hyde Hall'

Raymond Evison's Guernsey Clematis

(Des R. Evison. Litho Cartor)

2004 (29 Jan). Self-adhesive. Perf 12½ (die-cut).

1017	**956**	(22p.) multicoloured	75	75
		a. Sheetlet. Nos. 1017/26	8·00	
		b. Booklet pane. Nos. 1017/21, each ×2	7·00	
		c. Booklet pane. Nos. 1017/21, each ×2	7·00	
1018	**957**	(22p.) multicoloured	75	75
1019	**958**	(22p.) multicoloured	75	75
1020	**959**	(22p.) multicoloured	75	75
1021	**960**	(22p.) multicoloured	75	75
1022	**961**	(27p.) multicoloured	85	85
		a. Booklet pane. Nos. 1022/6, each ×2	8·75	
		b. Booklet pane. Nos. 1022/6, each ×2	8·75	
1023	**962**	(27p.) multicoloured	85	85
1024	**963**	(27p.) multicoloured	85	85
1025	**964**	(27p.) multicoloured	85	85
1026	**965**	(27p.) multicoloured	85	85
1017/26 *Set of 10*			8·00	8·00
First Day Cover				9·00
Presentation Pack			9·00	

Nos. 1017/21 were intended for postage within the Bailiwick and are inscribed "GY". They were each initially sold at 22p. Nos. 1022/6 were intended for postage to Great Britain and are inscribed "UK". They were each initially sold at 27p.

Sheets: 10 (5×2). Nos. 1017/26 were printed in sheetlets of ten containing Nos. 1017/26 and in booklets of ten or 100, all with the surplus self-adhesive paper around each stamp retained. The booklets of ten contain either Nos. 1017/21×2 (pane No. 1017b) or Nos. 1022/6×2 (pane No. 1022a), and the stamps are peeled directly from the cover in two blocks 3×2 and 2×2, the blocks separated by a gutter containing text. The booklets of 100 contain ten panes of either Nos. 1017/21×2 (pane No. 1017c) or Nos. 1022/6×2 (pane No. 1022b). These panes have the stamps in one block 5×2, on plain white backing paper, the panes being separated from the booklet by a line of rouletting.

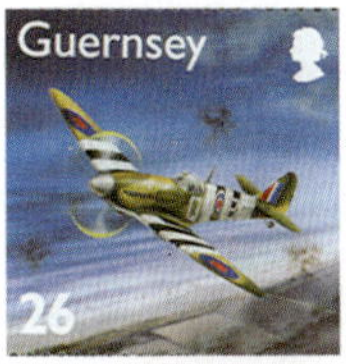

966 Supermarine Spitfire

967 Landing Craft and Ship

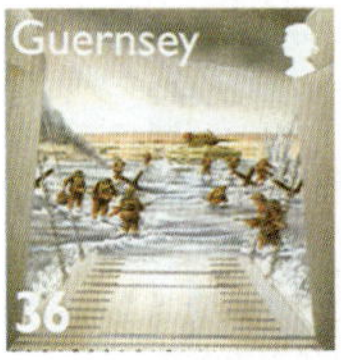

968 Troops going Ashore at Gold Beach

969 Troops in Water

970 *Vega* (Red Cross supply ship)

Memories of the Second World War (2nd issue). 60th Anniv of D-Day Landings

(Des N. Watton. Litho BDT)

2004 (12 May). Perf 15×14 (£1.50) or 14 (others) (both comb).

1027	**966**	26p. multicoloured	85	85
1028	**967**	32p. multicoloured	1·00	1·00
1029	**968**	36p. multicoloured	1·20	1·20
1030	**969**	40p. multicoloured	1·30	1·30
1031	**970**	£1.50 multicoloured	5·00	5·00
1027/31		*Set of 5*	9·25	9·25
First Day Cover				11·50
Presentation Pack			11·50	

Plate Nos.: All values 1A (×4).
Sheets: 50 (5×10).
Imprint: Upper side margins.
Withdrawn: 11.5.2005.

971 Sandcastle, Rider, Bucket and Spade, Deckchair and Canoeist

972 Pathway Sign, Walking Trails, Bench and Guernsey Landscapes

973 Lighthouse and Yachts in Marina, St. Peter Port

974 Glasses of Red Wine and Meals on Table

975 Statue-menhir at Castel and Loop Holed Tower, Le Gran'mere Statue-menhir, Little Chapel and Victor Hugo Statue

976 Guernsey Lily, Wildflowers and Robin

Europa. Holidays

(Des P. Furness. Litho BDT)

2004 (12 May). Perf 13½ (C).

1032	**971**	26p. multicoloured	85	85
1033	**972**	32p. multicoloured	1·10	1·10
1034	**973**	36p. multicoloured	1·20	1·20
1035	**974**	40p. multicoloured	1·30	1·30
1036	**975**	45p. multicoloured	1·50	1·50
1037	**976**	65p. multicoloured	2·10	2·10
1032/7		*Set of 6*	8·00	8·00
First Day Cover				10·00
Presentation Pack			10·00	

Sheets: 10 (2×5) with enlarged illustrated margins at right.
Imprint: Central, left-hand margin.
Withdrawn: 11.5.2005.

977 Three Crowns (Loyalty)

978 Three Ships (Trade)

979 Knotted Rope (Unity)

980 Three Castle Turrets (Protection)

981 Three Scrolls (Justice)

982 Three Leaping Fish (Industry)

800th Anniv of Allegiance to England

(Des Charlotte Barnes. Litho Enschedé)

2004 (24 June). Perf 13½×14 (C).

1038	**977**	26p. multicoloured	85	85
1039	**978**	32p. multicoloured	1·10	1·10
1040	**979**	36p. multicoloured	1·20	1·20
1041	**980**	40p. multicoloured	1·30	1·30
1042	**981**	45p. multicoloured	1·50	1·50
1043	**982**	65p. multicoloured	2·10	2·10
1038/43		*Set of 6*	8·00	8·00
First Day Cover				10·00
Presentation Pack			10·00	
MS1044		140×80 mm. Nos. 1038/43. P 14×13½	8·00	8·00
First Day Cover				10·00

Plate Nos.: All values 1A (×5).
Sheets: 50 (10×5).
Imprint: Upper side margins.
Withdrawn: 23.6.2005.

983 Discus Thrower

984 Javelin Thrower

985 Runners

986 Wrestlers

987a Olympic Sports (*Illustration reduced. Actual size 152×98 mm*)

Olympic Games, Athens, Greece

(Des A. Fothergill. Litho BDT)

2004 (29 July). Perf 13½ (C).

1045	**983**	32p. multicoloured	1·00	1·00
		a. Booklet pane. No. 1045×2 and Nos. 1046/7 with margins all round	4·75	
		b. Booklet pane. No. 1045, No. 1047×2 and No. 1048 with margins all round	6·00	
		c. Booklet pane. Nos. 1045/6 and 1048×2 with margins all round	6·50	
		d. Booklet pane. Nos. 1045/8 with margins all round	5·75	
1046	**984**	36p. multicoloured	1·20	1·20
		a. Booklet pane. No. 1046×2 and Nos. 1047/8 with margins all round	6·00	
1047	**985**	45p. multicoloured	1·50	1·50
1048	**986**	65p. multicoloured	2·10	2·10
1045/8 *Set of 4*			5·75	5·75
First Day Cover				7·75
Presentation Pack			5·25	
MS1049 152×98 mm. **987a** £1 multicoloured. Perf 15×14 (C)			3·50	3·50
a. Booklet pane. As No. **MS**1049, but with line of roulettes at left			3·50	
First Day Cover				5·25
Presentation Pack			7·75	

Plate Nos.: All values 1A (×4).
Sheets: 50 (10×5).
Imprint: Upper side margins.
Withdrawn: 28.7.2005.

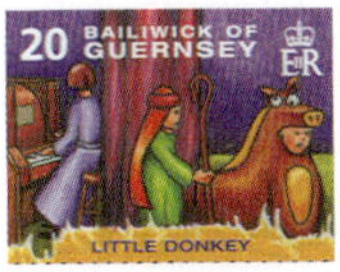

988 'Little Donkey'

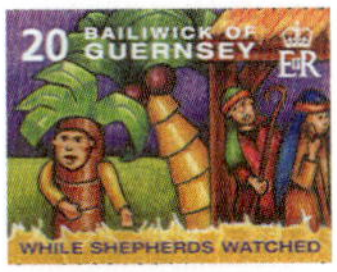

989 'While Shepherds Watched'

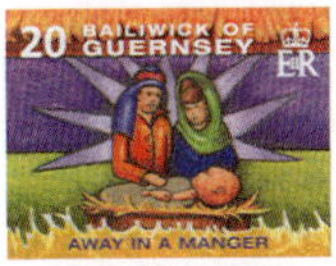

990 'Away in a Manger'

991 'Unto Us a Child is Born'

992 'We Three Kings'

993 Angels Wings

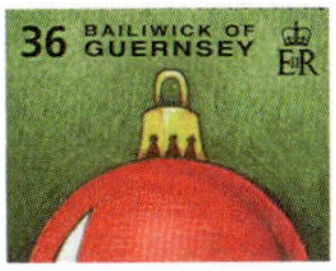

994 Bauble

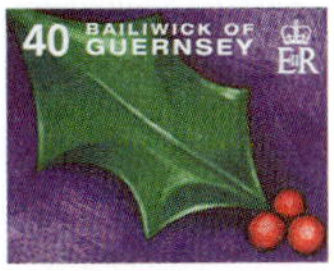

995 Holly

996 Detail of Snowman

997 Star atop Tree

'The Innocence of Christmas'

(Des J. Almer. Litho Cartor)

2004 (28 Oct). Perf 13 (C).

1050	**988**	20p. multicoloured	65	25
		a. Horiz strip of 5. Nos. 1050/4	3·25	3·50
1051	**989**	20p. multicoloured	65	25
1052	**990**	20p. multicoloured	65	25
1053	**991**	20p. multicoloured	65	25
1054	**992**	20p. multicoloured	65	25
1055	**993**	32p. multicoloured	1·10	1·10
1056	**994**	36p. multicoloured	1·20	1·20
1057	**995**	40p. multicoloured	1·30	1·30
1058	**996**	45p. multicoloured	1·50	1·50
1059	**997**	65p. multicoloured	2·20	2·20
1050/9 *Set of* 10			150	150
First Day Covers (2)				14·50
Presentation Pack			13·50	

Plate Nos.: All values 1A (×4).
Sheets: 50 (5×10). The 20p. values were printed together, *se-tenant*, in horizontal strips of 5 with the backgrounds forming a composite design.
Imprint: Upper and lower side margins.
Withdrawn: 27.10.2005.

Yearbook 2004

2004 (1 Dec). Comprises Nos. **MS**1016/59 and A223/47.

Yearbook	65·00

998 British Soldiers in Landrover and welcoming Crowd

999 Guernsey Woman waving and Liberty Sign and Flags on Building

1000 Parents and Children reunited

1001 Return of Local Men from Hampshire Regiment

1002 Winston Churchill

Memories of the Second World War (3rd issue). 60th Anniv of Liberation

(Des N. Watton. Litho BDT)

2005 (3 Feb). Perf 15×14½ (£1.50) or 14½ (others) (both comb).

1060	**998**	26p. multicoloured	50	55
1061	**999**	32p. multicoloured	65	70
1062	**1000**	36p. multicoloured	70	75
1063	**1001**	40p. multicoloured	80	85
1064	**1002**	£1.50 multicoloured	3·00	3·25
1060/4 *Set of 5*			5·50	6·00
First Day Cover				7·00
Presentation Pack			7·00	

Plate Nos.: All values 1A (×4).
Sheets: 50 (5×10).
Imprint: Upper left-hand margin.
Withdrawn: 2.2.2006.

1003 Iris 'Dorothea' and 'Royal'

1004 Nerine Fothergilli 'Major'

1005 Iris 'Garnet'

1006 Narcissus 'Sir Watkin'

1007 Narcissus 'Rip van Winkle'

1008 Narcissus 'Sulphur Pheonix'

Birth Centenary of William J. Caparne (artist and iris breeder). Watercolour Paintings of Flowers

(Litho Enschedé)

2005 (3 Feb). Perf 13½ (C).

1065	**1003**	26p. multicoloured	50	55
1066	**1004**	32p. multicoloured	65	70
1067	**1005**	36p. multicoloured	70	95
1068	**1006**	40p. multicoloured	85	1·00
1069	**1007**	45p. multicoloured	1·00	1·10
1070	**1008**	65p. multicoloured	1·50	1·50
1065/70 *Set of 6*			5·00	5·00
First Day Cover				6·00
Presentation Pack			6·00	
MS1071 140×85 mm. Nos. 1065/70			5·00	5·50
First Day Cover				6·00

Plate Nos.: All values 1A (×4).
Sheets: 50 (10×5).
Imprint: Upper left-hand margin.
Withdrawn: 2.2.2006.

1009 Spider Crab

1010 Seared Red Mullet and Crab Cake

1011 Lobster Salad

1012 Brill on Spinach with Local Moules

1013 Prawn Salad

1014 Salmon Wrapped in Spinach with Local Moules

Europa. Gastronomy. Seafood and Coastal Scenes

(Des P. Furness. Litho Enschedé)

2005 (9 May). Perf 14×13½ (C).

1072	**1009**	26p. multicoloured	50	55
1073	**1010**	32p. multicoloured	65	70
1074	**1011**	36p. multicoloured	70	75
1075	**1012**	40p. multicoloured	80	85
1076	**1013**	45p. multicoloured	90	95
1077	**1014**	65p. multicoloured	1·30	1·40
1072/7 *Set of 6*			4·75	5·00
First Day Cover				6·25
Presentation Pack			6·25	

Plate Nos.: All values 1A (×4).
Sheets: 10 (2×5) with enlarged illustrated right-hand margins.
Imprint: Lower left-hand margin.
Withdrawn: 8.5.2006.

1015 King George VI

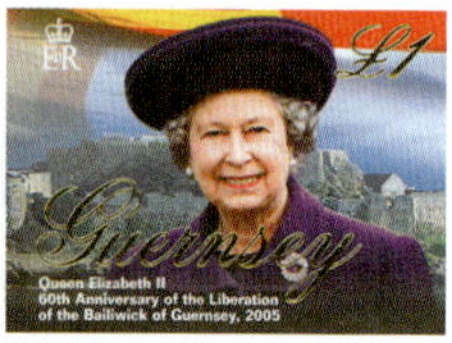

1016 Queen Elizabeth II 60th

60th Anniv of Liberation of Guernsey

(Des Keren Le Patourel. Litho and embossed BDT)

2005 (9 May). Perf 15×14½ (C).

1078	**1015**	£1 multicoloured	1·80	1·30
		a. Horiz pair. Nos. 1078/9	4·00	4·00
1079	**1016**	£1 multicoloured	1·80	1·30
1078/9 *Set of 2*			4·00	4·00
First Day Cover				5·50
Presentation Pack			5·50	

Nos. 1078/9 were retained in use as definitive stamps.
Plate Nos.: 1A (×5).
Sheets: 20 (4×5); the two designs printed together, *se-tenant*, in horizontal pairs throughout the sheet, each pair forming a composite background design.
Imprint: Central, side margins.

1017 Fishing Boat

1018 Yacht off Herm Harbour

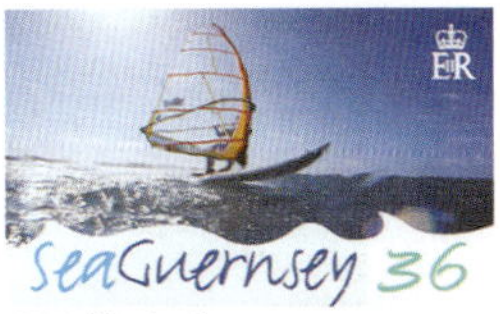

1019 Windsurfer

1020 Sea Angler on Rocks at Albecq

1021 Horse and Rider on Beach, Vazon Bay

'Sea Guernsey' (1st series)

(Des Sally Diamond. Litho Enschedé)

2005 (21 July). Perf 13½×14 (C).

1080	**1017**	26p. multicoloured	50	55
		a. Booklet pane. Nos. 1080/1, each ×2, with margins all round	2·30	
		b. Booklet pane. Nos. 1080 and 1084, each ×2, with margins all round	3·50	
1081	**1018**	32p. multicoloured	65	70
		a. Booklet pane. Nos. 1081/2, each ×2, with margins all round	2·75	
		b. Booklet pane. Nos. 1081/4 with margins all round	3·50	
1082	**1019**	36p. multicoloured	70	75
		a. Booklet pane. Nos. 1082/3, each ×2, with margins all round	3·00	
1083	**1020**	40p. multicoloured	80	85
		a. Booklet pane. Nos. 1083/4, each ×2, with margins all round	4·50	
1084	**1021**	65p. multicoloured	1·50	1·40
1080/4 *Set of 5*			4·00	4·00
First Day Cover				5·25
Presentation Pack			5·25	

Plate Nos.: All values 1A (×4).
Sheets: 10 (2×5).
Imprint: Lower right-hand margin.
Withdrawn: 20.7.2006.

1022 Basking Shark (*Illustration reduced. Actual size* 185×65 mm)

Endangered Species (2nd series). Basking Shark

(Des J. Kirk. Litho BDT)

2005 (21 July). Sheet 185×65 mm. Perf 13½ (C).

MS1085 **1022** £2 multicoloured	5·00	5·00
First Day Cover		6·00
Presentation Pack	6·00	

Withdrawn: 20.7.2006.

1023 Christ holding Guernsey Flag, St. Pierre du Bois

1024 Madonna and Child, St. Saviour

1025 John baptising Christ, St. Martin

1026 Christ the Light of the World, Torteval

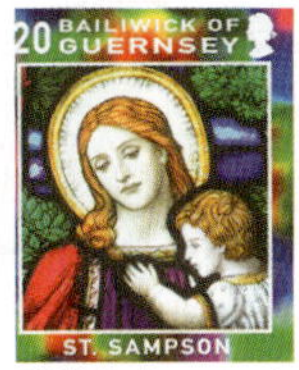

1027 Madonna and Child, St. Sampson

1028 Madonna and Child, Vale

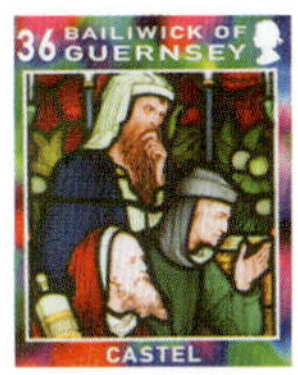

1029 Three Kings, Castel

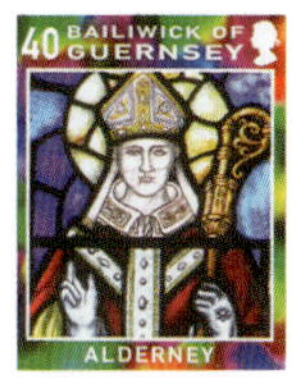

1030 St. Nicholas, Alderney

1031 Madonna and Child, St. Andrew

1032 St. Marguerite Forest

Christmas. Stained-glass Windows from Guernsey and Alderney Parish Churches

(Des K. Taylor. Litho Austrian State Ptg Wks, Vienna)

2005 (27 Oct). Perf 14×14½ (C).

1086	**1023**	20p. multicoloured	40	45
		a. Horiz strip of 5. Nos. 1086/90	2·00	2·20
1087	**1024**	20p. multicoloured	40	45
1088	**1025**	20p. multicoloured	40	45
1089	**1026**	20p. multicoloured	40	45
1090	**1027**	20p. multicoloured	40	45
1091	**1028**	32p. multicoloured	65	70
1092	**1029**	36p. multicoloured	70	75
1093	**1030**	40p. multicoloured	80	85
1094	**1031**	45p. multicoloured	90	95
1095	**1032**	65p. multicoloured	1·30	1·40
1086/95 *Set of 10*			6·25	6·75
First Day Covers (2)				9·00
Presentation Pack			7·75	

Plate Nos.: All values 1A (×4).
Sheets: 50 (10×5). The 20p. values were printed together, *se-tenant*, in horizontal strips of 5 with the backgrounds forming a composite design.
Imprint: Lower side margins.
Withdrawn: 26.10.2006.

Yearbook 2005

2005 (1 Dec). Comprises Nos. 802, 1060/95 and A248/**MS**A266.

Yearbook	65·00

1033 Atlantic Leatherback Turtle; American Wood Ibis
(Illustration reduced. Actual size 110×90 mm)

Endangered Species of the Florida Everglades

(Des J. Kirk. Litho BDT)

2006 (16 Feb). Sheet 110×90 mm. Perf 14×15 (C).

MS1096 £1 £1.50 multicoloured	6·00	6·00
First Day Cover		7·00
Presentation Pack	7·00	

Withdrawn: 15.2.2007.

1034 Iraq Conflict, 2004

1035 Falklands War, 1982

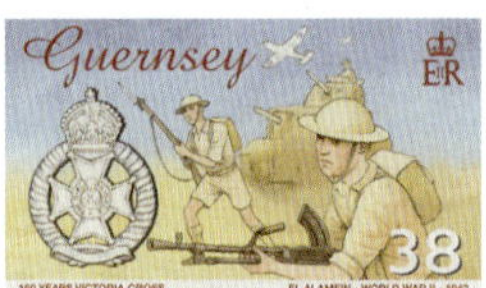

1036 Battle of El Alamein, 1942

1037 Gallipoli Campaign, 1915

1038 Battle of Rorke's Drift, 1879

1039 Charge of the Light Brigade, 1854

150th Anniversary of the Victoria Cross

(Des M. Hargreaves. Litho Austrian State Ptg Wks, Vienna)

2006 (16 Feb). Perf 14×13½ (C).

1097	**1034**	29p. multicoloured	60	65
1098	**1035**	34p. multicoloured	70	75
1099	**1036**	38p. multicoloured	75	80
1100	**1037**	42p. multicoloured	85	90
1101	**1038**	47p. multicoloured	95	1·00
1102	**1039**	68p. multicoloured	1·40	1·50
1097/102 *Set of 6*			5·25	5·50
First Day Cover				6·50
Presentation Pack			6·50	

Plate Nos.: All values 1A (×4).
Sheets: 50 (5×10).
Imprint: Upper left-hand margin.
Withdrawn: 15.2.2007.

1040 Pilbeam MP58, British Speed Hill Climb Championship, 1995

1041 Renault Spider Cup, 1999

1042 British Formula 3, 2001

1043 FIA European Touring Car Championship, 2004

1044 Nürburgring, Germany, 2005

1045 FIA World Touring Car Championship, 2005

Andy Priaulx's Motor Racing Victories

(Des P. Furness. Litho BDT)

2006 (20 May). Perf 13½ (C).

1103	**1040**	29p. multicoloured	60	65
1104	**1041**	34p. multicoloured	70	75
1105	**1042**	42p. multicoloured	85	90
1106	**1043**	45p. multicoloured	90	95
1107	**1044**	47p. multicoloured	1·20	1·20
1108	**1045**	68p. multicoloured	1·70	1·70
1103/8 *Set of 6*			5·75	6·00
First Day Cover				7·00
Presentation Pack			6·50	
MS1109 160×100 mm. Nos. 1103/8			6·00	6·00
First Day Cover				7·00

Plate Nos.: All values 1A (×4).
Sheets: 10 (2×5) with enlarged illustrated right margins.
Imprint: Central, left-hand margin.
Withdrawn: 19.5.2007.

1046 Brunel and Mailbags at Paddington Station

1047 Duke Class Locomotive No. 3258 *King Arthur* at Paddington Station

1048 *King Arthur* on Wharncliffe Viaduct

1049 Loading Mail from Train onto *Ibex* at Weymouth Harbour

1050 Weymouth & Channel Island Steam Packet *Ibex*

1051 Unloading Mail from *Ibex* at St. Peter Port Harbour

Birth Bicentenary of Isambard Kingdom Brunel (engineer)

(Des N. Watton. Litho Cartor)

2006 (20 May). Perf 13½×13 (C).

1110	**1046**	29p. multicoloured	60	65
		a. Booklet pane. Nos. 1110/13	3·00	
		b. Booklet pane. Nos. 1110 and 1113/15	3·75	
		c. Booklet pane. Nos. 1110/11 and 1114/15	5·00	
		d. Booklet pane. Nos. 1110/12 and 1115	4·00	
1111	**1047**	34p. multicoloured	70	75
		a. Booklet pane. Nos. 1111/14	4·00	
1112	**1048**	42p. multicoloured	85	90
		a. Booklet pane. Nos. 1112/15	5·00	
1113	**1049**	45p. multicoloured	90	95
1114	**1050**	47p. multicoloured	1·20	1·20
1115	**1051**	68p. multicoloured	1·70	1·70
1110/15 *Set of 6*			5·75	6·00
First Day Cover				7·00
Presentation Pack			7·00	

Plate Nos.: All values 1A (×4).
Sheets: 50 (5×10).
Imprint: Upper and lower left-hand margins.
Withdrawn: 19.5.2007.

1052 Student working as Waiter in Paris

1053 Sphinx, Egypt

1054 Great Wall of China

1055 Student and Aborigines at Ayers Rock, Australia

1056 Head of Statue of Liberty, New York

1057 Students at Taj Mahal, India

Europa. Integration. Student's Gap Year Travels

(Des R. Carter. Litho Cartor)

2006 (20 May). Perf 13½×14 (C).

1116	**1052**	29p. multicoloured	60	65
1117	**1053**	34p. multicoloured	70	75
1118	**1054**	42p. multicoloured	85	90
1119	**1055**	45p. multicoloured	1·00	95
1120	**1056**	47p. multicoloured	1·20	1·00
1121	**1057**	68p. multicoloured	1·50	1·50
1116/21 *Set of 6*			5·50	5·75
First Day Cover				6·50
Presentation Pack			6·50	

Plate Nos.: All values 1A (×4).
Sheets: 10 (2×5) with enlarged illustrated margins at right and foot.
Imprint: Lower left-hand margin.
Withdrawn: 19.5.2007.

1058 Queen Elizabeth II

80th Birthday of Queen Elizabeth II

(Des P. Furness. Litho and embossed Cartor)

2006 (17 June). Perf 14½ (C).

1122	**1058**	£10 multicoloured	22·00	22·00
First Day Cover				24·00
Presentation Pack			24·00	
Souvenir Folder (No. 1122 & complete sheets of Nos. A274/81)			65·00	

Sheets: 5 (5×1).
Imprint: Top, right-hand margin.
No. 1122 was retained in use as a definitive stamp.

1059 Grey Seal

1060 Ormer

1061 Common Blenny

1062 Le Creux és Faies (Neolithic grave)

1063 Yellow Horned Poppy

1064 Oystercatcher

Designation of L'Erée Wetland as Ramsar Site

(Des Wendy Bramall. Litho Enschedé)

2006 (27 July). Perf 14×13½ (C).

1123	**1059**	29p. multicoloured	60	65
1124	**1060**	34p. multicoloured	70	75
1125	**1061**	42p. multicoloured	85	90
1126	**1062**	45p. multicoloured	1·00	95
1127	**1063**	47p. multicoloured	1·20	1·00
1128	**1064**	68p. multicoloured	1·50	1·50
1123/8 *Set of 6*			5·50	5·75
First Day Cover				6·50
Presentation Pack			6·50	
MS1129 140×95 mm. Nos. 1123/8			6·50	5·75
First Day Cover				6·50

Plate Nos.: All values 1A (×4).
Sheets: 10 (2×5) with enlarged illustrated margins at right and foot.
Imprint: Central, left-hand margin.
Withdrawn: 26.7.2007.

1065 A Partridge in a Pear Tree

1066 Two Turtle Doves

1067 Three French Hens

1068 Four Calling Birds

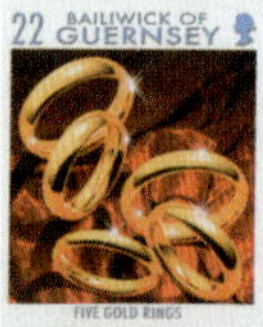

1069 Five Gold Rings

1070 Six Geese a-laying

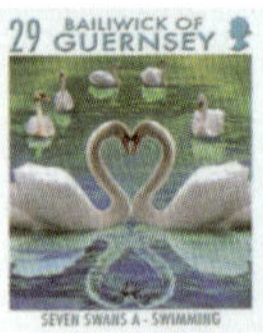

1071 Seven Swans a-swimming

1072 Eight Maids a-milking

1073 Nine Ladies Dancing

1074 Ten Lords a-leaping

1075 Eleven Pipers Piping

1076 Twelve Drummers Drumming

Christmas. 'The Twelve Days of Christmas' (carol)

(Des M. Wilkinson. Litho Austrian State Ptg Wks, Vienna)

2006 (2 Nov). Perf 15 (C).

1130	**1065**	22p. multicoloured	45	50
		a. Horiz strip of 6. Nos. 1130/5	2·50	
1131	**1066**	22p. multicoloured	45	50
1132	**1067**	22p. multicoloured	45	50
1133	**1068**	22p. multicoloured	45	50
1134	**1069**	22p. multicoloured	45	50
1135	**1070**	22p. multicoloured	45	50
1136	**1071**	29p. multicoloured	60	65
1137	**1072**	34p. multicoloured	70	75
1138	**1073**	42p. multicoloured	85	90
1139	**1074**	45p. multicoloured	90	95
1140	**1075**	47p. multicoloured	95	1·00
1141	**1076**	68p. multicoloured	1·40	1·50
1130/41 *Set of* 12			8·00	8·75
First Day Covers (2)				11·00
Presentation Pack			9·25	

Plate Nos.: All values 1A (×4).
Sheets: 22p. 60 (6×10); 29p. to 68p. 50 (10×5). The 22p. values were printed together, *se-tenant*, in horizontal strips of 6.
Imprint: Upper side margins.
Withdrawn: 1.11.2007.

Yearbook 2006.

2006 (1 Dec). Comprises Nos. **MS**1096/141, A267/97 and A306/7.
Yearbook £100

1077 Departure of Troops on *Queen Elizabeth 2*, Southampton

1078 Troops landing at San Carlos Bay

1079 Sea Harriers flying over SS *Canberra*

1080 Lt. Col. H. Jones firing Machine Gun

1081 Helicoper and H.M.S. *Invincible*

1082 Troops marching with Union Jack towards Port Stanley

25th Anniversary of the Battle for the Falklands

(Des R. Carter. Litho BDT)

2007 (8 Mar). Perf 13½ (C).

1142	**1077**	32p. multicoloured	75	75
1143	**1078**	37p. multicoloured	90	90
1144	**1079**	45p. multicoloured	1·10	1·10
1145	**1080**	48p. multicoloured	1·10	1·10
1146	**1081**	50p. multicoloured	1·20	1·50
1147	**1082**	71p. multicoloured	1·70	2·00
1142/7 *Set of* 6			6·75	7·00
First Day Cover				8·50
Presentation Pack			8·00	
MS1148 150×100 mm. Nos. 1142/7			6·75	7·00
First Day Cover				8·50

Plate Nos.: All values 1A (×4).
Sheets: 10 (2×5) with enlarged illustrated margins at right and foot.
Imprint: Central, left-hand margin.
Withdrawn: 7.3.2008.

1083 Rocks at Albecq

1084 Ivy Bee

1085 Vale Church

1086 Common Frog

1087 Parasol Mushroom

1088 Southern Marsh Orchid

1089 Shore Crab

1090 Alderney Blonde Hedgehog

1091 Barn Owl

1092 Le Trépied Dolmen

125th Anniversary of La Société Guernesiaise

(Des A. Wallace. Litho Cartor)

2007 (8 Mar). Self-adhesive. Perf 12½ (die-cut).

1149	**1083**	(32p.) multicoloured	80	80
		a. Sheetlet. Nos. 1149/58	8·00	
		b. Booklet pane. Nos. 1149/53, each ×2	7·50	
		c. Booklet pane. Nos. 1149/53, each ×2	7·50	
1150	**1084**	(32p.) multicoloured	80	80
1151	**1085**	(32p.) multicoloured	80	80
1152	**1086**	(32p.) multicoloured	80	80
1153	**1087**	(32p.) multicoloured	80	80
1154	**1088**	(37p.) multicoloured	80	80
		a. Booklet pane. Nos. 1154/8, each ×2	8·75	
		b. Booklet pane. Nos. 1154/8, each ×2	8·75	
1155	**1089**	(37p.) multicoloured	80	80
1156	**1090**	(37p.) multicoloured	80	80
1157	**1091**	(37p.) multicoloured	80	80
1158	**1092**	(37p.) multicoloured	80	80
1149/58 *Set of* 10			8·00	8·00
First Day Cover				9·00
Presentation Pack			9·00	

Nos. 1149/53 were intended for postage within the Bailiwick, are inscribed "GY" and sold for 32p. each. Nos. 1154/8 were intended for postage to Great Britain, are inscribed "UK" and sold for 37p. each.

Sheets: 10 (5×2). Nos. 1149/58 were printed in sheetlets of ten containing Nos. 1149/58 and in booklets of ten or 100, all with the surplus self-adhesive paper around each stamp retained. The booklets of ten contain either Nos. 1149/53×2 (pane No. 1149b) or Nos. 1154/8×2 (pane No. 1154a), and the stamps are peeled directly from the cover in two blocks 3×2 and 2×2, the blocks separated by a gutter containing text. The booklets of 100 contain ten panes of either Nos. 1149/5332 (pane No. 1149c) or Nos. 1154/832 (pane No. 1154b). These panes have the stamps in one block 5×2, on plain white backing paper.

1093 Scouts camping, 1907

1094 Scout sailing, 1924

1095 Two Scouts fishing from Rocks, 1947

1096 Scouts making and flying Model Aircraft, 1968

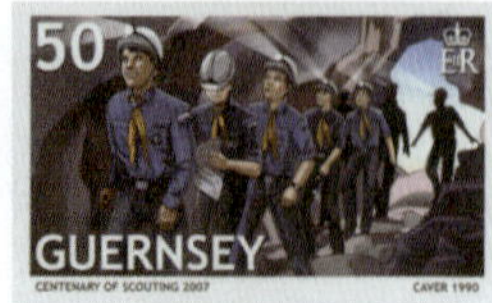

1097 Scouts on Caving Expedition, 1990

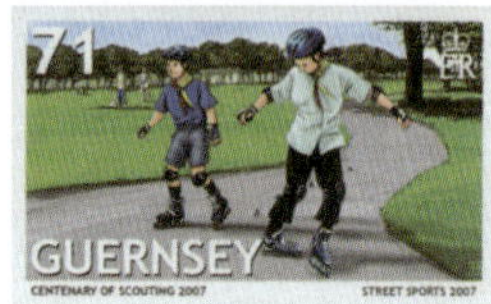

1098 Scouts rollerblading, Cambridge Park, St. Peter Port, 2007

Europa. Centenary of Scouting

(Des Björn Von Schlippe. Litho Cartor)

2007 (24 May). Perf 13½ (C).

1159	**1093**	32p. multicoloured	75	75
1160	**1094**	37p. multicoloured	90	90
1161	**1095**	45p. multicoloured	1·10	1·10
1162	**1096**	48p. multicoloured	1·10	1·10
1163	**1097**	50p. multicoloured	1·50	1·20
1164	**1098**	71p. multicoloured	2·00	1·70
1159/64 *Set of* 6			7·00	6·75
First Day Cover				8·50
Presentation Pack			8·50	

Sheets: 10 (2×5) with enlarged illustrated margins at right and foot.

Imprint: Central, left-hand margin.

Withdrawn: 23.5.2008.

1099 Mike Hawthorn, 1958

1100 Jackie Stewart, 1971

1101 Graham Hill, 1962

1102 James Hunt, 1976

1103 Jim Clark, 1963

1104 Nigel Mansell, 1992

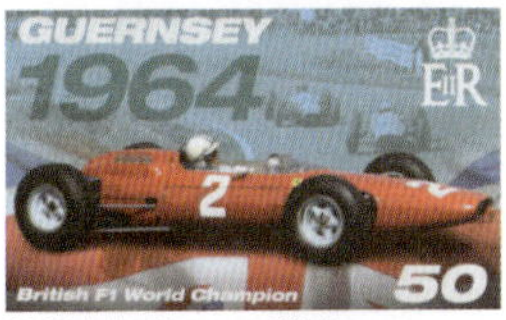

1105 John Surtees, 1964

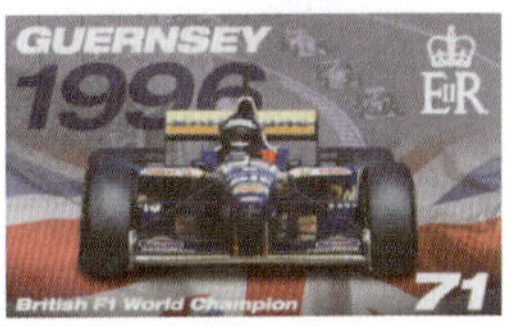

1106 Damon Hill, 1996

British Formula One World Champions

(Des Chris Griffiths. Litho Austrian State Ptg Wks, Vienna)

2007 (24 May). Perf 14 (C).

1165	**1099**	32p. multicoloured	75	75
1166	**1100**	32p. multicoloured	75	75
1167	**1101**	37p. multicoloured	85	85
1168	**1102**	37p. multicoloured	85	85
1169	**1103**	45p. multicoloured	1·20	1·10
1170	**1104**	48p. multicoloured	1·50	1·10
1171	**1105**	50p. multicoloured	1·70	1·20
1172	**1106**	71p. multicoloured	2·50	1·70
1165/72 *Set of 8*			9·00	8·25
First Day Cover				10·00
Presentation Pack			150	

Plate Nos.: All values 1A (×4).
Sheets: 10 (2×5) with enlarged illustrated margins at left and foot.
Imprint: Lower right-hand margin.
Withdrawn: 23.5.2008.

1107 Mountain Gorillas (*Illustration reduced. Actual size 118×84 mm*)

Endangered Species (4th series). Mountain Gorilla (*Gorilla beringei beringei*)

(Des Joel Kirk. Litho Austrian State Ptg Wks, Vienna)

2007 (2 Aug). Sheet 118×84 mm. Perf 14 (C).

MS1173 **1107** £2.50 multicoloured	7·00	7·00
First Day Cover		7·75
Presentation Pack	7·75	

Withdrawn: 1.8.2008.

1108 Engagement, 1947

1109 With Baby Princess Anne

1110 Off-duty

1111 On Tour

1112 With Princes William and Harry

1113 In Recent Years

Diamond Wedding of Queen Elizabeth II and Duke of Edinburgh

(Des Mark Whyte. Litho Enschedé)

2007 (2 Aug). Perf 13½×14 (C).

1174	**1108**	32p. multicoloured	75	75
		a. Booklet pane. Nos. 1174/5, each ×2, with margins all round	3·25	
		b. Booklet pane. Nos. 1174 and 1179, each×2, with margins all round	5·00	
1175	**1109**	37p. multicoloured	90	90
		a. Booklet pane. Nos. 1175/6, each ×2, with margins all round	4·00	
1176	**1110**	45p. multicoloured	1·10	1·10
		a. Booklet pane. Nos. 1176/7, each ×2, with margins all round	4·50	
1177	**1111**	48p. multicoloured	1·10	1·10
		a. Booklet pane. Nos. 1177/8, each ×2, with margins all round	4·50	
1178	**1112**	50p. multicoloured	1·20	1·50
		a. Booklet pane. Nos. 1178/9, each ×2, with margins all round	5·75	
1179	**1113**	71p. multicoloured	1·70	1·90
1174/9 *Set of 6*			6·75	7·00
First Day Cover				8·50
Presentation Pack			8·50	

Plate Nos.: All values 1A (×4).
Sheets: 10 (2×5) with enlarged illustrated margins at right and foot.
Imprint: Central, left-hand margin.
Withdrawn: 1.8.2008.

1114 St. Peter Port Harbour

1115 Fort Grey, Rocquaine Bay

1116 Point Robert Lighthouse, Sark

1117 Brecqhou seen from Sark

1118 Vazon Bay

1119 Fontenelle Bay

Sea Guernsey (2nd series)

(Litho Austrian State Ptg Wks, Vienna)

2007 (1 Oct). Perf 14×13½ (C).

1180	**1114**	32p. multicoloured	75	75
1181	**1115**	37p. multicoloured	90	90
1182	**1116**	45p. multicoloured	1·10	1·10
1183	**1117**	48p. multicoloured	1·10	1·10
1184	**1118**	50p. multicoloured	1·50	1·50
1185	**1119**	71p. multicoloured	2·00	1·90
1180/5 *Set of 6*			7·00	7·00
First Day Cover				8·50
Presentation Pack			8·50	

The 45p. value includes the 'sepac' emblem. This value was also available in a souvenir folder with ten other 'sepac' logo stamps issued by other participating administrations.

Plate Nos.: All values 1A (×4).
Sheets: 50 (5×10).
Imprint: Upper side margins.
Withdrawn: 30.9.2008.

1120 Crystal Angel

1121 Crystal Decoration

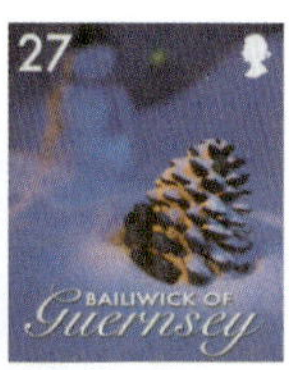

1122 Pine Cone

1123 Bauble

1124 Snowflake

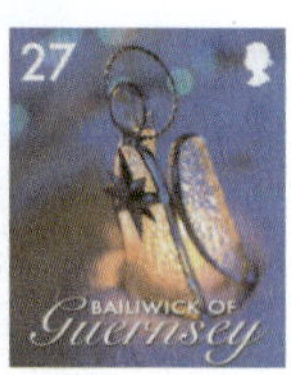

1125 Decoration with Star

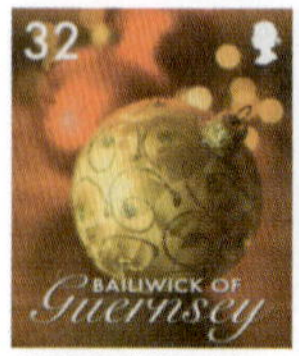

1126 Gold Bauble

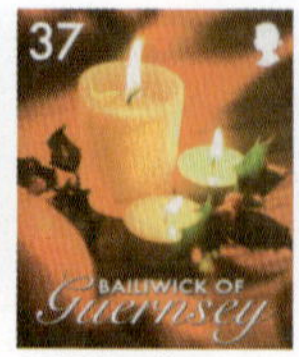

1127 Candles

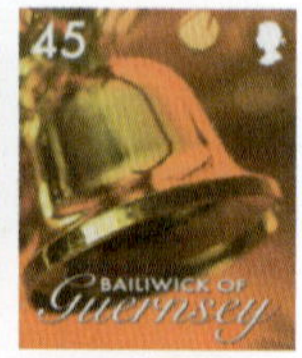

1128 Gold Bell

1129 Wrapped

1130 Spiky Star

1131 Fairy Present

Christmas. Decorations

(Litho Austrian State Ptg Wks, Vienna)

2007 (25 Oct). Perf 14½×15 (C).

1186	**1120**	27p. multicoloured	60	60
1187	**1121**	27p. multicoloured	60	60
1188	**1122**	27p. multicoloured	60	60
1189	**1123**	27p. multicoloured	60	60
1190	**1124**	27p. multicoloured	60	60
1191	**1125**	27p. multicoloured	60	60
1192	**1126**	32p. multicoloured	75	75
1193	**1127**	37p. multicoloured	90	90
1194	**1128**	45p. multicoloured	1·10	1·10
1195	**1129**	48p. multicoloured	1·10	1·10
1196	**1130**	50p. multicoloured	1·20	1·20
1197	**1131**	71p. multicoloured	1·70	1·70
1186/97 *Set of 12*			10·00	10·00
First Day Cover				11·50
Presentation Pack			11·50	

Plate Nos.: All values 1A (×4).
Sheets: 50 (10×5).
Imprint: Upper side margins.
Withdrawn: 24.10.2008.

Yearbook 2007

2007 (1 Dec). Comprises Nos. 1142/97, A298, A301, A304, A308 and A309/28.

Yearbook	85·00

1132 World Touring Car Championship, 2005; 2006; 2007 (*Illustration reduced. Actual size 140×95 mm*)

Andy Priaulx Triple World Touring Car Champion 2005–2007

(Des Chris Griffiths. Litho Walsall)

2008 (18 Jan). Sheet 140×95 mm. Perf 14×14½ (C).

MS1198 **1132** £1×3 multicoloured	7·00	7·50
First Day Cover		8·75
Presentation Pack	8·75	

Withdrawn: 17.1.2009.

1133 Beadlet Anemones

1134 Sand Crocus

1135 Fulmar

1136 Sheep's-bit

1137 Thick-lipped Grey Mullet

1138 Light Bulb Sea-Squirt

Designation of Gouliot Headland and Caves, Sark as RAMSAR Site

(Des Wendy Bramall. Litho BDT)

2008 (28 Feb). Perf 13½ (C).

1199	**1133**	34p. multicoloured	80	80
1200	**1134**	40p. multicoloured	95	95
1201	**1135**	48p. multicoloured	1·10	1·10
1202	**1136**	51p. multicoloured	1·20	1·20
1203	**1137**	53p. multicoloured	1·30	1·30
1204	**1138**	74p. multicoloured	1·70	1·70
1199/204 *Set of 6*			7·00	7·00
First Day Cover				8·75
Presentation Pack			8·75	
MS1205 140×95 mm. Nos. 1199/204			7·00	7·00
First Day Cover				8·75

Plate Nos.: All values 1A (×4).
Sheets: 10 (2×5) with enlarged illustrated margins at right and foot.
Imprint: Central, left-hand margin.
Withdrawn: 27.2.2009.

1139 Red Campion

1140 Great Bindweed

1141 Spear Thistle

1142 Greater Bird's-foot Trefoil

1143 Sheep's-bit

1144 Marguerite

1145 Sea Campion

Wild Flowers (1st series)

(Litho (£1, £2 also embossed) Austrian State Ptg Wks)

2008 (28 Feb). Perf 14 (C).

1211	**1139**	10p. multicoloured	25	25
1212	**1140**	20p. multicoloured	45	45
1213	**1141**	30p. multicoloured	70	70
1214	**1142**	40p. multicoloured	95	95
1215	**1143**	50p. multicoloured	1·20	1·20
1216	**1144**	£1 multicoloured	2·30	2·30
1217	**1145**	£2 multicoloured	4·75	4·75
1211/17 *Set of 7*			10·50	10·50
First Day Cover				14·00
Presentation Pack			12·50	
Set of 7 Gutter Pairs			21·00	

Nos. 1206/10 and 1218/19 are left for possible additions to this definitive series.

A miniature sheet containing Nos. 1210/11 and inscr 'Jersey Post Stamps–2009 Bonus Gift' was distributed by Jersey Post to customers purchasing more than £150 worth of stamp products in 2009.

Plate Nos.: All values 1A (×4).
Sheets: 50 (2 panes 5×5).
Imprint: Upper side margins.

1153 'À la perchôine' ('Till the next time')

1154 'Banjour' ('Hello')

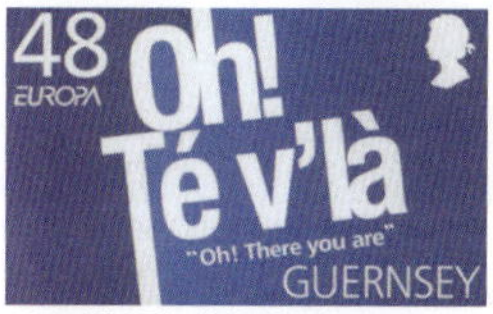

1155 'Oh! Té v'là' ('Oh! There you are')

1156 'Mais oy-ous!' ('Good gracious!')

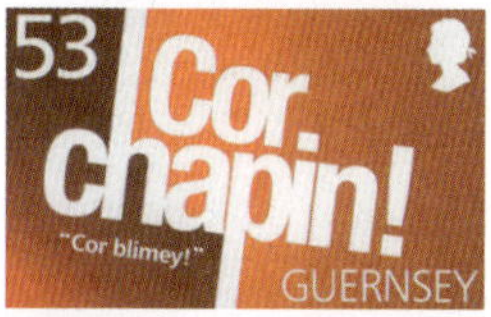

1157 'Cor chapin!' ('Gor blimey!')

1158 'L'affaire va-t-alle?' ('How are things?')

Europa. The Letter. Quotations in Guernsiasis (Guernsey French) and their English Translations

(Des Chris Griffiths. Litho Cartor)

2008 (15 May). Perf 13½×13 (C).

1220	**1153**	34p. multicoloured	80	80
1221	**1154**	40p. multicoloured	95	95
1222	**1155**	48p. multicoloured	1·10	1·10
1223	**1156**	51p. multicoloured	1·20	1·20
1224	**1157**	53p. multicoloured	1·30	1·30
1225	**1158**	74p. multicoloured	1·70	1·70
1220/5 *Set of 6*			7·00	7·00

First Day Cover		8·75
Presentation Pack	8·75	

The new blue plate number/colour dab on the sheet margin of the 40p. value is invisible because of the matching background colour.

Plate Nos.: All values 1A (×4).
Sheets: 10 (2×5) with enlarged illustrated left margins.
Imprint: Upper right-hand margin.
Withdrawn; 14.5.2009.

1159 *Mr. Happy*

1160 *Mr. Bump*

1161 *Little Miss Naughty*

1162 *Mr. Greedy*

1163 *Mr. Strong*

1164 *Mr. Tickle*

Mr. Men and Little Miss Series of Children's Books by Roger Hargreaves

(Des Andrew Fothergill. Litho Enschedé)

2008 (15 May). Perf 14×13½ (C).

1226	**1159**	34p. Type **242**	80	80
1227	**1160**	40p. *Mr. Bump*	95	95
1228	**1161**	48p. *Little Miss Naughty*	1·10	1·10
1229	**1162**	51p. *Mr. Greedy*	1·20	1·20
1230	**1163**	53p. *Mr. Strong*	1·30	1·30
1231	**1164**	74p. *Mr. Tickle*	1·70	1·70
1226/31 *Set of 6*			7·00	7·00
First Day Cover				8·75
Presentation Pack			8·75	

Plate Nos.: All values 1A (×4).
Sheets: 10 (2×5) with enlarged illustrated margins at left and foot.
Imprint: Lower right-hand margin.
Withdrawn: 14.5.2009.

1165 Pleimont Point

1166 Saint's Harbour

1167 Rocks at Albecq

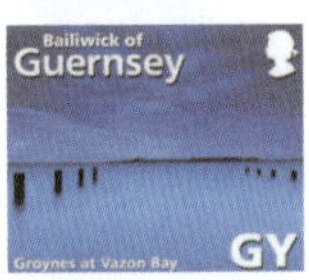

1168 Groynes at Vazon Bay

1169 La Bette Bay

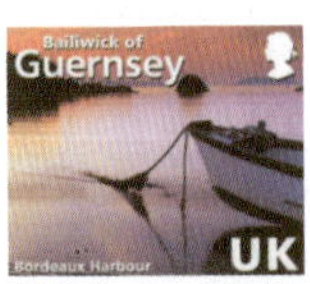

1170 Bordeaux Harbour

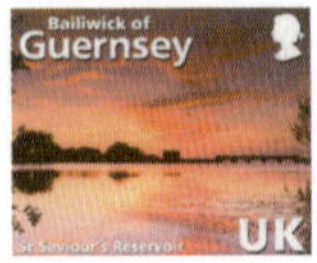

1171 St. Saviour's Reservoir

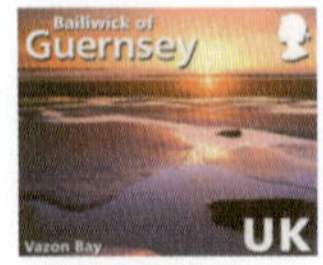

1172 Vazon Bay

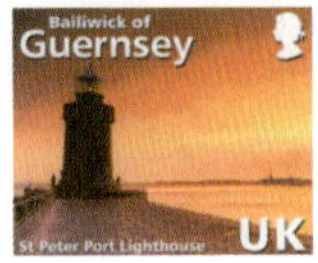

1173 St. Peter Port Lighthouse

1174 Petit Port

'Abstract Guernsey' (1st series). Photographs of Guernsey Coastline

(Litho Walsall)

2008 (9 June). Self-adhesive. Perf 12½ (die-cut).

1232	**1165**	(34p.) multicoloured	80	80
		a. Sheetlet. Nos. 1232/41	8·75	
		b. Booklet pane. Nos. 1232/6, each x2	8·00	
		c. Booklet pane. Nos. 1232/6, each x2	8·00	
1233	**1166**	(34p.) multicoloured	80	80
1234	**1167**	(34p.) multicoloured	80	80
1235	**1168**	(34p.) multicoloured	80	80
1236	**1169**	(34p.) multicoloured	80	80
1237	**1170**	(40p.) multicoloured	95	95
		a. Booklet pane. Nos. 1237/41, each x2	9·50	
		b. Booklet pane. Nos. 1237/41, each x2	9·50	
1238	**1171**	(40p.) multicoloured	95	95
1239	**1172**	(40p.) multicoloured	95	95
1240	**1173**	(40p.) multicoloured	95	95
1241	**1174**	(40p.) multicoloured	95	95
1232/41 *Set of 10*			8·75	8·75
First Day Cover				150
Presentation Pack			150	

Nos. 1232/6 were intended for postage within the Bailiwick and are inscribed 'GY'. They were each initially sold at 34p. Nos. 1237/41 were intended for postage to Great Britain and are inscribed 'UK'. They were each initially sold at 40p.

Stamps from the sheetlet 1232a measure 12.4 all round, but stamps from booklet panes have a slightly different perforation, 12.4×12.7.

Sheets: (5×2). Nos. 1232/41 were printed in sheetlets of ten containing Nos. 1232/41 (available only from the Philatelic Bureau) and also in booklets of ten or 100, all with the surplus self-adhesive paper around each stamp retained. The booklets of ten contain either Nos. 1232/632 (pane no. 1232b) or Nos. 1237/4132 (pane No. 1237a), and the stamps are peeled directly from the cover in two blocks 3×2 and 2×2, the blocks separated by a gutter containing text. The booklets of 100 contain ten panes of either Nos. 1232/6×2 (pane No. 1232c) or 1237/41×2 (pane No. 1237b). These panes have the stamps in one block 5×2, with plain white backing paper and are stitched at left.

1175 Ford Model T Touring Car, 1913

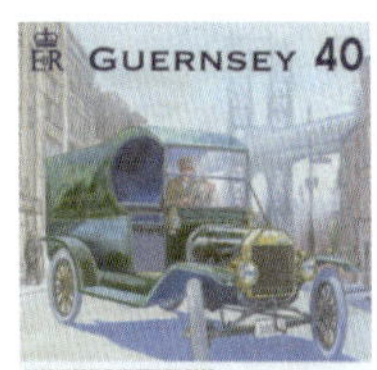

1176 Delivery Van, 1912

1177 Pick-up, 1925

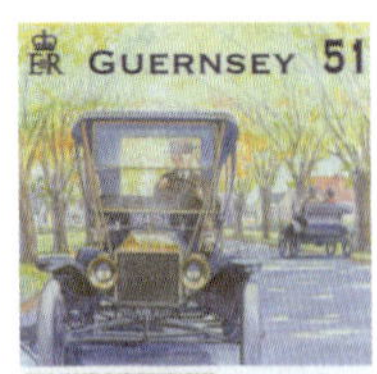

1178 Couplet, 1917

1179 First World War Army Ambulance

1180 Roadster, 1912

Centenary of the Model T Ford

(Des Robin Carter. Litho BDT)

2008 (31 July). Perf 13½ (C).

1242	**1175**	34p. multicoloured	80	80
		a. Booklet pane. Nos. 1242/5 with margins all round	4·00	
		b. Booklet pane. Nos. 1242/3 and 1246/7 with margins all round	4·75	
		c. Booklet pane. Nos. 1242, 1244/5 and 1247 with margins all round	4·75	
		d. Booklet pane. Nos. 1242/3 and 1245/6 with margins all round	4·25	
1243	**1176**	40p. multicoloured	95	95
		a. Booklet pane. Nos. 1243/4 and 1246/7 with margins all round	5·00	
1244	**1177**	48p. multicoloured	1·10	1·10
		a. Booklet pane. Nos. 1244/7 with margins all round	5·25	
1245	**1178**	51p. multicoloured	1·20	1·20
1246	**1179**	53p. multicoloured	1·30	1·30
1247	**1180**	74p. multicoloured	1·70	1·70
1242/7 *Set of 6*			7·00	7·00
First Day Cover				8·75
Presentation Pack			8·75	

Plate Nos.: All values 1A (×4).
Sheets: 10 (2×5) with enlarged illustrated margins at right and foot.
Imprint: Central, left-hand margin.
Withdrawn: 30.7.2009.

1181 Early Drawing of St. Paul's Cathedral

1182 Cathedral and River Thames, 1860s

1183 Cathedral during World War II Blitz

1184 Cathedral illuminated at Night

1185 Close-up of St. Paul's Cathedral

1186 Cathedral seen from Millennium Bridge

Guernsey Granite at St. Paul's Cathedral, London

(Des Mark Whyte. Litho Cartor)

2008 (31 Oct). Perf 13½ (C).

1248	**1181**	34p. multicoloured	80	80
1249	**1182**	40p. multicoloured	95	95
1250	**1183**	48p. multicoloured	1·10	1·10
1251	**1184**	51p. multicoloured	1·20	1·20
1252	**1185**	53p. multicoloured	1·30	1·30
1253	**1186**	74p. multicoloured	1·70	1·70
1248/53 *Set of 6*			7·00	7·00
First Day Cover				8·75
Presentation Pack			8·75	

Nos. 1248/53 commemorate the 300th anniversary of St. Paul's Cathedral.

They all have powdered Guernsey granite applied to the value tablets.

Plate Nos.: All values 1A (×4).
Sheets: 25 (5×5).
Imprint: Upper left margin.
Withdrawn; 29.10.2099.

1187 Spruce

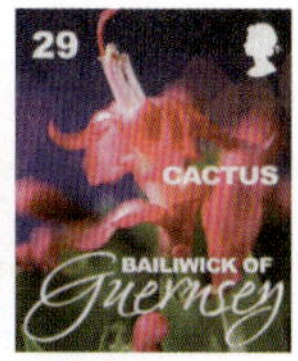

1188 Christmas Cactus

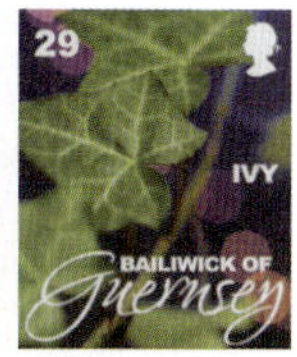

1189 Ivy

1190 Cyclamen

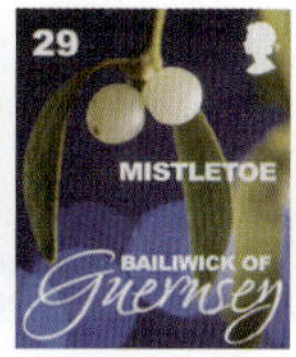

1191 Mistletoe

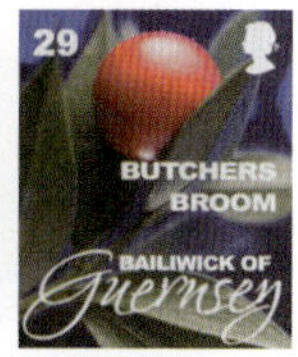

1192 Butchers Broom

1193 Holly

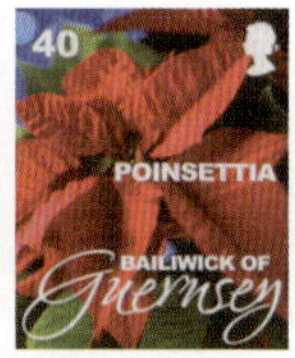

1194 Poinsettia

1195 Bracken

1196 Hawthorn

1197 Clematis 'Peppermint'

1198 Pyracantha

Christmas. Festive Foliage

(Des Andrew Fothergill. Litho Enschedé)

2008 (31 Oct). Perf 14×13½ (C).

1254	**1187**	29p. multicoloured	70	70
1255	**1188**	29p. multicoloured	70	70
1256	**1189**	29p. multicoloured	70	70
1257	**1190**	29p. multicoloured	70	70
1258	**1191**	29p. multicoloured	70	70
1259	**1192**	29p. multicoloured	70	70
1260	**1193**	34p. multicoloured	80	80
1261	**1194**	40p. multicoloured	95	95
1262	**1195**	48p. multicoloured	1·10	1·10
1263	**1196**	51p. multicoloured	1·20	1·20
1264	**1197**	53p. multicoloured	1·20	1·20
1265	**1198**	74p. multicoloured	1·70	1·70
1254/65 *Set of 12*			11·00	11·00
First Day Cover				14·50
Presentation Pack			13·00	

Plate Nos.: All value 1A (×4).
Sheets: 50 (10×5).
Imprint: Upper side margins.
Withdrawn:29.10.2009.

Yearbook 2008

2008 (1 Dec). Comprises Nos. 1199/265 and A329/55.

Yearbook	£110	

1199 Amur Leopard (*Illustration reduced. Actual size* 116×84 mm)

Endangered Species (5th series). Amur Leopard (Panthera pardus orientalis)

(Des Joel Kirk. Litho Enschedé)

2009 (26 Feb). Sheet 116×84 mm. Perf 13½×14 (C).

MS1266 **1199** multicoloured	8·50	8·50
First Day Cover		8·75
Presentation Pack	8·75	

Withdrawn: 27.2.2010.

1200 Land Iguana

1201 Wallaby

1202 Giant Tortoise

1203 Marine Iguana

1204 Guanaco

1205 Komodo Dragon

'Darwin's Discoveries'

(Des Andrew Fothergill. Litho Austrian State Ptg Wks, Vienna)

2009 (26 Feb). Perf 14 (C).

1267	**1200**	36p. multicoloured	85	85
1268	**1201**	43p. multicoloured	1·00	1·00
1269	**1202**	51p. multicoloured	1·25	1·25
1270	**1203**	54p. multicoloured	1·25	1·25
1271	**1204**	56p. multicoloured	1·25	1·25
1272	**1205**	77p. multicoloured	1·75	1·75
1267/72 *Set of* 6			7·25	7·25
First Day Cover				9·25
Presentation Pack			9·25	
MS1273 144×80 mm. Nos. 1267/72			7·50	7·50
First Day Cover				9·25

Nos. 1267/72 commemorate the birth bicentenary of Charles Darwin.

Plate Nos.: All values 1A (×4).
Sheets: 10 (2×5) with enlarged illustrated left margins.
Imprint: Lower right-hand margin.
Withdrawn: 27.2.2010.

1206 Stinking Onion

1207 Common Mallow

1208 Primrose

1209 Loose-flowered Orchid

1210 Common Centaury

1211 Yellow Horned-poppy

1212 Sea Kale

1213 Bluebell

1214 Sea Bindweed

1215 Common Poppy

Wild Flowers (2nd series)

(Des Raymond Evison. Litho (£3 also embossed) Cartor)

2009 (28 May). Perf 13 (C).

1274	**1206**	1p. multicoloured	10	10
1275	**1207**	2p. multicoloured	10	10
1276	**1208**	3p. multicoloured	10	10
1277	**1209**	4p. multicoloured	10	10
1278	**1210**	5p. multicoloured	10	10
1279	**1211**	6p. multicoloured	15	15
1280	**1212**	7p. multicoloured	20	20
1281	**1213**	8p. multicoloured	25	25
1282	**1214**	9p. multicoloured	25	25
1283	**1215**	£3 multicoloured	8·50	8·50
1274/83 *Set of* 10			8·50	8·50
First Day Cover				9·75
Presentation Pack			9·75	

Plate Nos.: All values 1A (each ×4).
Sheets: 50 1p to 9p (5×10) £3 (10×5).

1216 Quasar (digital enhancement)

1217 Asteroid

1218 Satellite View of Sunrays falling on the Earth's Surface

1219 Jupiter, Sun in Background (digital composite)

1220 The Moon touches the Sun before a Total Eclipse

1221 Solar Eruption from the Sun (satellite image)

Europa. Astronomy. 400th Anniversary of the Telescope

(Des Mark Totty. Litho Enschedé)

2009 (28 May). Perf 13 (C).

1284	**1216**	36p. multicoloured	85	85
1285	**1217**	43p. multicoloured	1·00	1·00
1286	**1218**	51p. multicoloured	1·25	1·25
1287	**1219**	54p. multicoloured	1·25	1·25
1288	**1220**	56p. multicoloured	1·40	1·40
1289	**1221**	77p. multicoloured	1·75	1·75
1283/8		*Set of 6*	7·25	7·25
		First Day Cover		9·00
		Presentation Pack	9·00	

Plate Nos.: All values 1A (each ×4).
Sheets: 10 (2×5) with enlarged illustrated right margins.
Imprint: Central, left-hand margin.

1222 Henry VIII as Young Man

1223 Coronation of Henry VIII and Katherine of Aragon, 1509

1224 Meeting of Henry VIII and Francis I, Field of the Cloth of Gold, 1520

1225 Thomas Wolsey presenting Hampton Court Palace to Henry VIII

1226 Henry VIII dancing with Anne Boleyn

1227 Henry VIII watching his Navy as *Mary Rose* sinks, 1545

500th Anniversary of the Coronation of King Henry VIII

(Des Gail Armstrong. Litho BDT)

2009 (30 July). Perf 13 (C).

1290	**1222**	36p. multicoloured	85	85
		a. Booklet pane. No. 1290×4 with margins all round	3·25	
1291	**1223**	43p. multicoloured	1·00	1·00
		a. Booklet pane. No. 1291×4 with margins all round	4·00	
1292	**1224**	51p. multicoloured	1·25	1·25
		a. Booklet pane. No. 1292×4 with margins all round	4·75	
1293	**1225**	54p. multicoloured	1·25	1·25
		a. Booklet pane. No. 1293×4with margins all round	5·00	
1294	**1226**	56p. multicoloured	1·40	1·40
		a. Booklet pane. No. 1294×4 with margins all round	5·00	
1295	**1227**	77p. multicoloured	1·75	1·75
		a. Booklet pane. No. 1295×4 with margins all round	7·00	
1290/5		*Set of 6*	7·25	7·25
		First Day Cover		9·00
		Presentation Pack	9·00	

Plate Nos.: All values 1A (×4).
Sheets: 10 (2×5) with enlarged illustrated right margins.
Imprint: Central, left-hand margin.

1228 'The Psychedelic 60's'

1229 'God Save the 70's'

1230 'The POPular 80's'

1231 'The Urban 90's'

1232 'The Seductive 00's'

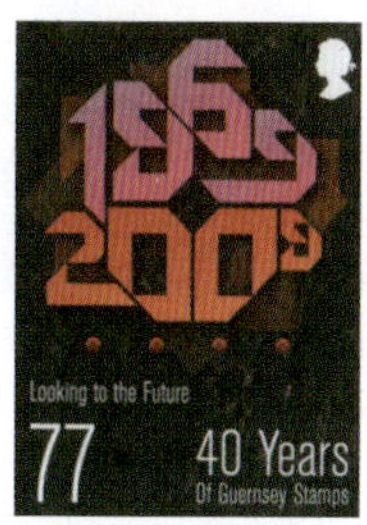

1233 'Looking to the Future'

40th Anniversary of Postal Independence

(Des Paul Mason-Barney. Litho Cartor)

2009 (30 July). Perf 14×13½ (C).

1296	**1228**	36p. multicoloured	85	85
1297	**1229**	43p. multicoloured	1·00	1·00
1298	**1230**	51p. multicoloured	1·25	1·25
1299	**1231**	54p. multicoloured	1·25	1·25
1300	**1232**	56p. multicoloured	1·40	1·40
1301	**1233**	77p. multicoloured	1·75	1·75

1296/301 Set of 6	7·25	7·25
First Day Cover		9·00
Presentation Pack	9·00	

Plate Nos.: All values 1A (each ×4).
Sheets: 10 (5×2).
Imprint: Central, top margin.

1234 Jerbourg Point

1235 Vazon Bay

1236 Saints Bay Moorings

1237 Le Jaonnet Bay

1238 Rocquaine Bay

1239 Bordeaux Harbour

Sea Guernsey (3rd series)

(Litho Enschedé)

2009 (16 Sept). Perf 13½ (C).

1302	**1234**	36p. multicoloured	85	85
1303	**1235**	43p. multicoloured	1·00	1·00
1304	**1236**	51p. multicoloured	1·25	1·25
1305	**1237**	54p. multicoloured	1·25	1·25
1306	**1238**	56p. multicoloured	1·40	1·40
1307	**1239**	77p. multicoloured	1·75	1·75
1302/7 *Set of 6*			7·25	7·25
First Day Cover				9·00
Presentation Pack			9·00	

The 51p value includes the 'sepac' emblem.
Plate Nos.: All values 1A (×4).
Sheets: 50 (5×10).
Imprint: Upper side margins.

1240 Castel Church

1241 Torteval Church

1242 St. Martin's Church

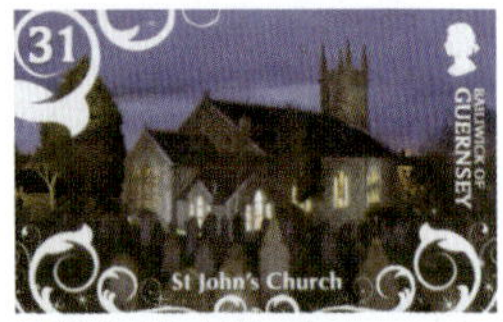

1243 St. John's Church

1244 St. Sampson's Church

1245 St. Peter Port Church

1246 St. Mathew's Church

1247 St. Saviour's Church

1248 Forest Church

1249 St. Andrew's Church

1250 Vale Church

1251 St. Peter's Church

Christmas. Churches

(Litho BDT)

2009 (29 Oct). Perf 13½ (C).

1308	**1240**	31p. multicoloured	75	75
1309	**1241**	31p. multicoloured	75	75
1310	**1242**	31p. multicoloured	75	75
1311	**1243**	31p. multicoloured	75	75
1312	**1244**	31p. multicoloured	75	75
1313	**1245**	31p. multicoloured	75	75
1314	**1246**	36p. multicoloured	85	85
1315	**1247**	43p. multicoloured	1·00	1·00
1316	**1248**	51p. multicoloured	1·25	1·25
1317	**1249**	54p. multicoloured	1·25	1·25
1318	**1250**	56p. multicoloured	1·40	1·40
1319	**1251**	77p. multicoloured	1·75	1·75
1308/19 *Set of 12*			11·50	11·50
First Day Covers (2)				15·00
Presentation Pack			13·50	

Plate Nos.: All values 1A (×4).
Sheets: 50 (5×10).
Imprint: Central, bottom margin.

Yearbook 2009

2009 (1 Dec). Comprises Nos. **MS**1266/319 *and* A356/80.

Yearbook .... 90·00

1252 Asian Elephant (*Illustration reduced. Actual size* 118×84 mm)

Endangered Species (6th series). Asian Elephant (*Elephas maximus*)

(Des Joel Kirk. Litho Austrian State Ptg Wks, Vienna)

2010 (25 Feb). *Sheet* 118×84 mm. Perf 14 (C).

MS1320 **1252** multicoloured	7·25	7·25
First Day Cover		9·00
Presentation Pack	9·00	

1253 Port à la Jument, Sark

1254 The Dog and Lion Rocks

1255 Fort Grey

1256 Sunset on West Coast of Guernsey

1257 Slipway at Havelet Bay at Sunrise

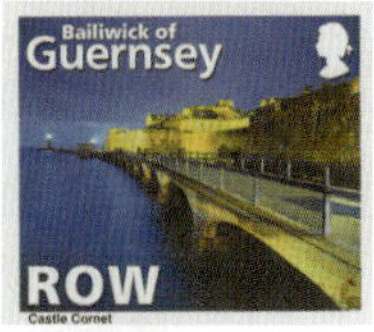

1258 Castle Cornet

Abstract Guernsey (2nd series). Photographs of Guernsey Coastline

(Litho Cartor)

2010 (18 Mar).

(a) Ordinary gum. Perf 13 (C).

1321	**1253**	(48p.) multicoloured	1·10	1·10
		a. Pair. Nos. 1321/2	2·25	2·25
1322	**1254**	(48p.) multicoloured	1·10	1·10
1323	**1255**	(50p.) multicoloured	1·25	1·25
1324	**1256**	(58p.) multicoloured	1·40	1·40
		a. Pair. Nos. 1324/5	2·75	2·75
1325	**1257**	(58p.) multicoloured	1·40	1·40
1326	**1258**	(80p.) multicoloured	1·90	1·90
1321/6 Set of 6			8·00	8·00
First Day Cover				10·00

(b) Self-adhesive. Perf 12½ (die-cut)

1327	**1253**	(48p.) multicoloured	1·10	1·10
		a. Sheetlet. Nos. 1327/32	8·00	
		b. Booklet pane. Nos. 1327/8, each ×2	4·50	
		c. Booklet pane. Nos. 1327/8, each ×5	10·00	
1328	**1254**	(48p.) multicoloured	1·10	1·10
1329	**1255**	(50p.) multicoloured	1·25	1·25
1330	**1256**	(58p.) multicoloured	1·40	1·40
		a. Booklet pane. Nos. 1330/1, each ×2	5·50	
		b. Booklet pane. Nos. 1330/1, each ×5	12·00	
1331	**1257**	(58p.) multicoloured	1·40	1·40
1332	**1258**	(80p.) multicoloured	1·90	1·90
1327/32 Set of 6			8·00	8·00
First Day Cover				10·00
Presentation Pack			17·00	

Nos. 1321/2 and 1324/5 were each printed together, *se-tenant*, as horizontal and vertical pairs in sheets of 20.

Nos. 1321/2 and 1327/8 were intended for postage within the Bailiwick and are inscribed 'GY LARGE'. They were each initially sold at 48p.

Nos. 1324/5 and 1330/1 were intended for postage to Great Britain and are inscribed 'UK LARGE'. They were each initially sold at 58p.

Nos. 1323 and 1329 for postage to Europe are inscribed 'EUR' and were initially sold at 50p. each.

Nos. 1326 and 1332 for postage to rest of world are inscribed 'ROW' and were initially sold at 80p. each.

Nos. 1327/32 were printed together in sheetlets of ten. Nos. 1327/8 and 1330/1 were also available from booklets of four, Nos. SB91/2, originally sold at £1.92 or £2.32, and booklets of 50, Nos. Sb93/4, originally sold at £24 and £29.

Nos. 1327/8 and 1330/1 were also issued in booklets of 50, not yet received.

Plate Nos.: All values 1A (each ×4).

Sheets: 20 (5×4). Nos. 1321/2 and 1324/5 (the GY LARGE and UK LARGE values) were each printed together, *se-tenant*, in vertical pairs throughout the sheets.

Imprint: Top margin at left.

1259 Penny the Postie and Pirate Captain Titch in Boat made from Wooden Chest

1260 Captain Titch spies enemy Captain Bullybones

1261 Captain Titch reclaiming his Stolen Ship

Europa. Children's Books. The Adventures of Penny the Postie by Keith Robinson

(Des Keith Robinson. Litho BDT)

2010 (4 May). Perf 13 (45p.) or 14 (50p., £2) (both comb).

1333	**1259**	45p multicoloured	1·00	1·00
1334	**1260**	50p multicoloured	1·25	1·25
1335	**1261**	£2 multicoloured	4·50	4·50
1333/5 *Set of 3*			6·75	6·75
First Day Cover				9·50
Presentation Pack			8·50	
MS1336 149×96 mm. Nos. 1333/5			6·75	6·75
First Day Cover				9.50

No. **MS**1336 is cut around in the shape of a scroll.

Plate Nos.: All values 1A (each ×4).

Sheets: 10 (5×2).

Imprint: Top margin at left.

1262 Guide kayaking ('Outdoor Activities')

1263 Spitfire crossing Searchlights ('Help during WW1&2')

1264 Crystal Palace Maze (renovated to celebrate Centenary)

1265 Agnes Baden-Powell (founder) wearing First Guide Uniform

1266 Mount Everest (Guide trek to base camp, 2009)

1267 Queen's Guide Award

Centenary of Girl Guiding. Embroidered Badges

(Des Paul Mason-Barney. Litho Enschedé)

2010 (27 May). Perf 13½ (C).

1337	**1262**	36p multicoloured	80	80
1338	**1263**	45p multicoloured	1·00	1·00
1339	**1264**	48p multicoloured	1·10	1·10
1340	**1265**	50p multicoloured	1·25	1·25
1341	**1266**	58p multicoloured	1·40	1·40
1342	**1267**	80p multicoloured	1·75	1·75
1337/42 Set of 6			7·25	7·25
First Day Cover				10·00
Presentation Pack			17·00	

Plate Nos.: All values 1A (each ×4).

Sheets: 10 (5×2).

Imprint: Top margin at left.

POSTAGE DUE STAMPS

D **1** Castle Cornet

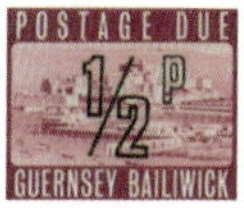

D **2** Castle Cornet

(Des R. Barrett. Photo Delrieu)

1969 (1 Oct). Face value in black; background colour given. No wmk. Perf 12½×12 (C).

D1	D **1**	1d. plum	2·00	1·20
D2		2d. bright green	2·00	1·20
D3		3d. vermilion	3·00	4·00
D4		4d. ultramarine	4·00	5·00
D5		5d. yellow-ochre	6·00	4·00
D6		6d. turquoise-blue	6·00	4·50
D7		1s. lake-brown	10·00	8·00
D1/7 *Set of 7*			30·00	25·00

Sheets: 60 (10×6).
Quantities sold: 1d. 82,802; 2d. 75,340; 3d. 74,532; 4d. 74,659; 5d. 71,129; 6d. 72,912; 1s 71,659.
Withdrawn and Invalidated: 14.2.72.

Decimal Currency

(Des R. Granger Barrett. Photo Delrieu)

1971 (15 Feb)–**76**. No wmk. Perf 12½×12 (C).

D8	D **2**	½p. plum (a)	10	10
D9		1p. bright green (a)	10	10
D10		2p. vermilion (a)	10	10
D11		3p. ultramarine (a)	10	10
D12		4p. yellow-ochre (a)	10	10
D13		5p. turquoise-blue (a)	10	10
D14		6p. violet (c)	10	10
D15		8p. yellow-orange (b)	20	40
D16		10p. lake-brown (a)	20	20
D17		15p. grey (c)	30	50
D8/17 *Set of 10*			1·20	1·50
D1/13, 16 *Presentation Pack* (a)			75·00	
D8/17 *Presentation Pack* (c)			2·00	

Printings: (a) 15.2.71; (b) 7.10.75; (c) 10.2.76.
Sheets: 60 (10×6).
Withdrawn: 14.2.72 *Presentation Pack* (Nos. D1/13 and D16); 1.8.78 ½p. to 15p. (½ and 1p. sold out by 6.78).

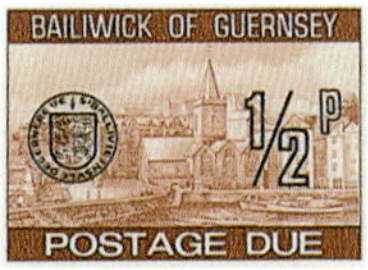

D **3** St. Peter Port

(Photo Delrieu)

1977 (2 Aug)–**80**. Face value in black; background colour given. Perf 13 (C).

D18	D **3**	½p. lake-brown (a)	10	10
D19		1p. bright purple (a)	10	10
D20		2p. bright orange (a)	10	10
D21		3p. vermilion (a)	10	10
D22		4p. turquoise-blue (a)	10	10
D23		5p. yellow-green (a)	10	10
D24		6p. turquoise-green (a)	10	10
D25		8p. brown-ochre (a)	10	10
D26		10p. ultramarine (a)	10	10
D27		14p. green (b)	20	20
D28		15p. bright violet (a)	20	20
D29		16p. rose-red (b)	30	30
D18/29 *Set of 12*			1·50	1·50
D18/26, 28 *Presentation Pack*			2·00	

Printings: (a) 2.8.77; (b) 5.2.80.
Sheets: 50 (5×10).
Withdrawn: 12.7.83.
(Presentation Pack sold out earlier)

D **4** Milking Cow

D **5** Vale Mill

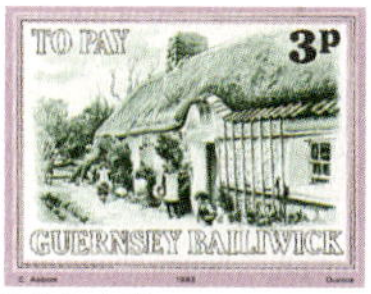

D **6** Sark Cottage

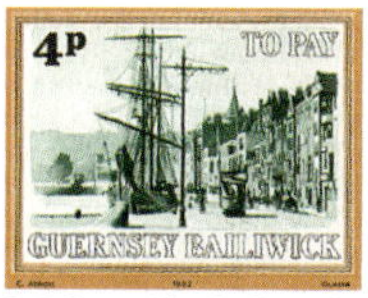

D **7** Quay-side, St. Peter Port

D **8** Well, Water Lane, Moulin Huet

D **9** Seaweed Gathering

D **10** Upper Walk, White Rock

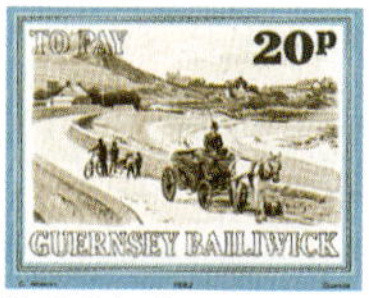

D **11** Cobo Bay

D **12** Saint's Bay

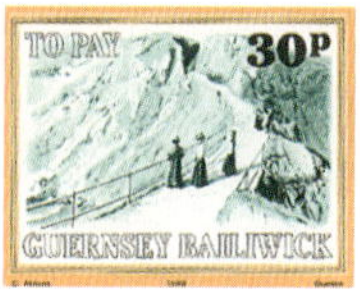

D **13** La Coupée, Sark

D **14** Old Harbour, ST. Peter Port

D **15** Greenhouse, Doyle Road, ST. Peter Port

Guernsey Scenes, c. 1900

(Des C. Abbott. Litho Questa)

1982 (13 July). Perf 14½ (C).

D30	D **4**	1p. indigo, blue-black & brt grn	10	10
D31	D **5**	2p. yellow-brown, sepia & azure	10	10
D32	D **6**	3p. blackish green, black & lilac	10	10
D33	D **7**	4p. bottle green, blk & dull orge	10	10
D34	D **8**	5p. deep violet-blue, blue-black and turquoise-green	10	10
D35	D **9**	16p. dp grey-blue, dp bl & cobalt	30	35
D36	D **10**	18p. steel bl, indigo & apple grn	35	40
D37	D **11**	20p. brown-olive, agate & pale bl	40	45
D38	D **12**	25p. Prussian blue, blue-black and rose-pink	50	55
D39	D **13**	30p. deep bluish green, blackish olive and bistre-yellow	60	65
D40	D **14**	50p. olive-brown, sepia and dull violet-blue	1·00	1·10
D41	D **15**	£1 lt brown, brown & pale brn	2·00	2·10
D30/41 *Set of 12*			5·25	5·75
Presentation Pack			6·00	

Sheets: 50 (5×10).
Imprint: Bottom corner, right-hand margin.
Withdrawn: 30.9.2001.

STAMP BOOKLETS

Prices given are for complete booklets. Booklets Nos. SB1/12 are stitched.

B **1** Military Uniforms

1969 (12 Dec). White covers as Type B **1**, printed in black.

SB1	2s. booklet containing 3×4d. (No. 18a), 2×5d. (No. 19a) and 2×1d. (No. 14c) (cover showing Trooper, Royal Guernsey Cavalry (Light Dragoons), 1814)	50
SB2	4s. booklet containing 6×4d. (No. 18a), 4×5d. (No. 19a) and 4×1d. (No. 14c) (cover showing Officer, St. Martin's Company (La Milice Bleue), Guernsey, 1720)	1·50
SB3	6s. booklet containing 9×4d. (No. 18a), 6×5d. (No. 19a) and 6×1d. (No. 14c) (cover showing Colour Sergeant of Grenadiers and Rifleman, East (Town) Regiment, Guernsey, 1833)	1·50

Withdrawn: 14.2.72.

1970 (29 June). White covers as Type B **1**. Printed in black (SB4), green (SB5) or red (SB6). Same composition as Nos. SB1/3.

SB4	2s. booklet (cover showing Officer, Royal Guernsey Horse Artillery, 1793)	2·00
SB5	4s. booklet (cover showing Gunner, Royal Guernsey Artillery, 1743)	12·00
SB6	6s. booklet (cover showing Sergeant, Royal Guernsey Light Infantry, 1832)	12·00

Quantities sold: 2s (SB1, SB4), 81,928; 4s (SB2, SB5), 23,817; 6s (SB3, SB6), 25,123.
Withdrawn: 14.2.72.

Decimal Currency

1971 (15 Feb). White covers as Type B **1**. Printed in black (SB7), green (SB8) or red (SB9).

SB7	10p. booklet containing 2×½p. (No. 44a), 2×2p. (No. 47a) and 2×2½p. (No. 48b) (cover showing Officer, Royal Guernsey Horse Artillery, 1850)	85
SB8	20p. booklet containing 4×½p. (No. 44a), 4×2p. (No. 47a) and 4×2½p. (No. 48b) (cover showing Sergeant, Guernsey Light Infantry (Grenadiers), 1826)	70
SB9	30p. booklet containing 6×½p. (No. 44a), 6×2p. (No. 47a) and 6×2½p. (No 48b) (cover showing Sergeant and Bandsman, Royal Guernsey Light Infantry (North Regiment), 1866)	1·00

Withdrawn: 27.6.73 (SB7); 12.3.75 (SB8); 15.1.75 (SB9).

1973 (2 Apr). White covers as Type B **1**. Printed in black (SB10), green (SB11) or red (SB12).

SB10	10p. booklet containing 2×½p. (No. 44ab), 2×2p. (No. 47ab) and 2×2½p. (No. 48ba) (cover showing Officer, Guernsey Horse Artillery, 1828)	40
SB11	20p. booklet containing 4×½p. (No. 44ab), 4×2p. (No. 47ab) and 4×2½p. (No. 48ba) (cover showing Grenadier, Guernsey Light Infantry, 1792)	45
SB12	30p. booklet containing 6×½p. (No. 44ab), 6×2p. (No. 47ab) and 6×2½p. (No. 48ba) (cover showing Insignia, Royal Guernsey Light Infantry)	70

Nos. SB10/12 are inscribed 'January 1973' on back cover.
Withdrawn: 1.4.75.

B **2** Arms of Guernsey

1974 (2 Apr). Silver (SB13) or gold cover (SB140 as Type B 2).

SB13	10p. booklet containing five ½p. stamps and three 2½p. in se-tenant strip (No. 98a)	35
SB14	35p. booklet containing four ½p. stamps, six 2½p. and six 3p. in se-tenant pane (No. 98b)	75

The strips and panes have the left-hand selvedge stuck into booklet covers and then folded and supplied in plastic wallets.
Withdrawn: 6.2.79.

1977 (8 Feb). Green cover as Type B **2**.

SB15	20p. booklet containing No. 99a	55

The note beneath No. SB14 also applies here.
Withdrawn: 12.2.80.

BOOKLET PANES from Nos. SB16/18 are loose within card covers supplied in plastic sachets.

1978 (7 Feb). Blue cover as Type B **2**.

SB16	10p. booklet containing No. 99b	35

Withdrawn: 12.2.80.

1979 (13 Feb). Covers as Type B **2**.

SB17	10p. booklet containing No. 178a (black and green cover)	40
SB18	30p. booklet containing No. 179a (black and red cover)	90

Withdrawn: 23.2.82.

B **3** Castle Cornet (*Illustration reduced. Actual size* 88×54 mm)

1980 (6 May). Horiz covers as Type B **3**. Folded.

SB19	30p. booklet containing No. 177a (blue printed cover, Type C)	60
SB20	50p. booklet containing No. 177b (brown printed cover showing view from the sea)	90

Withdrawn: 4.5.83.

1981 (24 Feb). Covers similar to Type B **3**, but vert. Folded.

SB21	60p. booklet containing No. 180a (red printed cover showing Fort Grey)	1·20
SB22	£1.20. booklet containing No. 180b (green printed cover showing Rokaine Castle)	2·50

Withdrawn 23.2.84.

1982 (2 Feb). Covers similar to Type B **3** showing Fort George. Folded.

SB23	70p. booklet containing No. 181b (orange printed cover showing main entrance)	1·50
SB24	£1.30. booklet containing No. 181c (magenta printed cover showing aerial view of Citadel)	2·20

Withdrawn: 22.7.85.

1983 (14 Mar). Covers similar to Type B **3**. Folded.

SB25	£1 booklet containing No. 180c (new blue printed cover showing States Office, St. Peter Port)	1·90
SB26	£1.30 booklet containing No. 180d (sepia printed cover showing Constable's Office, St. Peter Port)	2·50

Withdrawn: 22.7.85.

BOOKLET PANES from Nos. SB27/38 are loose within card covers.

B **4** View of Post Office Headquarters, St. Peter Port (*Illustration reduced. Actual size* 86×51 mm)

1984 (18 Sept). Multicoloured covers as Type B **4**.

SB27 £1 booklet containing No. 299a .... 2·00
SB28 £1.30 booklet containing No. 299b (cover showing Head Post Office, St. Peter Port) .... 2·50
Quantities sold: SB27 50,393; SB28 25,372.
Withdrawn: 1.87.

1985 (19 Mar). Multicoloured covers as Type B **4**.

SB29 £1.20 booklet containing No. 304a (cover showing French Halles, St. Peter Port) .... 2·50
SB30 £1.30 booklet containing No. 304b (cover showing Market Halls, St. Peter Port) .... 2·50
Quantities sold: SB29 49,248; SB30 45,463.
Withdrawn: 8.87.

1985 (2 Dec). Multicoloured cover as Type B **4**, but vert.

SB31 50p. booklet containing No. 297a (cover showing Victoria Tower, St. Peter Port) .... 1·60
Quantity sold: 55,768.
Withdrawn: 8.87.

1986 (1 Apr). Multicoloured cover as Type B **4**, but vert.

SB32 £1.20 booklet containing No. 305a (cover showing St. James-the-Less, St. Peter Port) .... 3·00
Quantity sold: 32,627.
Withdrawn: 2.89.

1987 (30 Mar). Multicoloured covers as Type B **4**, but vert.

SB33 £1 booklet containing No. 298a (cover showing Lukis Observatory, St. Peter Port) .... 2·50
SB34 £1.30 booklet containing No. 306a (cover showing Weighbridge, St. Peter Port) .... 3·00
Quantities sold: SB33 42,478; SB34 36,369.
Withdrawn: 2.89.

1988 (28 Mar). Multicoloured covers as Type B **4**, but vert.

SB35 £1 booklet containing No. 299c (cover showing North Pier Light, St. Peter Port) .... 2·75
SB36 £1.40 booklet containing No. 306ba (cover showing Castle Light, St. Peter Port) .... 3·00
Quantities sold: SB35 41,092; SB36 39,478.
Withdrawn: 2.90.

1989 (28 Feb). Multicoloured covers as Type B **4**, but vert.

SB37 £1 booklet containing No. 299d (cover showing Town Church, St. Peter Port) .... 3·00
SB38 £1.20 booklet containing No. 306bb (cover showing St. Barnabas Church, St. Peter Port) .... 3·50
Quantities sold: SB37 47,175; SB38 41,235.
Withdrawn: 12.90.

B **5** Opening Ceremony, 1939 (*Illustration reduced. Actual size* 163×97 mm)

50th Anniversary of Guernsey Airport

1989 (5 May). Multicoloured cover, Type B **5**. Booklet contains text and Illustrations on panes and interleaving pages. Stitched.

SB39 £3.90 booklet containing Nos. 456a, 458a and 460a .. 8·00
Quantity sold: 38,025 Sold out: By 11.89.

1989 (27 Dec). Multicoloured covers as Type B **4**, but vert.

SB40 £1.20 booklet containing No. 301a (cover showing Fish Market, St. Peter Port) .... 3·00

HAVE YOU READ THE NOTES AT THE BEGINNING OF THIS CATALOGUE?

These often provide answers to the enquiries we receive

SB41 £1.70 booklet containing No. 308a (cover showing Lloyds Bank, St. Peter Port) .... 3·75
Quantities sold: SB40 31,736; SB41 31,743.
Withdrawn: 21.5.92.

B **6** Crown Hotel (*Illustration reduced. Actual size* 163×97 mm)

50th Anniversary of First Guernsey Stamps

1991 (18 Feb). Multicoloured cover, Type B **6**. Booklet contains text on panes and text and illustrations on interleaving pages. Stitched.

SB42 £4.41 booklet containing No. 517a×3 .... 10·00
Quantity sold: 31,955.
Withdrawn: 17.2.92.

1991 (2 Apr). Multicoloured covers as Type B **4**, but vert.

SB43 £1.30 booklet containing No. 300a (cover showing Golden Lion Inn, St. Peter Port) .... 3·75
SB44 £1.80 booklet containing No. 309a (cover showing National Trust Building, St. Peter Port .... 5·50
Quantities sold: SB43 36,066; SB44 26,029.
Withdrawn: 21.5.92.

B **7** Carnations

1992 (22 May). Multicoloured covers as Type B **7**. Without barcode on the reverse. Panes attached by selvedge.

SB45 £1.45 booklet containing pane No. 572ac (cover Type B**7**) .... 4·00
SB46 £1.80 booklet containing pane No. 574ac (cover showing mixed freesias) .... 6·00
Withdrawn: 31.8.99.

B **8** Bow of Ship and Relics (*Illusration reduced. Actual size* 163×97 mm)

'Operation Asterix'

1992 (18 Sept). Multicoloured cover, Type B **8**. Booklet contains text and illustrations on interleaving pages. Stitched.

SB47 £5.60 booklet containing No. 583a×4 .... 15·00
Quantity sold: 24,211.
Withdrawn: 17.9.93.

1993 (2 Mar)–**95**. Multicoloured covers as Type B **7**, but different Guernsey Post Office logo. Without barcode on the reverse. Panes attached by selvedge.

SB48 £1.12 booklet containing pane No. 577ab (cover showing Lisianthus) .... 3·50

SB49 £1.28 booklet containing pane No. 572ad (cover Type B 7) .... 3·25
  a. With barcode sticker on reverse (6.95) .... 7·00
  b. Barcode printed on reverse (10.95) .... 4·00

SB50 £1.92 booklet containing pane No. 575ab (cover showing standard roses) .... 5·50
  a. With barcode sticker on reverse (3.95) .... 9·00
  b. Barcode printed on reverse (6.95) .... 5·25

Withdrawn: 31.8.99.

B **9** Thomas de la Rue (*Illustration reduced. Actual size* 163×97 mm)

Birth Bicentenary of Thomas de la Rue (printer)

1993 (27 July). Multicoloured cover as Type B **9**. Booklet contains text and illustrations on interleaving pages. Stapled.

SB51 £5.60 booklet containing panes Nos. 617a/21a .... 13·00

Withdrawn: 26.7.94.

1994 (18 Feb). Multicoloured cover as Type B **7**, but different Guernsey Post Office logo. With barcode on reverse. Pane attached by selvedge.

SB52 £1 booklet containing pane No. 576ab (cover showing Iris 'Ideal') .... 3·00

Withdrawn: 31.8.99.

B **10** Guernsey View 1936 Bently (*Illustration reduced. Actual size* 162×97 mm)

Centenary of First Car in Guernsey

1994 (19 July). Black and grey cover as Type B **10**. Booklet contains text and Illustrations on labels attached to panes and on interleaving pages. Stitched.

SB53 £7 booklet containing panes Nos. 639a/43a 19·00

Withdrawn 18.7.95.

B **11** Coins, Postbox and Stamps 'Face'

Greetings Stamps. 'The Welcoming Face of Guernsey'

1995 (28 Feb). Multicoloured cover as Type B **11**. Miniature sheet folded and attached by selvedge.

SB54 £1.92 booklet containing No. **MS**671 .... 4·50

Withdrawn: 27.2.96.

B **12** Stamps and Magnifying Glass (*Illustration reduced. Actual size* 97×163 mm)

Centenary of Cinema. Screen Detectives

1996 (6 Nov). Multicoloured cover as Type B **12**. Booklet contains text and illustrations on margins of panes and interleaving pages. Stitched.

SB55 £7.04 booklet containing panes Nos. 711a/15a .... 19·00

Quantity sold: 18,370.

Withdrawn: 5.11.97.

B **13** Freesia 'Pink Glow'

1997 (2 Jan). Multicoloured covers as Type B **13**. With barcode on reverse. Panes attached by selvedge.

SB56 £1.04 booklet containing pane No. 576bb (cover Type B **13**) .... 4·50

SB57 £1.44 booklet containing pane No. 572bb (cover showing Standard Rose) .... 4·75

SB58 £2 booklet containing No. 576ab×2 (cover showing Iris 'Ideal') .... 14·00

Withdrawn: 31.8.99.

B **14** Castle Conet, Guernsey

Guernsey Scenes (1st series)

1997 (24 Apr). Multicoloured covers as Type B **14**. Self- adhesive.

SB59	£1.04 booklet containing pane No. 739a (cover as Type B **14**)	6·00
SB60	£1.44 booklet containing pane No. 737a (cover showing Shell Beach, Herm)	7·50
SB61	£2 booklet containing pane No. 738a (cover showing La Seigneurie, Sark)	8·50

Withdrawn: 31.3.98.

B **15** Queen Elizabeth and Prince Philip (*Illustration reduced. Actual size* 162×95 mm)

Golden Wedding

1997 (20 Nov). Multicoloured cover as Type B **15**. Booklet contains text and illustrations on panes and interleaving pages. Stitched.

SB62	£8.48 booklet containing Nos. 754a/b, 756a and 758a	22·00

Withdrawn: 19.11.98.

B **16** Milennium Tapestry (*Illustration reduced. Actual size* 162×97 mm)

The Millennium Tapestries Project

1998 (10 Feb). Multicoloured cover as Type B **16**. Booklet contains text and illustrations on pane margins and inter- leaving pages. Stitched.

SB63	£7.50 booklet containing Nos. 760b/c, 762a, 764a and 766a	18·00

Withdrawn: 9.2.99.

B **17** Fort Grey

Guernsey Scenes (2nd series)

1998 (25 Mar). Multicoloured covers as Type B **17**. Self-adhesive.

SB64	£1.60 booklet containing pane No. 770b (cover as Type B **17**)	7·00
SB65	£2 booklet containing pane No. 772b (cover showing Guernsey cow)	8·00

Sold out: 6.2001.

B **18** Queen Elizabeth the Queen Mother (*Illustration reduced. Actual size* 160×100 mm)

Life and Times of Queen Elizabeth the Queen Mother

1999 (4 Feb). Multicoloured cover as Type B **18**. Booklet contains text and Illustrations on pane margins and interleaving pages. Stitched.

SB66	£7.50 booklet containing panes Nos. 817b/c, 819b, 821b and 923b	18·00

Withdrawn: 3.2.2000.

B **19** Supermarine Spitfire over St. Peter Port (*Illustration reduced. Actual size* 163×97 mm)

60th Anniversary of Battle of Britain

2000 (28 Apr). Multicoloured cover as Type B **19**. Booklet contains text and Illustrations on interleaving pages. Stitched.

SB67	£6.99 booklet containing pages Nos. 857a/c, 858a and 862a	18·00

Withdrawn: 27.4.2001.

B **20** Albecq (*Illustration reduced. Actual size* 100×60 mm)

Island Scenes

2001 (26 Apr). Multicoloured covers as Type B **20**. Self- adhesive.

SB68 (£2.20) booklet containing pane No. 901b (cover as Type B **20**) ..... 5·00

SB69 (£2.70) booklet containing pane No. 906b (cover showing Telegraph Bay, Alderney) ..... 7·50

Sold out: By 7.2004.

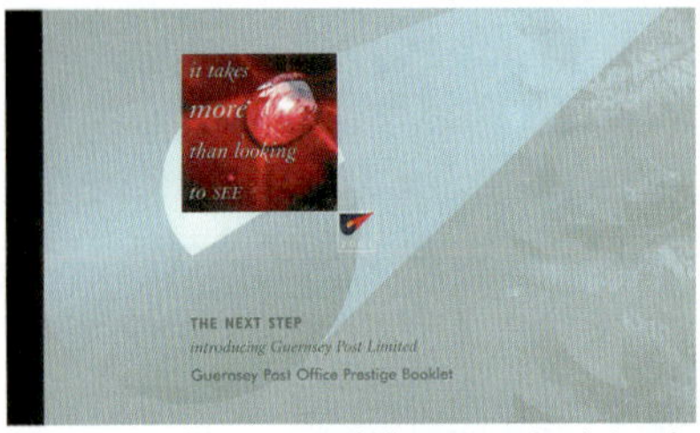

B **21** Droplet of Water on Leaf (*Illustration reduced. Actual size* 160×95 mm)

Incorporation of Guernsey Post Ltd

2001 (1 Aug). Multicoloured cover as Type B **21**. Booklet contains text on panes and transparent interleaves. Stitched.

SB70 £8.05 booklet containing panes Nos. 921a/7a ..... 18·00

Withdrawn: 31.7.02.

B **22** Queen Elizabeth carrying Bouquet (*Illustration reduced. Actual size* 165×98 mm)

Golden Jubilee

2002 (30 Apr). Multicoloured cover as Type B **22**. Booklet contains text and photographs on interleaving panes. Stitched.

SB71 £9.05 booklet containing panes Nos. 948a/c and 949a with Alderney No. **MS**A184 ..... 20·00

Withdrawn: 29.4.2003.

B **23** Prince William and His Coat of arms (*Illustration reduced. Actual size* 162×98 mm)

21st Birthday of Prince William of Wales

2003 (21 June). Multicoloured cover as Type B **23**. Booklet contains text and photographs on panes and interleaving pages. Stitched.

SB72 £8.10 booklet containing panes Nos. 998ba/bc and 999ba/bb ..... 18·00

Withdrawn: 20.6.2004.

B **24** Clematis 'Pistachio' (*Illustration reduced. Actual size* 100×60 mm)

Raymond Evison's Guernsey Clematis

2004 (29 Jan). Multicoloured covers as Type B **24**. Self-adhesive (Nos. SB73/4) or stitched (Nos. SB75/6).

SB73 (£2.20) booklet containing pane No. 1017b (cover Type B **24**) ..... 7·00

SB74 (£2.70) booklet containing pane No. 1022a) (cover showing Clematis 'Anna Louise') ..... 8·75

SB75 (£22) booklet containing ten panes of No. 1017c (cover as Type B **24**, but 181×59 mm) .. 50·00

SB76 (£27) booklet containing ten panes of No. 1022b) (cover showing Clematis 'Anna Louise', 181×59 mm) ..... 60·00

Sold out: By 10.2007.

B **25** Ruins of Ancient Greece (*Illustration reduced. Actual size* 163×98 mm)

Olympic Games, Athens, Greece

2004 (29 July). Multicoloured cover as Type B **25**. Booklet contains text and illustrations on panes and interleaving pages. Stitched.

SB77 £9.90 booklet containing panes Nos. 1045a/d, 1046a and **MS**1049a ..... 22·00

Withdrawn: 28.7.2005.

B **26** St. Peter Port Harbour and Castle Cornet at Dawn (*Illustration reduced. Actual size* 164×98 mm)

'Sea Guernsey 2005'

2005 (21 July). Multicoloured cover as Type B **26**. Booklet contains text and illustrations on panes and interleaving pages. Stitched.

SB78 £9.69 booklet containing panes Nos. 1080a/b, 1081a/b, 1082a and 1083a .... 22·00

Withdrawn: 20.7.2006.

B **27** Isambard Kingdom Brunel (*Illustration reduced. Actual size* 163×98 mm)

Birth Bicentenary of Isambard Kingdom Brunel (engineer)

2006 (20 May). Multicoloured cover as Type B **27**. Booklet contains text and illustrations on panes and interleaving pages. Stitched.

SB79 £10.60 booklet containing panes Nos. 1110a/d, 1111a and 1112a .... 25·00

Withdrawn: 19.5.2007.

B **28** Seashore (*Illustration reduced. Actual size* 101×59 mm)

125th Anniversary of La Société Guernesiaise

2007 (8 Mar). Multicoloured covers as Type B **28**. Self-adhesive (Nos. SB80/1) or stitched (Nos. SB82/3).

SB80 (£3.20) booklet containing pane No. 1149b (cover Type B **28**) .... 8·00

SB81 (£3.70) booklet containing pane No. 1154a (cover showing lighthouse) .... 8·75

SB82 (£32) booklet containing ten panes of No. 1149c (cover as Type B **28**, but 180×59 mm) .... 65·00

SB83 (£37) booklet containing ten panes of No. 1154b (cover showing lighthouse, 180×59 mm) .... 75·00

B **29** Queen Elizabeth II and Duke of Edinburgh (*Illustration reduced. Actual size* 161×98 mm)

Diamond Wedding of Queen Elizabeth II and Duke of Edinburgh

2007 (2 Aug). Cover as Type B **29** showing black/white photograph. Booklet contains text and illustrations on panes and interleaving pages. Stitched.

SB84 £11.32 booklet containing panes Nos. 1174a/b and 1175a/8a .... 27·00

Withdrawn: 1.8.2008.

B **30** Coastal Rocks (*Illustration reduced. Actual size* 101×59 mm)

'Abstract Guernsey'

2008 (8 June). Multicoloured covers as Type B **30**. Self-adhesive (Nos. SB85/6) or stitched (Nos. SB87/8).

SB85 (£3.40) booklet containing pane No. 1232c (cover Type B **30**) .... 8·00

SB86 (£4) booklet containing pane No. 1237b (cover showing coastal rocks at sunset) .... 9·50

SB87 (£34) booklet containing ten panes of No. 1232c. (cover as Type B **30**, but 182×58 mm) .... 65·00

SB88 (£40) booklet containing ten panes of No. 1237b (cover showing coastal rocks at sunset, 182×58 mm) .... 75·00

B **31** Ford Model T Production Line (*Illustration reduced. Actual size* (161×97 mm)

Centenary of the Model T Ford

2008 (31 July). Multicoloured cover as Type B **31**. Booklet contains text and illustrations on panes and interleaving pages. Stitched.

SB89 £12 booklet containing panes Nos. 1242a/d, 1243a and 1244a .... 28·00

B **32** Henry VIII watching his Navy as *Mary Rose* sinks, 1545 (*Illustration reduced. Actual size* 163×99 mm)

500th Anniversary of the Coronation of King Henry VIII

2009 (30 July). Multicoloured cover as Type B **32**. Booklet contains text and illustrations on panes and interleaving pages. Stitched.

SB90 £12.68 booklet containing panes Nos. 1290a/5a .... 29·00

B **33** Beach and Headland (*Illustration reduced. Actual size* 100×70 *mm*)

Abstract Guernsey (2nd series)

2010 (18 Mar). Multicoloured covers as Type B **33**. Self-adhesive.

SB91	(£1.92)	booklet containing pane No. 1327b (cover Type B **33**)	4·50
SB92	(£2.32)	booklet containing pane No. 1330a (cover showing rocky headlands at sunset)	5·50
SB93	(£24)	booklet containing pane No. 1327c (cover showing rocky bay, 180×59 mm)	50·00
SB94	(£29)	booklet conataining pane No. 1330b (cover showing rocky headlands and off shore rocks at sunset, 180×59 mm)	60·00

ALDERNEY

The following issues are provided by the Guernsey Post Office for use on Alderney. They are also valid for postal purposes throughout the rest of the Bailiwick of Guernsey.

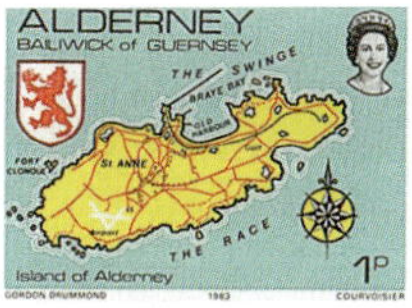

A **1** Island Map

A **2** Hanging Rock

A **3** States' Building, St. Anne

A **4** St. Anne's Church

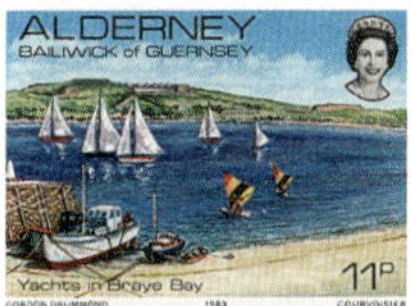

A **5** Yachts in Braye Bay

A **6** Victoria St, St. Anne

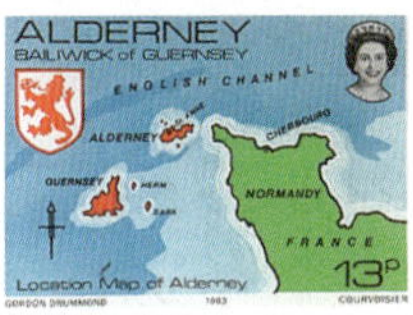

A **7** Map of Channel

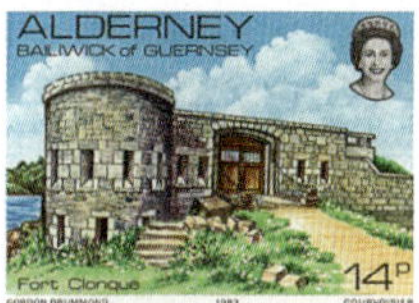

A **8** Fort Clonque

A **9** Corblets Bay and Fort

A **10** Old Tower, St. Anne

A **11** Golf Course and Essex Castle

A **12** Old Harbour

A **12a** Quesnard Lighthouse

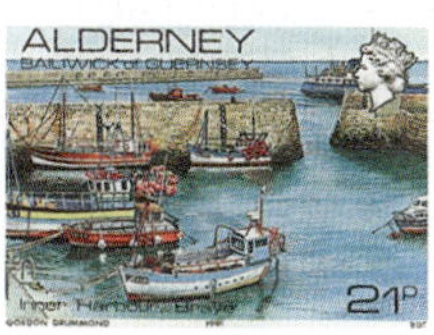

A **12b** Braye Harbour

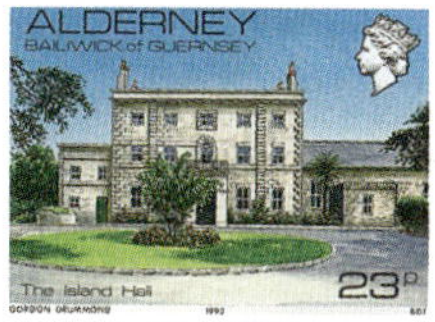

A **12c** The Island Hall

A **12d** *J. T. Daly* (steam locomotive)

A **12e** *Louis Marchesi of Round Table* (lifeboat)

Island Scenes

(Des G. Drummond. Litho B.D.T. (20p. to 28p.) or photo Courvoisier (others))

1983 (14 June)–**93**. Granite paper (1p to 18p.). Perf 15×14 (20p. to 28p.) or 11½ (others), both comb.

A1	A **1**	1p. multicoloured (a)	10	10
A2	A **2**	4p. multicoloured (a)	10	10
A3	A **3**	9p. multicoloured (a)	15	15
A4	A **4**	10p. multicoloured (a)	20	15
A5	A **5**	11p. multicoloured (a)	20	20
A6	A **6**	12p. multicoloured (a)	25	20
A7	A **7**	13p. multicoloured (a)	25	20
A8	A **8**	14p. multicoloured (a)	30	20
A9	A **9**	15p. multicoloured (a)	35	20
A10	A **10**	16p. multicoloured (a)	35	25
A11	A **11**	17p. multicoloured (a)	40	30
A12	A **12**	18p. multicoloured (a)	40	30
A12*a*	A **12a**	20p. multicoloured (b)	1·00	90
A12*b*	A **12b**	21p. multicoloured (c)	1·00	90
A12*c*	A **12c**	23p. multicoloured (d)	95	85
A12*d*	A **12d**	24p. multicoloured (e)	1·70	1·70
A12*e*	A **12e**	28p. multicoloured (e)	2·20	2·20
A1/12e *Set of 17*			9·00	8·00
First Day Covers (6)				22·00
Presentation Pack (2)			10·00	
Set of 17 Gutter Pairs			18·00	

Printings: (a) 14.6.83; (b) 27.12.89; (c) 2.4.91; (d) 6.2.92; (e) 2.3.93.
Plate and Cylinder Nos.: 1p., 12p., 13p., 17p., 20p. to 28p. 1A, 1B, 1C, 1D (each ×4); others 1A, 1B, 1C, 1D (each ×5).
Sheets: 40 (2 panes 5×4).
Imprint: Central, bottom margin.
Quantities sold: 1p. 1,337,865; 4p. 465,887; 9p. 680,896; 10p. 709,197; 11p. 778,483; 12p. 573,124; 13p. 671,772; 14p. 1,027,248; 15p. 740,519; 16p. 542,970; 17p. 404,323; 18p. 491,877; 20p. 248,694; 21p 233,975; 23p. 237,345; 24p 311,144; 28p 134,765.
Withdrawn: 4.6.94.

A **13** Oystercatcher

A **14** Ruddy Turnstone

A **15** Ringed Plover

A **16** Dunlin

A **17** Curlew

Birds

(Des and photo Harrison)

1984 (12 June). Perf 14½ (C).

A13	A **13**	9p. multicoloured	1·10	60
A14	A **14**	13p. multicoloured	1·10	75
A15	A **15**	26p. multicoloured	2·50	2·75
A16	A **16**	28p. multicoloured	2·50	2·75
A17	A **17**	31p. multicoloured	2·50	1·70
A13/17 *Set of 5*			8·75	7·75
First Day Cover				9·00
Presentation Pack			10·00	
Set of 5 Gutter Pairs			18·00	

Cylinder Nos.: All values 1A, 1B (each ×5).
Sheets: 50 (2 panes 5×5).
Imprint: Bottom margin, right-hand corner.
Quantities sold: 9p. 285,931; 13p. 360,619; 26p. 246,916; 28p. 261,370; 31p. 334,484.
Withdrawn: 11.6.85.

A **18** Westland Wessex HCC.4 Helicopter of the Queen's Flight

A **19** Britten Norman 'long-nose' Trislander

A **20** De Havilland D.H.114 Heron 1B

A **21** De Havilland D.H.89A Dragon Rapide *Sir Henry Lawrence*

A **22** Saro A.21 Windhover Amphibian *City of Portsmouth*

50th Anniversary of Alderney Airport

(Des A. Theobald. Photo Courvoisier)

1985 (19 Mar). Granite paper. Perf 11½ (C).

A18	A **18**	9p. multicoloured	1·40	70
A19	A **19**	13p. multicoloured	1·70	1·00
A20	A **20**	29p. multicoloured	3·00	2·75
A21	A **21**	31p. multicoloured	3·50	3·50
A22	A **22**	34p. multicoloured	3·50	3·50
A18/22 *Set of 5*			12·00	11·00
First Day Cover				14·00
Presentation Pack			14·00	

Cylinder Nos.: All values A1–1–1–1–1–1, B1–1–1–1–1–1.
Sheets: 25 (5×5).
Quantities sold: 9p. 294,437; 13p. 321,276; 29p. 231,422; 31p. 171,528; 34p. 162,429.
Withdrawn: 18.3.86.

A **23** Royal Engineers, 1890

A **24** Duke of Albany's Own Highlanders (72nd Highland Regt), 1856

A **25** Royal Artillery, 1855

A **26** South Hampshire Regiment, 1810

A **27** Royal Irish Regiment, 1782

Regiments of the Alderney Garrison

(Des E. Stemp. Litho Harrison)

1985 (24 Sept). Perf 14½ (C).

A23	A **23**	9p. multicoloured	25	20
A24	A **24**	14p. multicoloured	80	40
A25	A **25**	29p. multicoloured	80	70
A26	A **26**	31p. multicoloured	1·10	1·10
A27	A **27**	34p. multicoloured	1·40	1·50
A23/7 *Set of 5*			4·00	3·75
First Day Cover				6·00
Presentation Pack			6·00	
Set of 5 Gutter Pairs			8·00	

No. A24 shows the tartan and insignia of the 78th Highland Regiment in error.

Plate Nos.: All values 1A, 1B, 1C, 1D (each ×5).
Sheets: 50 (2 panes 5×5).
Imprint: Central, left-hand margin of each pane.
Quantities sold: 9p. 286,572; 14p.283,493; 29p. 224,196; 31p. 151,948; 34p. 145,422.
Withdrawn: 23.9.86.

A **28** Fort Grosnez

A **29** Fort Tourgis

A **30** Fort Clonque

A **31** Fort Albert

Alderney Forts

(Des R. Reed. Litho Cartor)

1986 (23 Sept). Perf 13×13½ (C).

A28	A **28**	10p. multicoloured	80	20
A29	A **29**	14p. multicoloured	90	80
A30	A **30**	31p. multicoloured	2·50	3·00
A31	A **31**	34p. multicoloured	2·50	3·00
A28/31 *Set of 4*			6·00	6·25
First Day Cover				8·00
Presentation Pack			7·00	
Set of 4 Gutter Pairs			12·00	

Plate Nos.: All values 1A, 1B, 1C, 1D (each ×5).
Sheets: 50 (2 panes 5×5).
Imprint: Left-hand margin of left-hand pane.
Quantities sold: 10p. 325,706; 14p. 231,891; 31p. 143,423; 34p. 138,556.
Withdrawn: 22.9.87.

A **32** *Liverpool* (full-rigged ship), 1902

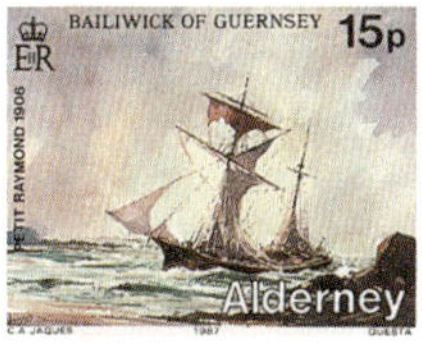

A **33** *Petit Raymond* (schooner), 1906

A **34** *Maina* (yacht), 1910

A **35** *Burton* (steamer), 1911

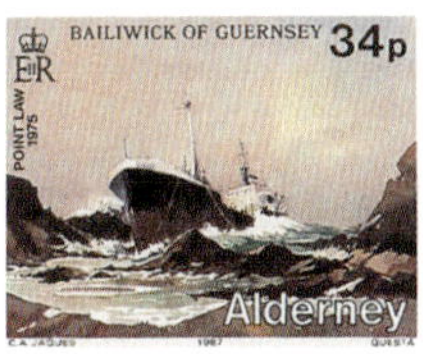

A **36** *Point Law* (oil tanker), 1975

Alderney Shipwrecks

(Des C. Jacques. Litho Questa)

1987 (5 May). Perf 14×14½ (C).

A32	A **32**	11p. multicoloured	1·60	50
A33	A **33**	15p. multicoloured	1·70	60
A34	A **34**	29p. multicoloured	3·00	3·50
A35	A **35**	31p. multicoloured	3·75	3·50
A36	A **36**	34p. multicoloured	4·00	4·25
A32/6 *Set of 5*			12·00	11·00
First Day Cover				11·00
Presentation Pack			15·00	
Set of 5 Gutter Pairs			24·00	

Plate Nos.: All values 1A, 1B, 1C, 1D (each ×4).
Sheets: 50 (2 panes 5×5).
Imprint: Bottom, right-hand margin of each pane.
Quantities sold: 11p. 228,998; 15p. 233,861; 29p. 139,453; 31p. 148,572; 34p. 145,641.
Withdrawn: 4.5.88.

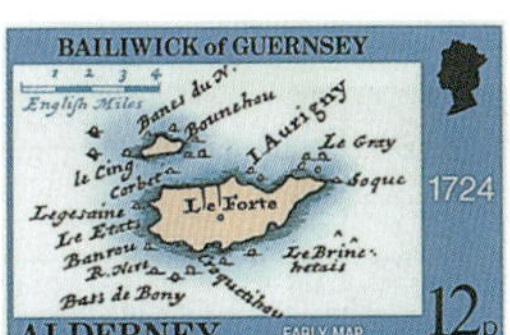

A **37** Moll's Map of 1724

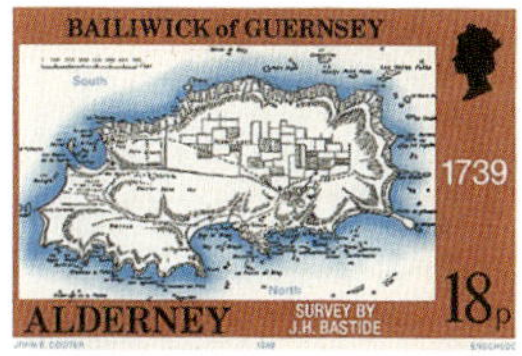

A **38** Bastide's Survey of 1739

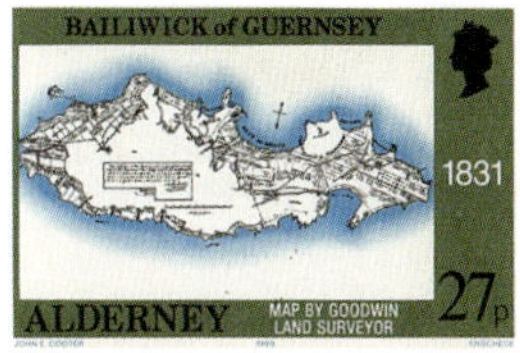

A **39** Goodwin's Map of 1831

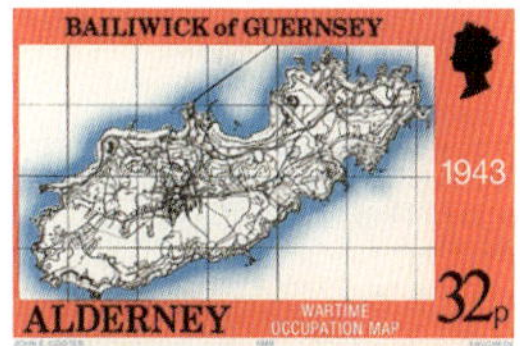

A **40** General Staff Map of 1943

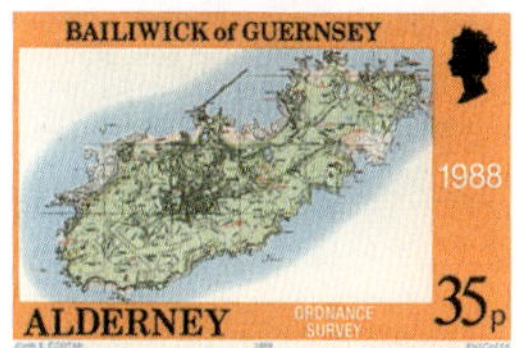

A **41** Ordnance Survey Map of 1988

250th Anniversary of Bastide's Survey of Alderney

(Des J. Cooter. Litho Enschedé)

1989 (7 July). Perf 13½×14 (C).

A37	A **37**	12p. multicoloured	25	25
A38	A **38**	18p. blk, greenish blue & orge-brn	45	30
A39	A **39**	27p. black, greenish blue and dull yellow-green	95	1·10
A40	A **40**	32p. black, greenish blue & brt rose-red	1·10	1·10
A41	A **41**	35p. multicoloured	1·50	1·40
A37/41 *Set of 5*			3·75	3·75
First Day Cover				4·75
Presentation Pack			5·00	
Set of 5 Gutter Pairs			7·50	

Plate Nos.: 12p. 1–1–1–1; 18p., 27p., 32p. 1–1–1; 35p. 1–1–1–1–1.
Sheets: 50 (2 panes 5×5).
Imprint: Central, both margins of each pane.
Quantities sold: 12p. 169,993; 18p. 194,667; 27p. 148,621; 32p. 158,600; 35p. 153,544.
Withdrawn: 6.7.90.

A **42** H.M.S. *Alderney* (bomb ketch), 1738

A **43** H.M.S. *Alderney* (frigate), 1742

A **44** H.M.S. *Alderney* (sloop), 1755

A **45** H.M.S. *Alderney* (submarine), 1945

A **46** H.M.S. *Alderney* (patrol vessel), 1979

Royal Navy Ships named after Alderney

(Des A. Theobald. Litho B.D.T.)

1990 (3 May). Perf 13½ (C).

A42	A **42**	14p. black and olive-bistre	25	20
A43	A **43**	20p. black and orange-brown	45	35
A44	A **44**	29p. black and cinnamon	1·00	1·00
A45	A **45**	34p. black & pale turquoise-blue	1·10	1·50
A46	A **46**	37p. black and cobalt	1·40	1·50
A42/6 *Set of 5*			3·75	4·00
First Day Cover				5·50
Presentation Pack			4·50	
Set of 5 Gutter Pairs			7·50	

Plate Nos.: 14p., 20p., 29p, 34p. 1A–1A, 1B–1B; 37p. 1A–1A, 1B–1B, 1C–1C, 1D–1D.
Sheets: 50 (2 panes 5×5).
Imprint: Central, side margins of each pane.
Quantities sold: 14p. 290,801; 20p. 291,996; 29p. 142,011; 34p. 146,711; 37p. 151,711.
Withdrawn: 4.5.91.

A **47** Wreck of H.M.S. *Victory*, 1744

A **48** Lighthouse Keeper's Daughter rowing back to the Casquets

A **49** MBB-Bolkow Bo105D Helicopter leaving pad on St. Thomas Tower

A **50** Migrating Birds over Lighthouse

A **51** Trinity House Vessel *Patricia* and Arms

Automation of the Casquets Lighthouse

(Des A. Theobald. Litho Cartor)

1991 (30 Apr). Perf 14×13½ (C).

A47	A **47**	21p. multicoloured	80	50
A48	A **48**	26p. multicoloured	1·90	1·70
A49	A **49**	31p. multicoloured	2·00	2·20
A50	A **50**	37p. multicoloured	2·75	3·25
A51	A **51**	50p. multicoloured	3·75	3·50
A47/51 *Set of 5*			10·00	9·00
First Day Cover				9·00
Presentation Pack			10·50	
Set of 5 Gutter Pairs			20·00	

Plate Nos.: All values 1A, 1B, 1C, 1D (each ×4).
Sheets: 50 (2 panes 5×5).
Imprint: Central, side margins.
Quantities sold: 21p. 280,555; 26p. 164,155; 31p. 158,465; 37p. 158,375; 50p. 238,825.
Withdrawn: 29.4.92.

A **52** Two French Warships on Fire

A **53** Crews leaving burning Ships

A **54** French Warship sinking

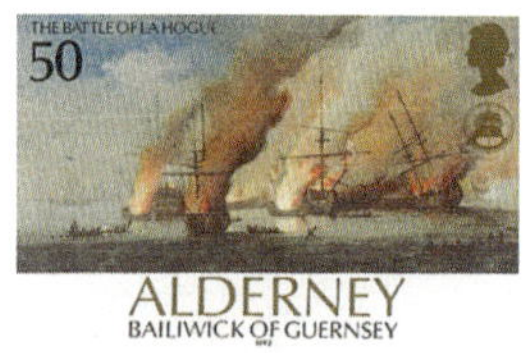

A **55** 'The Battle of La Hogue'

300th Anniversary of Battle of La Hogue

(Des C. Abbott. Litho B.D.T.)

1992 (18 Sept). Perf 14×15 (50p) or 13½ (others), both comb.

A52	A **52**	23p. multicoloured	1·10	1·00
A53	A **53**	28p. multicoloured	2·40	2·50
A54	A **54**	33p. multicoloured	2·75	3·00
A55	A **55**	50p. multicoloured	3·00	3·50
A52/5 *Set of 4*			8·00	9·00
First Day Cover				8·50
Presentation Pack			9·00	
Set of 4 Gutter Pairs			16·00	

Nos. A52/4 show details of the painting on the 50p value.
Plate Nos.: All values 1A, 1B (each ×5).
Sheets: 50 (2 panes 5×5).
Imprint: Central, right-hand margin (50p.) or central, side margins (others).
Quantities sold: 23p. 238,820; 28p. 188,685; 33p. 172,565; 50p. 186,096.
Withdrawn: 17.9.93.

A **56** Spiny Lobster

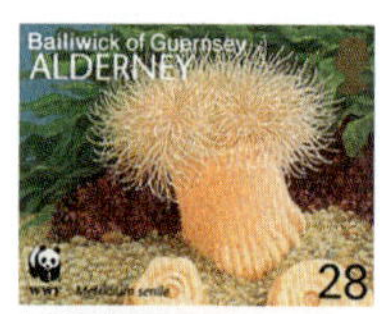

A **57** Plumrose Anemone

A **58** Starfish

A **59** Sea Urchin

Endangered Species. Marine Life

(Des A. Peck. Litho Questa)

1993 (2 Nov). Perf 14½ (C).

A56	A **56**	24p. multicoloured	60	30
		a. Horiz strip of 4. Nos. A56/9	5·50	6·00
A57	A **57**	28p. multicoloured	60	35
A58	A **58**	33p. multicoloured	70	40
A59	A **59**	39p. multicoloured	90	60
A56/9 *Set of 4*			5·50	6·00
First Day Cover				6·00
Presentation Pack			6·50	

Plate Nos.: All values 1A, 1B (each ×5).
Sheets: 16 (4×4). Nos. A56/9 were printed together, *se-tenant*, in horizontal strips of 4 throughout the sheet.
Imprint: Central, right-hand margin.
Quantity sold: 216.788 strips.
Withdrawn: 1.11.94.

A **60** Blue-tailed Damselfly, Dark Hair Water Crowfoot and Branched Bur-reed

A **61** White-toothed Shrew and Flax-leaved St. John's Wort

A **62** Fulmar and Kaffir Fig

A **63** Clouded Yellow (butterfly) and Red Clover

A **64** Bumble Bee, Prostrate Broom and Giant Broomrape

A **65** Dartford Warbler and Lesser Dodder

A **66** Peacock (butterfly) and Stemless Thistle

A **67** Mole and Bluebell

A **68** Great Green Grasshopper and Common Gorse

A **69** Six-spot Burnet (moth) and Viper's Bugloss

A **70** Common Blue (butterfly) and Pyramidal Orchid

A **70a** Small Tortoiseshell (butterfly) and Buddleia

A **71** Common Rabbit and Creeping Buttercup

A **72** Greater Black-backed Gull and Sand Crocus

A **72a** Rock Pipit and Sea Stock

A **72b** Sand Digger Wasp and Sea Bindweed

A **73** Atlantic Puffin and English Stonecrop

A **74** Emperor (moth) and Bramble

A **75** Pale-spined Hedgehog and Pink Oxalis

A **76** Common Tern and Bermuda Grass

A **77** Northern Gannet and *Fucus vesiculosus* (seaweed)

Flora and Fauna

(Des Wendy Bramall. Litho B.D.T. (No. A71a) or Questa (others))

1994 (5 May)–**98**. Perf 14½ (C).

A60	A **60**	1p. multicoloured (a)	10	10
A61	A **61**	2p. multicoloured (a)	10	10
A62	A **62**	3p. multicoloured (a)	10	10
A63	A **63**	4p. multicoloured (a)	10	10
A64	A **64**	5p. multicoloured (a)	10	10
A65	A **65**	6p. multicoloured (a)	15	20
A66	A **66**	7p. multicoloured (a)	15	20
A67	A **67**	8p. multicoloured (a)	15	20
A68	A **68**	9p. multicoloured (a)	20	25
A69	A **69**	10p. multicoloured (a)	20	25
A70	A **70**	16p. multicoloured (a)	55	40
		a. Perf 14×15	55	50
		ab. Booklet pane of 8	4·00	
A70*b*	A **70a**	18p. multicoloured (c)	35	40
		ba. Perf 14×15	35	40
		bb. Booklet pane of 8	3·00	
A71	A **71**	20p. multicoloured (a)	40	45
		a. Perf 14×15 (d)	40	45
		ab. Booklet pane of 8	3·75	
A72	A **72**	24p. multicoloured (a)	50	55
		a. Perf 14×15	50	55
		ab. Booklet pane of 8	4·25	
A72*b*	A **72a**	25p. multicoloured (c)	50	55
		ba. Perf 14×15	50	55
		bb. Booklet pane of 8	4·00	
A72*c*	A **72b**	26p. multicoloured (c)	50	55
A73	A **73**	30p. multicoloured (a)	60	65
A74	A **74**	40p. multicoloured (a)	80	85
A75	A **75**	50p. multicoloured (a)	1·50	1·20
A76	A **76**	£1 multicoloured (a)	2·50	2·20
A77	A **77**	£2 multicoloured (b)	5·00	4·50
A60/77 *Set of 21*			12·50	13·00
First Day Covers (5)				17·00
Presentation Packs (3)			16·00	
Stamp-cards (set of 21)			4·50	18·00
Set of 21 Gutter Pairs			25·00	

Nos. A70a, A70ba, A71a, A72a and A72ba were issued in booklets with the upper and lower edges of the panes imperforate. Unfolded booklet panes were also available from the Philatelic Bureau and Head Post Office.

Printings: (a) 5.5.94; (b) 28.2.95; (c) 2.1.97; (d) 25.3.98.

Plate Nos.: 1p., 3p., 5p., 7p., 9p., 16p., 18p., 20p., 25p., 26p., 40p. 1A, 1B (each ×4); 2p., 4p., 6p., 8p., 10p., 24p., 30p., 50p. 1C, 1D (each ×4); £1, £2 1A, 1B, 1C, 1D (each ×4).

Sheets: 50 (2 panes 5× 5).

Imprint: £1, £2 Central left margin of each pane; others central left or right margin of each pane.

Sold out: 4.2001 (1p. to 16p., 20p., 24p., 30p to £1); by 10.2006 (18p., 25p., 26p. and £2).

A **78** Royal Aircraft Factory SE5A

A **79** Miles Master II and other Miles Aircraft

A **80** Miles Aerovan and Miles Monitor

A **81** Miles Falcon Six winning King's Cup Air Race, 1935

A **82** Miles Hawk Speed Six winning Manx Air Derby, 1947

A **83** Mles Falcon Six breaking U.K.–Cape Record, 1936

Birth Centenary of Tommy Rose (aviator)

(Des C. Abbott. Litho B.D.T.)

1995 (1 Sept). Perf 14×15 (C).

A78	A **78**	35p. multicoloured	95	95
		a. Horiz strip of 3. Nos. A78/80	2·75	2·75
A79	A **79**	35p. multicoloured	95	95
A80	A **80**	35p. multicoloured	95	95
A81	A **81**	41p. multicoloured	1·10	1·10
		a. Horiz strip of 3. Nos. A81/3	3·25	3·25
A82	A **82**	41p. multicoloured	1·10	1·10
A83	A **83**	41p. multicoloured	1·10	1·10
A78/83 *Set of 6*			6·00	6·00

First Day Cover		6·75
Presentation Pack	7·50	
Gutter strips of 6 (2)	12·00	

Plate Nos.: Both values 1A, 1B, 1C (each ×5).
Sheets: 12 (2 panes 3×2). Nos. A78/80 and A81/3 were printed together, *se-tenant*, as horizontal strips of 3 throughout the sheet.
Imprint: Central, bottom margin.
Quantities sold: 35p. 361,895 strips; 41p. 362,801 strips.
Withdrawn: 31.8.96.

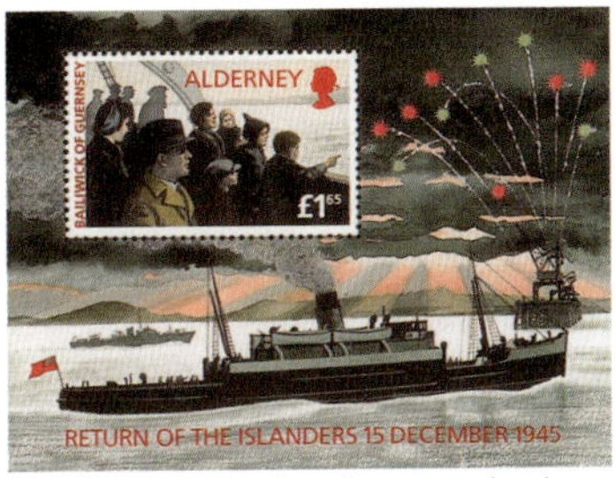

A **84a** Returning Islanders (*Illustration reduced. Actual size* 93×70 mm)

50th Anniversary of Return of Islanders to Alderney

(Des C. Abbott. Litho B.D.T.)

1995 (16 Nov). Sheet 93×70 mm. Perf 13½ (C).

MSA84 A **84a** £1.65 multicoloured	5·00	5·00
First Day Cover		5·50
Presentation Pack	5·50	

Quantity sold: 139,665.
Withdrawn: 15.11.96.

A **85** Signallers training on Alderney

A **86** Communications Station, Falkland Islands

A **87** Dish Aerial and Land Rover, Gulf War

A **88** Sevice with United Nations

25th Anniversary of Adoption of 30th Signal Regiment by Alderney

(Des A. Theobald. Litho Walsall)

1996 (24 Jan). Perf 14 (C).

A85	A **85**	24p. multicoloured	45	35
		a. Horiz strip of 4. Nos. A85/8	5·50	5·50
A86	A **86**	41p. multicoloured	75	55
A87	A **87**	60p. multicoloured	1·10	80
A88	A **88**	75p. multicoloured	1·10	1·10
A85/8 *Set of 4*			5·50	5·50
First Day Cover				6·00
Presentation Pack			6·75	
Gutter strip of 8			11·00	

Plate Nos.: All values 1A, 1B, 1C, 1D, 1E, 1F (each ×4).
Sheets: 16 (2 panes 4×2). Nos. A85/8 were printed in *se-tenant* strips of 4 across the sheet, each strip forming a composite design.
Imprint: Central, bottom margin.
Quantities sold: 24p. 141,697; 41p. 141,631; 60p. 141,679; 75p. 141,680.
Withdrawn: 28.1.97.

A **89** Cat with Butterfly

A **90** Blue and White on Table

A **91** Tabby Kitten grooming Blue and White Persian Kitten

A **92** Red Persian under Table

A **93** White Cat with Tortoiseshell in Toy Cart

A **94** Siamese playing with Wool

Cats

(Des P. le Vasseur. Litho B.D.T.)

1996 (19 July). Perf 13½ (C).

A89	A **89**	16p. multicoloured	45	35
A90	A **90**	24p. multicoloured	65	40
A91	A **91**	25p. multicoloured	65	65
A92	A **92**	35p. multicoloured	1·20	1·20
A93	A **93**	41p. multicoloured	1·50	1·70
A94	A **94**	60p. multicoloured	2·00	2·00
A89/94 *Set of 6*			6·00	6·00
First Day Cover				8·00
Presentation Pack			7·00	
Set of 6 Gutter Pairs			12·00	
MSA95 144×97 mm. Nos. A89/94			6·50	6·50
First Day Cover				12·00

Plate Nos.: All values 1A, 1B (each ×4).
Sheets: 50 (2 panes 5×5).
Imprint: Central, right-hand margin of top pane.
Quantities sold: 16p. 243,841; 24p. 243,457; 25p. 193,625; 35p. 193,393; 41p. 192,612; 60p. 191,587; miniature sheet 83,144.
Withdrawn: 18.7.97.

A **95** Harold Larwood

A **96** John Arlott

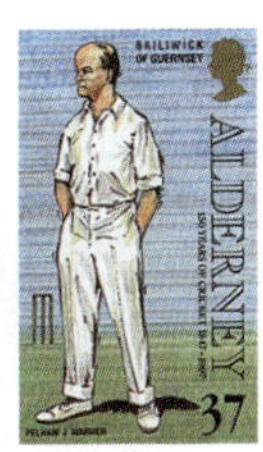

A **97** Pelham J. Warner

A **98** W. G. Grace

A **99** John Wisden

150th Anniversary of Cricket on Alderney

(Des R. Ollington. Litho Walsall)

1997 (21 Aug). Perf 13½ (C).

A96	A **95**	18p. multicoloured	50	30
A97	A **96**	25p. multicoloured	65	35
A98	A **97**	37p. multicoloured	1·00	1·20
A99	A **98**	43p. multicoloured	1·20	1·50
A100	A **99**	63p. multicoloured	1·60	1·70
A96/100 *Set of 5*			4·50	4·50
First Day Cover				5·50
Presentation Pack			8·00	
Set of 5 Gutter Pairs			9·00	
MSA101 190×75 mm. Nos. A96/100 and label			9·00	9·00
First Day Cover				12·00

Plate Nos.: All values 1A, 1B (each ×5).
Sheets: 50 (2 panes 5×5).
Imprint: Central, top and bottom margins.
Quantities sold: 18p. 246,846; 25p. 246,765; 37p. 146,969; 43p. 146,886; 63p 148,816; miniature sheet 87,220.
Withdrawn: 20.8.98.

A **100** Railway under Construction

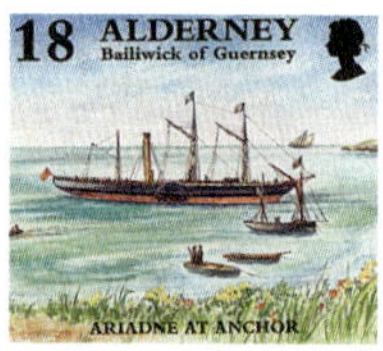

A **101** *Ariadne* (paddle steamer) at Anchor

A **102** Quarrying Stone

A **103** Quarry Railway

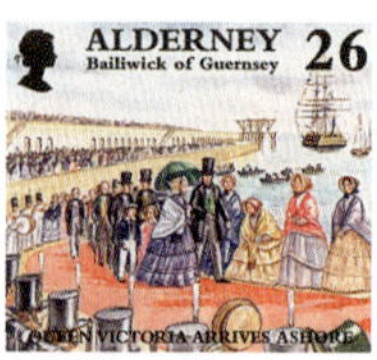

A **104** Queen Victoria and Prince Albert on Alderney

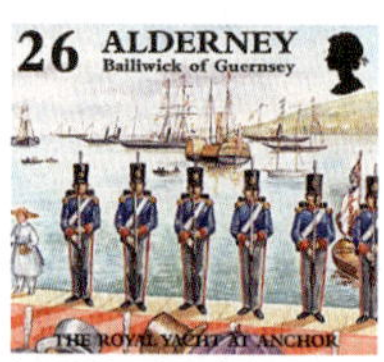

A **105** Royal Yacht *Victoria and Albert* and Guard of Honour

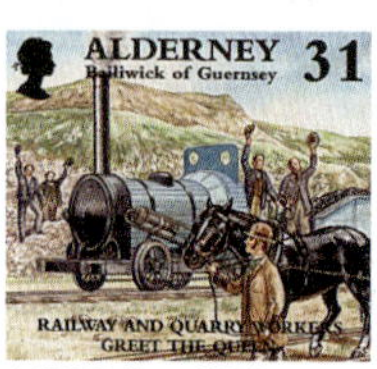

A **106** Railway Workers greet Queen Victoria

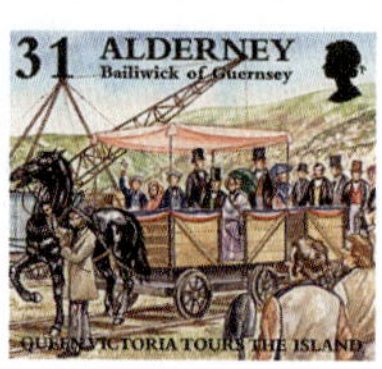

A **107** Royal Party in Railway Wagons

Garrison Island (1st series). 150th Anniversary of Harbour

(Des R. Carter. Litho Questa)

1997 (20 Nov)–**98**. Perf 14½×14 (C).

A102	A **100**	18p. multicoloured	45	20
		a. Horiz pair. Nos. A102/3	1·10	1·10
		b. Booklet pane. Nos. A102/5 with margins all round (10.11.98)	2·50	
		c. Booklet pane. Nos. A102/3 and A106/7 with margins all round (10.11.98)	2·75	
A103	A **101**	18p. multicoloured	45	20
A104	A **102**	25p. multicoloured	65	30
		a. Horiz pair. Nos. A104/5	1·50	1·50
		b. Booklet pane. Nos. A104/5 and A108/9 with margins all round (10.11.98)	3·50	
A105	A **103**	25p. multicoloured	65	30
A106	A **104**	26p. multicoloured	70	30
		a. Horiz pair. Nos. A106/7	1·70	1·70
		b. Booklet pane. Nos. A106/9 with margins all round (10.11.98)	3·75	
A107	A **105**	26p. multicoloured	70	30
A108	A **106**	31p. multicoloured	80	35
		a. Horiz pair. Nos. A108/9	2·00	2·00
A109	A **107**	31p. multicoloured	80	35
A102/9 *Set of 8*			6·00	6·00
First Day Cover				6·50
Presentation Pack			6·50	

See also Nos. A116/23, A132/9, A154/61 and A176/83.

Plate Nos.: All values 1A, 1B (each ×4).
Sheets: 20 (4×5), the two designs for each value printed together, *se-tenant*, in horizontal pairs throughout the sheets, each pair forming a composite design.
Imprint: Central, side margins.
Quantities sold: 18p. 145,264; 25p. 145,364; 26p. 145,464; 31p. 115,164.
Withdrawn: 19.11.98.

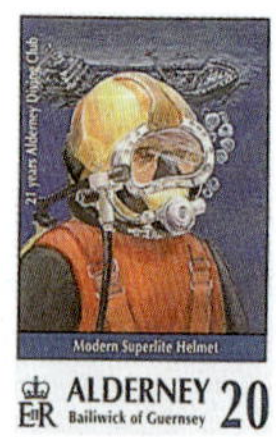

A **108** Modern Superlite Helmet and Wreck of *Point Law* (oil tanker)

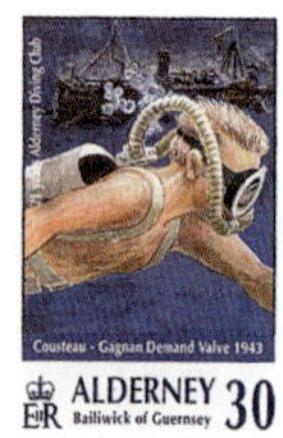

A **109** Cousteau-Gagnan Demand Valve and Wreck of *Stella* (steamer)

A **110** Heinke Closed Helmet and *Liverpool* (full-rigged ship)

A **111** Siebe Closed Helmet

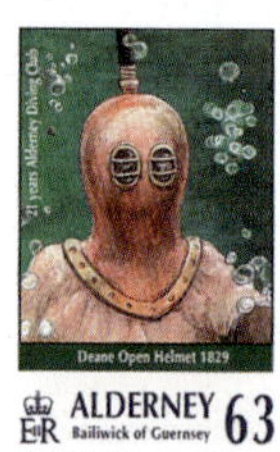

A **112** Deane Open Helmet

21st Anniversary of Alderney Diving Club

(Des Victoria Kinnersly. Litho B.D.T.)

1998 (10 Feb). Perf 13 (C).

A110	A **108**	20p. multicoloured	60	40
A111	A **109**	30p. multicoloured	85	85
A112	A **110**	37p. multicoloured	1·20	1·20
A113	A **111**	43p. multicoloured	1·70	1·70
A114	A **112**	63p. multicoloured	2·20	2·30
A110/14 *Set of 5*			6·00	6·00
First Day Cover				6·50
Presentation Pack			7·00	
Set of 5 Gutter Pairs			12·00	
MSA115 190×75 mm. Nos. A110/14 and label			8·00	8·00
First Day Cover				12·00

Plate Nos.: All values 1A, 1B (each ×5).
Sheets: 50 (2 panes 5×5).
Imprint: Central, side margins.
Withdrawn: 9.2.99.

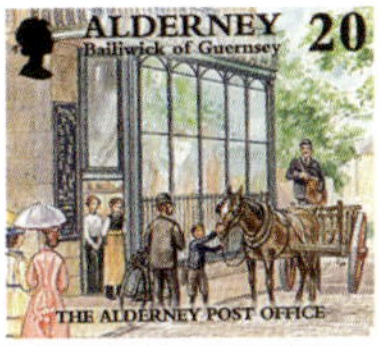

A **113** Alderney Post Office

A **114** Traders in Victoria Street

A **115** Court House

A **116** Police Station and Fire Engine

A **117** St. Anne's Church

A **118** Wedding Party at Albert Gate

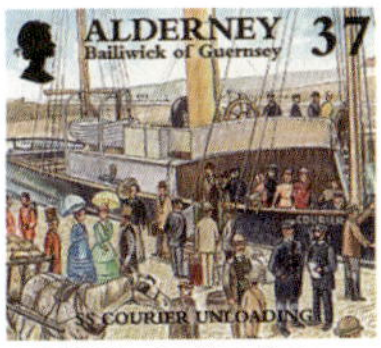

A **119** *Courier* (ferry) at Braye Bay

A **120** Fisherman at Quay

Garrison Island (2nd series)

(Des R. Carter. Litho Questa)

1998 (10 Nov). Perf 14½×14 (C).

A116	A **113**	20p. multicoloured	50	25
		a. Horiz pair. Nos. A116/17	1·10	1·10
		b. Booklet pane. Nos. A116/19 with margins all round	2·50	
		c. Booklet pane. Nos. A116/17 and A120/1 with margins all round	2·75	
A117	A **114**	20p. multicoloured	50	25
A118	A **115**	25p. multicoloured	60	30
		a. Horiz pair. Nos. A118/19	1·50	1·50
		b. Booklet pane. Nos. 118/19 and A122/3 with margins all round	3·50	
A119	A **116**	25p. multicoloured	60	30
A120	A **117**	30p. multicoloured	70	35
		a. Horiz pair. Nos. A120/1	1·70	1·70
		b. Booklet pane. Nos. A120/3 with margins all round	3·75	
A121	A **118**	30p. multicoloured	70	35
A122	A **119**	37p. multicoloured	85	40
		a. Horiz pair. Nos. A122/3	2·00	2·00
A123	A **120**	37p. multicoloured	85	40
A116/23 *Set of 8*			6·00	6·00
First Day Cover				5·50
Presentation Pack			6·00	

Plate Nos.: 20p., 30p. 1A (×4); 25p., 37p. 1B (×4).
Sheets: 20 (4×5), the two designs for each value were printed together, *se-tenant*, in horizontal pairs throughout the sheets, each pair forming a composite design.
Imprint: Central, side margins.
Withdrawn: 9.11.99.

A **121a** Stained Glass Window commemorating Mary Rogers (Chief Stewardess) (25p.); *Stella* leaving Southampton (£1.75)
(*Illustration reduced. Actual size* 110×90 mm)

Centenary of the Wreck of *Stella* (mail steamer)

(Des Joanna Brehaut. Litho B.D.T.)

1999 (5 Feb). Sheet 110×90 mm. Perf 14 (C).

MSA124 A **121a** 25p., £1.75, multicoloured	6·00	6·00
First Day Cover		8·00
Presentation Pack	6·50	

Withdrawn: 3.2.2000.

A **122** Solar Eclipse at 10.15 am

A **123** At 10.51 am

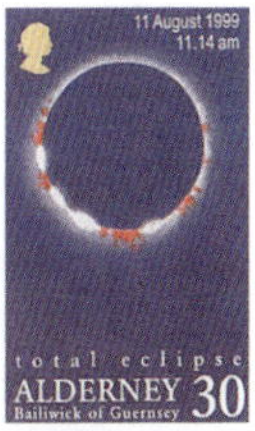

A **124** At 11.14 am

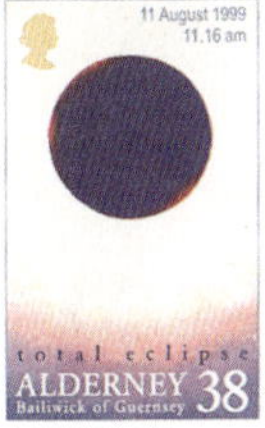

A **125** 11.16 am

A **126** At 11.17 am

A **127** At 11.36 am

Total Eclipse of the Sun on 11 August

(Des Victoria Kinnersly. Litho Enschedé)

1999 (27 Apr). Perf 13½×13 (C).

A125	A **122**	20p. multicoloured	50	50
A126	A **123**	25p. multicoloured	60	60
A127	A **124**	30p. multicoloured	70	70
A128	A **125**	38p. multicoloured	1·00	1·00
A129	A **126**	44p. multicoloured	1·50	1·50
A130	A **127**	64p. multicoloured	1·70	1·90
A125/30 *Set of 6*			6·00	6·00
First Day Cover				8·00
Presentation Pack			8·00	
Set of 6 Gutter Pairs			12·00	
MSA131 191×80 mm. Nos. A125/30 and label			6·50	6·50
First Day Cover				10·00
Postcard			1·00	

No. **MS**A131 also includes the 'PHILEXFRANCE '99', Paris, and the 'iBRA '99', Nuremberg, emblems on the sheet margin.
Plate Nos.: All values 1A, 1B (each ×4).
Sheets: 50 (2 panes 5×5).
Imprint: Central, side margins.
Withdrawn: 26.4.2000.

A **128** Field Gun and Crew, Fort Grosnez, c 1855

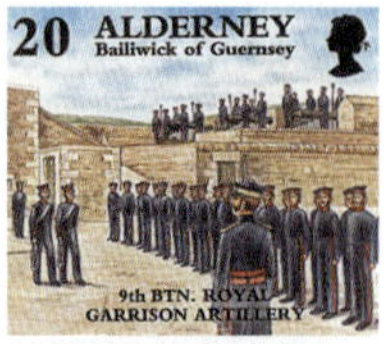

A **129** Parade of 9th Bn, Royal Garrison Artillery

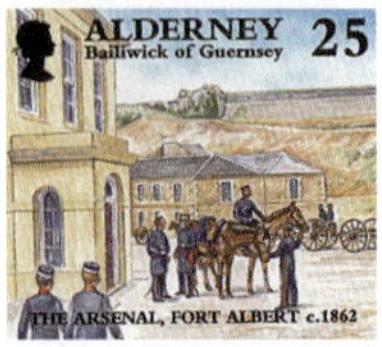

A **130** The Arsenal, Fort Albert, c 1862

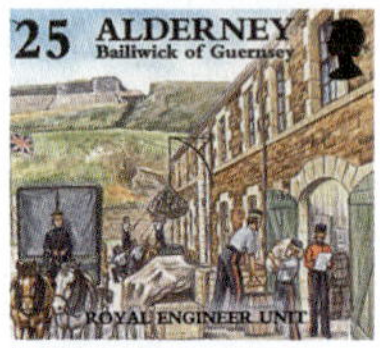

A **131** Royal Engineers loading Wagons

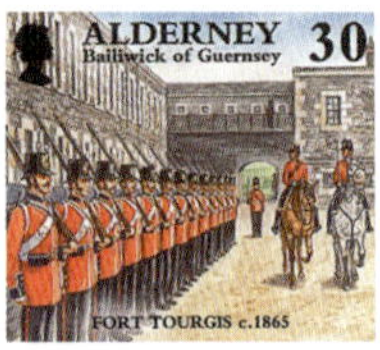

A **132** 2nd Bn, Royal Scots on Parade

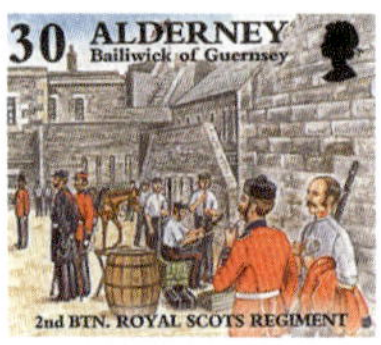

A **133** Garrison at Work, Fort Tourgis, c 1865

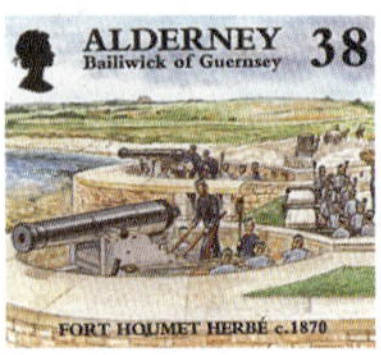

A **134** Gun Emplacement, Fort Houmet Herbé, c 1870

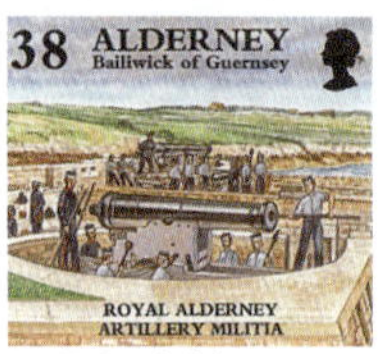

A **135** Royal Alderney Artillery Militia loading Cannon

Garrison Island (3rd series). Forts

(Des R. Carter. Litho Questa)

1999 (19 Oct). Perf 14½×14 (C).

A132	A **128**	20p. multicoloured	45	25
		a. Horiz pair. Nos. A132/3	1·10	1·10
		b. Booklet pane. Nos. A132/5, with margins all round	2·50	
		c. Booklet pane. Nos. A132/3 and A136/7, with margins all round	3·00	
		d. Booklet pane. Nos. A132/3 and A138/9, with margins all round	2·75	
A133	A **129**	20p. multicoloured	45	25
A134	A **130**	25p. multicoloured	55	30
		a. Horiz pair. Nos. A134/5	1·50	1·50
		b. Booklet pane. Nos. A134/7, with margins all round	3·25	
		c. Booklet pane. Nos. A134/5 and A138/9, with margins all round	3·50	
A135	A **131**	25p. multicoloured	55	30
A136	A **132**	30p. multicoloured	65	35
		a. Horiz pair. Nos. A136/7	1·70	1·70
		b. Booklet pane. Nos. A136/9, with margins all round	3·75	
A137	A **133**	30p. multicoloured	65	35
A138	A **134**	38p. multicoloured	80	40
		a. Horiz pair. Nos. A138/9	2·00	2·00
A139	A **135**	38p. multicoloured	80	40
A132/9 *Set of 8*			6·00	6·00
First Day Cover				8·00
Presentation Pack			8·50	

Plate Nos.: All values 1A, 1B (each ×4).
Sheets: 20 (4×5), the two designs for each value were printed together, *se-tenant*, in horizontal pairs throughout the sheets, each pair forming a composite design.
Imprint: Central, right-hand margin.
Withdrawn: 18.10.2000.

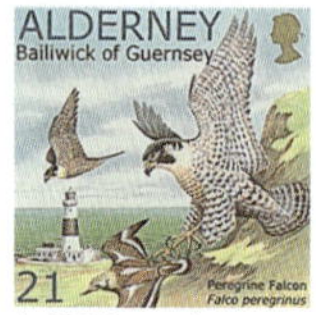

A **136** Peregrine Falcon attacking Ruddy Turnstone

A **137** Two Falcons and Prey

A **138** Falcon guarding Eggs

A **139** Falcon feeding Young

A **140** Falcon and Prey

A **141** Two Young Falcons

Endangered Species. Peregrine Falcon

(Des R. Gorringe. Litho Questa)

2000 (4 Feb). Perf 14½×14 (C).

A140	A **136**	21p. multicoloured	50	45
		a. Booklet pane of 10	5·00	
A141	A **137**	26p. multicoloured	55	55
		a. Booklet pane of 10	5·75	
A142	A **138**	34p. multicoloured	95	95
A143	A **139**	38p. multicoloured	1·00	1·00
A144	A **140**	44p. multicoloured	1·50	1·50
A145	A **141**	64p. multicoloured	2·00	2·00
		a. Black printed Quadruple		
A140/5 *Set of 6*			6·00	6·00
First Day Cover				6·50
Presentation Pack			6·50	

Nos. A142/5 include the W.W.F. emblem.
Booklet panes Nos. A140a and A141a show the upper and lower edges of the panes imperforate and have margins at left and right.
Plate Nos.: All values 1A (×6).
Sheets: 10 (2×5) with enlarged illustrated margin at left.
Imprint: Central, right-hand margin.
Withdrawn: 3.2.2001.

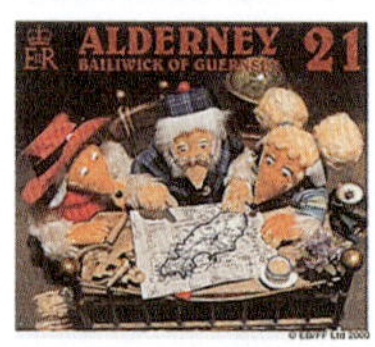

A **142** Wombles around Map of Alderney

A **143** Alderney and Shansi on Beach

A **144** Wellington by Lighthouse

A **145** Madame Cholet and Bungo having Picnic

A **146** Tomsk playing Golf

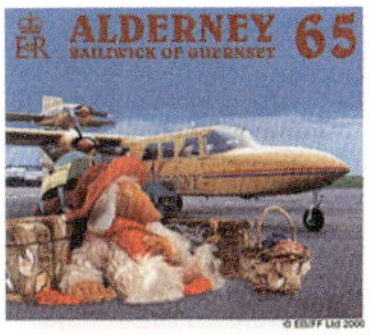

A **147** Orinoco at Airport

'A Wombling Holiday' (characters from children's television programme)

(Des Sally Diamond. Litho Questa)

2000 (28 Apr). Perf 14½×14 (C).

A146	A **142**	21p. multicoloured	45	45
A147	A **143**	26p. multicoloured	55	55
A148	A **144**	36p. multicoloured	95	95
A149	A **145**	40p. multicoloured	1·10	1·10
A150	A **146**	45p. multicoloured	1·50	1·50
A151	A **147**	65p. multicoloured	2·00	2·00
A146/51 *Set of 6*			6·00	6·00
First Day Cover				6·50
Presentation Pack			6·50	
Set of 6 Gutter Pairs			12·00	
MSA152 160×86 mm. Nos. A146/51			6·50	6·50
First Day Cover				12·00

No. **MS**A152 also includes the logo for 'The Stamp Show 2000', International Stamp Exhibition, London, on the sheet margin.

Plate Nos.: All values 1A (×4).
Sheets: 50 (2 panes 5×5).
Imprint: Lower right-hand margin.
Withdrawn: 27.4.2001.

A **148a** Queen Elizabeth the Queen Mother on Alderney, 1984 (*Illustration reduced. Actual size 93×70 mm*)

Queen Elizabeth the Queen Mother's 100th Birthday

(Des M. Whyte. Litho Walsall)

2000 (4 Aug). Sheet 93×70 mm. Perf 13½ (C).

MSA153 A **148a** £1.50. multicoloured	4·00	4·50
First Day Cover		6·00
Presentation Pack	6·00	

Withdrawn: 3.8.2001.

A **149** Regimental Boxing Tournament

A **150** Sports Day, Alderney Gala Week, 1924

A **151** Regimental Orchestra playing at Ball

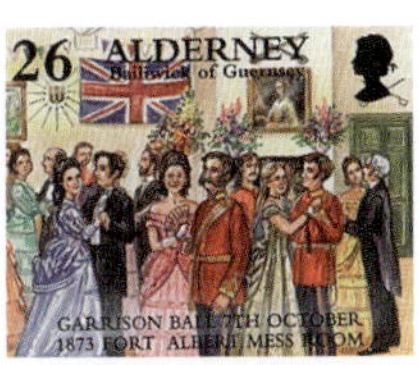

A **152** Garrison Ball in Fort Albert Mess, 1873

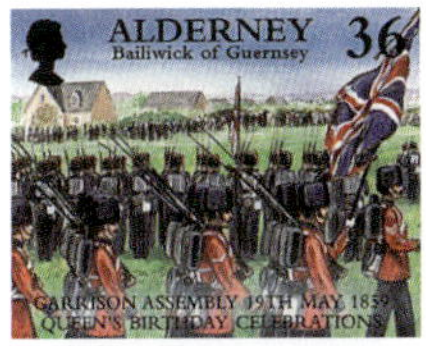

A **153** Royal Engineers' Colour Party, 1859

A **154** Royal Artillery on Parade, Queen's 40th Birthday, 1859

A **155** Royal Artillery Guard of Honour

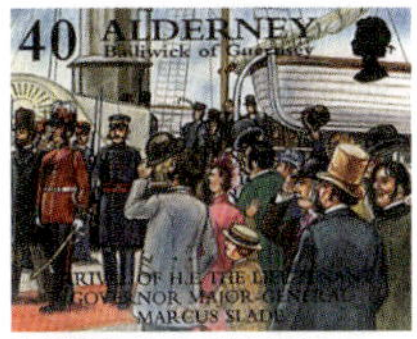

A **156** Arrival of Maj.-Gen. Marcus Slade, 1863

Garrison Island (4th series). Events

(Des R. Carter. Litho Cartor)

2000 (19 Oct). Perf 13 (C).

A154	A **149**	21p. multicoloured	45	25
		a. Horiz pair. Nos. A154/5	90	85
		b. Booklet pane. Nos. A154/7 with margins all round	2·40	
		c. Booklet pane. Nos. A154/5 and A160/1 with margins all round	3·00	
A155	A **150**	21p. multicoloured	45	25
A156	A **151**	26p. multicoloured	55	30
		a. Horiz pair. Nos. A156/7	1·10	1·10
		b. Booklet pane. Nos. A156/9 with margins all round	3·00	
A157	A **152**	26p. multicoloured	55	30
A158	A **153**	36p. multicoloured	75	40
		a. Horiz pair. Nos. 158/9	2·00	2·00
		b. Booklet pane. Nos. A158/61 with margins all round	4·50	
A159	A **154**	36p. multicoloured	75	40
A160	A **155**	40p. multicoloured	90	45
		a. Horiz pair. Nos. A160/1	2·50	2·50
A161	A **156**	40p. multicoloured	90	45
A154/61 *Set of 8*			6·00	6·00
First Day Cover				6·25
Presentation Pack			6·25	

Plate Nos.: All values 1A (×4).
Sheets: 20 (4×5), the two designs for each value were printed together, *se-tenant*, in horizontal pairs throughout the sheets, each pair forming a composite design.
Imprint: Central, right-hand margin.
Withdrawn: 18.10.2001.

A **157a** Queen Elizabeth II (*Illustration reduced. Actual size 70×70 mm*)

75th Birthday of Queen Elizabeth II

(Des C. Abbott. Litho and die-stamped. B.D.T.)

2001 (1 Feb). Sheet 70×70 mm. Perf 14 (C).

MSA162 A **157a** £1.75, multicoloured	4·50	4·50
First Day Cover		6·00
Presentation Pack	5·50	

Withdrawn: 31.1.2002.

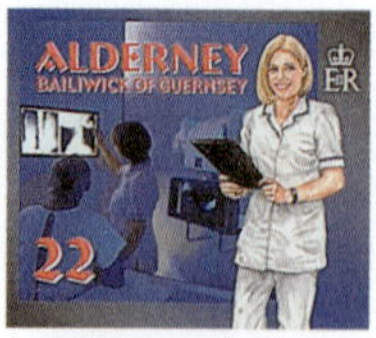

A **158** Nurse with Clipboard and Patient in X-Ray

A **159** Nurse with Tray and Mignot Memorial Hospital

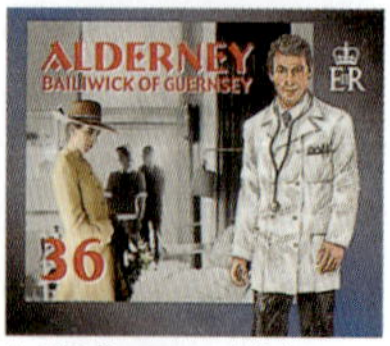

A **160** Doctor and Princess Anne visiting Hopital, 1972

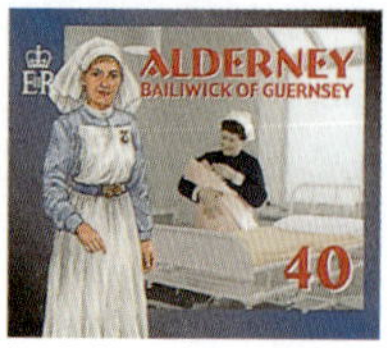

A **161** Nurse from 1960s and Maternity Unit

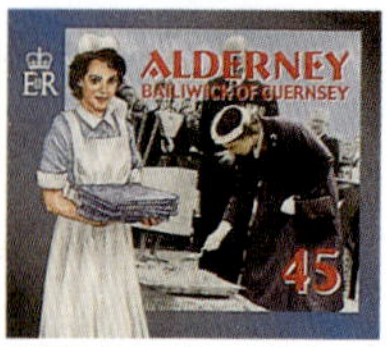

A **162** Nurse from 1957 and Queen Elizabeth II laying Hospital Foundation Stone

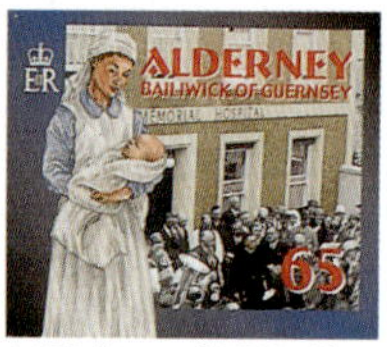

A **163** Nurse of 1926 with Baby and opening of Original Hospital

Community Services (1st series). Healthcare

(Des Sally Diamond. Litho Walsall)

2001 (26 Apr)–**02**. Perf 14×14½ (C).

A163	A **158**	22p. multicoloured (a)	45	50
		a. Perf 13½×13 (b)	60	80
		ab. Booklet pane. Nos. A163a/6a with margins all round	3·75	
		ac. Booklet pane. Nos. A163a/4a and A167a/8a with margins all round	4·50	
A164	A **159**	27p. multicoloured (a)	55	60
		a. Perf 13½×13 (b)	55	60
A165	A **160**	36p. multicoloured (a)	70	75
		a. Perf 13½×13 (b)	70	75
		ab. Booklet pane. Nos. A165a/8a with margins all round	4·50	
A166	A **161**	40p. multicoloured (a)	80	85
		a. Perf 13½×13 (b)	1·00	1·20
A167	A **162**	45p. multicoloured (a)	90	95
		a. Perf 13½×13 (b)	1·30	1·50
A168	A **163**	65p. multicoloured (a)	1·20	1·40
		a. Perf 13½×13 (b)	1·50	2·00
A163/8 *Set of 6*			4·50	5·00
First Day Cover				6·00
Presentation Pack			7·50	

Nos. A163a/8a were only issued in £9.40 stamp booklets.

See also Nos. A197/202.

Printings: (a) 26.4.01; (b) 17.10.02.
Plate Nos.: All values 1A (×4).
Sheets: 10 (2×5) with enlarged illustrated margin at left (22, 27, 36p.) or right (40, 45, 65p.).
Imprint: Central, right-hand margin (22, 27, 36p.) or central, left-hand margin (40, 45, 65p.).
Withdrawn: 25.4.2002 (sheets).

A **164** 'Feathery' Golf Ball, 1901

A **165** Golfing Fashions of the 1920s

A **166** Alderney Golf Course in 1970s

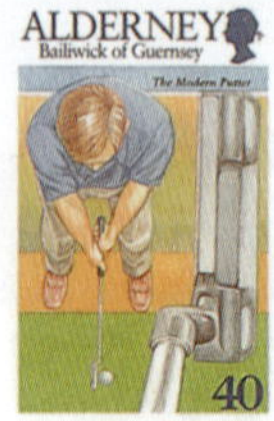

A **167** Modern Putter

A **168** Modern Golf Gloves and Shoes

A **169** Modern 'lofted wood'

30th Anniversary of Alderney Golf Club

(Des Colleen Corlett. Litho Questa)

2001 (1 Aug). Perf 14½ (C).

A169	A **164**	22p. multicoloured	45	50
A170	A **165**	27p. multicoloured	55	60
A171	A **166**	36p. multicoloured	80	75
A172	A **167**	40p. multicoloured	1·10	1·10
A173	A **168**	45p. multicoloured	1·50	1·50
A174	A **169**	65p. multicoloured	1·70	1·70
A169/74 *Set of 6*			6·00	6·00
First Day Cover				7·50
Presentation Pack			7·50	
Set of 6 Gutter Pairs			12·00	
MSA175 190×75 mm. Nos. A169/74			6·50	6·50
First Day Cover				9·00

No. **MS**A175 shows the 'Philanippon '01' logo on the margin.

Plate Nos.: All values 1A (×5).
Sheets: 50 (2 panes 5×5).
Imprint: Upper right-hand margin.
Withdrawn: 31.7.2002.

A **170** Construction of New Breakwater, 1853

A **171** Official Party inspecting Harbour, 1853

A **172** H.M.S. *Emerald* (steam frigate) aground, 1860

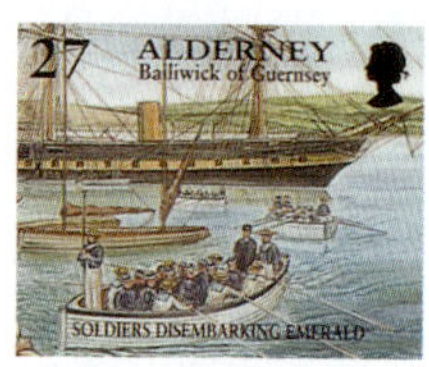

A **173** Disembarking Troops from H.M.S. *Emerald*, 1860

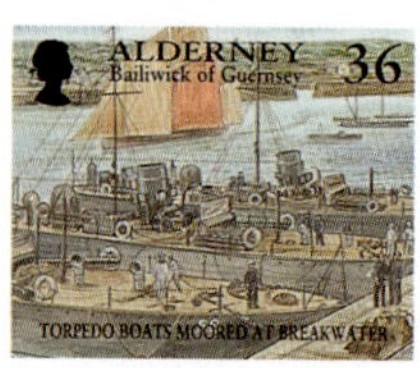

A **174** Moored Torpedo Boats, 1890

A **175** Quick-firing Gun on Railway Wagon, 1890

A **176** H.M.S. *Majestic* (battleship) at Anchor, 1901

A **177** Torpedo Boats outside Harbour, 1901

Garrison Island (5th series). The Royal Navy

(Des R. Carter. Litho Cartor)

2001 (16 Oct). Perf 13 (C).

A176	A **170**	22p. multicoloured	45	25
		a. Horiz pair. Nos. A176/7	1·00	1·00
		b. Booklet pane. Nos. A176/9 with margins all round	2·50	
		c. Booklet pane. Nos. A176/7 and A182/3 with margins all round	3·00	
A177	A **171**	22p. multicoloured	45	25
A178	A **172**	27p. multicoloured	55	30
		a. Horiz pair. Nos. A178/9	1·20	1·20
		b. Booklet pane. Nos. A178/81 with margins all round	3·00	
		c. Booklet pane. Nos. A178/9 and A182/3 with margins all round	3·75	
A179	A **173**	27p. multicoloured	55	30
A180	A **174**	36p. multicoloured	70	40
		a. Horiz pair. Nos. A180/1	1·60	1·60
		b. Booklet pane. Nos. A180/3 with margins all round	3·50	
A181	A **175**	36p. multicoloured	70	40
A182	A **176**	40p. multicoloured	80	45
		a. Horiz pair. Nos. A182/3	2·00	2·00
A183	A **177**	40p. multicoloured	80	45
A176/83 *Set of 8*			6·00	6·00
First Day Cover				8·00
Presentation Pack			8·00	

Plate Nos: All values 1A (×4).
Sheets: 20 (4×5), the two designs for each value were printed together, *se-tenant*, in horizontal pairs throughout the sheets, each pair forming a composite design.
Imprint: Central, right-hand margin.
Withdrawn: 15.10.2002.

A **178a** Queen Elizabeth and Prince Philip arriving at London Airport, Feb 1952 (*Illustration reduced. Actual size* 159×98 mm)

Golden Jubilee

(Des A. Fothergill. Litho B.D.T.)

2002 (6 Feb). Sheet 159×98 mm. Perf 13½ (C).

MSA184 A **178a** £2 blackish purple and gold		4·00	4·25
	a. Black omitted	£1150	
	b. Booklet pane. No. **MS**A184	4·00	
First Day Cover			7·50
Presentation Pack		5·50	

Booklet pane **MS**A18b comes from Guernsey booklet **SB**71.
Withdrawn: 5.2.2003.

A **179** Northern Hobby

A **180** Black Kite

A **181** Merlin

A **182** Honey Buzzard

A **183** Osprey

A **184** Marsh Harrier

Migrating Birds (1st series). Raptors

(Des G. Austin. Litho Questa)

2002 (30 Apr). Perf 14 (C).

A185	A **179**	22p. multicoloured	45	50
A186	A **180**	27p. multicoloured	55	60
A187	A **181**	36p. multicoloured	85	85
A188	A **182**	40p. multicoloured	1·00	1·00
A189	A **183**	45p. multicoloured	1·20	1·20
A190	A **184**	65p. multicoloured	1·70	1·70
A185/90 *Set of 6*			6·00	6·00
First Day Cover				6·50
Presentation Pack			7·50	
MSA191 170×80 mm. Nos. A185/90			6·50	6·50
First Day Cover				7·50

Plate Nos.: All values 1A (×4).
Sheets: 10 (2×5).
Imprint: Central, left-hand margin.
Withdrawn: 29.4.2003.

A **185** Coal Fire Beacon, 1725

A **186** Oil Lantern, 1779

A **187** Argand Lamp, 1790

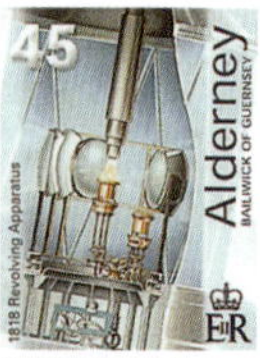

A **188** Revolving Light, 1818

A **189** Electric Light, 1952

50th Anniversary of Electrification of Les Casquets Lighthouse

(Des N. Watton. Litho Enschedé)

2002 (30 July). Perf 13×13½ (C).

A192	A **185**	22p. multicoloured	50	50
A193	A **186**	27p. multicoloured	60	60
A194	A **187**	36p. multicoloured	75	75
A195	A **188**	45p. multicoloured	1·10	1·10
A196	A **189**	65p. multicoloured	1·50	1·50
A192/6 *Set of 5*			4·50	4·50
First Day Cover				7·50
Presentation Pack			7·50	
Set of 5 Gutter Pairs			8·00	

No. A196 is inscribed 'Elictrification' in error.
Plate Nos.: All values 1A (×4).
Sheets: 50 (2 panes 5×5).
Imprint: Lower left-hand margin.
Withdrawn: 29.7.2003.

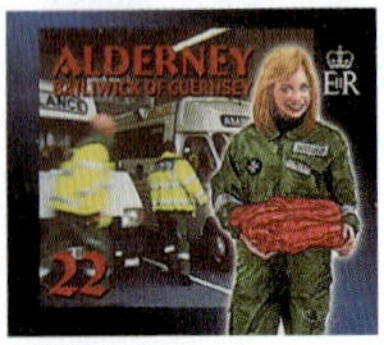

A **190** Ambulance Technician, and Ambulance Station

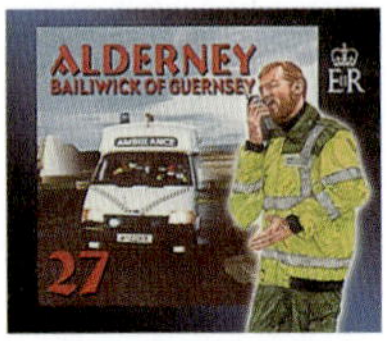

A **191** Ambulance Technician using Radio, and Ambulance

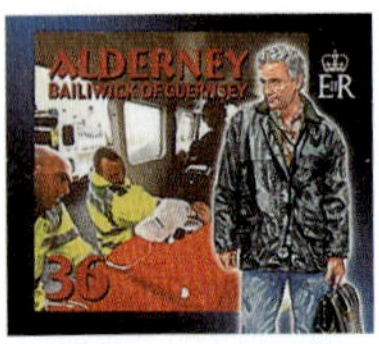

A **192** Doctor, and loading Patient onto Aircraft

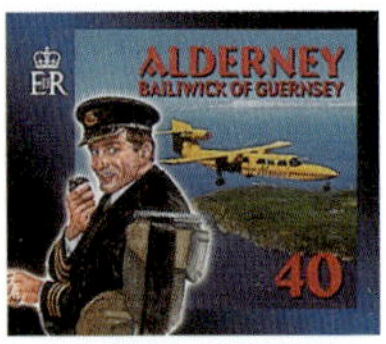

A **193** Pilot, and Trislander over Alderney

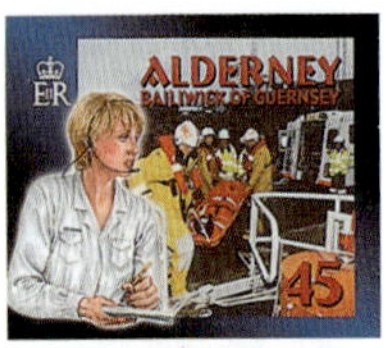

A **194** Emergency Operator, and Patient on Stretcher

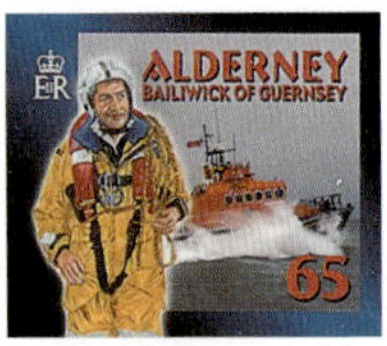

A **195** Lifebaotman, and *Roy Barker One* (lifeboat)

Community Services (2nd series). Emergency Medical Aid

(Des Sally Diamond. Litho Walsall)

2002 (17 Oct). Perf 14×14½ (C).

A197	A **190**	22p. multicoloured	45	50
		a. Perf 13½×13	90	90
		ab. Booklet pane. Nos. A197a/200a, with margins all round	5·75	
		ac. Booklet pane. Nos. A197a/200a and A201a/2a, with margins all round	11·00	
A198	A **191**	27p. multicoloured	55	60
		a. Perf 13½×13	1·00	1·00
A199	A **192**	36p. multicoloured	95	95
		a. Perf 13½×13	1·70	1·70
		ab. Booklet pane. Nos. A199a/202a, with margins all round	11·00	
A200	A **193**	40p. multicoloured	1·10	1·10
		a. Perf 13½×13	2·00	2·00
A201	A **194**	45p. multicoloured	1·70	1·70
		a. Perf 13½×13	3·00	3·00
A202	A **195**	65p. multicoloured	2·00	2·00
		a. Perf 13½×13	4·00	4·00
A197/202 *Set of 6*			6·00	6·00
First Day Cover				7·50
Presentation Pack			7·50	

Nos. A197a/202a were only issued in £9.40 stamp booklets.
Plate Nos.: All values 1A (×4).
Sheets: 10 (2×5) with enlarged illustrated margin at left.
Imprint: Central, right-hand margin.
Withdrawn: 16.10.2003.

A **196** St. Edward's Crown *(Illustration reduced. Actual size* 128×90 mm)

50th Anniversary of Coronation

(Des A. Fothergill. Litho and embossed Enschedé)

2003 (30 Jan). Sheet 128×90 mm. Perf 13½ (C).

MSA203	A **196**	£2 multicoloured	4·50	4·50
First Day Cover				7·50
Presentation Pack			6·00	

Withdrawn: 29.1.2004.

A **197** Wright Brothers' *Flyer I*, 1903

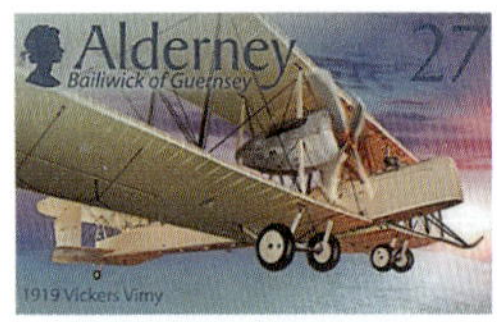

A **198** Alcock and Brown's Vickers FB-27 Vimy, 1919

A **199** Douglas DC-3, 1936

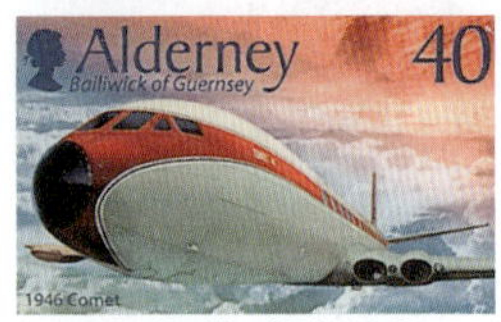

A **200** De Havilland DH106 Comet 4, 1946

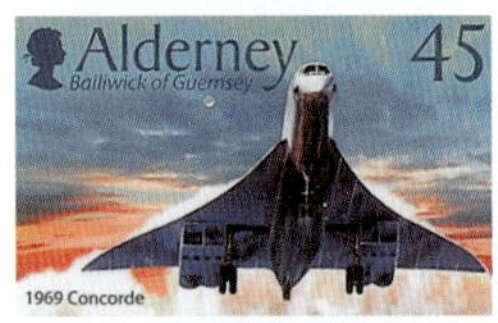

A **201** British Aerospace/Aerospatiale Concorde, 1969

A **202** Projected Airbus Industrie A380

Centenary of Powered Flight

(Des M. Wilkinson. Litho B.D.T.)

2003 (10 Apr). Perf 13½ (C).

A204	A **197**	22p. multicoloured	50	50
A205	A **198**	27p. multicoloured	75	75
A206	A **199**	36p. multicoloured	85	85
A207	A **200**	40p. multicoloured	1·00	1·00
A208	A **201**	45p. multicoloured	1·20	1·20
A209	A **202**	65p. multicoloured	1·50	1·50
A204/9 *Set of 6*			6·00	6·00
First Day Cover				7·50
Presentation Pack			7·50	
Set of 6 Gutter Pairs			12·00	

Plate Nos.: All values 1A (×4).
Sheets: 50 (2 panes 5×5).
Imprint: Central, left-hand margin.
Withdrawn: 9.4.2004.

A **203** Arctic Tern

A **204** Great Skua

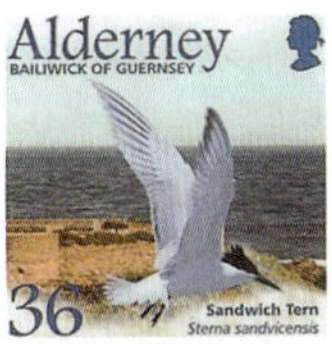

A **205** Sandwich Tern

A **206** Sooty Shearwater

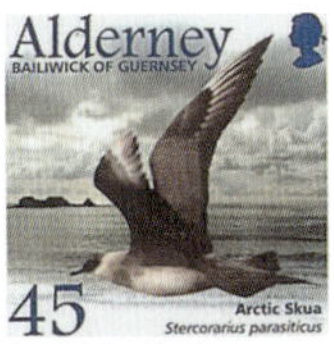

A **207** Arctic Skua

A **208** Manx Shearwater

Migrating Birds (2nd series). Seabirds

(Des G. Austin. Litho Questa)

2003 (3 July). Perf 14 (C).

A210	A **203**	22p. multicoloured	45	50
A211	A **204**	27p. multicoloured	55	60
A212	A **205**	36p. multicoloured	75	75
A213	A **206**	40p. multicoloured	1·00	1·00
A214	A **207**	45p. multicoloured	1·50	1·50
A215	A **208**	65p. multicoloured	2·00	2·00
A210/15 *Set of 6*			6·00	6·00
First Day Cover				7·50
Presentation Pack			7·50	
MSA216 80×170 mm. Nos. A210/15			6·00	6·00
First Day Cover				7·50

Plate Nos.: All values 1A (×4).
Sheets: 10 (2×5) with enlarged illustrated margin at right.
Imprint: Central, left-hand margin.
Withdrawn: 2.7.2004.

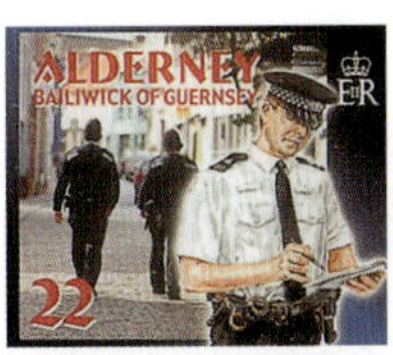

A **209** Policeman with Clipboard and Constable on Beat

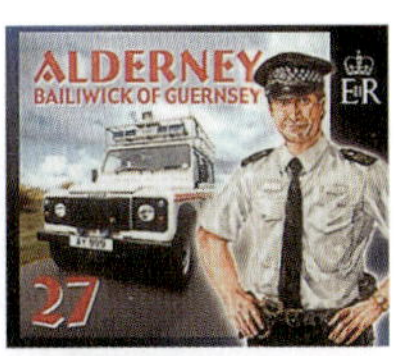

A **210** Policeman and Land Rover

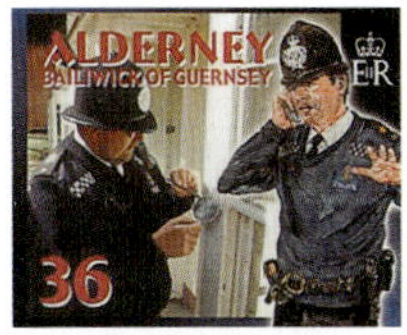

A **211** Forensic Team

A **212** Police Constable and Policeman with Child Cyclist

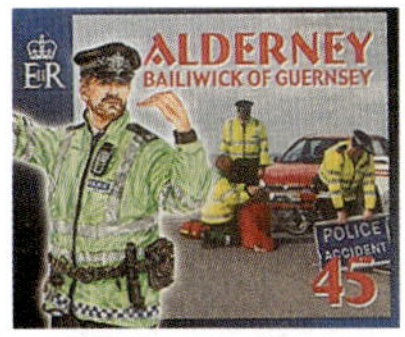

A **213** Policeman directing Traffic and Police at Scene of Accident

A **214** Policewoman and Policeman with Customs Officer

Community Services (3rd series). Alderney Police

(Des Sally Diamond. Litho Walsall)

2003 (16 Oct). Perf 13½×13 (C).

A217	A **209**	22p. multicoloured	50	50
		a. Booklet pane. Nos. A217/20	4·00	
		b. Booklet pane. Nos. A217/18 and A221/2	4·75	
		c. Booklet pane. Nos. A217/19 and A221	4·00	
		d. Booklet pane. Nos. A217/18, A220 and A222	4·50	
A218	A **210**	27p. multicoloured	60	60
A219	A **211**	36p. multicoloured	80	80
		a. Booklet pane. Nos. A219/22	5·50	
A220	A **212**	40p. multicoloured	1·00	1·00
A221	A **213**	45p. multicoloured	1·50	1·50
A222	A **214**	65p. multicoloured	2·00	2·00
A217/22 *Set of 6*			6·00	6·00
First Day Cover				7·50
Presentation Pack			6·50	

Plate Nos.: All values 1A (×4).
Sheets: 10 (2×5) with enlarged illustrated margin at left.
Imprint: Central, right-hand margin.
Withdrawn: 15.10.2004.

A **215** *Hypholoma fasciculare*

A **216** *Aleuria aurantia*

A **217** *Coprinus micaceus*

A **218** *Langermannia gigantea*

HAVE YOU READ THE NOTES AT THE BEGINNING OF THIS CATALOGUE?

These often provide answers to the enquiries we receive

A **219** *Macrolepiota procera*

A **220** *Xylaria hypoxylon*

Fungi

(Des Petula Stone. Litho Enschedé)

2004 (29 Jan). Perf 13½ (C).

A223	A **215**	22p. multicoloured	70	70
A224	A **216**	27p. multicoloured	85	85
A225	A **217**	36p. multicoloured	1·20	1·20
A226	A **218**	40p. multicoloured	1·30	1·30
A227	A **219**	45p. multicoloured	1·40	1·40
A228	A **220**	65p. multicoloured	2·10	2·10
A223/8 *Set of 6*			7·50	7·50
First Day Cover				9·75
Presentation Pack			8·50	
Set of 6 Gutter Pairs			12·00	

Plate Nos.: All values 1A (×4).
Sheets: 50 (2 panes 5×5).
Imprint: Upper side margins.
Withdrawn: 28.1.2005.

A **221** Boys playing Football, Tourgis Close

A **222** Three Children playing Football, Braye Beach

A **223** Two Boys playing Football in Playground

A **224** Teenagers playing Football, Arch Bay

A **225** Football Match

A **226** Father and Two Children playing Football, Arch Bay

Centenary of FIFA (Fédération Internationale de Football Association)

(Des A. Robinson. Litho Cartor)

2004 (12 May). Perf 13½ (C).

A229	A **221**	26p. multicoloured	85	85
A230	A **222**	32p. multicoloured	1·10	1·10
A231	A **223**	36p. multicoloured	1·20	1·20
A232	A **224**	40p. multicoloured	1·30	1·30
A233	A **225**	45p. multicoloured	1·50	1·50
A234	A **226**	65p. multicoloured	2·10	2·10
A229/34 *Set of 6*			8·00	8·00
First Day Cover				10·00
Presentation Pack			10·00	

Nos. A229/34 were each perforated in a circle contained within an outer perforated square which continued the design.

Plate Nos.: All values 1A (×4).
Sheets: 50 (5×10).
Imprint: Upper and lower side margins.
Withdrawn: 11.5.2005.

A **227** Northern Wheatear

A **228** Common Redstart

A **229** Yellow Wagtail

A **230** Hoopoe

A **231** Ring Ousel ('Ouzel')

A **232** Sand Martin

Migrating Birds (3rd series). Passerines

(Des A. Robinson. Litho Enschedé)

2004 (29 July). Perf 13½ (C).

A235	A **227**	26p. multicoloured	85	85
A236	A **228**	32p. multicoloured	1·10	1·10
A237	A **229**	36p. multicoloured	1·20	1·20
A238	A **230**	40p. multicoloured	1·30	1·30
A239	A **231**	45p. multicoloured	1·50	1·50
A240	A **232**	65p. multicoloured	2·10	2·10
A235/40 *Set of 6*			8·00	8·00
First Day Cover				10·00
Presentation Pack			10·00	
MSA241 170×80 mm. Nos. A235/40			8·00	8·00
First Day Cover				10·00

Plate Nos.: All values 1A, 1B, 1C, 1D (each ×4).
Sheets: 10 (2×5) with enlarged illustrated right-hand margin.
Imprint: Central, left-hand margin.
Withdrawn: 28.7.2005.

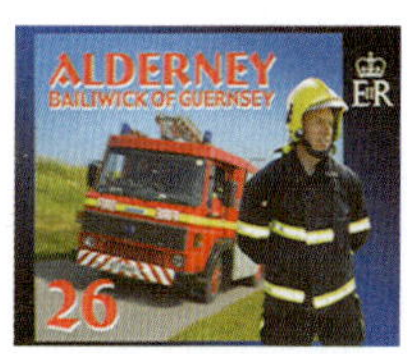

A **233** Fire Engine

A **234** Fireman up Ladder and Fire Engine at Fort Tourgis

A **235** Airport Service Fire Truck

A **236** Alderney Fire Station

A **237** Airport Training Ground

A **238** Road Accident Training Exercise

Community Services (4th series). Fire Service

(Des M. Legg. Litho Walsall)

2004 (28 Oct). Perf 13½×13 (C).

A242	A **233**	26p. multicoloured	85	85
		a. Booklet pane. Nos. A242/5 with margins all round	4·50	
		b. Booklet pane. Nos. A242/3 and A246/7 with margins all round	5·50	
		c. Booklet pane. Nos. A242/4 and A246 with margins all round	4·50	
		d. Booklet pane. Nos. A242/3, A245 and A247 with margins all round	5·50	
A243	A **234**	32p. multicoloured	1·10	1·10
A244	A **235**	36p. multicoloured	1·20	1·20
		a. Booklet pane. Nos. A244/7 with margins all round	6·00	
A245	A **236**	40p. multicoloured	1·30	1·30
A246	A **237**	45p. multicoloured	1·50	1·50
A247	A **238**	65p. multicoloured	2·10	2·10
A242/7 *Set of 6*			8·00	8·00
First Day Cover				10·00
Presentation Pack			10·00	

Plate Nos.: All values 1A×4.
Sheets: 10 (2×5) with enlarged illustrated left-hand margin.
Imprint: Central, right-hand margin.
Withdrawn: 27.10.2005.

A **239** Mermaid at her Undersea Home

A **240** Mermaid rescuing drowning Prince

A **241** Mermaid with Sea Witch bargaining her voice for a Human Life

A **242** Mermaids waving to Prince and his Lover on Seashore

A **243** Mermaid carried away by Angels

Birth Bicentenary of Hans Christian Andersen. Scenes from *The Little Mermaid*

(Des N. Watton. Litho Enschedé)

2005 (3 Feb). Perf 13½×14 (C).

A248	A **239**	26p. multicoloured	50	55
A249	A **240**	32p. multicoloured	65	70
A250	A **241**	36p. multicoloured	1·00	1·00
A251	A **242**	40p. multicoloured	2·00	2·00
A252	A **243**	65p. multicoloured	3·00	3·00
A248/52 *Set of 5*			7·00	7·00
First Day Cover				8·00
Presentation Pack			7·50	

Plate Nos.: All values 1A (×4).
Sheets: 50 (5×10).
Imprint: Upper left-hand margin.
Withdrawn: 2.2.2006.

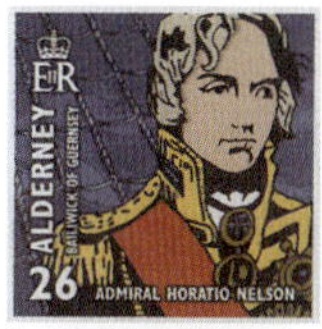

A **244** Admiral Horatio Nelson

A **245** H.M.S. *Victory*

A **246** Marine firing musket

A **247** Wounded Nelson with Captain Hardy

A **248** H.M.S. *Victory* in battle with *Redoutable*

A **249** Admiral James Lord de Saumarez

Bicentenary of the Battle of Trafalgar

(Des S. Shackleton. Litho Enschedé)

2005 (9 May). Perf 14×13½ (C).

A253	A **244**	26p. multicoloured	50	55
		a. Booklet pane. Nos. A253/6 with margins all round	2·50	
		b. Booklet pane. Nos. A253/4 and A257/8 with margins all round	4·75	
		c. Booklet pane. Nos. A253 and A256/8 with margins all round	5·00	
A254	A **245**	32p. multicoloured	65	70
		a. Booklet pane. Nos. A254/5 and A257/8	5·00	
A255	A **246**	36p. multicoloured	70	75
		a. Booklet pane. Nos. A255/8 with margins all round	5·00	
A256	A **247**	40p. multicoloured	80	85
A257	A **248**	45p. multicoloured	1·50	1·70
A258	A **249**	65p. multicoloured	2·00	2·50
A253/8 *Set of 6*			6·00	6·50
First Day Cover				7·50
Presentation Pack			7·50	

Plate Nos.: All values 1A (×4).
Sheets: 10 (2×5) with enlarged illustrated left margins.
Imprint: Central right-hand margins.
Withdrawn: 8.5.2006.

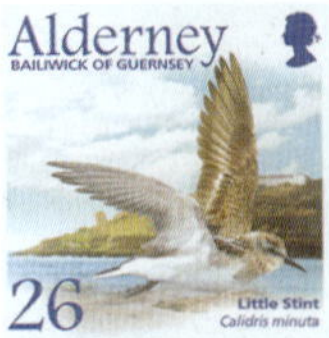

A **250** Little Stint

A **251** Common Greenshank

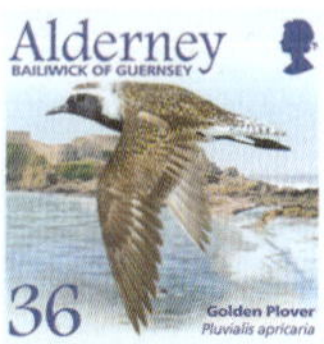

A **252** Golden Plover

A **253** Bar-tailed Godwit

A **254** Green Sandpiper

A **255** Sanderling

Migrating Birds (4th series). Waders

(Des A. Robinson. Litho Enschedé)

2005 (21 July). Perf 13½ (C).

A259	A **250**	26p. multicoloured	50	55
A260	A **251**	32p. multicoloured	65	70
A261	A **252**	36p. multicoloured	70	75
A262	A **253**	40p. multicoloured	1·00	85
A263	A **254**	45p. multicoloured	2·00	2·00
A264	A **255**	65p. multicoloured	3·00	3·00
A259/64 *Set of 6*			7·50	7·50
First Day Cover				8·50
Presentation Pack			8·50	
MSA265 170×80 mm. Nos. A259/64			8·00	8·00
First Day Cover				9·00

Plate Nos.: All values 1A (×4).
Sheets: 10 (2×5) with enlarged illustrated right margins.
Imprint: Lower left-hand margins.
Withdrawn: 20.7.2006.

A **256** Alderney Arms and Sunset (*Illustration reduced. Actual size 140×80 mm*)

60th Anniversary of Return of War Evacuees

(Des P. Furness. Litho BDT)

2005 (27 Oct). Sheet 140×80 mm. Perf 14 (C).

MSA266 A **256** £2 multicoloured	6·00	7·50
First Day Cover		8·50
Presentation Pack	8·50	

Withdrawn: 26.10.2006.

A **257** Young King Arthur

A **258** Merlyn

A **259** Morgause

A **260** Queen Guenever

A **261** Lancelot

A **262** Mordred

'The Once and Future King'

(Des N. Watton. Litho Enschedé)

2006 (16 Feb). Perf 13½×14 (C).

A267	A **257**	29p. multicoloured	60	65
A268	A **258**	34p. multicoloured	70	75
A269	A **259**	38p. multicoloured	1·00	1·00
A270	A **260**	42p. multicoloured	1·50	1·50
A271	A **261**	47p. multicoloured	1·90	1·90
A272	A **262**	68p. multicoloured	2·20	2·20
A267/72 *Set of 6*			8·00	8·00
First Day Cover				9·00
Presentation Pack			9·00	
MSA273 120×90 mm. Nos. A267/72			8·50	8·50
First Day Cover				9·50

Nos. A267/**MS**A273 commemorate the birth centenary of Terence Hanbury White, author of 'The Once and Future King'.
Plate Nos.: All values 1A (×4).
Sheets: 10 (2×5) with enlarged illustrated right margins.
Imprint: Lower left-hand margin.
Withdrawn: 15.2.2007.

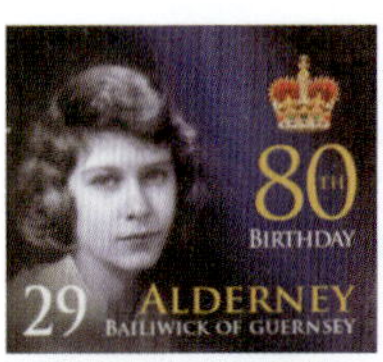

A **263** Princess Elizabeth

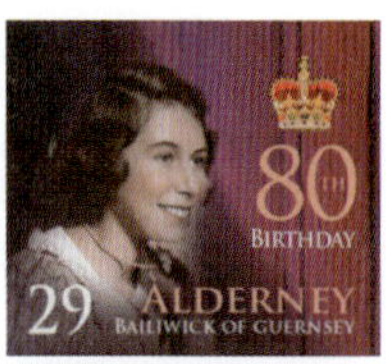

A **264** Princess Elizabeth

A **265** Queen Elizabeth II, c. 1955

A **266** Wearing Brown Coat and Hat

A **267** Wearing Tiara

A **268** Wearing Red Jacket and Red and White Hat

A **269** Wearing Pale Pink Hat

A **270** Wearing Mauve Dress and Hat

80th Birthday of Queen Elizabeth II

(Des P. Furness. Litho Austrian State Ptg Wks, Vienna)

2006 (21 Apr). Perf 14 (C).

A274	A **263**	29p. multicoloured	30	30
		a. Horiz pair. Nos. A274/5	1·30	1·30
A275	A **264**	29p. multicoloured	30	30
A276	A **265**	34p. multicoloured	50	50
		a. Horiz pair. Nos. A276/7	1·50	1·50
A277	A **266**	34p. multicoloured	50	50
A278	A **267**	42p. multicoloured	85	90
		a. Horiz pair. Nos. A278/9	2·50	2·50
A279	A **268**	42p. multicoloured	85	90
A280	A **269**	45p. multicoloured	90	95
		a. Horiz pair. Nos. A280/1	3·00	3·00
A281	A **270**	45p. multicoloured	90	95
A274/81 *Set of 8*			8·00	8·00
First Day Cover				9·50
Presentation Pack			9·50	

Nos. A274/81 in sheets of ten were included in a souvenir folder, together with the £10 stamp issued by Guernsey to celebrate The Queen's birthday (see Guernsey No. 1122).

Plate Nos.: All values 1A (×4).

Sheets: 10 (2×5) with enlarged illustrated left margins. Nos. A274/5, A276/7, A278/9 and A280/1 were each printed together, *se-tenant*, in horizontal pairs throughout the sheets.

Imprint: Lower right-hand margin.

Withdrawn: 20.4.2007.

A **271** Fulmar

A **272** Gannet

A **273** Lesser Black-backed Gull

A **274** Storm Petrel

A **275** Kittiwake

A **276** Puffin

Resident Birds (1st series). Seabirds

(Des A. Robinson. Litho BDT)

2006 (27 July). Perf 14 (C).

A282	A **271**	29p. multicoloured	65	65
		a. Booklet pane. No. A282×4 with margins all round	2·50	
A283	A **272**	34p. multicoloured	75	75
		a. Booklet pane. No.A283×4 with margins all round	3·00	
A284	A **273**	42p. multicoloured	1·00	1·00
		a. Booklet pane. No. A284×4 with margins all round	4·00	
A285	A **274**	45p. multicoloured	1·50	1·50
		a. Booklet pane. No. 285×4 with margins all round	6·00	
A286	A **275**	47p. multicoloured	2·00	2·00
		a. Booklet pane. No. A286×4 with margins all round	8·00	
A287	A **276**	68p. multicoloured	3·00	3·00
		a. Booklet pane. No. A287×4 with margins all round	12·00	
A282/7 *Set of 6*			8·00	8·00
First Day Cover				9·50
Presentation Pack			9·50	

Plate Nos.: All values 1A (×4).

Sheets: 10 (2×5) with enlarged illustrated margins at right and foot.

Imprint: Upper left-hand margin.

Withdrawn: 26.7.2007.

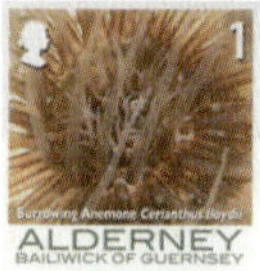

A **277** *Cerianthus lloydii* (burrowing anemone)

A **278** *Parazoanthus axinellae* (colonial anemone)

A **279** *Corynactis viridis* (jewel anemone colony)

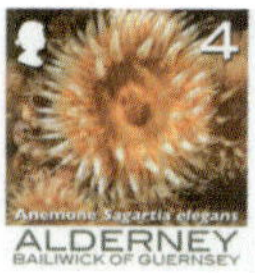

A **280** *Sagartia elegans* (elegant anemone)

A **281** *Alcyonium glomeratum* (red fingers)

A **282** *Metridium senile* (plumose anemone)

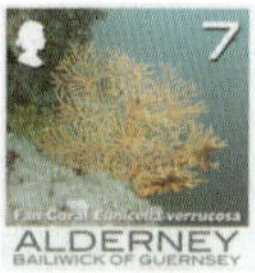

A **283** *Eunicella verrucosa* (fan coral)

A **284** *Corynactis viridis* (jewel anemone)

A **285** *Actinothoe sphyrodeta* (sandalled anemone)

A **286** *Anemonia viridis* (snakelocks anemone)

A **287** *Caryophyllia smithii* (Devonshire cup coral)

A **290** *Actinothoe sphyrodeta* (fried egg anemone)

A **293** *Calliactis parasitica* (parasitic anemone)

A **295** *Actinia equina* (beadlet anemone)

A **296** *Leptopsammia pruvoti* (sunset cup coral)

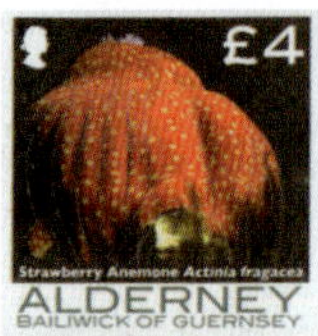

A **297** *Actinia fragacea* (strawberry anemone)

Corals and Anemones

(Des Sue Daly. Litho (£4 also embossed) Austrian State Ptg Wks, Vienna (20p. to 50p., £4) or Enschedé (others))

2006 (2 Nov)–**07**. Perf 14 (20p. to 50p., £4) or 13×13½ (others), both comb.

A288	A **277**	1p. multicoloured	10	10
A289	A **278**	2p. multicoloured	10	10
A290	A **279**	3p. multicoloured	10	10
A291	A **280**	4p. multicoloured	10	15
A292	A **281**	5p. multicoloured	10	15
A293	A **282**	6p. multicoloured	10	15
A294	A **283**	7p. multicoloured	15	20
A295	A **284**	8p. multicoloured	15	20
A296	A **285**	9p. multicoloured	20	25
A297	A **286**	10p. multicoloured	20	25
A298	A **287**	20p. multicoloured (b)	45	45
A301	A **290**	40p. multicoloured (b)	95	95
A304	A **293**	50p. multicoloured (b)	1·20	1·20
A306	A **295**	£1 multicoloured	2·00	2·10
A307	A **296**	£2 multicoloured	4·00	4·25
A308	A **297**	£4 multicoloured (b)	9·50	9·50
A288/308 *Set of 16*			19·00	20·00
First Day Covers (4)				23·00
Presentation Packs (2)			22·00	
Set of 16 Gutter Pairs			38·00	

Nos. A299/300, A302/3 and A305 are left for additions to these definitive stamps.

Printings: (a) 2.11.2006; (b) 2.8.2007.
Plate Nos.: All values 1A (×4).
Sheets: 50 (2 panes 5×5).
Imprint: Central, side margins.

A **298** Cushion Starfish

A **299** Gannet Colony at Les Etacs

A **300** Spiny Squat Lobster

A **301** Grey Seal

A **302** Golden Samphire near Fort Clonque

A **303** Little Egret and Oystercatchers

Designation of Alderney West Coast and the Burhou Islands as Ramsar Site

(Des Wendy Bramall. Litho BDT)

2007 (8 Mar). Perf 13½ (C).

A309	A **298**	32p. multicoloured	75	75
A310	A **299**	37p. multicoloured	90	90
A311	A **300**	45p. multicoloured	1·10	1·10
A312	A **301**	48p. multicoloured	1·10	1·10
A313	A **302**	50p. multicoloured	1·20	1·20
A314	A **303**	71p. multicoloured	1·70	1·70
A309/14 *Set of 6*			6·75	6·75
First Day Cover				8·50
Presentation Pack			8·50	
MSA315 140×95 mm. Nos. A309/14			6·75	6·75
First Day Cover				8·50

Plate Nos.: All values 1A (×4).
Sheets: 10 (2×5) with enlarged illustrated margins at right and foot.
Imprint: Central, left-hand margin.
Withdrawn: 7.3.2007.

A **304** Balckbird

A **305** Dartford Warbler

A **306** Blue Tit

A **307** Wren

A **308** House Sparrow

A **309** Jackdaw

Resident Birds (2nd series). Passerines

(Des Andrew Robinson. Litho BDT)

2007 (24 May). Perf 14 (C).

A316	A **304**	32p. multicoloured	75	75
		a. Booklet pane. No. A316×4 with margins all round	3·00	
A317	A **305**	37p. multicoloured	90	90
		a. Booklet pane. No. A317×4 with margins all round	3·50	
A318	A **306**	45p. multicoloured	1·10	1·10
		a. Booklet pane. No. A318×4 with margins all round	4·50	
A319	A **307**	48p. multicoloured	1·25	1·25
		a. Booklet pane. No. A319×4 with margins all round	4·75	
A320	A **308**	50p. multicoloured	1·25	1·25
		a. Booklet pane. No. A320×4 with margins all round	5·25	
A321	A **309**	71p. multicoloured	1·75	1·75
		a. Booklet pane. No. A321×4 with margins all round	7·50	
A316/21 *Set of 6*			7·00	7·00

First Day Cover		8·50
Presentation Pack	8·50	

Plate Nos.: All values 1A (×4).
Sheets: 10 (2×5) with enlarged illustrated margins at right and foot.
Imprint: Central, left margin.
Withdrawn: 23.5.2008.

A **310** 'How the Camel got his Hump'

A **311** 'How the Whale got his Throat'

A **312** 'The Elephant's Child'

A **313** 'How the Leopard got his Spots'

A **314** 'The Cat that walked by Himself'

A **315** 'How the Rhinoceros got his Skin'

'Rudyard Kipling's Just So Stories

(Des Nick Watton. Litho BDT)

2007 (25 Oct). Rudyard Kipling's Just So Stories. Perf 13½ (C).

A322	A **310**	32p. multicoloured	75	75
A323	A **311**	37p. multicoloured	90	90
A324	A **312**	45p. multicoloured	1·10	1·10
A325	A **313**	48p. multicoloured	1·25	1·25
A326	A **314**	50p. multicoloured	1·25	1·25
A327	A **315**	71p. multicoloured	1·75	1·75
A322/7 *Set of 6*			7·00	7·00
First Day Cover				8·50
Presentation Pack			8·50	
MSA328 140×95 mm. Nos. A322/7			7·00	7·00
First Day Cover				8·50

Sheets: 10 (2×5) with enlarged illustrated margins at right and foot.
Imprint: Central, left-hand margin.
Withdrawn: 24.10.2008.

A **316** *Vanessa cardui* (painted lady)

A **317** Hipparchia semele (grayling)

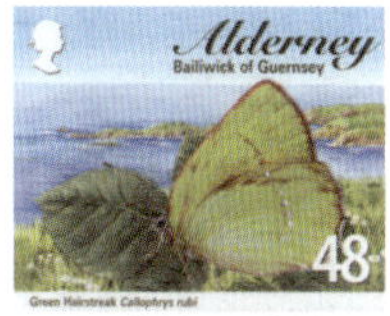

A **318** callophrys rubi (green hairstreak)

A **319** Pararge aegeria (speckled wood)

A **320** Polymmatus icarus (common blue)

A **321** Melitaea cinxia (Glanvile fritillary)

Butterflies

(Des Petula Stone. Litho BDT)

2008 (28 Feb). Perf 14 (C).

A329	A **316**	34p. multicoloured	80	80
A330	A **317**	40p. multicoloured	95	95
A331	A **318**	48p. multicoloured	1·10	1·10
A332	A **319**	51p. multicoloured	1·20	1·20
A333	A **320**	53p. multicoloured	1·30	1·30
A334	A **321**	74p. multicoloured	1·70	1·70
A329/34 *Set of 6*			7·00	7·00
First Day Cover				8·75
Presentation Pack			8·75	
MSA335 140×100 mm. Nos. A329/34			7·00	7·00
First Day Cover				8·75

Plate Nos.: All values 1A (×4).
Sheets: 10 (2×5) with enlarged illustrated margins at right and foot.
Imprint: Central, left-hand margin.
Withdrawn: 27.2.2009.

A **322** Common Buzzard

A **323** Peregrine Falcon

A **324** Kestrel

A **325** Barn Owl

A **326** Long-eared Owl

A **327** Sparrowhawk

Resident Birds (3rd series). Raptors

(Des Andrew Robinson. Litho BDT)

2008 (15 May). Perf 14 (C).

A336	A **322**	34p. multicoloured	80	80
		a. Booklet pane. No. A336×4 with margins all round	3·25	
A337	A **323**	40p. multicoloured	95	95
		a. Booklet pane. No. A337×4 with margins all round	3·75	

A338	A **324**	48p. multicoloured	1·10	1·10
		a. Booklet pane. No. A338×4 with margins all round	4·50	
A339	A **325**	51p. multicoloured	1·20	1·20
		a. Booklet pane. No. A339×4 with margins all round	4·75	
A340	A **326**	53p. multicoloured	1·30	1·30
		a. Booklet pane. No. A340×4 with margins all round	5·00	
A341	A **327**	74p. multicoloured	1·70	1·70
		a. Booklet pane. No. A341×4 with margins all round	7·00	
A336/41 *Set of 6*			7·00	7·00
First Day Cover				8·75
Presentation Pack			8·75	

Plate Nos.: All values 1A (×4).
Sheets: 10 (2×5) with enlarged illustrated margins at right and foot.
Imprint: Central, left-hand margin.
Withdrawn: 14.5.2009.

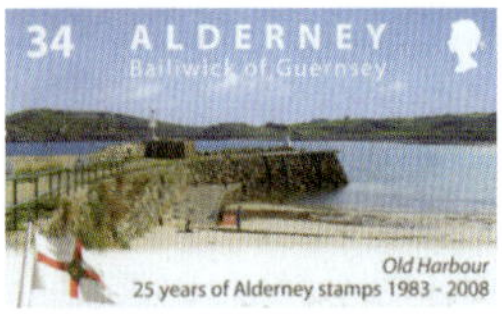

A **328** Old Harbour

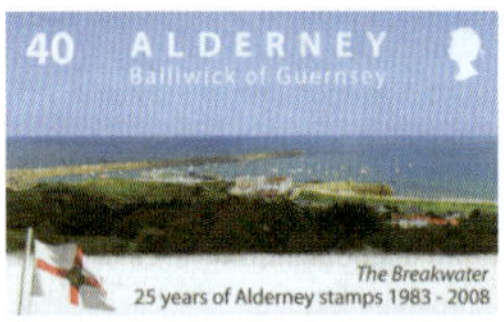

A **329** The Breakwater

A **330** Fort Clonque Causeway

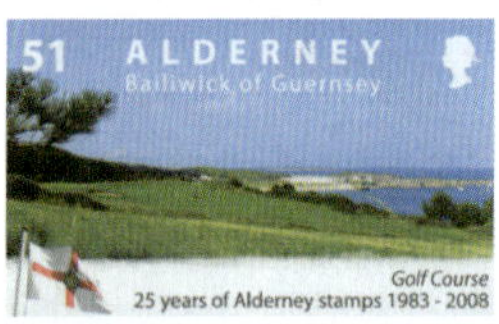

A **331** Golf Course

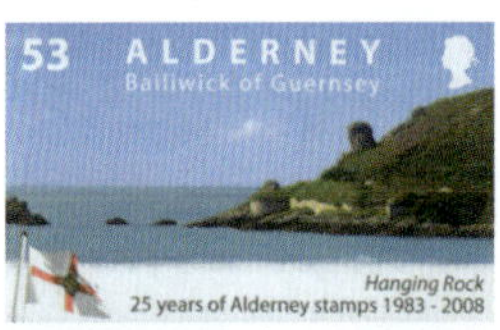

A **332** Hanging Rock

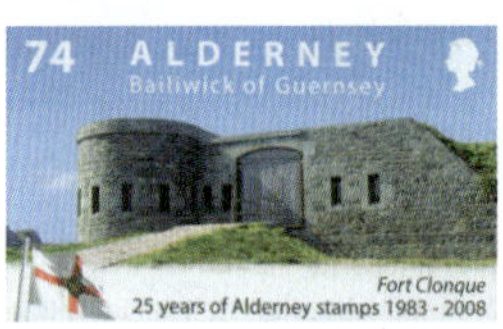

A **333** Fort Clonque

25th Anniversary of Alderney Stamps

(Des Andrew Fothergill. Litho Austrian State Ptg Wks, Vienna)

2008 (14 June). Perf 14 (C).

A342	A **328**	34p. multicoloured	80	80
A343	A **329**	40p. multicoloured	95	95
A344	A **330**	48p. multicoloured	1·10	1·10
A345	A **331**	51p. multicoloured	1·20	1·20
A346	A **332**	53p. multicoloured	1·30	1·30
A347	A **333**	74p. multicoloured	1·70	1·70
A342/7 *Set of 6*			7·00	7·00
First Day Cover				8·75
Presentation Pack			8·75	
Souvenir Folder (Nos. A342/8)			55·00	

Plate Nos.: All values 1A (×4).
Sheets: 10 (2×5) with enlarged illustrated margins at left and foot.
Imprint: Lower right-hand margin.
Withdrawn: 13.6.2009.

A **334** Lion Rampant from Alderney Flag

(Des Andrew Fothergill. Litho and embossed Austrian State Ptg Wks, Vienna)

2008 (14 June). Perf 14½×13½ (C).

A348	A **334**	£5 multicoloured	12·00	12·00
First Day Cover				13·50
Presentation Pack			13·50	

No. A348 was retained as a definitive stamp.
Sheets: 5 (5×1) with enlarged illustrated margins.
Imprint: Top margin.

A **335** Britten-Norman Islander

A **336** Britten-Norman Trislander

A **337** DHC-6 Twin Otter

A **338** Short 360

A **339** Saab 340

A **340** ATR 72

40th Anniv of Aurigny Air Services

(Des Mark Wilkinson. Litho BDT)

2008 (31 Oct). Perf 13½ (C).

A349	A **335**	34p. multicoloured	80	80
A350	A **336**	40p. multicoloured	95	95
A351	A **337**	48p. multicoloured	1·10	1·10
A352	A **338**	51p. multicoloured	1·20	1·20
A353	A **339**	53p. multicoloured	1·30	1·30
A354	A **340**	74p. multicoloured	1·70	1·70
A349/54 *Set of 6*			7·00	7·00
First Day Cover				8·75
Presentation Pack			8·75	
MSA355 140×95 mm. Nos. A349/54			7·00	7·00
First Day Cover				8·75

Plate Nos.: All values 1A (×4).
Sheets: 10 (2×5) with enlarged illustrated margins at right and foot.
Imprint: Central, left-hand margin.
Withdrawn: 29.10.2009.

A **341** Tawny Mining Bee (*Andrena fulva*)

A **342** Early Bumble Bee (*Bombus pratorum*)

A **343** Bug Mining Bee (*Colletes daviesanus*)

A **344** Cuckoo Bee (*Nomada goodeniana*)

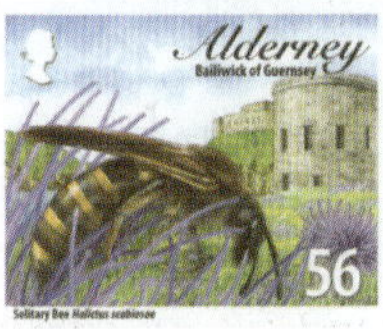

A **345** Solitary Bee (*Halictus scabiosae*)

A **346** Honey Bee (*Apis mellifera*)

Alderney Bees

(Des Petula Stone. Litho BDT)

2009 (26 Feb). Perf 13½ (C).

A356	A **341**	36p. multicoloured	90	90
A357	A **342**	43p. multicoloured	1·00	1·00
A358	A **343**	51p. multicoloured	1·25	1·25
A359	A **344**	54p. multicoloured	1·25	1·25
A360	A **345**	56p. multicoloured	1·40	1·40
A361	A **346**	77p. multicoloured	1·75	1·75
A356/61 *Set of 6*			7·25	7·25
First Day Cover				9·25
Presentation Pack			9·25	
MSA362 140×100 mm. Nos. A356/61			8·00	8·00
First Day Cover				9·25

Plate Nos.: All values 1A (×4).
Sheets: 10 (2×5) with enlarged illustrated right margins.
Imprint: Central, left-hand margin.

A **347** Turnstone

A **348** Curlew

A **349** Oystercatcher

A **350** Snipe

A **351** Dunlin

A **352** Ringed Plover

Resident Birds (4th series). Waders

(Des Andrew Robinson. Litho BDT)

2009 (28 May). Perf 13½ (C).

A363	A **347**	36p. multicoloured	85	75
		a. *Booklet pane. No. A363×4 with margins allround*	3·25	
A364	A **348**	43p. multicoloured	1·10	1·10
		a. *Booklet pane. No. A364×4 with margins allround*	4·00	
A365	A **349**	51p. multicoloured	1·25	1·25
		a. *Booklet pane. No. A365×4 with margins allround*	4·75	
A366	A **350**	54p. multicoloured	1·25	1·25
		a. *Booklet pane. No. A366×4 with margins allround*	5·00	
A367	A **351**	56p. multicoloured	1·40	1·40
		a. *Booklet pane. No. A367×4 with margins allround*	5·00	
A368	A **352**	77p. multicoloured	1·60	1·60
		a. *Booklet pane. No. A368×4 with margins allround*	7·00	
A363/8 *Set of 6*			7·25	7·25
First Day Cover				9·00
Presentation Pack			9·00	

Plate Nos.: All values 1A (×4).
Sheets: 10 (2×5) with enlarged illustrated right margins.
Imprint: Central, left-hand margin.

A **353** Felixstowe F2A Flying Boat with 'Dazzle' Paint over Castle Cornet, 1918

A **354** Fairey Swordfish NE874 attacking U-boat

A **355** Blackburn Skuas dive bombing *Scharnhorst*

A **356** Hawker Sea Fury FB11 (VR930) over Alderney

A **357** Hawker Seahawk and Sea Fury

A **358** Agusta Westland HM101 Merlin Helicopter landing on HMS *Daring*

Centenary of Naval Aviation

(Des Robin Carter. Litho Enschedé)

2009 (30 July). Perf 14×13½ (C).

A369	A **353**	36p. multicoloured	85	85
A370	A **354**	43p. multicoloured	1·00	1·00
A371	A **355**	51p. multicoloured	1·25	1·25
A372	A **356**	54p. multicoloured	1·25	1·25
A373	A **357**	56p. multicoloured	1·40	1·40
A374	A **358**	77p. multicoloured	1·75	1·75
A369/74 Set of 6			7·25	7·25
First Day Cover				9·00
Presentation Pack			9·00	
Souvenir Album (complete sheets of A369/74, *first day cover and prints of artwork)*			80·00	

Plate Nos.: All values 1A, 1B (each×4).
Sheets: 10 (2×5) with enlarged illustrated right margins.
Imprint: Central, left-hand margin.

A **359** Alice West reporting Theft of Bull to Sherlock Holmes

A **360** Holmes studying Coded Message and Arrest of Herdsman

A **361** Holmes studying Message on Harbour Wall

A **362** Sherlock Holmes and Farmer West

A **363** Holmes and Watson observing Half-built LIghthouse

A **364** Arrest of Thief

150th Birth Anniversary of Sir Arthur Conan Doyle. Scenes from new story *Sherlock Holmes and the Curious Case of the Alderney Bull*

(Des Keith Robinson. Litho Cartor)

2009 (29 Oct). Perf 13½×13 (C).

A375	A **359**	36p. multicoloured	85	85
A376	A **360**	43p. multicoloured	1·00	1·00
A377	A **361**	51p. multicoloured	1·25	1·25
A378	A **362**	54p. multicoloured	1·25	1·25
A379	A **363**	56p. multicoloured	1·40	1·40
A380	A **364**	77p. multicoloured	1·75	1·75
A375/80 *Set of 6*			7·25	7·25
First Day Cover				9·00
Presentation Pack			9·00	

Plate Nos.: All values 1A (×4).
Sheets: 10 (2×5) with enlarged illustrated right margins.
Imprint: Central, left-hand margin.

A miniature sheet containing Nos. A375/80 was only available in a 'mystery pack' sold for £9·99.

A **365** Common Darter (*Sympetrum striolatum*)

A **366** Emperor Dragonfly (*Anax imperator*)

A **367** Blue-tailed Damselfly (*Ischnura elegans*)

A **368** Brown Hawker (*Aeshna grandis*)

A **369** Black-tailed Skimmer (*Orthetrum cancellatum*)

A **370** Red Veined Darter (*Sympetrum fonscolumbii*)

Dragonflies

(Des Petula Stone. Litho BDT)

2010 (25 Feb). Perf 13½ (C).

A381	A **365**	36p. multicoloured	85	85
A382	A **366**	45p. multicoloured	1·10	1·10
A383	A **367**	56p. multicoloured	1·40	1·40
A384	A **368**	66p. multicoloured	1·50	1·50
A385	A **369**	75p. multicoloured	1·75	1·75
A386	A **370**	83p. multicoloured	2·00	2·00
A381/6 *Set of 6*			8·50	8·50
First Day Cover				10·50
Presentation Pack			10·50	
MS387 140×100 mm. Nos. A381/6			8·50	8·50
First Day Cover				10·50

Plate Nos.: All values 1A (each ×4).
Sheets: 10 (2×5) with enlarged illustrated right margins.
Imprint: Central, left-hand margin.

A **371** Pilot Keith Gilman

A **372** Hurricanes

A **373** Pilots Scramble

A **374** Spitfire Sortie

A **375** Air Raid Warden

A **376** Evacuees

A **377** Sir Douglas Bader (birth centenary) (*Illustration reduced. Actual size* 110×70 mm)

70th Anniversary of the Battle of Britain

(Des The Westminster Collection. Litho BDT)

2010 (4 May). Perf 14 (C).

A388	A **371**	36p. black and brownish grey	80	80
A389	A **372**	45p. black and brownish grey	1·00	1·00
A390	A **373**	48p. black and brownish grey	1·10	1·10
A391	A **374**	50p. black and brownish grey	1·25	1·25
A392	A **375**	58p. black and brownish grey	1·40	1·40
A393	A **376**	80p. black and brownish grey	1·75	1·75
A388/93 *Set of 6*			7·25	7·25
First Day Cover				7·50
Presentation Pack			6·50	
MS394 110×70 mm. A **377** £2 black and brownish grey			4·50	4·50
First Day Cover				10·00
Presentation Pack			9·00	

Plate Nos.: 1A (each ×4).
Sheets: 6 (2×6) with enlarged illustrated margins.

STAMP BOOKLETS

PRICES given are for complete booklets.

AB **1** Common Blue and Pyramidal Orchid (*Illustration reduced. Actual size* 99×60 mm)

1994 (5 May)–**95**. Multicoloured covers as Type AB **1**. Without barcode on the reverse. Panes attached by selvedge.

ASB1 £1.28 booklet containing pane No. A70ab (cover Type AB **1**) .... 4·00
a. With barcode sticker on reverse (1995) .... 8·50
ASB2 £1.92 booklet containing pane No. A72ab (cover showing Great Black-backed Gull and Sand Crocus) .... 4·50
Withdrawn: By 10.2006.

1997 (2 Jan). Multicoloured covers as Type AB **1**. Without barcode on the reverse. Panes attached by selvedge.

ASB3 £1.44 booklet containing pane No. A70bb (cover showing Small Tortoiseshell (butterfly) and Buddleia) .... 3·00
ASB4 £2 booklet containing pane No. A72bb (cover showing Rock Pipit and Sea Stock) .... 4·00
Sold out: 9.99 (No. ASB3);
Withdrawn by 10.2006 (No. ASB4).

1998 (25 Mar). Multicoloured cover as Type AB **1**. With barcode on the reverse. Pane attached by selvedge.

ASB5 £1.60 booklet containing pane No. A71ab (cover showing Common Rabbit and Creeping Buttercup) .... 4·00
Sold out: By 11.2006.

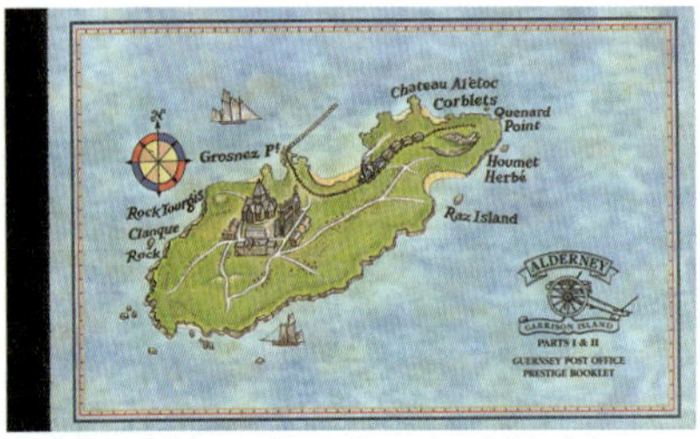

AB **2** Map of Alderney (*Illustration reduced. Actual size* 164×98 mm)

Garrison Island (1st and 2nd series)

1998 (10 Nov). Multicoloured cover as Type AB **2** containing text and illustrations on panes and interleaving pages. Stitched.

ASB6 £8.48 booklet containing panes Nos. A102b/c, A104b, A106b, A116b/c, A118b and 120b .... 20·00
Withdrawn: 9.11.99.

Garrison Island (3rd series). Forts

1999 (19 Oct). Multicoloured cover as Type AB **2** containing text and illustrations on panes and interleaving pages. Stitched.

ASB7 £6.78 booklet containing panes Nos. A132b/d, A134b/c. and A136b (cover showing view of fortified coastline) .... 17·00
Withdrawn: 18.10.2000.

NEW INFORMATION

The editor is always interested to correspond with people who have new information that will improve or correct this catalogue

AB **3** Peregrine Falcon (*Illustration reduced*). *Actual size* 105×60 mm)

Endangered Species. Peregrine Falcon

2000 (4 Feb). Multicoloured covers as Type AB **3**. Panes attached by selvedge.

ASB8 £2.10 booklet containing pane No. A140a (cover Type AB **3**) .... 5·00
ASB9 £2.60 booklet containing pane No. A141a (cover showing falcon with prey) .... 6·00
Withdrawn: 3.2.2001.

Garrison Island (4th series). Events

2000 (19 Oct). Multicoloured cover as Type AB **2** containing text and illustrations on panes and interleaving pages. Stitched.

ASB10 £7.38 booklet containing panes Nos. A154b, A154c×2, A156b×2 and A158b (cover showing Braye Road with Fort Albert in the distance) .... 18·00
Withdrawn: 18.10.2001.

Garrison Island (5th series). The Royal Navy

2001 (16 Oct). Multicoloured cover as Type AB **2** containing text and illustrations on panes and interleaving pages. Stitched.

ASB11 £7.50 booklet containing panes Nos. A176b, A176c×2, A178b/c, and A180b (cover showing Alderney Harbour) .... 19·00
Withdrawn: 15.10.2002.

AB **4** Medical and Rescue Services (*Illustration reduced. Actual size* 162×98 mm)

Community Services (1st and 2nd series)

2002 (17 Oct). Multicoloured cover as Type AB **4** containing text and illustrations on panes and interleaving pages. Stitched.

ASB12 £9.40 booklet containing panes Nos. A163ab/ac, A165ab, A197ab/ac and A199ab .... 30·00
Withdrawn: 16.10.2003.

Community Services (3rd series)

(Des M. Legg)

2003 (16 Oct). Multicoloured cover as Type AB **4** containing text and illustrations on panes and interleaving pages. Stitched.

ASB13 £9.40 booklet containing panes Nos. A217a/d and A219a .... 25·00
Withdrawn: 15.10.2004.

Community Services (4th series)

(Des M. Legg)

2004 (28 Oct). Multicoloured cover as Type AB **4** containing text and illustrations on panes and interleaving pages. Stitched.

ASB14 £9.76 booklet containing panes Nos. A242a/d and A244a32 .... 30·00
Withdrawn: 27.10.2005.

AB **5** Gun Carriage (*Illustration reduced. Actiual size* 162×98 mm)

Bicentenary of the Battle of Trafalgar

2005 (9 May). Multicoloured cover as Type AB **5**. Booklet contains text and Illustrations on panes and interleaving pages. Stitched.

ASB15 £9.76 booklet containing panes Nos. A253ax2, A253b/c, A254a and A255a .... 25·00

Withdrawn: 8.5.2006.

AB **6** Gannet (*Illustration reduced. Actual size* 164×98 mm)

Resident Birds (1st series). Seabirds

2006 (27 July). Multicoloured cover as Type AB **6**. Booklet contains text and Illustrations on panes and interleaving pages. Stitched.

ASB16 £10.60 booklet containing panes Nos. A282a/7a .... 30·00

Withdrawn: 26.7.2007.

Resident Birds (2nd series). Passerines

2007 (24 May). Multicoloured cover as Type AB **6**. Booklet contains text and Illustrations on panes and interleaving pages. Stitched.

ASB17 £11.32 booklet containing panes Nos. A316a/21a .... 30·00

Withdrawn: 23.5.2008.

Resident Birds (3rd series). Raptors

2008 (15 May). Multicoloured cover as Type AB **6**. Booklet contains text and Illustrations on panes and interleaving pages. Stitched.

ASB18 £12 booklet containing panes Nos. A337a/41a .... 30·00

Resident Birds (4th series). Waders

2009 (28 May). Multicoloured cover as Type AB **6**. Booklet contains text and illustrations on panes and interleaving pages. Stitched.

ASB19 £12.68 booklet containing panes Nos. A363a/8a .... 29·00

Isle of Man

REGIONAL ISSUES

Although specifically issued for regional use, these issues were initially valid for use throughout the U.K. Regional issues ceased to be valid in the Isle of Man from 5 July 1973 when the island established its own independent postal administration and introduced its own stamps.

DATES OF ISSUE. Conflicting dates of issue have been announced for some of the regional issues, partly explained by the stamps being released on different dates by the Philatelic Bureau in Edinburgh or the Philatelic Counter in London and in the regions. We have adopted the practice of giving the earliest known dates, since once released the stamps could have been used anywhere in the U.K.

INVALIDATION. Nos. 1/7 were invalidated as from 1 March 1972 in common with other British '£sd' stamps. Nos. 8/11 were invalidated for use in the Isle of Man on 5 July 1973, but, together with other British stamps, were accepted for the prepayment of postage on letters from the island until 5 August 1973. The Manx Regionals remained valid for use in the rest of the United Kingdom and were withdrawn from sale at the British Post Office Philatelic Sales counters on 4 July 1974.

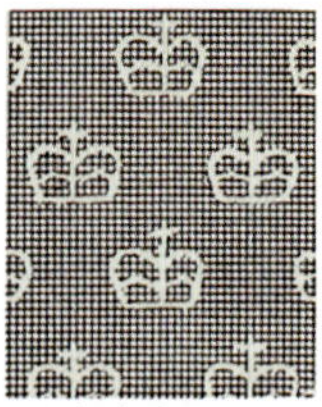

1 Multiple Crowns

2

3

(Des J. Nicholson. Portrait by Dorothy Wilding Ltd. Photo Harrison)

1958–68. Wmk Type **1**. Perf 15×14 (C).

1	**2**	2½d. carmine-red (8.6.64)	50	1·20
2	**3**	3d. deep lilac (18.8.58)	50	20
		a. Chalk-surfaced paper (17.5.63)	12·00	12·00
		p. One centre phosphor band (27.6.68)	20	50
3		4d. ultramarine (7.2.66)	1·50	1·50
		p. Two phosphor bands (5.7.67)	20	30
1/3p. *Set of 3*			80	1·60
First Day Cover 1				45·00
First Day Cover 2				32·00
First Day Cover 3				15·00

Cylinder Nos.: 2½d 1; 3d. (ord and phos) 1; 4d. (ord and phos) 1.
Sheets: 240 (12×20).
Quantities sold (ordinary only): 2½d. 4,298,160; 3d. 35,959,420 (up to 31.3.68 and including 1,080,000 on chalky paper); 4d. 4.,353,840.
Withdrawn: 31.8.66 2½d.
Sold out: 11.67 4d. ordinary; 12.68 3d. ordinary, 4d. phosphor; 4.69 3d. phosphor.

1968–69. No wmk. Chalk-surfaced paper. One centre phosphor band (Nos. 5/6) or two phosphor bands (others). Perf 15×14 (C).

4	**3**	4d. blue (24.6.68)	25	30
5		4d. olive-sepia (4.9.68)	25	30
		Ey. Phosphor omitted	22·00	
6		4d. bright vermilion (26.2.69)	45	75
7		5d. royal blue (4.9.68)	45	75
		Ey. Phosphor omitted	£175	
4/7 *Set of 4*			1·20	2·00
5, 7*First Day Cover*				4·00

Cylinder Nos.: 4d (blue) 1; 4d. (olive-sepia) 1; 4d. (bright vermilion) 1; 5d. 1.
Sheets: 240 (12×20).
Sold out: 16.7.69 4d. blue.
Withdrawn: 14.3.71 (locally), 25.11.71 (British Philatelic Counters) 4d.

4

Decimal Currency

(Des J. Matthews. Portrait after plaster cast by Arnold Machin. Photo Harrison)

1971 (7 July). Chalk-surfaced paper. One centre phosphor band (2½p.) or two phosphor bands (others). Perf 15×14 (C).

8	**4**	2½p. bright magenta	20	15
		Ey. Phosphor omitted	£1500	
9		3p. ultramarine	20	15
10		5p. reddish violet	80	80
		Ey. Phosphor omitted	£275	
11		7½p. chestnut	90	90
8/11 *Set of 4*			1·10	1·50
First Day Cover				3·00
Presentation Pack				

All values were originally issued on ordinary cream paper, but the 2½p. and 3p. later appeared on white fluorescent paper.

Cylinder Nos.: (dot and no dot): 2½p. 3, phos 5; 3p. 1, phos 4; 5p. 4, phos 12; 7½p. 4, phos 10.
Sheets: 200 (10×20).
Withdrawn: 4.7.73 (locally), 4.7.74 (British Philatelic Counters).

INDEPENDENT POSTAL ADMINISTRATION

The Isle of Man established an independent postal admini-stration on 5 July 1973 and introduced its own stamps.

NO WATERMARK. All the following issues are on unwatermarked paper *unless otherwise stated.*

5 Castletown

6 Port Erin

7 Snaefell

8 Laxey

9 Tynwald Hill

10 Douglas Promenade

11 Port St. Mary

12 Fairy Bridge

13 Peel

14 Cregneish

15 Ramsey Bay

16 Douglas Bay

17 Manx Cat

18 Monk's Bridge, Ballasalla

19 Derbyhaven

20 Manx Loaghtyn Ram

21 Manx Shearwater

22 Viking Longship

(Des J. Nicholson. Photo Courvoisier)

1973 (5 July)–**75**. Granite paper. Perf 11½ (C).

12	**5**	½p. multicoloured (ab)	10	10
13	**6**	1p. multicoloured (ae)	10	10
14	**7**	1½p. multicoloured (ak)	10	10
15	**8**	2p. multicoloured (aj)	10	10
16	**9**	2½p. multicoloured (a)	10	10
17	**10**	3p. mult (sage-green border) (ac)	10	10
		a. Error. Olive-bistre border †	£125	85·00
18	**11**	3½p. mult (olive-brown border) (ad)	10	10
		a. Error. Grey-brown border †	£125	85·00
19	**12**	4p. multicoloured (a)	10	10
20	**9**	4½p. multicoloured (f)	20	15
21	**13**	5p. multicoloured (ah)	15	10
22	**10**	5½p. multicoloured (g)	20	15
23	**14**	6p. multicoloured (al)	20	15
24	**8**	7p. multicoloured (g)	20	15
25	**15**	7½p. multicoloured (a)	20	20
26		8p. multicoloured (f)	25	25
27	**16**	9p. multicoloured (an)	20	20
28	**17**	10p. multicoloured (an)	35	20
29	**18**	11p. multicoloured (i)	35	30
30	**19**	13p. multicoloured (i)	40	35
31	**20**	20p. multicoloured (an)	50	50
32	**21**	50p. multicoloured (an)	1·00	1·10
33	**22**	£1 multicoloured (am)	2·00	2·00
12/33 Set of 22			6·00	6·00
First Day Covers (7)				7·75
Presentation Packs (6)			9·00	

† These errors occur on printings (c) and (d). That on the 3p. resembles the border colour of the ½p. and that on the 3½p. the 2p. Intermediate shades also exist, but are not covered by the listing.

Printings: (a) 5.7.73; (b) 1.11.73; (c) 16.4.74; (d) 29.7.74; (e) 2.9.74; (f) 8.1.75; (g) 28.5.75; (h) 16.6.75; (i) 29.10.75; (j) 1.12.75; (k) 2.2.76; (l) 20.9.76; (m) 16.2.77; (n) 7.7.77.

Printings (a) and (i) have thick shiny gum, but all the other printings have matt, almost invisible gum. Printings (f), (g) and (i) are inscribed '1975'. The remainder are inscribed '1973'.

Sheets: 50 (5×10) ½p. to 9p., 11p., 13p.; (10×5) 10p., 20p. to £1.

Withdrawn: 31.12.78 (except ½p., 3p. and 3½p. values in booklets withdrawn 15.5.79. In addition 2p and 3½p. values were kept available for use on postal orders after 31.12.78 until finally withdrawn on 30.6.83 (2p.) or 31.12.85 (3½p.)).

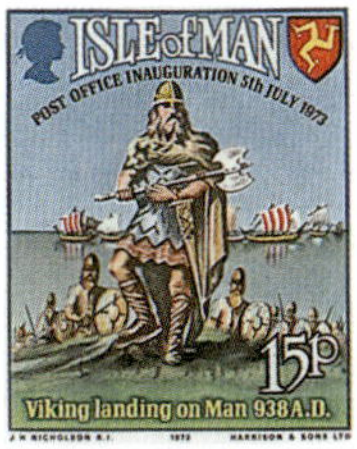

23 Vikings Landing on Man, A.D. 938

Inauguration of Postal Independence

(Des J. Nicholson. Photo Harrison)

1973 (5 July). Perf 14 (C).

34	**23**	15p. multicoloured	35	30
First Day Cover				1·10
Presentation Pack			1·40	

For 15p. inscr 'POST OFFICE DECENNIUM' 1983 see No. 256.
Cylinder Nos.: 1A (×4).
Sheets: 50 (10×5).
Quantity sold: 350,000.
Sold out: Soon after issue.

24 No. 1 *Sutherland*, 1873

25 No. 4 *Caledonia*, 1885

26 No. 13 *Kissack*, 1910

27 No. 3 *Pender*, 1873

Centenary of Steam Railway

(Des J. Nicholson. Photo Harrison)

1973 (4 Aug). Perf 15×14 (C).

35	**24**	2½p. multicoloured	15	10
36	**25**	3p. multicoloured	15	15
37	**26**	7½p. multicoloured	25	25
38	**27**	9p. multicoloured	25	25
35/8 Set of 4			70	70
First Day Cover				1·90
Presentation Pack			1·50	

Cylinder Nos.: All values 1A (×5).
Sheets: 50 (5×10).
Quantities sold: 2½p. 617,122; 3p. 808,173; 7½p. 331,695; 9p. 324,414.
Withdrawn: 3.8.74.

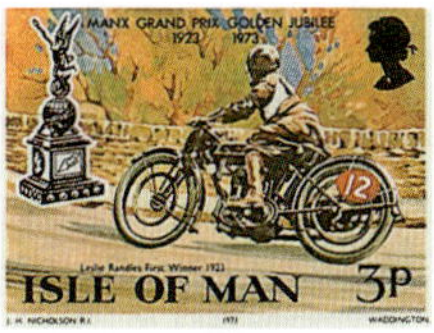

28 Leonard Randles, First Winner, 1923 on Sumbeam motorcycle

29 Alan Holmes, Double Winner, 1957 on Norton motorcycle

Golden Jubilee of Manx Grand Prix

(Des J. Nicholson. Litho John Waddington)

1973 (4 Sept). Perf 14 (C).

39	**28**	3p. multicoloured	10	15
40	**29**	3½p. multicoloured	15	15
39/40 Set of 2			25	25

First Day Cover		90
Presentation Pack	70	
Set of 2 Gutter Pairs	60	

Plate Nos.: Both values 1A, 1B, 1C, 1D (each ×4).
Sheets: (2 panes 5×5).
Imprint: Central, bottom margin.
Quantities sold: 3p. 550,347; 3½p. 653,355.
Withdrawn: 3.9.74.

30 Princess Anne and Capt. Mark Philips

Royal Wedding

(Des A. Larkins and litho De La Rue)

1973 (14 Nov). Perf 13½ (C).

41	**30**	25p. multicoloured	45	50
First Day Cover				85
Presentation Pack			90	
Gutter Pair			90	

Plate Nos.: 1A, 1B (each ×4).
Sheets: 50 (5 panes 5×5).
Imprint: Right-hand corner, bottom margin.
Quantity sold: 400,813.
Withdrawn: 13.11.74.

31 Badge, Citation and Sir Wiliam Hillary (founder)

32 Wreck of *St. George*, 1830

33 *Manchester & Salford*, 1868–87

34 *Osman Gabriel*

150th Anniversary of Royal National Lifeboat Institution

(Des J. Nicholson. Photo Courvoisier)

1974 (4 Mar). Granite paper. Perf 11½ (C).

42	**31**	3p. multicoloured	10	10
43	**32**	3½p. multicoloured	15	10
44	**33**	8p. multicoloured	25	25
45	**34**	10p. multicoloured	30	25
42/5 *Set of 4*			70	60
First Day Cover				1·00
Presentation Pack			1·00	

Sheets: 100 (10×10).
Quantities sold: 3p. 674,984; 3½p. 849,990; 8p. 374,941; 10p. 375,043.
Withdrawn: 3.3.75.

35 Stanley Woods, 1935 on Motoguzzi motorcycle

36 Freddy Frith, 1937 on Norton motorcycle

37 Max Deubel and Emil Horner, 1961 on BMW 500 with Sidecar

38 Mike Hailwood, 1961 on Honda 125 motorcycle

Tourist Trophy Motorcycle Races (1st issue)

(Des J. Nicholson. Litho De La Rue)

1974 (29 May). Perf 13×13½ (C).

46	**35**	3p. multicoloured	10	10
47	**36**	3½p. multicoloured	10	10
48	**37**	8p. multicoloured	25	20
49	**38**	10p. multicoloured	25	20
46/9 *Set of 4*			60	55
First Day Cover				1·00
Presentation Pack			1·00	
Set of 4 Gutter Pairs			1·20	

See also Nos. 63/6.

Plate Nos.: All values 1A, 1B, 1C, 1D (each ×6); 3p. also 1A (×4)–2A–2A, 1B (×4)–2B–2B, 1C (×4)–2C–2C, 1D (×4)–2D–2D; 8p. also 1A–1A–2A–1A (×3), 1B–1B–2B–1B (×3), 1C–1C–2C–1C (×3), 1D–1D–2D–1D (×3).
Sheets: 50 (2 panes 5×5).
Imprint: Right-hand corner, bottom margin.
Quantities sold: 3p. 578,045; 3½p. 816,235; 8p. 334,760; 10p. 403,177.
Withdrawn: 28.5.75.

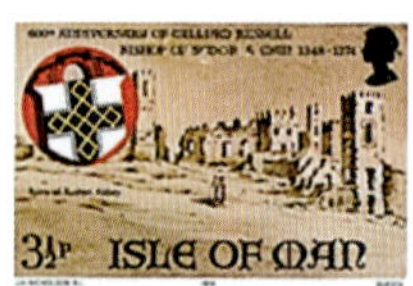

39 Rushen Abbey and Arms

40 Magnus Haraldson rows King Edgar on the Dee

41 King Magnus and Norse Fleet

42 Bridge at Avignon and Bishop's Mitre

Historical Anniversaries

(Des J. Nicholson, from ideas by G. Kneale. Litho Questa (3½p., 10p.) or John Waddington (others))

1974 (18 Sept). Perf 14 (C).

50	**39**	3½p. multicoloured	10	10
51	**40**	4½p. multicoloured	10	10
52	**41**	8p. multicoloured	15	15
53	**42**	10p. multicoloured	20	20
50/3 *Set of 4*			50	50
First Day Cover				85
Presentation Pack			85	
Set of 4 Gutter Pairs			85	

Plate Nos.: All values 1A, 1B, 1C, 1D (each ×4).
Sheets: 50 (2 panes 5×5).
Imprint: Right-hand corner, bottom margin and left-hand corner, top margin.
Quantities sold: 3½p. 931,610; 4½p. 1,025,044; 8p. 450,418; 10p. 425,305.
Withdrawn: 17.9.75.

43 Churchill and Bugler Dunne at Colenso, 1899

44 Churchill and Government Buildings, Douglas

45 Churchill and Manx A.A Gun Crew

46 Churchill as Freeman of Douglas

Birth Centenary of Sir Winston Churchill

(Des G. Kneale. Photo Courvoisier)

1974 (22 Nov). Granite paper. Perf 11½ (C).

54	**43**	3½p. multicoloured	10	10
55	**44**	4½p. multicoloured	10	10
56	**45**	8p. multicoloured	15	15
57	**46**	20p. multicoloured	30	25
54/7 *Set of 4*			60	55
First Day Cover				85
Presentation Pack			1·40	
MS58 121×91 mm. Nos. 54/7			75	75
First Day Cover				1·50

No. **MS**58 is inscribed '30th NOV. 1974.
Sheets: 25 (5×5).
Quantities sold: 3½p. 916,748; 4½p. 853,537; 8p. 424,691; 20p. 429,586; miniature sheet 362,089.
Withdrawn: 21.11.75.

47 Cabin School and Names of Pioneers

48 Terminal Tower Building, John Gill and Robert Carran

49 Clague House Museum and Robert and Margaret Clague

50 *William T. Graves* and Thomas Quayle

Manx Pioneers in Cleveland, Ohio

(Des J. Nicholson. Photo Courvoisier)

1975 (14 Mar). Granite paper. Perf 11½ (C).

59	**47**	4½p. multicoloured	10	10
60	**48**	5½p. multicoloured	10	10
61	**49**	8p. multicoloured	15	15
62	**50**	10p. multicoloured	25	25
59/62 *Set of 4*			55	55
First Day Cover				75
Presentation Pack			80	

Sheets: 50 (5×10).
Quantities sold: 4½p. 473,352; 5½p. 999,802; 8p. 433,352; 10p. 447,945.
Withdrawn: 13.3.76 (5½p. sold out 12.75).

51 Tom Sheard, 1923 and Douglas motorcycle

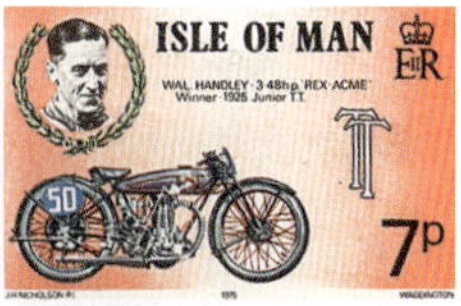

52 Walter Handley, 1925 and Rex-Acme motorcycle

53 Geoff Duke, 1955 and Gilera motorcycle

54 Peter Williams, 1973 and Norton motorcycle

Tourist Trophy Motorcycle Races (2nd issue)

(Des J. Nicholson. Litho John Waddington)

1975 (28 May). Perf 13½ (C).

63	**51**	5½p. multicoloured	10	10
64	**52**	7p. multicoloured	15	15
65	**53**	10p. multicoloured	15	15
66	**54**	12p. multicoloured	25	20
63/6 *Set of 4*			60	55
First Day Cover				2·40
Presentation Pack			1·00	
Set of 4 Gutter Pairs			1·20	

Plate Nos.: 5½p., 7p. 1B, 1D (each ×5); 10p. 1A, 1B, 1C, 1D (each ×5); 12p. 1A, 1B, 1C, 1D (each ×5).
Sheets: 50 (2 panes 5×5).
Imprint: Right-hand corner, bottom margin.
Quantities sold: 5½p. 633,250; 7p. 520,285; 10p. 399,710; 12p. 440,208.
Withdrawn: 27.5.76.

55 Sir George Goldie and Birthplace

56 Goldie and Map of Africa

57 Goldie as President of Royal Geographical Society

58 River Scene on the Niger

50th Death Anniversary of Sir George Goldie

(Des G. Kneale. Photo Courvoisier)

1975 (9 Sept). Granite paper. Perf 11½ (C).

67	**55**	5½p. multicoloured	10	10
68	**56**	7p. multicoloured	15	15
69	**57**	10p. multicoloured	15	15
70	**58**	12p. multicoloured	25	25
67/70 *Set of 4*			65	65
First Day Cover				90
Presentation Pack			1·00	

Sheets: 50 (10×5) 7p., 10p.; (5×10) others.
Quantities sold: 5½p. 488,317; 7p. 426,849; 10p. 373,771; 12p. 439,843.
Withdrawn: 8.9.76.

59 Title Page of Manx Bible

60 Rev. Philip Moore and Ballaugh Old Church

61 Bishop Hildesley and Bishops Court

62 John Kelly saving Bible Manuscript

Christmas and Bicentenary of Manx Bible

(Des J. Nicholson. Litho Questa)

1975 (29 Oct). Perf 14 (C).

71	**59**	5½p. multicoloured	10	10
72	**60**	7p. multicoloured	15	15
73	**61**	11p. multicoloured	20	20
74	**62**	13p. multicoloured	25	25
71/4 *Set of 4*			60	60
First Day Cover				1·00
Presentation Pack			1·00	
Set of 4 Gutter Pairs			1·20	

Plate Nos. 13p. 1A, 1B, 1C, 1D (each ×4); others 1A, 1B (each ×4).
Sheets: 50 (2 panes 5×5).
Quantities sold: 5½p. 738,774; 7p. 607,377; 11p. 405,126; 13p. 402,463.

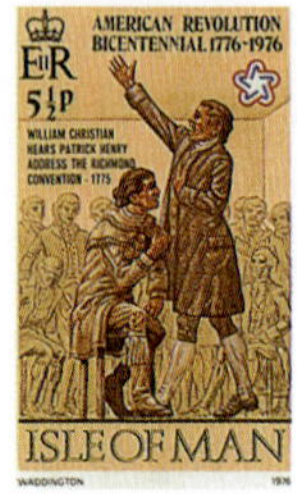

63 William Christian listening to Patrick Henry

64 Conveying the Fincastle Resolutions

65 Patrick Henry and William Christian

66 Christian as an Indian Fighter

Bicentenary of American Revolution and Col. William Christian Commemoration

(Des and litho John Waddington)

1976 (12 Mar). Perf 13½ (C).

75	**63**	5½p. multicoloured	10	10
76	**64**	7p. multicoloured	15	15
77	**65**	13p. multicoloured	30	30
		a. Black (face value and inscr) printed double	£500	
78	**66**	20p. multicoloured	35	35
75/8 *Set of 4*			75	80
Set of 4 Gutter Pairs			1·50	
MS79 150×90 mm. Nos. 75/8. Perf 14 (C)			90	1·00
First Day Cover				4·00
Presentation Pack			1·90	

Plate Nos.: 5½p., 20p. 1A, 1C (each ×4); others 1B, 1D (each ×4).
Sheets: 50 (2 panes 5×5).
Quantities sold: 5½p. 487,310; 7p. 524,144; 13p. 558,348; 20p. 424,728; miniature sheet 209,367.
Withdrawn: 11.3.77.

67 First Horse Tram, 1876

68 'Toast-rack' Tram, 1890

69 Horse-bus, 1895

70 Royal Tram, 1972

Douglas Horse Trams Centenary

(Des J. Nicholson. Photo Courvoisier)

1976 (26 May). Granite paper. Perf 11½ (C).

80	**67**	5½p. multicoloured	10	10
81	**68**	7p. multicoloured	15	15
82	**69**	11p. multicoloured	20	20
83	**70**	13p. multicoloured	25	25
80/3 *Set of 4*			65	65
First Day Cover				1·00
Presentation Pack			1·00	

Sheets: 25 (5×5).
Quantities sold: 5½p. 627,083; 7p. 480,417; 11p. 391,871; 13p. 389,604.
Withdrawn: 25.5.77.

71 Barroose Beaker

72 Souvenir Teapot

73 Laxey Jug

74 Cronk Aust Food Vessel

75 Sansbury Bowl

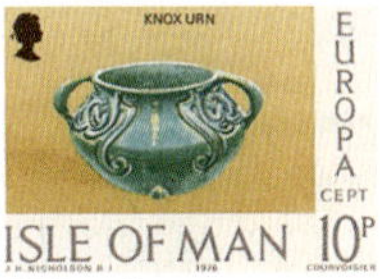

76 Knox Urn

Europa. Ceramic Art

(Des J. Nicholson. Photo Courvoisier)

1976 (28 July). Granite paper. Perf 11½ (C).

84	**71**	5p. multicoloured	20	10
		a. Strip of 3. Nos. 84/6	60	60
85	**72**	5p. multicoloured	20	10
86	**73**	5p. multicoloured	20	10
87	**74**	10p. multicoloured	20	10
		a. Strip of 3 Nos. 87/9	60	60
88	**75**	10p. multicoloured	20	10
89	**76**	10p. multicoloured	20	10
84/9 *Set of 6*			1·10	1·10
First Day Cover				2·10
Presentation Pack			1·50	

Sheets: 9 (3×3) containing the three designs of each value horizontally and vertically *se-tenant*.
Quantities sold: 5p. 256,400 of each design; 10p. 262,900 of each design.
Sold out: 20.11.76 (5p.); 12.76 (10p.).

77 Diocesan Banner

78 Onchan Banner

79 Castletown Banner

80 Ramsey Banner

Christmas and Centenary of Mothers' Union

(Des G. Kneale. Litho Questa)

1976 (14 Oct). Perf 14½ (C).

90	**77**	6p. multicoloured	10	10
91	**78**	7p. multicoloured	15	15
92	**79**	11p. multicoloured	20	20
93	**80**	13p. multicoloured	25	25
90/3 *Set of 4*			65	65
First Day Cover				80
Presentation Pack			1·00	

Plate Nos.: All values 1A, 1B, 1C, 1D (each ×5).
Sheets: 50 (10×5).
Imprint: Right-hand corner, bottom margin and left-hand corner, top margin.
Quantities sold: 6p. 905,752; 7p. 890,762; 11p. 397,807; 13p. 390,057.
Withdrawn: 13.10.77.

81 Queen Elizabeth II

82 Queen Elizabeth and Prince Philip

83 Queen Elizabeth II

Silver Jubilee

(Des A. Larkins. Litho and recess De La Rue)

1977 (1 Mar). Perf 14×13 (7p.) or 13×14 (others), both comb.

94	**81**	6p. multicoloured	10	10
95	**82**	7p. multicoloured	20	20
96	**83**	25p. multicoloured	50	50
94/6 *Set of 3*			70	70
First Day Cover				85
Presentation pack			1·00	
Set of 3 Gutter Pairs			1·40	

Plate Nos.: 6p., 7p. 1A (×6), 1A (×5)–2A, 1B (×6), 1B (×5)–2B, 1C (×6), 1C (×5)–2C, 1D (×6), 1D (×5)–2D 25p. 1A, 1B, 1C, 1D (each ×6).
Sheets: 50 (2 panes 5×5).
Imprint: Right-hand corner, bottom margin.
Quantities sold: 6p. 942,356; 7p. 911,191; 25p. 651,101.
Withdrawn: 28.2.78.

84 Carrick Bay from 'Tom-the-Dipper'

85 View from Ramsey

Europa. Landscapes

(Des J. Nicholson. Litho Questa)

1977 (26 May). Perf 13½×14 (C).

97	**84**	6p. multicoloured	15	15
98	**85**	10p. multicoloured	25	25
97/8 *Set of 2*			40	40
First Day Cover				75
Presentation Pack			75	
Set of 2 Gutter Pairs			80	

Plate Nos.: 6p. 1A, 1B, 1C, 1D, 2A, 2B, 2C, 2D (each ×4); 10p. 1A, 1B, 1C, 1D (each ×5), 2A–1A–1A–2A–1A, 2B–1B–1B–2B–1B, 2C–1C–1C–2C–1C, 2D–1D–1D–2D–1D.
Sheets: 40 (2 panes 4×5).
Imprint: Right-hand corner, bottom margin and left-hand corner, top margin.
Quantities sold: 6p. 778,685; 10p. 843,525.
Withdrawn: 25.5.78.

86 F. A. Applebee, 1912 riding Scott motorcycle

87 St. John Ambulance Brigade at Governor's Bridge, c. 1938

88 Scouts working Scoreboard

89 John Williams, 1976 on Norton motorcycle

Linked Anniversaries

(Des J. Nicholson. Litho John Waddington)

1977 (26 May). Perf 13½ (C).

99	**86**	6p. multicoloured	15	10
100	**87**	7p. multicoloured	15	15
101	**88**	11p. multicoloured	25	25
102	**89**	13p. multicoloured	25	30
99/102 *Set of 4*			70	65
First Day Cover				85
Presentation Pack			1·00	
Set of 4 Gutter Pairs			1·40	

The events commemorated are: 70th anniversary of Manx TT; 70th anniversary of Boy Scouts; centenary of St. John Ambulance Brigade.
Plate Nos.: 11p. 1A, 1C (each ×4); others 1B, 1D (each ×4).
Sheets: 50 (2 panes 5×5).
Imprint: Right-hand corner, bottom margin.
Quantities sold: 6p. 525,703; 7p. 875,303; 11p. 431,053; 13p. 440,403.
Withdrawn: 25.5.78.

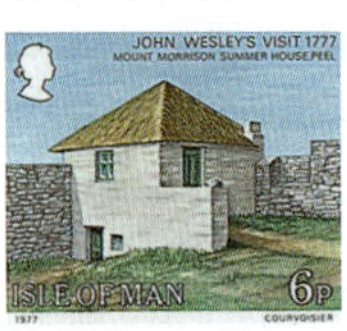

90 Old Summer House, Mount Morrison, Peel

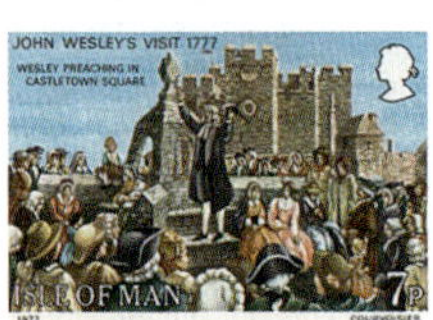

91 Wesley preaching in Castletown Square

92 Wesley preaching outside Bradden Church

93 New Methodist Church, Douglas

Bicentenary of the First Visit of John Wesley

(Des and photo Courvoisier)

1977 (19 Oct). Granite paper. Perf 11½ (C).

103	**90**	6p. multicoloured	15	10
104	**91**	7p. multicoloured	15	15
105	**92**	11p. multicoloured	25	25
106	**93**	13p. multicoloured	25	25
103/6 *Set of 4*			70	65
First Day Cover				85
Presentation Pack			1·00	

Sheets: 50 (5×10).
Quantities sold: 6p. 661,755; 7p. 976,155; 11p. 373,805; 13p. 366,905.
Withdrawn: 18.10.78.

94 Short Type 184 Seaplane and H.M.S. *Ben-My-Chree*, 1915

95 Bristol Scout C and H.M.S. *Vindex*, 1915

96 Boulton Paul Defiant over Douglas Bay, 1941

97 Sepecat Jaguar over Ramsey, 1977

R.A.F. Diamond Jubilee

(Des A. Theobald. Litho John Waddington)

1978 (28 Feb). Perf 13½×14 (C).

107	**94**	6p. multicoloured	15	10
108	**95**	7p. multicoloured	15	15
109	**96**	11p. multicoloured	25	25
110	**97**	13p. multicoloured	25	25
107/10 *Set of 4*			70	65
First Day Cover				1·20
Presentation Pack			1·00	
Set of 4 Gutter Pairs			1·40	

Plate Nos.: All values 1A, 1C (each ×4).
Sheets: 50 (2 panes 5×5).
Quantities sold: 6p. 690,536; 7p. 875,811; 11p. 416,082; 13p. 422,797.
Withdrawn: 27.2.79.

98 Watch Tower, Langness

99 Jurby Church

100 Government Buildings

101 Tynwald Hill

102 Milner's Tower

103 Laxey Wheel

104 Castle Rushen

105 St. Ninian's Church

106 Tower of Refuge

107 St. German's Cathedral

108 Point of Ayre Lighthouse

109 Corrin's Tower

110 Douglas Head Lighthouse

111 Fuchsia

112 Manx Cat

113 Red-billed Chough

114 Viking Warrior

114a Queen Elizabeth II

Landmarks and Queens Portrait (£2)

(Des G. Kneale (£2), J. Nicholson (others). Litho Questa (½p. to 16p.), photo Courvoisier (20p. to £2))

1978 (28 Feb)–**81**.

		(a) Perf 14 (C)		
111	**98**	½p. multicoloured (a)	10	10
		a. Perf 14½	20	10
112	**99**	1p. multicoloured (a)	10	10
		a. Perf 14½	20	10
113	**100**	6p. multicoloured (a)	30	30
114	**101**	7p. multicoloured (a)	35	35
		a. Perf 14½	8·50	6·50
115	**102**	8p. multicoloured (a)	25	25
		a. Perf 14½	35	35
116	**103**	9p. multicoloured (a)	35	35
		a. Perf 14½	3.50	35
117	**104**	10p. multicoloured (a)	40	40
		a. Perf 14½	35	35
118	**105**	11p. multicoloured (a)	40	40
		a. Perf 14½	40	40
119	**106**	12p. multicoloured (a)	40	25
		a. Perf 14½	50	40
120	**107**	13p. multicoloured (a)	60	60
		a. Perf 14½	30	25
121	**108**	14p. multicoloured (a)	60	60
		a. Perf 14½	30	25
122	**109**	15p. multicoloured (a)	75	75
		a. Perf 14½	30	25
123	**110**	16p. multicoloured (a)	55	30
		a. Perf 14½	26·00	21·00
		(b) Granite paper. Perf 11½ (C)		
124	**111**	20p. multicoloured (b)	50	35
125	**112**	25p. multicoloured (b)	65	45
126	**113**	50p. multicoloured (b)	90	75
127	**114**	£1 multicoloured (b)	1·90	2·00
128	**114a**	£2 multicoloured (c)	3·50	3·50
111/28 *Set of 18 (cheapest)*			9·00	10·00
*First Day Covers** (5)				12·00
Presentation Packs (4)			14·00	

*The most common versions of the three low and medium value first day covers prepared by the Philatelic Bureau were franked with Nos. 111a, 112/15, 116a, 117/18, 119a, 120, 121a, 122 and 123a. Some examples can be found with the ½p. as No. 111, the 11p. as No. 118a or the 13p. as No. 120a. First day covers prepared by dealers or collectors on the island were franked with Nos. 111/18, 119a/20a, 121, 122a and 123.

Printings: (a) 28.2.78; (b) 18.10.78; (c) 29.9.81.

Although both perforations of Nos. 111/23 were printed at the same time, some did not appear in use until some time after 28 February 1978. Earliest dates for these are as follows: 1p. (112a) 8.79, 7p. (114a) 8.78, 8p. (115a) 6.80, 10p. (117a) 8.79, 12p. (119) 9.80.

Plate Nos.: ½, 6, 8, 9, 10, 11, 12, 13, 14, 15, 16p. 1A, 1B, 1C, 1D (each ×4); 1p. 1A, 1B, 1C, 1D (each ×4) (No. 112), 1A–1A–2A–1A, 1B–1B–2B–1B, 1C–1C–2C–1C, 1D–1D–2D–1D; 6p. 1D–1D–2D–1D; 7p. 1A, 1B, 1C, 1D (each ×4) (No. 114); 2A, 2B, 2C, 2D (each ×4), 2B–2B–3B–2B, 2C–2C–3C–2C (No. 114a); £2 A1–1–1–1, B1–1–1–1, others none.

Sheets: 25 (5×5) (£2); 50 (1, 7, 10, 12, 13, 14, 15, 16p. 5×10; others 10×5).

Imprint: ½p. to 16p. left-hand corner, top margin and right-hand corner, bottom margin; 20p. to £1 none; £2 central bottom margin.

Withdrawn: 30.6.83 1p to 16p.; 31.12.83 20p. to £1; 31.12.85 ½p.; 30.6.90 £2.

115 Queen Elizabeth in Coronation Regalia

25th Anniversary of Coronation

(Des G. Kneale. Litho Questa)

1978 (24 May). Perf 14½×14 (C).

132	**115**	25p. multicoloured	50	45
First Day Cover				65
Presentation Pack			85	
Gutter Pair			1·00	

Plate Nos.: 1A, 1B, 1C, 1D (each ×6).
Sheets: 50 (2 panes 5×5).
Imprint: Left-hand corner, top margin and right-hand corner, bottom margin.
Quantity sold: 575,996.
Withdrawn: 23.5.79.

116 Wheel-headed Cross-slab

117 Celtic Wheel-Cross

118 Keeil Chiggyrt Stone

119 Olaf Liotulfson Cross

120 Odd's and Thorleif's Crosses

121 Thor Cross

Europa. Celtic and Norse Crosses

(Des J. Nicholson. Photo Courvoisier)

1978 (24 May). Granite paper. Perf 11½ (C).

133	**116**	6p. multicoloured	10	10
		a. Strip of 3. Nos. 133/5	25	25
134	**117**	6p. multicoloured	10	10
135	**118**	6p. multicoloured	10	10
136	**119**	11p. multicoloured	20	15
		a. Strip of 3. Nos. 136/8	60	60
137	**120**	11p. multicoloured	20	15
138	**121**	11p. multicoloured	20	15
133/8 *Set of 6*			85	80
First Day Cover				1·10
Presentation Pack			1·20	

Sheets: 9 (3×3) The three designs of each value were printed together, *se-tenant*, in horizontal and vertical strips throughout.
Quantities sold: 6p. 3,821,152; 11p. 3,788,667.
Withdrawn: 23.5.79.

122 J. K. Ward and Ward Library, Peel

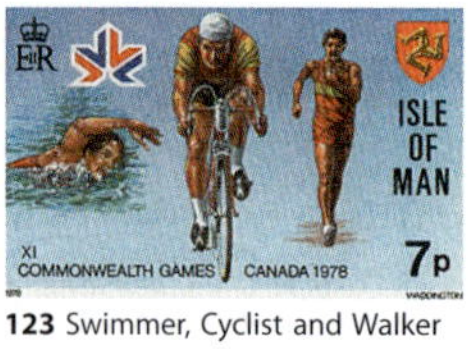

123 Swimmer, Cyclist and Walker

124 American Bald Eagle, Manx Arms and Maple Leaf

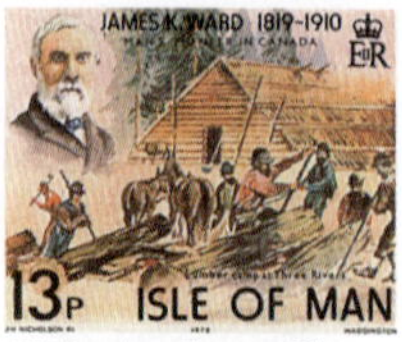

125 Lumber Camp at Three Rivers, Quebec

Anniversaries and Events

(Des John Waddington (7p.), G. Kneale (11p.), J. Nicholson (others). Litho John Waddington)

1978 (10 June). Invisible gum. Perf 13½ (C).

139	**122**	6p. multicoloured	10	10
140	**123**	7p. multicoloured	20	15
141	**124**	11p. multicoloured	25	25
142	**125**	13p. multicoloured	25	25
139/42 *Set of 4*			70	65
First Day Covers (3)				1·00
Presentation Packs (2)			1·00	
Set of 4 Gutter Pairs			1·40	

Plate Nos.: 6p. 1A, 1B, 1C, 1D (each ×4); others 1B, 1D (each ×4).
Sheets: 50 (2 panes 5×5).
Imprint: Central, bottom margin.
Quantities sold: 6p. 629,041; 7p. 873,067; 11p. 393,907; 13p. 383,048.
Withdrawn: 9.6.79.

126 Hunt the Wren

Christmas

(Des J. Nicholson. Litho John Waddington)

1978 (18 Oct). Perf 13 (C).

143	**126**	5p. multicoloured	20	20
First Day Cover				40
Presentation Pack			45	
Gutter Pair			40	

Plate Nos.: 1A, 1B, 1C, 1D (each ×4).
Sheets: 50 (2 panes 5×5).
Imprint: Central, bottom margin.
Quantity sold: 1,000,000.
Sold out: 4.79 (stamp) or 8.79 (presentation pack).

127 P. M. C. Kermode (founder) and *Nassa kermodei*

128 Peregrine Falcon

129 Fulmar

130 *Epitriptus cowini* (fly)

Centenary of Natural History and Antiquarian Society

(Des J. Nicholson. Litho Questa)

1979 (27 Feb). Perf 14 (C).

144	**127**	6p. multicoloured	10	10
145	**128**	7p. multicoloured	25	15
146	**129**	11p. multicoloured	25	30
147	**130**	13p. multicoloured	25	35
144/7 *Set of 4*			80	80

First Day Cover 90
Presentation Pack .... 1·00
Set of 4 Gutter Pairs .... 1·60

Plate Nos.: 6p. 1A, 1B, 1C, 1D (each ×4); 13p. 1A, 1B (each ×4); others 1C, 1D (each ×4).
Sheets: 50 (2 panes 5×5).
Imprint: Left-hand corner, top margin and right-hand corner, bottom margin.
Quantities sold: 6p. 642,126; 7p. 790,515; 11p. 411,863; 13p. 390,454.
Withdrawn: 26.2.80.

131 Postman, 1859

132 Postman, 1979

Europa. Communications

(Des A. Theobald. Litho Questa)

1979 (16 May). Perf 14½ (C).

148	**131**	6p. multicoloured	15	10
149	**132**	11p. multicoloured	40	45
148/9 *Set of 2*			50	50
First Day Cover				75
Presentation Pack			85	

Plate Nos.: 6p. 1A, 1B, 1C, 1D (each ×6); 11p. 1A, 1B, 1C, 1D (each ×5).
Sheets: 20 (4×5).
Imprint: Right-hand corner, bottom margin.
Quantities sold: 6p. 1,301,039; 11p. 1,290,318.
Sold out: By 10.79 (stamps).
Withdrawn: 15.5.80 (presentation pack).

133 Viking Longship Emblem

134 'Three Legs of Man' Emblem

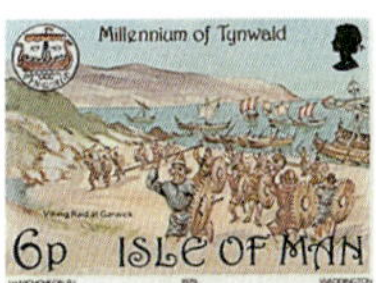

135 Viking Raid at Garwick

136 10th-century Meeting of Tynwald

137 Tynwald Hill and St. John's Church

138 Procession to Tynwald Hill

Two types of 3p.:

Type I. Wrongly inscribed 'INSULAREM'. '1979' imprint date.

Type II. Inscription corrected to 'INSULARUM'. '1980' imprint date.

Millennium of Tynwald

(Des J. Nicholson. Litho Harrison (3, 4p.), John Waddington (others))

1979 (16 May)–**80**.

(a) Perf 14½×14 (C)

150	**133**	3p. multicoloured (Type I) (a)	10	10
		a. Booklet pane. Nos. 150×4, 151×2 (4p. stamps at top)	60	
		ab. Do. (4p. stamps in centre)	1·20	
		b. Type II (b)	10	10
		ba. Booklet pane. Nos. 150b×4, 151×2 (4p stamps at bottom)	50	
151	**134**	4p. multicoloured (ab)	10	10

(b) Perf 13 (C)

152	**135**	6p. multicoloured (a)	15	10
153	**136**	7p. multicoloured (a)	20	20
154	**137**	11p. multicoloured (a)	25	25
155	**138**	13p. multicoloured (a)	30	30
150/5 *Set of 6*			1·00	1·00
First Day Cover				95
Presentation Pack			1·20	
Set of 6 Gutter Pairs			2·00	

See also Nos. 188/9.

Printings: (a) 16.5.79; (b) 29.9.80. Inscribed 1980.
Plate Nos.: 3, 4p. 1A (×6); 13p. 1G (×4); others 1E (×4).
Sheets: 3, 4p. 80 (10 panes 2×3, 5 panes 2×2); others 40 (2 panes 4×5). The 3 and 4p. values were printed together, *se-tenant*, each pane of 6 containing four 3p. and two 4p, the 4p being in either positions 1 and 2 or 3 and 4. The panes of 4 contain the 4p value only. For details of No. 150ba see after No. 189.
Imprint: 3, 4p. right-hand corner, bottom margin; others central, bottom margin.
Quantities sold: 6p. 381,334; 7p. 465,473; 11p. 341,204; 13p. 241,162.
Withdrawn: 15.5.80 6p. to 13p.; 25.3.87 3p., 4p.

139 Queen and Court on Tynwald Hill

140 Queen and Procession from St. John's Church to Tynwald Hill

Royal Visit

(Des G. Kneale. Litho Questa)

1979 (5 July). Perf 14½ (C).

156	**139**	7p. multicoloured	15	15
157	**140**	13p. multicoloured	25	25
156/7 *Set of 2*			40	40
First Day Cover				50
Presentation pack			75	
Set of 2 Gutter Pairs			80	

Plate Nos.: 7p. 1A, 1B, 1C, 1D (each ×4); 13p. 1A, 1B, 1C, 1D (each ×4).
Sheets: 50 (2 panes 5×5).
Imprint: Right-hand corner, bottom margin.
Quantities sold: 7p. 641,930; 13p. 436,516.
Withdrawn: 4.7.80.

141 *Odin's Raven*

Voyage of Odin's Raven

(Des J. Nicholson. Litho Questa)

1979 (19 Oct). Perf 14×14½ (C).

158	**141**	15p. multicoloured	45	30

First Day Cover		70
Presentation Pack	75	
Gutter Pair	90	

See also No. **MS**180.

Plate Nos.: 1A, 1B, 1C, 1D (each ×4).
Sheets: 50 (2 panes 5×5).
Imprint: Right-hand corner, bottom margin.
Quantity sold: 412,631.
Withdrawn: 18.10.80.

142 John Quilliam seized by Press Gang

143 Steering H.M.S. *Victory*, Battle of Trafalgar

144 Captain John Quilliam and H.M.S. *Spencer*

145 Captain John Quilliam (member of the House of Keys)

150th Death Anniversary of Captain John Quilliam

(Des A. Theobald. Litho Questa)

1979 (19 Oct). Perf 14 (C).

159	**142**	6p. multicoloured	15	15
160	**143**	8p. multicoloured	20	15
161	**144**	13p. multicoloured	25	25
162	**145**	15p. multicoloured	30	25
159/62 *Set of 4*			80	70
First Day Cover				85
Presentation Pack			1·00	
Set of 4 Gutter Pairs			1·60	

Plate Nos.: 6p. 1C, 1D (each ×4); others 1A, 1B (each ×4).
Sheets: 50 (2 panes 5×5).
Imprint: Right-hand corner, bottom margin.
Quantities sold: 6p. 608,876; 8p. 858,665; 13p. 360,821; 15p. 360,400.
Withdrawn: 18.10.80.

146 Young Girl with Teddybear and Cat

147 Father Christmas with Young Children

Christmas and International Year of the Child

(Des Mrs. E. Moore. Litho John Waddington)

1979 (19 Oct). Perf 13 (C).

163	**146**	5p. multicoloured	10	10
164	**147**	7p. multicoloured	20	20
163/4 *Set of 2*			30	30
First Day Cover				50
Presentation Pack			60	
Set of 2 Gutter Pairs			60	

Plate Nos.: Both values 1A, 1B, 1C, 1D (each ×4).
Sheets: 50 (2 panes 5×5).
Imprint: Central, left-hand margin.
Quantities sold: 5p. 1,036,495; 7p. 1,087,734.
Withdrawn: 18.10.80.

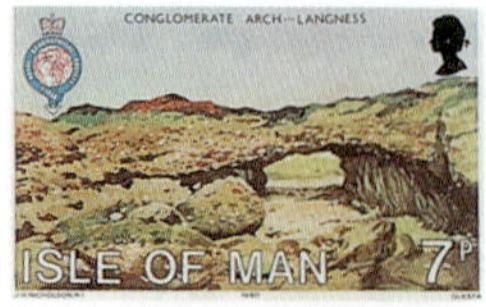

148 Conglomerate Arch, Langness

149 Braaid Circle

150 Cashtal-yn-Ard

151 Volcanic Rocks at Scarlett

152 Sugar-loaf Rock

150th Anniversary of Royal Geographical Society

(Des J. Nicholson. Litho Questa)

1980 (5 Feb). Perf 14½ (C).

165	**148**	7p. multicoloured	15	15
166	**149**	8p. multicoloured	20	20
167	**150**	12p. multicoloured	25	25
168	**151**	13p. multicoloured	25	25
169	**152**	15p. multicoloured	30	25
165/9 *Set of 5*			1·00	1·00
First Day Cover				1·10
Presentation Pack			1·40	
Set of 5 Gutter Pairs			2·00	

Plate Nos.: 12p. 1A, 1B, 1C, 1D (each ×4); 15p. 1C, 1D (each ×4); others 1A, 1B (each ×4).
Sheets: 50 (2 panes 5×5).
Imprint: Right-hand corner, bottom margin.
Quantities sold: 7p. 842,859; 8p. 837,710; 12p. 361,362; 13p. 360,261; 15p. 360,310.
Withdrawn: 4.2.81.

153 *Mona's Isle I*

154 *Douglas I*

155 H.M.S. *Mona's Queen II* sinking U-boat

156 H.M.S. *King Orry III* at Surrender of German Fleet

157 *Ben-My-Chree IV*

158 *Lady of Mann II*

150th Anniversary of Isle of Man Steam Packet Company

(Des J. Nicholson. Photo Courvoisier)

1980 (6 May). Granite paper. Perf 11½ (C).

170	**153**	7p. multicoloured	15	15
171	**154**	8p. multicoloured	20	20
172	**155**	11½p. multicoloured	20	25
173	**156**	12p. multicoloured	25	25
174	**157**	13p. multicoloured	35	25
175	**158**	15p. multicoloured	40	25
170/5		*Set of 6*	1·20	1·10
		First Day Cover		1·00
		Presentation Pack	2·40	
		Set of 6 Gutter Pairs	2·40	
MS176		180×125 mm. Nos. 170/5	1·20	1·20
		First Day Cover		4·50

No. **MS**176 was issued to commemorate the 'London 1980' International Stamp Exhibition.

Cylinder Nos.: All values A1–1–1–1, B1–1–1–1, C1–1–1–1, D1–1–1–1.
Sheets: 40 (2 panes 5×4).
Imprint: Central, bottom margin.
Quantities sold: 7p. 512,449; 8p. 624,090; 11½p. 381,466; 12p. 367,943; 13p. 368,138; 15p. 376,596; miniature sheet 300,678.
Withdrawn: 5.5.81.

159 Stained Glass Window, T. E. Brown Room, Manx Museum

160 Clifton College, Bristol

Europa. Personalities. Thomas Edward Brown (poet and scholar) Commemoration

(Des G. Kneale. Photo Courvoisier)

1980 (6 May). Granite paper. Perf 11½ (C).

177	**159**	7p. multicoloured	15	15
178	**160**	13½p. multicoloured	25	25
177/8		*Set of 2*	50	50
		First Day Cover		60
		Presentation Pack	75	
		Set of 2 Gutter Pairs	1·00	

Cylinder Nos.: Both values A1–1–1–1–1, B1–1–1–1–1, C1–1–1–1–1, D1–1–1–1–1.
Sheets: 20 (2 panes 2×5).
Imprint: Bottom margin at right-hand corner of left-hand pane.
Quantities sold: 7p. 1,726,009; 13½p. 1,708,590.
Withdrawn: 5.5.81.

161 King Olav V and *Norge* (Norwegian royal yacht)

Visit of King Olav V of Norway, August 1979

(Des J. Nicholson. Litho Questa)

1980 (13 June). Perf 14×14½ (C).

179	**161**	12p. multicoloured	30	30
MS180		125×157 mm. Nos. 158 and 179	75	75
		First Day Cover		1·75

No. **MS**180 also commemorates the 'NORWEX 80' stamp exhibition, Oslo.

Plate Nos.: 1A, 1B, 1C, 1D (each ×4).
Sheets: 40 (2 panes 5×4).
Imprint: Right-hand corner, bottom margin.
Quantities sold: 12p. 449,267; miniature sheet 401,424.
Withdrawn: 12.6.81.

162 Winter Wren and View of Calf of Man

163 European Robin and View of Port Erin Marine Biological Station

Christmas and Wildlife Conservation Year

(Des J. Nicholson. Litho John Waddington)

1980 (29 Sept). Perf 13½×14 (C).

181	**162**	6p. multicoloured	15	10
182	**163**	8p. multicoloured	30	35
181/2		*Set of 2*	45	40
		First Day Cover		1·20
		Presentation Pack	80	
		Set of 2 Gutter Pairs	90	

Plate Nos.: 6p. 1B, 1D (each ×4); 8p. 1A, 1C (each ×4).
Sheets: 40 (2 panes 4×5).
Imprint: Right-hand corner, bottom margin.
Quantities sold: 6p. 967,976; 8p. 942,323.
Withdrawn: 28.9.81.

164 William Kermode and Brig *Robert Quayle*, 1819

165 'Mona Vale', Van Diemen's Land, 1834

166 Ross Bridge, Tasmania

167 'Mona Vale', Tasmania (completed 1868)

168 Robert Q. Kermode and Parliament Buildings, Tasmania

Kermode Family in Tasmania Commemoration

(Des A. Theobald. Litho Questa)

1980 (29 Sept). Perf 14½ (C).

183	**164**	7p. multicoloured	15	15
184	**165**	9p. multicoloured	20	20
185	**166**	13½p. multicoloured	25	25
186	**167**	15p. multicoloured	30	25
187	**168**	17½p. multicoloured	30	30
183/7		*Set of 5*	1·10	1·00
		First Day Cover		1·00
		Presentation Pack	1·50	
		Set of 5 Gutter Pairs	2·20	

Plate Nos.: All values 1C, 1D (each ×4).
Sheets: 40 (2 panes 5×4).
Imprint: Right-hand corner, bottom margin.
Quantities sold: 7p. 416,487; 9p. 498,880; 13½p. 318,353; 15p. 314,837; 17½p. 315,107.
Withdrawn: 28.9.81.

169 Peregrine Falcon

170 Loaghtyn Ram

Booklet stamps

(Des J. Nicholson. Litho Harrison)

1980 (29 Sept). Perf 14½×14 (C).

188	**169**	1p. multicoloured	20	20
		a. Booklet pane. Nos. 151, 188 and 189, each x2	60	
189	**170**	5p. multicoloured	30	30
188/9		*Set of 2*	50	50
		First Day Cover (Nos. 150b x2, 151×2, 188 and 189)		1·10
		Presentation Pack (Nos. 150b x2, 151×2, 188 and 189)	1·20	

In addition to Booklets SB11/12 Nos. 188/9 also come from special booklet sheets of 60. These sheets contain No. 150ba×5 and No. 188a×5.
Plate Nos.: 1A, 1B (each x7).
Withdrawn: 25.3.87.

171 Luggers passing Red Pier, Douglas

172 Peel Lugger *Wanderer* rescuing survivors from the *Lusitania*

173 Nickeys leaving Port St. Mary Harbour

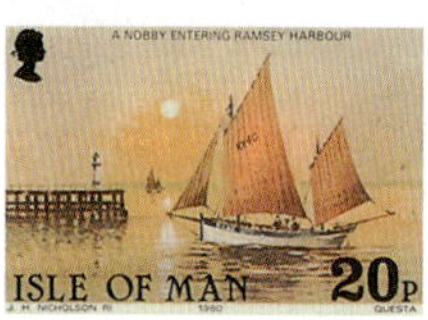

174 Nobby entering Ramsey Harbour

175 Nickeys *Sunbeam* and *Zebra* at Port Erin

Centenary of Royal National Mission to Deep Sea Fishermen

(Des J. Nicholson. Litho Questa)

1981 (24 Feb). Perf 14 (C).

190	**171**	8p. multicoloured	15	15
191	**172**	9p. multicoloured	20	20
192	**173**	18p. multicoloured	30	30
193	**174**	20p. multicoloured	30	30
194	**175**	22p. multicoloured	35	35
190/4		*Set of 5*	1·20	1·20
		First Day Cover		1·50
		Presentation pack	1·50	
		Set of 5 Gutter Pairs	2·50	

Plate Nos.: 8p. 1E, 1F (each ×4); 9p. 1G, 1H (each ×4); 22p. 1A, 1B (each ×4); others 1C, 1D (each ×4).
Sheets: 40 (2 panes 5×4).
Imprint: Right-hand corner, bottom margin.
Quantities sold: 8p. 566,522; 9p. 583,358; 18p. 334,765; 20p. 315,511; 22p 324,607.
Withdrawn: 23.2.82.

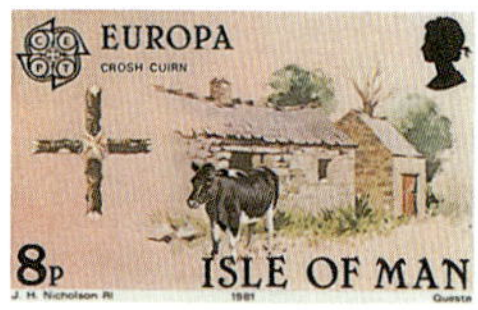

176 'Crosh Cuirn' Superstition

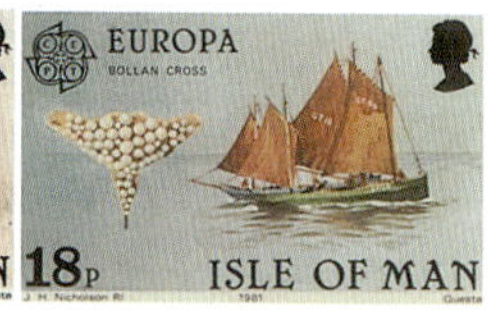

177 'Bollan Cross' Superstition

Europa. Folklore

(Des J. Nicholson. Litho Questa)

1981 (22 May). Perf 14½ (C).

195	**176**	8p. multicoloured	15	10
196	**177**	18p. multicoloured	30	35
195/6		*Set of 2*	45	45
		First Day Cover		65
		Presentation Pack	75	
		Set of 2 Gutter Pairs	90	

Plate Nos.: 1A, 1B (each ×4).
Sheets: 24 (2 panes 3×4).
Imprint: Right-hand corner, bottom margin.
Quantities sold: 8p. 1,261,267; 18p. 1,243,459.
Withdrawn: 21.5.82.

178 Lt. Mark Wilks (Royal Manx Fencibles) and Peel Castle

179 Ensign Mark Wilks and Fort St. George, Madras

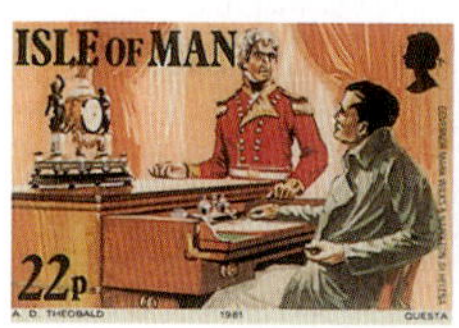

180 Governor Mark Wilks and Napoleon, St. Helena

181 Col. Mark Wilks (speaker of the House of Keys) and Estate, Kirby

150th Death Anniversary of Colonel Mark Wilks

(Des A. Theobald. Litho Questa)

1981 (22 May). Perf 14 (C).

197	**178**	8p. multicoloured	20	20
198	**179**	20p. multicoloured	30	30

199	**180**	22p. multicoloured	40	35
200	**181**	25p. multicoloured	45	35
197/200 *Set of 4*			1·20	1·10
First Day Cover				2·50
Presentation Pack			1·60	
Set of 4 Gutter Pairs			2·50	

Plate Nos.: 8, 20p. 1A, 1B (each ×5); others 1A, 1B (each ×4).
Sheets: 40 (2 panes 5×4).
Imprint: 22p none; others right-hand corner, bottom margin.
Quantities sold: 8p. 371,280; 20p. 278,840; 22p. 294,480; 25p. 272,640.
Withdrawn: 21.5.82.

182 Miss Emmeline Goulden (Mrs. Pankhurst) and Mrs. Sophia Jane Goulden

Centenary of Manx Women's Suffrage

(Des A. Theobald. Litho Questa)

1981 (22 May). Perf 14 (C).

201	**182**	9p. black, olive-grey and stone	20	20
First Day Cover				60
Presentation Pack			50	
Gutter Pair			40	

Plate Nos.: 1C, 1D (each ×3).
Sheets: 40 (2 panes 5×4).
Imprint: Right-hand corner, bottom margin.
Quantity sold: 657,760.
Withdrawn: 21.5.82.

183 Prince Charles and Lady Diana Spencer

Royal Wedding

(Des G. Kneale. Litho Harrison)

1981 (29 July). Perf 14 (C).

202	**183**	9p. black, bright blue & pale blue	15	20
203		25p. black, bright blue and pink	75	80
202/3 *Set of 2*			90	1·00
First Day Cover				1·70
Presentation Pack			1·70	
Set of 2 Gutter Pairs			2·00	
MS204 130×183 mm. Nos. 202/3×2			2·00	2·00
First Day Cover				9·00

Plate Nos.: 9p. 1C, 1D (each ×3); 25p. 1A, 1B (each ×3).
Sheets: 50 (2 panes 5×5).
Imprint: Central, bottom margin.
Quantities sold: 9p. 668,864; 25p. 474,364; miniature sheet 327,094.
Withdrawn: 28.7.82.

184 Douglas War Memorial, Poppies and Inscription

185 Major Robert Cain (war hero)

186 Festival of Remembrance, Royal Albert Hall

187 T.S.S. *Tynwald* at Dunkirk, May, 1940

60th Anniversary of the Royal British Legion

(Des A. Theobald. Photo Courvoisier)

1981 (29 Sept). Granite paper. Perf 11½ (C).

205	**184**	8p. multicoloured	20	20
206	**185**	10p. multicoloured	25	25
207	**186**	18p. multicoloured	30	30
208	**187**	20p. multicoloured	35	35
205/8 *Set of 4*			1·00	1·00
First Day Cover				1·20
Presentation Pack			1·40	
Set of 4 Gutter Pairs			2·00	

Cylinder Nos.: 8p. A1-1-1-1, B1-1-1-1; others A1-1-1-1-1, B1-1-1-1-1.
Sheets: 40 (2 panes 4×5).
Imprint: Central, bottom margin.
Quantities sold: 8p. 314,794; 10p. 799,326; 18p. 284,059; 20p. 261,194.
Withdrawn: 28.9.82.

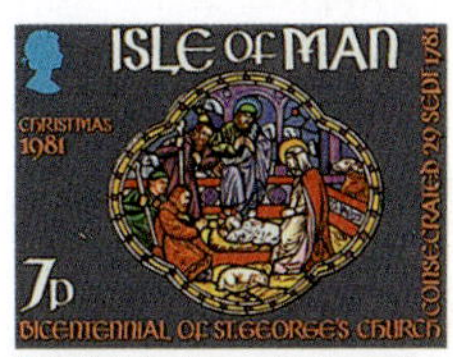

188 Nativity Scene (stained glass window, St. Georges Church)

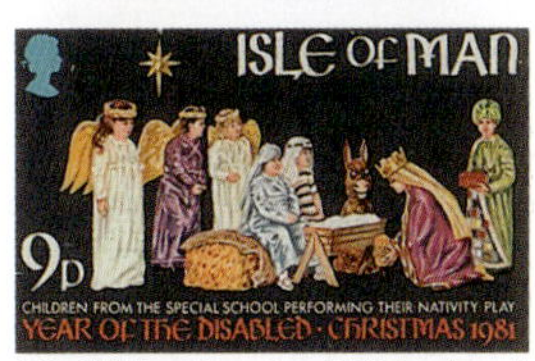

189 Children from Special School performing Nativity Play

Christmas

(Des John Waddington (7p.), G. Kneale (9p.). Litho John Waddington)

1981 (29 Sept). Perf 14 (C).

209	**188**	7p. multicoloured	15	15
210	**189**	9p. multicoloured	20	20

209/10 *Set of 2*	35	35
First Day Cover		55
Presentation pack	75	
Set of 2 Gutter Pairs	70	

The 7p. value also commemorates the bicentenary of St. George's Church, Douglas and the 9p. the International Year for Disabled Persons.

Plate Nos.: 7p. 1A, 1B (each ×6); 9p. 1A, 1B, 1C, 1D (each ×6).
Sheets: 40 (2 panes 2×10).
Imprint: Right-hand corner, bottom margin.
Quantities sold: 7p. 855,407; 9p. 862,892.
Withdrawn: 28.9.82.

190 Joseph and William Cunningham (founders of Manx Boy Scout Movement) and Cunningham House Headquarters

191 Baden-Powell visiting Isle of Man, 1911

192 Baden-Powell and Scout Emblem

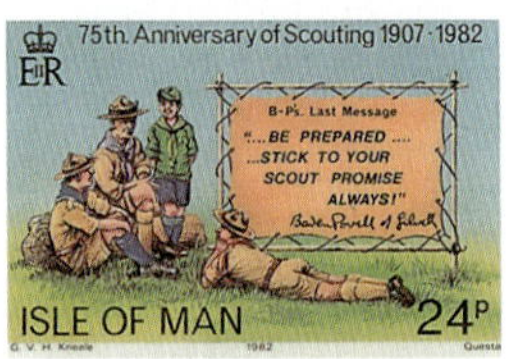

193 Scouts and Baden-Powell's Last Message

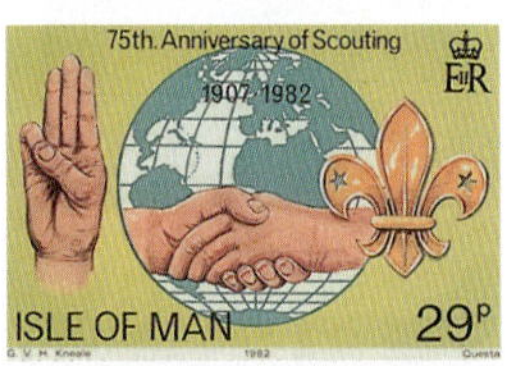

194 Scout Salute, Handshake, Emblem and Globe

75th Anniversary of Boy Scout Movement and 125th Birth Anniversary of Lord Baden-Powell

(Des G. Kneale. Litho Questa)

1982 (23 Feb). Perf 14×14½ (19½p.) or 13½×14 (others), all comb.

211	**190**	9p. multicoloured	20	15
212	**191**	10p. multicoloured	25	25
213	**192**	19½p. multicoloured	45	40
214	**193**	24p. multicoloured	50	45
215	**194**	29p. multicoloured	70	60
211/15 *Set of 5*			1·90	1·70
First Day Cover				2·00
Presentation Pack			2·40	
Set of 5 Gutter Pairs			4·00	

Plate Nos.: 9p. 1A, 1B (each ×4); 29p. 1A, 1B (each ×5); others 1C, 1D (each ×4).
Sheets: 40 (2 panes 5×4).
Imprint: Right-hand corner, bottom margin.
Quantities sold: 9p. 748,353; 10p. 868,401; 19½p. 364,487; 24p. 368,346; 29p. 370,466.
Withdrawn: 22.2.83.

195 *The Principals and Duties of Christianity* (first book printed in Manx, 1707), and Bishop T. Wilson

196 Landing at Derbyhaven (visit of Thomas, 2nd Earl of Derby, 1507)

Europa. Historic Events

(Des A. Theobald. Photo Courvoisier)

1982 (1 June). Granite paper. Perf 12×12½ (C).

216	**195**	9p. multicoloured	15	10
217	**196**	19½p. multicoloured	40	40
216/17 *Set of 2*			55	50
First Day Cover				85
Presentation Pack			85	
Set of 2 Gutter Pairs			1·10	

Cylinder Nos.: Both values A1–1–1–1–1, B1–1–1–1–1.
Sheets: 24 (2 panes 3×4).
Imprint: Right-hand corner, bottom margin.
Quantities sold: 9p. 1,120,457; 19½p. 1,129,315.
Withdrawn: 31.5.83.

197 Charlie Collier (first TT race (single cylinder) winner) and Tourist Trophy Race, 1907

198 Freddie Dixon (Sidecar and Junior TT winner) and Junior TT race, 1927

199 Jimmie Simpson (TT winner and first to lap at 60, 70 and 80 mph) and Senior TT, 1932

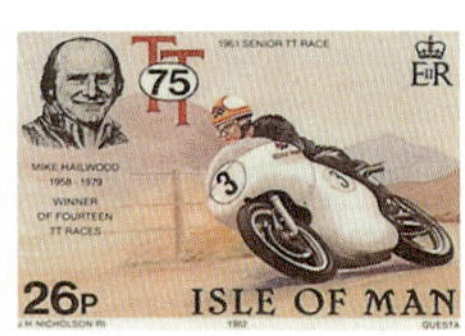

200 Mike Hailwood (winner of fourteen TTs) and Senior TT, 1961

201 Jock Taylor (Sidecar TT winner, 1978, 1980 and 1981) and Sidecar TT (with Benga Johansson), 1980

75th Anniversary of Tourist Trophy Motorcycle Races

(Des J. Nicholson. Litho Questa)

1982 (1 June). Perf 14 (C).

218	**197**	9p. multicoloured	15	15
219	**198**	10p. multicoloured	15	15
220	**199**	24p. multicoloured	60	55
221	**200**	26p. multicoloured	60	50
222	**201**	29p. multicoloured	60	60
218/22 *Set of 5*			1·90	1·80
First Day Cover				2·10
Presentation Pack			3·00	
Stamp Cards (set of 5)			1·20	4·00
Set of 5 Gutter Pairs			4·00	

Plate Nos.: All values 1B, 1C, 1D (each ×4).
Sheets: 40 (2 panes 5×4).
Imprint: Right-hand corner, bottom margin.
Quantities sold: 9p. 837,930; 10p. 866,223; 24p. 351,406; 26p. 361,063; 29p. 355,690.
Withdrawn: 11.6.83.

202 *Mona I*

203 *Manx Maid II*

150th Anniversary of Isle of Man Steam Packet Company Mail Contract

(Des J. Nicholson. Litho Questa)

1982 (5 Oct). Perf 13½ (C).

223	**202**	12p. multicoloured	30	25
224	**203**	19½p. multicoloured	45	45
223/4 *Set of 2*			75	70
First Day Cover				90
Presentation Pack			1·20	
Set of 2 Gutter Pairs			1·50	

Plate Nos.: Both values 1A (×4).
Sheets: 40 (2 panes 5×4).
Imprint: Right-hand bottom margin.
Quantities sold: 12p. 701,044; 19½p. 291,100.
Withdrawn: 4.10.83.

204 The Three Wise Men

205 Snow Scene and European Robin

Christmas

(Des and litho John Waddington)

1982 (5 Oct). Perf 13 (C).

225	**204**	8p. multicoloured	15	15
226	**205**	11p. multicoloured	30	30
225/6 *Set of 2*			45	45
First Day Cover				70
Presentation Pack			85	
Set of 2 Gutter Pairs			1·00	

Plate Nos.: 8p.: 1A, 1C (each ×4), 11p. 1B, 1D (each ×4).
Sheets: 40 (8p. 2 panes 5×4), (11p. 2 panes 4×5).
Imprint: Right-hand corner, bottom margin (8p.); Top right-hand margin (11p.).

Quantities sold; 8p. 740,651; 11p. 787,552.
Withdrawn: 4.10.83.

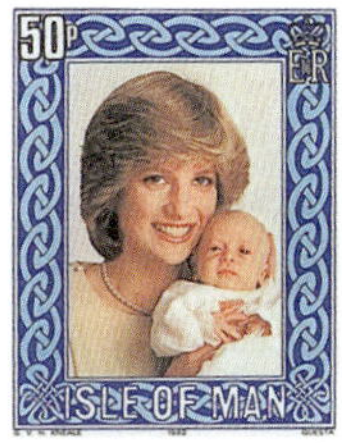

206 Princess Diana with Prince William

21st Birthday of the Princess of Wales and Birth of Prince William

(Des G. Kneale. Litho Questa)

1982 (12 Oct). Sheet 100×83 mm. Perf 14½×14 (C).

MS227 **206** 50p multicoloured	1·50	1·50
First Day Cover		4·50
Presentation Pack	1·70	

Quantity sold: 218,759.
Withdrawn: 11.10.83.

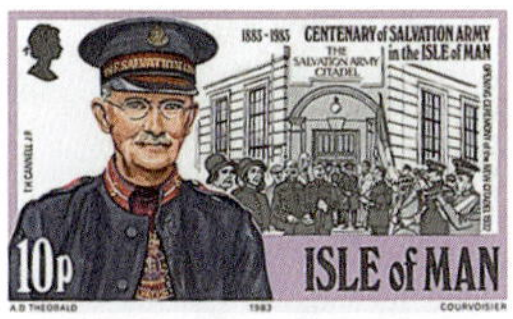

207 Opening of Salvation Army Citadel, and T. H. Cannell, J.P.

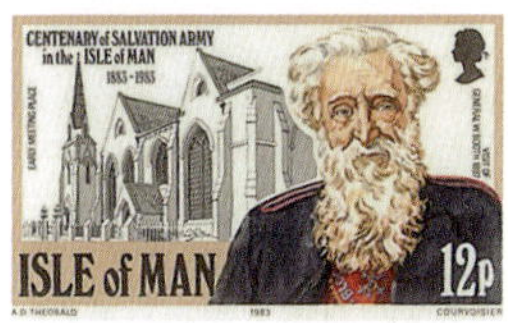

208 Early Meeting Place and Gen. William Booth

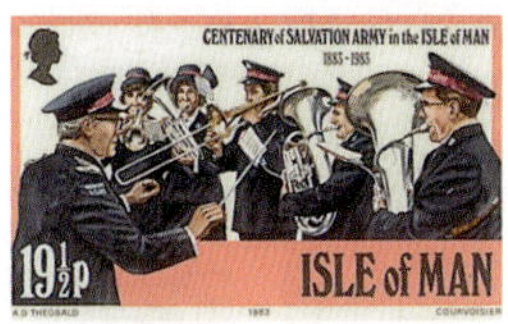

209 Salvation Army Band

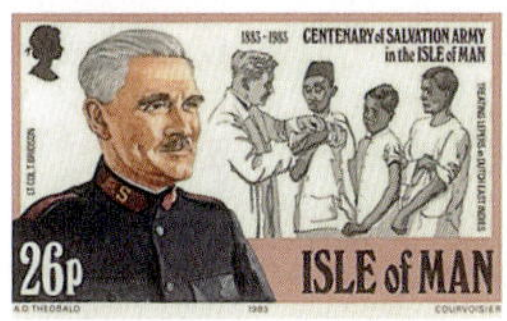

210 Treating Lepers, and Lt.-Col. Thomas Bridson

Centenary of Salvation Army in Isle of Man

(Des A. Theobald. Photo Courvoisier)

1983 (15 Feb). Granite paper. Perf 11½ (C).

228	**207**	10p. multicoloured	20	15
229	**208**	12p. multicoloured	30	25
230	**209**	19½p. multicoloured	45	45
231	**210**	26p. multicoloured	65	60
228/31 *Set of 4*			1·40	1·20
First Day Cover				1·60
Presentation Pack			2·10	
Set of 4 Gutter Pairs			2·75	

Cylinder Nos.: All values B1–1–1–1–1.
Sheets: 40 (2 panes 4×5).
Imprint: Central, bottom margin.
Quantities sold: 10p. 467,665; 12p. 567,863; 19½p. 267,929; 26p. 288,069.
Withdrawn: 14.2.84.

211 Atlantic Puffins

212 Northern Gannets

213 Lesser Black-backed Gulls

214 Great Cormorants

215 Black-legged Kittiwakes

216 Shags

217 Grey Herons

218 Herring Gulls

219 Razorbills

220 Greater Black-backed Gulls

221 Common Shelducks

222 Oystercatchers

223 Arctic Terns

224 Common Guillemots

225 Common Redshanks

226 Mute Swans

227 'Queen Elizabeth II' (Ricardo Macarron)

Sea Birds and Queen's Portrait (£5)

(Des Colleen Corlett (£5), J. Nicholson (others). Litho Questa)

1983 (15 Feb)–**85**. Perf 14 (20p. to £1), 14×13½ (£5) or 14½ (others), all comb.

232	**211**	1p. multicoloured (a)	30	30
233	**212**	2p. multicoloured (a)	30	30
234	**213**	5p. multicoloured (a)	60	40
235	**214**	8p. multicoloured (a)	60	40
236	**215**	10p. multicoloured (a)	60	35
237	**216**	11p. multicoloured (a)	60	35
238	**217**	12p. multicoloured (a)	70	40
239	**218**	13p. multicoloured (a)	70	40
240	**219**	14p. multicoloured (a)	70	40
241	**220**	15p. multicoloured (a)	80	50
242	**221**	16p. multicoloured (a)	80	50
243	**222**	18p. multicoloured (a)	80	50
244	**223**	20p. multicoloured (b)	1·00	70
245	**224**	25p. multicoloured (b)	1·20	75
246	**225**	50p. multicoloured (b)	1·70	1·50
247	**226**	£1 multicoloured (b)	2·50	2·75
248	**227**	£5 multicoloured (c)	8·00	8·50
232/48 *Set of 17*			18·00	19·00
First Day Covers (4)				25·00
Presentation Packs (4)			20·00	

Printings: (a) 15.2.83; (b) 14.9.83; (c) 31.1.85.
Plate Nos.: 1p. to £1 1A, 1B, 1C, 1D (each ×4); £5 1A, 1B (each ×4).
Sheets: 10 (5×2) £5; 50 (5×10) others.
Imprint: £5 Right-hand margin; others right-hand corner, bottom margin.
Withdrawn: 30.6.88 1p. to 18p.; 31.12.88 20p. to £1; 4.7.94 £5.

228 Design Drawings by Robert Casement for the Great Laxey Wheel

229 Robert Casement and the Great Laxey Wheel

Europa. The Great Laxey Wheel

(Des J. Nicholson. Litho Questa)

1983 (18 May). Perf 14 (C).

249	**228**	10p. black, azure and buff	25	20
250	**229**	20½p. multicoloured	50	55
249/50 *Set of 2*			75	75
First Day Cover				1·00
Presentation Pack			1·10	
Set of 2 Gutter Pairs			1·50	

Plate Nos.: 10p. 1A, 1B (each ×3); 20½p. 1A, 1B (each ×4).
Sheets: 12 (2 panes 2×3).
Imprint: Right-hand corner, bottom margin.
Quantities sold: 10p. 653,743; 20½p. 686,084.
Withdrawn 17.5.84.

230 Nick Keig (international yachtsman) and Trimaran *Three Legs of Man III*

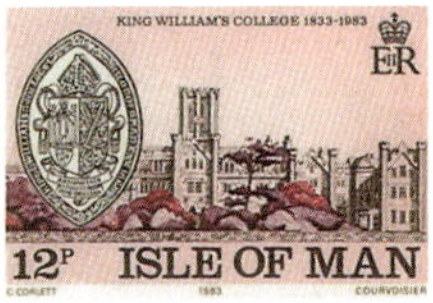

231 King William's College, Castletown

232 Sir William Bragg (winner of Nobel Prize for Physics) and Spectrometer

233 General Sir George White V.C. and Action at Charasiah

150th Anniversary of King William's College

(Des J. Nicholson (10p., 31p.), Colleen Corlett (12p., 28p.). Photo Courvoisier)

1983 (18 May). Granite paper. Perf 11½ (C).

251	**230**	10p. multicoloured	15	15
252	**231**	12p. multicoloured	20	20
253	**232**	28p. multicoloured	55	55
254	**233**	31p. multicoloured	65	65
251/4 *Set of 4*			1·40	1·40
First Day Cover				1·50
Presentation Pack			2·00	
Set of 4 Gutter Pairs			3·00	

Cylinder Nos.: 10p. C1–1–1–1, D1–1–1–1; 12p. C1–1–1–1, D1–1–1–1; 28p. A1–1–1–1, B1–1–1–1; 31p. A1–1–1–1–1, B1–1–1–1–1.
Sheets: 40 (2 panes 5×4).
Imprint: Central, bottom margin.
Quantities sold: 10p. 552,573; 12p. 693,004; 28p. 263,814; 31p. 242,393.
Withdrawn: 17.5.84.

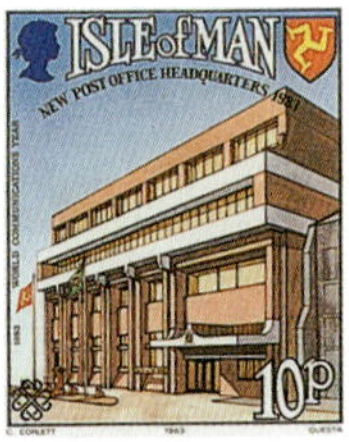

234 New Post Office Headquarters, Douglas

235 Vikings Landing on Man, AD 938

World Communications Year and 10th Anniversary of Isle of Man Post Office Authority

(Des Colleen Corlett (10p.), J. Nicholson (15p.). Litho Questa)

1983 (5 July). Perf 14½ (C).

255	**234**	10p. multicoloured	25	25
256	**235**	15p. multicoloured	35	40
255/6 *Set of 2*			60	65
First Day Cover				90
Presentation Pack			90	
Stamp Cards (set of 2)			90	1·40
Set of 2 Gutter Pairs			1·20	

Plate Nos.: Both values 1A, 1B, 1C, 1D (each ×5).
Sheets: 40 (2 panes 4×5).
Imprint: Central, right-hand margin.
Quantities sold: 10p. 269,843; 15p. 222,013.
Withdrawn: 4.7.84.

236 Shepherds

237 Three Kings

Christmas

(Des Colleen Corlett. Litho John Waddington)

1983 (14 Sept). Perf 13 (C).

257	**236**	9p. multicoloured	20	20
258	**237**	12p. multicoloured	30	30
257/8 *Set of 2*			50	50
First Day Cover				85
Presentation Pack			85	
Set of 2 Gutter Pairs			1·00	

Plate Nos.: Both values 1A, 1B, 1C, 1D (each ×5).
Sheets: 40 (2 panes 5×4).
Imprint: Right-hand corner, bottom margin.
Quantities sold: 9p. 642,763; 12p. 656,060.
Withdrawn: 13.9.84.

238 *Manx King* (full-rigged ship)

239 *Hope* (barque)

240 *Rio Grande* (brig)

241 *Lady Elizabeth* (barque)

242 *Sumatra* (barque)

243 Wreck of *Lady Elizabeth* as shown on Falkland Islands Stamp

The Karran Fleet

(Des J. Nicholson (10p. to 31p.); Colleen Corlett, J. Nicholson and J. Smith (miniature sheet). Litho Questa)

1984 (14 Feb). Perf 14 (C).

259	**238**	10p. multicoloured	20	15
260	**239**	13p. multicoloured	30	20
261	**240**	20½p. multicoloured	45	35
262	**241**	28p. multicoloured	65	50
263	**242**	31p. multicoloured	75	65
259/63 *Set of 5*			2·20	1·50
First Day Cover				2·00
Presentation Pack			2·75	
Set of 5 Gutter pairs			4·25	
MS264 103×94 mm. 28p. Type **241**; 31p. Type **243** (sold at 60p.)			2·20	1·50
First Day Cover				3·00
Presentation Pack			2·75	

No. **MS**264 was issued to commemorate links between the Isle of Man and the Falkland Islands.

Plate Nos.: All values 1A, 1B (each ×4).
Sheets: 40 (2 panes 5×4).
Imprint: Right-hand corner, bottom margin.
Quantities sold: 10p. 389,728; 13p. 417,637; 20½p. 253,949; 28p. 238,292; 31p. 236,196; miniature sheet 137,031.
Withdrawn: 13.2.85.

244 C.E.P.T. 25th Anniversary Logo

Europa

(Des J. Larrivière, adapted Colleen Corlett. Photo Courvoisier)

1984 (27 Apr). Granite paper. Perf 12×11½ (C).

265	**244**	10p. dull orange, deep reddish brown and pale orange	30	25

266	20½p. lt blue, dp blue & pale blue	50	50
265/6 *Set of 2*		80	75
First Day Cover			2·00
Presentation Pack		2·50	

Cylinder Nos.: 10p. B1–1–1; 20½p. A1–1–1.
Sheets: 20 (4×5).
Imprint: Central, right-hand margin.
Quantities sold: 10p. 705,410; 20½p. 715,479.
Withdrawn: 26.4.85.

245 Railway Air Services De Havilland D.H.84 Dragon Mk 2

246 West Coast Air Services De Havilland D.H.86A Dragon Express *Ronaldsway*

247 B.E.A. Douglas DC-3

248 B.E.A. Vickers Viscount 800

249 Telair Britten Norman Islander

50th Anniversary of First Official Airmail to the Isle of Man and 40th Anniversary of International Civil Aviation Organization

(Des A. Theobald. Litho Questa)

1984 (27 Apr). Perf 14 (C).

267	**245**	11p. multicoloured	35	30
268	**246**	13p. multicoloured	40	30
269	**247**	26p. multicoloured	70	65
270	**248**	28p. multicoloured	70	65
271	**249**	31p. multicoloured	70	65
267/71 *Set of 5*			2·50	2·50
First Day Cover				2·75
Presentation Pack			2·75	
Set of 5 Gutter Pairs			5·00	

Plate Nos.: All values 1C, 1D (each ×4).
Sheets: 40 (2 panes 5×4).
Imprint: Right-hand corner, bottom margin.
Quantities sold: 11p. 399,155; 13p. 440,623; 26p. 234,165; 28p. 173,841; 31p. 171,890.
Withdrawn: 26.4.85.

Year Pack 1983

1984. Comprises Nos. 228/47, 249/58.

Year Pack	15·00	

Withdrawn: 31.3.85.

250 Window from Glencrutchery House, Douglas

251 Window from Lonan Old Church

Christmas. Stained-glass Windows

(Des D. Swinton. Litho John Waddington)

1984 (21 Sept). Perf 14 (C).

272	**250**	10p. multicoloured	20	20
273	**251**	13p. multicoloured	40	40
272/3 *Set of 2*			60	60
First Day Cover				1·25
Presentation Pack			90	
Set of 2 Gutter Pairs			1·20	

Plate Nos.: Both values 1A, 1C (each ×6).
Sheets: 40 (2 panes 4×5).
Imprint: Top right-hand margin.
Quantities sold: 10p. 652,870; 13p. 668,084.
Withdrawn: 20.9.85.

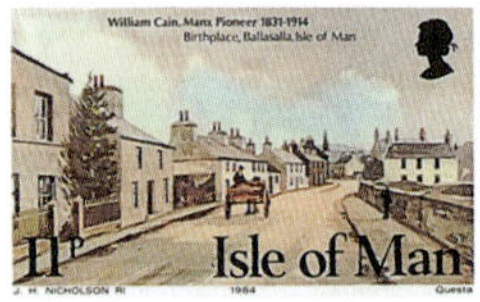

252 William Cain's Birthplace, Ballasalla

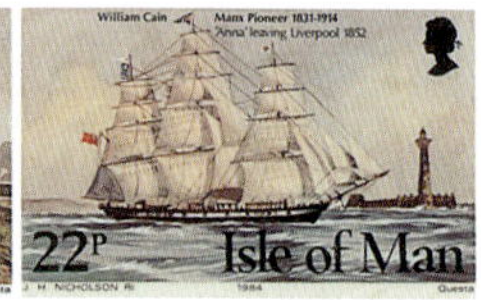

253 The *Anna* Leaving Liverpool, 1852

254 Early Australian Railway

255 William Cain as Mayor of Melbourne, and Town Hall

256 Royal Exhibition Buildings, Melbourne

William Cain (civic leader, Victoria) Commemoration

(Des J. Nicholson. Litho Questa)

1984 (21 Sept). Perf 14½×14 (C).

274	**252**	11p. multicoloured	25	20
275	**253**	22p. multicoloured	50	50
276	**254**	28p. multicoloured	70	65
277	**255**	30p. multicoloured	75	65
278	**256**	33p. multicoloured	70	65
274/8 *Set of 5*			2·50	2·40
First Day Cover				2·75
Presentation Pack			2·50	
Set of 5 Gutter Pairs			5·00	

Plate Nos.: All values 1B (×4).
Sheets: 40 (2 panes 5×4).
Imprint: Right-hand corner, bottom margin.
Quantities sold: 11p. 393,219; 22p. 280,598; 28p. 223,515; 30p. 220,913; 33p. 213,933.
Withdrawn: 20.9.85.

257 Queen Elizabeth II and Commonwealth Parliamentary Association Badge

258 Queen Elizabeth II and Manx Emblem

Links with the Commonwealth. 30th Commonwealth Parliamentary Association Conference

(Des and litho John Waddington)

1984 (21 Sept). Perf 14 (C).

279	**257**	14p. multicoloured	35	35
280	**258**	33p. multicoloured	65	65
279/80 *Set of 2*			1·00	1·00

First Day Cover			1·50
Presentation Pack		2·75	
Set of 2 Gutter Pairs		2·00	

Plate Nos.: Both values 1A, 1C (each x7).
Sheets: 40 (2 panes 5×4).
Imprint: Right-hand corner, bottom margin.
Quantities sold: 14p. 373,204; 33p. 231,073.
Withdrawn: 20.9.85.

Year Pack 1984

1985 (1 Jan). Comprises Nos. 259/80.

Year Pack	17·00	

Withdrawn: 31.12.85.

259 Cunningham House Headquarters, and Mrs. Willie Cunningham and Mrs. Joseph Cunningham (former Commissioners)

260 Princess Margaret, Isle of Man Standard and Guides

261 Lady Olave Baden-Powell opening Guide Headquarters, 1955

262 Guide Uniforms from 1910 to 1985

263 Guide Handclasp, Salute and Early Badge

75th Anniversary of Girl Guide Movement

(Des Colleen Corlett. Photo Courvoisier)

1985 (31 Jan). Granite paper. Perf 11½ (C).

281	**259**	11p. multicoloured	30	25
282	**260**	14p. multicoloured	35	30
283	**261**	29p. multicoloured	70	60
284	**262**	31p. multicoloured	75	75
285	**263**	34p. multicoloured	90	85
281/5 *Set of 5*			2·75	2·50
First Day Cover				3·00
Presentation Pack			3·00	
Set of 5 Gutter Pairs			5·50	

Cylinder Nos.: 11p., 34p. A1–1–1–1–1–1, B1–1–1–1–1–1; others A1–1–1–1–1, B1–1–1–1–1.
Sheets: 40 (2 panes 4×5).
Imprint: Central, bottom margin of each pane.
Withdrawn: 30.1.86.

264 Score of Manx National Anthem

265 William H. Gill (lyricist)

266 Score of Hymn 'Crofton'

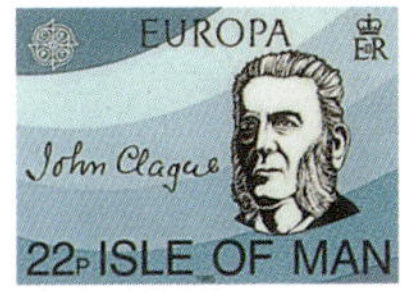

267 Dr. John Clague (composer)

Europa. European Music Year

(Des D. Swinton. Photo Courvoisier)

1985 (24 Apr). Granite paper. Perf 11½ (C).

286	**264**	12p. black, orange-brn & chestnut	30	15
		a. Horiz pair. Nos. 286/7	75	75
287	**265**	12p. black, orange-brn & chestnut	30	15
288	**266**	22p. black, brt blue & new bl	80	25
		a. Horiz pair. Nos. 288/9	1·60	1·60
289	**267**	22p. black, brt new blue & new bl	80	25
286/9 *Set of 4*			2·10	2·10
First Day Cover				2·75
Presentation Pack			2·50	

Cylinder Nos.: Both values A1–1–1, B1–1–1.
Sheets: 20 (4×5). The two designs for each value printed together, *se-tenant*, in horizontal pairs throughout the sheets.
Imprint: Central, bottom margin.
Withdrawn: 23.4.86.

268 Charles Rolls in 20 h.p. Rolls Royce Light Twenty tourer (1906 Tourist Trophy Race)

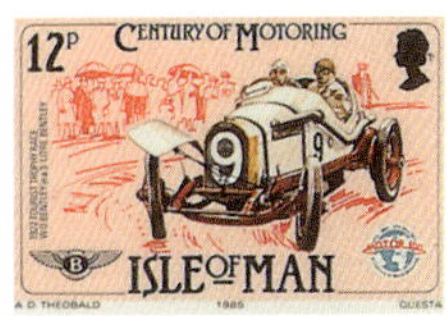

269 W. Bentley in 3 litre Bentley (1922 Tourist Trophy Race)

270 F. Gerard in E.R.A. (1950 British Empire Trophy Race)

271 Brian Lewis in Alfa Romeo (1934 Mannin Moar Race)

272 Jaguar XJ-SC ('Roads Open' Car, 1984 Motorcycle T.T. Races)

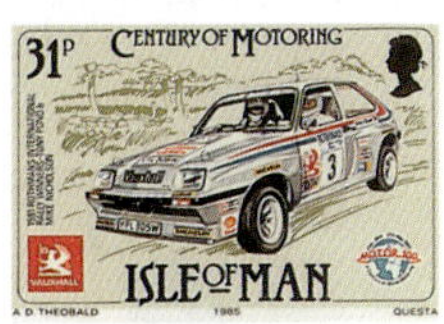

273 Tony Pond and Mike Nicholson in Vauxhall Chevette (1981 Rothmans International Rally)

Century of Motoring

(Des A. Theobald. Litho Questa)

1985 (25 May). Perf 14 (C).

290	**268**	12p. multicoloured	25	15
		a. Horiz pair. Nos. 290/1	60	60

291	**269**	12p. multicoloured	25	15
292	**270**	14p. multicoloured	25	15
		a. Horiz pair. Nos. 292/3	60	60
293	**271**	14p. multicoloured	25	15
294	**272**	31p. multicoloured	60	40
		a. Horiz pair. Nos. 294/5	2·00	2·00
295	**273**	31p. multicoloured	60	40
290/5 *Set of 6*			2·50	2·50
First Day Cover				2·75
Presentation Pack			3·25	
Stamp Cards (set of 6)			3·00	7·25
Set of 3 Gutter Blocks of 4			5·00	

Plate Nos.: All values 1A, 1B (each ×6).
Sheets: 40 (2 panes 4×5). The two designs for each value printed together, *se-tenant*, in horizontal pairs throughout the sheets.
Imprint: Right-hand corner, bottom margin of each pane.
Withdrawn: 24.5.86.

274 Queen Alexandra and Victorian Sergeant with Wife

275 Queen Mary and Royal Air Force Family

276 Earl Mountbatten and Royal Navy Family

277 Prince Michael of Kent and Royal Marine with Parents, 1982

Centenary of the Soldiers', Sailors' and Airmens Familie's Association

(Des Colleen Corlett. Litho Questa)

1985 (4 Sept). Perf 14 (C).

296	**274**	12p. multicoloured	25	20
297	**275**	15p. multicoloured	35	30
298	**276**	29p. multicoloured	65	55
299	**277**	34p. multicoloured	90	85
296/9 *Set of 4*			1·90	1·70
First Day Cover				3·00
Presentation Pack			2·50	
Set of 4 Gutter Pairs			4·00	

Plate Nos. 12p., 34p. 1A, 1B, 1C, 1D, 1E, 1F, 1G, 1H (each ×6); others 1A, 1B, 1C, 1D, 1E, 1F, 1G, 1H (each ×5).
Sheets: 40 (2 panes 5×4).
Imprint: Right-hand corner, bottom margin of each pane.
Withdrawn: 3.9.86.

278 Kirk Maughold (Birthplace)

279 Lieut. Gen. Sir Mark Cubbon

280 Memorial Statue, Bangalore, India

Birth Bicentenary of Lieut.-Gen. Sir Mark Cubbon (Indian administrator)

(Des A. Theobald. Litho Questa)

1985 (2 Oct). Perf 14 (C).

300	**278**	12p. multicoloured	30	25
301	**279**	22p. multicoloured	70	65
302	**280**	45p. multicoloured	1·00	95
300/2 *Set of 3*			1·70	1·60
First Day Cover				2·00
Presentation Pack			2·50	
Set of 3 Gutter pairs			3·50	

Plate Nos.: All values 1A, 1B, 1C, 1D (each ×4).
Sheets: 40 (2 panes 5×4) 12p. or (2 panes 4×5) others.
Imprint: Right-hand corner, bottom margin of each pane.
Withdrawn: 1.10.86.

281 St. Peter's Church, Onchan

282 Royal Chapel of St. John, Tynwald

283 Bride Parish Church

Christmas. Manx Churches

(Des A. Theobald. Litho John Waddington)

1985 (2 Oct). Perf 13×13½ (C).

303	**281**	11p. multicoloured	30	25
304	**282**	14p. multicoloured	40	35
305	**283**	31p. multicoloured	1·00	90
303/5 *Set of 3*			1·50	1·40
First Day Cover				1·70
Presentation Pack			2·00	
Set of 3 Gutter Pairs			3·00	

Plate Nos.: All values 1A, 1B, 1C, 1D (each ×4).
Sheets: 40 (2 panes 5×4).
Imprint: Right-hand corner, bottom margin of each pane.
Withdrawn: 1.10.86.

Post Office Yearbook

1985 (9 Dec). Comprises Nos. 248 and 281/305 in slipcase.

Yearbook	25·00

Withdrawn: 9.92.

Year Pack 1985

1986 (1 Jan). Comprises Nos. 281/305 with or without No. 248.

Year Pack with No. 248	29·00
Year Pack without No. 248	21·00

Withdrawn: 30.12.86.

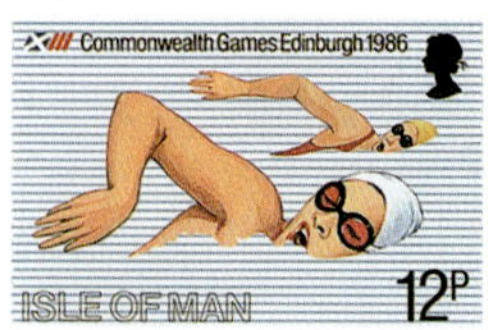

284 Swimming

285 Race Walking

286 Rifle-shooting

287 Cycling

Commonwealth Games, Edinburgh

(Des C. Abbott. Litho Questa)

1986 (5 Feb). Perf 14½ (C).

306	**284**	12p. multicoloured	20	15
307	**285**	15p. multicoloured	25	30
308	**286**	31p. multicoloured	90	95
309	**287**	34p. multicoloured	1·00	95
306/9 *Set of 4*			2·10	2·10
First Day Cover				2·50
Presentation Pack			3·00	
Set of 4 Gutter Pairs			4·25	

No. 309 also commemorates the 50th anniversary of Manx International Cycling Week.

Plate Nos.: All values 1A, 1B, 1C, 1D (each ×5).
Sheets: 40 (2 panes 5×4).
Imprint: Right-hand corner, bottom margin of each pane.
Withdrawn: 4.2.87.

288 Viking Necklace and Peel Castle

289 Meayll Circle, Rushen

290 Skeleton of Great Deer and Manx Museum

291 Viking Longship Model

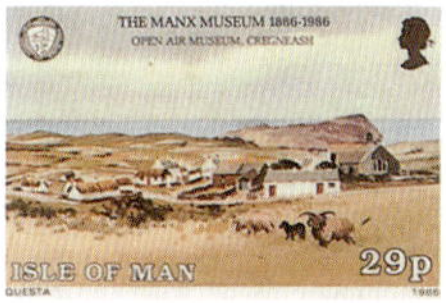

292 Open Air Museum, Cregneash

Centenary of Manx Museum

(Des J. Nicholson. Litho Questa)

1986 (5 Feb). Perf 14 (C).

310	**288**	12p. multicoloured	20	15
311	**289**	15p. multicoloured	25	20
312	**290**	22p. multicoloured	65	50
313	**291**	26p. multicoloured	80	60
314	**292**	29p. multicoloured	90	60
310/14 *Set of 5*			2·50	1·90
First Day Cover				2·50
Presentation Pack			2·75	
Set of 5 Gutter Pairs			5·00	

Plate Nos.: All values 1A, 1B, 1C, 1D (each ×6).
Sheets: 40 (2 panes 5×4) 12p., 15p., 29p.; (2 panes 4×5) others.
Imprint: Right-hand corner, bottom margin (12p., 15p., 29p.) or bottom left-hand margin (others).
Withdrawn: 4.2.87.

293 Viking Longship

294 Celtic Cross Logo

Manx Heritage Year. Booklet stamps

(Des Colleen Corlett. Litho Harrison)

1986 (10 Apr). Perf 14½×14 (C).

315	**293**	2p. multicoloured	40	40
		a. Booklet pane. Nos. 315×2 and 316×4	2·00	
316	**294**	10p. black, apple green and brownish grey	35	35
		a. Booklet pane. No. 316×3 and 3 stamp size labels	1·20	
315/16 *Set of 2*			90	90
First Day Cover (Nos. 315×1 and 316×2)				2·00
Presentation Pack (Nos. 315×1 and 316×2)			1·90	

In addition to Booklets SB14/15 Nos. 315/16 also come from special booklet sheets of 60 containing five each of Nos. 315a and 316a.

Plate Nos.: 1A, 1B (each x7).
Withdrawn: 25.3.87.

295 *Usnea articulata* (lichen) and *Neotinea intacta* (orchid), The Ayres

296 Hen Harrier, Calf of Man

297 Manx Stoat, Eary Chuslin

298 *Stenobothus stigmaticus* (grasshopper), St. Michael's Isle

Europa. Nature and Environment Protection

(Des J. Nicholson and Nancy Corkish. Photo Courvoisier)

1986 (10 Apr). Granite paper. Perf 11½ (C).

317	**295**	12p. multicoloured	30	15
		a. Horiz pair. Nos. 317/18	60	75
318	**296**	12p. multicoloured	30	15
319	**297**	22p. multicoloured	60	25
		a. Horiz pair. Nos. 319/20	1·20	1·40
320	**298**	22p. multicoloured	60	25
317/20 *Set of 4*			1·60	1·60
First Day Cover				2·00
Presentation Pack			2·10	

Cylinder Nos.: Both values A1–1–1–1–1.
Sheets: 20 (4×5). The two designs for each value printed together, *se-tenant*, in horizontal pairs throughout the sheets.
Imprint: Central, right-hand margin.
Withdrawn: 9.4.87.

299 Ellanbane (home of Myles Standish)

300 *Mayflower* crossing the Atlantic, 1620

301 Pilgrim Fathers landing at Plymouth, 1620

302 Captain Myles Standish

'Ameripex '86' International Stamp Exhibition, Chicago. Captain Myles Standish of the *Mayflower*

(Des C. Abbott. Litho Cartor)

1986 (22 May). Perf 13½ (C).

321	**299**	12p. multicoloured	20	20
322	**300**	15p. multicoloured	25	25
323	**301**	31p. multicoloured	90	90
324	**302**	34p. multicoloured	95	95
321/4 *Set of 4*			2·10	2·10
First Day Cover				2·50
Presentation Pack			2·40	
MS325 100×75 mm. Nos. 323/4. Perf 12½			2·10	2·10
First Day Cover				3·75
Presentation Pack			2·50	

No. **MS**325 also commemorates the 75th anniversary of the World Manx Association.

Plate Nos.: All values 1A, 1B, 1C, 1D (each ×5).
Sheets: 20 (5×4).
Imprint: Right-hand corner, bottom margin.
Withdrawn: 21.5.87.

303 Prince Andrew in Naval Uniform and Miss Sarah Ferguson

304 Engagement Photograph

Royal Wedding

(Des Colleen Corlett. Litho B.D.T.)

1986 (23 July). Perf 15×14 (C).

326	**303**	15p. multicoloured	25	25
327	**304**	40p. multicoloured	1·50	1·50
326/7 *Set of 2*			1·50	1·50
First Day Cover				2·00
Presentation Pack			2·00	

Plate Nos.: Both values 1A, 1B (each ×5).
Sheets: 20 (4×5).
Imprint: Right-hand corner, bottom margin.
Withdrawn: 22.7.87.

305 Prince Philip

306 Queen Elizabeth II

307 Queen Elizabeth II and Prince Philip

Royal Birthdays

(Des Colleen Corlett from photos by Karsh. Photo Courvoisier)

1986 (28 Aug). Granite paper. Perf 11½ (C).

328	**305**	15p. multicoloured	30	30
		a. Horiz pair. Nos. 328/9	70	70
329	**306**	15p. multicoloured	30	30
330	**307**	34p. multicoloured	1·10	1·10
328/30 *Set of 3*			1·60	1·60
First Day Cover				2·00
Presentation Pack			2·40	
Souvenir Folder (complete sheets)			14·00	

Nos. 328/30 also commemorate 'Stockholmia '86' and 350th anniversary of Swedish Post Office.

Cylinder Nos.: 15p. A1–1–1–1–1–1, B1–1–1–1–1–1, C1–1–1–1–1–1, D1–1–1–1–1–1; 34p. A1–1–1–1–1, B1–1–1–1–1, C1–1–1–1–1, D1–1–1–1–1.
Sheets: 15p. 12 (4×3). The two designs printed together, *se-tenant*, in horizontal pairs throughout the sheets; 34p. 6 (2×3).
Imprint: Central, bottom margin.
Withdrawn: 27.8.87.

308 European Robins on Globe and 'Peace and Goodwill' in Braille

309 Hands releasing Peace Dove

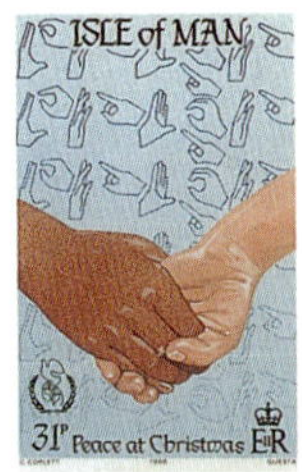

310 Clasped Hands and 'Peace' in Sign Language

Christmas and International Peace Year

(Des Colleen Corlett. Litho Questa)

1986 (25 Sept). Perf 14 (C).

331	**308**	11p. multicoloured	30	30
332	**309**	14p. multicoloured	30	30
333	**310**	31p. multicoloured	80	80
331/3 *Set of 3*			1·20	1·20
First Day Cover				1·50
Presentation Pack			1·70	
Set of 3 Gutter Pairs			2·50	

No. 331 also commemorates the 50th anniversary of Manx Blind Welfare Society.

Plate Nos.: All values 1A, 1B, 1C, 1D (each ×5).
Sheets: 40 (2 panes 4×5).
Imprint: Right-hand corner, bottom margin of each pane.
Withdrawn: 24.9.87.

Year Pack 1986

1986 (25 Sept). Comprises Nos. 306/33.

Year Pack	27·00

Withdrawn: 31.12.87.

Post Office Yearbook

1986 (Dec). Comprises Nos. 306/14, 315a, 316a, 317/27, 328/30 in complete sheets, and 331/3 in slipcase.

Yearbook	49·00

Sold out 9.90.

311 North Quay

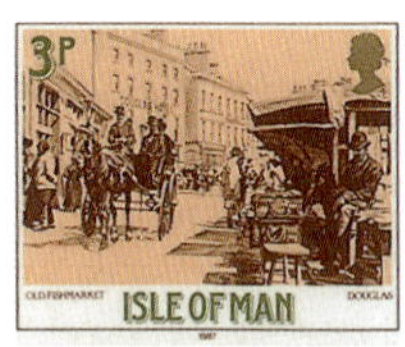

312 Old Fishmarket

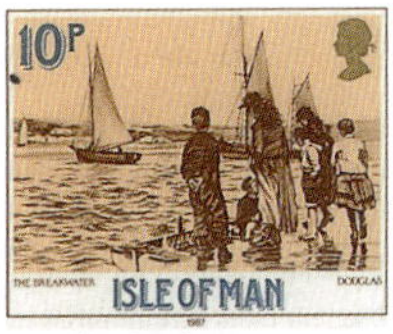

313 The Breakwater

314 Jubilee Clock

315 Loch Promenade

316 Beach

Victorian Douglas

(Des A. Theobald. Litho Questa)

1987 (21 Jan–26 Mar). Perf 14×14½ (C).

334	**311**	2p. multicoloured (a)	10	10
		a. Booklet pane. Nos. 334×2, 335×2 and 336×4 (2p. stamps at top) (b)	1·70	
		ab. Ditto, but 2p. stamps at bottom (b)	1·70	
		b. Booklet pane. Nos. 334/7, each ×2 (b)	2·00	
		ba. Ditto, but 2p stamps at bottom (b)	2·00	
335	**312**	3p. multicoloured (a)	10	10
336	**313**	10p. multicoloured (a)	25	25
337	**314**	15p. multicoloured (a)	30	30
338	**315**	31p. multicoloured (a)	90	80
339	**316**	34p. multicoloured (a)	1·00	90
334/9 *Set of 6*			2·40	2·20
First Day Cover (Nos. 334/9)				2·50
First Day Covers (2) (se-tenant strips)				5·0
Presentation Pack (Nos. 334/9)			3·00	
Set of 6 Gutter Pairs			5·00	

Printings: (a) 21.1.87; (b) 26.3.87.
Plate Nos.: All values 1A, 1B, 1C, 1D (each ×4).
Sheets: 40 (2 panes 5×4). In addition to booklets SB16/17 Nos. 334/7 also come from special booklet sheets of 48 (6×8), containing either 3 each of Nos. 334a/ab or 3 each of Nos. 334b/ba.
Imprint: Right-hand corner, bottom margin of each pane.
Withdrawn: 20.1.88 sheets; 15.3.88 booklets.

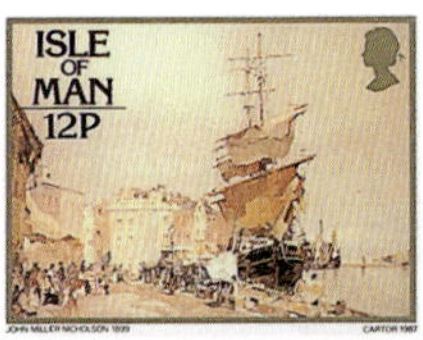

317 'The Old Fishmarket and Harbour, Douglas'

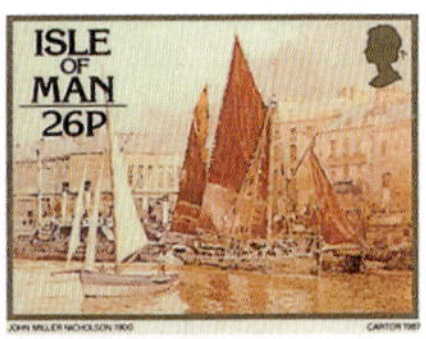

318 'Red Sails at Douglas'

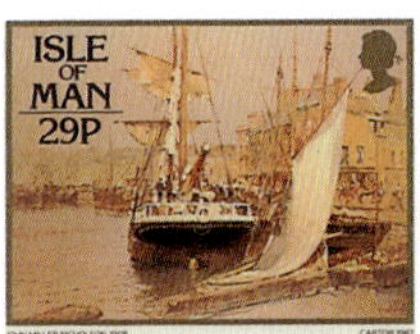

319 'The Double Corner, Peel'

320 'Peel Harbour'

Paintings by John Miller Nicholson

(Des A. Theobald. Litho Cartor)

1987 (18 Feb). Perf 13½ (C).

340	**317**	12p. multicoloured	20	20
341	**318**	26p. multicoloured	70	60
342	**319**	29p. multicoloured	90	80
343	**320**	34p. multicoloured	1·00	1·00
340/3 *Set of 4*			2·50	2·40
First Day Cover				2·75
Presentation Pack			3·00	
Set of 4 Gutter Pairs			5·00	

Plate Nos.: All values 1A, 1B, 1C, 1D (each ×5).
Sheets: 40 (2 panes 5×4).
Imprint: Right-hand corner, bottom margin of each pane.
Withdrawn: 17.2.88.

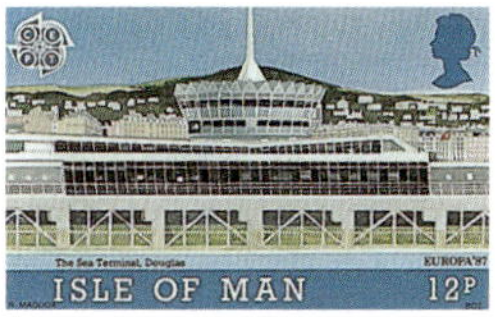

321 Sea Terminal, Douglas

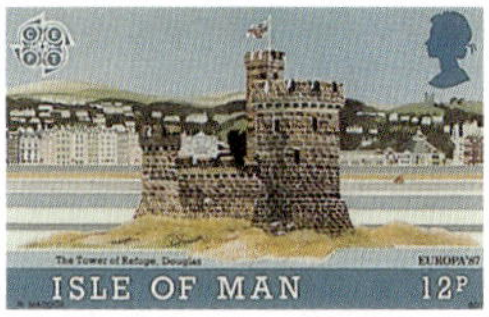

322 Tower of Refuge, Douglas

323 Gaiety Theatre, Douglas

324 Villa Marina, Douglas

Europa. Architecture

(Des R. Maddox. Litho B.D.T.)

1987 (29 Apr). Perf 13½ (C).

344	**321**	12p. multicoloured	45	15
		a. Horiz pair. Nos. 344/5	90	1·70
345	**322**	12p. multicoloured	45	15
346	**323**	22p. multicoloured	65	25
		a. Horiz pair. Nos. 346/7	1·50	2·50
347	**324**	22p. multicoloured	65	25
344/7 *Set of 4*			2·20	3·50
First Day Cover				2·00
Presentation Pack			2·50	

Plate Nos.: Both values 1A, 1B (each ×5).
Sheets: 10 (2×5). The two designs for each value printed together, *se-tenant*, in horizontal pairs throughout the sheets.
Imprint: Central, right-hand margin.
Withdrawn: 28.4.88.

325 Supercharged BMW 500cc, 1939

326 Manx Kneeler Norton 350cc, 1953

327 MV Agusta 500cc 4, 1956

328 Moto Guzzi 500cc V8, 1957

329 Honda 250cc 6, 1967

80th Anniversary of Tourist Trophy Motor-cycle Races

(Des B. Dix. Litho Cartor)

1987 (27 May). Perf 13½×13 (C).

348	**325**	12p. multicoloured	45	25
349	**326**	15p. multicoloured	50	35
350	**327**	29p. multicoloured	90	70
351	**328**	31p. multicoloured	90	75
352	**329**	34p. multicoloured	1·00	90
348/52 *Set of 5*			2·75	2·75
First Day Cover				4·00
Presentation Pack			4·00	
Stamp Cards (Set of 5)			3·25	4·00
Set of 5 Gutter Pairs			7·00	
MS353 150×140 mm. Nos. 348/52. Perf 14×13½ (C)			3·00	3·50
Souvenir Folder				6·00

Nos. 348/53 also commemorate the centenary of the St. John Ambulance Brigade and the miniature sheet also carries the logo of 'Capex '87' International Stamp Exhibition, Toronto on its margin.

Plate Nos.: 12p., 15p., 29p., 31p., 34p. 1A, 1B, 1C, 1D (each ×4); miniature sheet 1A (×4).
Sheets: 40 (2 panes 5×4).
Imprint: Right-hand corner, bottom margin of each pane (sheets) or bottom, right-hand margin (miniature sheet).
Withdrawn: 11.6.88.

330 Fuchsia and Wild Roses

331 Field Scabious and Ragwort

332 Wood Anemone and Celandine

333 Violets and Primroses

Wild Flowers

(Des Nancy Corkish. Litho Enschedé)

1987 (9 Sept). Perf 14½×13 (C).

354	**330**	16p. multicoloured	50	30
355	**331**	29p. multicoloured	90	80
356	**332**	31p. multicoloured	90	1·00
357	**333**	34p. multicoloured	1·00	1·20
354/7 *Set of 4*			3·00	3·00
First Day Cover				3·00
Presentation Pack			4·00	

Plate Nos.: All values 1A, 1B (each ×4).
Sheets: 20 (5×4).
Imprint: Right-hand corner, bottom margin.
Withdrawn: 8.9.88.

334 Stirring the Christmas Pudding

335 Bringing Home the Christmas Tree

336 Decorating the Christmas Tree

Christmas. Victorian Scenes

(Des Colleen Corlett. Litho Questa)

1987 (16 Oct). Perf 14 (C).

358	**334**	12p. multicoloured	40	35
359	**335**	15p. multicoloured	50	55
		a. Black printed triple	£500	
360	**336**	31p. multicoloured	90	90
358/60 *Set of 3*			1·60	1·60
First Day Cover				2·10
Presentation Pack			2·50	
Set of 3 Gutter Pairs			3·25	

Plate Nos.: All values 1A, 1B, 1C, 1D (each ×4).
Sheets: 40 (2 panes 4×5).
Imprint: Right-hand corner, bottom margin of each pane.
Withdrawn: 15.10.88.

Year Pack 1987

1987 (16 Oct). Comprises Nos. 334/52 and 354/60.

Year Pack	31·00

Withdrawn: 31.12.88.

Post Office Yearbook

1987 (Dec). Comprises Nos. 334/43, 344/7 in complete sheets, and **MS**353/60 in slipcase.

Yearbook	40·00

Sold out: 5.91.

337 Russell Brookes in Vauxhall Opel (Manx Rally winner, 1985)

338 Ari Vatanen in Ford Escort RS2000 Mk 1 (Manx Rally winner, 1976)

339 Terry Smith in Repco March 761 (Hill Climb winner, 1980)

340 Nigel Mansell in Williams/Honda FW1B F1 (British Grand Prix winner, 1986 and 1987)

Motor Sport

(Des C. Abbott. Litho Enschedé)

1988 (10 Feb). Perf 13½×14½ (C).

361	**337**	13p. multicoloured	75	35
362	**338**	26p. multicoloured	1·20	1·20
		a. *Black* printed double	£500	
363	**339**	31p. multicoloured	1·40	1·50
364	**340**	34p. multicoloured	1·60	1·70
361/4 *Set of 4*			4·50	4·50
First Day Cover				5·00
Presentation Pack			4·75	

Plate Nos.: All values 1A, 1B (each ×4).
Sheets: 10 (2×5).
Imprint: Central, right-hand margin.
Withdrawn: 9.2.89.

341 Horse Tram Terminus, Douglas Bay Tramway

342 Snaefell Mountain Railway

343 Marine Drive Tramway

343a Douglas Cable Tramway

344 Douglas Head Incline Railway

345 Douglas and Laxey Coast Electric Tramway Car at Maughold Head

346 Douglas Cable Tramway

347 Manx Northern Railway No. 4, *Caledonia*, at Gob-y-Deigan

348 Laxey Mine Railway Lewin Locomotive *Ant*

349 Port Erin Breakwater Tramway Locomotive *Henry B. Loch*

350 Ramsey Harbour Tramway

351 Locomotive No. 7, *Tynwald*, on Foxdale Line

351a T.P.O. Special leaving Douglas, 3 July 1991

352 Baldwin Reservoir Tramway Steam Locomotive No. 1, *Injebreck*

353 I.M.R. No. 13, *Kissack*, near St. Johns

353a Manx Northern Railway No. 4, *Caledonia*, at Gob-y-Deigan

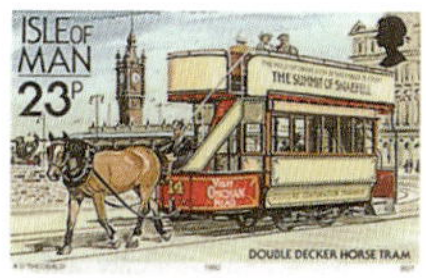

353b Double-deck Horse Tram, Douglas

354 I.M.R. No. 12, *Hutchinson*, leaving Douglas

355 Groudle Glen Railway Locomotive *Polar Bear*

356 I.M.R. No. 11, *Maitland*, pulling Royal Train, 1963

356a Queen Elizabeth II taking Salute at Trooping the Colour

Manx Railways and Tramways, and Queen's Portrait (£2)

(Des Colleen Corlett (£2), A. Theobald (others). Litho B.D.T. (1p. to 19p., 21p., 23p.), Questa (20p., 25p. to £2))

1988 (10 Feb)–**92**. Perf 13 (1p. to 19p., 21p., 23p.), 14½×15 (20p., 25p. to £1) or 14½ (£2), all comb.

365	**341**	1p. multicoloured (a)	10	10
366	**342**	2p. multicoloured (a)	10	10
367	**343**	3p. multicoloured (a)	10	10
		a. Booklet pane. Nos. 367×2, 370 and 373×2 (b)	3·00	
		b. Booklet pane. Nos. 367×2, 371×2 and 374 (d)	2·50	
367*c*	**343a**	4p. multicoloured (g)	20	10
		ca. Booklet pane. Nos. 367*c*×3, 374 and 377*a*		
		cb. Booklet pane. Nos. 367*c*×3, 374×4 and 377*a*		
368	**344**	5p. multicoloured (a)	20	20
369	**345**	10p. multicoloured (a)	30	30
370	**346**	13p. multicoloured (a)	50	50
		a. Booklet pane. Nos. 370×4 and 373×6 (b)	4·00	

371	**347**	14p. multicoloured (a)	50	50
		a. Booklet pane. Nos. 371×4 and 374×6 (d)	4·00	
372	**348**	15p. multicoloured (af)	50	50
		a. Booklet pane. Nos. 372 and 376×2 (e)	2·75	
		b. Booklet pane. Nos. 372×4 and 376×6 (e)	6·25	
373	**349**	16p. multicoloured (a)	50	50
374	**350**	17p. multicoloured (ag)	50	50
375	**351**	18p. multicoloured (a)	55	55
375*a*	**351a**	18p. multicoloured (h)	70	70
		ab. Booklet pane. Nos. 375*a*×3 and 377*b*×2	4·00	
		ac. Booklet pane. Nos. 375*a*×6 and 377*b*×4	7·00	
376	**352**	19p. multicoloured (af)	60	60
377	**353**	20p. multicoloured (c)	60	60
377*a*	**353a**	21p. multicoloured (g)	60	60
377*b*	**353b**	23p. multicoloured (h)	80	80
378	**354**	25p. multicoloured (c)	60	60
379	**355**	50p. multicoloured (ci)	1·30	1·20
380	**356**	£1 multicoloured (ci)	2·50	2·50
380*a*	**356a**	£2 multicoloured (e)	5·00	5·00
365/80a *Set of 21*			15·00	14·00
First Day Covers (6)				18·00
First Day Covers (se-tenant strips) (5)				18·00
Presentation Packs (4) (ex 4p., 18p. (No. 375*a*), 21p., 23p.)			18·00	
Stamp Cards (1p. to £1 ex 4p., 18p. (No. 375*a*), 21p., 23p.)			8·00	22·00
Souvenir Folder (1p. to £1 ex 4p., 18p. (No. 375*a*), 21p. 23p.)			11·00	

Printings: (a) 10.2.88. Inscribed '1988'; (b) 16.3.88. Inscribed '1988'; (c) 21.9.88. Inscribed '1988'; (d) 16.10.89. Inscribed '1989'; (e) 14.2.90. Inscribed '1990'; (f) 1.3.90. Inscribed '1990'; (g) 9.1.91. Inscribed '1991'; (h) 8.1.92. Inscribed '1992'; (i) 16.11.92. Inscribed '1992'.

Plate Nos.: 20p., 25p., 50p., £1 1A, 1B (each ×4); £2 1A, 1B (each ×5); others 1A, 1B, 1C, 1D (each ×4).

Sheets: 25 (5×5) (£2) or 50 (5×10) (others). In addition to Booklets Nos. SB18/19 and SB21/4 Nos. 367 and 370/4 also come from special booklet sheets of 50 containing either ten examples of the strips of five or five examples of the strips of ten. No. 372*a*, a strip of three, was taken from the top or bottom of the strip of ten, No. 372*b*. The 4p. value was issued in Booklets Nos. SB26/7 and special booklet sheets of 50 containing five vertical strips of No. 367cb, from which No. 367ca could also be obtained, and five extra examples of both Nos. 367c and 377a. In addition to Booklets Nos. SB29/30 No. 375*ac* was also issued in special booklet sheets of 50 from which No. 375ab could also be obtained. Nos. 367c and 377a were also issued in a miniature sheet, No. **MS**484.

Imprints: Left-hand margin (£2) or right-hand corner, bottom margin (others).

Withdrawn: 31.12.93 1p. to £1; 11.1.94 £2.

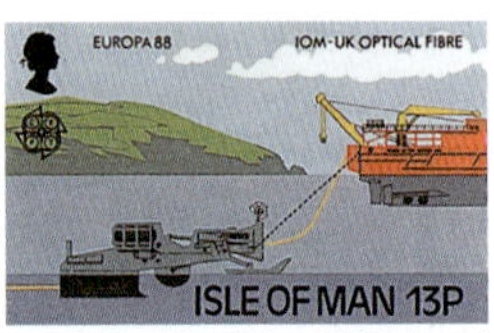

357 Laying Isle of Man–U.K. Submarine Cable

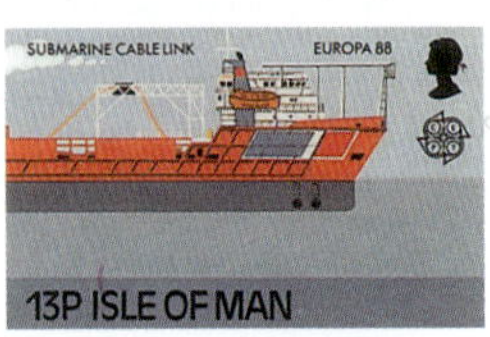

358 *Flex Service 3* (cable ship)

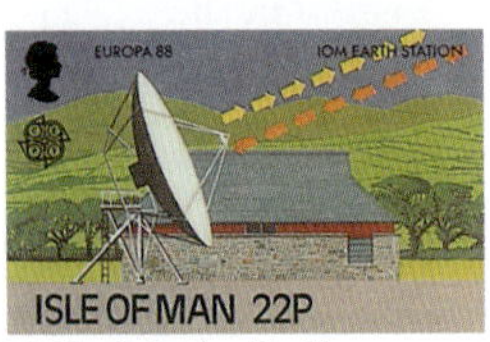

359 Earth Station, Braddan

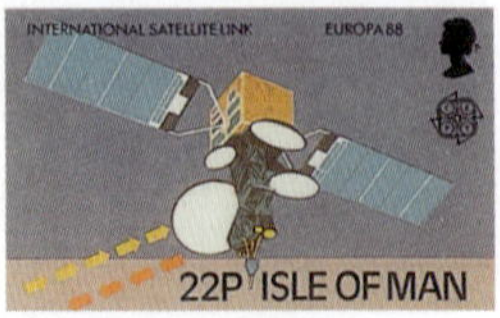

360 'INTELSAT 5' Satellite

Europa. Transport and Communications

(Des C. Abbott. Litho Cartor)

1988 (14 Apr). Perf 14×13½ (C).

381	**357**	13p. multicoloured	50	45
		a. Horiz pair. Nos. 381/2	1·00	90
382	**358**	13p. multicoloured	50	45
383	**359**	22p. multicoloured	75	75
		a. Horiz pair. Nos. 383/4	1·50	1·50
384	**360**	22p. multicoloured	75	75
381/4 *Set of 4*			2·20	2·20
First Day Cover				4·00
Presentation Pack			3·00	

Plate Nos.: Both values 1A, 1B, 1C, 1D (each ×4).

Sheets: 16 (4×4). The two designs of each value printed together, *se-tenant*, in horizontal pairs throughout the sheets.

Imprint: Central, right-hand margin.

Withdrawn: 13.4.89.

361 *Euterpe* (full-rigged ship) off Ramsey, 1863

362 *Vixen* (topsail schooner) leaving Peel for Australia, 1853

363 *Ramsey* (full-rigged ship) off Brisbane, 1870

364 *Star of India* (formerly *Euterpe*) (barque) off San Diego, 1976

Manx Sailing Ships

(Des J. Nicholson. Litho Questa)

1988 (11 May). Perf 14 (C).

385	**361**	16p. multicoloured	45	30
386	**362**	29p. multicoloured	90	90
387	**363**	31p. multicoloured	90	90
388	**364**	34p. multicoloured	1·10	1·10
385/8 *Set of 4*			3·00	3·00
First Day Cover				3·25
Presentation Pack			3·75	
MS389 110×85 mm. Nos. 385 and 388			1·90	2·00
First Day Cover				3·50
Presentation Pack			2·50	

Nos. 386/7 also commemorate the Bicentenary of Australian Settlement.

Plate Nos.: All values 1A, 1B (each ×5).

Sheets: 15 (3×5).

Imprint: Bottom, left-hand margin.

Withdrawn: 10.5.89.

365 'Magellanica'

366 'Pink Cloud'

367 'Leonora'

368 'Satellite'

369 'Preston Guild'

370 'Thalia'

50th Anniversary of British Fuchsia Society

(Des Colleen Corlett. Litho Enschedé)

1988 (21 Sept). Perf 13½×14 (C).

390	**365**	13p. multicoloured	40	25
391	**366**	16p. multicoloured	45	35
392	**367**	22p. multicoloured	65	50
393	**368**	29p. multicoloured	90	90
394	**369**	31p. multicoloured	1·00	1·00
395	**370**	34p. multicoloured	1·10	1·20
390/5	*Set of 6*		4·00	3·50
First Day Cover				3·75
Presentation Pack			5·00	

Plate Nos.: All values 1A, 1B (each ×5).
Sheets: 20 (4×5).
Imprint: Right-hand margin.
Withdrawn: 20.9.89.

371 Long-eared Owl

372 European Robin

373 Grey Partridge

Christmas. Manx Birds

(Des Audrey North. Litho Questa)

1988 (12 Oct). Perf 14 (C).

396	**371**	12p. multicoloured	40	30
397	**372**	15p. multicoloured	60	65
398	**373**	31p. multicoloured	1·20	1·20
396/8	*Set of 3*		2·00	2·00
First Day Cover				2·50
Presentation Pack			2·50	
Set of 3 Gutter Pairs			4·00	

Plate Nos.: All values 1A, 1B, 1C, 1D (each ×5).
Sheets: 40 (2 panes 5×4).
Imprint: Right-hand corner, bottom margin of each pane.
Withdrawn: 11.10.89.

Year Pack 1988

1988 (1 Nov). Comprises Nos. 361/7, 368/75, 376/7, 378/80 and 381/98.

Year Pack	40·00

Withdrawn: 31.12.89.

Post Office Yearbook

1988 (1 Dec). Comprises Nos. 361/7, 368/75, 376/7, 378/80 and 381/98 in slipcase.

Yearbook	45·00

Sold out: By 9.93.

374 Ginger Cat

375 Black and White Cat

376 Tortoiseshell and White Cat

377 Tortoiseshell Cat

Manx Cats

(Des P. Layton. Litho Questa)

1989 (8 Feb). Perf 14 (C).

399	**374**	16p. multicoloured	50	25
400	**375**	27p. multicoloured	90	85
401	**376**	30p. multicoloured	1·20	85
402	**377**	40p. multicoloured	1·50	1·20
399/402	*Set of 4*		3·75	2·75
First Day Cover				3·50
Presentation Pack			4·50	
Stamp Cards (set of 4)			3·00	8·00
Set of 4 Gutter Pairs			7·50	

Plate Nos.: 16p., 27p. 1C, 1D, 1G, 1H (each ×4); 30p., 40p. 1A, 1B, 1E, 1F (each ×4).
Sheets: 40 (2 panes 5×4).
Imprint: Right-hand corner, bottom margin of each pane.
Withdrawn: 7.2.90.

378 Tudric Pewter Clock, c. 1903

379 'Celtic Cross' Watercolour

380 Silver Cup and Cover, 1902–03

381 Gold and Silver Brooches from Liberty's Cymric Range

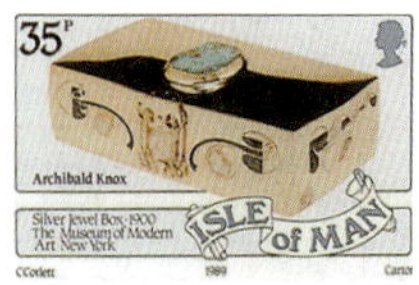

382 Silver Jewel Box, 1900

125th Birth Anniversary of Archibald Knox (artist and designer)

(Des Colleen Corlett. Litho Cartor)

1989 (8 Feb). Perf 13 (C).

403	**378**	13p. multicoloured	20	20
404	**379**	16p. multicoloured	30	25
405	**380**	23p. multicoloured	50	50
406	**381**	32p. multicoloured	1·20	1·00
407	**382**	35p. multicoloured	1·40	1·00
403/7	*Set of 5*		3·00	2·75
First Day Cover				3·00
Presentation Pack			4·00	
Set of 5 Gutter Pairs			6·00	

Plate Nos.: All values 1A, 1B, 1C, 1D (each ×5).
Sheets: 40 (2 panes 4×5) 13p., 16p., 23p.; (2 panes 5×4) others.
Imprint: Bottom, left-hand margin of each pane (13p., 16p., 23p.) or right-hand corner, bottom margin of each pane.
Withdrawn: 7.2.90.

383 William Bligh and Old Church, Onchan

384 Bligh and Loyal Crew cast Adrift

385 Pitcairn Islands 1989 Bicentenary 90c. Stamp

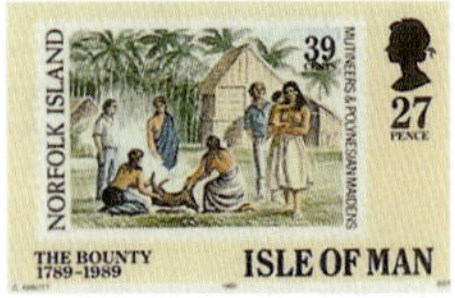

386 Norfolk Island 1989 39c. *Bounty* Stamp

387 Midshipman Peter Heywood and Tahiti

388 H.M.S. *Bounty* anchored off Pitcairn

389 Fletcher Christian and Pitcairn Island

Bicentenary of the Mutiny on the *Bounty*

(Des C. Abbott. Litho B.D.T.)

1989 (28 Apr). Perf 14 (C).

408	**383**	13p. multicoloured	30	20
		a. Booklet pane. Nos. 408/10 and 412/14	4·25	
		b. Booklet pane. Nos. 408/9 and 411/14	4·00	
409	**384**	16p. multicoloured	35	30
410	**385**	23p. multicoloured	1·00	1·00
		a. Booklet pane. Nos. 410/11, each ×3	5·50	
411	**386**	27p. multicoloured	1·00	1·00
412	**387**	30p. multicoloured	50	60
413	**388**	32p. multicoloured	50	60
414	**389**	35p. multicoloured	50	60
408/14 *Set of 7*			3·75	4·00
First Day Cover (ex Nos. 410/11)				4·75
Presentation Pack (ex Nos. 410/11)			5·50	
MS415 110×85 mm. Nos. 410/11 and 414			3·75	3·75
First Day Cover				5·00
		a. Booklet pane. As No. **MS**415, but 147×101 mm with line of roulettes at left	4·00	

Plate Nos.: 13p., 16p., 30p., 32p., 35p. 1A, 1B (each ×4).
Sheets: 20 (4×5) 13p., 16p., 30p., 32p., 35p. The 23p. and 27p. values were only issued in £5.30 booklets and in the miniature sheet. Booklet panes Nos. 408a/b and 410a each contain two vertical rows of three stamps, separated by a central gutter.
Imprint: 13p., 16p., 30p., 32p., 35p. Central, left-hand margin.
Withdrawn: 27.4.90 13, 16, 30, 32, 35p.

390 Skipping and Hopscotch

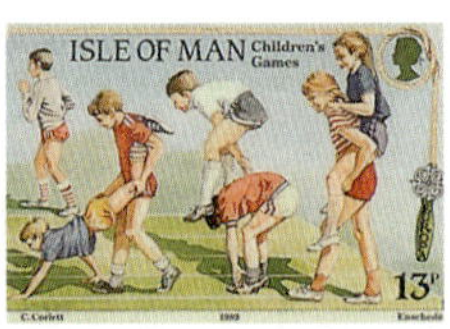

391 Wheelbarrow, Leapfrog and Piggyback

392 Building Model House and Blowing Bubbles

393 Girl and Doll and Doll's House

Europa. Childrens Games

(Des Colleen Corlett. Litho Enschedé)

1989 (17 May). Perf 13½ (C).

416	**390**	13p. multicoloured	45	50
		a. Horiz pair. Nos. 416/17	90	1·00
417	**391**	13p. multicoloured	45	50
418	**392**	23p. multicoloured	70	75
		a. Horiz pair. Nos. 418/19	1·40	1·50
419	**393**	23p. multicoloured	70	75
416/19 *Set of 4*			2·10	2·20
First Day Cover				2·75
Presentation Pack			2·50	

Plate Nos.: Both values 1A, 1B (each ×4).
Sheets: 20 (4×5). The two designs for each value printed together, *se-tenant*, in horizontal pairs throughout the sheets.
Imprint: Central, right-hand margin.
Withdrawn: 16.5.90.

394 Atlantic Puffin

395 Black Guillemot

396 Great Cormorant

397 Black-legged Kittiwake

World Wide Fund for Nature, Sea Birds

(Des W. Oliver. Litho Questa)

1989 (20 Sept). Perf 14 (C).

420	**394**	13p. multicoloured	55	55
		a. Strip of 4. Nos. 420/3	2·20	
		ab. Black ptd double	£375	
421	**395**	13p. multicoloured	55	55
422	**396**	13p. multicoloured	55	55
423	**397**	13p. multicoloured	55	55
420/3 *Set of 4*			2·20	2·20
First Day Cover				2·75
Presentation Pack			2·50	

In addition to a double image of the black printing on the design some examples of No. 420ab also show three additional impressions of the imprint at the foot of each stamp.

Examples of Nos. 420/3 sold at World Stamp Expo 89, held at Washington D.C. between 17 November and 3 December 1989, carried a commemorative inscription on the bottom sheet margin.

Plate Nos.: 1A, 1B, 1C, 1D (each ×4).
Sheets: 16 (4×4). The four designs were printed together, *se-tenant*, in horizontal and vertical strips throughout the sheet which exists with or without perforations across the side margins.
Imprint: Central, right-hand margin.
Withdrawn: 19.9.90.

398 Red Cross Cadets learning Resuscitation

399 Anniversary Logo

400 Signing Geneva Convention, 1864

401 Red Cross Ambulance

402 Henri Dunant (founder)

125th Anniversary of International Red Cross and Centenary of Noble's Hospital, Isle of Man

(Des A. Theobald. Litho Questa)

1989 (16 Oct). Perf 14 (C).

424	**398**	14p. multicoloured	40	30
425	**399**	17p. grey and orange-vermilion	60	35
426	**400**	23p. multicoloured	75	85
427	**401**	30p. multicoloured	1·00	1·10
428	**402**	35p. multicoloured	1·20	1·20
424/8 *Set of 5*			2·75	3·00
First Day Cover				2·75
Presentation Pack			3·50	
Set of 5 Gutter Pairs			5·50	

Plate Nos.: 14p., 30p. 1A, 1B, 1C, 1D (each ×5); 17p. 1A, 1B, 1C, 1D (each ×2); 23p., 35p. 1A, 1B, 1C, 1D (each ×4).
Sheets: 40 (2 panes 5×4).
Imprint: Right-hand corner, bottom margin of each pane.
Withdrawn: 15.10.90.

403 Mother with Baby, Jane Crookall Maternity Home

404 Mother with Child

405 Madonna and Child

406 Baptism, St. Ninian's Church

Christmas. 50th Anniversary of Jane Crookall Maternity Home and 75th Anniversary of St. Ninian's Church, Douglas

(Des Colleen Corlett. Litho Questa)

1989 (16 Oct). Perf 14½ (C).

429	**403**	13p. multicoloured	50	45
430	**404**	16p. multicoloured	60	60
431	**405**	34p. multicoloured	1·10	1·20
432	**406**	37p. multicoloured	1·20	1·40
429/32 *Set of 4*			2·50	3·00
First Day Cover				2·75
Presentation Pack			3·00	
Set of 4 Gutter Pairs			5·00	

Plate Nos.: 13p., 34p. 1A, 1B, 1C, 1D (each ×5); 16p., 37p. 1A, 1B, 1C, 1D (each ×4).
Sheets: 40 (2 panes 4×5).
Imprint: Right-hand corner, bottom margin of each pane.
Withdrawn: 15.10.90.

Year Pack 1989

1989 (16 Oct). Comprises Nos. 399/409 and 412/32.

Year Pack	33·00

Withdrawn: 31.12.90.

Post Office Yearbook

1989 (Nov). Comprises Nos. 399/409, 412/19, 420/3 in complete sheet, and 424/32 in slipcase.

Yearbook	41·00

Sold out: By 9.93.

407 'The Isle of Man Express going up a Gradient'

408 'A way we have in the Isle of Man'

409 'Douglas – waiting for the Male Boat'

410 'The Last Toast Rack Home, Douglas Parade'

411 'The Last Isle of Man Boat'

Isle of Man Edwardian Postcards

(Des D. Swinton. Litho B.D.T.)

1990 (14 Feb). Perf 14 (C).

433	**407**	15p. multicoloured	35	35
434	**408**	19p. multicoloured	60	50
435	**409**	32p. multicoloured	1·10	1·10
436	**410**	34p. multicoloured	1·50	1·50
437	**411**	37p. multicoloured	1·60	1·60
433/7 *Set of 5*			4·50	4·50
First Day Cover				4·50
Presentation Pack			5·50	
Stamp Cards (set of 5)			3·00	6·50
Set of 5 Gutter Pairs			9·00	

Plate Nos.: All values 1A, 1B, 1C, 1D (each ×4).
Sheets: 40 (2 panes 5×4).
Imprint: Right-hand corner, bottom margin of each pane.
Withdrawn: 13.2.91.

412 Modern Postman

413 Ramsey Post Office, 1990

414 Postman, 1890

415 Douglas Post Office, 1890

Europa. Post Office Buildings

(Des A. Kellett. Litho Cartor)

1990 (18 Apr). Perf 13½ (C).

No.	Type	Description	Unused	Used
438	**412**	15p. multicoloured	55	20
		a. Horiz pair. Nos. 438/9	1·10	1·10
439	**413**	15p. multicoloured	55	20
440	**414**	24p. multicoloured	90	25
		a. Horiz pair. Nos. 440/1	1·90	1·75
441	**415**	24p. multicoloured	90	25
438/41 *Set of 4*			2·75	2·40
First Day Cover				3·00
Presentation Pack			3·25	

Plate Nos.: Both values 1A, 1B (each ×4).
Sheets: 20 (4×5). The two designs for each value printed together, *se-tenant*, in horizontal pairs throughout the sheets.
Withdrawn 17.4.91.

416 Penny Black

417 Wyon Medal, 1837

418 Wyon's Stamp Essay

419 Perkins Bacon Engine-turned Essay, 1839

420 Twopence Blue, 1840

421 Marginal Block of Four Penny Blacks

150th Anniversary of the Penny Black

(Des Colleen Corlett. Eng Inge Madlé (No. **MS**447). Recess and litho (No. **MS**447) or litho (others) Enschedé)

1990 (3 May). Perf 14×13½ (C).

No.	Type	Description	Unused	Used
442	**416**	1p. black, buff and gold	15	15
		a. Sheetlet. Horiz strip of 5. Nos. 442/6	3·00	
		b. Sheetlet. No. 442×25	2·20	
		c. Booklet pane. No. 442×8 with margins all round	1·10	
443	**417**	19p. gold, black and buff	60	50
		a. Booklet pane. Nos. 443/6×2 with margins all round	6·00	
444	**418**	32p. multicoloured	1·20	1·10
445	**419**	34p. multicoloured	1·40	1·10
446	**420**	37p. multicoloured	1·50	1·10
442/6 *Set of 5*			3·00	3·00
First Day Cover				5·50
Presentation Pack			3·50	
MS447 100×71 mm. **421** £1 black, gold and buff			3·00	3·50
		a. Booklet pane. As No. **MS**447, but 115×75 mm with line of roulettes at left	3·00	
First Day Cover				4·75
Presentation Pack			3·75	

Sheetlet No. 442a was reissued on 24 August 1990 overprinted 'From STAMP WORLD LONDON '90 to NEW ZEALAND 1990' for sale at the New Zealand exhibition.

The Penny Black stamps shown on Nos. 442b/c each have different corner letters at foot. The sheetlet of 25 was issued in conjunction with a special postal concession which allowed hand-addressed personal mail for the island to be posted for 1p. between 10 am and 12 noon on 6 May 1990.

No. **MS**447 also commemorates 'Stamp World London '90' International Stamp Exhibition, London.

Plate Nos.: No. 442b, 1A, 1B (each ×3).
Sheets: 5 (5×1) containing Nos. 442/6 *se-tenant*, or 25 (5×5) No. 442 only.
Imprint: No. 442a. Bottom margin, right-hand corner. No. 442b. Central, bottom margin.
Withdrawn: 2.5.91.

422 Queen Elizabeth the Queen Mother

90th Birthday of Queen Elizabeth the Queen Mother

(Des Colleen Corlett. Litho B.D.T.)

1990 (4 Aug). Perf 13×13½ (C).

No.	Type	Description	Unused	Used
448	**442**	90p. multicoloured	3·00	3·00
First Day Cover				3·75
Presentation Pack			4·00	

Plate Nos.: 1A, 1B (each ×5).
Sheets: 20 (5×4) containing ten stamps and ten *se-tenant* inscribed labels.
Imprint: Central, right-hand margin.
Withdrawn: 3.8.91.

423 Hawker Hurricane Mk1, Bristol Type 142 Blenheim Mk 1 and Home Defence

424 Supermarine Spitfire, Westland Lysander Mk I and Vickers Walrus with Launch

425 Rearming Hawker Hurricane Mk I Fighters

426 Ops Room and Scramble

427 Civil Defence Personnel

428 Anti-aircraft Battery

50th Anniversary of the Battle of Britain

(Des A. Theobald. Litho Questa)

1990 (5 Sept). Perf 14 (C).

449	**423**	15p. multicoloured	35	20
		a. Horiz pair. Nos. 449/50	70	70
450	**424**	15p. multicoloured	35	20
451	**425**	24p. multicoloured	80	25
		a. Horiz pair. Nos. 451/2	1·60	1·60
452	**426**	24p. multicoloured	80	25
453	**427**	29p. multicoloured	1·00	30
		a. Horiz pair. Nos. 453/4	2·00	2·00
454	**428**	29p. multicoloured	1·00	30
449/54 Set of 6			4·00	4·00
First Day Cover				5·00
Presentation Pack			4·75	
Souvenir Folder (complete sheets)			18·00	

Plate Nos.: All values 1A, 1B (each ×4).
Sheets: 8 (2×4). The two designs of each value were printed together, *se-tenant*, in horizontal pairs throughout the sheet, each showing composite panel at foot of Dover cliffs (15p.), Weald landscape (24p.) or London skyline (29p.).
Withdrawn: 4.9.91.

429 Churchill with Freedom of Douglas Casket

430 Churchill and London Blitz

431 Churchill and Searchlights over Westminster

432 Chuchill with Hawker Hurricane Mk I Fighters

25th Death Anniversary of Sir Winston Churchill

(Des C. Abbott. Litho Cartor)

1990 (5 Sept). Perf 13½ (C).

455	**429**	19p. multicoloured	45	45
456	**430**	32p. multicoloured	1·00	1·00
457	**431**	34p. multicoloured	1·20	1·20
458	**432**	37p. multicoloured	1·20	1·20
455/8 Set of 4			3·50	3·50
First Day Cover				4·00
Presentation Pack			4·00	
Set of 4 Gutter Pairs			7·00	

Plate Nos.: All values 1A, 1B, 1C, 1D (each ×5).
Sheets: 40 (2 panes 5×4).
Imprint: Right-hand corner, bottom margin of each pane.
Withdrawn: 4.9.91.

433 Boy on Toboggan and Girl posting Letter

434 Girl on Toboggan and Skaters

435 Boy with Snowman

436 Children throwing Snowballs

Christmas

(Des C. Abbott. Litho B.D.T.)

1990 (10 Oct). Perf 13×13½ (C).

459	**433**	14p. multicoloured	40	40
460	**434**	18p. multicoloured	50	50
461	**435**	34p. multicoloured	1·00	1·00
462	**436**	37p. multicoloured	1·20	1·20
459/62 Set of 4			2·75	2·75
First Day Cover				3·50
Presentation Pack			3·75	
Set of 4 Gutter Pairs			5·50	
MS463 123×55 mm. As Nos. 459/62 but face values in black			3·00	3·75
		a. Blue (inscriptions) omitted	£3250	£2000
First Day Cover				3·50
Presentation Pack			3·75	

Plate Nos.: 18p. 1A, 1B, 1C, 1D (each ×5); others 1A, 1B, 1C, 1D (each ×6).
Sheets: 40 (2 panes 4×5).
Imprint: Right-hand corner, bottom margin of each pane.
Withdrawn: 9.10.91.

Year Pack 1990

1990 (10 Oct). Comprises Nos. 380a and 433/63.

Year Pack ... 41·00

Withdrawn: 31.12.91.

Post Office Yearbook

1990 (Dec). Comprises Nos. 380a, 433/41, 422a/b, **MS**447 and 448/63 in slipcase.

Yearbook ... 50·00

Sold out: By 9.93.

437 Henry Bloom Noble and Orphans (Marshall Wane)

438 Douglas (Frederick Frith)

439 Studio Portrait of Three Children (Hilda Newby)

440 Cashtal yn Ard (Christopher Killip)

441 Peel Castle (Colleen Corlett)

Manx Photography

(Des Colleen Corlett. Litho Walsall)

1991 (9 Jan). Perf 14 (C).

464	**437**	17p. blackish brn, pale brownish grey and black	35	35
465	**438**	21p. deep brown and ochre	50	50
466	**439**	26p. blackish brown, stone and brownish black	65	65
467	**440**	31p. agate, pale grey-brown & blk	90	90
468	**441**	40p. multicoloured	1·10	1·10
464/8 Set of 5			3·25	3·25
First Day Cover				3·50
Presentation Pack			3·75	

Plate Nos: 21p. 1A–1A, 1B–AB, 40p. 1A, 1B (each ×4); others 1A, 1B (each ×3).
Sheets: 20 (4×5).
Imprint: Central, right-hand margin.
Withdrawn: 8.1.92.

442 Lifeboat, *Sir William Hillary*, Douglas

443 *Osman Gabriel*, Port Erin

444 *Ann and James Ritchie*, Ramsey

445 *The Gough Ritchie*, Port St. Mary

446 *John Batstone*, Peel

Manx Lifeboats

(Des A. Peck. Litho Questa)

1991 (13 Feb). Perf 14 (C).

469	**442**	17p. multicoloured	45	45
470	**443**	21p. multicoloured	55	55
		a. Black ptg double	£225	
471	**444**	26p. multicoloured	90	90
472	**445**	31p. multicoloured	1·20	1·20
473	**446**	37p. multicoloured	1·40	1·40
469/73 *Set of 5*			3·00	4·00
First Day Cover				4·50
Presentation Pack			4·50	
Set of 5 Gutter Pairs			6·00	

No. 469 is inscribed 'HILARY' and No. 471 'JAMES & ANN RITCHIE', both in error.

Plate Nos.: All values 1A, 1B, 1C, 1D (each ×4).
Sheets: 40 (2 panes 5×4).
Imprint: Right-hand corner, bottom margin of each pane.
Withdrawn: 12.2.92.

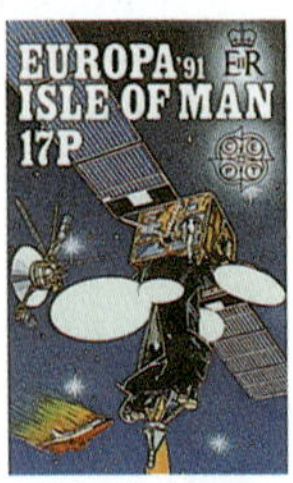

447 'Intelsat' Communications Satellite

448 'Ariane' Rocket Launch and Fishing Boats in Douglas Harbour

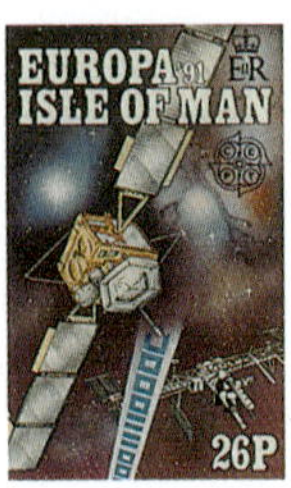

449 Weather Satellite and Space Station

450 Ronaldsway Airport, Manx Radio Transmitter and Space Shuttle Launch

Europa. Europe in Space

(Des D. Miller. Litho B.D.T.)

1991 (24 Apr). Perf 14 (C).

474	**447**	17p. multicoloured	70	20
		a. Vert pair. Nos. 474/5	1·40	1·40
475	**448**	17p. multicoloured	70	20
476	**449**	26p. multicoloured	1·00	30
		a. Vert pair. Nos. 476/7	2·00	2·00
477	**450**	26p. multicoloured	1·00	30
474/7 *Set of 4*			3·00	3·00
First Day Cover				3·75
Presentation Pack			3·75	

Plate Nos.: Both values 1A, 1B (each ×4).
Sheets: 20 (5×4). The two designs for each value printed together, *se-tenant*, in vertical pairs throughout the sheets, each pair forming a composite design.
Imprint: Central, right-hand margin.
Withdrawn: 23.4.92.

451 Oliver Godfrey with Indian 500cc at Start, 1911

452 Freddie Dixon on Douglas 'Banking' Sidecar, 1923

453 Bill Ivy on Yamaha 125cc, 1968

454 Giacomo Agostini on MV Agusta 500cc, 1972

455 Joey Dunlop on RVF Honda 750cc, 1985

80th Anniversary of Tourist Trophy Mountain Course

(Des A. Theobald. Litho Enschedé)

1991 (30 May). Perf 14½×13 (C).

478	**451**	17p. multicoloured	50	40
479	**452**	21p. multicoloured	65	60
480	**453**	26p. multicoloured	80	80
481	**454**	31p. multicoloured	1·20	1·10
482	**455**	37p. multicoloured	1·50	1·50
478/82 *Set of 5*			4·25	4·00
First Day Cover				4·50
Presentation Pack			4·75	
Stamp Cards (set of 5)			3·00	6·00
Set of 5 Gutter Pairs			8·50	
MS483 149×144 mm. Nos. 478/82			4·00	4·00
First Day Cover				9·00
Souvenir Folder			5·50	

No. **MS**483 was reissued on 16 November 1991 overprinted for the Phila Nippon exhibition, Japan.

Plate Nos.: All values 1A, 1B, 1C, 1D (each ×4).
Sheets: 40 (2 panes 5×4).
Imprint: Right-hand corner, bottom margin of each pane.
Withdrawn: 29.5.92.

Ninth Conference of Commonwealth Postal Administrations, Douglas

(Des Colleen Corlett. Litho B.D.T.)

1991 (1 July). Perf 13 (C).

MS484 119×77 mm. Nos. 367c and 377a, each x2	1·90	2·00
First Day Cover		2·50
Presentation Pack	2·75	

Withdrawn: 30.6.92.

456 Laxey Hand-cart, 1920

457 Horse-drawn Steamer, Douglas, 1909

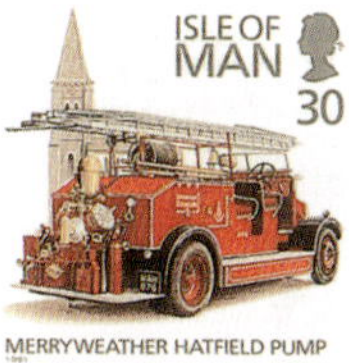

458 Merryweather Hatfield Pump, 1936

459 Dennis F8 Pumping Appliance, Peel, 1953

460 Volvo Turntable Ladder, Douglas, 1989

Fire Engines

(Des C. Abbott. Litho Questa)

1991 (18 Sept). Perf 14½ (C).

485	**456**	17p. multicoloured	45	40
486	**457**	21p. multicoloured	65	65
487	**458**	30p. multicoloured	85	90
488	**459**	33p. multicoloured	1·20	1·20
489	**460**	37p. multicoloured	1·40	1·50
485/9 *Set of 5*			4·25	4·25
First Day Cover				4·75
Presentation Pack			4·75	
Set of 5 Gutter Pairs			8·50	

Plate Nos.: All values 1A, 1B, 1C, 1D (each ×5).
Sheets: 40 (2 panes 4×5).
Imprint: Central, gutter margin.
Withdrawn: 17.9.92.

461 Mute Swans, Douglas Harbour

462 Black Swans, Curraghs Wildlife Park

463 Whooper Swans, Bishop's Dub, Ballaugh

464 Tundra ('Bewick's') Swans, Eairy Dam, Foxdale

465 Coscoroba Swans, Curraghs Wildlife Park

466 Whopper ('Trumpeter') Swans, Curraghs Wildlife Park

Swans

(Des Colleen Corlett. Litho Cartor)

1991 (18 Sept). Perf 13 (C).

490	**461**	17p. multicoloured	40	20
		a. Horiz pair. Nos. 490/1	80	1·00
491	**462**	17p. multicoloured	40	20
492	**463**	26p. multicoloured	1·10	30
		a. Horiz pair. Nos. 492/3	2·10	2·20
493	**464**	26p. multicoloured	1·10	30
494	**465**	37p. multicoloured	1·20	40
		a. Horiz pair. Nos. 494/5	2·40	2·75
		ab. Black ptg double		
495	**466**	37p. multicoloured	1·20	40
490/5 *Set of 6*			4·50	5·00
First Day Cover				6·00
Presentation Pack			5·25	

Plate Nos: All values 1A, 1B (each ×4).
Sheets: 20 (4×5). The two designs of each value were printed together, *se-tenant*, in horizontal pairs throughout the sheets, with the backgrounds forming composite designs.
Imprint: Central, bottom margin.
Withdrawn: 17.9.92.

467 The Three Kings

468 Mary with Manger

469 Shepherds with Sheep

470 Choir of Angels

Christmas. Paper Sculptures

(Des D. Swinton. Litho Walsall)

1991 (14 Oct).

(a) Sheet stamps. Perf 14×14½ (C)

496	**467**	16p. multicoloured	45	35
497	**468**	20p. multicoloured	65	70
498	**469**	26p. multicoloured	85	85
499	**470**	37p. multicoloured	1·10	1·10
496/9 *Set of 4*			2·75	2·50
First Day Cover				3·25
Presentation Pack			3·50	

Plate Nos: All values 1A, 1B, 1C, 1D (each ×4).
Sheets: 40 (2 panes 4×5).
Imprint: Central, gutter margin.
Withdrawn: 13.10.92.

(b) Booklet stamps. Self-adhesive. Stamps die-cut

500	**467**	16p. multicoloured	60	60
		a. Booklet pane. Nos. 500×8 and 501×4	7·50	
501	**468**	20p. multicoloured	1·20	1·20

Year Pack 1991

1991 (14 Oct). Comprises Nos. 367c, 377a, 464/82 and **MS**484/99.

Year Pack	40·00

Withdrawn: 31.12.92.

Post Office Yearbook

1991 (14 Oct). Comprises Nos. 367c, 377a, 464/82 and **MS**484/99.

Yearbook	45·00

Withdrawn: 30.11.94.

471 North African and Italian Campaigns, 1942–43

472 D-Day, 1944

473 Arnhem, 1944

474 Rhine Crossing, 1945

475 Operations in Near, Middle and Far East, 1945–68

476 Liberation of Falkland Islands, 1982

50th Anniversary of Parachute Regiment

(Des A. Theobald. Litho Questa)

1992 (6 Feb). Perf 14 (C).

502	**471**	23p. multicoloured	70	25
		a. Horiz pair. Nos. 502/3	1·50	1·50
503	**472**	23p. multicoloured	70	25
504	**473**	28p. multicoloured	80	30
		a. Horiz pair. Nos. 504/5	1·60	1·70
505	**474**	28p. multicoloured	80	30
506	**475**	39p. multicoloured	1·20	40
		a. Horiz pair. Nos. 506/7	2·50	2·75
507	**476**	39p. multicoloured	1·20	40
502/7 *Set of 6*			5·00	5·00
First Day Cover				6·00
Presentation Pack			6·00	
Souvenir Folder (complete sheets)			24·00	

Plate Nos: All values 1A, 1B (each ×5).
Sheets: 8 (2×4). The two designs of each value were printed together, *se-tenant*, in horizontal pairs throughout the sheets.
Imprint: Top, left-hand margin.
Withdrawn: 5.2.93.

477 Quenn Elizabeth II at Coronation, 1953

478 Queen visiting Isle of Man, 1979

479 Queen in Evening Dress

480 Queen visiting Isle of Man, 1989

481 Queen arriving for Film Premiere, 1990

40th Anniversary of Accession

(Des D. Miller. Litho B.D.T.)

1992 (6 Feb). Perf 14 (C).

508	**477**	18p. multicoloured	45	40
509	**478**	23p. multicoloured	60	60
510	**479**	28p. multicoloured	70	70
511	**480**	33p. multicoloured	1·20	1·40
512	**481**	39p. multicoloured	1·40	1·40
508/12 *Set of 5*			4·00	4·00
First Day Cover				5·00
Presentation Pack			5·00	

Plate Nos: All values 1A, 1B (each ×5).
Sheets: 20 (5×4).
Imprint: Central, bottom margin.
Withdrawn: 5.2.93.

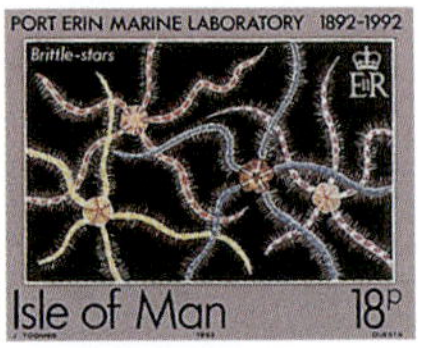

482 Brittle-stars

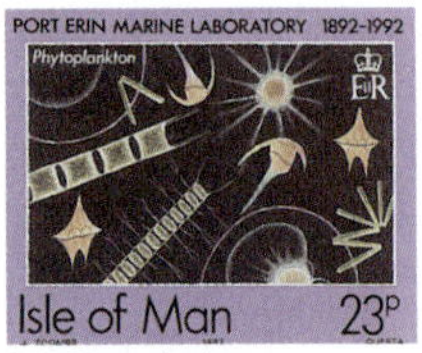

483 Phytoplankton

484 Atlantic Herring

485 Great Scallop

486 Dahlia Anemone and Delesseria

Centenary of Port Erin Marine Laboratory

(Des Jennifer Toombs. Litho Questa)

1992 (16 Apr). Perf 14×14½ (C).

513	**482**	18p. multicoloured	40	35
514	**483**	23p. multicoloured	60	55
515	**484**	28p. multicoloured	60	60
516	**485**	33p. multicoloured	1·20	1·20
517	**486**	39p. multicoloured	1·50	1·50
513/17 *Set of 5*			4·00	4·00
First Day Cover				4·50
Presentation Pack			4·75	
Set of 5 Gutter Pairs			8·00	

Plate Nos.: All values 1A, 1B, 1C, 1D (each ×4).
Sheets: 40 (2 panes 5×4).
Imprint: Top right-hand side, gutter margin.
Withdrawn: 15.4.93.

487 The Pilgrim Fathers embarking at Delfshaven

488 *Speedwell* leaving Delfshaven

489 *'Mayflower and Speedwell* at Dartmouth' **490** (L. Wilcox)

Europa. 500th Anniversary of Discovery of America by Columbus

(Des C. Abbott. Litho Enschedé)

1992 (16 Apr). Perf 14×13½ (C).

518	**487**	18p. multicoloured	40	20
		a. Horiz pair. Nos. 518/19	1·60	1·60
519	**488**	18p. multicoloured	40	30
520	**489**	28p. multicoloured	75	30
		a. Horiz pair. Nos. 520/1	3·50	3·50
521	**490**	28p. multicoloured	75	30
518/21 *Set of 4*			4·50	4·50
First Day Cover				5·00
Presentation Pack			5·25	

Plate Nos.: Both values 1A, 1B (each ×5).
Sheets: 20 (4×5). The two designs of each value were printed together, *se-tenant*, in horizontal pairs throughout the sheets, each pair forming a composite design.
Imprint: Central, bottom margin.
Withdrawn: 15.4.93.

491 Central Pacific Locomotive *Jupiter*, 1869

492 Union Pacific Locomotive No. 119, 1869

493 Union Pacific Locomotive No. 844, 1992

494 Union Pacific Locomotive No. 3985, 1992

495 Golden Spike Ceremony, 10 May 1869 (*Illustration reduced. Actual size* 105×73 mm)

Construction of Union Pacific Railroad, 1866–69

(Des A. Peck. Litho Enschedé)

1992 (22 May). Perf 13½×14 (C).

522	**491**	33p. multicoloured	90	35
		a. Horiz pair. Nos. 522/3 plus label	2·50	2·50
		b. Booklet pane. Nos. 522/5×2 and **MS**526	12·00	
523	**492**	33p. multicoloured	90	35
524	**493**	39p. multicoloured	1·20	40
		a. Horiz pair. Nos. 524/5 plus label	3·00	3·00
525	**494**	39p. multicoloured	1·20	40
522/5 *Set of 4*			4·00	4·50
First Day Cover				5·00
Presentation Pack			5·50	
Souvenir Folder (sheets of 10)			22·00	
Stamp Cards (set of 4)			3·25	
MS526 105×73 mm. **495** £1.50, mult			3·75	4·50
First Day Cover				6·00
Presentation Pack			5·50	
Stamp Card			70	

Nos. 522b and **MS**526 also commemorated the 'World Columbian Stamp Expo'.

Booklet pane No. 522b contains two blocks of four of Nos. 522/5 with No. **MS**526 between them. Miniature sheets from the booklet show a white margin and line of roulettes at left and right. In the blocks of four each horizontal pair is separated by a half stamp-size label.

Plate Nos.: Both values 1A, 1B (each ×4).
Sheets: 10 (2×5). The two designs for each value were printed together in horizontal pairs separated by a half stamp-size label showing Union Pacific emblem or portraits of Dan and Jack Casement (railroad contractors).
Imprint: Central, right-hand margin.
Withdrawn: 21.5.93.

496 *King Orry V* in Douglas Harbour

497 Castletown

498 Port St. Mary

499 Ramsey

Manx Harbours

(Des Colleen Corlett. Litho Walsall)

1992 (18 Sept). Perf 14½×14 (C).

527	**496**	18p. multicoloured	45	45
528	**497**	23p. multicoloured	55	55
529	**498**	37p. multicoloured	1·20	1·20
530	**499**	40p. multicoloured	1·40	1·40
527/30 *Set of 4*			3·25	3·25
First Day Cover				3·75
Presentation Pack			4·00	

Plate Nos.: All values 1A, 1B (each ×4).
Sheets: 10 (2×5).
Imprint: Right-hand corner, bottom margin.
Withdrawn: 17.9.93.

500 *King Orry V* (ex *Saint Eloi*) in 1972 and 1992 (*Illustration reduced. Actual size* 111×68 mm)

'Genova '92' International Thematic Stamp Exhibition

(Des Colleen Corlett. Litho Walsall)

1992 (18 Sept). Sheet 111×68 mm. Perf 14½×14 (C).

MS531 **500** 18p, £1 multicoloured		3·25	3·50
First Day Cover			3·75
Presentation Pack		3·75	

Withdrawn: 17.9.93.

501 Window, St. German's Cathedral, Peel

502 Reredos, St. Matthew the Apostle, Douglas

503 Window, St. George's, Douglas

504 Reredos, St. Mary of the Isle Catholic Church, Douglas

505 Window, Trinity Methodist Church, Douglas

Christmas. Manx Churches

(Des Colleen Corlett, Litho Questa)

1992 (13 Oct). Perf 14½ (C).

532	**501**	17p. multicoloured	45	40
533	**502**	22p. multicoloured	65	65
534	**503**	28p. multicoloured	80	80
535	**504**	37p. multicoloured	95	95
536	**505**	40p. multicoloured	1·00	1·00
		a. Gold ptg double		
532/6 *Set of 5*			3·50	3·50
First Day Cover				4·00
Presentation Pack			4·00	
Set of 5 Gutter Pairs			7·00	

Plate Nos.: 17p., 22p. 1A, 1B, 1C, 1D (each×5); others 1A, 1B (each×5).
Sheets: 40 (2 panes 4 ×5).
Imprint: Right-hand corner, bottom margin of each pane.
Withdrawn: 12.10.93.

Year Pack 1992

1992 (13 Oct). Comprises Nos. 502/36.
Year Pack .... 40·00
Withdrawn: 31.12.93.

Post Office Yearbook

1992 (13 Oct). Comprises Nos. 375a, 377b, 502/36 and D25.
Yearbook .... 45·00
Withdrawn: 30.11.94.

506 Mansell on Lap of Honour, British Grand Prix, 1992

507 Mansell in French Grand Prix, 1992

Nigel Mansell's Victory in Formula 1 World Motor Racing Championship

(Des A. Theobald. Litho Walsall)

1992 (8 Nov). Perf 13½ (C).

537	**506**	20p. multicoloured	80	80
538	**507**	24p. multicoloured	1·00	1·00
537/8 *Set of 2*			1·80	1·80
First Day Cover				2·75
Presentation Pack			2·75	

Plate Nos.: Both values 1A, 1B (each ×4).
Sheets: 50 (5×10).
Imprint: Bottom margin.
Withdrawn: 7.11.93.

508 H.M.S. *Amazon* (frigate)

509 *Fingal* (lighthouse tender)

510 *Sir Winston Churchill* (cadet schooner)

511 *Dar Mlodziezy* (full-rigged cadet ship)

512 *Tynwald I* (paddle-steamer)

513 *Ben Veg* (freighter)

514 *Waverley* (paddle-steamer)

515 Royal Yacht *Britannia*

516 *Francis Drake* (ketch)

517 *Royal Viking Sky* (liner)

518 *Lord Nelson* (cadet barque)

519 *Europa* (liner)

520 *Snaefell V* (ferry) leaving Androssan

520a *Seacat* (catamaran ferry)

521 *Lady of Man I* (ferry) off Ramsey

522 *Mona's Queen II* (paddle ferry) leaving Fleetwood

523 *Queen Elizabeth 2* (liner) and *Mona's Queen V* (ferry) off Liverpool

523a Manx Red Ensign

523b Queen Elizabeth II (hologram)

Ships

(Des A. Theobald (1p. to 27p.), J. Nicholson (30p., 35p., 40p., 50p., £1), Colleen Corlett (£2, £5). Litho Questa (£2), Walsall (£5) (hologram by Applied Holographics), Enschedé others))

1993 (4 Jan)–**97**. Perf 14½ (£2), 14½×14 (£5) or 13½×13 (others), all comb.

539	**508**	1p. multicoloured (a)	10	10
540	**509**	2p. multicoloured (a)	10	10
541	**510**	4p. multicoloured (a)	10	10
		a. Booklet pane. Nos. 541, 544 and 548 each ×2 (g)	5·00	
542	**511**	5p. multicoloured (a)	10	10
543	**512**	20p. multicoloured (ae)	40	25
		a. Booklet pane. Nos. 543×2 and 547×3	3·00	
		b. Booklet pane. Nos. 543×4 and 547×6	6·50	
544	**513**	21p. multicoloured (ag)	50	50
545	**514**	22p. multicoloured (a)	50	50
546	**515**	23p. multicoloured (a)	55	55
547	**516**	24p. multicoloured (ae)	50	35
548	**517**	25p. multicoloured (ag)	60	60
549	**518**	26p. multicoloured (a)	65	65
550	**519**	27p. multicoloured (a)	65	65
551	**520**	30p. multicoloured (b)	75	75
552	**520a**	35p. multicoloured (f)	85	85
553	**521**	40p. multicoloured (b)	1·00	90
554	**522**	50p. multicoloured (b)	1·20	1·10
555	**523**	£1 multicoloured (bg)	2·50	2·40
556	**523a**	£2 multicoloured (c)	3·75	4·00
557	**523b**	£5 multicoloured (d)	10·00	12·00
539/57 *Set of 19*			22·00	23·00
First Day Covers (6)				30·00
Presentation Packs (6)			30·00	
Stamp Cards (Nos. 539/51, 553/5)			8·00	22·00
Souvenir Folder (Nos. 539/51, 553/5)			12·00	

For 4p., 20p. and 24p. in similar designs, but smaller, see Nos. 687/93.

Printings: (a) 4.1.93. Inscribed '1993'; (b) 15.9.93. Inscribed '1993'; (c) 12.1.94. Inscribed '1994'; (d) 5.7.94. Inscribed 1994; (e) 8.2.95. Inscribed '1995'; (f) 11.1. '1996'. Inscribed '1996'; (g) 14.5.97. Inscribed '1997'.

Plate Nos.: £2, £5 1A, 1B (each ×4); others 1A, 1B, 1C, 1D (each ×4).

Sheets: 25 (5×5) (£2), 10 (5×2) (£5) or 50 (5×10) (others). In addition to stamp booklets Nos. 543a/b also come from a special booklet sheet of 50 (5×10) which provides either 10 examples of No. 543a or 5 of 543b. No. 541a comes from a special booklet sheet of 30 (5×6).

Imprint: Central, bottom margin (£2, £5) or right-hand corner, bottom margin (others).

Withdrawn: 30.11.98 1p. to £1; 12.1.99 £2; 5.7.99 £5.

524 No. 1 Motor Car and No. 13 Trailer at Groudle Glen Hotel

525 No. 9 Tunnel Car and No. 19 Trailer at Douglas Bay Hotel

526 No. 19 Motor Car and No. 59 Royal Trailer Special at Douglas Bay

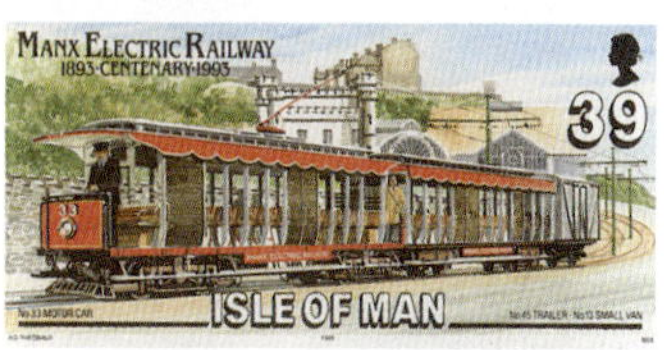

527 No. 33 Motor Car, No. 45 Trailer and No. 13 Van at Derby Castle

Centenary of Manx Electric Railway

(Des A. Theobald. Litho B.D.T.)

1993 (3 Feb). Perf 14 (C).

559	**524**	20p. multicoloured	60	60
		a. Boolet pane. Nos. 559/62	3·50	
560	**525**	24p. multicoloured	90	90
561	**526**	28p. multicoloured	1·00	1·00
562	**527**	39p. multicoloured	1·40	1·40
559/62 *Set of 4*			3·50	3·50
First Day Cover				3·75
Presentation Pack			3·75	

Booklet pane No. 559a exists in four versions, which differ in the order of the stamps within the block of four and in the information printed on the pane margin.

Plate Nos.: All values 1A, 1B (each ×4).

Sheets: 10 (2×5).

Imprint: Central, left-hand margin.
Withdrawn: 2.2.94.

528 'Sir Hall Caine' (statue)

529 'The Brass Bedstead' (painting)

530 Abstract Bronze Sculpture

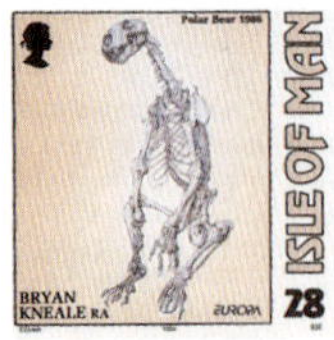

531 'Polar Bear Skeleton' (drawing)

Europa. Contemporary Art by Bryan Kneale

(Des Colleen Corlett. Litho B.D.T.)

1993 (14 Apr). Perf 14 (C).

563	**528**	20p. multicoloured	40	20
		a. Horiz pair. Nos. 563/4	1·20	1·20
564	**529**	20p. multicoloured	40	20
565	**530**	28p. multicoloured	75	30
		a. Horiz pair. Nos. 565/6	2·00	2·00
566	**531**	28p. multicoloured	75	30
563/6 *Set of 4*			3·00	3·00
First Day Cover				3·50
Presentation Pack			3·75	

Plate Nos.: Both values 1A, 1B, 1C (each ×4).
Sheets: 20 (4×5). The two designs for each value printed together, *se-tenant*, in horizontal pairs throughout the sheets.
Imprint: Central, right-hand margin.
Withdrawn: 13.4.94.

532 Graham Oates and Bill Marshall (1933 International Six Day Trial) on Ariel Square Four

533 Sergeant Geoff Duke (1947 Royal Signals Display Team) on Triumph 3T Twin

534 Dennis Parkinson (1953 Senior Manx Grand Prix) on Manx Norton

535 Richard Swallow (1991 Junior Classic MGP) on Aermacchi

536 Steve Colley (1992 Scottish Six Day Trial) on Beta Zero

Manx Motor Cycling Events

(Des C. Abbott. Litho Walsall)

1993 (3 June). Perf 13½×14 (C).

567	**532**	20p. multicoloured	35	35
568	**533**	24p. multicoloured	45	45
569	**534**	28p. multicoloured	70	60
570	**535**	33p. multicoloured	90	90
571	**536**	39p. multicoloured	1·00	95
567/71 *Set of 5*			3·00	3·00
First Day Cover				4·00
Presentation Pack			4·00	
Stamp Cards (set of 5)			3·00	6·00
MS572 165×120 mm. Nos. 567/71			4·50	4·50
Souvenir Folder			4·75	

Plate Nos.: All values 1A, 1B, 1C, 1D (each ×4).
Sheets: 20 (4×5).
Imprint: Right-hand corner, bottom margin.
Withdrawn: 2.6.94.

537 *Inachis io* (Peacock)

538 *Argynnis aglaja* (Dark Green Fritillary)

539 *Cynthia cardui* (Painted Lady)

540 *Celastrina argiolus* (Holly Blue)

541 *Vanessa atalanta* (Red Admiral)

Butterflies

(Des Colleen Corlett. Litho Questa)

1993 (15 Sept). Perf 14½ (C).

573	**537**	24p. multicoloured	75	65
		a. Horiz strip of 5. Nos. 573/7	3·50	
574	**538**	24p. multicoloured	75	65
575	**539**	24p. multicoloured	75	65
576	**540**	24p. multicoloured	75	65
577	**541**	24p. multicoloured	75	65
573/7 *Set of 5*			3·50	3·00
First Day Cover				4·25
Presentation Pack			4·00	

Examples of Nos. 573/7 sold at 'Philakorea '94' and 'Singpex '94' come with commemorative cachets on the bottom margin.

Plate Nos.: 1A, 1B (each ×4).

Sheets: 20 (5×4). The five designs for each value printed together, *se-tenant*, in horizontal strips throughout the sheets.

Imprint: Right-hand corner, bottom margin.

Withdrawn: 14.9.94.

542 Children decorating Christmas Tree

543 Girl with Snowman

544 Boy opening Presents

545 Girl with Teddy Bear

546 Children with Toboggan

Christmas

(Des Christine Haworth. Litho Questa)

1993 (12 Oct). Perf 14 (C).

578	**542**	19p. multicoloured	50	50
579	**543**	23p. multicoloured	60	60
580	**544**	28p. multicoloured	70	70
581	**545**	39p. multicoloured	1·10	1·10
582	**546**	40p. multicoloured	1·10	1·10
578/82 *Set of 5*			3·50	3·50
First Day Cover				4·00
Presentation Pack			4·25	
Set of 5 Gutter Pairs			7·00	

Nos. 578 and 579 were also issued in booklets, SB35 and SB36.

Plate Nos.: All values 1A, 1B, 1C, 1D (each ×4).

Sheets: 40 (2 panes 4×5).

Imprint: Bottom, right-hand margin of each pane.

Withdrawn: 11.10.94.

Year Pack 1993

1993 (12 Oct). Comprises Nos. 539/51, 553/5, 559/71 and 573/82.

Year Pack	32·00

Withdrawn: 31.12.94.

Post Office Yearbook

1993 (12 Oct). Comprises Nos. 539/51, 553/5, 559/71 and 573/82.

Yearbook	40·00

Sold out: 8.95.

547 White-throated Robin

548 Black-eared Wheatear

549 Goldcrest

550 Northern Oriole

551 River Kingfisher

552 Hoopoe

553 Black-billed Magpie (*Illustration reduced. Actual size 100×71 mm*)

Calf of Man Bird Observatory

(Des Colleen Corlett. Litho B.D.T.)

1994 (18 Feb). Perf 13½×13 (No. **MS**589) or 14 (others), both comb.

583	**547**	20p. multicoloured	50	20
		a. Pair. Nos. 583/4	1·00	1·20
584	**548**	20p. multicoloured	50	20
585	**549**	24p. multicoloured	80	25
		a. Pair. Nos. 585/6	1·60	1·70
586	**550**	24p. multicoloured	80	25
587	**551**	30p. multicoloured	1·00	30
		a. Pair. Nos. 587/8	2·00	2·00
588	**552**	30p. multicoloured	1·00	30
583/8 *Set of 6*			4·25	4·75
First Day Cover				5·50
Presentation Pack			5·00	
Souvenir Folder (complete sheets)			20·00	
MS589 100×71 mm. **553** £1 multicoloured			3·00	3·50
First Day Cover				4·50
Presentation Pack			4·50	

No. **MS**589 also commemorates the 'Hong Kong '94' philatelic exhibition.

Plate Nos.: All values 1A, 1B (each ×4).

Sheets: 10 (2×5). The two designs for each value printed together, *se-tenant*, in horizontal and vertical pairs throughout the sheets.

Imprint: Central, right-hand margin.

Withdrawn: 17.2.95.

554 Gaiety Theatre, Douglas

555 Sports

556 Artist at work and Yachts racing

557 T.T. Races and British Aerospace Hawk T.1s of Red Arrows

558 Musical Instruments

559 Laxey Wheel and Manx Cat

560 Tower of Refuge, Douglas, with Bucket and Spade

561 Cyclist

562 Tynwald Day and Bentley 3 Litre Racing Car (1922)

563 Santa Mince Pie Train, Groudle Glen

Manx Tourism Centenary. Booklet Stamps

(Des Colleen Corlett. Litho Cartor)

1994 (18 Feb). Perf 13½ (C).

590	**554**	24p. multicoloured	65	60
		a. Booklet pane. Nos. 590/9 with margins all round	6·00	
591	**555**	24p. multicoloured	65	60
592	**556**	24p. multicoloured	65	60
593	**557**	24p. multicoloured	65	60
594	**558**	24p. multicoloured	65	60
595	**559**	24p. multicoloured	65	60
596	**560**	24p. multicoloured	65	60
597	**561**	24p. multicoloured	65	60
598	**562**	24p. multicoloured	65	60
599	**563**	24p. multicoloured	65	60
590/9 *Set of 10*			6·00	5·50
First Day Cover				6·50
Presentation Pack			6·50	
Stamp Cards (set of 3)			1·50	

Nos. 590/9 were issued in £2.40 stamp booklets, but were also available from the Philatelic Bureau as a loose pane, which was also inserted into the*Presentation Pack*.

Withdrawn: 17.2.95.

564 *Eubranchus tricolor* (sea slug)

565 *Loligo forbesii* (common squid)

566 Edward Forbes and Signature

567 *Solaster moretonis* (fossil starfish)

568 *Adamsia carciniopados* (anemone) on Hermit Crab

569 *Solaster endeca* (starfish)

Europa. Discoveries of Edward Forbes (marine biologist)

(Des Jennifer Toombs. Litho Enschedé)

1994 (5 May). Perf 13×14½ (C).

600	**564**	20p. multicoloured	40	20
		a. Horiz strip of 3. Nos. 600/2	1·50	1·50
601	**565**	20p. multicoloured	40	20
602	**566**	20p. multicoloured	40	20
603	**567**	30p. multicoloured	75	30
		a. Horiz strip of 3. Nos. 603/5	2·75	2·75
604	**568**	30p. multicoloured	75	30
605	**569**	30p. multicoloured	75	30
600/5 *Set of 6*			3·75	3·75
First Day Cover				4·25
Presentation Pack			4·50	

Plate Nos.: Both values 1A, 1B (each ×4).

Sheets: 15 (3×5). The three designs for each value printed together, *se-tenant*, in horizontal strips of 3 throughout the sheets.

Imprint: Central, bottom margin.

Withdrawn: 4.5.95.

570 Maj.-Gen. Bedell Smith and Naval Landing Force including *Ben-My-Chree IV* (ferry)

571 Admiral Ramsay and Naval Ships including *Victoria* and *Lady of Man* (ferries)

572 Gen. Motogomery and British Landings

573 Lt.-Gen. Dempsey and 2nd Army Landings

574 Air Chief Marshal Leigh-Mallory, U.S. Paratroops and Aircraft

575 Air Chief Marshal Tedder, British Paratroops and Aircraft

576 Lt.-Gen. Bradley and U.S. 1st Army Landings

577 Gen. Eisenhower and American Landings

50th Anniversary of D-Day

(Des A. Theobald. Litho Questa)

1994 (6 June). Perf 14 (C).

606	**570**	4p. multicoloured	10	10
		a. Horiz pair. Nos. 606/7	30	30
607	**571**	4p. multicoloured	10	10
608	**572**	20p. multicoloured	50	20
		a. Horiz pair. Nos. 608/9	1·40	1·40
609	**573**	20p. multicoloured	50	20
610	**574**	30p. multicoloured	75	30
		a. Horiz pair. Nos. 610/11	2·00	2·00
611	**575**	30p. multicoloured	75	30
612	**576**	41p. multicoloured	85	45
		a. Horiz pair. Nos. 612/13	2·50	2·50
613	**577**	41p. multicoloured	85	45
606/13 *Set of 8*			5·50	5·50
First Day Cover				6·00
Presentation Pack			6·25	
Souvenir Folder (complete sheets)			26·00	

Plate Nos.: All values 1A, 1B (each ×5).
Sheets: 8 (2×4). The two designs for each value printed together, *se-tenant*, in horizontal pairs throughout the sheets.
Imprint: Central, left-hand margin.
Withdrawn: 5.6.95.

578 Postman Pat, Jess and Ffinlo at Sea Terminal, Douglas

579 Laxey Wheel

580 Cregneash

581 Manx Electric Railway Trains

582 Peel Harbour

583 Douglas Promenade

584 Postman Pat, Jess, Policeman and Children at Zebra Crossing (*Illustration reduced. Actual size* 110×85 mm)

Postman Pat visits the Isle of Man

(Des Colleen Corlett. Litho B.D.T.)

1994 (14 Sept). Perf 13 (No. **MS**620) or 15×14 (others), both comb.

614	**578**	1p. multicoloured	15	15
		a. Booklet pane of 2 with margins all round	50	
615	**579**	20p. multicoloured	60	60
		a. Booklet pane of 2 with margins all round	1·70	
616	**580**	24p. multicoloured	80	80
		a. Booklet pane of 2 with margins all round	2·20	
617	**581**	30p. multicoloured	90	90
		a. Booklet pane of 2 with margins all round	2·50	
618	**582**	36p. multicoloured	1·10	1·10
		a. Booklet pane of 2 with margins all round	2·75	
619	**583**	41p. multicoloured	1·20	1·20
		a. Booklet pane of 2 with margins all round	3·25	
614/19 *Set of 6*			4·25	4·25
First Day Cover				4·50
Presentation Pack			4·50	
Stamp Cards (set of 6)			3·00	7·50
MS620 110×85 mm. **584** £1 multicoloured			2·20	2·20
		a. Booklet pane. As No. **MS**620 but with line of roulettes at left	2·20	
First Day Cover				3·50
Presentation Pack			3·00	

Examples of No. **MS**620 from stamp booklets show a line of roulettes at left.

Plate Nos.: All values 1A, 1B (each ×4).
Sheets: 10 (2×5).
Imprint: Right-hand corner, bottom margin.
Withdrawn: 13.9.95.

585 Cycling

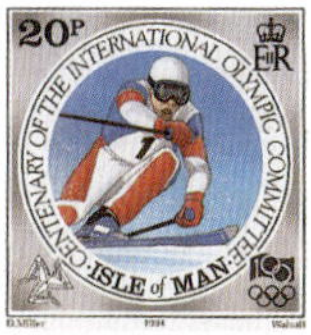

586 Downhill Skiing

587 Swimming

588 Hurdling

589 Centenary Logo

Centenary of International Olympic Committee

(Des D. Miller. Litho Walsall)

1994 (11 Oct). Perf 14×14½ (C).

621	**585**	10p. multicoloured	35	25
622	**586**	20p. multicoloured	55	50
623	**587**	24p. multicoloured	70	65
624	**588**	35p. multicoloured	95	1·00
625	**589**	48p. multicoloured	1·60	1·80
621/5 *Set of 5*			3·75	3·75
First Day Cover				3·75
Presentation Pack			4·00	

Plate Nos.: 10p. 1A (×4); 20p. 1B (×4); 24p. 1C (×4); 35p. 1D (×4); 48p. 1E (×4).
Sheets: 20 (5×4).
Imprint: Central, left-hand margin.
Withdrawn: 10.10.95.

590 Santa Train to Santon

591 Father Christmas and Postman Pat on Mini Tractor, Douglas

592 Father Christmas and Majorettes in Sleigh, Port St. Mary

Christmas. Father Christmas in the Isle of Man

(Des Colleen Corlett. Litho Cartor)

1994 (11 Oct). Perf 13½×14 (23p.) or 14×13½ (others), all comb.

626	**590**	19p. multicoloured	60	60
627	**591**	23p. multicoloured	80	80
628	**592**	60p. multicoloured	2·00	2·00
626/8 *Set of 3*			3·00	3·00
First Day Cover				3·50
Presentation Pack			3·75	
Set of 3 Gutter Pairs			6·00	

Plate Nos.: All values 1A, 1B, 1C, 1D (each ×4).
Sheets: 40 (2 panes 5×4).
Imprint: Central, side margins of each pane.
Withdrawn: 10.10.95.

Year Pack 1994

1994 (11 Oct). Comprises Nos. 556 and 583/628, with or without No. 557.

Year Pack with No. 557	50·00
Year Pack without No. 557	40·00

Withdrawn: 31.12.95.

Post Office Yearbook

1994 (Nov). Comprises Nos. 556/7 and 583/628.

Yearbook	55·00

Sold out: 3.96.

593 Foden Steam Wagon, Highway Board Depot, Douglas

594 Clayton & Shuttleworth and Fowler engines pulling Dead Whale

595 Wallis & Steevens at Ramsey Harbour

596 Marshall Engine with Threshing Machine, Ballarhenny

597 Marshall Convertible Steam Roller

Steam Traction Engines

(Des A. Peck. Litho Enschedé)

1995 (8 Feb). Perf 13½×13 (C).

629	**593**	20p. multicoloured	55	60
630	**594**	24p. multicoloured	60	70
631	**595**	30p. multicoloured	80	85
632	**596**	35p. multicoloured	1·10	1·10
633	**597**	41p. multicoloured	1·10	1·20
629/33 *Set of 5*			3·75	4·00
First Day Cover				4·50
Presentation Pack			4·50	

Plate Nos.: 35p. 1A, 1B, 1C, 1D (each ×4); others 1A, 1B (each ×4).
Sheets: 20 (4×5).
Withdrawn: 7.2.96.

598 Car No. 2 and First Train, 1895

599 Car No. 4 in Green Livery and Car No. 3 in Laxey Valley

600 Car No. 6 and Car No. 5 in 1971

601 Goods Car No. 7 and *Caledonia* Steam Locomotive pulling Construction Train

602 Passenger Car and Argus Char-a-banc at Bungalow Hotel (*Illustration reduced. Actual size* 110×87 mm)

Centenary of Snaefell Mountain Railway

(Des A. Theobald. Litho B.D.T.)

1995 (8 Feb). Perf 14 (C).

634	**598**	20p. multicoloured	70	70
		a. Booklet pane. Nos. 634/7 with margins all round	3·50	
635	**599**	24p. multicoloured	80	80
636	**600**	35p. multicoloured	1·10	1·10
637	**601**	42p. multicoloured	1·20	1·20
634/7 *Set of 4*			3·50	3·50
First Day Cover				4·25
Presentation Pack			4·50	
MS638 110×87 mm. **602** £1 multicoloured			3·25	3·25
		a. Booklet pane. As No. **MS**638 with additional margins all round showing further inscriptions at right and left	3·75	
First Day Cover				4·25
Presentation Pack			4·00	

Booklet pane No. 634a exists in three versions which differ in the order of the stamps within the block of four.

Examples of No. **MS**638 from booklet No. SB39 show a white margin, description of the design and line of roulettes at left and an additional inscription, '1895. CENTENARY SNAEFELL MOUNTAIN RAILWAY. 1995', vertically in the margin at right.

Plate Nos.: All values 1A, 1B (each ×4).
Sheets: 10 (2×5).
Imprint: Central, left-hand margin.
Withdrawn: 7.2.96.

603 Peace Doves forming Wave and Tower of Refuge, Douglas Bay

604 Peace Dove breaking Barbed Wire

Europa. Peace and Freedom

(Des Colleen Corlett and M. Magleby (20p.), Colleen Corlett (30p.). Litho Enschedé)

1995 (28 Apr). Perf 14×13½ (C).

639	**603**	20p. multicoloured	60	75
640	**604**	30p. multicoloured	1·00	1·00
639/40 *Set of 2*			1·60	1·70
First Day Cover				2·20
Presentation Pack			2·40	

Plate Nos.: Both values 1A, 1B (each ×5).
Sheets: 10 (5×2).
Imprint: Central, bottom margin.
Withdrawn: 27.4.96.

605 Spitfire, Tank and Medals

606 Typhoon, Anti-aircraft Gun and Medals

607 Lancaster, H.M.S. *Biter* (escort carrier) and Medals

608 Grumman Avenger, Jungle Patrol and Medals

609 Celebrations in Parliament Square

610 V.E. Day Bonfire

611 Street Party

612 King George VI and Queen Elizabeth on Isle of Man in July, 1945

50th Anniversary of End of Second World War

(Des A. Theobald. Litho B.D.T.)

1995 (8 May). Perf 14 (C).

641	**605**	10p. multicoloured	30	15
		a. Horiz pair. Nos. 641/2	60	60
642	**606**	10p. multicoloured	30	15
643	**607**	20p. multicoloured	55	25
		a. Horiz pair. Nos. 643/4	1·10	1·10
644	**608**	20p. multicoloured	55	25
645	**609**	24p. multicoloured	70	25
		a. Horiz pair. Nos. 645/6	1·40	1·40
646	**610**	24p. multicoloured	70	25
647	**611**	40p. multicoloured	1·10	50
		a. Horiz pair. Nos. 647/8	2·20	2·20
648	**612**	40p. multicoloured	1·10	50
641/8 *Set of 8*			4·75	4·75
First Day Cover				5·50
Presentation Pack			6·00	
Souvenir Folder (complete sheets)			19·00	

Plate Nos.: All values 1A, 1B, 1C (each ×4).
Sheets: 8 (2×4). The two designs for each value printed together, *se-tenant*, in horizontal pairs throughout the sheets.
Imprint: Central, left-hand margin.
Withdrawn: 7.5.96.

613 Reg Parnell in Maserati 4 CLT, 1951

614 Stirling Moss in Frazer Nash Le Mans Replica car, 1951

615 Richard Seaman in Delage, 1936

616 Prince Bira in ERA R2B Romulus, 1937

617 Kenelm Guinness in Sunbeam 1, 1914

618 Freddie Dixon in Riley 6 Cylinder Special Racing Car, 1934

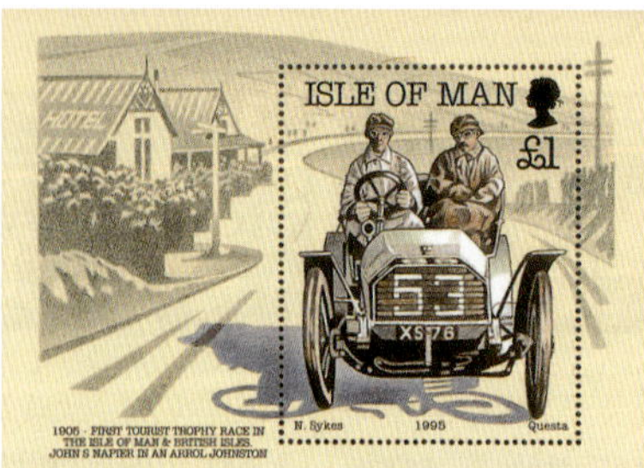

619 John Napier in Arrol Johnston 18 h.p. Racing Car, 1905 (*Illustration reduced. Actual size* 103×73 mm)

90th Anniversary of Motor Racing on Isle of Man

(Des N. Sykes. Litho Questa)

1995 (8 May). Perf 14 (C).

649	**613**	20p. multicoloured	65	60
650	**614**	24p. multicoloured	80	75
651	**615**	30p. multicoloured	90	85
652	**616**	36p. multicoloured	1·10	1·00
653	**617**	41p. multicoloured	1·20	1·20
654	**618**	42p. multicoloured	1·20	1·50
649/54 *Set of* 6			5·50	5·50
First Day Cover				5·75
Presentation Pack			6·00	
MS655 103×73 mm. **619** £1 multicoloured			3·00	3·00
First Day Cover				3·25
Presentation Pack			3·25	

Plate Nos.: All values 1A, 1B (each ×5).
Sheets: 20 (5×4).
Imprint: Right-hand corner, bottom margin.
Withdrawn: 7.5.96.

620 Thomas the Tank Engine and Bertie Bus being Unloaded

621 Mail Train

622 Bertie and Engines at Ballasalla

623 Viking the Diesel Engine, Port Erin

624 Thomas and Railcar at Snaefell Summit

625 Engines racing past Laxey Wheel

50th Anniversary of Thomas the Tank Engine Stories by Revd. Awdry. 'Thomas the Tank Engines Dream'

(Des O. Bell. Litho B.D.T.)

1995 (15 Aug). Perf 14 (C).

656	**620**	20p. multicoloured	65	60
		a. Booklet pane. Nos. 656/7 with margins all round	1·70	
		b. Booklet pane. Nos. 656 and 661 with margins all round	2·20	
657	**621**	24p. multicoloured	80	75
		a. Booklet pane. Nos. 657/8 with margins all round	1·70	
658	**622**	30p. multicoloured	90	85
		a. Booklet pane. Nos. 658/9 with margins all round	2·00	
659	**623**	36p. multicoloured	1·10	1·10
		a. Booklet pane. Nos. 659/60 with margins all round	2·20	
660	**624**	41p. multicoloured	1·20	1·10
		a. Booklet pane. Nos. 660/1 with margins all round	2·50	
661	**625**	45p. multicoloured	1·50	1·20
656/61 *Set of* 6			5·50	5·00
First Day Cover				5·50
Presentation Pack			6·00	
Stamp Cards (*set of* 6)			3·00	9·00

Plate Nos.: All values 1A, 1B (each ×4).
Sheets: 10 (2×5).
Imprint: Central, bottom margin.
Withdrawn: 14.8.96.

626 *Amanita muscaria*

627 *Boletus edulis*

628 *Coprinus disseminatus*

629 *Pleurotus ostreatus*

630 *Geastrum triplex*

631 Shaggy Ink Cap and Bee Orchid (*Illustration reduced. Actual size* 100×71 mm)

Fungi

(Des Colleen Corlett. Litho Enschedé)

1995 (1 Sept). Perf 13½ (C).

662	**626**	20p. multicoloured	40	40
663	**627**	24p. multicoloured	50	50
664	**628**	30p. multicoloured	60	60
665	**629**	35p. multicoloured	75	75
666	**630**	45p. multicoloured	1·20	1·20
662/6 *Set of 5*			3·25	3·25
First Day Cover				4·00
Presentation Pack			4·75	
MS667 100×71 mm. **631** £1 multicoloured			3·00	3·00
First Day Cover				3·50
Presentation Pack			3·50	

No. **MS**667 is inscribed 'Singapore World Stamp Exhibition 1st–10th September 1995' on the sheet margin.

Plate Nos.: All values 1A, 1B, 1C (each ×4).
Sheets: 20 (4×5).
Imprint: Right-hand corner, bottom margin.
Withdrawn: 31.8.96.

632 St. Catherine's Church, Port Erin

633 European Robin on Holly Branch

634 St. Peter's Church and Wild Flowers

635 Hedgehog hibernating under Farm Machinery

Christmas

(Des Colleen Corlett. Litho B.D.T.)

1995 (10 Oct). Perf 14 (C).

668	**632**	19p. multicoloured	55	55
669	**633**	23p. multicoloured	70	70
670	**634**	42p. multicoloured	1·50	1·50
671	**635**	50p. multicoloured	1·70	1·70
668/71 *Set of 4*			4·00	4·00
First Day Cover				4·50
Presentation Pack			4·50	
Set of 4 Gutter Pairs			8·00	

Plate Nos.: All values 1A, 1B, 1C (each ×4).
Sheets: 40 (2 panes 5×4) Imprint: Right-hand corner, bottom margin.
Withdrawn: 9.10.96.

Year Pack 1995

1995 (10 Oct). Comprises Nos. 629/71.

Year Pack .... 42·00

Withdrawn: 31.12.96.

Post Office Yearbook

1995 (Oct). Comprises Nos. 629/38, 639/40 in sheets of 10 and 641/71.

Yearbook .... 45·00

Sold out: By 5.97.

636 Langness Lighthouse

637 Point of Ayre Lighthouse

638 Chicken Rock Lighthouse

639 Calf of Man Lighthouse

640 Douglas Head Lighthouse

641 Maughold Head Lighthouse

Lighthouses

(Des D. Swinton. Litho Questa)

1996 (24 Jan). Perf 14 (C).

672	**636**	20p. multicoloured	50	50
		a. Booklet pane. No. 672×4 with margins all round	2·20	
673	**637**	24p. multicoloured	60	60
		a. Booklet pane. No. 673×4 with margins all round	3·00	
674	**638**	30p. multicoloured	90	90
		a. Booklet pane. Nos. 674 and 676, each ×2, with margins all round	3·75	
675	**639**	36p. multicoloured	1·00	1·00
		a. Booklet pane. Nos. 675 and 677, each ×2, with margins all round	4·00	
676	**640**	41p. multicoloured	1·10	1·10
677	**641**	42p. multicoloured	1·20	1·20
672/7 *Set of 6*			5·00	5·00
First Day Cover				5·50
Presentation Pack			5·50	
Set of 6 Gutter Pairs			10·00	

Plate Nos.: All values 1A, 1B (each ×5).
Sheets: 40 (2 panes 4×5) 20p., 30p., 41p.; (2 panes 5×4) others.
Imprint: Central, left-hand margin (20p., 30p., 41p.) or central, bottom margin (others).
Withdrawn: 22.1.97.

642 White Manx Cat and Celtic Interlaced Ribbons

643 Cat and Union Jack Ribbons

644 Cat on Rug in German Colours, Mouse and Brandenburg Gate

645 Cat, U.S.A. Flag and Statue of Liberty

646 Cat, Map of Australia and Kangaroo

647 Cat and Kittens (*Illustration reduced. Actual size 100×71 mm*)

Manx Cats

(Des Nancy Corkish. Litho B.D.T.)

1996 (14 Mar). Perf 13×13 (No. **MS**683) or 14 (others), both comb.

678	**642**	20p. multicoloured	50	50
679	**643**	24p. multicoloured	60	60
680	**644**	36p. multicoloured	90	90
681	**645**	42p. multicoloured	1·10	1·10
682	**646**	48p. multicoloured	1·20	1·20
678/82 *Set of 5*			4·00	4·00
First Day Cover				5·00
Presentation Pack			5·00	
Stamp Cards (set of 5)			2·50	6·50
MS683 100×71 mm. **647** £1.50, mult			3·50	3·50
First Day Cover				4·50
Presentation Pack			4·50	

For No. **MS**683 with 'CAPEX '96' logo see No. **MS**712.
Plate Nos.: All values 1A, 1B (each ×4).
Sheets: 10 (2×5).
Imprint: Central, left-hand margin.
Withdrawn: 13.3.97.

648 Douglas Borough Arms

Centenary of Douglas Borough

(Des Colleen Corlett. Litho B.D.T.)

1996 (14 Mar). Self-adhesive. Die-cut perf 9×10.

684	**648**	(20p.) multicoloured	70	1·00
First Day Cover				1·50
Presentation Pack			1·50	

No. 684 was printed in sheets of 40, each stamp surrounded by white backing paper divided by roulettes. The actual stamps are separated from the backing paper by die-cut perforations. It was initially sold for 20p. and was only valid for postage within the Isle of Man.

Plate Nos.: 1A, 1B (each ×4).
Sheets: 40 (8×5).
Imprint: Right-hand corner, bottom margin.
Withdrawn: 30.11.98.

651 *Sir Winston Churchill* (cadet schooner)

653 *Tynwald I* (paddle-steamer), 1846

657 *Francis Drake* (ketch)

Ships

(Des A. Theobald. Litho Walsall)

1996 (21 Apr). As Nos. 541, 543 and 547, but smaller as T **651/7**. Perf 14 (C).

687	**651**	4p. multicoloured	20	15
		a. Booklet pane. Nos. 687, 689 and 693, each ×2	10·00	
689	**653**	20p. multicoloured	60	70
693	**657**	24p. multicoloured	90	90
687/93 *Set of 3*			1·50	1·60
First Day Cover				2·50
Presentation Pack			2·50	

The 20p. and 24p. show the positions of the face value and Queens head reversed.

Plate Nos.: All values 1A, 1B (each ×4).
Sheets: 100 (10×10).
Imprint: Right-hand corner, bottom margin.
Withdrawn: 30.11.98.

665 Princess Anne (President, Save the Children Fund) and Children

666 Queen Elizabeth II and People of the Commonwealth

Europa. Famous Women

(Des D. Miller. Litho B.D.T.)

1996 (21 Apr). Perf 14 (C).

701	**665**	24p. multicoloured	70	75
702	**666**	30p. multicoloured	90	1·00
701/2 *Set of 2*			1·60	1·70
First Day Cover				2·20
Presentation Pack			3·50	

The background designs of Nos. 701/2 continue onto the vertical sheet margins.

Plate Nos.: Both values 1A, 1B (each ×4).
Sheets: 10 (2×5).
Withdrawn: 20.4.97.

667 Alec Bennett

668 Stanley Woods

669 Artie Bell

670 Joey and Robert Dunlop

671 R.A.F. Red Arrows Display Team (*Illustration reduced. Actual size* 100×70 mm)

Tourist Trophy Motorcycle Races. Irish Winners

(Des J. Dunne. Litho Questa)

1996 (30 May). Perf 14 (C).

703	**667**	20p. multicoloured	50	45
704	**668**	24p. multicoloured	60	60
705	**669**	45p. multicoloured	90	90
706	**670**	60p. multicoloured	1·40	1·40
703/6 *Set of 4*			3·00	3·00
First Day Cover				3·75
Presentation Pack			4·00	
Souvenir Folder			12·00	
Set of 4 Gutter Pairs			6·00	
MS707 100×70 mm. **671** £1 multicoloured			3·00	3·00
First Day Cover				4·00
Presentation Pack			4·00	

The souvenir folder contains Nos. 703/7, together with the stamps and miniature sheet in similar designs issued by Ireland.

Plate Nos.: 20p. 1A, 1B (each ×4); 24p. 1A (×4); 45p. 1C (×4); 60p. 1D (×4).

Sheets: 40 (2 panes 2×10).
Imprint: Right-hand corner, bottom margin.
Withdrawn: 29.5.97.

672 National Poppy Appeal Trophy

673 Manx War Memorial, Braddan

674 Poppy Appeal Collection Box

675 Royal British Legion Badge

75th Anniversary of Royal British Legion

(Des C. Abbott. Litho B.D.T.)

1996 (8 June). Perf 14 (C).

708	**672**	20p. multicoloured	65	55
709	**673**	24p. multicoloured	70	60
710	**674**	42p. multicoloured	1·10	1·20
711	**675**	75p. multicoloured	2·00	2·00
708/11 *Set of 4*			4·00	4·00
First Day Cover				4·25
Presentation Pack			4·50	

Plate Nos.: 75p. 1A, 1B, 1C (each ×4): others 1A (×4).
Sheets: 40 (8×5).
Imprint: Right-hand corner, bottom margin.
Withdrawn: 7.6.97.

'CAPEX '96' International Stamp Exhibition, Toronto

1996 (8 June). No. **MS**683 additionally inscribed with 'CAPEX '96' exhibition logo on sheet margin.

MS712 100×71 mm. **647** £1.50, mult	6·00	6·50
First Day Cover		8·00

Withdrawn: 31.7.97.

676 U.N.I.C.E.F. Projects in Mexico

677 Projects in Sri Lanka

678 Projects in Colombia

679 Projects in Zambia

680 Projects in Afghanistan

681 Projects in Vietnam

50th Anniv of U.N.I.C.E.F.

(Des C. Abbott. Litho Enschedé)

1996 (18 Sept). Perf 13½×14 (C).

713	**676**	24p. multicoloured	50	30
		a. Horiz pair. Nos. 713/14	1·30	1·20
714	**677**	24p. multicoloured	50	30
715	**678**	30p. multicoloured	60	60
		a. Horiz pair. Nos. 715/16	1·60	1·60
716	**679**	30p. multicoloured	60	60
717	**680**	42p. multicoloured	80	80
		a. Horiz pair. Nos. 717/18	2·50	2·50
718	**681**	42p. multicoloured	80	08
713/18 *Set of 6*			4·75	4·75
First Day Cover				5·50
Presentation Pack			5·25	

Plate Nos.: All values 1A, 1B (each ×4).
Sheets: 40 (10×4). The two designs for each value printed together, *se-tenant*, in horizontal pairs throughout the sheets.
Imprint: Right-hand corner, bottom margin.
Withdrawn: 17.9.97.

682 Labrador

683 Border Collie

684 Dalmatian

685 Mongrel

686 English Setter

687 Alsatian

688 Dogs at Work (*Illustration reduced. Actual size* 100×71 mm)

Dogs

(Des Colleen Corlett. Litho Questa)

1996 (18 Sept). Perf 13½×14 (No. **MS**725) or 14½ (others), both comb.

719	**682**	20p. multicoloured	60	55
		a. Booklet pane. No. 719×4 with margins all round	2·00	
720	**683**	24p. multicoloured	70	65
		a. Booklet pane. No. 720×4 with margins all round	2·20	
721	**684**	31p. multicoloured	1·00	90
		a. Booklet pane. Nos. 721/4 with margins all round	3·75	
722	**685**	38p. multicoloured	1·10	1·10
723	**686**	43p. multicoloured	1·50	1·50
724	**687**	63p. multicoloured	2·00	2·00
719/24 *Set of 6*			6·25	6·25
First Day Cover				6·50
Presentation Pack			6·75	
MS725 100×71 mm. **688** £1.20, mult			3·75	3·75
		a. Booklet pane. As No. **MS**725, but with additional white margins all round separated by roulette	4·00	
First Day Cover				4·25
Presentation Pack			4·50	

Plate Nos.: All values 1A (×4).
Sheets: 10 (2×5).
Imprint: Left-hand corner, bottom margin.
Withdrawn: 17.9.97.

689 'Snowman and Pine Trees' (David Bennett)

690 'Three-legged Father Christmas' (Louis White)

691 'Family around Christmas Tree' (Robyn Whelan)

692 'Father Christmas in Sleigh' (Claire Bradley)

Christmas. Children's Paintings

(Adapted Colleen Corlett. Litho Walsall)

1996 (2 Nov). Perf 14×14½ (C).

726	**689**	19p. multicoloured	55	50
727	**690**	23p. multicoloured	70	65
728	**691**	50p. multicoloured	1·60	1·60
729	**692**	75p. multicoloured	2·10	2·20
726/9 *Set of 4*			4·50	4·50
First Day Cover				4·50
Presentation Pack			5·00	

Plate Nos.: All values 1A, 1B (each ×4).
Sheets: 40 (5×8).
Imprint: Right-hand corner, bottom margin.
Withdrawn: 1.11.97.

Year Pack 1996

1996 (Nov). Comprises Nos. 552 and 672/729.

Year Pack	45·00

Withdrawn: 30.11.98.

Post Office Yearbook

1996 (Nov). Comprises Nos. 552 and 672/729.

Yearbook	48·00

Withdrawn: 30.11.98.

693 Primroses and Cashtyl ny Ard

694 Lochtan Sheep and Lambs

695 Daffodils, Mallard and Ducklings

696 Little Grebe with Young and Frog on Lily Pad

Spring in Man

(Des Colleen Corlett. Litho B.D.T.)

1997 (12 Feb). Perf 14 (C).

730	**693**	20p. multicoloured	50	50
731	**694**	24p. multicoloured	70	70
732	**695**	43p. multicoloured	1·10	1·10
733	**696**	63p. multicoloured	1·60	1·60
730/3 *Set of 4*			3·50	3·50
First Day Cover				4·25
Presentation Pack			4·25	
Set of 4 Gutter Pairs			7·00	

Plate Nos.: All values 1A, 1B (each ×4).
Sheets: 40 (2 panes 5×4).
Imprint: Right-hand corner, bottom margin.
Withdrawn: 11.2.98.

697 Barn Owl

698 Short-eared Owl

699 Long-eared Owl

700 Little Owl

701 Snowy Owl

702 Eurasian Tawny Owl

703a Long-eared Owl (*Illustration reduced. Actual size 100×71 mm*)

Owls

(Des J. Paul. Litho B.D.T.)

1997 (12 Feb). Perf 13 (No. **MS**740) or 14 (others), both comb.

734	**697**	20p. multicoloured	65	60
		a. Booklet pane. No. 734×4 with margins all round	1·60	
735	**698**	24p. multicoloured	80	75
		a. Booklet pane. No. 735×4 with margins all round	2·00	
736	**699**	31p. multicoloured	1·00	90
		a. Booklet pane. Nos. 736/9 with margins all round	3·75	
737	**700**	36p. multicoloured	1·20	1·10
738	**701**	43p. multicoloured	1·40	1·50
739	**702**	56p. multicoloured	1·60	1·70
734/9 Set of 6			6·00	6·00
First Day Cover				6·50
Presentation Pack			6·75	
Stamp Cards (set of 6)			2·75	7·00
MS740 100×71 mm. **703a** £1.20, mult			4·00	4·25
		a. Booklet pane. As No. **MS**740 but with additional white margins all round and with line of roulettes at left	4·75	
First Day Cover				5·50
Presentation Pack			5·00	

No. **MS**740 includes the 'HONG KONG '97' International Stamp Exhibition logo on the sheet margin.

Plate Nos.: All values 1A, 1B (each ×4).
Sheets: 10 (5×2).
Imprint: Bottom, right-hand margin.
Withdrawn: 11.2.98.

704 Moddey Dhoo, Peel Castle

705 Fairies in Tree and Cottage

706 Fairies at Fairy Bridge

707 Giant Finn Maccoil and Calf of Man

708 The Buggane of St. Trinian's

709 Fyonderee and Farm

Europa. Tales and Legends

(Des Colleen Corlett. Litho Enschedé)

1997 (24 Apr). Perf 13½×14 (C).

741	**704**	21p. multicoloured	55	55
742	**705**	25p. multicoloured	65	65
743	**706**	31p. multicoloured	85	85
744	**707**	36p. multicoloured	1·10	1·10
745	**708**	37p. multicoloured	1·10	1·10
746	**709**	43p. multicoloured	1·40	1·40
741/6 Set of 6			5·00	5·00
First Day Cover				5·50
Presentation Pack			5·75	

Nos. 742/3 include the 'EUROPA' emblem.
Plate Nos.: All values 1A, 1B, 1C, 1D (each ×4).
Sheets: 10 (2×5).
Withdrawn: 23.4.98.

710 Sopwith Tabloid

711 Grumman Tiger (1996 Schneider Trophy)

712 BAe ATP (15th anniv of Manx Airlines)

713 BAe 146-200 (15th anniv of Manx Airlines)

714 Boeing 757-200 (largest aircraft to land on Isle of Man)

715 Farman Biplane (1st Manx flight, 1911)

716 Supermarine Spitfire

717 Hawker Hurricane

Manx Aircraft

(Des R. Carter. Litho Questa)

1997 (24 Apr). Perf 14 (C).

747	**710**	21p. multicoloured	30	25
		a. Horiz pair. Nos. 747/8	90	90
748	**711**	21p. multicoloured	30	25
749	**712**	25p. multicoloured	35	25
		a. Horiz pair. Nos. 749/50	1·10	1·10
750	**713**	25p. multicoloured	35	25
751	**714**	31p. multicoloured	70	35
		a. Horiz pair. Nos. 751/2	1·50	1·50
752	**715**	31p. multicoloured	70	35
753	**716**	36p. multicoloured	75	40
		a. Horiz pair. Nos. 753/4	1·70	1·70
754	**717**	36p. multicoloured	75	40
747/54 Set of 8			5·00	5·00
First Day Cover				5·50
Presentation Pack			6·00	
Souvenir Folder (complete sheets)			20·00	

No. 752 is inscribed 'EARMAN' in error.

Plate Nos.: All values 1A (×4).

Sheets: 8 (2×4) the two designs for each value printed together, *se-tenant*, in horizontal pairs throughout the sheets, the backgrounds forming composite designs.

Withdrawn: 23.4.98.

718 14th Hole, Ramsey Golf Club

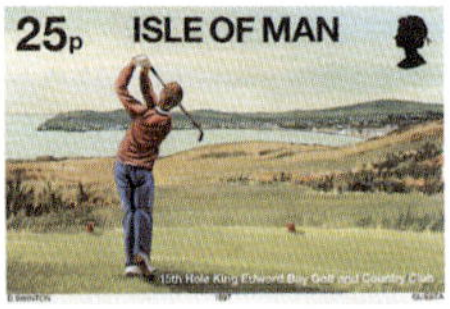

719 15th Hole, King Edward Bay Golf and Country Club

720 17th Hole, Rowany Golf Club

721 8th Hole, Castletown Golf Links

722a Golf Ball (*Illustration reduced. Actual size* 100×71 mm)

Golf

(Des D. Swinton. Litho Questa)

1997 (29 May). Perf 14 (C).

755	**718**	21p. multicoloured	50	50
		a. Booklet pane. No. 755×3 with margins all round	1·70	
756	**719**	25p. multicoloured	60	60
		a. Booklet pane. No. 756×3 with margins all round	2·00	
757	**720**	43p. multicoloured	1·10	1·10
		a. Booklet pane. Nos. 757/8 each ×2 with margins all round	4·25	
758	**721**	50p. multicoloured	1·50	1·50
755/8 Set of 4			3·25	3·25
First Day Cover				4·00
Presentation Pack			3·75	
Set of 4 Gutter Pairs			6·50	
MS759 100×71 mm. **722a** £1.30, mult			3·50	3·50
		a. Booklet pane. As No. **MS**759, but with additional white margins all round	4·00	
First Day Cover				3·75
Presentation Pack			3·75	

No. **MS**759 includes the 'PACIFIC '97' International Stamp Exhibition logo on the sheet margin.

Plate Nos.: All values 1A, 1B (each ×4).

Sheets: 40 (2 panes 5×4).

Imprint: Right-hand corner, bottom margin of each pane.

Withdrawn: 28.5.98.

723a Royal Yacht *Britannia* (*Illustration reduced. Actual size* 130×90 mm)

Return of Hong Kong to China

(Litho Walsall)

1997 (1 July). Sheet 130×90 mm containing stamp as No. 546 with changed imprint date. Wmk Mult Crown CA Diagonal. Perf 13×13½ (C).

MS760 **723a** 23p. multicoloured		1·40	1·60

Withdrawn: 30.6.98.

724 Steve Colley

725 Steve Saunders

726 Sammy Miller

727 Don Smith

F.I.M. 'Trial des Nations' Motorcycle Team Trials

(Des R. Organ. Litho Cartor)

1997 (17 Sept). Perf 13½ (C).

761	**724**	21p. multicoloured	55	50
762	**725**	25p. multicoloured	65	60
763	**726**	37p. multicoloured	1·20	1·00
764	**727**	44p. multicoloured	1·50	1·20
761/4 Set of 4			3·50	3·00
First Day Cover				4·00
Presentation Pack			4·50	
Set of 4 Gutter Pairs			7·00	

Plate Nos.: All values 1A, 1B (each ×4).
Sheets: 40 (2 panes 5×4) 21p., 44p.; (2 panes 4×5) 25p., 37p.
Imprint: Central, gutter margin.
Withdrawn: 16.9.98.

728 Angel and Shepherd

729 Angel and King

730 The Nativity

Christmas

(Des Jennifer Toombs. Litho B.D.T.)

1997 (3 Nov). Perf 14 (C).

765	**728**	20p. multicoloured	65	55
766	**729**	24p. multicoloured	75	70
767	**730**	63p. multicoloured	1·80	1·80
765/7 *Set of 3*			3·00	3·00
First Day Cover				3·00
Presentation Pack			3·50	

Plate Nos.: 20p., 24p. 1A (×5); 63p. 1A, 1B (each ×5).
Sheets: 40 (8×5) 20p., 24p.; 20 (4×5) 63p.
Imprint: Central, left-hand margin.
Withdrawn: 2.11.98.

731 Engagement of Princess Elizabeth and Lieut. Philip Mountbatten, 1947

732 Wedding Photograph, 1947

733 At Ascot, 1952

734 Golden Wedding Photograph, 1997

735a Queen Elizabeth and Prince Philip at Peel, 1989

Golden Wedding of Queen Elizabeth and Prince Philip

(Des Colleen Corlett. Litho and die-stamped Questa)

1997 (3 Nov). Perf 14 (No. **MS**772) or 14×14½, both comb.

768	**731**	50p. sepia and gold	1·00	1·00
		a. Strip of 4. Nos. 768/71	5·00	5·00
769	**732**	50p. multicoloured	1·00	1·00
770	**733**	50p. multicoloured	1·00	1·00
771	**734**	50p. multicoloured	1·00	1·00
768/71 *Set of 4*			5·00	5·00
First Day Cover				5·50
Presentation Pack			5·50	
Souvenir Folder (complete sheet and **MS**772)			21·00	
MS772 100×72 mm. **735a** £1 multicoloured			3·00	3·00
First Day Cover				3·50

Plate Nos.: 1A (x5).
Sheets: 16 (4×4). Nos. 768/71 were printed together, *se-tenant*, as horizontal or vertical strips of 4 throughout the sheets.
Imprint: Right-hand corner, bottom margin.
Withdrawn: 2.11.98.

Year Pack 1997

1997 (3 Nov). Comprises Nos. 730/72.

Year Pack	37·00

Withdrawn: 30.11.98.

Post Office Yearbook

1997 (3 Nov). Comprises Nos. 730/72.

Yearbook	40·00

Sold out: By 8.2001.

736 Bearded Iris

737 Daisy

738 Shamrock

739 Silver Jubilee Rose

740 Oriental Poppy

741 Heath Spotted Orchid

742 Cushag

743 Gorse

744 Princess of Wales Rose

745 Dog Rose

746 Fuchsia 'Lady Thumb'

747 Daffodil

748 Spear Thistle

753 Queen Elizabeth II and Queen Elizabeth the Queen Mother

Two Types of 4p.:—

I. 'WSP' imprint aligns with 'N of 'MAN' (sheet stamps and 1998 booklet)

II. WSP ends to right of 'N' of 'MAN' (1999 booklet)

Flowers

(Des Colleen Corlett (1p. to £1). Litho Cartor (£2.50), Walsall (others))

1998 (12 Feb)–**99**. Perf 13 (1p., 2p, 10p., 20p., 30p.) or 13×13½ (others), both comb.

773	**736**	1p. multicoloured (b)	10	10
774	**737**	2p. multicoloured (b)	10	10
775	**738**	4p. multicoloured (I) (a)	10	10
		a. Booklet pane. Nos. 775, 779 and 781, each ×2 (a)	4·00	
		b. Type II (c)	50	60
		ba. Booklet pane. Nos. 775bx2, 780×3 and 782 (c)	3·00	
776	**739**	5p. multicoloured (c)	10	15
777	**740**	10p. multicoloured (b)	20	25
778	**741**	20p. multicoloured (b)	40	30
779	**742**	21p. multicoloured (a)	40	45
780	**743**	22p. multicoloured (c)	45	50
781	**744**	25p. multicoloured (a)	50	40
782	**745**	26p. multicoloured (c)	50	40
783	**746**	30p. multicoloured (b)	60	60
784	**747**	50p. multicoloured (a)	1·00	1·00
785	**748**	£1 multicoloured (a)	2·00	2·00
790	**753**	£2.50 multicoloured (b)	5·00	4·75
773/90 *Set of 14*			10·50	10·00
First Day Covers (4)				13·50
Presentation Packs (4)			13·50	
Souvenir Folder (Nos. 773/85)			8·00	
Gutter Pair (No. 790)			10·00	

Printings: (a) 12.2.98. Inscribed '1998'; (b) 2.7.98. Inscribed '1998'; (c) 26.4.99. Inscribed '1999'.

Plate Nos.: 4p., 21p., 25p., 50p., £1, £2.50 1A, 1B (each ×4); others 1A (×4).

Sheets: 40 (2 panes 5×4) £2.50, 50 (10×5) (others). In addition to stamp booklets Nos. 775a and 775ba also come from separate special booklet sheets of 36 (6×5), each containing five strips.

Imprint: Central, bottom margin.

756 Viking Figurehead

757 Viking Longship at Sea

758 Viking Longship on Beach

759 Stern of Ship

760a Viking Ship at Peel Castle (*Illustration reduced. Actual size* 100×71 mm)

Viking Longships

(Des A. Bell. Litho B.D.T.)

1998 (14 Feb). Perf 14 (C).

793	**756**	21p. multicoloured	55	50
794	**757**	25p. multicoloured	75	75
795	**758**	31p. multicoloured	90	90
796	**759**	75p. multicoloured	2·20	2·50
793/6 *Set of 4*			4·00	4·25
First Day Cover				4·25
Presentation Pack			5·00	
Set of 4 Gutter Pairs			8·00	
MS797 100×71 mm. **760a** £1 multicoloured			3·00	3·00
First Day Cover				4·50
Presentation Pack			4·75	

Plate Nos.: All values 1A, 1B (each ×4).

Sheets: 40 (2 panes 4×5).

Imprint: Central, right-hand margin.

Withdrawn: 13.2.99.

761 Bottle-nosed Dolphins

762 Basking Shark

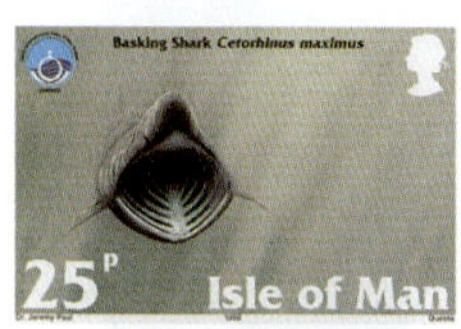

763 Front View of Basking Shark

764 Minke Whale

765 Killer Whale and Calf

U.N.E.S.C.O. International Year of the Ocean

(Des J. Paul. Litho Questa)

1998 (14 Mar). Perf 14 (C).

798	**761**	10p. multicoloured	30	30
		a. Booklet pane. Nos. 798/9, each ×3 and 3 labels with margins all round	2·75	
		b. Booklet pane. Nos. 798/9 and 800/2, each ×2, and 1 central label with margins all round	7·00	
799	**762**	21p. multicoloured	50	50
800	**763**	25p. multicoloured	65	65
801	**764**	31p. multicoloured	75	75
802	**765**	63p. multicoloured	1·60	1·60
798/802 *Set of 5*			3·50	3·50
First Day Cover				4·25
Presentation Pack			5·00	
Souvenir Folder			25·00	
Stamp Cards (set of 5)			3·00	6·00

Plate Nos.: All values 1A, 1B (each ×4).
Sheets: 10 (2×5).
Withdrawn: 13.3.99.

766 Locomotive No. 12 *Hutchinson*

767 Locomotive No. 10 *G. H. Wood*

768 Locomotive No. 11 *Maitland*

769 Locomotive No. 4 *Loch*

770a Pillar Box and Train at Douglas Station (25p.); Locomotive No. 1 *Sutherland* (£1) (*Illustration reduced. Actual size* 120×54 mm)

125th Anniversary of Isle of Man Steam Railway

(Des A. Peck. Litho Questa)

1998 (2 May). Perf 14½×14 (C).

803	**766**	21p. multicoloured	60	50
		a. Booklet pane. Nos. 803/6 with margins all round	3·50	
804	**767**	25p. multicoloured	70	60
805	**768**	31p. multicoloured	90	80
806	**769**	63p. multicoloured	1·60	1·60
803/6 *Set of 4*			3·50	3·25
First Day Cover				3·50
Presentation Pack			4·00	
Souvenir Folder			25·00	
MS807 199×54 mm. **770a** 25p. mult; £1 mult			3·00	3·00
		a. Booklet pane. As No. **MS**807, but with additional margins showing diagram all round	3·00	
First Day Cover				4·00
Presentation Pack			4·00	

Booklet pane No. 803a exists in two versions, which differ in the order of the stamps within the block of four.
Plate Nos.: All values 1A (×4).
Sheets: 40 (5×8).
Imprints: Right-hand corner, bottom margin.
Withdrawn: 31.5.99.

771 Purple Helmets Display Team

772 Joey Dunlop

773 Dave Molyneux

774 Naomi Taniguchi

775 Mike Hailwood

Isle of Man T.T. Races and 50th Anniversary of Honda (motorcycle manufacturer)

(Des The Agency. Litho B.D.T.)

1998 (1 June). Perf 14 (C).

808	**771**	21p. multicoloured	40	45
809	**772**	25p. multicoloured	50	55
810	**773**	31p. multicoloured	65	65
811	**774**	43p. multicoloured	1·00	1·00
812	**775**	63p. multicoloured	1·40	1·50
808/12 *Set of 5*			3·50	3·75
First Day Cover				4·50
Presentation Pack			4·50	
Souvenir Folder			20·00	
Set of 5 Gutter Pairs			7·00	

Plate Nos.: All values 1A (×4).
Sheets: 40 (2 panes 5×4 with double gutter).
Withdrawn: 31.5.99.

776 Princess Diana wearing Protective Clothing, Angola

777 Receiving Award from United Cerebral Palsy Charity, New York, 1995

778 With Children, South Korea, 1992

779 Wearing Blue Jacket, July 1993

Diana, Princess of Wales Commemoration

(Litho Cartor)

1998 (19 June). Perf 13½×13 (C).

813	**776**	25p. multicoloured	50	30
		a. Strip of 4. Nos. 813/16	2·50	2·50

814	**777**	25p. multicoloured	50	30
815	**778**	25p. multicoloured	50	30
816	**779**	25p. multicoloured	50	30
813/16 *Set of 4*			2·50	2·50
First Day Cover				3·00
Presentation Pack			3·00	
Souvenir Folder			20·00	

Plate Nos.: 1A (×4).
Sheets: 16 (4×4). Nos. 813/16 were printed together, *se-tenant*, as horizontal or vertical strips of 4 throughout the sheet.
Withdrawn: 18.6.99.

780 Tynwald Day Ceremony

781 Traditional Dancers, Tynwald Fair

Europa. Festivals

(Des M. Thompson. Litho Cartor)

1998 (2 July). Perf 13×13½ (C).

817	**780**	25p. multicoloured	50	45
818	**781**	30p. multicoloured	1·10	1·20
817/18 *Set of 2*			1·50	1·50
First Day Cover				2·00
Presentation Pack			2·20	

Plate Nos.: Both values 1A (×4).
Sheets: 10 (2×5).
Withdrawn: 30.10.99.

782 Father Christmas at North Pole

783 Father Christmas checking List

784 Flying over Spring Valley Sorting Office

785 Passing through Baldrine Village

786 Father Christmas delivering Presents

Christmas. 'A Very Special Delivery'

(Des A. Bell. Litho Enschedé)

1998 (25 Sept). Perf 14½×14 (C).

819	**782**	20p. multicoloured	40	30
820	**783**	24p. multicoloured	50	45
821	**784**	30p. multicoloured	75	75
822	**785**	43p. multicoloured	95	95
823	**786**	63p. multicoloured	1·40	1·40
819/23 *Set of 5*			3·75	3·75
First Day Cover				4·50
Presentation Pack			4·50	
Set of 5 Gutter Pairs			7·50	

Plate Nos.: All values 1A (×4).
Sheets: 40 (2 panes 5×4).
Imprint: Right-hand corner, bottom margin.
Withdrawn: 30.10.99.

Year Pack 1998

1998 (25 Sept). Comprises Nos. 773/823.
Year Pack .... 36·00
Sold out: 9.99.

Post Office Yearbook

1998 (25 Sept). Comprises Nos. 773/823.
Yearbook .... 38·00
Sold out: 8.2000.

787 Large Oval Pillar Box, Kirk Onchan

788 Wall Box, Ballaterson

789 King Edward VII Pillar Box, Laxey Station

790 Wall Box, Spaldrick

791 Small Oval Pillar Box, Derby Road, Douglas

792 Wall Box, Baldrine Station

Local Post Boxes

(Des The Agency. Litho Walsall)

1999 (4 Mar). Perf 14 (C).

824	**787**	10p. multicoloured	25	25
825	**788**	20p. multicoloured	45	45
826	**789**	21p. multicoloured	50	50
827	**790**	25p. multicoloured	85	85
828	**791**	44p. multicoloured	1·50	1·50
829	**792**	63p. multicoloured	1·75	1·75
824/9 *Set of 6*			4·50	4·50
First Day Cover				5·00
Presentation Pack			5·50	
Set of 6 Gutter Pairs			9·00	

Plate Nos.: All values 1A, 1B (each ×4).
Sheets: 50 (2 panes 5×5).
Imprint: Right-hand corner, bottom margin.
Withdrawn: 3.3.2000.

793 Cottage, Ballaglass Glen

794 Glen Maye Waterfall

Europa. Parks and Gardens

(Des Julia Ashby-Smyth. Litho B.D.T.)

1999 (4 Mar). Perf 14 (C).

830	**793**	25p. multicoloured	50	50
831	**794**	30p. multicoloured	75	80
830/1 *Set of 2*			1·20	1·30
First Day Cover				2·00
Presentation Pack			2·00	

Plate Nos.: Both values 1A, 1B (each ×4).
Sheets: 10 (5×2).
Withdrawn: 3.3.2000.

795 *Ann and James Ritchie*, Ramsey

796 *Sir William Hillary*, Douglas

797 *Ruby Clery*, Peel

798 *Herbert and Edith* (inshore lifeboat), Port Erin

799 1974 150th Anniversary 8p. Stamp

800 *Gough Ritchie II*, Port St. Mary

801 1991 Manx Lifeboats 21p. Stamp

802a Sir William Hillary (founder) (*Illustration reduced. Actual size* 100×70 mm)

175th Anniversary of Royal National Lifeboat Institution

(Des Mainstream Media (No. **MS**839), R. Tomlinson (others). Litho Questa)

1999 (4 Mar). Perf 13½×14 (No. **MS**839) or 14, both comb.

832	**795**	21p. multicoloured	50	50
		a. Booklet pane. Nos. 832/5 and 837, plus four printed labels, with margins all round	4·00	
		b. Booklet pane. Nos. 832/4, 836 and 838, plus four printed labels, with margins all round	5·00	
833	**796**	25p. multicoloured	55	55
834	**797**	37p. multicoloured	80	80
835	**798**	43p. multicoloured	90	90
836	**799**	43p. multicoloured	1·00	1·00
837	**800**	56p. multicoloured	1·20	1·20
838	**801**	56p. multicoloured	1·50	1·50
832/8 *Set of 7*			4·00	4·00
First Day Cover (Nos. 832/5, 837)				4·50
Presentation Pack (Nos. 832/5, 837)			5·00	
Set of 5 Gutter Pairs (Nos. 832/5, 837)			8·00	
MS839 100×70 mm. **802a** £1 multicoloured			4·00	4·00
		a. Booklet pane. As No. **MS**839, but with additional margins showing lifeboats all round	3·50	
First Day Cover				4·50
Presentation Pack			5·00	

Nos. 836 and 838 were available in £4.64 stamp booklets or as a single pane (with no stitch holes), obtainable from the Philatelic Bureau.

No. 832b includes an' iBRA' Stamp Exhibition label and No. **MS**839 the 'Australia '99' World Stamp Exhibition emblem on the sheet margin.

Plate Nos.: All values 1A (×4).
Sheets: 40 (2 panes 5×4).
Withdrawn: 3.3.2000.

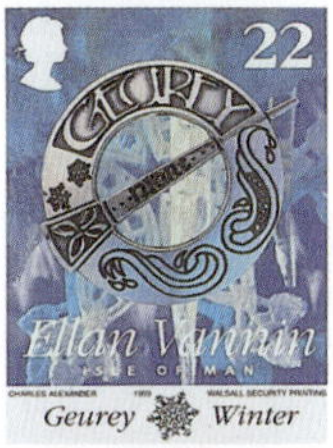

803 Winter

804 Spring

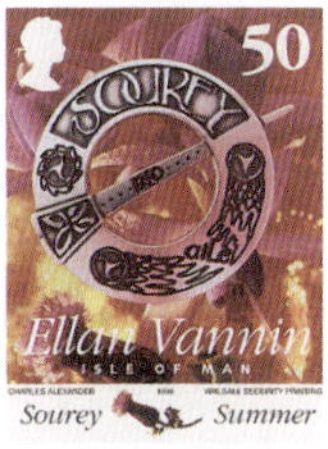

805 Summer

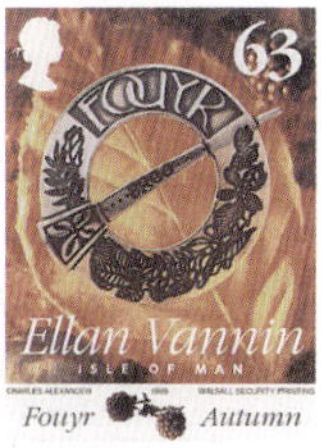

806 Autumn

Centenary of Yn Cheshaght Ghailckagh (Manx Gaelic Society). The Seasons

(Des C. Alexander. Litho Walsall)

1999 (11 May). Perf 14½×14 (C).

840	**803**	22p. multicoloured	60	60
841	**804**	26p. multicoloured	65	65

842	**805**	50p. multicoloured	1·10	1·10
843	**806**	63p. multicoloured	1·60	1·60
840/3 *Set of 4*			3·50	3·50
First Day Cover				4·25
Presentation Pack			4·50	
Set of 4 Gutter Pairs			7·00	

Nos. 840/3 are inscribed 'Ellan Vannin', the Manx name for the Isle of Man.

Plate Nos.: All values 1A, 1B (each ×4).
Sheets: 50 (2 panes 5×5).
Imprint: Right-hand corner, bottom margin.
Withdrawn: 10.5.2000.

807a Queen Victoria; King Edward VII; King George V; King Edward VIII; King George VI; Queen Elizabeth II (*Illustration reduced. Actual size* 170×75 mm)

British Monarchs of the 20th Century

(Des Colleen Corlett. Litho Walsall)

1999 (2 June). Sheet 170×75 mm. Perf 14 (C).

MS844 **807a** 26p.×6, multicoloured	4·00	4·00
First Day Cover		6·00
Presentation Pack	5·00	
Souvenir Folder (Nos. 824/9, **MS**844)	25·00	

Withdrawn: 1.6.2000.

808 Tilling-Stevens Double Deck Bus, 1922

809 Thornycroft BC Single Deck, 1928

810 Cumberland ADC 416 Single Deck, 1927

811 Straker-Squire Single Deck, 1914

812 Thornycroft A2 Single Deck, 1927

813 Leyland Lion LT9 Single Deck, 1938

Manx Buses

(Des P. Hearsey. Litho B.D.T.)

1999 (18 June). Perf 14 (C).

845	**808**	22p. multicoloured	50	50
		a. Booklet pane. Nos. 845/6 and 847×2, with margins all round	2·50	
		b. Booklet pane. Nos. 845/6 and 848×2, with margins all round	3·50	
		c. Booklet pane. Nos. 845/6 and 849×2, with margins all round	4·00	
		d. Booklet pane. Nos. 845/6 and 850×2, with margins all round	4·50	
846	**809**	26p. multicoloured	55	55
847	**810**	28p. multicoloured	65	65
848	**811**	37p. multicoloured	1·00	1·00
849	**812**	38p. multicoloured	1·20	1·20
850	**813**	40p. multicoloured	1·50	1·50
845/50 *Set of 6*			4·00	4·00
First Day Cover				4·50
Presentation Pack			4·50	
Stamp Cards (set of 6)			3·00	7·50

Plate Nos.: All values 1A (×4).
Sheets: 25 (5×5).
Imprint: Central, bottom margin.
Withdrawn: 17.6.2000.

814 Miss Sophie Rhys-Jones

815 Leaving St. George's Chapel, Windsor

816 Prince Edward

817 Miss Sophie Rhys-Jones and Prince Edward

818 In Landau

Royal Wedding

(Des Catherine James. Litho B.D.T.)

1999 (19 June–1 Sept). Perf 14 (C).

851	**814**	22p. multicoloured (a)	55	55
852	**815**	26p. multicoloured (b)	55	55
853	**816**	39p. multicoloured (a)	80	80
854	**817**	44p. multicoloured (a)	1·10	1·10
855	**818**	53p. multicoloured (b)	1·20	1·20
851/5 *Set of 5*			3·75	3·75
First Day Covers (2)				5·00
Presentation Pack			4·50	

Printings: (a) 19.6.99; (b) 1.9.99.
Plate Nos.: All values 1A, 1B (each ×4).
Sheets: 25 (5×5).
Imprint: Central, bottom margin.
Withdrawn: 31.8.2000.

'PhilexFrance 99' International Stamp Exhibition, Paris

1999 (2 July). No. **MS**807 additionally inscribed with 'PhilexFrance' exhibition logo on sheet margin.

MS856 119×54 mm. **770a** 25p. mult; £1 mult	8·00	8·00

Withdrawn: 1.7.2000.

819 St. Luke's Church, Baldwin

820 St. Mark's Chapel, Malew

821 St. German's Parish Church and Cathedral, Peel

822 Kirk Christ Church, Rushen

Christmas. Churches

(Des N. Sayle. Litho Cartor)

1999 (22 Sept). Perf 13½ (C).

857	**819**	21p. multicoloured	45	45
858	**820**	25p. multicoloured	60	60
859	**821**	30p. multicoloured	70	70
860	**822**	64p. multicoloured	1·50	1·50
857/60 *Set of 4*			3·00	3·00
First Day Cover				4·00
Presentation Pack			4·50	
Set of 4 Gutter Pairs			6·00	

Plate Nos.: All values 1A (×4).
Sheets: 40 (2 panes 4×5).
Imprint: Central, bottom margin.
Withdrawn: 21.9.2000.

823 'Massachusetts', 1967

824 'Words', 1968

825 I've Gotta Get a Message to You', 1968

826 'Ellan Vannin', 1998

827 'You Win Again', 1987

828 'Night Fever', 1978

829a 'Immortality', 1998 (*Illustration reduced. Actual size* 119×108 mm)

830a 'Stayin' Alive', 1978 (*Illustration reduced. Actual size* 119×108 mm)

Legends of Music. The Bee Gees (pop group)

(Des The Agency. Litho Cartor (Nos. 861/6), Walsall (No. **MS**867))

1999 (12 Oct). Perf 15 (No. **MS**867) or 13½, both comb.

861	**823**	22p. multicoloured	60	50
862	**824**	26p. multicoloured	70	65
863	**825**	29p. multicoloured	75	75
864	**826**	37p. multicoloured	90	90
865	**827**	38p. multicoloured	90	90
866	**828**	66p. multicoloured	1·50	1·70
861/6 *Set of 6*			4·75	5·00
First Day Cover				5·50
Presentation Pack			6·00	
Souvenir Folder (complete sheets)			45·00	
MS867 Two sheets, each 119×108 mm. (a) **829a** 60p. multicoloured (circular, 40 mm diam). (b) **830a** 90p. multicoloured, (circular 40 mm diam)			8·00	10·00
Set of 2 sheets			8·00	10·00
First Day Cover				25·00

Sheets: 9 stamps and three labels, arranged 3×4, with the labels in the third horizontal row.
Withdrawn: 11.10.2000.

Year Pack 1999

1999 (12 Oct). Comprises Nos. 776, 780, 782, 824/35, 837 and 840/67.

Year Pack .... 50·00

Withdrawn: 2.8.2001.

Post Office Yearbook

1999 (12 Oct). Comprises Nos. 776, 780, 782, 824/35, 837 and **MS**839/67.

Yearbook .... 58·00

Sold out: 8.2000.

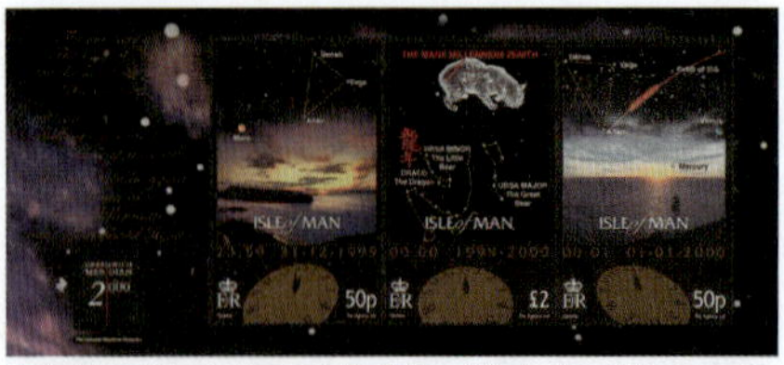

831a Sky at Sunset over Calf of Man (50p.); Sky at Dawn over Maughold Head (50p.); Constellations over Man at Start of New Millennium (£2) (*Illustration reduced. Actual size* 169×74 mm)

New Millennium

(Des H. Parkin and R. Berry. Litho Questa)

1999 (31 Dec). Sheet 169×74 mm. Perf 14½ (C).

MS868 **831a** 50p., 50p., £2 multicoloured	8·00	8·00
First Day Cover		10·00
Presentation Pack	9·00	

The first day cover has three cancellations, one on each stamp, running in a two minute sequence from 23.59 on 31 Dec 99 to 00.01 on 01 Jan 00.

Withdrawn: 30.12.2000.

832 Harrison's Chronometer, 1735, and Map

833 Daniel's Chronometer, 2000, and Clock Face

834 Harrison's Chronometer, 1767, Map and Clock

835 Mudge's Chronometer, 1769, and Steam Locomotives

836 Arnold's Chronometer, 1779, and Map of Africa

837 Earnshaw's Chronometer, 1780, and Map of Caribbean

'The Story of Time'

(Des E. Cassidy. Litho Cartor)

2000 (24 Jan). Perf 13×13½ (C).

869	**832**	22p. multicoloured	50	55
870	**833**	26p. multicoloured	55	60
871	**834**	29p. multicoloured	65	70
872	**835**	34p. multicoloured	90	90
873	**836**	38p. multicoloured	1·20	1·20
874	**837**	44p. multicoloured	1·50	1·50
869/74 *Set of* 6			5·00	5·00
First Day Cover				5·50
Presentation Pack			5·50	

Plate Nos.: 29p., 38p. 1A, 1B (each ×4); others 1A (×4).
Sheets: 25 (5×5).
Imprint: Top left-hand margin and bottom right-hand margin.
Withdrawn: 23.1.2001.

838 Duke and Duchess of York on Wedding Day, 1923

839 Queen Elizabeth with Princess Elizabeth, 1940

840 King George VI and Queen Elizabeth visting Troops, 1944

841 Queen Mother and Queen Elizabeth, 1954

842 Queen Mother with Prince Charles, 1985

843 Queen Mother, 1988

844a Queen Mother visiting Isle of Man

'Queen Elizabeth the Queen Mothers Century'

(Des E.D.L. Litho B.D.T.)

2000 (29 Feb). Perf 14 (C).

875	**838**	22p. multicoloured	50	55
		a. Horiz strip of 3. Nos. 875/7	2·00	2·00
876	**839**	26p. sepia and black	55	60
877	**840**	30p. sepia and black	65	70
878	**841**	44p. multicoloured	95	80
		a. Horiz strip of 3. Nos. 878/80	3·50	3·50
879	**842**	52p. multicoloured	1·00	1·00
880	**843**	64p. multicoloured	1·10	1·10
875/80 *Set of* 6			5·00	5·00
First Day Cover				5·75
Presentation Pack			5·50	
Souvenir Folder (complete sheets and **MS**881)			21·00	
MS881 100×70 mm. **844a** £1 multicoloured			2·50	2·50
First Day Cover				3·00
Presentation Pack			3·00	

Plate Nos.: All values 1A (×4).
Sheets: 12 (3×4). Nos. 875/7 and 878/80 were each printed together, *se-tenant*, as horizontal strips of 3 throughout the sheets.
Withdrawn: 28.2.2001.

845 Barn Swallow

846 Spotted Flycatcher

847 Eurasian Sky Lark

848 Yellowhammer

Endangered Species. Song Birds

(Des Catherine James. Litho Walsall)

2000 (5 May). Perf 14½ (C).

882	**845**	22p. multicoloured	50	55
		a. Strip of 4. Nos. 882/5	4·50	4·50
883	**846**	26p. multicoloured	55	60
884	**847**	64p. multicoloured	80	80
885	**848**	77p. multicoloured	1·00	1·00
882/5 Set of 4			4·50	4·50
First Day Cover				5·50
Presentation Pack			6·00	

Plate Nos.: All values 1A (×4).
Sheets: 20 (4×5). Nos. 882/5 were printed together, *se-tenant*, both horizontally and vertically, within the sheets.
Withdrawn: 4.5.2001.

'The Stamp Show 2000' International Stamp Exhibition, London

2000 (22 May). As No. **MS**881, but with 'The Stamp Show 2000' multicoloured logo added to the bottom sheet margin. Perf 14 (C).

MS886 100×70 mm. **844a** £1 multicoloured		5·00	5·00

Withdrawn: 21.5.2001.

849 Lieut. John Quilliam and Admiral Lord Nelson, Battle of Trafalgar

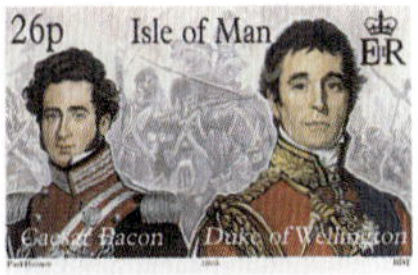

850 Ensign Caesar Bacon and Duke of Wellington, Battle of Waterloo

851 Col. Thomas Leigh Goldie and Earl of Cardigan, Crimea

852 Bugler John Dunne and Sir Robert Baden-Powell, Boer War

853 George Kneale and Viscount Kitchener of Khartoum, First World War

854 First Oficer Alan Watterson and Sir Winston Churchill, Second World War

855a Two Supermarine Spitfires (60p.); Spitfire on Ground, Battle of Britain (60p.) (*Illustration reduced. Actual size 170×75 mm*)

Isle of Man at War

(Des P. Hannon (Nos. 887/92), P. Hearsey (No. **MS**893). Litho B.D.T.)

2000 (22 May). Perf 15×14 (No. **MS**893) or 13, both comb.

887	**849**	22p. multicoloured	50	55
		a. Booklet pane. Nos. 887/91	4·75	
		b. Booklet pane. Nos. 887 and 890/2	5·00	
888	**850**	26p. multicoloured	55	60
889	**851**	36p. multicoloured	75	80
890	**852**	48p. multicoloured	1·00	1·10
891	**853**	50p. multicoloured	1·10	1·20
892	**854**	77p. multicoloured	1·50	1·60
887/92 Set of 6			4·75	5·25
First Day Cover				6·00
Presentation Pack			6·00	
MS893 170×75 mm. **855a** 60p. multi- coloured; 60p. multicoloured			2·75	2·75
		a. Booklet pane. As No. **MS**893, but with line of roulettes at left	2·75	
First Day Cover				3·50
Presentation Pack			3·50	

Plate Nos.: All values A1 (×4).
Sheets: 8 (2×4). Nos. 887/8, 889/90 and 891/2 were each printed in sheets containing vertical strips of the two designs separated by a gutter margin.
Imprint: Lower left-hand margin.
Withdrawn: 21.5.2001.

856a Prince William as a Child (22p.); With Queen Mother (26p.); As a teenager (45p.); With Prince Charles and Prince Harry (52p.); Wearings ski-suit (56p.) (*Illustration reduced. Actual size* 170×75 mm)

18th Birthday of Prince William

(Des The Agency. Litho B.D.T.)

2000 (21 June). Sheet 170×75 mm. Perf 14 (C).

MS894 **856a** 22p., 26p., 45p., 52p., 56p. multicoloured	4·50	4·50
First Day Cover		5·25
Presentation Pack	5·25	

Withdrawn: 20.6.2001.

857 Ballet Shoes and Painted Ceiling

858 Comedy Mask and Box Decoration

859 Drama Mask and Statue

860 Pantomime Dame with Wig and Mosaic

861 Opera Glasses and Decoration

862 Top Hat with Cane and Painted Ceiling

Centenary of Gaiety Theatre, Douglas

(Des The Agency. Litho B.D.T.)

2000 (16 July). Perf 14 (C).

895	**857**	22p. multicoloured	50	55
896	**858**	26p. multicoloured	55	60
897	**859**	36p. multicoloured	75	80
898	**860**	45p. multicoloured	95	1·00
899	**861**	52p. multicoloured	1·10	1·20
900	**862**	65p. multicoloured	1·40	1·50
895/900 *Set of 6*			4·75	5·25
First Day Cover				6·25
Presentation Pack			6·25	
Stamp Cards (set of 6)			3·50	9·50

Plate Nos.: All values 1A (×4).
Sheets: 20 (4×5) with enlarged illustrated margin at left.
Imprint: Central, right-hand margin.
Withdrawn: 14.7.2001.

863 Map of Great Britain, Union Jack and Liner

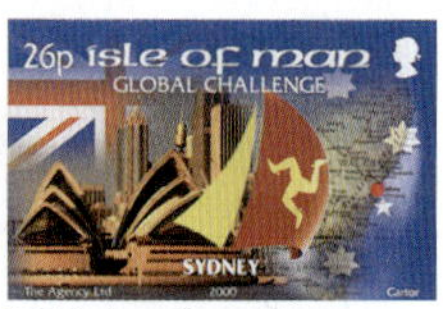

864 Sydney Opera House, Australian Flag and Map

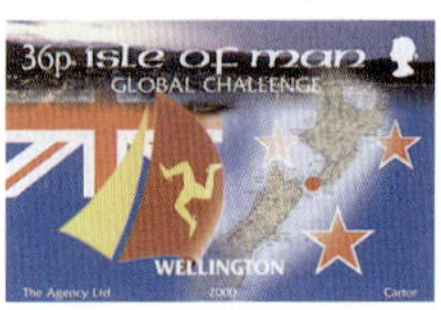

865 New Zealand Map and Flag

866 Map of Buenos Aires and Waterfront

867 U.S. Flag, Map of Boston and Harbour

868 South African Flag, Map and Table Mountain

'BT Global Challenge' Round the World Yacht Race

(Des The Agency. Litho Cartor)

2000 (10 Sept). Perf 13½ (C).

901	**863**	22p. multicoloured	50	55
902	**864**	26p. multicoloured	55	60
903	**865**	36p. multicoloured	75	80
904	**866**	40p. multicoloured	85	90
905	**867**	44p. multicoloured	95	1·00
906	**868**	65p. multicoloured	1·40	1·50
901/6 *Set of 6*			4·50	4·75
First Day Cover				5·75
Presentation Pack			5·75	
Set of 6 Gutter Pairs			9·00	

Plate Nos.: All values 1A (×4).
Sheets: 40 (2 panes 2×10).
Imprint: Centre, side margins.
Withdrawn: 8.9.2001.

869 Sailing and Holiday Tours Poster, 1925

870 Isle of Man for Happy Holidays

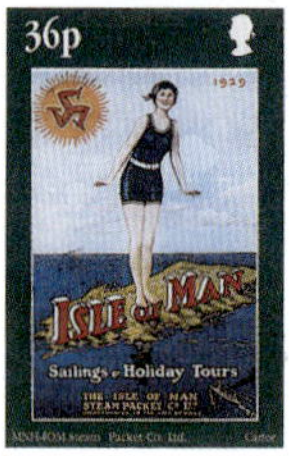

871 Woman in Swimsuit standing on Isle of Man, 1929

872 Stewardess and Ferry

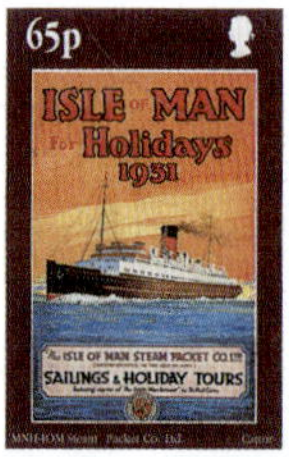

873 'Isle of Man for Holidays 1931' and Ferry

170th Anniversary of Steam Packet Company. Tourism Posters

(Litho Cartor)

2000 (6 Oct). Perf 13½ (C).

907	**869**	22p. multicoloured	50	55
908	**870**	26p. multicoloured	55	60
909	**871**	36p. multicoloured	75	80
910	**872**	45p. multicoloured	1·50	1·50
911	**873**	65p. multicoloured	1·90	2·00
907/11 *Set of 5*			4·75	5·00
First Day Cover				5·00
Presentation Pack			5·00	

Plate Nos.: All values 1A (×4).
Sheets: 20 (5×4).
Imprint: Centre, side margins.
Withdrawn: 5.10.2001.

874 Girl with Christingle Candle

875 Children dancing around Christmas Tree

876 'Building Europe'

877 Girl hugging Teddy Bear

878 Children with Stars

Christmas and Europa

(Des R. Wetherall (36p. after J.-P. Cousin). Litho Questa)

2000 (7 Nov). Perf 14 (C).

912	**874**	21p. multicoloured	45	50
913	**875**	25p. multicoloured	55	60
914	**876**	36p. multicoloured	75	80
		a. Sheetlet of 10	7·50	
915	**877**	45p. multicoloured	1·50	1·50
916	**878**	65p. multicoloured	1·90	2·00
912/16 *Set of 5*			4·75	5·00
First Day Cover				5·00
Presentation Pack			5·00	
Set of 5 Gutter Pairs			7·50	

Plate Nos.: All values 1A (×4).
Sheets: 40 (2 panes 4×5); 36p. also 10 (5×2).
Imprint: Right-hand corner, bottom margin.
Withdrawn: 6.11.2001.

Year Pack 2000

2000 (7 Nov). Comprises Nos. **MS**868/85 and 887/916.

Year Pack	55·00

Sold out: By 10.2002.

Post Office Yearbook

2000 (7 Nov). Comprises Nos. **MS**868/85 and 887/916.

Yearbook	58·00

Sold out: By 10.2003.

879 Wyon Medal, Penny Black and Queen Victoria

880 Great Exhibition Medal and Albert Tower, Ramsey

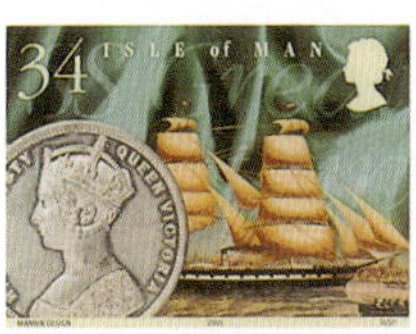

881 Silver Coin and *Great Britain* (early steamship)

882 Manx Coin of 1839, *Oliver Twist* and St. Thomas' Church, Douglas

883 Silver Coin of 1887, Arrival of First Train at Vancouver and Jubilee Lamp Standard

884 Silver Coin of 1893, Joe Mylchreest at Kimberley Diamond Mine and Foxdale Clock Tower

Death Centenary of Queen Victoria

(Des Mannin Design. Litho Walsall)

2001 (22 Jan). Perf 13½ (C).

917	**879**	22p. multicoloured	50	55
918	**880**	26p. multicoloured	55	60
919	**881**	34p. multicoloured	75	80
920	**882**	39p. multicoloured	1·10	1·20
921	**883**	40p. multicoloured	1·10	1·20
922	**884**	52p. multicoloured	1·60	1·70
917/22 *Set of 6*			5·25	5·50
First Day Cover				5·50
Presentation Pack			6·00	

Plate Nos.: All values 1A (×4).
Sheets: 20 (4×5).
Imprint: Right-hand corner, bottom margin.
Withdrawn: 21.1.2002.

885a St. Patrick and Snakes (Illustration reduced. Actual size 110×85 mm)

Chinese New Year (Year of the Snake)

(Des The Agency. Litho and die-stamped Questa)

2001 (22 Jan). Sheet 110×85 mm. Perf 13½×14 (C).

MS923 **885a** £1 multicoloured	3·00	3·50
First Day Cover		4·00
Presentation Pack	4·00	

No. **MS**923 includes the 'Hong Kong 2001' logo on the sheet margin.
Withdrawn: 21.1.2002.

886 White-tailed Bumble Bee

887 Seven-spot Ladybird

888 Lesser Mottled Grasshopper

889 Manx Robber Fly

890 Elephant Hawkmoth

Insects

(Des R. Lewington. Litho Questa)

2001 (1 Feb). Perf 14 (C).

924	**886**	22p. multicoloured	50	55
925	**887**	26p. multicoloured	55	60
926	**888**	29p. multicoloured	80	90
927	**889**	59p. multicoloured	1·50	1·60
928	**890**	66p. multicoloured	1·90	2·00
924/8 *Set of 5*			5·00	5·25
First Day Cover				5·00
Presentation Pack			5·50	

Plate Nos.: All values 1A, 1B (each ×4).
Sheets: 10 (5×2).
Imprint: Right-hand corner, bottom margin.
Withdrawn: 31.1.2002.

891 Letter-carrier, 1805

892 Postman, 1859

893 Postman, 1910

894 Postman, 1933

895 Postman, 1983

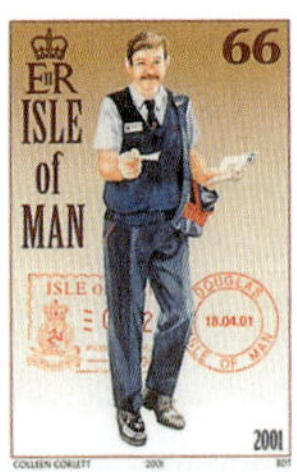

896 Postman, 2001

Postal Uniforms

(Des Colleen Corlett. Litho B.D.T.)

2001 (18 Apr). Perf 14 (C).

929	**891**	22p. multicoloured	50	55
930	**892**	26p. multicoloured	55	60
931	**893**	36p. multicoloured	75	80
932	**894**	39p. multicoloured	1·10	1·20
933	**895**	40p. multicoloured	1·10	1·20
934	**896**	66p. multicoloured	1·90	2·00
929/34 *Set of 6*			5·50	5·75
First Day Cover				5·50
Presentation Pack			6·00	

Plate Nos.: All values 1A (×4).
Sheets: 20 (5×4).
Imprint: Central, bottom margin.
Withdrawn: 17.4.2002.

897a 1967–70 Great Britain ½d. Machin (29p.); 1952–1954 Great Britain 6d. Wilding (34p.); 1971 Isle of Man 2½p. Regional (37p.); 1958–68 Isle of Man 4d. Regional (50p.) (*Illustration reduced. Actual size* 170×75 mm)

75th Birthday of Queen Elizabeth II

(Des The Agency. Litho B.D.T.)

2001 (18 Apr). Sheet 170×75 mm. Perf 14 (C).

MS935 **897a** 29p., 34p., 37p., 50p. multicoloured	3·75	4·00
First Day Cover		4·50
Presentation Pack	4·50	

Withdrawn: 17.4.2002.

898 Joey Dunlop on Rea Yamaha, Parliament Square, 1977 TT Races

899 At Governor's, 1983 TT Races

900 Leaving Ramsey, 1988 TT Races

901 On Honda motorbike, 1991

902 On 250cc Honda at Ballaspur, 1999

903 On the Mountain

Joey Dunlop (motorcycle champion) Commemoration

(Des Ruth Sutherland. Litho B.D.T.)

2001 (17 May). Perf 14 (C).

936	**898**	22p. multicoloured	50	55
937	**899**	26p. multicoloured	55	60
938	**900**	36p. multicoloured	75	80
939	**901**	45p. multicoloured	95	1·00
940	**902**	65p. multicoloured	1·40	1·50
941	**903**	77p. multicoloured	1·60	1·70
936/41 *Set of 6*			5·25	5·75
First Day Cover				6·50
Presentation Pack			7·00	
Souvenir Folder (containing 5 sets of Nos. 936/41, 6 Postcards (PC20/5) and special commemorative cover)			40·00	
Set of 6 Gutter Pairs			10·50	

Sheets: 20 (2 panes 2×5).
Withdrawn: 16.5.2002.

904 'The Manx Derby, 1627' (Johnny Jonas)

905 'Post Haste' (Johnny Jonas)

906 'Red Rum' (Hamilton-Rennick)

907 'Hyperion' (Sir Alfred Munnings)

908 'Isle of Man' (Johnny Jonas)

Horse Racing Paintings

(Des The Agency. Litho Cartor)

2001 (18 May). Perf 13½ (C).

942	**904**	22p. multicoloured	50	55
943	**905**	26p. multicoloured	55	60
944	**906**	36p. multicoloured	85	80
945	**907**	52p. multicoloured	1·50	1·60
946	**908**	63p. multicoloured	1·70	1·70
942/6 *Set of 5*			4·50	4·75
First Day Cover				5·00
Presentation Pack			5·00	

Plate Nos: All values 1A (×4).
Sheets: 20 (4×5).
Withdrawn: 17.5.2002.

909 Beef

910 Queenies with Salmon Caviar

911 Seafood

912 Lamb

913 Kipper Tart

914 Lemon Tart with Raspberries

Europa. Water, a Natural Treasure, Local Dishes prepared by Kevin Woodford

(Des The Agency. Litho B.D.T.)

2001 (10 Aug). Perf 14 (C).

947	**909**	22p. multicoloured	50	55
948	**910**	26p. multicoloured	55	60
		a. Panel at foot of stamp in pale lilac (R. 2/1)	20·00	
		b. Sheetlet of 10	5·50	
949	**911**	36p. multicoloured	75	80
		b. Sheetlet of 10	7·75	
950	**912**	45p. multicoloured	1·20	1·20
951	**913**	50p. multicoloured	1·30	1·50
952	**914**	66p. multicoloured	1·90	2·00
947/52 *Set of 6*			5·75	6·25
First Day Cover				6·50
Presentation Pack			7·00	
Recipe Cards (set of 6)			20·00	

The 26p. and 36p. show the inscription 'EUROPA 2001' at bottom right.

On Nos. 947/52 the panel at the foot of each stamp, on which the designer and printer imprints occur, is normally white. On R. 2/1 of the 26p. in sheets of 25 this panel is in pale lilac.

The set of recipe cards show a strip of 4 stamps plus label and first day of issue postmark.

Plate Nos.: All values 1A (×4).
Sheets: 30 (6×5) containing 25 stamps and 5 stamp-size labels, different for each value, in the first vertical row; 26p., 36p. also 10 (2×10).
Withdrawn: 9.8.2002.

915 Castletown Police Station

916 Leafield (semi-detached house)

917 'The Red House' (Baillie Scott's home)

918 'Ivydene' (detached house)

919 Onchan Village Hall

The Architecture of Mackay Hugh Baillie Scott

(Des Tracey Harding. Litho Cartor)

2001 (3 Sept). Perf 13½ (C).

953	**915**	22p. multicoloured	50	55
954	**916**	26p. multicoloured	55	60
955	**917**	37p. multicoloured	80	85
956	**918**	40p. multicoloured	1·00	1·10
957	**919**	80p. multicoloured	2·00	2·10
953/7 *Set of 5*			4·50	4·75
First Day Cover				5·50
Presentation Pack			6·00	

Nos. 953/7 are inscribed 'HUGH MACKAY' in error.
Plate Nos.: All values 1A (×4).
Sheets: 20 (4×5) with a further view of the building depicted on the sheet margins.
Withdrawn: 2.9.2002.

'Hafnia '01' International Stamp Exhibition, Denmark

2001 (16 Oct). No. **MS**935 additionally inscribed with 'Hafnia '01' logo in red on sheet margin.

MS958 170×75 mm. **897a** 29p., 34p., 37p., 50p. multicoloured	6·50	7·00
First Day Cover		7·50

Sold out: By 8.2003.

920 Royal Refreshments at Glasgow

921 Queen on Visit to Lancaster

922 Queen with Labradors, Sandringham

923 Queen meeting Scottish Korean War Veterans

924 Queen at Desk, Sandringham

925 Queen with Bouquet, Oxford

Golden Jubilee (1st issue). 'The Daily Life of the Queen—An Artists Diary' (paintings by Michael Noakes)

(Adapted The Agency. Litho Questa)

2001 (29 Oct)–**02**. Perf 14 (C).

959	**920**	22p. multicoloured (a)	50	55
		a. Booklet pane. Nos. 959/61 with margins all round (b)	2·20	
960	**921**	26p. multicoloured (a)	55	60
961	**922**	39p. multicoloured (a)	85	90
962	**923**	40p. multicoloured (a)	85	90
		a. Booklet pane. Nos. 962/4 with margins all round (b)	4·00	
963	**924**	45p. multicoloured (a)	95	1·00
964	**925**	65p. multicoloured (a)	1·90	2·00
959/64 *Set of 6*			5·00	5·50
First Day Cover				6·00
Presentation Pack			6·25	
Souvenir Folder (*complete sheets*)			42·00	

See also Nos. 970/5.
Printings: (a) 29.10.2001; (b) 6.2.2002.
Plate Nos.: All values 1A (×4).
Sheets: 8 (4×2) with enlarged illustrated margin at left.
Withdrawn: 28.10.2002 (sheets).

926 Christmas Tree Wall Decoration

927 Traditional Wreath

928 Table Decoration

929 Topiary Tree

930 Contemporary Wreath

Christmas. Decorations by Isle of Man Floreat Workshop

(Des The Agency. Litho Questa)

2001 (5 Nov). Perf 14×14½ (C).

965	**926**	21p. multicoloured	45	50
966	**927**	25p. multicoloured	55	60
967	**928**	37p. multicoloured	1·00	1·10
968	**929**	45p. multicoloured	1·20	1·30
969	**930**	65p. multicoloured	1·90	2·00
965/9 *Set of 5*			4·75	5·00
First Day Cover				5·25
Presentation Pack			5·50	

Plate Nos.: All values 1A, 1B (each ×4).
Sheets: 25 (5×5) with horizontal rows of stamps interspersed by rows of inscribed greetings labels. The 21p. and 25p values were also available with personal photographs shown on these labels.
Withdrawn: 4.11.2002.

Year Folder 2001

2001 (5 Nov). Comprises Nos. 917/57 and 959/69.

Year Folder	45·00

Sold out: By 11.2003.

Year Pack 2001

2001 (5 Nov). Comprises Nos. 917/57 and 959/69.

Year Pack	55·00

Sold out: By 11.2003.

Post Office Yearbook

2001 (5 Nov). Comprises Nos. 917/57 and 959/69.

Yearbook	60·00

Sold out: By 4.2002.

931 'The Coronation, 1953' (Terence Cuneo)

932 'Queen Elizabeth II as Colonel-in-Chief of Grenadier Guards on Imperial, 1962' (Terence Cuneo)

933 'Queen Elizabeth II in Evening Dress, 1981' (June Mendoza)

934 'Queen Elizabeth II in Garter Robes, 2000' (Chen Yan Ning)

935 'The Royal Family' (John Wonnacott)

936a Sculpture of Queen Elizabeth II by David Cregeen
(Illustration reduced. Actual size 110×85 mm)

Golden Jubilee (2nd issue). Royal Paintings

(Des The Agency. Litho and die-stamped Questa)

2002 (6 Feb). Perf 14½×14 (No. **MS**975) or 14 (others), both comb.

970	**931**	50p. multicoloured	80	60
		a. Vert strip of 5. Nos. 970/4	5·00	5·50
		b. Booklet pane. Nos. 970/2 with margins all round	3·50	
971	**932**	50p. multicoloured	80	60
972	**933**	50p. multicoloured	80	60
973	**934**	50p. multicoloured	80	60
		b. Booklet pane. Nos. 973/4 with margins all round	2·40	
974	**935**	50p. multicoloured	80	60
970/4 *Set of 5*			5·00	5·50
First Day Cover				6·00
Presentation Pack			6·00	
Souvenir Folder (complete sheet)			20·00	
Gutter Strip			10·50	
MS975 110×85 mm. **936a** £1 multicoloured			2·00	2·10
		b. Booklet pane. As No. **MS**975, but 152×97 mm with a line of roulettes at left	2·40	2·50
First Day Cover				5·50
Presentation Pack			3·00	

Plate Nos.: 1A (×4).
Sheets: 20 (2 panes 2×5). Nos. 970/4 were printed together, *se-tenant*, as vertical strips of 5. The panes are separated by an enlarged vertical gutter illustrated with further royal portraits.
Withdrawn: 5.2.2003.

937 Cycling

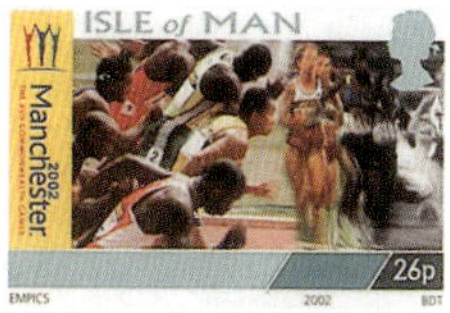

938 Running

939 Javelin and High Jump

940 Swimming

941 Decathlon

942 Wheelchair Racing

17th Commonwealth Games, Manchester. Photographic Montages

(Des The Agency. Litho B.D.T.)

2002 (11 Mar). Perf 14 (C).

976	**937**	22p. multicoloured	45	50
977	**938**	26p. multicoloured	50	55
978	**939**	29p. multicoloured	60	65
979	**940**	34p. multicoloured	70	75
980	**941**	40p. multicoloured	1·00	1·10
981	**942**	45p. multicoloured	1·10	1·20
976/81 *Set of 6*			4·25	4·75
First Day Cover				5·25
Presentation Pack			5·50	

Plate Nos.: All values 1A (×4).
Sheets: 9 (3×3) with an illustrated gutter between the second and third horizontal rows, and an enlarged right margin.
Withdrawn: 10.3.2003.

943 'Queen Elizabeth the Queen Mother' (Johnny Jonas)

Queen Elizabeth the Queen Mother Commemoration

(Des The Agency. Litho Cartor)

2002 (23 Apr). Perf 13×13½ (C).

982	**943**	£3 multicoloured	6·00	6·25
First Day Cover				7·00
Presentation Pack			7·00	

No. 982 was retained in use as a definitive stamp.
Plate Nos.: 1A (×4).
Sheets: 10 (5×2).

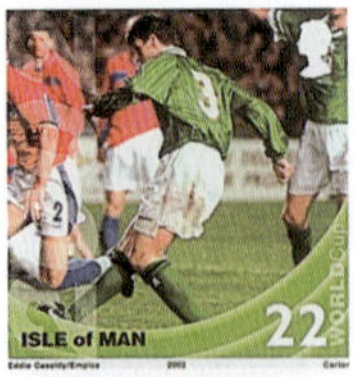

944 Ireland v Czech Republic

945 England v Greece

946 Italy v Belgium

947 France v Portugal

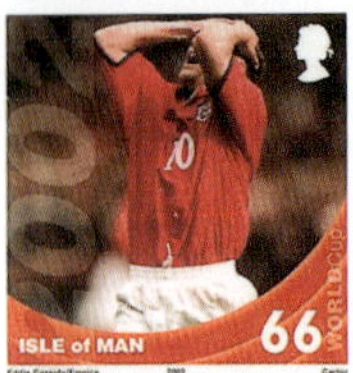

948 England v Brazil

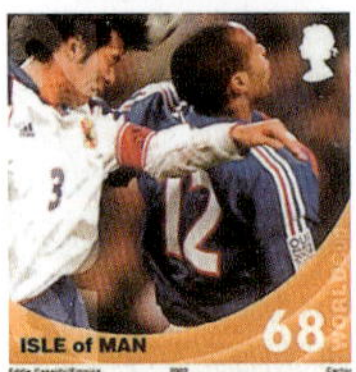

949 France v Japan

World Cup Football Championship, Japan and Korea

(Des E. Cassidy. Litho Cartor)

2002 (1 May). Perf 13½ (C).

983	**944**	22p. multicoloured	45	50
984	**945**	26p. multicoloured	50	55
985	**946**	39p. multicoloured	80	85
986	**947**	40p. multicoloured	80	85
987	**948**	66p. multicoloured	1·20	1·40
988	**949**	68p. multicoloured	1·40	1·50
983/8 *Set of 6*			5·00	5·50
First Day Cover				6·00
Presentation Pack			6·25	

Plate Nos.: All values 1A (×4).
Sheets: 25 (5×5).
Withdrawn: 30.4.2003.

950 'Monk's Bridge, Ballasalla'

951 'Laxey'

952 'Langness Lighthouse'

953 'King William's College'

954 'The Mull Circle and Bradda Head'

Watercolours by Toni Onley

(Des The Agency. Litho Cartor)

2002 (1 May). Perf 13½ (C).

989	**950**	22p. multicoloured	45	50
990	**951**	26p. multicoloured	50	55
991	**952**	37p. multicoloured	75	80
992	**953**	45p. multicoloured	1·10	1·20
993	**954**	65p. multicoloured	1·50	1·60
989/93 *Set of 5*			4·25	4·50
First Day Cover				5·25
Presentation Pack			5·50	

Plate Nos.: All values 1A (×4).
Sheets: 25 (5×5).
Withdrawn: 30.4.2003.

Golden Jubilee Celebrations

2002 (4 June). No. **MS**975 additionally inscribed 'THE ISLE OF MAN CELEBRATES THE JUBILEE 4th June 2002' in purple on the sheet margin.

MS994 110×85 mm. **935a** £1 multicoloured .... 6·50 6·50

Withdrawn: 3.6.2003.

955 Magenta Flower on Yellow Background

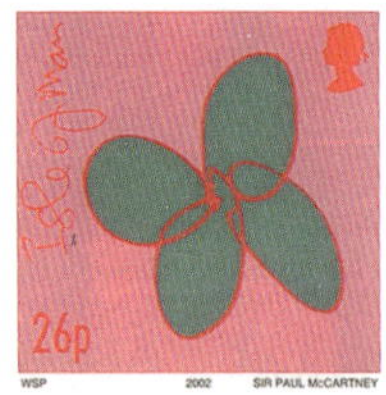

956 Green Flower on Pink Background

957 Purple Flower on Green Background

958 Maroon Flower on Brown Background

959 Red Flower on Blue Background

960 Orange Flowr on Yellow Background

Memories of the Isle of Man

(Des Sir Paul McCartney. Litho Walsall)

2002 (1 July). Perf 13½×13 (C).

995	**955**	22p. multicoloured	45	50
996	**956**	26p. multicoloured	50	55
997	**957**	29p. multicoloured	60	65
998	**958**	52p. multicoloured	1·00	1·10
999	**959**	63p. multicoloured	1·20	1·40
1000	**960**	77p. multicoloured	1·50	1·60
995/1000 *Set of 6*			5·25	5·75
First Day Cover				6·25
Presentation Pack			6·50	
Souvenir Folder (complete sheets and first day cover)			50·00	

Plate Nos.: All values 1A (×4).
Sheets: 8 (4×2) with inscribed margins and a photograph of Sir Paul McCartney at left.
Withdrawn: 30.6.2003.

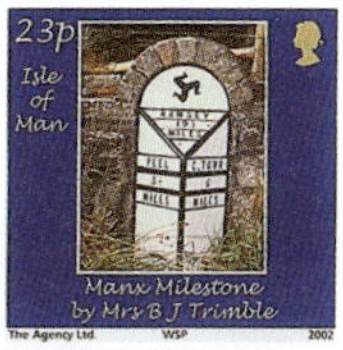

961 Manx Milestone (Mrs. B. Trimble)

962 Plough Horses (Miss D. Flint)

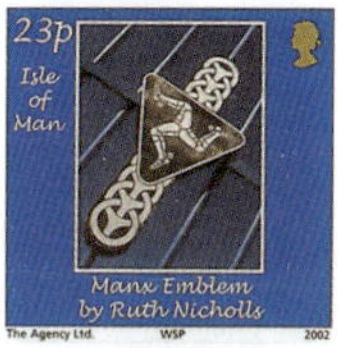

963 Manx Emblem (Ruth Nicholls)

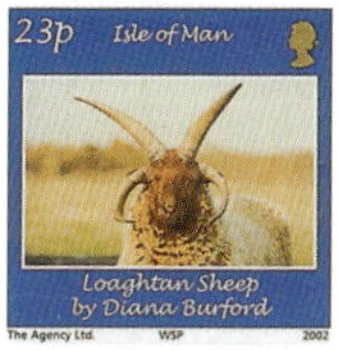

964 Loaghtan Sheep (Diana Burford)

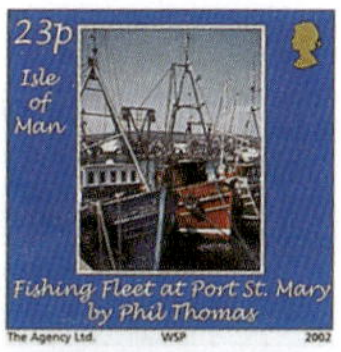

965 Fishing Fleet, Port St. Mary (Phil Thomas)

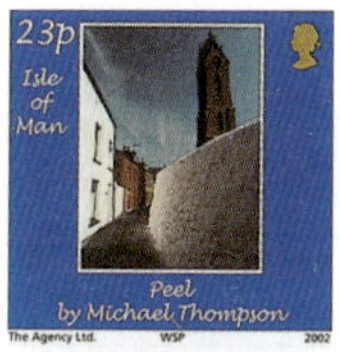

966 Peel (Michael Thompson)

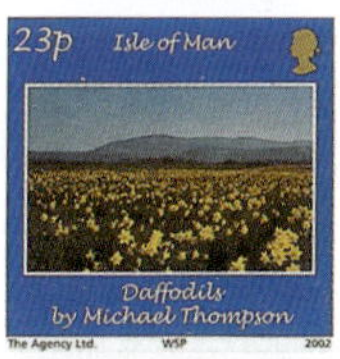

967 Daffodils (Michael Thompson)

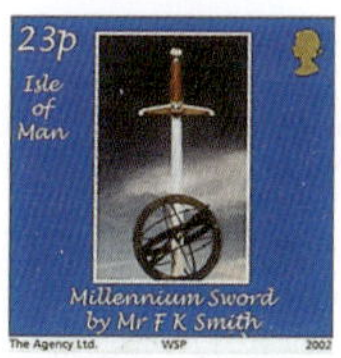

968 Millennium Sword (Mr. F. K. Smith)

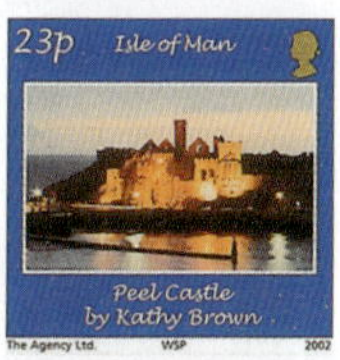

969 Peel Castle (Kathy Brown)

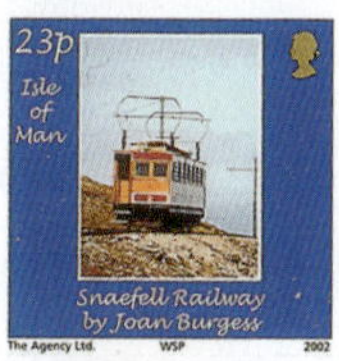

970 Snaefell Railway (Joan Burgess)

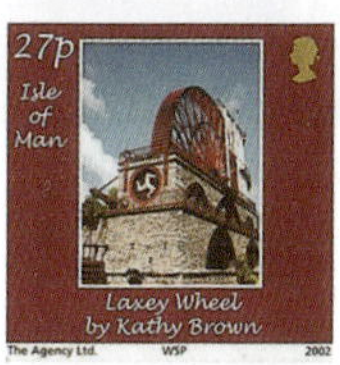

971 Laxey Wheel (Kathy Brown)

972 Sheep at Druidale (John Hall)

973 Carousel at Silverdale (Colin Edwards)

974 Grandma (Stephanie Corkhill)

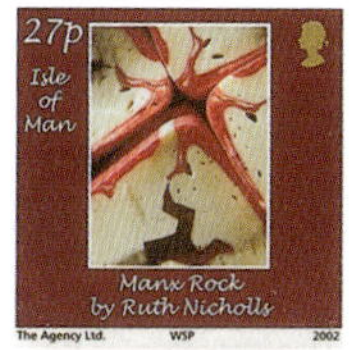

975 Manx Rock (Ruth Nicholls)

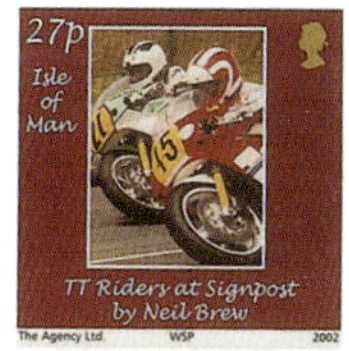

976 T.T. Riders at Signpost (Neil Brew)

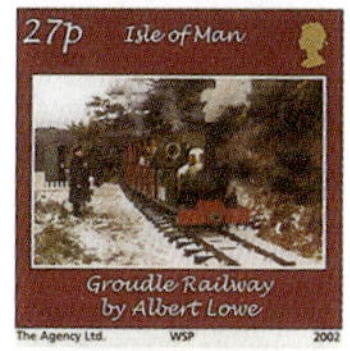

977 Groudle Railway (Albert Lowe)

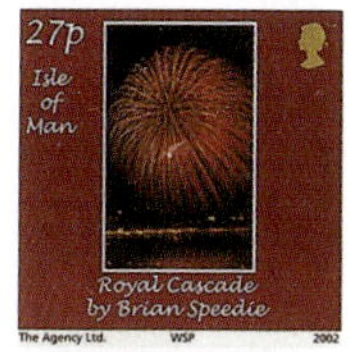

978 Royal Cascade (Brian Speedie)

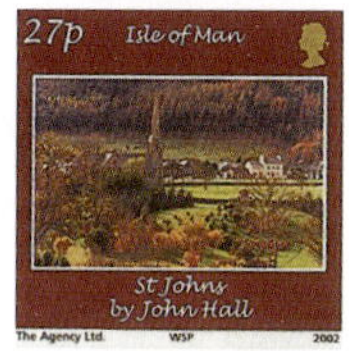

979 St. Johns (John Hall)

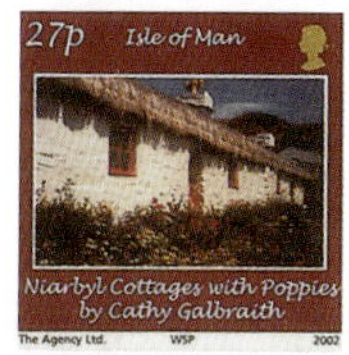

980 Niarbyl Cottages with Poppies (Cathy Galbraith)

Photography – The People's Choice. Competition Winners

(Des The Agency. Litho Walsall)

2002 (30 Aug–1 Oct).

(a) PVA gum. Perf 14 (C)

1001	**961**	23p. multicoloured (b)	30	25
		a. Block of 10. Nos. 1001/10	5·00	5·00
1002	**962**	23p. multicoloured (b)	30	25
1003	**963**	23p. multicoloured (b)	30	25
1004	**964**	23p. multicoloured (b)	30	25
1005	**965**	23p. multicoloured (b)	30	25
1006	**966**	23p. multicoloured (b)	30	25
1007	**967**	23p. multicoloured (b)	30	25
1008	**968**	23p. multicoloured (b)	30	25
1009	**969**	23p. multicoloured (b)	30	25
1010	**970**	23p. multicoloured (b)		
1011	**971**	27p. multicoloured (a)	35	30
		a. Block of 10. Nos. 1011/20	6·00	6·00
1012	**972**	27p. multicoloured (a)	35	30
1013	**973**	27p. multicoloured (a)	35	30
1014	**974**	27p. multicoloured (a)	35	30
1015	**975**	27p. multicoloured (a)	35	30
1016	**976**	27p. multicoloured (a)	35	30
1017	**977**	27p. multicoloured (a)	35	30
1018	**978**	27p. multicoloured (a)	35	30
1019	**979**	27p. multicoloured (a)	35	30
1020	**980**	27p. multicoloured (a)	35	30
1001/20 *Set of 20*			11·00	11·00
First Day Covers (2)				12·00
Presentation Packs (2)			12·00	

(b) Booklet stamps. Self-adhesive. Perf 6½ (die-cut)

1021	**961**	23p. multicoloured (b)	45	50
		a. Booklet pane. Nos. 1021/30	6·50	
1022	**962**	23p. multicoloured (b)	45	50
1023	**963**	23p. multicoloured (b)	45	50
1024	**964**	23p. multicoloured (b)	45	50
1025	**965**	23p. multicoloured (b)	45	50
1026	**966**	23p. multicoloured (b)	45	50
1027	**967**	23p. multicoloured (b)	45	50
1028	**968**	23p. multicoloured (b)		
1029	**969**	23p. multicoloured (b)	45	50
1030	**970**	23p. multicoloured (b)	45	50
1031	**971**	27p. multicoloured (b)	55	60
		a. Booklet pane. Nos. 1031/40	8·00	
1032	**972**	27p. multicoloured (b)	55	60
1033	**973**	27p. multicoloured (b)	55	60
1034	**974**	27p. multicoloured (b)	55	60
1035	**975**	27p. multicoloured (b)	55	60
1036	**976**	27p. multicoloured (b)	55	60
1037	**977**	27p. multicoloured (b)	55	60
1038	**978**	27p. multicoloured (b)	55	60
1039	**979**	27p. multicoloured (b)	55	60
1040	**980**	27p. multicoloured (b)	55	60

1021/40 *Set of* 20 .... 10·00 11·00

Nos. 1021/30 and 1031/40 were only available in £2.30 and £2.70 stamp booklets with the surplus self-adhesive paper around each stamp retained.

Printings: (a) 30.8.02; (b) 1.10.02.
Plate Nos.: Both values 1A (×5).
Sheets: 40 (5×8) Nos. 1001/10 and 1011/20 were each printed together, *se-tenant*, as blocks of 10, in sheets of 40.
Withdrawn: 29.8.2003 27p. sheets; 30.9.2003 23p. sheets.

981 Father Christmas

982 Virgin Mary and Jesus

983 Clown

984 Bandsman playing Cymbals

985 Fairy

986a 'CHRISTMAS' and Festive Characters (*Illustration reduced. Actual size* 125×55 *mm*)

Christmas. Entertainment

(Des Anthea Radcliffe. Litho Questa)

2002 (5 Nov). Perf 15×14½ (No. **MS**1046) or 14×14½ (others), both comb.

1041	**981**	22p. multicoloured	45	50
1042	**982**	26p. multicoloured	50	55
1043	**983**	37p. multicoloured	75	80
1044	**984**	47p. multicoloured	95	1·00
1045	**985**	68p. multicoloured	1·40	1·50
1041/5 *Set of* 5			4·00	4·25
First Day Cover				5·00
Presentation Pack			5·00	
MS1046 123×55 mm. **986a** £1.30, multicoloured			3·00	3·25
First Day Cover				4·00
Presentation Pack			4·25	

The 37p. value includes the 'EUROPA' emblem.
Plate Nos.: All values 1A (each ×4).
Sheets: 40 (5×8). The 37p. Europa stamp also exists in a sheetlet of ten (5×2).
Withdrawn: 4.11.2003.

Year Folder 2002

2002 (5 Nov). Comprises Nos. 970/93, 995/1020 and 1041/5.
Year Folder .... 45·00
Sold out: By 31.7.2004.

Year Pack 2002

2002 (5 Nov). Comprises Nos. 970/93, 995/1020 and 1041/5.
Year Pack .... 55·00
Sold out: By 31.7.2004.

Post Office Yearbook

2002 (5 Nov). Comprises Nos. 970/93, 995/1020 and 1041/5.
Yearbook .... 60·00
Sold out: By 5.2005.

987 Dish Aerial and Peel Castle

988 Dish Aerial, Tromode Teleport

989 Camp on Moon and lunar vehicle

990 Astronaut exploring lunar service

991 *Sea Launch Odyssey* (marine launch platform)

992 *Sea Launch Commander* (assembly and command ship)

993 Loral Telstar 1 satellite

994 Loral Telstar 8 satellite

995a Phobos and American Spaceship (75p.); Mars, Astronauts and Transfer Vehicle (75p.) (*Illustration reduced. Actual size* 110×85 *mm*)

Isle of Man Involvement in Space Exploration

(Des E. McCall (27p., 75p.), E. Gignac (others). Litho Cartor)

2003 (14 Feb). Perf 13½×13 (**MS**1055) or 13½ (others), both comb.

1047	**987**	23p. multicoloured	45	50
		a. Horiz pair. Nos. 1047/8	90	1·00
1048	**988**	23p. multicoloured	45	50
1049	**989**	27p. multicoloured	55	60
		a. Horiz pair. Nos. 1049/50	1·10	1·10
1050	**990**	27p. multicoloured	55	60
1051	**991**	37p. multicoloured	75	80
		a. Horiz pair. Nos. 1051/2	1·50	1·60
1052	**992**	37p. multicoloured	75	80
1053	**993**	42p. multicoloured	85	90
		a. Horiz pair. Nos. 1053/4	2·10	2·20
1054	**994**	42p. multicoloured	85	90
1047/54 *Set of* 8			6·00	6·00
First Day Cover				6·50

Presentation Pack	6·75	
MS1055 110×85 mm. **995a** 75p. multicoloured	4·00	4·00
First Day Cover		4·50
Presentation Pack	4·50	

Plate Nos.: All values 1A (×4).
Sheets: 8 (2×4). Nos. 1047/8, 1049/50, 1051/2 and 1053/4 were each printed together, as horizontal *se-tenant* pairs forming composite designs, in sheets with enlarged illustrated right margins.
Withdrawn: 13.2.2004.

996 Delivery Handcart (1900-45)

997 Morris Z Van (1942)

998 Morris L Diesel Van (1960s)

999 DI BSA Bantam Telephone Delivery Motorbikes

1000 Ford Escort 55 Van

Van Post Office Vehicles

(Des P. Hearsey. Litho Questa)

2003 (14 Feb). Perf 14½ (C).

1056	**996**	23p. multicoloured	45	50
1057	**997**	27p. multicoloured	55	60
1058	**998**	37p. multicoloured	1·00	1·10
1059	**999**	42p. multicoloured	1·10	1·20
1060	**1000**	89p. multicoloured	2·20	2·40
1056/60 *Set of 5*			5·25	5·50
First Day Cover				6·00
Presentation Pack			6·00	

Plate Nos.: All values 1A (×4).
Sheets: 25 (5×5).
Imprint: Right-hand side, bottom margin.
Withdrawn: 13.2.2004.

1001 Queen Elizabeth II wearing St. Edward's Crown

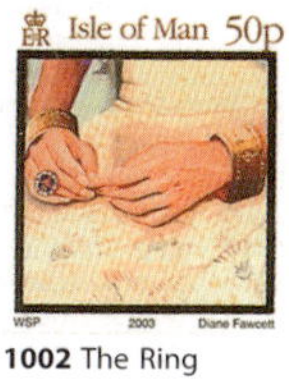

1002 The Ring

1003 The Orb

1004 Royal Sceptre and Rod of Equity and Mercy

1005 Queen Elizabeth II wearing Imperial State Crown

1006 State Coach

50th Anniversary of Coronation

(Des Diane Fawcett. Litho Walsall)

2003 (12 Apr). Perf 13½ (C).

1061	**1001**	50p. multicoloured	70	75
		a. Block of 6. Nos. 1061/6	6·00	6·50
1062	**1002**	50p. multicoloured	70	75
1063	**1003**	50p. multicoloured	70	75
1064	**1004**	50p. multicoloured	70	75
1065	**1005**	50p. multicoloured	70	75
1066	**1006**	50p. multicoloured	70	75
1061/6 *Set of 6*			6·00	6·50
First Day Cover				7·00
Presentation Pack			7·00	
Souvenir Folder			25·00	

Plate Nos.: 1A (×5).
Sheets: 24. Nos. 1061/6 were printed together, *se-tenant*, as four blocks of six with Nos. 1061 and 1065 at either end, 1062/4 in the top row and 1066 at the bottom.
Withdrawn: 10.4.2004.

1007 De Havilland D.H.83 Fox Moth and Saro Cloud (amphibian)

1008 De Havilland D.H.61 Giant Moth and D.H.80 Puss Moth

1009 Avro Anson Type 652 and Boeing B-17 Flying Fortress

1010 Eurofighter Typhoon and Avro Vulcan

1011 Handley Page Herald and Bristol Wayfarer

1012 Aerospatiale Concorde and projected Airbus Industrie A380

Centenary of Powered Flight

(Des K. Woodcock. Litho B.D.T.)

2003 (9 May). Perf 13½ (C).

1067	**1007**	23p. multicoloured	45	50
		a. Horiz strip of 3. Nos. 1067/9	1·80	2·00
1068	**1008**	27p. multicoloured	60	60
1069	**1009**	37p. multicoloured	70	80
1070	**1010**	40p. multicoloured	70	85
		a. Horiz strip of 3. Nos. 1070/2	4·00	4·50
1071	**1011**	67p. multicoloured	80	1·50
1072	**1012**	89p. multicoloured	1·20	1·90
1067/72 *Set of 6*			5·50	6·00
First Day Cover				6·50
Presentation Pack			6·75	
Souvenir Folder (complete sheets and **MS**1073)			28·00	

Plate Nos.: All values 1A (×4).
Sheets: 12 (2 panes 3×2). Nos. 1067/9 and 1070/2 were each printed together, *se-tenant*, as horizontal strips of three, within sheets containing two blocks of six separated by large illustrated gutters.
Withdrawn: 8.5.2004.

1012a Avro Lancaster attacking Mohne Dam (*Illustration reduced. Actual size 75×50 mm*)

60th Anniversary of Attack on German Dams by No. 617 ('Dambusters) Squadron

(Des R. Taylor. Litho B.D.T.)

2003 (9 May). Sheet 170×75 mm. Perf 13 (C).

MS1073 **1012a** £2 multicoloured	4·00	4·25
First Day Cover		6·00
Presentation Pack	5·00	

Withdrawn: 8.5.2004.

1013 Prince William

1014 Prince William

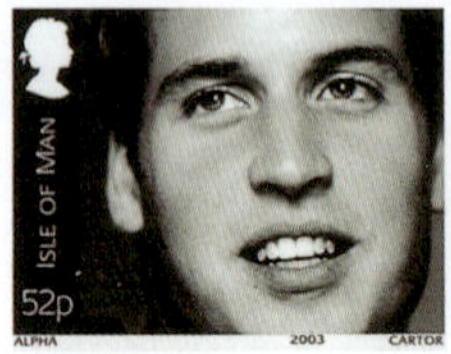

1015 Prince William

1016 Prince William

21st Birthday of Prince William of Wales

(Des The Agency Ltd. Litho Cartor)

2003 (9 June). Perf 13½ (C).

1074	**1013**	42p. black and grey	85	90
1075	**1014**	47p. black and grey	95	1·00
1076	**1015**	52p. black and grey	1·50	1·60
1077	**1016**	68p. black and grey	1·90	2·00
1074/7 *Set of 4*			5·00	5·50
First Day Cover				6·00
Presentation Pack			6·25	

Plate Nos.: All values 1A (×4).
Sheets: 25 (5×5).
Imprint: Central, side margins.
Withdrawn: 8.6.2004.

Trilaterale Ticino Exhibition, Locarno, Switzerland

2003 (18 June). No. **MS**1073 additionally inscribed with 'Ticino 2003' logo in blue on sheet Margin.

MS1078 £2 multicoloured	4·75	4·75

Withdrawn: 17.6.2004.

1017 *Manx Gold* (Agatha Christie)

1018 *Quatermass and the Pit* (Nigel Kneale)

1019 *Flashman at the Charge* (George MacDonald Fraser)

1020 *The Eternal City* (Hall Caine)

1021 *Peveril of the Peak* (Sir Walter Scott)

1022 *Emmas Secret* (Barbara Taylor Bradford)

'The Manx Bookshelf'. Book Covers

(Des D. Macdonald. Litho Walsall)

2003 (5 July). Perf 13½ (C).

1079	**1017**	23p. multicoloured	45	50
1080	**1018**	27p. multicoloured	55	60
1081	**1019**	30p. multicoloured	60	65
1082	**1020**	38p. multicoloured	75	80
1083	**1021**	40p. multicoloured	1·00	1·10
1084	**1022**	53p. multicoloured	1·20	1·30

1079/84 *Set of 6*	4·50	5·00
First Day Cover		5·75
Presentation Pack	5·75	

The 38p. value includes the 'EUROPA 2003' emblem.
Plate Nos: All values 1A (×4).
Sheets: 20 (5×4) with small *se-tenant* label giving the author's name at the foot of each stamp; 38p. also 10 (5×2).
Withdrawn: 3.7.2004.

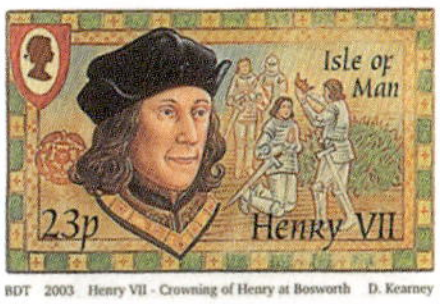

1023 King Henry VII and Henry Tudor crowned by Sir Thomas Stanley on Bosworth Battlefield

1024 King Henry VIII and Manx Church (Dissolution of the Monasteries)

1025 Queen Elizabeth I and Globe showing Route of Drake's Circumnavigation

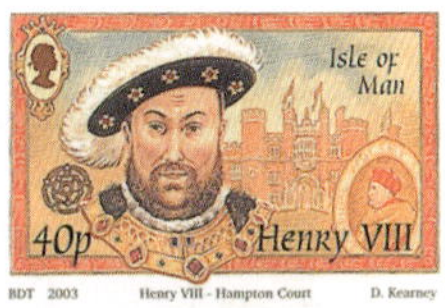

1026 King Henry VIII, Cardinal Wolsey and Hampton Court Palace

1027 Queen Mary I and Tudor Rose

1028 Queen Elizabeth I and Ships of Spanish Armada

400th Anniversary of End of the Tudor Reign

(Des D. Kearney. Litho BDT)

2003 (15 Sept). Perf 14 (C).

1085	**1023**	23p. multicoloured	45	50
1086	**1024**	27p. multicoloured	55	60
1087	**1025**	38p. multicoloured	75	80
1088	**1026**	40p. multicoloured	80	85
1089	**1027**	47p. multicoloured	95	1·00
1090	**1028**	67p. multicoloured	1·40	1·50
1085/90 *Set of 6*			4·75	5·25
First Day Cover				5·75
Presentation Pack			5·50	
Stamp Cards (set of 6)			4·25	10·00

Plate Nos.: All values 1A (×4).
Sheets: 25 (5×5).
Withdrawn: 14.9.2004.

1029 Henry Bloom Noble and Orphanage Boys

1030 Nurse and Ramsey Cottage Hospital

1031 Children and Children's Home

1032 Bathers at Noble's Baths

1033 Scout and Headquarters

1034 Noble's Hospital c.1912

1035 Villa Marina

1036 Noble's Park

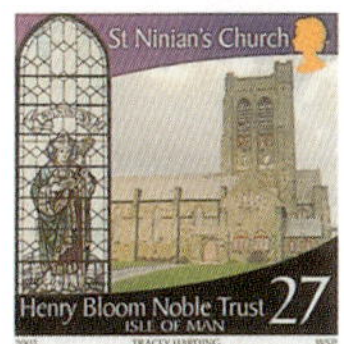

1037 St. Ninian's Church

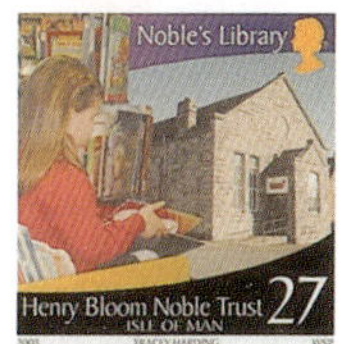

1038 Noble's Library

Centenary of Henry Bloom Noble Trust

(Des Tracey Harding. Litho Walsall)

2003 (1 Oct).

(a) PVA gum. Perf 14 (C)

1091	**1029**	23p. multicoloured	40	25
		a. Horiz strip of 5. Nos. 1091/5	2·50	2·75
1092	**1030**	23p. multicoloured	40	25
1093	**1031**	23p. multicoloured	40	25
1094	**1032**	23p. multicoloured	40	25
1095	**1033**	23p. multicoloured	40	25
1096	**1034**	27p. multicoloured	45	30
		a. Horiz strip of 5. Nos. 1096/1100	3·00	3·25
1097	**1035**	27p. multicoloured	45	30
1098	**1036**	27p. multicoloured	45	30
1099	**1037**	27p. multicoloured	45	30
1100	**1038**	27p. multicoloured	45	30
1091/1100 *Set of 10*			5·00	5·50
First Day Cover				6·00
Presentation Pack			6·00	

(b) Self-adhesive booklet stamps. Roul 6½

1101	**1029**	23p. multicoloured		
		a. Booklet pane. Nos. 1101/5, each ×2		
1102	**1030**	23p. multicoloured	45	50
1103	**1031**	23p. multicoloured	45	50
1104	**1032**	23p. multicoloured	45	50
1105	**1033**	23p. multicoloured	45	50
1106	**1034**	27p. multicoloured	55	60
		a. Booklet pane. Nos. 1106/1110, each ×2		
1107	**1035**	27p. multicoloured		
1108	**1036**	27p. multicoloured	55	60
1109	**1037**	27p. multicoloured	55	60
1110	**1038**	27p. multicoloured	55	60
1101/10 *Set of 10*			5·00	5·50

Plate Nos.: Both values 1A (×4).
Sheets: 50 (5×10). Nos. 1091/5 and 1096/1100 were each printed together, *se-tenant*, in horizontal strips of 5 throughout the sheets. Nos. 1101/5 and 1106/1110 were only issued in £2.30 and £2.70 booklets, Nos. SB57/8.
Withdrawn: 30.9.2004 (sheets).

1039 Boy tying Scarf on Snowman

1040 Snowman (wearing black hat and scarf)

1041 Boy and Snowman holding Hands

1042 Snowman (wearing brown hat and scarf)

1043 Boy flying with Snowman

Christmas. *The Snowman* by Raymond Briggs.

(Litho DLR)

2003 (5 Nov). Perf 14½ (C).

1111	**1039**	22p. multicoloured	45	50
1112	**1040**	26p. multicoloured	50	55
1113	**1041**	38p. multicoloured	75	80
1114	**1042**	47p. multicoloured	95	1·00
1115	**1043**	68p. multicoloured	1·40	1·50
1111/15 *Set of 5*			4·00	4·25
First Day Cover				5·00
Presentation Pack			5·25	

Plate Nos.: All values 1A (×4).
Sheets: 40 (5×8).
Withdrawn: 4.11.2004.

Year Folder 2003

2003 (12 Nov). Comprises Nos. 1047/77, 1079/1100 and 1111/15.
Year Folder .... 50·00
Sold out: By 12.2004.

Year Pack 2003

2003 (12 Nov). Comprises Nos. 1047/77, 1079/1100 and 1111/15.
Year Pack .... 60·00
Sold out: By 5.2005.

Post Office Yearbook

2003 (12 Nov). Comprises Nos. 1047/77, 1079/1100 and 1111/15.
Yearbook .... 60·00
Sold out: By 12.2006.

1044 Aragorn

1045 Gimli

1046 Gandalf

1047 Legolas on Horseback

1048 Gollum

1049 Frodo and Sam

1050 Legolas drawing Bow

1051 Aragon on Horseback

1052a The Ring (*Illustration reduced. Actual size*120×78 mm)

Making of *The Lord of the Rings* Film Trilogy: *The Return of the King*

(Des The Agency Ltd. Litho BDT)

2003 (17 Dec). Perf 13½ (C).

1116	**1044**	23p. multicoloured	45	50
1117	**1045**	27p. multicoloured	55	60
1118	**1046**	30p. multicoloured	60	65
1119	**1047**	38p. multicoloured	1·00	90
1120	**1048**	42p. multicoloured	1·50	1·00
1121	**1049**	47p. multicoloured	2·00	2·00
1122	**1050**	68p. multicoloured	3·00	3·50
1123	**1051**	85p. multicoloured	3·50	3·00
1116/23 *Set of 8*			9·75	9·75
First Day Cover				11·00
Presentation Pack			11·00	
Souvenir Folder (complete sheets and **MS**1124)			50·00	
Stamp Cards (pre-paid) (set of 8)			9·50	9·50
MS1124 120×78 mm. **1052a** £2 The Ring (44×40 mm)			5·00	5·50
First Day Cover				6·00
Presentation Pack			6·00	

Plate Nos.: All values 1A (×4).
Sheets: 6 (3×2) with enlarged illustrated margins.
Withdrawn: 16.12.2004.

1053 *Maitland* (Simon Hall)

1054 *Evening Star* (Terence Cuneo)

1055 *Pen-y-Darren* Tramroad Locomotive (Terence Cuneo)

1056 *Duchess of Hamilton* (Craig Tiley)

1057 *City of Truro* (B. J. Freeman)

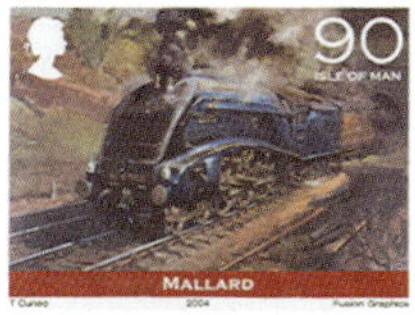

1058 *Mallard* (Terence Cuneo)

Bicentenary of Running of First Steam Locomotive. Paintings of Steam Locomotives.

(Des Fusion Graphics from paintings. Litho Cartor)

2004 (21 Feb). Perf 13×13½ (C).

1125	**1053**	23p. multicoloured	75	75
1126	**1054**	27p. multicoloured	90	90
1127	**1055**	40p. multicoloured	1·30	1·30
1128	**1056**	57p. multicoloured	1·80	1·80
1129	**1057**	61p. multicoloured	2·00	2·00
1130	**1058**	90p. multicoloured	3·00	3·00
1125/30 *Set of* 6			9·75	9·75
First Day Cover				11·00
Presentation Pack			11·50	

Plate Nos.: All values 1A (×4).
Sheets: (5×5).
Withdrawn: 20.2.2005.

1059 Troops on Landing Craft and Tanks going Ashore

1060 Troops leaving Landing Craft and Tanks going Ashore

1061 Troops leaving Landing Craft

1062 Landing Craft and Troops wading Ashore

1063 *Lady of Mann* (ferry used as landing craft carrier)

1064 *Ben-my-Chree* (ferry used as landing craft carrier)

1065 Consolidated B-24 Liberators (bombers) and North American P-51 Mustang (fighter)

1066 Airspeed A.S.51 Horsa Gliders (troop carriers)

1067a Winston Churchill; Troops and Aircraft; Military Vehicles on Street; Soldiers with *France* Guidebook (*Illustration reduced. Actual size* 170×75 mm)

60th Anniversary of D-Day

(Des B. Sanders (Nos. 1131/8 only) and The Agency Ltd. Litho DLR (Nos. 1131/8) or Enschedé **MS**1139))

2004 (6 Apr). Perf 14 (C).

1131	**1059**	23p. multicoloured	50	25
		a. Horiz pair. Nos. 1131/2	1·50	1·50
1132	**1060**	23p. multicoloured	50	25
1133	**1061**	27p. multicoloured	60	30
		a. Horiz pair. Nos. 1133/4	1·80	1·80
1134	**1062**	27p. multicoloured	60	30
1135	**1063**	47p. multicoloured	1·00	50
		a. Horiz pair. Nos. 1135/6	3·00	3·00
1136	**1064**	47p. multicoloured	1·00	50
1137	**1065**	68p. multicoloured	1·20	70
		a. Horiz pair. Nos. 1137/8	5·00	5·00
1138	**1066**	68p. multicoloured	1·20	70
1131/8 *Set of* 8			10·50	10·50
First Day Cover				12·50
Presentation Pack			12·50	
Collectors Folder (complete sheets and **MS**1139)			40·00	
MS1139 170×75 mm. **1067a** 50p. 34,multicoloured. Perf 13½×14 (C)			6·50	6·50
First Day Cover				8·00
Presentation Pack			8·25	

Plate Nos.: All values 1A (×4).
Sheets: 10 (2×5) Nos. 1131/2, 1133/4, 1135/6 and 1137/8 were each printed together, *se-tenant*, in horizontal pairs throughout the sheets, each pair forming a composite design.
Withdrawn: 5.4.2005.

1068 Lesser Celandine

1069 Red Campion

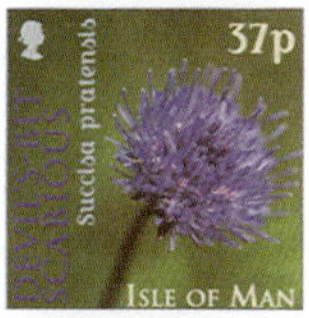

1070 Devil's-bit Scabious

1071 Northern Harebell

1072 Wood Anemone

1073 Common Spotted Orchid

Bicentenary of Royal Horticultural Society. Wild Flowers

(Des The Agency Ltd. Litho Cartor)

2004 (3 May). Perf 13½ (C).

1140	**1068**	25p. multicoloured	85	85
1141	**1069**	28p. multicoloured	95	95
1142	**1070**	37p. multicoloured	1·20	1·20
1143	**1071**	40p. multicoloured	1·30	1·30
1144	**1072**	68p. multicoloured	2·20	2·20
1145	**1073**	85p. multicoloured	2·75	2·75
1140/5 *Set of* 6			9·25	9·25
First Day Cover				11·00
Presentation Pack			11·00	

Plate Nos.: All values 1A (×4).
Sheets: 40 (5×8).
Withdrawn: 2.5.2005.

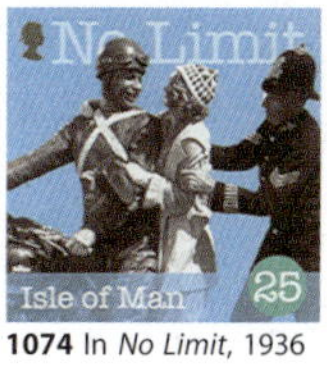

1074 In *No Limit*, 1936

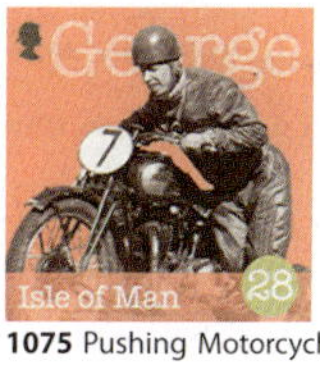

1075 Pushing Motorcycle

1076 Riding in TT Race

1077 With Florence Desmond

1078 On Motorcycle

1079 Close-up of George Formby

Birth Centenary of George Formby (entertainer). Scenes from *No Limit* (film)

(Des Ruth Sutherland. Litho BDT)

2004 (26 May). Perf 13½ (C).

1146	**1074**	25p. multicoloured	80	80
1147	**1075**	28p. multicoloured	90	90
1148	**1076**	40p. multicoloured	1·30	1·30
1149	**1077**	43p. multicoloured	1·40	1·40
1150	**1078**	50p. multicoloured	1·70	1·70
1151	**1079**	74p. multicoloured	2·40	2·40
1146/51		*Set of* 6	8·50	8·50
First Day Cover				10·00
Presentation Pack			10·00	

Sheets: (5×5).
Withdrawn: 25.5.2005.

1080 Johnny Weissmuller (gold, 100m & 400m freestyle), Paris, 1924

1081 Jesse Owens (gold, 100m, 200m, long jump), Berlin, 1936

1082 John Mark carrying Olympic Flame, London, 1948

1083 Fanny Blankers-Koen (gold, 100m, 200m, 80m hurdles), London, 1948

1084 James Cracknell, Steven Redgrave, Tim Foster and Matthew Pinsent (gold, men's coxless fours), Sydney, 2000

Olympic Games, Athens. Olympic Legends

(Des Fusion Graphics. Litho BDT)

2004 (1 July). Perf 14 (C).

1152	**1080**	25p. multicoloured	85	85
1153	**1081**	28p. multicoloured	95	95
1154	**1082**	43p. multicoloured	1·40	1·40
1155	**1083**	55p. multicoloured	1·80	1·80
1156	**1084**	91p. multicoloured	3·00	3·00
1152/6		*Set of* 5	8·00	8·00
First Day Cover				9·75
Presentation Pack			10·00	

Plate Nos.: All values 1A (×4).
Sheets: (5×5).
Imprint: Central, bottom margin.
Withdrawn: 30.6.2005.

1085 Celtic Islanders and Viking Invaders

1086 Fisherman ('Ships and the Sea')

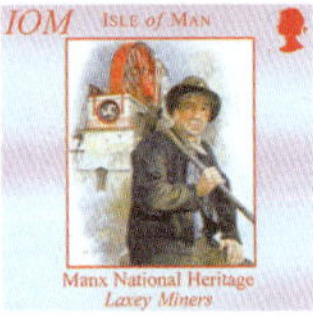

1087 Miner and Laxey Wheel ('Laxey Miners')

1088 Soldier with Longbow and Castle ('Kings and Lords of Mann')

1089 Woman with Spinning Wheel ('Farmers and Crofters')

1090 Calf of Man

1091 Peel Castle

1092 Laxey Wheel

1093 Castle Rushen

1094 Cregneash

Manx National Heritage 'The Story of Mann'

(Des The Agency Ltd. Litho BDT)

2004 (3 Aug).

(a) PVA gum. Perf 14 (C)

1157	**1085**	(25p.) multicoloured	50	25
		a. Horiz strip of 5. Nos. 1157/61	4·00	4·00
1158	**1086**	(25p.) multicoloured	50	25
1159	**1087**	(25p.) multicoloured	50	25
1160	**1088**	(25p.) multicoloured	50	25
1161	**1089**	(25p.) multicoloured	50	25
1162	**1090**	(28p.) multicoloured	60	30
		a. Horiz strip of 5. Nos. 1162/6	5·00	5·00
1163	**1091**	(28p.) multicoloured	60	30

1164	**1092** (28p.) multicoloured	60	30
1165	**1093** (28p.) multicoloured	60	30
1166	**1094** (28p.) multicoloured	60	30
1157/66 *Set of* 10		8·50	8·50
First Day Cover			10·50
Presentation Pack		10·50	

(b) Self-adhesive booklet stamps. Perf 12½ (die-cut)

1167	**1085** (25p.) multicoloured	60	60
	a. Booklet pane. Nos. 1167/71, each ×2	8·00	
1168	**1086** (25p.) multicoloured	60	60
1169	**1087** (25p.) multicoloured	60	60
1170	**1088** (25p.) multicoloured	60	60
1171	**1089** (25p.) multicoloured	60	60
1172	**1090** (28p.) multicoloured	75	75
	a. Booklet pane. Nos. 1172/6, each ×2	9·00	
1173	**1091** (28p.) multicoloured	75	75
1174	**1092** (28p.) multicoloured	75	75
1175	**1093** (28p.) multicoloured	75	75
1176	**1094** (28p.) multicoloured	75	75
1167/76 *Set of* 10		8·50	8·50

Nos. 1157/61 and 1167/71 are inscribed 'IOM' and were initially sold at 25p. Nos. 1162/6 and 1172/6 are inscribed 'UK' and were initially sold at 28p.

Plate Nos. Both values 1A (×4).

Sheets: 50 (5×10). Nos. 1157/61 and 1162/6 were each printed together, *se-tenant*, in horizontal strips of 5 throughout the sheets. Nos. 1167/71 and 1172/6 were only issued in £2.50 and £2.80 booklets, Nos. SB59/60.

Withdrawn: 2.8.2005.

1095a Laxey Wheel (*Illustration reduced. Actual size* 120×78 *mm*)

150th Anniversary of the Great Laxey Wheel

(Des The Agency Ltd. Litho BDT)

2004 (3 Aug). Perf 14 (C).

MS1177 **1095a** £2 multicoloured		6·50	6·50
First Day Cover			8·50
Presentation Pack		8·50	

Withdrawn: 2.8.2005.

1096 'Maughold Church'

1097 'Port St. Mary'

1098 'Ballaugh Old Church'

1099 'Douglas Bay (A Midsummer's Night)'

1100 'Point of Ayre'

1101 'Peel Harbour and Castle'

The Isle of Man Watercolours by Alfred Heaton Cooper

(Des The Agency Ltd. Litho Enschedé)

2004 (21 Oct). Perf 13½×13 (C).

1178	**1096**	25p. multicoloured	80	80
1179	**1097**	28p. multicoloured	90	90
1180	**1098**	40p. multicoloured	1·30	1·30
1181	**1099**	41p. multicoloured	1·30	1·30
1182	**1100**	43p. multicoloured	1·40	1·40
1183	**1101**	74p. multicoloured	2·40	2·40
1178/83 *Set of* 6			8·00	8·00
First Day Cover				10·00
Presentation Pack			8·75	

The 28p. and 40p. values include the 'EUROPA 2004' emblem.

Plate Nos.: All values 1A (×4).

Sheets: 25 (5×5); 28p. and 40p. also 10 (2×5).

Withdrawn: 20.10.2005.

Sindelfingen International Stamp Exhibition, Sindelfingen, Germany

2004 (29 Oct). No. **MS**1177 additionally inscribed with SINDELFINGEN logo on the sheet margin.

MS1184 **1095a** £2 multicoloured		6·50	6·50

Withdrawn: 28.10.2005.

1102 Robin on Flower Pot

1103 Robin at Foot of Tree

1104 Robin perched on Branch among Bracken

1105 Robin on Window Ledge

1106 Robin on Snowy Logs

Robins—'Winters Friends'

(Des Dr. J. Paul. Litho Lowe-Martin, Canada)

2004 (9 Nov). Perf 12½×13 (C).

1185	**1102**	25p. multicoloured	80	80
1186	**1103**	28p. multicoloured	90	90
1187	**1104**	40p. multicoloured	1·30	1·30
1188	**1105**	47p. multicoloured	1·50	1·50
1189	**1106**	68p. multicoloured	2·30	2·30
1185/9 *Set of* 5			6·75	6·75
First Day Cover				8·75
Presentation Pack			8·75	
Collectors Folder (**MS**1190 *and signed first day cover*)			30·00	
MS1190 148×200 mm. Nos. 1185/9×2			8·50	8·50

Plate Nos.: All values 1A (×7).

Sheets: 40 (5×8).

Withdrawn: 8.11.2005.

Year Folder 2004

2004 (9 Nov). Comprises Nos. 1116/66, **MS**1177/83 and 1185/9.
Year Folder ..... 60·00
Sold out: By 7.2005.

Year Pack 2004

2004 (9 Nov). Comprises Nos. 1116/66, **MS**1177/83 and 1185/9.
Year Pack ..... 75·00
Sold out: By 8.2006.

Post Office Yearbook

2004 (9 Nov). Comprises Nos. 1116/66, **MS**1177/83 and 1185/9.
Yearbook ..... 60·00
Sold out: By 12.2006.

1107 Harry Potter, Ron Weasley and Hermione Granger

1108 Snowy Owl delivering Owl Post

1109 Harry Potter and White Stag

1110 *Hogwarts Express*

1111 Rubeus Hagrid

1112 Purple Triple-decker Bus

1113 Dementor and Harry Potter flying

1114 Harry Potter on the Hippogriff Buckbeak

***Harry Potter and the Prisoner of Azkaban* (film)**

(Des The Agency Ltd. Litho Enschedé)

2004 (7 Dec). Perf 13½ (C).

1191	**1107**	25p. multicoloured	80	80
1192	**1108**	28p. multicoloured	90	90
1193	**1109**	39p. multicoloured	1·30	1·30
1194	**1110**	40p. multicoloured	1·30	1·30
1195	**1111**	49p. multicoloured	1·60	1·60
1196	**1112**	55p. multicoloured	1·80	1·80
1197	**1113**	57p. multicoloured	1·90	1·90
1198	**1114**	68p. multicoloured	2·20	2·20
1191/8 *Set of 8*			11·50	11·50
First Day Cover				13·50
Presentation Pack			13·50	
Collectors Folder (contains complete sheets and Owl Post Office first day cover)			50·00	

Stamp Cards (pre-paid) (set of 8) ..... 11·50 11·50
Plate Nos.: All values 1A (×5).
Sheets: 5 (1×5). with enlarged illustrated right margins.
Withdrawn: 6.12.2005.

1115 'The Nile Campaign'

1116 'The Battle of Copenhagen'

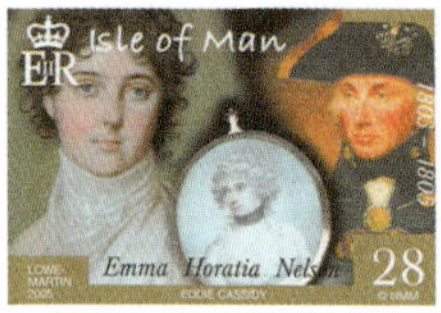

1117 Emma, Horatia and Nelson

1118 Band of Brothers

1119 'Prepare for Battle'

1120 'Victory in Sight'

1121 'The Fall of Nelson'

1122 'The Death of Nelson'

1123 2000 Isle of Man at War 22p. Stamp (£1); 1979 150th Death Anniversary of Captain John Quilliam 8p. Stamp (£1)
(*Illustration reduced. Actual size 170×75 mm*)

Bicentenary of the Battle of Trafalgar

(Des E. Cassidy. Litho Enschedé Nos. 1199/1206) or Lowe-Martin (**MS**1207))

2005 (9 Jan). Perf 12½×13 (C).

1199	**1115**	25p. multicoloured	50	55
		a. Horiz pair. Nos. 1199/1200	1·00	1·10
1200	**1116**	25p. multicoloured	50	55
1201	**1117**	28p. multicoloured	55	60
		a. Horiz pair. Nos. 1201/2	1·10	1·20
1202	**1118**	28p. multicoloured	55	60
1203	**1119**	50p. multicoloured	1·00	1·10
		a. Horiz pair. Nos. 1203/4	2·00	2·20
1204	**1120**	50p. multicoloured	1·00	1·10
1205	**1121**	65p. multicoloured	1·30	1·40
		a. Horiz pair. Nos. 1205/6	2·50	2·75
1206	**1122**	65p. multicoloured	1·30	1·40
1199/206 *Set of 8*			6·50	7·00
First Day Cover				8·00
Presentation Pack			8·00	
Collectors Folder (complete sheets and **MS**1207)			30·00	
MS1207 170×75 mm. **1123** £1 multicoloured; £1 multicoloured			4·00	4·25
First Day Cover				5·00
Presentation Pack			5·00	

Plate Nos.: All values 1A (×5).

Sheets: 8 (2×4). Nos. 1199/1200, 1201/2, 1203/4 and 1205/6 were each printed together, *se-tenant*, in horizontal pairs throughout the sheets.
Withdrawn: 8.1.2006.

1124 Two Couples by Waterside

1125 Group celebrating in the Street

1126 Man trying on Hat

1127 Civil Service Personnel

1128 King George VI and Winston Churchill on Balcony of Buckingham Palace

1129 King George VI and Queen Elizabeth in Carriage

1130 Servicemen

1131 War Graves

1132 The Manx Regiment (£1); Royal Visit, 1945 (£1) (*Illustration reduced. Actual size* 170×75 mm)

60th Anniversary of the End of World War II

(Des The Agency Ltd. Litho Enschedé)

2005 (15 Apr). Perf 13½×14 (C).

1208	**1124**	26p. multicoloured	45	30
		a. Horiz pair. Nos. 1208/9	1·00	1·10
1209	**1125**	26p. multicoloured	45	30
1210	**1126**	29p. multicoloured	50	30
		a. Horiz pair. Nos. 1210/11	1·20	1·30
1211	**1127**	29p. multicoloured	50	30
1212	**1128**	60p. multicoloured	75	70
		a. Horiz pair. Nos. 1212/13	2·50	2·50
1213	**1129**	60p. multicoloured	75	70
1214	**1130**	65p. multicoloured	85	70
		a. Horiz pair. Nos. 1214/15	2·75	2·75
1215	**1131**	65p. multicoloured	85	70
1208/15 *Set of 8*			7·00	7·75
First Day Cover				8·25
Presentation Pack			8·25	
Collectors Folder (complete sheets)			40·00	
MS1216 170×75 mm. **1132** £1 multicoloured; £1 multicoloured			4·50	4·50
First Day Cover				6·00
Presentation Pack			5·50	

Plate Nos.: All values 1A (×4).
Sheets: 10 (2×5). Nos. 1208/9, 1210/11, 1212/13 and 1214/15 were each printed together, *se-tenant*, in horizontal pairs throughout the sheets.
Withdrawn: 14.4.2006.

1133 *'Mona's Isle'* (Samuel Walters)

1134 *'Viking'* (Norman Wilkinson)

1135 *'King Orry'* (Robert Lloyd)

1136 *'Mona's Queen'* (Arthur Burgess)

1137 *'Ben-my-Chree'*(John Nicholson)

1138 *'King Orry'* (Robert Lloyd)

1139 *'Ben-my-Chree'* (Robert Lloyd)

1140 *'Lady of Mann'* (Robert Lloyd)

175th Anniversary of Steam Packet Company

(Des Tracey Harding. Litho BDT)

2005 (6 May). Perf 14 (C).

1217	**1133**	26p. multicoloured	45	30
		a. Horiz pair. Nos. 1217/18	1·00	1·00
		b. Booklet pane. Nos. 1217/20 with margins all round	2·20	
		c. Booklet pane. Nos. 1217/18 and 1221/2 with margins all round	2·50	
1218	**1134**	26p. multicoloured	45	30
1219	**1135**	29p. multicoloured	50	30
		a. Horiz pair. Nos. 1219/20	1·20	1·50
		b. Booklet pane. Nos. 1219/20 and 1223/4 with margins all round	3·75	
1220	**1136**	29p. multicoloured	50	30
1221	**1137**	40p. multicoloured	75	45
		a. Horiz pair. Nos. 1221/2	1·70	1·70
		b. Booklet pane. Nos. 1221/4 with margins all round	4·00	
1222	**1138**	40p. multicoloured	75	45
1223	**1139**	66p. multicoloured	1·00	70
		a. Horiz pair. Nos. 1223/4	2·75	2·75
		b. Booklet pane. Nos. 1223/4 with margins all round	2·50	
1224	**1140**	66p. multicoloured	1·00	70
1217/24 *Set of 8*			6·25	6·75
First Day Cover				7·50
Presentation Pack			7·50	
Set of 4 Gutter Pairs			13·00	

Plate Nos.: All values 1A (×4).
Sheets: 40 (2 panes 2×10). Nos. 1217/18, 1219/20, 1221/2 and 1223/4 were each printed together, *se-tenant*, as horizontal pairs in sheets containing two vertical columns of pairs separated by an illustrated and inscribed gutter.
Withdrawn: 5.5.2006.

1141 Bill Ivy and Phil Read

1142 Joey Dunlop and Ray McCullough

1143 Steve Hislop

1144 Carl Fogarty

1145 David Jefferies

1146 John McGuinness

50th Anniversary of Yamaha

(Des Ruth Sutherland. Litho Enschedé)

2005 (17 May). Perf 14 (C).

1225	**1141**	26p. multicoloured	50	55
		a. Sheetlet. Nos. 1225/30×2	11·50	
1226	**1142**	29p. multicoloured	60	65
1227	**1143**	40p. multicoloured	80	85
1228	**1144**	42p. multicoloured	85	90
1229	**1145**	68p. multicoloured	1·40	1·50
1230	**1146**	78p. multicoloured	1·60	1·70
1225/30 *Set of 6*			5·75	6·00
First Day Cover				6·75
Presentation Pack			6·75	
Carl Fogarty Folder (sheetlet & signed first day cover)			40·00	

Plate Nos.: All values 1A (×4) (sheets of 25 only).
Sheets: 25 (5×5) or 12 (2 columns 6×1). Nos. 1225/30 were issued in separate sheets of 25 and *se-tenant* in sheetlets of 12 containing two vertical columns separated by an illustrated gutter.
Withdrawn: 16.5.2006.

1147 Paul Harris (founder)

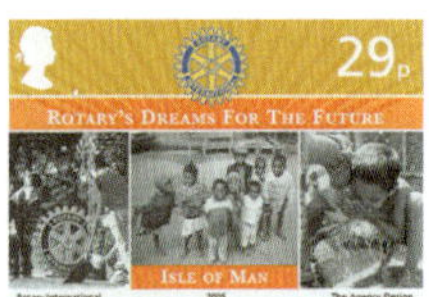

1148 Planting Tree, Children grouped and Child drinking

1149 Child being immunised and Boy with Leg Braces and Crutches

1150 Food Preparations

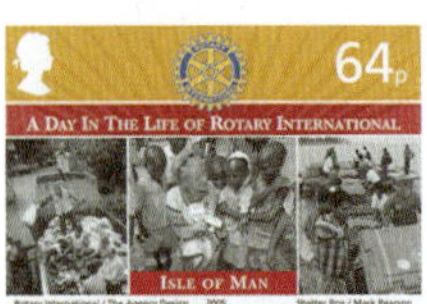

1151 Supply Truck, Children with Volunteer and loading Cases

1152 Child having Eye Test, Group under Rotary Banner and Family

Centenary of Rotary International and Europa Gastronomy

(Des The Agency Ltd. Litho Cartor)

2005 (15 June). Perf 13½×14 (C).

1231	**1147**	26p. multicoloured	50	55
1232	**1148**	29p. multicoloured	60	65
1233	**1149**	40p. multicoloured	80	85
1234	**1150**	42p. multicoloured	85	90
1235	**1151**	64p. multicoloured	1·30	1·40
1236	**1152**	68p. multicoloured	1·40	1·50
1231/6 *Set of 6*			5·25	5·75
First Day Cover				6·75
Presentation Pack			6·75	

The 42p. value includes the 'EUROPA 2005' emblem.
Plate Nos.: All values 1A (×4).
Sheets: 25 (5×5); 42p. also 10 (2×5).
Withdrawn: 14.6.2006.

1153 Guttin' Herrin'

1154 Pickin' Spuds

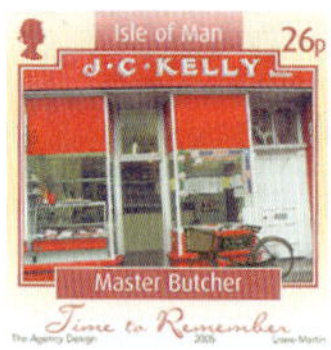

1155 J. C. Kelly, Master Butcher

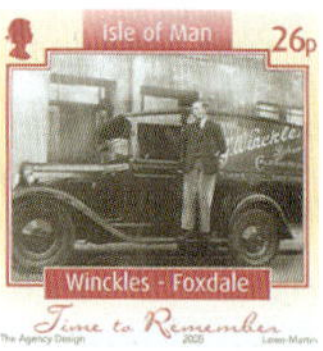

1156 Winckles, Foxdale

1157 Palace Ballroom

1158 Land Army

1159 Farmyard, Glen Maye

1160 Eva Kane, Summer Season Stars

1161 Donkey Rides

1162 Alfie Gilmour, 'Give us a go Mister!'

'Time to Remember'

(Des The Agency Ltd. Litho Lowe-Martin)

2005 (12 Aug).

(a) PVA gum. Perf 12½×13 (C)

1237	**1153**	26p. multicoloured	45	30
		a. Horiz strip of 5. Nos. 1237/41	2·50	2·50
1238	**1154**	26p. multicoloured	45	30

1239	**1155**	26p. multicoloured	45	30
1240	**1156**	26p. multicoloured	45	30
1241	**1157**	26p. multicoloured	45	30
1242	**1158**	29p. multicoloured	50	30
		a. Horiz strip of 5. Nos. 1242/6	3·50	3·75
1243	**1159**	29p. multicoloured	50	30
1244	**1160**	29p. multicoloured	50	30
1245	**1161**	29p. multicoloured	50	30
1246	**1162**	29p. multicoloured	50	30
1237/46 *Set of* 10			5·50	6·00
First Day Cover				6·75
Presentation Pack			6·75	

(b) Self-adhesive. Perf 12½×13

1247	**1153**	26p. multicoloured	50	55
		a. Horiz strip of 5. Nos. 1247/51	2·50	
		b. Die cut perf 10½	50	55
		ba. Booklet pane. Nos. 1247b/51b, each ×2	5·00	
1248	**1154**	26p. multicoloured	50	55
		b. Die-cut perf 10½	50	55
1249	**1155**	26p. multicoloured	50	55
		b. Die-cut perf 10½	50	55
1250	**1156**	26p. multicoloured	50	55
		b. Die-cut perf 10½	50	55
1251	**1157**	26p. multicoloured	50	55
		b. Die-cut perf 10½	50	55
1252	**1158**	29p. multicoloured	60	65
		a. Horiz strip of 5. Nos. 1252/6	3·75	
		b. Die-cut perf 10½	60	65
		ba. Booklet pane. Nos. 1252b/6b, each ×2	5·75	
1253	**1159**	29p. multicoloured	60	65
		b. Die-cut perf 10½	60	65
1254	**1160**	29p. multicoloured	60	65
		b. Die-cut perf 10½	60	65
1255	**1161**	29p. multicoloured	60	65
		b. Die-cut perf 10½	60	65
1256	**1162**	29p. multicoloured	60	65
		b. Die-cut perf 10½	60	65
1247/56 *Set of* 10			5·50	6·00

Plate Nos.: All values 1A (×5).

Sheets: 50 (5×10). Nos. 1237/41, 1242/6, 1247/51 and 1252/6 were each printed together, *se-tenant*, in horizontal strips of five stamps throughout the sheets.

Nos. 1247b/51b and 1252b/6b were only available from £2.60 and £2.90 booklets, Nos. SB62/3.

Withdrawn: 11.8.2006.

1163 Obelisk in St. Peter's Square (42p.); St. Peter's Basilica (£1.50) (*Illustration reduced. Actual size 170×75 mm*)

20th World Youth Day

(Des E. Cassidy. Litho BDT)

2005 (15 Aug). Sheet 170×75 mm. Perf 14×15 (C).

MS1257 **1163** multicoloured; £1.50 multicoloured		4·00	4·00
First Day Cover			5·00
Presentation Pack		5·00	

The stamps within No. **MS**1257 each have labels at left showing Pope John Paul II (42p.) and Pope Benedict XVI (£1.50).

Withdrawn: 14.8.2006.

1164 Harry Potter

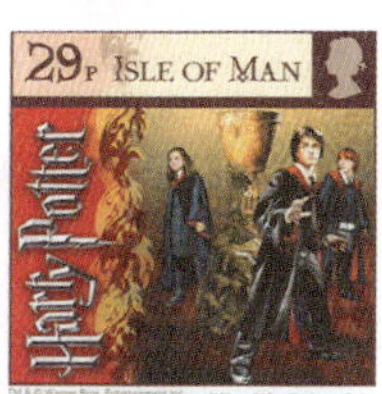

1165 Harry Potter, Hermione, Ron Weasley and Goblet of Fire

1166 Trophy

1167 Hungarian Horntail Dragon

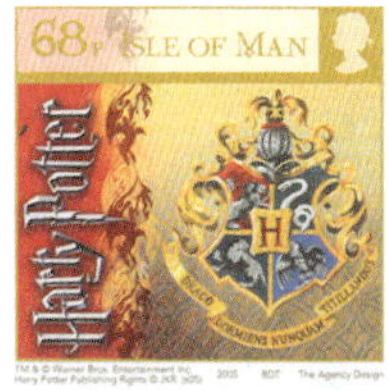

1168 Hogwarts Coat of Arms

1169 Murcus, Chieftainess of the Merpeople

***Harry Potter and the Goblet of Fire* (film)**

(Des The Agency. Litho BDT)

2005 (21 Oct). Perf 13½ (C).

1258	**1164**	26p. multicoloured	50	55
1259	**1165**	29p. multicoloured	60	65
1260	**1166**	33p. multicoloured	65	70
1261	**1167**	64p. multicoloured	1·30	1·40
1262	**1168**	68p. multicoloured	1·40	1·50
1263	**1169**	75p. multicoloured	1·50	1·60
1258/63 *Set of* 6			5·75	6·25
First Day Cover				7·00
Presentation Pack			7·00	
Collectors Folder (complete sheets & special first day cover (silver post mark))			50·00	

Plate Nos.: All values 1A (×5).

Sheets: 5 (1×5) with enlarged illustrated right margins.

Withdrawn: 20.10.2006.

1170 Death of Nelson (Gibraltar £1); Arrival of Nelson's funeral procession at St. Paul's Cathedral, London (£1) (*Illustration reduced. Actual size 170×75 mm*)

Death Bicentenary of Admiral Lord Nelson

(Des and litho Lowe-Martin, Canada)

2005 (21 Oct). Sheet 170×75 mm. Perf 13½ (C).

MS1264 **1170** Gibraltar £1 multicoloured; £1 multicoloured	4·50	4·50
First Day Cover		5·25
Presentation Pack	5·25	
Collectors Folder (**MS**1264, *Gibraltar miniature sheet, Isle of Man & Gibraltar first day covers)*	35·00	

The miniature sheet contains a £1 Gibraltar stamp and a £1 Isle of Man stamp. The same miniature sheet was also issued by Gibraltar.

Withdrawn: 20.10.2006.

1171 Mary and Jesus

1172 Angel with the Crown of Glory

1173 Shepherds worshipping Christ Child

1174 Nativity

1175 Three Kings

Christmas. Stained-glass Windows from Manx Churches

(Des E. Cassidy. Litho Cartor)

2005 (7 Nov). Perf 13½×13 (C).

1265	**1171**	26p. multicoloured	50	55
1266	**1172**	29p. multicoloured	60	65
1267	**1173**	42p. multicoloured	85	90
1268	**1174**	60p. multicoloured	1·20	1·30
1269	**1175**	68p. multicoloured	1·40	1·50
1265/9 *Set of 5*			4·50	4·75
First Day Cover				5·75
Presentation Pack			5·75	

Nos. 1265/7 show windows from St. German's Cathedral, Peel and Nos. 1268/9 windows from Kirk Christ, Rushen.

Plate Nos.: All values 1A (×4).
Sheets: 50 (10×5) .
Withdrawn: 6.11.2006.

Year Folder 2005

2005 (7 Nov). Comprises Nos. 1191/246 and **MS**1257/69.
Year Folder .... 70·00
Sold out: By 12.2006.

Year Pack 2005

2005 (7 Nov). Comprises Nos. 1191/246 and **MS**1257/69.
Year Pack .... 85·00
Sold out: By 12.2006.

Post Office Yearbook

2005 (7 Nov). Comprises Nos. 1191/246, **MS**1257/69 and 'Time to Remember' CD including booklets SB62/3.
Yearbook .... 70·00
Sold out: By 8.2008.

1176 Princess Elizabeth aged Five with Duke and Duchess of York and Princess Margaret, 1931

1177 Princess Elizabeth wearing ATS Uniform, c. 1944

1178 Queeen Elizabeth wearing Diadem, 1952

1179 With Princes Philip, Andrew, Edward, Charles and Princess Anne, 1972

1180 With Prince Philip at Balmoral on Silver Wedding Anniversary, 1972

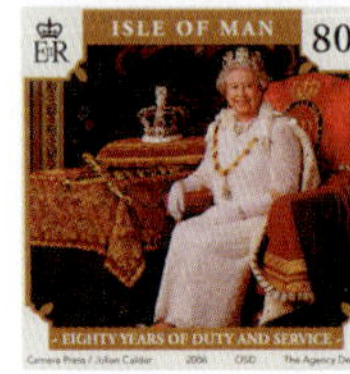

1181 With Regalia in Throne Room, Buckinghan Palace, 2001

1182 With Prince William on Buckingham Palace Balcony

1183 With Crowd at Aylesbury, Buckinghamshire on Golden Jubilee Tour, 2002

80th Birthday of Queen Elizabeth II (1st issue)

(Des The Agency. Litho Austrian State Ptg Wks, Vienna)

2006 (16 Jan). Perf 14 (C).

1270	**1176**	20p. multicoloured	40	30
		a. Horiz strip of 4. Nos. 1270/3	1·70	1·70
1271	**1177**	20p. multicoloured	40	30
1272	**1178**	20p. multicoloured	40	30
1273	**1179**	20p. multicoloured	40	30
1274	**1180**	80p. multicoloured	1·60	1·00
		a. Horiz strip of 4. Nos. 1274/7	6·75	6·75
1275	**1181**	80p. multicoloured	1·60	1·00
1276	**1182**	80p. multicoloured	1·60	1·00
1277	**1183**	80p. multicoloured	1·60	1·00
1270/7 *Set of 8*			8·00	8·50
First Day Cover				9·25
Presentation Pack			9·50	
Collectors Folder (complete sheets)			32·00	
Set of 2 Gutter Strips			16·00	

See also No. **MS**1304.

Plate Nos.: Both values 1A (×4).
Sheets: 16 (2 blocks 2×4). Nos. 1270/3 and 1274/7 were each printed together, *se-tenant*, as horizontal strips of four stamps in sheets containing two blocks of 8 separated by a large illustrated gutter.
Withdrawn: 15.1.2007.

1184 Jurby Chalice and Jurby Church

1185 Viking Period Gold Pin Head and Peel Castle

1186 Fragment of Early Neolithic Bowl and Meayll Hill, Rushen

1187 Manx Stoat and Cronk Sumark Late Iron Age Hill Fort

1188 Hen Harrier and South Barrule Hill, Malew

1189 Fossil Ammonite, Scarlett Point and Castletown

Manx—Study Isle of Man Natural History and Antiquarian Society

(Des Icon Imaging. Litho Enschedé)

2006 (15 Feb). Perf 14 (C).

1278	**1184**	26p. multicoloured	50	55
1279	**1185**	29p. multicoloured	60	65
1280	**1186**	64p. multicoloured	1·30	1·40
1281	**1187**	68p. multicoloured	1·40	1·50
1282	**1188**	78p. multicoloured	1·60	1·70
1283	**1189**	97p. multicoloured	1·90	2·00
1278/83 *Set of* 6			7·75	7·75
First Day Cover				8·50
Presentation Pack			9·50	

Plate Nos.: All values 1A (×4).
Sheets: 25 (5×5).
Withdrawn: 14.2.2007.

1190 Peregrine Falcon

1191 Puffin

1192 Manx Shearwater

1193 Chough

1194 Guillemot

1195 Whinchat

1196 Hen Harrier

1197 Goldcrest

1198 Grey Wagtail

1199 Wren

Manx Bird Atlas

(Des Dr. J. Paul and The Agency. Litho Cartor)

2006 (17 Apr).

(a) PVA gum. Perf 12½ (C)

1284	**1190**	28p. multicoloured	55	35
		a. Horiz strip of 5. Nos. 1284/8	3·00	3·00
1285	**1191**	28p. multicoloured	55	35
1286	**1192**	28p. multicoloured	55	35
1287	**1193**	28p. multicoloured	55	35
1288	**1194**	28p. multicoloured	55	35
1289	**1195**	31p. multicoloured	60	40
		a. Horiz strip of 5. Nos. 1289/93	3·50	3·25
1290	**1196**	31p. multicoloured	60	40
1291	**1197**	31p. multicoloured	60	40
1292	**1198**	31p. multicoloured	60	40
1293	**1199**	31p. multicoloured	60	40
1284/93 *Set of* 10			6·00	6·25
First Day Cover				7·00
Presentation Pack			7·25	

(b) Self-adhesive. Perf 12½ (die-cut)

1293*a*	**1190**	28p. multicoloured	55	60
		ab. Horiz strip of 5. Nos. 1293*a*/*e*	5·50	5·50
1293*b*	**1191**	28p. multicoloured	55	60
1293*c*	**1192**	28p. multicoloured	55	60
1293*d*	**1193**	28p. multicoloured	55	60
1293*e*	**1194**	28p. multicoloured	55	60
1293*f*	**1195**	31p. multicoloured	60	65
		fa. Horiz strip of 5. Nos. 1293*f*/*j*	6·00	6·00
1293*g*	**1196**	31p. multicoloured	60	65
1293*h*	**1197**	31p. multicoloured	60	65
1293*i*	**1198**	31p. multicoloured	60	65
1293*j*	**1199**	31p. multicoloured	60	65
1293*a*/*j* *Set of* 10			10·00	10·00

Nos. 1293a/j include the RSPB logo in the margin.

Plate Nos.: Both values 1A (×4).
Sheets: 50 (5×10). Nos. 1284/8, 1289/93, 1293*a*/*e* and 1293*f*/*j* were each printed together, *se-tenant*, in horizontal strips of five stamps throughout the sheets.
Withdrawn: 16.4.2007.

1200 Queen Elizabeth II at Tynwald Ceremony, 2003 (£1); In 1972 (£1) (*Illustration reduced. Actual size* 120×78 *mm*)

80th Birthday of Queen Elizabeth II (2nd issue)

(Des The Agency. Litho BDT)

2006 (21 Apr). Sheet 120×78 mm. Perf 14 (C).

MS1294 £1 multicoloured; £1 multicoloured	4·00	4·25
First Day Cover		5·50
Presentation Pack	5·50	

Withdrawn: 20.4.2007.

1201 West German Player

1202 West German Team

1203 Bobby Moore (England captain) with Trophy and Alf Ramsey (manager)

1204 Bobby Moore holding Trophy aloft

1205 West German Players

1206 Victorious England Team

World Cup Football Championship, Germany. 40th Anniversary of England's World Cup Victory

(Des E. Cassidy. Litho Lowe-Martin, Canada)

2006 (2 May). Perf 12½×13 (C).

1295	**1201**	28p. multicoloured	55	60
1296	**1202**	31p. multicoloured	60	65
1297	**1203**	44p. multicoloured	90	95
1298	**1204**	72p. multicoloured	1·40	1·50
1299	**1205**	83p. multicoloured	1·70	1·80
1300	**1206**	94p. multicoloured	1·90	2·00
1295/300 *Set of 6*			7·00	7·50
First Day Cover				8·50
Presentation Pack			8·50	

Nos. 1295/300 each contained a circle of gold imitation perforations.

Plate Nos. All values 1A ×5.
Sheets: 20 (4×5).
Withdrawn: 1.5.2007.

1207 1977 Isle of Man 10p. Europa Stamp (42p.); 1990 Isle of Man 15p. Europa Stamp (83p.) (*Illustration reduced. Actual size 170×75 mm*)

50th Anniversary of First Europa Stamp

(Des D. Clague. Litho Enschedé)

2006 (2 May). Sheet 170×75 mm. Perf 13½×14 (C).

MS1301 42p. multicoloured; 83p multicoloured	2·50	2·75
First Day Cover		4·00
Presentation Pack	4·00	

Withdrawn: 1.5.2007.

1208 Letitia Tyler (First Lady 1841–2)

1209 Joseph Gurney 'Czar' Cannon (Speaker of House of Representatives 1903–11)

1210 Matthew Quay (Civil War hero and Republican Party National Committee chairman)

1211 Mary Clemmer (19th-century journalist)

1212 Ewan Clague (economist)

1213 Henry 'Marse' Watterson (advisor to Pres. Roosevelt)

Manx Links with Washington

(Des Fusion Design. Litho BDT)

2006 (23 May). Perf 14 (C).

1302	**1208**	28p. multicoloured	55	60
1303	**1209**	31p. multicoloured	60	65
1304	**1210**	45p. multicoloured	90	95
1305	**1211**	50p. multicoloured	1·00	1·10
1306	**1212**	76p. multicoloured	1·50	1·60
1307	**1213**	83p. multicoloured	1·70	1·80
1302/7 *Set of 6*			6·25	6·50
First Day Cover				7·75
Presentation Pack			7·75	

Nos. 1302/7 were issued to coincide with the Washington 2006 Stamp Exhibition.

Plate Nos.: All values 1A (×4).
Sheets: 25 (5×5).
Withdrawn: 22.5.2007.

1214 Peel P50

1215 Trident

1216 Viking Sport

1217 BMC GRP Mini

1218 Manxcar

1219 P1000

Peel Cars

(Des Fusion Design. Litho Lowe-Martin, Canada)

2006 (23 July). Perf 13½ (C).

1308	**1214**	28p. multicoloured	55	60
1309	**1215**	31p. multicoloured	60	65
1310	**1216**	38p. multicoloured	75	80
1311	**1217**	41p. multicoloured	1·00	85
1312	**1218**	54p. multicoloured	1·50	1·20
1313	**1219**	94p. multicoloured	2·00	2·00
1308/13 *Set of 6*			6·00	6·00
First Day Cover				7·00
Presentation Pack			7·25	
Collectors Folder (top row of 5 and sheet top of each value)			35·00	

Plate Nos.: All values 1A (×4).
Sheets: 25 (5×5).
Withdrawn: 21.7.2007.

1220 'Ewan Christian'

1221 'Dame Agatha Christie' (John Gay)

1222 'Sir Hall Caine' (Harry Furniss)

1223 'William Bligh' John Condé, after John Russell)

1224 'Lady Maria Callcott' (Sir Thomas Lawrence)

1225 'John Martin' (Henry Warren)

1226 'Sir John Betjeman' (Stephen Hyde)

1227 'Sir Edward Elgar' (Herbert Lambert)

150th Anniversary of National Portrait Gallery, London

(Des The Agency. Litho Lowe-Martin, Canada)

2006 (25 Aug). Perf 13½ (C).

1314	**1220**	28p. multicoloured	55	60
1315	**1221**	31p. multicoloured	60	65
1316	**1222**	38p. multicoloured	75	80
1317	**1223**	41p. multicoloured	80	85
1318	**1224**	44p. multicoloured	90	95
1319	**1225**	54p. multicoloured	1·10	1·20
1320	**1226**	64p. multicoloured	1·30	1·40
1321	**1227**	96p. multicoloured	1·90	2·00
1314/21 *Set of 8*			7·75	8·25
First Day Cover				9·25
Presentation Pack			9·50	

Plate Nos.: All values 1A (×4).
Sheets: 25 (5×5).
Withdrawn: 24.8.2007.

1228 Christmas Tree and Gifts

1229 Tree with Three Legs of Mann Decoration at Top

1230 Tree with White Decorations

1231 Monkey-puzzle Tree and Three Legs of Mann Symbols

1232 Tree with Yellow Three Legs of Mann Decorations

1233 Tree with Brown Three Legs of Mann Decorations

Christmas. Trees

(Des Emma Cooke and The Agency. Litho and die-stamped BDT)

2006 (11 Oct).

(a) PVA gum. Perf 14 (C)

1322	**1228**	28p. multicoloured	55	60
1323	**1229**	31p. multicoloured	60	65
1324	**1230**	41p. multicoloured	80	85
1325	**1231**	44p. multicoloured	90	95
1326	**1232**	72p. multicoloured	1·40	1·50
1327	**1233**	94p. multicoloured	1·90	2·00
1322/7 *Set of 6*			6·00	6·50
First Day Cover				7·50
Presentation Pack			7·75	

(b) Size 28×39 mm. Self-adhesive booklet stamps. Perf 9×9½ (die-cut)

1328	**1228**	28p. multicoloured	55	60
		a. Booklet pane. No. 1328×10	5·50	
1329	**1229**	31p. multicoloured	60	65
		a. Booklet pane.No. 1329×10	6·00	

Nos. 1323, 1325 and 1329 include the 'EUROPA 2006' emblem.

Nos. 1328/9 were only available in £2.80 and £3.10 booklets, Nos. SB64/5.

Plate Nos.: All values 1A (×5).
Sheets: 25 (5×5); 31p., 44p. also 10 (5×2).
Withdrawn: 10.10.2007.

1234 Benjamin Bunny (28p.); Jemima Puddle-duck (50p.); Peter Rabbit (72p.); Jeremy Fisher (75p.) (*Illustration reduced. Actual size* 170×75 mm)

The Tales of Beatrix Potter

(Litho Lowe-Martin, Canada)

2006 (11 Oct). Sheet 170×75 mm. Perf 13 (C).

MS1330 28p. multicoloured; 50p. multicoloured; 72p. multicoloured; 75p. multicoloured	4·50	4·75
First Day Cover		6·00
Presentation Pack	6·00	

The logos for Belgica '06 and the RSPB are included in the margin of **MS**1331.
Withdrawn: 10.10.2007.

Belgica '06 International Stamp Exhibition, Brussels

2006 (11 Oct). Sheet 148×210 mm. Perf 12½ (C).

MS1331 Nos. 1284/93	8·50	10·00

Withdrawn: 10.10.2007.

Year Folder 2006

2006 (11 Oct). Comprises Nos. 1270/93, **MS**1294/327 and **MS**1330.
Year Folder .... 65·00
Sold out: By 5.2008.

Year Pack 2006

2006 (11 Oct). Comprises Nos. 1270/93, **MS**1294/327 and **MS**1330.
Year Pack .... 80·00
Sold out: By 5.2008.

Post Office Yearbook

2006 (11 Oct). Comprises Nos. 1270/93, **MS**1294/327 and **MS**1330/1.
Yearbook .... 70·00
Sold out: By November 2007.

1235 Steve Hislop

1236 Joey Dunlop

1237 David Jefferies

1238 Dave Molyneux

1239 John McGuinness

1240 Stanley Woods

1241 Geoff Duke

1242 Bob McIntyre

1243 Giacomo Agostini

1244 Mike Hailwood

Centenary of Isle of Man TT Motor Cycle Races

(Des Ruth Sutherland. Litho BDT)

2007 (1 Jan). Perf 14½ (C).

1332	**1235**	(31p.) multicoloured	65	50
		a. Horiz strip of 5. Nos. 1332/6	4·00	4·00
1333	**1236**	(31p.) multicoloured	65	50
1334	**1237**	(31p.) multicoloured	65	50
1335	**1238**	(31p.) multicoloured	65	50
1336	**1239**	(31p.) multicoloured	65	50
1337	**1240**	(44p.) multicoloured	85	80
		a. Horiz strip of 5. Nos. 1337/41	5·25	5·25
1338	**1241**	(44p.) multicoloured	85	80
1339	**1242**	(44p.) multicoloured	85	80
1340	**1243**	(44p.) multicoloured	85	80
1341	**1244**	(44p.) multicoloured	85	80
1332/41 *Set of 10*			8·75	8·75
First Day Cover				9·25
Presentation Pack			9·25	
Collectors Folder (complete sheets)			45·00	
Set of 2 Gutter Strips			20·00	
Stamp Cards (pre-paid) (set of 10)			16·00	16·00
Deluxe Stamp Cards (set of 14 Nos. 1332/41 and 4 TT trophy cards) (mint)			25·00	

Nos. 1332/6 are inscribed 'UK' and were sold at 31p. each. Nos. 1337/41 are inscribed 'E' and were sold at 44p. each.
Plate Nos.: Both values 1A (×4).
Sheets: 20 (2 blocks 5×2). Nos. 1332/6 and 1337/41 were each printed together, *se-tenant*, as horizontal strips of five stamps in sheets containing two blocks of 10 separated by a large illustrated gutter.
Withdrawn: 31.12.2007.

1245 Scouts hiking near South Barrule

1246 Scout Investiture on Douglas Beach

1247 Backpacking below Cronk-ny-Arrey-Laa

1248 Manx Scouts on Parade at St. Johns

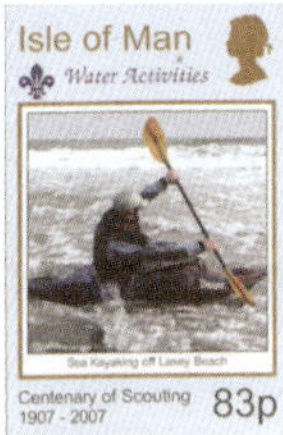

1249 Sea kayaking off Laxey Beach

1250 Manx Scouts operating the TT Scoreboard

1251 Two Scouts at Camp, 1913 (50p.); Scout Camp with Bell Tent and Open Fire, 1913 (£1.50) (*Illustration reduced. Actual size* 135×85 mm)

Centenary of Scouting

(Des M. J. Southall. Litho BDT)

2007 (22 Feb). Perf 14 (C).

1342	**1245**	28p. multicoloured	65	65
		a. Booklet pane. Nos. 1342/4 with margins all round	3·00	
		b. Booklet pane. Nos. 1342, 1344 and 1346 with margins all round	4·50	
1343	**1246**	31p. multicoloured	75	75
		a. Booklet pane. Nos. 1343, 1345 and 1347 with margins all round	6·00	
1344	**1247**	44p. multicoloured	1·00	1·00
1345	**1248**	72p. multicoloured	1·70	1·70
		a. Booklet pane. Nos. 1345/7 with margins all round	7·50	
1346	**1249**	83p. multicoloured	2·00	2·00
1347	**1250**	£1 multicoloured	2·40	2·40
1342/7 *Set of* 6			8·50	8·50
First Day Cover				9·00
Presentation Pack			9·00	
Collectors Folder			45·00	
MS1348 135×85 mm. **1251** 50p., £1.50 multicoloured			4·75	4·75
a. Booklet pane. As No. **MS**1348, but 155×96 mm with additional margins showing Scout emblems and a line of roulettes at left			4·75	
First Day Cover				5·25
Presentation Pack			5·25	

Nos. 1343/4 include the 'EUROPA 2007' emblem.

Plate Nos.: All values 1A (×4).

Sheets: 25 (5×5); 31p., 44p. also 10 (5×2).

Withdrawn: 21.2.2008.

1252 Wedding, 1947

1253 Queen and Duke of Edinburgh, c 1955

1254 Queen and Duke of Edinburgh, c 1965

1255 Queen and Duke of Edinburgh, c 1977

1256 Queen and Duke of Edinburgh, c 1997

1257 Queen and Duke of Edinburgh, c 2002

Diamond Wedding of Queen Elizabeth II and Duke of Edinburgh

(Des EDL Design. Litho BDT)

2007 (22 Feb). Perf 14 (C).

1349	**1252**	60p. multicoloured	1·00	1·00
		a. Horiz strip of 6. Nos. 1349/54	8·50	8·50
1350	**1253**	60p. multicoloured	1·00	1·00
1351	**1254**	60p. multicoloured	1·00	1·00
1352	**1255**	60p. multicoloured	1·00	1·00
1353	**1256**	60p. multicoloured	1·00	1·00
1354	**1257**	60p. multicoloured	1·00	1·00
1349/54 *Set of* 6			8·50	8·50
First Day Cover				9·00
Presentation Pack			9·00	

Plate Nos.: 1A (×4).

Sheets: 30 (6×5). Nos. 1349/54 were printed together, *se-tenant*, as horizontal strips of six stamps in sheets of 30.

Withdrawn: 21.2.2008.

1258 'Headland, Cornaa'

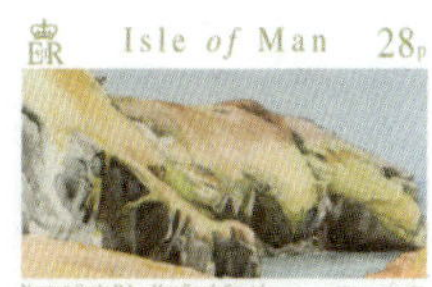

1259 'Headland, Sound'

1260 'St Marks Church'

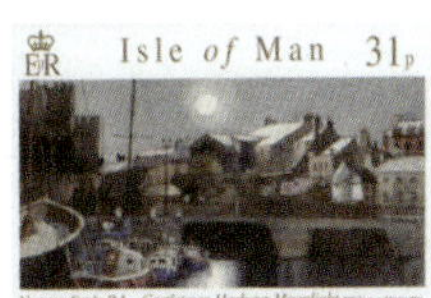

1261 'Castletown Harbour Moonlight'

1262 'Bridge House, Castletown'

1263 'Winter Sun'

1264 'In Ancient Times'

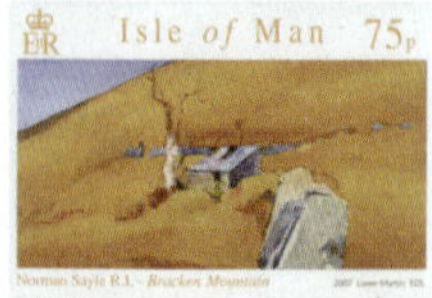

1265 'Bracken Mountain'

Watercolour Paintings by Norman Sayle

(Des EDL. Litho Lowe-Martin, Canada)

2007 (12 Apr).

(a) PVA gum. Perf 12½×13

1355	**1258**	28p. multicoloured	65	65
1356	**1259**	28p. multicoloured	65	65
1357	**1260**	31p. multicoloured	75	75
1358	**1261**	31p. multicoloured	75	75
1359	**1262**	42p. multicoloured	1·00	1·00
1360	**1263**	44p. multicoloured	1·00	1·00
1361	**1264**	65p. multicoloured	1·50	1·50
1362	**1265**	75p. multicoloured	1·70	1·70
1355/62 *Set of 8*			8·00	8·00
First Day Cover				8·50
Presentation Pack			8·50	

(b) Self-adhesive. Die-cut perf 10

1363	**1258**	28p. multicoloured	85	85
		a. Booklet pane. Nos. 1363/4, each ×5	8·50	
1364	**1259**	28p. multicoloured	85	85
1365	**1260**	31p. multicoloured	95	95
		a. Booklet pane. Nos. 1365/6, each ×5	9·25	
1366	**1261**	31p. multicoloured	95	95
1363/6 *Set of 4*			3·50	3·50

Nos. 1363/4 and 1365/6 were only issued in £2.80 or £3.10 stamp booklets, Nos. SB67/8.

Plate Nos.: All values 1A (each ×4).
Sheets: 25 (5×5).
Withdrawn: 11.4.2008.

1266 King John granting Royal Charter

1267 Liverpool Cathedral and Liverpool Metropolitan Cathedral

1268 Statue of Capt. Noel Chavasse ('Liverpool war heroes')

1269 St. George's Hall

1270 Port of Liverpool

1271 The Wall of Fame

800th Anniversary of the Royal Charter of Liverpool

(Des Fusion Design. Litho BDT)

2007 (20 Apr). Perf 14 (C).

1367	**1266**	31p. multicoloured	70	70
1368	**1267**	48p. multicoloured	1·10	1·10
1369	**1268**	54p. multicoloured	1·30	1·30
1370	**1269**	74p. multicoloured	1·70	1·70
1371	**1270**	80p. multicoloured	1·90	1·90
1372	**1271**	£1 multicoloured	2·30	2·30
1367/72 *Set of 6*			9·00	9·00
First Day Cover				9·50
Presentation Pack			9·50	

The plate numbers for Nos. 1367/72 were omitted from the sheets in error.

Sheets: 20 (5×4).
Withdrawn: 18.4.2008.

1272 *Susan Constant* and Map showing Voyage from England to Virginia, 1607

1273 Capt. Christopher Newport and *Susan Constant*, *Godspeed* and *Discovery* on the James River

1274 James Fort and James River, 1607

1275 Algonquin Princess Pocahontas and Capt. John Smith

1276 Jamestown Settlement, 1607

1277 Powhatan Village

400th Anniversary of Jamestown, Virginia, USA

(Des Julia Ashby Smyth. Litho Cartor)

2007 (26 Apr). Perf 13½ (C).

1373	**1272**	28p. multicoloured	65	65
1374	**1273**	31p. multicoloured	75	75
1375	**1274**	44p. multicoloured	1·00	1·00
1376	**1275**	54p. multicoloured	1·30	1·30
1377	**1276**	78p. multicoloured	1·90	1·90
1378	**1277**	90p. multicoloured	2·20	2·20
1373/8 *Set of 6*			7·75	7·75
First Day Cover				8·25
Presentation Pack			8·25	

Plate Nos.: All values 1A (×4).
Sheets: 15 (3×5) with enlarged illustrated right margins.
Withdrawn: 25.4.2008.

1278 James Brown (25p.); Joseph Cunningham and Holiday Camp, c 1895 (40p.); William Gill and First Landing Stage at Liverpool, c 1857 (80p.); Dalrymple Maitland and 'Liverpool Echo' Newspaper (80p.) (*Illustration reduced. Actual size 170×75 mm*)

800 Years of Trade between Liverpool and the Isle of Man

(Des Fusion Design. Litho)

2007 (10 May). Sheet 170×75 mm. Perf 14 (C).

MS1379 25p., 40p., 80p., 80p. multicoloured	5·50	6·00
First Day Cover		7·00
Presentation Pack	7·00	

Withdrawn: 9.5.2008.

TT Race Winners

2007 (9 July). Sheet 180×235 mm. Perf 14½ (C).

MS1379*a* Nos. 1332/41	11·50	12·00
TT Race Winners Folder		

Plate Nos. 1A (x4).

Sheets: 10 (2 blocks 5×1). Nos. 1332/41 were printed together, *se-tenant*, as horizontal strips of five stamps in sheets containing two blocks of five stamps and five *se-tenant* labels separated by a large illustrated gutter.

Withdrawn: 8.7.2008.

21st World Scout Jamboree, Chelmsford, England

2007 (26 July). No. **MS**1348 additionally inscr with jamboree emblem on the margin.

MS1380 50p., £1.50 multicoloured	5·00	5·50
Stamp Cards (pre-paid) (Nos. 1342, 1344, 1346, as No. **MS**1380)	9·00	9·00

The miniature sheet depicted on the stamp card differs from Type **1251** and **MS**1380. The face value is omitted, the 'centenary of scouting 2007' inscription is at bottom left and the Jamboree emblem at top right.

Withdrawn: 25.7.2008.

1279 Map by John Speed, 1605

1280 Map by Capt. Greenville Collins, 1693

1281 Map published by John Drinkwater based on Trigonometrical Survey, 1826

1282 Ordnance Survey County Series Map, 1870

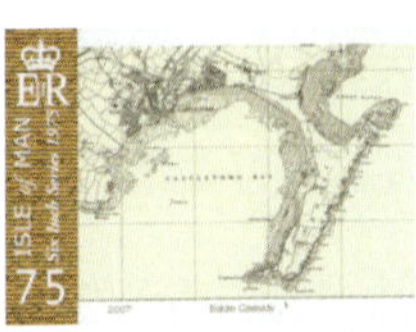

1283 Six-inch Series Map based on National Grid, 1975

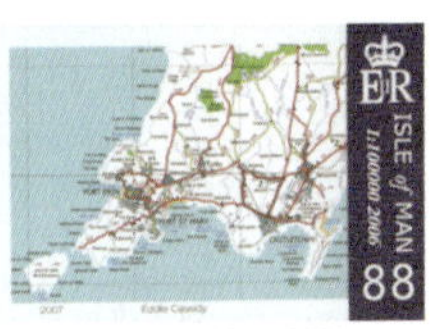

1284 1:100,000 Map, 2006

Maps of the Isle of Man

(Des Eddie Cassidy. Litho Lowe-Martin)

2007 (1 Aug). Perf 12½×13 (C).

1381	**1279**	28p. multicoloured	65	65
1382	**1280**	31p. multicoloured	75	75
1383	**1281**	44p. multicoloured	1·10	1·10
1384	**1282**	48p. multicoloured	1·10	1·10
1385	**1283**	75p. multicoloured	1·80	1·80
1386	**1284**	88p. multicoloured	2·10	2·10
1381/6 *Set of 6*			7·50	7·50
First Day Cover				8·00
Presentation Pack			8·00	

Plate Nos.: All values 1A (×4).

Sheets: 20 (5×4).

Imprint: Lower side margins.

Withdrawn: 31.7.2008.

1285 Captain John Ross and *Victory* trapped in Ice

1286 Flares from *Victory* guide returning Exploration Parties

1287 *Victory's* Crew hunting with Inuit

1288 Hunted Musk Ox

1289 Crew on 300 Mile Trek after abandoning *Victory*

1290 Crew in Whaleboats rescued by Whaler *Isabella*

International Polar Year (1st issue). Voyage of the *Victory* to the North Pole, 1829–33

(Des Peter Hearsey. Litho Lowe-Martin)

2007 (20 Aug). Perf 12½×13 (C).

1387	**1285**	28p. multicoloured	65	65
1388	**1286**	31p. multicoloured	70	70
1389	**1287**	55p. multicoloured	1·30	1·30
1390	**1288**	75p. multicoloured	1·80	1·80
1391	**1289**	90p. multicoloured	2·10	2·10
1392	**1290**	117p. multicoloured	2·75	2·75
1387/92 *Set of 6*			9·25	9·25
First Day Cover				9·75
Presentation Pack			9·75	

Plate Nos.: All values 1A (×4).

Sheets: 25 (5×5).

Withdrawn: 19.8.2008.

1291 'Ben-my-Chree' Log Cabin, Tagish Lake, British Columbia (50p.); Graham 'Jimmy' Oates taking Motorcycle and Sidecar along Railroad Track to Hudson Bay, 1932 (50p.); Kermode Bear (subspecies of Grizzly Bear) (75p.); Dog Sled and Hudson Bay Post Office, 1931–61) (75p.) (*Illustration reduced. Actual size 170×75 mm*)

International Polar Year (2nd issue). Manx Connections with Northern Canada

(Des Kcreative. Litho Lowe-Martin)

2007 (20 Aug). Sheet 170×75 mm. Perf 13 (C).

MS1393 50p., 50p., 75p., 75p. multicoloured	6·00	6·50
First Day Cover		9·50
Presentation Pack	9·50	

Withdrawn: 19.8.2008.

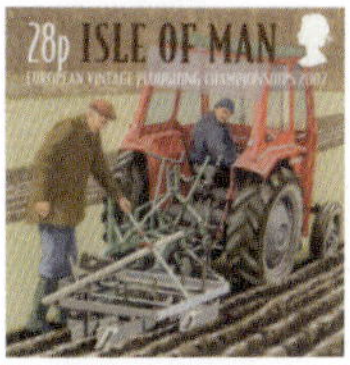

1292 Harold Leece ploughing Manx Style

1293 John Costain with 1947 Ferguson Tractor and Trailed Plough

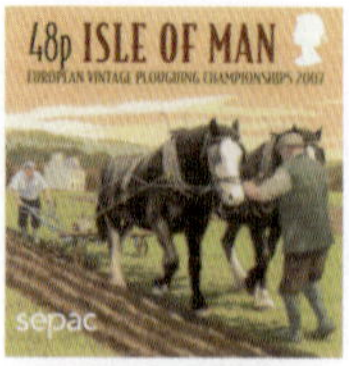

1294 Jim Caine with Digger Plough

1295 Herbie Moore with Swing Plough

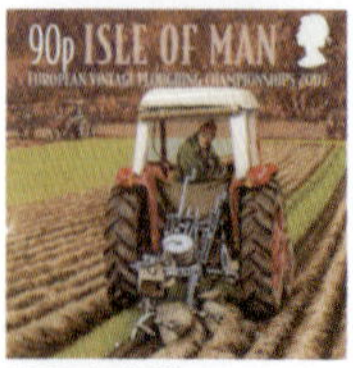

1296 Jack Clague ploughing World Style

1297 Jean Burns ploughing

European Vintage Ploughing Championships, Isle of Man

(Des Peter Hearsey and Eddie Cassidy. Litho Cartor)

2007 (1 Sept). Perf 13 (C).

1394	**1292**	28p. multicoloured (a)	65	65
1395	**1293**	31p. multicoloured (a)	70	70
1396	**1294**	48p. multicoloured (b)	1·10	1·10
1397	**1295**	71p. multicoloured (a)	1·70	1·70
1398	**1296**	90p. multicoloured (a)	2·10	2·10
1399	**1297**	£1.27 multicoloured (a)	3·00	3·00
1394/9 *Set of 6*			9·25	9·25
First Day Cover				9·75
Presentation Pack			9·75	

No. 1396 is inscr 'sepac'. This stamp was also available in a folder with 10 other 'sepac' logo stamps issued by other participating administrations.

Plate Nos.: All values 1A (×4).
Sheets: 25 (5×5).
Printings: (a) 1.9.07; (b) 1.10.07.
Withdrawn: 30.9.2008.

1298 Angel playing Trumpet

1299 Angel playing Lute

1300 Angel wearing Crown

1301 Angel with Harp

1302 Angel with Hands clasped in Prayer

Christmas. 'Hark the Herald Angels Sing'

(Des Julia Ashby Smyth. Litho Lowe-Martin, Canada)

2007 (19 Oct). Self-adhesive. Die-cut perf 13×13½.

1400	**1298**	28p. multicoloured	65	65
1401	**1299**	31p. multicoloured	75	75
1402	**1300**	69p. multicoloured	1·60	1·60
1403	**1301**	78p. multicoloured	1·80	1·80
1404	**1302**	£1.24 multicoloured	3·00	3·00
1400/4 *Set of 5*			7·75	7·75
First Day Cover				8·25
Presentation Pack			8·25	

The backing paper of Nos. 1400/4 is divided into rectangles by lines of rouletting.

Plate Nos.: All values 1A (each ×5).
Sheets: 20 (5×4).
Withdrawn: 17.10.2008.

Year Folder 2007

2007 (19 Oct). Comprises Nos. 1332/62, 1367/79 and 1381/404.
Year Folder .... 80·00

Year Pack 2007

2007 (19 Oct). Comprises Nos. 1332/62, 1367/79 and 1381/404.
Year Pack £100

Post Office Yearbook

2007 (19 Oct). Comprises Nos. 1332/62, 1367/79 and 1381/404.
Yearbook .... 80·00

1303 *Queen Elizabeth* 2

1304 *Queen Mary* 2

1305 *Queen Victoria*

Cunard Ocean Liners

(Des Kcreative. Litho Enschedé)

2008 (13 Jan). Perf 14×13½ (C).

1405	**1303**	£1 multicoloured	3·00	3·50
1405*a*	**1304**	£1 multicoloured	3·00	3·50
1405*b*	**1305**	£1 multicoloured	3·00	3·50
MS1405*c* 170×75 mm. Nos. 1405/*b*			7·00	8·00
1405/b *Set of 3*			7·00	8·00
First Day Cover				8·75
Presentation Pack			8·75	
QE2 Farewell Season Folder (full sheet of No. 1405 and special first day cover)			50·00	

Nos. 1405/*b* were only available from the Isle of Man Philatelic Bureau in complete sheetlets, sold for £10 each, or from the miniature sheet.

Plate Nos.: 1A (×6).
Sheets: 10 (2 columns 1×5). Nos. 1405/*b* were each printed in separate sheetlets of ten stamps and ten labels containing two vertical strips of stamps alternated with two columns of stamp-size labels showing the interior of the ship, so that each stamp is accompanied by a *se-tenant* label at left.
Withdrawn: 12.1.2009.

1306 H.P. 0/400 and Bristol F2B Fighter

1307 Avro 504N and Westland Wapiti

1308 Hawker Hurricane and Short Sunderland

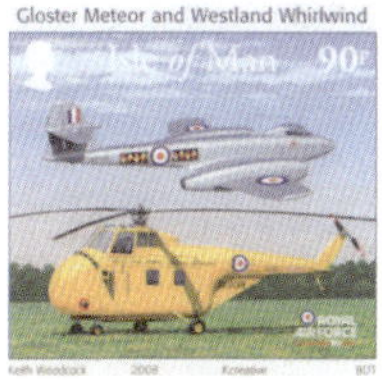

1309 Gloster Meteor and Westland Whirlwind

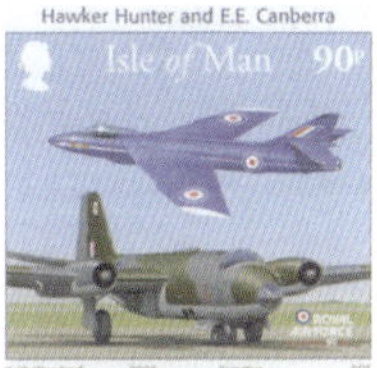

1310 Hawker Hunter and E.E. Canberra

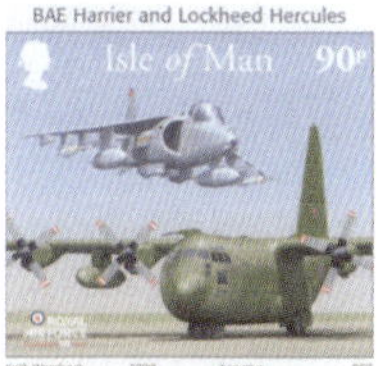

1311 BAE Harrier and Lockheed Hercules

90th Anniversary of the Royal Air Force

(Des Keith Woodcock and Kcreative. Litho BDT)

2008 (15 Jan). Perf 13½ (C).

1406	**1306**	31p. multicoloured	60	60
		a. Horiz strip of 3. Nos. 1406/8	2·20	2·20
		b. Booklet pane. Nos. 1406/9 with margins all round	4·25	
		c. Booklet pane. Nos. 1406/7 and 1409/10 with margins all round..	5·75	
		d. Booklet pane. Nos. 1406/7 and 1410/11 with margins all round..	5·75	
1407	**1307**	31p. multicoloured	60	60
1408	**1308**	31p. multicoloured	60	60
		a. Booklet pane. Nos. 1408/11 with margins all round	7·25	
1409	**1309**	90p. multicoloured	1·70	1·70
		a. Horiz strip of 3. Nos. 1409/11	6·50	6·50
1410	**1310**	90p. multicoloured	1·70	1·70
1411	**1311**	90p. multicoloured	1·70	1·70
1406/11 *Set of 6*			8·50	8·50
First Day Cover				10·00
Presentation Pack			10·00	
Souvenir Folder (full sheets)			35·00	

Plate Nos.: All values 1A (each ×4).
Sheets: 12 (2 blocks 3×2). Nos. 1406/8 and 1409/11 were each printed together, *se-tenant*, as horizontal strips of three stamps in sheets containing two blocks of 6 separated by a large illustrated gutter.
Withdrawn: 14.1.2009.

1312 The Pagan Lady of Peel

1313 Ship Burial

1314 Godred Crovan ('King Orry')

1315 Gautr Bjornsson the Sculptor

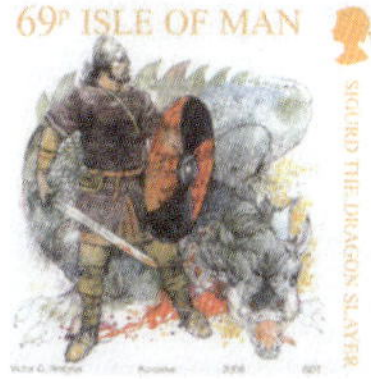

1316 Sigurd the Dragon Slayer

1317 Coming of Christianity

The Viking Age on the Isle of Man

(Des Victor Ambrus and Kcreative. Litho BDT)

2008 (18 Feb). Perf 13½ (C).

1412	**1312**	28p. multicoloured	65	65
1413	**1313**	31p. multicoloured	75	75
1414	**1314**	44p. multicoloured	1·00	1·00
1415	**1315**	54p. multicoloured	1·30	1·30
1416	**1316**	69p. multicoloured	1·60	1·60
1417	**1317**	£1.24 multicoloured	3·00	3·00
1412/17 *Set of 6*			8·25	8·25
First Day Cover				9·75
Presentation Pack			9·75	

Plate Nos.: All values 1A (each ×4).
Sheets: 25 (5×5).
Withdrawn: 17.2.2009.

1318 Isle of Man Bank £1 Note, 1956

1319 Isle of Man Govt £10 Note, 1972

1320 Manx Bank (1882–1900) £1 Note

1321 Isle of Man Govt 50p. Decimal Note, 1969

1322 Isle of Man Govt £50 Note, 1983

1323 Parr's Bank £1 Note, 1918

Bank Notes of the Isle of Man

(Des Kcreative. Litho BDT)

2008 (7 Apr).

(a) PVA gum. Perf 14

1418	**1318**	30p. multicoloured	70	70
1419	**1319**	31p. multicoloured	75	75
1420	**1320**	44p. multicoloured	1·00	1·00
1421	**1321**	56p. multicoloured	1·40	1·40
1422	**1322**	85p. multicoloured	2·00	2·00
1423	**1323**	114p. multicoloured	2·75	2·75
1418/23 *Set of 6*			8·50	8·50
First Day Cover				10·00
Presentation Pack			10·00	

(b) Self-adhesive. Die-cut perf 12×12½

1424	**1318**	30p. multicoloured	80	1·00
		a. Booklet pane. No. 1424×10	7·50	

No. 1424 was only issued in £3 stamp booklets, No. SB69.
Plate Nos.: All values 1A (each ×4).
Sheets: 20 (2 columns 1×10). Nos. 1418/23 were each printed in separate sheetlets containing two vertical strips of stamps alternated with two columns of stamp-size labels so that each stamp is accompanied by a *se-tenant* label at left.
Withdrawn: 6.4.2009.

1324 Archery (1p.); Show-jumping (2p.); Cycling (3p.); Hand holding Olympic Torch (94p.) (*Illustration reduced. Actual size 170×75 mm*)

Olympic Games, Beijing

(Des Pobjoy Mint Studio and Solus Strategic Limited. Litho Lowe-Martin, Canada)

2008 (21 Apr). Sheet 170×75 mm. Perf 13½ (C).

MS1425 1p., 2p., 3p., 94p. multicoloured	2·40	3·00
First Day Cover		4·00
Presentation Pack	4·00	

Withdrawn: 20.4.2009.

1325 Cornish Flag

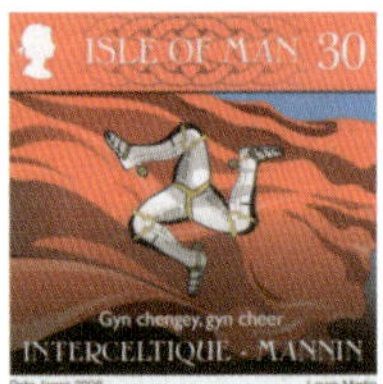

1326 Isle of Man Flag

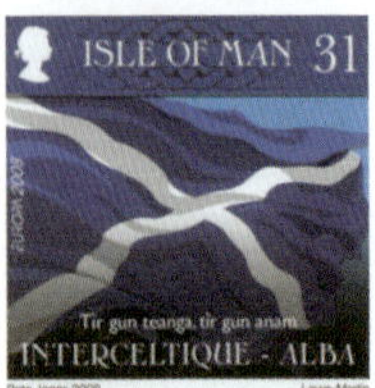

1327 Scottish Flag

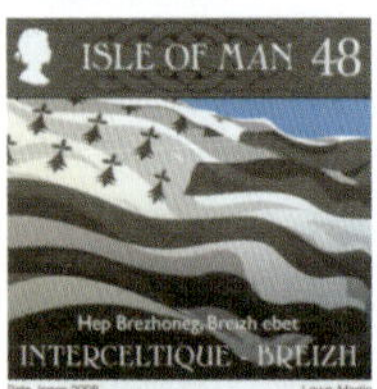

1328 Breton Flag

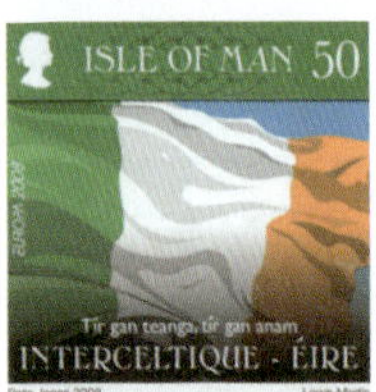

1329 Irish Flag

1330 Flag of Asturias

1331 Welsh Flag

1332 Flag of Galicia

Interceltique. Flags of Celtic Countries

(Des Pete Jones Design. Litho Lowe-Martin, Canada)

2008 (12 May). Perf 13½ (C).

1426	**1325**	20p. multicoloured	45	45
1427	**1326**	30p. multicoloured	70	70
1428	**1327**	31p. multicoloured	70	70
1429	**1328**	48p. multicoloured	1·10	1·10
1430	**1329**	50p. multicoloured	1·20	1·20
1431	**1330**	56p. multicoloured	1·30	1·30
1432	**1331**	72p. multicoloured	1·70	1·70
1433	**1332**	£1.13 multicoloured	2·75	2·75
1426/33 *Set of* 8			9·75	9·75
MS1434 174×210 mm. Nos. 1426/33 (1 Aug)			9·75	9·75
First Day Cover				11·50
Presentation Pack			11·50	
Stamp Cards (set of 8) (1 Aug)				13·00
Festival Postcard			1·90	1·90

Nos. 1428 and 1430 include the EUROPA emblem.
Plate Nos.: All values 1A (each ×4).
Sheets: 10 (2×5) with enlarged illustrated right margins.
Withdrawn: 11.5.2009.

1333 Reg Parnell in Maserati 4CLT

1334 Mike Hawthorn

1335 Tony Brooks in Vanwall

1336 Roy Salvadori in Aston Martin

1337 Stirling Moss at Pit Stop

1338 Jim Clark in Lotus-Climax 25 R4

1339 Aston Martin DB4 GT Zagato, 1961; Ferrari 250 LM, Le Mans, 1965; Ferrari 250 GTO, Goodwood Revival, 1962; Ford GT 40, Goodwood Festival of Speed, 1965; Mercedes-Benz 300 SLR, Mille Miglia Road Race, Italy, 1955; Shelby Cobra, Goodwood Revival, 1964 (*Illustration reduced. Actual size 170×75 mm*)

British Motor Racing

(Des Nick Sykes and Kreative (**MS**1441) or Peter Hearsey and Kreative (others). Litho BDT)

2008 (10 July). Perf 14 (C).

1435	**1333**	20p. multicoloured	45	45
1436	**1334**	30p. multicoloured	70	70
1437	**1335**	70p. multicoloured	1·60	1·60
1438	**1336**	81p. multicoloured	1·90	1·90
1439	**1337**	94p. multicoloured	2·20	2·20
1440	**1338**	£1.22 multicoloured	3·00	3·00
1435/40 *Set of* 6			9·75	9·75
First Day Cover				11·50
Presentation Pack			11·50	
MS1441 170×75 mm. **1339** 50p.×6 multicoloured. Perf 15×14 (C)			7·00	7·00
First Day Cover				8·75
Presentation Pack			8·75	

Plate Nos.: All values 1A (each ×4).
Sheets: 25 (5×5).
Imprint: Central, bottom margin.
Withdrawn: 9.7.2009.

1340 Miss M. L. Wood (founder of Manx Music Festival)

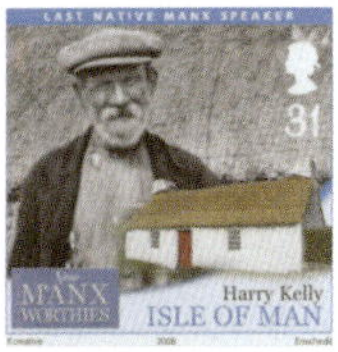

1341 Harry Kelly (last native Manx speaker) and Cottage at Cregneash Folk Museum

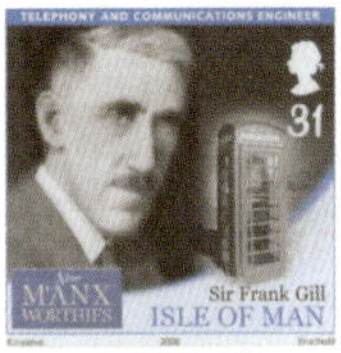

1342 Sir Frank Gill (telephony and communications engineer) and Phone Box

1343 Ramsey Gelling Johnson (second deemster (Manx judge), 1947–54)

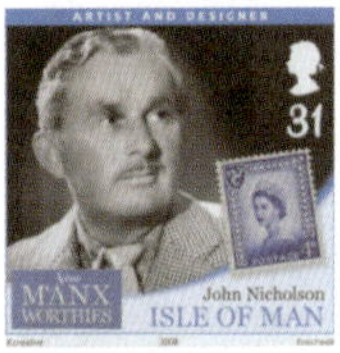

1344 John Nicholson (artist and designer of Manx stamps, currency notes and gold coinage)

1345 Dr. Dorothy Pantin (Island's first woman doctor and first medical supervisor of Jane Crookall Maternity Home)

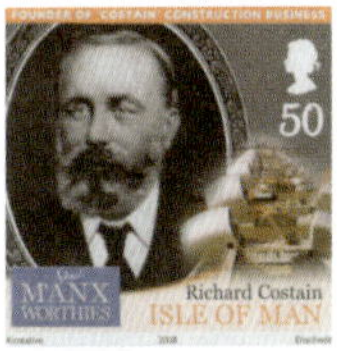

1346 Richard Costain (founder of construction company)

1347 Sir William Percy Cowley (first deemster and Clerk of the Rolls, 1947–58)

1348 Revd Fred Cubbon (philanthropist)

1349 William Henry Gill (author, musician and collector of Manx folk music)

New Manx Worthies. Personalities from Book

(Des Kreative. Litho Enschedé)

2008 (1 Aug). Perf 13½ (C).

1442	**1340**	31p. multicoloured	60	60
		a. Horiz strip of 5. Nos. 1442/6	3·75	3·75
1443	**1341**	31p. multicoloured	60	60
1444	**1342**	31p. multicoloured	60	60
1445	**1343**	31p. multicoloured	60	60
1446	**1344**	31p. multicoloured	60	60
1447	**1345**	50p. multicoloured	1·00	1·00
		a. Horiz strip of 5. Nos. 1447/51	6·00	6·00
1448	**1346**	50p. multicoloured	1·00	1·00
1449	**1347**	50p. multicoloured	1·00	1·00
1450	**1348**	50p. multicoloured	1·00	1·00
1451	**1349**	50p. multicoloured	1·00	1·00
1442/51 *Set of* 10			9·50	9·50
First Day Cover				11·00
Presentation Pack			11·00	

Plate Nos.: Both values 1A (each ×4).

Sheets 50 (5×10): Nos. 1442/6 and 1447/51 were each printed together, *se-tenant*, as horizontal strips of five stamps in sheets of 50.

Withdrawn: 31.7.2009.

Olympex Olympic Stamp Expo, Beijing

2008 (8 Aug). No. **MS**1425 additionally inscr with 'Beijing 2008' emblem and 'OLYMPEX, THE OLYMPIC EXPO' on the bottom margin.

MS1452 1p., 2p., 3p., 94p. multicoloured	2·40	2·75
Postcard (pre paid)	2·40	

Withdrawn: 7.8.2009.

Team GB Olympic Cyclists

2008 (9 Aug). Sheet 145×208 mm. Perf 13½ (C).

MS1453 3p Cycling; 94p. Hand holding Olympic torch	2·40	2·75

No. **MS**1453 contains 3p. and 94p. designs as in **MS**1425.

Withdrawn: 7.8.2009.

1350 Orange-tip Butterfly (*Anthocharis cardamines*)

1351 Curlew (*Numenius arquata*)

1352 Birch Bracket Fungus (*Piptoporus betulinus*)

1353 Large Red Damselfly (*Pyrrhosoma nymphula*)

1354 Marsh Cinquefoil (*Potentilla palustris*)

1355 Royal Fern (*Osmunda regalis*)

A Walk in the Ballaugh Curragh

(Des Richard Lewington and Kcreative. Litho Lowe-Martin)

2008 (1 Oct). Perf 13½ (C).

1454	**1350**	30p. multicoloured	70	70
1455	**1351**	31p. multicoloured	75	75
1456	**1352**	50p. multicoloured	1·20	1·20
1457	**1353**	70p. multicoloured	1·70	1·70
1458	**1354**	82p. multicoloured	1·90	1·90
1459	**1355**	£1.38 multicoloured	3·25	3·25
1454/9 *Set of* 6			9·50	9·50
First Day Cover				11·00
Presentation Pack			11·00	

Plate Nos.: All values 1A (each ×4).

Sheets: 25 (5×5).

Withdrawn: 30.9.2009.

1356 Second Lt. Roy F. Corlett, 1916

1357 Second Lt. John W. Lewis, 1916

1358 Pte Joseph Killey

1359 Lt. Col. W. A. W. Crellin, 1917

1360 Lance Cpl Tom Quilliam, 1918

1361 Pte Robert Oates, 1914

1362 Manx National War Memorial, St. John's (*Illustration reduced. Actual size* 110×70 mm)

90th Anniversary of the End of World War I. Manx Soldiers and their Letters Home

(Des Mannin Design. Litho BDT)

2008 (1 Oct). Perf 14 (C).

1460	**1356**	30p. multicoloured	70	70
1461	**1357**	31p. multicoloured	70	70
1462	**1358**	44p. multicoloured	1·00	1·00
1463	**1359**	56p. multicoloured	1·30	1·50
1464	**1360**	81p. multicoloured	1·90	2·00
1465	**1361**	94p. multicoloured	2·20	2·50
1460/5 *Set of 6*			7·75	8·00
First Day Cover				9·50
Presentation Pack			9·50	
MS1466 110×70 mm. **1362** £2 multicoloured			4·75	5·00
First Day Cover				6·25
Presentation Pack			6·50	

Plate Nos.: All values 1A (each ×4).
Sheets: 6 (3×2).
Withdrawn: 30.9.2009.

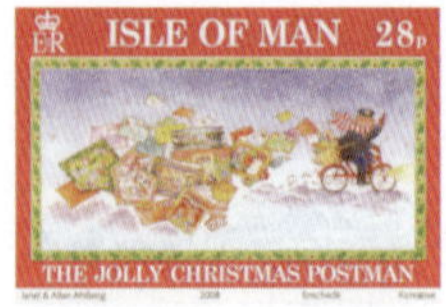

1363 Christmas Cards and Postman on Bicycle

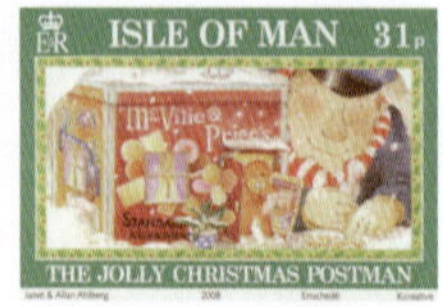

1364 Postman icing Biscuits and Giant Biscuit Tin

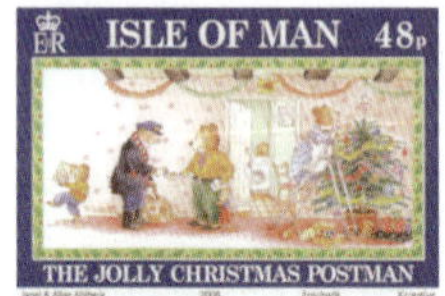

1365 Offering Postman Mince Pies and Decorating Christmas Tree

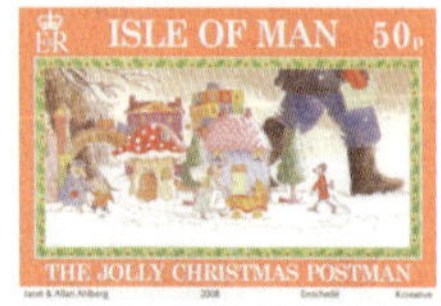

1366 Postman holding Card and Toy Town

1367 Postman on Bicycle and Winter Landscape

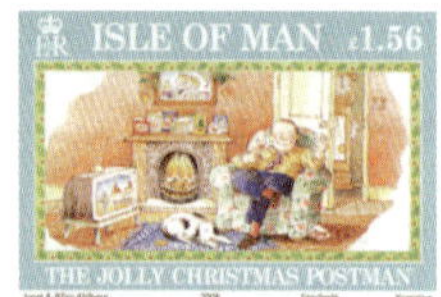

1368 Postman relaxing at Home

Christmas. Illustrations from *The Jolly Christmas Postman* by Janet and Allan Ahlberg

(Des Kcreative. Litho Enschedé)

2008 (20 Oct). Perf 14×14½ (C).

1467	**1363**	28p. multicoloured	65	65
1468	**1364**	31p. multicoloured	75	75
1469	**1365**	48p. multicoloured	1·10	1·10
1470	**1366**	50p. multicoloured	1·20	1·20
1471	**1367**	56p. multicoloured	1·30	1·30
1472	**1368**	£1.56 multicoloured	3·50	3·50
1467/72 *Set of 6*			8·50	8·50
First Day Cover				10·00
Presentation Pack			10·00	

Plate Nos.: All values 1A (each ×4).
Sheets: 25 (5×5).
Withdrawn: 19.10.2009.

Year Folder 2008

2008 (20 Oct). Comprises Nos. **MS**1405c/23, **MS**1425/33, 1435/51 and 1454/72.

Year Folder .... 85·00

Year Pack 2008

2008 (20 Oct). Comprises Nos. **MS**1405c/23, **MS**1425/33, 1435/51 and 1454/72.

Year Pack £100

Post Office Yearbook

2008 (20 Oct). Comprises Nos. **MS**1405c/23, **MS**1425/33, 1435/51 and 1454/72.

Yearbook .... 90·00

1369 Fairey Barracuda II

1370 Blackburn Buccaneer S.2

1371 Fairey Flycatcher

1372 EH101 Merlin Helicopter

1373 BAe Sea Harrier FRS.1

1374 Sea Scout SS.24 Airship

Centenary of Naval Aviation

(Des Keith Woodcock and Kcreative. Litho BDT)

2009 (15 Jan). Perf 14 (C).

1473	**1369**	30p. multicoloured	70	70
		a. Horiz strip of 3. Nos. 1473/5	3·25	3·25
		b. Booklet pane. Nos. 1473/4, each ×2 with margins all round	2·75	
		c. Booklet pane. Nos. 1473/6 with margins all round	5·00	
		d. Booklet pane. Nos. 1473/4 and 1477/8 with margins all round	6·50	
1474	**1370**	31p. multicoloured	70	70
1475	**1371**	72p multicoloured	1·75	1·75
		a. Booklet pane. Nos. 1475/8 with margins all round	9·00	
1476	**1372**	85p. multicoloured	2·00	2·00
		a. Horiz strip of 3. Nos. 1476/8	7·25	7·25
1477	**1373**	98p. multicoloured	2·25	2·25
1478	**1374**	£1.36 multicoloured	3·00	3·00
1473/8 *Set of 6*			10·50	10·50
First Day Cover			12·00	
Presentation Pack			12·00	

Plate Nos. Both values 1A (each ×4).

Sheets: 12 (2 blocks 3×2). Nos. 1473/5 and 1476/8 were each printed together, *se-tenant*, as horizontal strips of three stamps in sheetlets containing two blocks of 6 separated by a large illustrated gutter.

1375 McClaren Race Car

1376 Celebrating with Champagne

1377 Crossing Finishing Line

1378 Seated in Race Car

1379 Race Car

1380 With Arms Raised in Triumph

Lewis Hamilton, Formula One World Champion, 2008

(Des Home Strategic. Litho BDT)

2009 (15 Jan). Perf 14 (C).

1479	**1375**	30p. multicoloured	70	70
		a. Horiz pair. Nos. 1479/80	1·40	1·40
1480	**1376**	31p. multicoloured	70	70
1481	**1377**	56p. multicoloured	1·25	1·25
		a. Horiz pair. Nos. 1481/2	3·25	3·25
1482	**1378**	85p. multicoloured	2·00	2·00
1483	**1379**	98p. multicoloured	2·25	2·25
		a. Horiz pair. Nos. 1483/4	5·50	5·50
1484	**1380**	£1.42 multicoloured	3·25	3·25
1479/84 *Set of 6*			10·00	10·00
First Day Cover			12·00	
Presentation Pack			12·00	
Special Folder (complete sheets)			40·00	

Plate Nos.: All values 1A (each ×4).

Sheets: 10 (2×5). Nos. 1479/80, 1481/2 and 1483/4 were each printed together, *se-tenant*, as horizontal pairs in sheetlets of ten with enlarged illustrated right margins.

1381 Henry VIII

1382 Catherine of Aragon

1383 Anne Boleyn

1384 Jane Seymour

1385 Anne of Cleves

1386 Catherine Howard

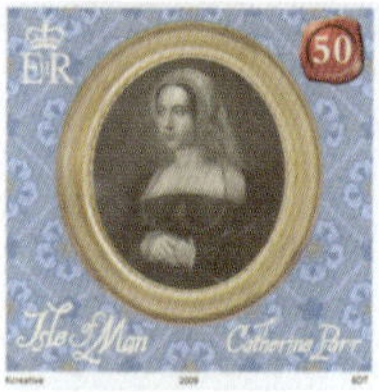

1387 Catherine Parr

1388 Hampton Court

500th Anniv of the Accession of King Henry VIII

(Des Kcreative. Litho BDT)

2009 (18 Feb). Perf 13 (C).

1485	**1381**	50p. multicoloured	1·25	1·25
		a. Horiz strip of 4. Nos. 1485/8	5·00	5·00
1486	**1382**	50p. multicoloured	1·25	1·25
1487	**1383**	50p. multicoloured	1·25	1·25
1488	**1384**	50p. multicoloured	1·25	1·25
1489	**1385**	50p. multicoloured	1·25	1·25
		a. Horiz strip of 4. Nos. 1489/92	5·00	5·00
1490	**1386**	50p. multicoloured	1·25	1·25
1491	**1387**	50p. multicoloured	1·25	1·25
1492	**1388**	50p. multicoloured	1·25	1·25
1485/92 *Set of 8*			9·50	9·50
First Day Cover			11·00	
Presentation Pack			11·00	
Special Folder (complete sheets)			30·00	

Plate Nos. Both sheets 1A (each ×4).

Sheets: 16 (2 blocks 4×2). Nos. 1485/8 and 1489/92 were each printed together, *se-tenant*, as horizontal strips of four in sheetlets containing two blocks of eight separated by a large illustrated gutter.

1389 Ballakilley Farm

1390 Grenaby Farm

1391 Mr. Cubbon

1392 Glenmoar Mill

1393 Golden Meadow Mill

1394 Bernie Mylcraine

1395 Golden Meadow Mill

1396 Loughtan Farm

Mills and Millers. Photographs by Chris Kilip

(Des Kcreative. Litho Cartor)

2009 (1 Apr).

(a) Ordinary gum. Perf 13 (C)

1493	**1389**	32p. black	70	70
		a. Pair. Nos. 1493/4	1·40	1·40
1494	**1390**	32p. black	70	70
1495	**1391**	33p. black	70	70
		a. Pair. Nos. 1495/6	1·50	1·50
1496	**1392**	33p. black	70	70
1497	**1393**	50p. black	1·25	1·25
		a. Pair. Nos. 1497/8	3·00	3·00
1498	**1394**	50p. black	1·25	1·25
1499	**1395**	78p. black	1·75	1·75
		a. Pair. Nos. 1499/500	4·00	4·00
1500	**1396**	78p. black	1·75	1·75
1493/500 *Set of 8*			9·00	9·00
First Day Cover			10·00	
Presentation Pack			10·00	

(b) Self-adhesive. Die-cut perf 12½

1501	**1389**	32p. multicoloured	70	70
		a. Booklet pane. Nos. 1501/2, each ×5	7·00	
1502	**1390**	32p. multicoloured	70	70
1503	**1392**	33p. multicoloured	70	70
		a. Booklet pane. Nos. 1503/4, each ×5	7·00	
1504	**1391**	33p. multicoloured	70	70
1501/4 *Set of 4*			2·75	2·75

Nos. 1501/2 and 1503/4 were only issued in separate booklets of ten stamps, Nos. SB72/3.

Plate Nos.: All values 1A (each ×1).

Sheets: 40 (5×8). Nos. 1493/4, 1495/6, 1497/8 and 1499/500 were each printed together, *se-tenant*, as horizontal and vertical pairs throughout the sheets.

1397 Peonies

China World Stamp Exhibition and Peony Festival, Luoyang

(Des YH Design. Litho Beijing Security Printers)

2009 (10 APR). Multicoloured; colours of face values and right-hand borders given. Perf 13 (C).

1505	**1397**	10p. multicoloured (gold)	25	25
		a. Sheetlet. Nos. 1505/12	2·00	
1506		10p. multicoloured (deep yellow-green)	25	25
1507		10p. multicoloured (dull rose)	25	25
1508		10p. multicoloured (blue)	25	25
1509		10p. multicoloured (mauve)	25	25
1510		10p. multicoloured (orange-vermilion)	25	25
1511		10p. multicoloured (deep turquoise-green)	25	25
1512		10p. multicoloured (yellow-olive)	25	25
1505/12 *Set of 8*			2·00	2·00
First Day Cover			3·00	
Presentation Pack			3·00	

Sheets: 10 (4×2). Nos. 1505/12 were printed together, *se-tenant*, in sheetlets of eight stamps.

1398 Boot Print and *Sunrise over Antares* (Apollo 14 lunar module)

1399 *Clan MacBean* (Alan Bean) *arrives on the Moon* and *Documenting the Sample*

1400 *Pete and Me* (Pete Conrad taking photograph)

1401 *Headed for the Last Parking Lot* (Gene Cernan and lunar roving vehicle)

1402 *The Eagle* (Apollo 11 lunar module) *is Headed Home* and *In the Beginning*

1403 *Ceremony on the Plain at Hadley* and *The Hoer* (Jim Irwin digging trench)

1404 *On the Rim* (John Young and Charlie Duke at North Ray Crater, 1972) (*Illustration reduced. Actual size* 109×84 *mm*)

40th Anniversary of First Manned Moon Landing. Paintings by Alan Bean

(Des Eddie Cassidy. Litho Lowe-Martin)

2009 (12 Apr). Perf 12½ (C).

1513	**1398**	33p. multicoloured	1·00	1·00
1514	**1399**	50p. multicoloured	1·50	1·50
1515	**1400**	56p. multicoloured	1·50	1·50
1516	**1401**	81p. multicoloured	2·00	2·00
1517	**1402**	105p. multicoloured	2·50	2·50
1518	**1403**	135p. multicoloured	3·00	3·00
1513/18 *Set of 6*			11·00	11·00
First Day Cover			12·00	

Presentation Pack		12·00	
MS1519 109×84 mm. **1404** £2.50 multicoloured		6·00	6·00
First Day Cover			7·00
Presentation Pack		7·00	

Plate Nos.: All values 1A (each ×4).
Sheets: 25 (5×5); 33p., 56p. also 10 (2×5).
Nos. 1513 and 1515 include the 'EUROPA' emblem.

1405 Naomi Taniguchi, 1959

1406 Mike Hailwood, 1960s

1407 Alex George, 1970s

1408 Joey Dunlop, 1980s

1409 Steve Hislop, 1990s

1410 John McGuinness, 2000s

50th Anniversary of Honda Motorcycles in World Championship Racing

(Des Peter Jones. Litho BDT)

2009 (11 May). Perf 14 (C).

1520	**1405**	32p. multicoloured	70	70
1521	**1406**	33p. multicoloured	75	75
1522	**1407**	56p. multicoloured	1·25	1·25
1523	**1408**	62p. multicoloured	1·60	1·60
1524	**1409**	90p. multicoloured	2·40	2·40
1525	**1410**	£1.77 multicoloured	3·75	3·75
1520/5 *Set of 6*			10·00	10·00
First Day Cover			11·00	
Presentation Pack			11·00	

Plate Nos.: All values 1A (each ×4).
Sheets: 25 (5×5).

1411 W. G. Grace at Lord's, 1895; MCC Ashes Trophy and Urn; England v. Australia, Lord's, 2005 (*Illustration reduced. Actual size* 170×75 mm)

The Ashes. England v. Australia 2009

(Des Karen Neale, Christina Pierce and Gautam Saha. Litho BDT)

2009 (29 JUNE). Sheet 170×75 mm. Perf 14 (horiz) or 14×14½ (vert) (both comb).

MS1526 **1411** £1×3 multicoloured	7·00	7·00
First Day Cover		8·50
Presentation Pack	8·50	

1412 Barry, Maurice and Robin Gibb as Boys

1413 *Children of the World* Album Cover

1414 *Bee Gees* Album Cover

1415 *Still Waters* Album

1416 *One Night Only* Album

1417 *This is Where I Came In* Album

1418 Bee Gees *Number Ones* Album

1419 Bee Gees *The Studio Albums* 1967–8

50th Anniversary of the Bee Gees (pop group)

(Des Kcreative. Litho Lowe-Martin)

2009 (1 July). Perf 13×12½ (C).

1527	**1412**	32p. multicoloured	75	75
		a. Horiz strip of 4 with central label. Nos. 1527/30	4·00	4·00
1528	**1413**	33p. multicoloured	75	75
1529	**1414**	50p. multicoloured	1·25	1·25
1530	**1415**	54p. multicoloured	1·25	1·25
1531	**1416**	56p. multicoloured	1·25	1·25
		a. Horiz strip of 4. Nos. 1531/4	7·50	7·50
1532	**1417**	62p. multicoloured	1·60	1·60
1533	**1418**	78p. multicoloured	1·75	1·75
1534	**1419**	£1.28 multicoloured	3·00	3·00
1527/34 *Set of 8*			11·50	11·50
First Day Cover			13·00	
Presentation Pack			13·00	

Plate Nos. Both values 1A (×5).
Sheets: 16 (2 blocks 4×2 with central labels). Nos. 1527/30 and 1531/4 were each printed together,*se-tenant* , as horizontal strips of four stamps with a central label, in sheets containing two blocks of eight stamps separated by a large illustrated gutter.

40th Anniv of First Manned Moon Landing (2nd issue)

2009 (20 July). No. **MS**1519 additionally inscr with '40th anniversary man on the moon' emblem on the bottom right margin.

MS1534*a* £2.50 *On the Rim* (John Young and Charlie Duke at North Ray Crater, 1972) (Alan Bean)	6·00	6·00

1420 Brown Hare

1421 Hedgehogs

1422 Pheasants

1423 Barn Owl

1424 Cockerel

1425 *On the Hill*

Country File. Paintings by Jeremy Paul

(Des Kcreative. Litho Lowe-Martin)

2009 (1 Sept). Perf 12½ (C).

1535	**1420**	32p. multicoloured	75	75
1536	**1421**	33p. multicoloured	75	75
1537	**1422**	54p. multicoloured	1·25	1·25
1538	**1423**	90p. multicoloured	2·40	2·40
1539	**1424**	92p. multicoloured	2·40	2·40
1540	**1425**	£1.58 multicoloured	3·50	3·50
1535/40 *Set of 6*			11·00	11·00
MS1541 148×210 mm. Nos. 1535/40			11·00	11·00
First Day Cover				12·00
Presentation Pack			12·00	

Plate Nos. All values 1A (each ×4).
Sheets: 25 (5×5).

1426 *Bridge*

1427 *Willows and Blue Mountain*

1428 *Kew*

1429 *Eairy Beg*

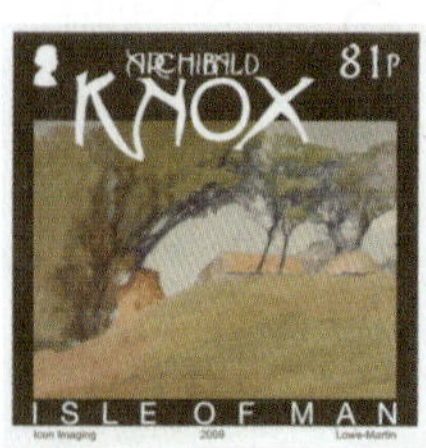

1430 *Leaning Trees*

1431 *Old Laxey*

Watercolour Paintings by Archibald Knox

(Des Icon Imaging. Litho Lowe-Martin)

2009 (16 Sept). Perf 12½ (C).

1542	**1426**	32p. multicoloured	75	75
1543	**1427**	33p. multicoloured	75	75
1544	**1428**	56p. multicoloured	1·25	1·25
1545	**1429**	62p. multicoloured	1·60	1·60
1546	**1430**	81p. multicoloured	1·90	1·90
1547	**1431**	182p. multicoloured	4·25	4·25
1542/7 *Set of 6*			10·50	10·50
First Day Cover				12·00
Presentation Pack			12·00	

No. 1544 is inscr 'sepac'. This stamp was also available in a folder with 10 other 'sepac' logo stamps issued by other participating administrations.

Plate Nos.: All values 1A (each ×4).
Sheets: 15 (5×3).

1432 Captain James Teare and SS *Ellan Vannin*; SS *Ellan Vannin* in Ramsey Harbour (*Illustrationreduced. Actual size 170×75 mm*)

Centenary of Sinking of the SS *Ellan Vannin* (steam packet)

(Des Peter Hearsey. Litho BDT)

2009 (1 Oct). Sheet 170×75 mm. Perf 14 (C).

MS1548 **1432** £1.50×2 multicoloured		7·00	7·00
First Day Cover			8·50
Presentation Pack		8·50	

1433 Father Christmas putting Present into Stocking

1434 Writing List

1435 Carrying Sack of Toys

1436 Carrying Wrapped Present

1437 With Archbishop's Staff, Mitre and Robes

1438 With Christmas Pudding and Wine Goblet

Christmas. Father Christmas

(Litho BDT)

2009 (20 Oct). Perf 14 (C).

1549	**1433**	30p. multicoloured	70	70
1550	**1434**	33p. multicoloured	75	75
1551	**1435**	56p. multicoloured	1·25	1·25
1552	**1436**	62p. multicoloured	1·60	1·60
1553	**1437**	81p. multicoloured	1·75	1·75
1554	**1438**	90p. multicoloured	2·40	2·40
1549/54 *Set of 6*			8·25	8·25
First Day Cover			10·00	
Presentation Pack			10·00	

(b) Self-adhesive. Size 26×37 mm. Die-cut perf 14

1555	**1433**	30p. multicoloured	70	70
1556	**1434**	33p. multicoloured	75	75

Plate Nos.: All values 1A (each ×4).
Sheets: Nos. 1549/54 25 (5×5); Nos. 1555/6 30 (6×5).

Year Folder 2009

2009 (20 Oct). Comprises Nos. 1473/500, 1505/34, 1535/40 and 1542/54.

Year Folder.. £100

Year Pack 2009

2009 (20 Oct). Comprises Nos. 1473/500, 1505/34, 1535/40 *and* 1542/54.

Year Pack.. £110

Post Office Yearbook

2009 (20 Oct). Comprises Nos. 1473/500, 1505/34, 1535/40 and 1542/54.

Yearbook.. £100

1439 Woman walking in Lane

1440 Angler

1441 Yachtsman

1442 Climber

1443 Children riding Ponies

1444 Apple picking

1445 Unloading Kayak

1446 Motorcyclist

1447 Children on Rocky Shore

1448 Horses Ploughing at Cregneash National Folk Museum

Island Life

(Des truly London. Litho Lowe-Martin)

2010 (12 Jan).

(a) Ordinary gum. Perf 12½ (C)

1557	**1439**	(32p.) multicoloured	75	75
		a. Horiz strip of 4. Nos. 1557/60	3·00	3·00
1558	**1440**	(32p.) multicoloured	75	75
1559	**1441**	(32p.) multicoloured	75	75
1560	**1442**	(32p.) multicoloured	75	75
1561	**1443**	(33p.) multicoloured	75	75
		a. Horiz strip of 4. Nos. 1561/4	3·00	3·00
1562	**1444**	(33p.) multicoloured	75	75
1563	**1445**	(33p.) multicoloured	75	75
1564	**1446**	(33p.) multicoloured	75	75
1565	**1447**	56p. multicoloured	1·25	1·25
1566	**1448**	90p. multicoloured	2·40	2·40
1557/66 *Set of 10*			9·50	9·50
First Day Cover			11·00	
Presentation Pack			11·00	

(b) Self-adhesive. Perf 13½×13 (die-cut)

1567	**1439**	(32p.) multicoloured	75	75
		a. Booklet pane. Nos. 1567/70, each ×3	9·00	
1568	**1440**	(32p.) multicoloured	75	75
1569	**1441**	(32p.) multicoloured	75	75
1570	**1442**	(32p.) multicoloured	75	75
1571	**1443**	(33p.) multicoloured	75	75
		a. Booklet pane. Nos. 1571/4, each ×3	9·00	
1572	**1444**	(33p.) multicoloured	75	75
1573	**1445**	(33p.) multicoloured	75	75
1574	**1446**	(33p.) multicoloured	75	75

Nos. 1557/60 and 1567/70 were inscribed 'IOM RATE' and originally sold for 32p. each.

Nos. 1561/4 and 1571/4 were inscribed 'UK RATE' and originally sold for 33p. each.

Nos. 1567/70 and 1571/4 were only issued in separate booklets of ten stamps, Nos. SB74/5.

Plate Nos.: All values 1A (each ×4).

Sheets: 40 (8×5). Nos. 1557/60 and 1561/4 were each printed together, *se-tenant*, as horizontal strips of four throughout the sheets.

1449 Two Rainbows

1450 Company of Rainbows and Leaders

1451 Brownies holding Badges

1452 Five Brownies

1453 Girl Guide

1454 Guides and Leaders on Parade

1455 Senior Section Members

1456 Queen Elizabeth II meeting Guide Leaders

1457 Manx Guide Leaders (£1.50); Trefoil Guild Members planting Tree, 1985 (£1.50) (*Illustration reduced. Actual size 170×75 mm*)

Centenary of Girlguiding

(Des Andrew Robinson. Litho BDT)

2010 (18 Feb). Perf 14 (C).

1575	**1449**	32p. multicoloured	75	75
		a. Horiz pair. Nos. 1575/6	1·50	1·50
1576	**1450**	32p. multicoloured	75	75
1577	**1451**	33p. multicoloured	75	75
		a. Horiz pair. Nos. 1577/8	1·50	1·50
1578	**1452**	33p. multicoloured	75	75
1579	**1453**	56p. multicoloured	1·25	1·25
		a. Horiz pair. Nos. 1579/80	2·50	2·50
1580	**1454**	56p. multicoloured	1·25	1·25
1581	**1455**	£1 multicoloured	2·25	2·25
		a. Horiz pair. Nos. 1581/2	4·50	4·50
1582	**1456**	£1 multicoloured	2·25	2·25
1575/82 *Set of 8*			10·00	10·00
First Day Cover				11·00
Presentation Pack			11·00	
MS1583 170×75 mm. **1457** £1.50×2 multicoloured			7·00	7·00
First Day Cover				8·50
Presentation Pack			8·50	

Nos. 1577 and 1579 include the 'EUROPA' emblem.

Plate Nos.: All values 1A (each ×4).

Sheets: 12 (2 blocks 2×3) 33p., 56p. also separate sheets of 10 (2×5). Nos. 1575/6, 1577/8, 1579/80 and 1581/2 were each printed together, *se-tenant*, as horizontal pairs in sheetlets of 12 containing two blocks of 6 separated by a large illustrated vertical gutter.

1458 Messerschmitt BF109 and Defiant

1459 Spitfire and Messerschmitt BF109

1460 Junkers Ju87 and Hurricane

1461 Messerschmitt BF110 and Hurricane

1462 Blenheim I and Junkers 88

1463 Heinkel III and Spitfire

1464 1981 60th Anniversary of Royal British Legion 20p. Stamp and Ship crowded with Evacuated Troops, Dunkirk, 1940 (£1.50); 1990 50th Anniversary of Battle of Britain Pair of 24p. Stamps and Aircrew running for Planes (£1.50) (*Illustration reduced. Actual size* 170×75 mm)

70th Anniversary of the Battle of Britain

(Des Keith Woodcock (Nos. 1584/9) and Kreative. Litho BDT)

2010 (20 Apr). Perf 13½ (C).

1584	**1458**	70p. multicoloured	1·60	1·60
		a. Horiz strip of 3. Nos. 1584/6	5·25	5·25
1585	**1459**	70p. multicoloured	1·60	1·60
1586	**1460**	70p. multicoloured	1·60	1·60
1587	**1461**	70p. multicoloured	1·60	1·60
		a. Horiz strip of 3. Nos. 1587/9	5·25	5·25
1588	**1462**	70p. multicoloured	1·60	1·60
1589	**1463**	70p. multicoloured	1·60	1·60
1584/9 *Set of 6*			10·00	10·00
First Day Cover				8·50
Presentation Pack			8·50	
Commemorative Folder (complete sheets)			40·00	
MS1590 170×75 mm. **1464** £1.50 multicoloured; £1.50 multicoloured			7·00	7·00
First Day Cover				11·00
Presentation Pack			11·00	

MS1590 also commemorates the 70th anniversary of Operations Dynamo and Ariel (evacuation of troops from Dunkirk).

Plate Nos.: Both sheets 1A (each ×4).

Sheets: 12 (2 blocks 3×2). Nos. 1584/6 and 1587/9 were each printed together, *se-tenant*, as horizontal strips of three stamps in sheets containing two blocks of six separated by a large illustrated horizontal gutter.

1465 King George V and Queen Mary at Grand Hall, Douglas, 1920 and Cast of Great Britain 1d. George V Stamp

1466 King George V and Queen Mary, Isle of Man, 1920 and Cape of Good Hope Tête-Bêche Pairs of 1861 1d. 'Hope' Stamps

1467 King George V and Queen Mary arriving at Queen's Pier, Ramsey, 1920 and Great Britain 1910 2d. Tyrian Plum Stamp

1468 King George V and Queen Mary with Nurses, Ramsey, and Oil Rivers Protectorate 1893 20s. on 1s. Stamp

1469 King George V planting Tree at Bishopscourt, 1920 and George V ½d. Green Stamp

1470 King George V and Queen Mary at Castletown and Mauritius 1847 2d. Deep Blue Stamp

Centenary of Accession of King George V

(Des Kcreative. Litho Enschedé)

2010 (6 May). Perf 14 (C).

1591	**1465**	55p. multicoloured	1·25	1·25
1592	**1466**	60p. multicoloured	1·50	1·50
1593	**1467**	67p. multicoloured	1·60	1·60
1594	**1468**	96p. multicoloured	2·50	2·50
1595	**1469**	97p. multicoloured	2·50	2·50
1596	**1470**	£1.10 multicoloured	3·00	3·00
1591/6 *Set of 6*			11·50	11·50
First Day Cover			12·00	
Presentation Pack			12·00	
Set of 6 Pre-Paid Postcards			5·50	15·00

Plate Nos.: All values 1A (each ×4).

Sheets: 25 (5×5).

1471 Model T Speedster, 1915

1472 Model T Coupe, 1926

1473 Model T 7cwt Van, 1923

1474 Model T Town Car, 1912

1475 Model T Charabanc, 1922

1476 Model T Tourer, 1912

50th Anniversary of Model T Ford Register

(Des Peter Hearsey and Eddie Cassidy. Litho BDT)

2010 (7 May). Perf 13½ (C).

1597	**1741**	35p. multicoloured	80	80
1598	**1742**	36p. multicoloured	85	85
1599	**1743**	60p. multicoloured	1·50	1·50
1600	**1744**	74p. multicoloured	1·75	1·75
1601	**1745**	97p. multicoloured	2·25	2·25
1602	**1746**	172p. multicoloured	4·00	4·00
1597/602 *Set of 6*			11·00	1·00
First Day Cover			12·00	
Presentation Pack			12·00	

Plate Nos.: 1A (each ×4).
Sheets: 25 (5×5).

SOUVENIR POSTAL STATIONERY POSTCARDS

The following postcards were issued by the Isle of Man Postal Authority often in connection with various philatelic exhibitions and, with the exception of Nos. PC8, PC11 and PC15/16 show imprinted stamp designs.

'San Marino 82'

1982 (1 Sept). Card showing imprinted stamp design as No. 217. Sold at 30p.
PC1 19½p. multicoloured .... 1·00 1·20
Withdrawn: 30.4.84.

' Tembal 83', Basel

1983 (21 May). Card showing imprinted stamp design as No. 250. Sold at 30p.
PC2 20½p. multicoloured .... 1·00 1·60
Withdrawn: 20.5.84.

'Espana 84', Madrid

1984 (27 Apr). Card showing imprinted stamp design as No. 266. Sold at 30p.
PC3 20½p. multicoloured .... 1·50 1·70
Withdrawn: 26.4.85.

'Ausipex 84', Melbourne
1984 (21 Sept). Card showing imprinted stamp design as No. 278. Sold at 40p.
PC4 33p. multicoloured .... 1·50 2·75
Withdrawn: 20.9.85.

'Italia 85', Rome

1985 (25 Oct). Card showing imprinted stamp designs as Nos. 292/3. Sold at 40p.
PC5 14p. +14p. multicoloured .... 1·50 3·25
Withdrawn: 24.10.86.

' Ameripex 86', Chicago

1986 (22 May). Card showing imprinted stamp design as No. 302. Sold at 40p.
PC6 34p. multicoloured .... 2·20 2·75
Withdrawn: 21.5.87.

'Stockholmia 86', Stockholm

1986 (28 Aug). Card showing imprinted stamp designs as Nos. 305/6. Sold at 40p.
PC7 15p. +15p. multicoloured .... 1·20 2·00
Withdrawn: 27.8.87.

'Hafnia 87', Copenhagen

1987 (16 Oct). Card with Nos. 358/9 affixed. Sold at 50p.
PC8 12p. +15p. multicoloured .... 1·20 1·70
Withdrawn: 15.10.88.

'Finlandia 88', Helsinki

1988 (1 June). Card showing imprinted stamp designs as Nos. 371 and 375. Sold at 50p.
PC9 14p. +18p. multicoloured .... 1·20 1·50
Withdrawn: 31.5.89.

'Sydpex 88', Sydney

1988 (30 July). Card showing imprinted stamp designs as Nos. 386/7. Sold at 60p.
PC10 29p. +31p. multicoloured .... 1·50 1·70
Withdrawn: 29.7.89.

' Filacept 88', The Hague

1988 (18 Oct). Card with Nos. 383/4 affixed. Sold at 50p.
PC11 22p. +22p. multicoloured .... 1·20 2·00
Withdrawn: 17.10.89.

'Belgica 90', Brussels

1990 (2 June). Card showing imprinted stamp designs as Nos. 442 and 446. Sold at 50p.
PC12 1p. +37p. multicoloured .... 1·20 1·50
Withdrawn: 2.93.

'Essen 94', Centenary of Picture Postcards

1994 (5 May). Cards showing imprinted stamp design as No. 338. Sold at 80p. the pair.
PC13 31p. multicoloured (Douglas) .... 1·20 1·50
PC14 31p. multicoloured (Ramsey) .... 1·20 1·50
Withdrawn: 4.5.95.

'Jakarta 95'

1995 (19 Aug). Sold at 15p.
PC15 Komodo Dragon .... 75 1·00
Withdrawn: 6.98.

'Beijing 95'

1995 (16 Sept). Sold at 15p.
PC16 Great Wall of China .... 75 1·00
Withdrawn: 6.98.

Isle of Man T.T. Races and 50th Anniversary of Honda

1998 (1 June). Card showing imprinted stamp design as No. 809. Sold at 50p.
PC17 25p. multicoloured .... 1·00 1·20
Withdrawn: 6.99.

' Espana 2000', Madrid

2000 (6 Oct). Card showing imprinted stamp design as No. 910.
PC18 45p. multicoloured .... 1·50 1·50
Withdrawn: 6.2002.

' Sindelfingen', Germany

2000 (6 Oct). Card showing imprinted stamp design as No. 911.
PC19 65p. multicoloured .... 1·50 1·50
Withdrawn: 6.2002.

Joey Dunlop (motorcycle champion) Commemoration

2001 (17 May). Cards showing stamp designs and enlarged photographs on the front and Douglas postage paid impression on the reverse. Sold at £5.71.

PC20/5 *Set of* 6 cards	11·50	11·50

Withdrawn: 16.5.2002.

MANX POSTAL MUSEUM POSTCARDS

1987 (23 Mar). Sold at 10p.

PM1	Reopening of Regent Street Post Office, Douglas	30	1·00

Sold out: By 2.90.

1989 (28 Apr). Sold at 15p.

PM2	Bicentenary of the Mutiny on the *Bounty*	40	1·50

Sold out: By 1.93.

1990 (10 Apr). Sold at 18p.

PM3	CUNARD 150 Exhibition, Liverpool. Sinking of *Lusitania* (as No. 191)	50	1·50

Sold out: By 2.94.

POSTAGE DUE STAMPS

D **1**

D **2**

D **3** Badge of Post Office Authority

(Des and litho Questa)

1973 (5 July). Perf 14×13½ (C).

D1	D **1**	½p. red, black & bistre-yellow (ab)	1·50	1·10
D2		1p. red, black and cinnamon (ab)	50	60
D3		2p. red, black & lt apple-green (ab)	15	20
		a. Positive offset of red ptg on back.		
D4		3p. red, black and grey (ab)	20	20
D5		4p. red, black & carmine-rose (ab)	30	35
D6		5p. red, black and cobalt (ab)	30	35
D7		10p. red, black & light lavender (ab)	40	40
D8		20p. red, black & pale turq-grn (ab)	75	60
D1/8 *Set of* 8			3·75	3·50
Presentation Pack (ptg b)			5·00	

Printings: (a) 5.7.73; (b) 1.9.73. Examples of printing (b) are known used from mid-August onwards.

Prices quoted above are for printing (b), which can be identified by the letter 'A' added after 1973 at the foot of the stamp. Collectors should beware of spurious examples with the 'A' removed. Price for set of 8 from printing (a) £24 mint or used.

Plate Nos.: All values 1A, 1B (each ×3).
Sheets: 100 (10×10).
Imprint: Right-hand corner, bottom margin, and left-hand corner, top margin.
Sold out: Printing (a) between 13.8.73 and 10.9.73. Printing (b) ½p. by 12.74; 1p. by 2.75; 2p. and 3p. by 5.75; others by 31.12.75.

(Des and litho Questa)

1975 (8 Jan). Perf 14×13½ (C).

D9	D **2**	½p. black, red & greenish yellow	10	10
D10		1p. black, red and flesh	10	10
D11		4p. black, red and rose-lilac	10	15
D12		7p. black, red & lt greenish blue	15	20
D13		9p. black, red and brownish grey	25	30
D14		10p. black, red and bright mauve	25	20
D15		50p. black, red and orange-yellow	90	90
D16		£1 black, red & turquoise-green	1·50	1·60
D9/16 *Set of* 8			3·00	3·25
First Day Cover				4·50
Presentation Pack			3·50	

Plate Nos.: All values 1A, 1B (each ×3).
Sheets: 100 (10×10).
Imprint: Left-hand corner, bottom margin.
Withdrawn: 31.12.82 (1p. to £1); 31.12.85 ½p.

(Litho B.D.T.)

1982 (5 Oct). Centres multicoloured; background colour given. Perf 14½×14 (C).

D17	D **3**	1p. turquoise-green	10	10
D18		2p. mauve	10	10
D19		5p. greenish blue	10	10
D20		10p. reddish lilac	20	25
D21		20p. grey	40	45
D22		50p. buff	90	1·10
D23		£1 salmon	1·60	2·10
D24		£2 bright blue	3·25	4·25
D17/24 *Set of* 8			6·00	7·75
First Day Cover				12·00
Presentation Pack Plate			8·00	

Plate Nos.: All values 1A (×5).
Sheets: 50 (10×5).
Imprint: Right-hand corner, bottom margin.

D **4**

(Des Colleen Corlett. Litho B.D.T.)

1992 (18 Sept). Perf 13×13½ (C).

D25	D **4**	£5 multicoloured	8·00	8·50

First Day Cover .... 8·00 8·50
Presentation Pack .... 9·50

Plate Nos.: 1A, 1B (each ×4).
Sheets: 50 (10×5).
Imprint: Right-hand corner, bottom margin.

STAMP BOOKLETS

PRICES are given for complete booklets. All booklets to No. SB7 are stitched.

B **1** Derbyhaven

1973 (5 July–17 Oct). Coloured covers as Type B **1**, printed in black Type B **1**. Yellow cover.

SB1 10p. booklet containing 2×2½p. (No. 16), 2×2p. (No. 15) and 2×½p (No. 12) (ab). 12·00

Ballaugh Church. Green cover.

SB2 25p. booklet containing 10×2½p. (No. 16) (ab) .... 3·00

Peel Castle. Stone cover.

SB3 30p. booklet containing 10×3p (No. 17) (a).. 15·00
SB3*a* As SB3 but cover in buff (b) .... 14·00

Quayside, Douglas. Lavender-grey cover.

SB4 50p. booklet containing 8×2½p. (No. 16) and 10×3p. (No. 17) (a) .... 6·00
SB4*a* As SB4 but grey-green cover (b) .... 5·50

Nos. SB1/4 were made up from ordinary sheets, the stamps being in vertical pairs with stitching through the side margins. Stamps from both sides of the sheets were used, so that panes come either upright or inverted.

Printings: (a) 5.7.73: (b) 17.10.73.

STAMP SACHETS. These are cardboard covers, with stamps loose inside, contained in clear plastic sachets.

B **2**

1973 (5 July–1 Nov). Stamp Sachets. Covers as Type B **2** 10p. sachet containing 5×½p (No. 12) and 3×2½p (No. 16) 10p. sachet containing 2×½p. (No. 12) and 3×3p (No. 17) (1 Nov) (Price 1·00 each).

B **3** Old Laxey Bridge (*Illustration reduced. Actual size* 89×51 mm)

1974 (1 Apr*). Coloured covers as Type B **3**, printed in black Type B **3**. Buff cover.

SB5 30p. booklet containing 8×½p. (No. 12), 4×3p. (No. 17) and 4×3½p. (No. 18) .... 2·00

Monk's Bridge, Ballasalla. Green cover.

SB6 40p. booklet containing 4×½p. (No. 12), 8×3p. (No. 17) and 4×3½p. (No. 18) .... 2·00

St. Michael's Chapel, Langness. Red cover.

SB7 50p. booklet containing 12×3p. (No. 17) and 4×3½p. (No. 18) .... 2·00

Nos. SB5/7 contain panes of four, and were produced in the same way as Nos. SB1/4. 3p. panes from SB5/7 exist with either shiny or matt gum. ½p. panes are shiny gum and 3½p. panes matt gum only (see note after No. 33).

*The booklets were placed on sale at the Interpex stamp exhibition in New York on 22 March 1974 and panes and covers exist cancelled with this date.

1974 (29 July–19 June). Stamp Sachets. Cover designs as Nos. SB5/7, but inscriptions redrawn. Contents unchanged.

30p. sachet. Pink cover (Price 1·50) ....
40p. sachet. Green cover (Price 1·60) ....
50p. sachet. Yellow cover (Price 1·90) ....

1975 (25 Apr–16 June). Stamp Sachets. Blue cover showing Post Office badge.

20p. sachet containing 3×2p. (No. 15) and 4×3½p. (No. 18) attached to cover by the selvedge (Price 2·20) ....
20p. sachet containing 1×½p. (No. 12), 2×1½p. (No. 14) and 3×5½p. (No. 22), loose or attached to selvedge (28 May) (Price 2·70)
20p. sachet containing 4×½p. (No. 12), 2×1½p. (No. 14) and 3×5p. (No. 21), loose or attached to selvedge (16 June) (Price 2·70) ....

1976 (20 Sept)–**79**. Stamp Sachet. Blue cover similar to Type B **3**, showing Rushen and Castletown Harbour.

20p. sachet containing 2×1p. (No. 13) and 3×6p. (No. 23) (Price 1·10) ....
20p. sachet containing 2×1p. (No. 13) and 3×6p. (No. 139) (3.79) (Price 2·40) ....

B **4** Viking Longship (*Illustration reduced. Actual size* 89×49 mm)

Millennium of Tynwald

1979 (16 May). Folded card covers as Type B **4**.

SB8 20p. booklet containing 4×3p. and 2×4p. (No. 150ab) (blue cover) .... 1·00
SB9 40p. booklet containing 8×3p. and 4×4p. (No. 150a×2) (pink cover) .... 1·20
SB10 60p. booklet containing 12×3p. and 6×4p. (No. 150a×3) (yellow cover) .... 1·50

Examples of Nos. SB8/9 are known containing the wrong pane.
Withdrawn: 28.9.80.

1980 (29 Sept). Folded card covers as Type B **4**.

SB11 40p. booklet containing 2×1p., 4×3p., 4×4p. and 2×5p. (Nos. 150ba and 188a) (pink cover showing Manx Loaghtyn Ram) .... 1·00
SB12 80p. booklet containing 4×1p., 8×3p., 8×4p. and 4×5p. (Nos. 150ba and 188a each ×2) (green cover showing Peregrine Falcon) .... 1·50

Withdrawn: 9.4.86.

1985 (12 June). Booklet No. SB11 with cover surcharged 50p. and an additional loose 10p. stamp inside.

SB13 50p. booklet containing Nos. 150ba, 188a and one 10p. (No. 236) .... 4·50

Withdrawn: 9.4.86.

HAVE YOU READ THE NOTES AT THE BEGINNING OF THIS CATALOGUE?
These often provide answers to the enquiries we receive

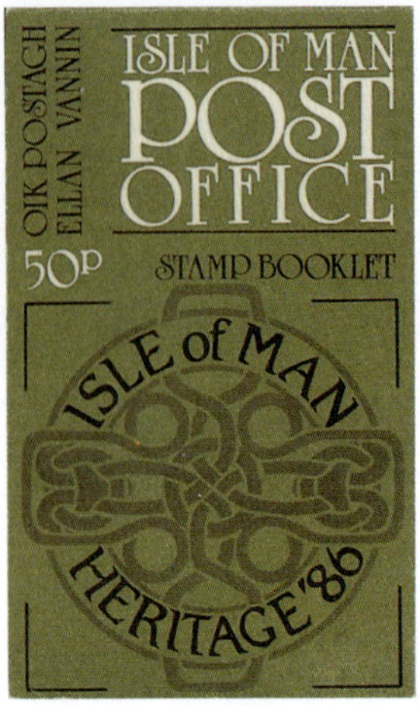

B **5** Celtic Cross Logo (*Illustration reduced. Actual size* 80×48 mm)

Manx Heritage Year

1986 (10 Apr). Folded card covers as Type B **5**.

SB14	50p. booklet containing 2×1p., 2×4p., 2×5p. and 3×10p. (Nos. 188a and 316a) olive-green cover)	1·40
SB15	£1.14 booklet containing 2×1p., 2×2p., 4×3p., 4×4p., 2×5p. and 7×10p. (Nos. 150ba, 188a, 315a and 316a) (greenish blue cover)	2·50

Withdrawn: 25.3.87.

B **6** Loch Promenade (*Illustration reduced. Actual size* 82×48 mm)

Victorian Douglas

1987 (26 Mar). Folded card covers as Type B **6**.

SB16	50p. booklet containing either No. 334a or 334ab (orange-brown and deep yellow-green cover Type B **6**)	1·50
SB17	£1.10 booklet containing either Nos. 334a or 334ab, and 334b or 334ba (orange-brown and bright scarlet cover showing The Breakwater)	2·50

Withdrawn: 15.3.88.

B **7** Baldwin Reservoir Tramway Steam Locomotive Injebreck (*Illustration reduced. Actual size* 82×48 mm)

Manx Railways and Tramways

1988 (16 Mar). Folded multicoloured card covers as Type B **7**.

SB18	50p. booklet containing No. 367a (cover Type B **7**)	2·00
SB19	£1.99 booklet containing Nos. 367a and 370a (cover showing Manx Electric Railway train at Maughold Head)	5·00

Withdrawn: 15.10.89.

B **8** 'Mutineers casting Bligh adrift' (Robert Dodd) (*Illustration reduced. Actual size* 155×100 mm)

Bicentenary of The Mutiny on the *Bounty*

1989 (28 Apr). Multicoloured cover as Type B **8**. Booklet contains text and Illustrations on interleaving pages. Stitched.

SB20	£5.30 booklet containing Nos. 408a/b, 410a and **MS**415a	10·00

Examples of No. **MS**415 from the booklet have wider margins than the normal miniature sheets.

Withdrawn: 2.92.

Manx Railways and Tramways

1989 (16 Oct). Folded multicoloured covers as Type B **7**.

SB21	50p. booklet containing No. 367b (cover showing Port Erin Breakwater Tramway Locomotive *Henry B. Loch*)	1·50
SB22	£2.09 booklet containing Nos. 367b and 371a (cover showing Douglas Cable Tramway)	4·50

Withdrawn: 13.2.90.

Manx Railways and Tramways

1990 (14 Feb). Folded multicoloured covers as Type B **7**.

SB23	50p. booklet containing No. 372a (cover showing Marine Drive Tramway)	2·00
SB24	£1.74 booklet containing No. 372b (cover showing Ramsey Harbour Tramway)	4·50

Withdrawn: 8.1.91.

B **9** Penny Black (*Illustration reduced. Actual size* 125×75 mm)

150th Anniversary of the Penny Black and 'Stamp World London 90' International Stamp Exhibition, London

1990 (3 May). Black and ochre cover as Type B **9**. Booklet contains text and Illustrations on interleaving pages. Stapled.

SB25	£3.50 booklet containing Nos. 442c, 443a and **MS**447a	6·00

Withdrawn: 23.9.93.

Manx Railway and Tramways

1991 (9 Jan). Folded multicoloured covers as Type B **7**.

SB26	50p. booklet containing No. 367ca (cover, 80×48 mm, showing Groudle Glen Railway steam locomotive *Polar Bear*)	3·00

SB27 £1 booklet containing No. 367cb (cover, 56×43 mm, showing I.M.R. No. 11 *Maitland* pulling Royal Train, 1963)......... 2·75
Withdrawn: 7.1.92.

B **10** Three Kings (*Illustration reduced. Actual size* 150×105 mm)

Christmas

1991 (14 Oct). Deep violet cover as Type B **10**. Stitched.
SB28 £4.16 booklet containing No. 500a×2............... 10·00
Withdrawn: 23.9.93.

Manx Railways and Tramways

1992 (8 Jan). Folded multicoloured covers as Type B **7**, but 56×43 mm.
SB29 £1 booklet containing No. 375ab (cover showing double-decker horse tram, Douglas).. 3·00
SB30 £2 booklet containing No. 375ac (cover showing T.P.O. Special)................................ 5·00
Withdrawn: 3.1.93.

B **11** Union Pacific No. 119, 1869 (*Illustration reduced. Actual size* 119×74 mm)

Construction of Union Pacific Railroad

1992 (22 May). Multicoloured cover as Type B **11**. Pane attached by selvedge.
SB31 £4.38 booklet containing pane No. 522b......... 8·50
Withdrawn: 27.4.94.

B **12** *Francis Drake* (ketch)

Ships

1993 (4 Jan). Multicoloured covers as Type B **12**. Panes attached by selvedge.
SB32 £1.10 booklet containing pane No. 543a (cover Type B **12**).. 3·00
SB33 £2.20 booklet containing pane No. 543b (cover showing *Tynwald I*)......................... 5·00
Withdrawn: 20.4.96.

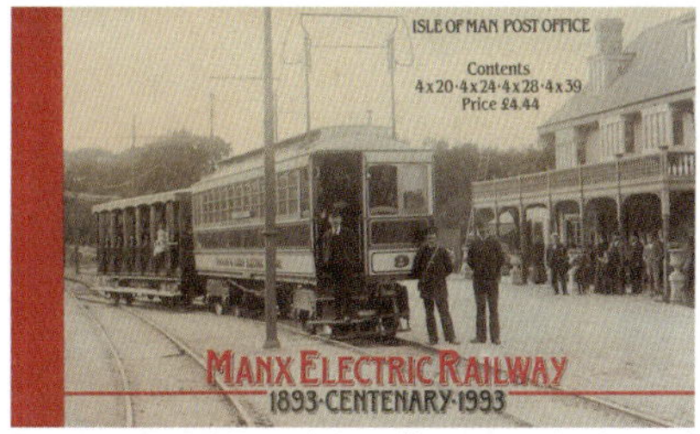

B **13** No. 9 Tunnel Car and Crew (*Illustration reduced. Actual size* 160×98 mm)

Centenary of Manx Electric Railway

1993 (3 Feb). Multicoloured cover as Type B **13**. Stitched.
SB34 £4.44 booklet containing pane No. 559a×4.... 10·00
Withdrawn: 27.4.94.

B **14** (*Illustration reduced. Actual size* 62×95 mm)

Christmas

1993 (12 Oct). Folded multicoloured covers as Type B **14**. Panes attached by selvedge.
SB35 £1.90 booklet containing No. 578×10 (cover Type B **14**).. 3·50
SB36 £2.30 booklet containing No. 579×10 (cover showing No. 579).. 5·00
Withdrawn: 10.10.95.

B **15** (*Illustration reduced. Actual size* 134×85 mm)

Manx Tourism Centenary

1994 (18 Feb). Multicoloured cover as Type B **15**. Pane attached by selvedge.
SB37 £2.40 booklet containing pane No. 590a and pane of 12 (3×4) greetings labels.......... 4·50
Sold out: By 9.95.

B **16** Postman Pat, Jess, Ferry and Aircraft (*Illustration reduced. Actual size* 152×85 mm)

Postman Pat visits the Isle of Man

1994 (14 Sept). Multicoloured cover as Type B **16** cut out to show stamps from first pane. Booklet contains text and Illustrations on labels attached to panes. Stitched.

SB38 £4.04 booklet containing Nos. 614a/19a, **MS**620a and pane of 8 character labels .... 9·00

Withdrawn: By 2.97.

B **17** Car and Passengers at Snaefell Summit (*Illustration reduced. Actual size* 162×97 mm)

Centenary of Snaefell Mountain Railway

1995 (8 Feb). Black, scarlet and grey cover as Type B **17**. Booklet contains text and Illustrations on labels attached to panes. Stitched.

SB39 £4.63 booklet containing No. 634a×3 and **MS**638a .... 10·00

Withdrawn: By 2.97.

B **18** Thomas the Tank Engine (*Illustration reduced. Actual size* 151×80 mm)

50th Anniversary of Thomas the Tank Engine Stories by Revd. Awdry. 'Thomas the Tank Engine's Dream'

1995 (15 Aug). Multicoloured cover as Type B **18** cut out to show stamps from first pane. Stitched.

SB40 £3.92 booklet containing Nos. 656a/b, 657a, 658a, 659a and 660a .... 8·50

Withdrawn: By 2.97.

B **19** Aerial view of Langness Lighthouse (*Illustration reduced. Actual size* 130×82 mm)

Lighthouses

1996 (24 Jan). Multicoloured cover as Type B **19**. Booklet contains text and Illustrations on interleaving pages. Stitched.

SB41 £4.74 booklet containing Nos. 672a/5a .... 8·00

Withdrawn: By 5.97.

Ships

1996 (21 Apr). Multicoloured cover as Type B **12**. Pane attached by selvedge.

SB42 96p. booklet containing pane No. 687a (cover showing *Sir Winston Churchill*) ..... 10·00

Sold out: 5.97.

B **20** (*Illustration reduced. Actual size* 118×81 mm)

Dogs

1996 (18 Sept). Multicoloured cover as Type B **20**. Booklet contains text and Illustrations on interleaving pages. Stitched.

SB43 £4.71 booklet containing Nos. 719a, 720a, 721a and **MS**725a .... 12·00

Withdrawn: 17.9.97.

B **21** Tawny Owl (*Illustration reduced. Actual size* 152×80 mm)

Owls

1997 (12 Feb). Multicoloured cover as Type B **21**. Booklet contains text and Illustrations on interleaving pages. Stitched.

SB44 £4.62 booklet containing Nos. 734a/6a and **MS**740a .... 10·00

Withdrawn: 11.2.98.

Ships

1997 (14 May). Multicoloured cover as Type B **12**. Pane attached by selvedge.

SB45 £1 booklet containing pane No. 541a (cover showing Royal Yacht *Britannia*)... 5·00

a. With extra loose 4p. stamp and optd inside front cover........ 6·00

No. SB45a was issued from booklet machines until 1 July 1997 when the postal rates were revised. The overprint inside the front cover was applied by handstamp.

Withdrawn: 31.12.97 No. SB45a; 30.11.98 No. SB45.

B **22** King Edward Bay Golf and Country Club (*Illustration reduced. Actual size* 160×98 mm)

Golf

1997 (29 May). Multicoloured cover as Type B **22**. Booklet contains text and Illustrations on panes and interleaving pages. Stitched.
SB46 £4.54 booklet containing Nos. 755a/7a and **MS**759a .... 10·00
Withdrawn: 28.5.98.

B **23** Cushag

Flowers

1998 (12 Feb). Multicoloured cover as Type B **23**. Pane attached by selvedge.
SB47 £1 booklet containing No. 775a .... 3·50
Withdrawn: 31.8.99.

B **24** Basking Shark (*Illustration reduced. Actual size* 157×105 mm)

U.N.E.S.C.O. International Year of the Ocean

1998 (16 Mar). Multicoloured cover as Type B **24**. Booklet contains text and Illustrations on interleaving pages. Stitched.
SB48 £3.62 booklet containing No. 798a/b........ 9·00
The price (£3.92) and content details of SB48 are incorrectly stated on the back cover.
Withdrawn: 13.3.99.

B **25** Steam Train at Douglas Station (*Illustration reduced. Actual size* 157×105 mm)

125th Anniversary of Isle of Man Steam Railway

1998 (2 May). Multicoloured cover as Type B **25**. Booklet contains text and Illustrations on interleaving pages. Stitched.
SB49 £4.05 booklet containing Nos. 803a×2 and **MS**807a .... 9·00
Sold out: 6.2000.

B **26** *Manchester & Salford*, 1868–1887 (*Illustration reduced. Actual size* 158×108 mm)

175th Anniversary of Royal National Lifeboat Institution

1999 (4 Mar). Multicoloured cover as Type B **26**. Booklet contains text and Illustrations on interleaving pages. Stitched.
SB50 £4.64 booklet containing Nos. 832a/b and **MS**839a .... 15·00
Withdrawn: 3.3.2000.

Flowers

1999 (26 Apr). Multicoloured cover as Type B **23**. Pane attached by selvedge.
SB51 £1 booklet containing pane No. 775ba (cover showing Dog Rose)........ 3·00
Sold out: By 31.8.2004.

B **27** Bus Radiator and Headlights (*Illustration reduced. Actual size* 158×100 mm)

Manx Buses

1999 (18 June). Multicoloured cover as Type B **27**. Booklet contains text and Illustrations on panes and interleaving pages. Stitched.
SB52 £4.78 booklet containing panes Nos. 845a/d. 13·00
Sold out: 8.2001.

B **28** Flags, Weapons and Military Headgear (*Illustration reduced. Actual size* 180×75 mm)

Isle of Man at War

2000 (22 May). Multicoloured cover as Type B **28**. Booklet contains text and Illustrations on interleaving pages. Stitched.
SB53 £4.99 booklet containing Nos. 887a/b and **MS**893a .... 12·00
Sold out: By 6.2003.

B **29** 'The Coronation, 1953' (Terence Cuneo) (*Illustration reduced. Actual size* 165×95 mm)

Golden Jubilee

2002 (6 Feb). Multicoloured cover as Type B **29**. Booklet contains text and Illustrations on panes and interleaving pages. Stitched.

SB54 £5.87 booklet containing panes Nos. 959a, 962a, 970b, 973b and **MS**975b .... 13·00

Withdrawn: 30.4.2004.

B **30** Aspects of the Isle of Man (*Illustration reduced. Actual size* 105×70 mm)

Photography–'The People's Choice

2002 (1 Oct). Multicoloured covers as Type B **30**. Self-adhesive.

SB55 £2.30 booklet containing No. 1021a .... 7·00

SB56 £2.70 booklet containing No. 1031a .... 8·50

Withdrawn: 30.4.2004.

B **31** Henry Bloom Noble and Original Villa Marina (*Illustration reduced. Actual size* 104×70 mm)

Centenary of Henry Bloom Noble Trust

2003 (1 Oct). Multicoloured covers as Type B **31**. Self-adhesive.

SB57 £2.30 booklet containing No. 1101a .... 6·00

SB58 £2.70 booklet containing No. 1106a .... 10·00

Withdrawn: 31.12.2004.

NEW INFORMATION

The editor is always interested to correspond with people who have new information that will improve or correct this catalogue

B **32** Soldier, Viking, Miner, Spinner and Fisherman (*Illustration reduced. Actual size* 102×70 mm)

Manx National Heritage The Story of Mann

2004 (3 Aug). Multicoloured covers as Type B **32**. Self-adhesive.

SB59 (£2.50) booklet containing pane No. 1167a (cover as Type B **32**) .... 8·00

SB60 (£2.80) booklet containing pane No. 1172a (cover showing Cregneash, Calf of Man, Castle Rushen, Laxey Wheel and Peel Castle) .... 9·00

Withdrawn: 2.8.2005.

B **33** 'Mona's Queen' (Arthur Burgess) (*Illustration reduced. Actual size* 165×95 mm)

175th Anniversary of Steam Packet Company

2005 (6 May). Multicoloured cover as Type B **33**. Booklet contains text and Illustrations on interleaving pages. Stitched.

SB61 £7.80 booklet containing panes Nos. 1217b/c, 1219b, 1221b and 1223b .... 14·00

Withdrawn: 5.5.2006.

B **34** Traditional Scenes (*Illustration reduced. Actual size* 107×76 mm)

' Time to Remember'

2005 (12 Aug). Multicoloured covers as Type B **34** showing portions of the stamp designs within. Self-adhesive.

SB62 £2.60 booklet containing pane No. 1247b (cover as Type B **34**) .... 5·50

SB63 £2.90 booklet containing pane No. 1252b (cover showing scenes from stamps) ..... 6·00

Sold out: By 12.2006.

B **35** Christmas Tree with Lights (*Illustration reduced. Actual size* 150×70 mm)

Christmas

2006 (11 Oct). Multicoloured covers as Type B **35**. Self-adhesive.
SB64 £2.80 booklet containing pane No. 1328a (Type B 35) .... 5·50
SB65 £3.10 booklet containing pane No. 1329a (cover showing tree with Three Legs of Mann decoration at top) .... 6·00
Withdrawn: 10.10.2007.

B **36** Scouts hiking near South Barrule (*Illustration reduced. Actual size* 165×96 mm)

Centenary of Scouting

2007 (22 Feb). Multicoloured cover as Type B **36**. Booklet contains text and Illustrations on interleaving pages. Stitched.
SB66 £9.16 booklet containing panes Nos. 1342a/b, 1343a, 1345a and **MS**1348a .... 20·00
Withdrawn: 21.2.2008.

B **37** 'Headland, Cornaa' (*Illustration reduced. Actual size* 132×67 mm)

Watercolour Paintings by Norman Sayle

2007 (12 Apr). Multicoloured covers as Type B **37**. Self-adhesive.
SB67 £2.80 booklet containing pane No. 1363a (Type B **37**) .... 8·50
SB68 £3.10 booklet containing pane No. 1365a (cover showing St. Mark"s Church) .... 9·25

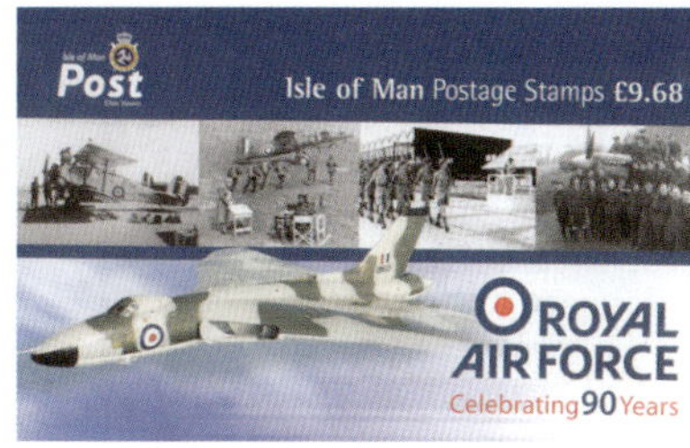

B **38** Aircraft (*Illustration reduced. Actual size* 166×96 mm)

90th Anniversary of the Royal Air Force

2008 (15 Jan). Multicoloured cover as Type B **38**. Booklet contains text and Illustrations on panes and interleaving pages. Stitched.
SB69 £9.68 booklet containing panes Nos. 1406b/d and 1408a .... 23·00

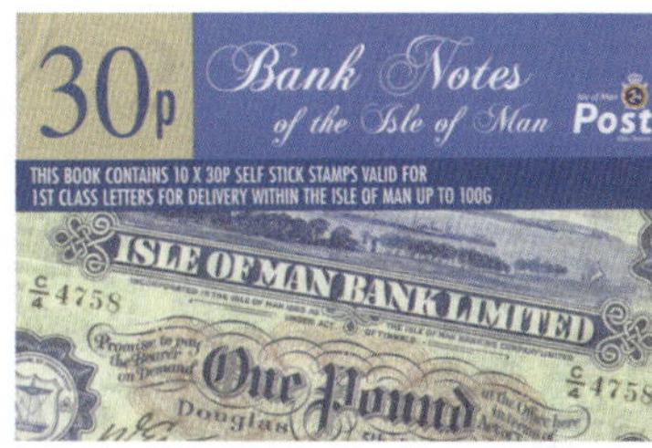

B **39** Isle of Man Bank £1 Note (*Illustration reduced. Actual size* 98×63 mm)

Bank Notes of the Isle of Man

2008 (7 Apr). Multicoloured cover as Type B **39**. Self-adhesive.
SB70 £3 booklet containing pane No. 1424a .... 7·00

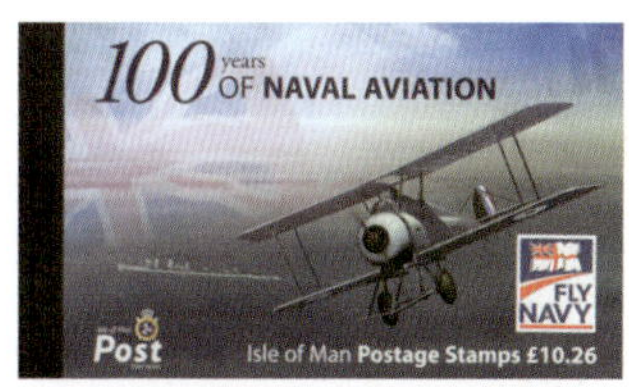

B **40** Biplane (*Illustration reduced. Actual size* 167×95 mm)

Centenary of Naval Aviation

2009 (15 Jan). Multicoloured cover as Type B **40**. Booklet contains text and Illustrations on panes and interleaving pages. Stitched.
SB71 £10.26 booklet containing panes Nos. 1473b/d and 1475a .... 23·00 23·00

B **41** Ballakilley Farm (*Illustration reduced. Actual size* 119×83 mm)

Mills and Millers. Photographs by Chris Kilip

2009 (1 Apr). Grey and black covers as Type B **41**. Self-adhesive.
SB72 £3.20 booklet containing pane No. 1501a .... 7·00 7·00
SB73 £3.30 booklet containing pane No. 1503a (cover showing *Mr. Cubbon*) .... 7·00 7·00

B **42** Horses Ploughing at Cregneash National Folk Museum (*Illustration reduced. Actual size 102×72 mm*)

Island Life

2010 (12 Jan). Multicoloured covers as Type B **42**. Self-adhesive.

SB74	(£3.84) booklet containing pane No. 1567a (cover as Type B **42**)	9·00	9·00
SB75	(£3.96) booklet containing pane No. 1571a (cover showing unloading of kayak)	9·00	9·00

JERSEY

THE GERMAN OCCUPATION

1940–1945

Soon after the commencement of the occupation of Jersey by German forces on 1 July 1940 orders were given by the German Commandant to the Islands Postmaster for stocks of the currently available stamps to be forwarded to the Jersey printers, J. T. Bigwood, for overprinting with a swastika and 'JERSEY 1940'. All values of the 1937–8 definitives from ½d. to 10s., excluding the 1d., were so overprinted as were the 1940 Postal Centenary stamps, excluding the 1d., but whilst this was in progress the Bailiff of Jersey protested to the German Commandant who referred the matter to Berlin and was ordered to destroy the stocks. Four complete sets to 1s., and a few singles, however, are known to exist. At the same time Bigwoods prepared a local 1d. stamp incorporating the ams of Jersey and the words 'ETATS DE JERSEY'. These were printed in imperforate sheets of thirty (10×3) and are known with and without a swastika and '1940' overprint. These also were destroyed with the exception of two sheets of each which have been cut up for collectors and a damaged sheet with the overprint which is complete. There is also a complete sheet of the unoverprinted stamp in the National Postal Museum.

Jersey eventually issued locally printed ½d. and 1d. stamps, the 1d. on 1 April 1941 and the ½d. on 29 January 1942. No distinct shades exist though both values come on newsprint paper and, in addition, the 1d. is known on chalk-surfaced paper.

In June 1943 a pictorial set of six stamps from ½d. to 3d. was issued, the designer being the well-known Jersey artist Edmund Blampied. Two values, the 1d. and 2½d., are known on newsprint paper.

Both these and the earlier issues remained on sale until 13 April 1946 after which date they could no longer be used.

1

2

The Swastika Overprints

1940. Prepared for use but not issued. Stamps of Great Britain overprinted by J. T. Bigwood, States Printers.

(a) On 1937–9 definitive issue

Cat. No.	*Type No.*		*Unused*
SW1	1	½d. green	£2500
SW2		1½d. red-brown	£2500
SW3		2d. orange	£2500
SW4		2½d. ultramarine	£2500
SW5		3d. violet	£2500
SW6		4d. grey-green	£2500
SW7		5d. brown	£2500
SW8		6d. purple	£2500
SW9		7d. emerald-green	£2500
SW10		8d. bright carmine	£2500
SW11		9d. deep olive-green	£2500
SW12		10d. turquoise-blue	£2500
SW13		1s. bistre-brown	£2500
		(b) On 1940 Stamp Centenary issue.	
SW14	2	½d. green	£2500
SW15		1½d. red-brown	£2500
SW16		2d. orange	£2500
SW17		2½d. ultramarine	£2500
SW18		3d. violet	£2500

3

4

(Des R. W. Cutland. Typo J. T. Bigwood)

1940. Prepared for use but not issued. No wmk. Imperforate.

SW19	3	1d. scarlet	£2200
SW20	4	1d. scarlet	£2200

5 Arms of Jersey

Stamps issued during the German Occupation

(Des Major N. V. L. Rybot. Typo Jersey Evening Post, St. Helier)

1941–43. White paper. No wmk. Perf 11 (L).

1	5	½d. bright green (29.1.42)	8·00	6·00
		a. Imperf between (vertical pair)	£850	
		b. Imperf between (horizontal pair)	£750	
		c. Imperf (pair)	£275	
		d. On greyish paper (1.43)	12·00	12·00
2		1d. scarlet (1.4.41)	8·00	5·00
		a. Imperf between (vertical pair)	£850	
		b. Imperf between (horizontal pair)	£750	
		c. Imperf (pair)	£300	
		d. On chalk-surfaced paper (9.41)	55·00	48·00
		e. On greyish paper (1.43)	14·00	14·00
1 *First Day Cover (plain)*				7·50
2 *First Day Cover (plain)*				8·00

Sheets: 60 (6×10).
Imprint: ½d. 'EVENING POST', JERSEY, JANUARY, 1942.
1d. 'EVENING POST', JERSEY, 17/3/41.
Quantities printed: ½d. 703,500; 1d. 1,030,620.
Withdrawn and invalidated: 13.4.46.

6 Old Jersey Farm

7 Portelet Bay

8 Corbière Lighthouse

9 Elizabeth Castle

10 Mont Orgueil Castle

11 Gathering Vraic (seaweed)

Pictorial Issue

(Des E. Blampied. Eng H. Cortot.
Typo French Govt Printing Works, Paris)

1943 (1 June)–**44**. No wmk. Perf 13½ (c).

3	6	½d. green	12·00	12·00
		a. Rough, grey paper (6.10.43)	15·00	14·00
4	7	1d. scarlet	3·00	50
		a. On newsprint (28.2.44)	3·50	75
5	8	1½d. brown (8.6.43)	8·00	5·75
6	9	2d. orange-yellow (8.6.43)	7·50	2·00
7	10	2½d. blue (29.6.43)	3·00	1·00
		a. On newsprint (25.2.44)	1·00	1·70
		ba. Thin paper (design shows through on reverse)	£225	
8	11	3d. violet (29.6.43)	3·00	2·75
3/8 Set of 6			30·00	21·00
First Day Covers (3)				36·00
Set of 6 Gutter Pairs			60·00	

Printings: The sheets of the various printings were dated in the sheet corners as follows:

½d.	1st Printing 1/5/43
	2nd Printing 3/5/43
	3rd Printing 6/10/43
1d.	1st Printing 7/5/43
	2nd Printing 8/5/43
	3rd Printing 7/10/43
	4th Printing 28/2/44
1½d.	1st Printing 17/5/43
	2nd Printing 18/5/43
2d.	1st Printing 20/5/43
	2nd Printing 21/5/43
2½d.	1st Printing 31/5/43
	2nd Printing 25/2/44
3d.	1st Printing 4/6/43
	2nd Printing 5/6/43

Sheets: 60 (2 panes 3×10).
Imprint: None.
Quantities printed: ½d. (No. 3) 360,000; ½d. (No. 3a) 120,000; 1d. (No. 4) 960,000; 1d. (No. 4a) 240,000; 1½d. 360,000; 2d. 360,000; 2½d. (No. 7) 360,000; 2½d. (Nos. 7a/b) 360,000; 3d. 360,000.
Withdrawn and invalidated: 13.4.46.

REGIONAL ISSUES

Although specifically issued for regional use, these issues were initially valid for use throughout Great Britain. However, they ceased to be valid in Jersey and Guernsey from 1 October 1969 when these islands each established their own independent postal administration and introduced their own stamps.

DATES OF ISSUE. Conflicting dates of issue have been announced for some of the regional issues, partly explained by the stamps being released on different dates by the Philatelic Bureau in Edinburgh or the Philatelic Counter in London and in the regions. We have adopted the practice of giving the earliest known dates, since once released the stamps could have been used anywhere in the U.K.

INVALIDATION. The regional issues of Jersey were invalidated for use in Jersey and Guernsey on 1 November 1969 (although Guernsey granted a further extension for British and regional stamps till the end of March 1970). The stamps continued to be valid for use in the rest of the United Kingdom until 29 February 1972. Those still current remained on sale at philatelic sales counters until 30 September 1970.

11a Multiple Crowns

12

13

(Des E. Blampied (Type **12**), W. Gardner (Type **13**). Portrait by Dorothy Wilding Ltd. Photo Harrison)

1958–67. Wmk Type **11a**. Perf 15×14 (c).

9	**12**	2½d. carmine-red (8.6.64)	30	45
		a. Imperf three sides (pair)	£2000	
10	**13**	3d. deep lilac (18.8.58)	30	25
		p. One centre phosphor band (9.6.67)	15	15
11		4d. ultramarine (7.2.66)	25	30
		p. Two phosphor bands (5.9.67)	15	25
9/11 *Set of 3*			50	75
9 *First Day Cover*				30·00
10 *First Day Cover*				20·00
11 *First Day Cover*				10·00

Cylinder Nos.: 2½d. 1; 3d. (ord) 1, 2; 3d. (phos) 2; 4d. (ord) 1; 4d. (phos) 1.
Sheets: 240 (12×20).
Quantities sold (ordinary only); 2½d. 4,770,000; 3d. 35,169,720; 4d. 6,623,040.
Withdrawn: 31.8.66 2½d.
Sold out: 10.67 3d. (ordinary); 11.67 4d. (ordinary); 10.68 3d. and 4d. (phosphor).

1968–69. No wmk. Chalk-surfaced paper. One centre phosphor band (4d. values) or two phosphor bands (5d.). Perf 15×14 (c).

12	**13**	4d. olive-sepia (4.9.68)	15	25
		Ey. Phosphoe omitted	£1000	
13		4d. bright vermilion (26.2.69)	15	25
14		5d. Royal blue (4.9.68)	15	50
12/14 *Set of 3*			40	1·00
12, 14 *First Day Cover*				3·00

Cylinder Nos.: 4d. (olive-sepia) 1; 4d. (bright vermilion) 1; 5d. 1.
Withdrawn: 30.9.69 (locally), 30.9.70 (British Philatelic Counters) 4d. olive-sepia, 4d. bright vermilion and 5d.

INDEPENDENT POSTAL ADMINISTRATION

Jersey established their own independent postal administration on 1 October 1969 and introduced their own stamps.

NO WATERMARK. All the following issues are on unwatermarked paper.

14 Elizabeth Castle

15 La Hougue Bie (Prehistoric Tomb)

16 Portelet Bay

17 La Corbière Lighthouse

18 Mont Orgueil Castle by Night

19 Arms and Royal Mace

20 Jersey Cow

21 Chart of the English Channel

22 Mont Orgueil Castle by Day

23 Queen Elizabeth II (after Cecil Beaton)

24 Jersey Airport

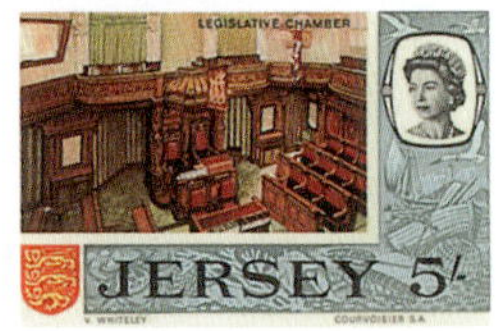

25 Legislative Chamber

26 The Royal Court

27 Queen Elizabeth II (after Cecil Beaton)

(Des V. Whiteley. Photo Harrison (½d. to 1s.9d.), Courvoisier (others))

1969 (1 Oct)–**70**. Granite paper (2s.6d. to £1). Multicoloured; frame colours given. Perf 14 (½d. to 1s.9d.) or 12 (others), all comb.

15	**14**	½d. ochre (a)	10	60
		a. Thick paper (a)	30	60
16	**15**	1d. brown (abc)	10	10
		a. Booklet stamp with blank margins* (a)	75	
		b. Thick paper (a)	80	90
17	**16**	2d. claret (a)	10	10
		a. Thinner paper (bc)	50	50
18	**17**	3d. ultramarine (a)	10	10
		a. Thinner paper (d)	75	75
		b. Orange omitted	£400	
19	**18**	4d. yellow-olive (a)	10	10
		a. Booklet stamp with blank margins* (a)	50	
		b. Thinner paper (c)	50	50
		c. Gold omitted		
20	**19**	5d. bistre (a)	10	10
		a. Thinner paper (c)	50	50
21	**20**	6d. yellow-brown (ab)	10	10
		a. Thinner paper (e)	9·00	9·00
22	**21**	9d. orange-brown (a)	10	20
		a. Thinner paper (d)	2·75	2·75
23	**22**	1s. reddish lilac (a)	25	25
		a. Thinner paper (c)	2·00	2·00
24	**21**	1s.6d. myrtle-green (a)	80	75
		a. Thinner paper (d)	3·50	3·50
25	**23**	1s.9d. pale myrtle-green (a)	1·00	1·00
		a. Thinner paper (c)	15·00	15·00
26	**24**	2s.6d. black and pale mauve (a)	1·60	1·00
27	**25**	5s. black and pale blue (a)	6·50	5·00
28	**26**	10s. black and pale slate-blue (a)	14·00	12·00
		a. Error. Green border †	£5250	
29	**27**	£1 pale bistre (af) ††	1·90	1·60
15/29 *Set of 15*			20·00	16·00
First Day Cover				20·00
15/29 *Presentation Packs* (3)			24·00	

*Nos. 16a and 19a are on medium paper. No. 16b on thick paper comes from 7s. and 10s. booklets.

†During the final printing of the 10s. a sheet was printed in the colours of the 50p., No. 56, ie. green border instead of slate.

††Printing (f) is the decimal issue which can be positively distinguished by the inscriptions in the left sheet margin which read 'Sheet value £25' at bottom and 'Value per row £5' at top instead of 'Sheet value £25 0s. 0d.' and 'Value per row £5 0s. 0d.' respectively. It exists with more blue in the Queen's dress and less red in the drapery but this printing also includes intermediate shades close to printing (a).

The thinner paper varieties result from a deliberate change as the thicker paper did not adhere well. The two types may be further distinguished by the gum which is creamy on the thicker paper and white on the thinner.

There are a number of shades in this issue which are in part due to the variation in the paper.

There was no postal need for the ½d. value as the ½d. coin had been withdrawn prior to its issue in anticipation of decimalisation.

Printings: (a) 1.10.69; (b) 18.2.70; (c) 15.4.70; (d) 5.5.70; (e) 27.5.70; (f) 3.73.

Cylinder Nos.: ½d., 1d., 2d., 4d., 1s. 1A (×5); 3d. 1A (37); 5d., 6d., 9d., 1s.6d., 1s.9d. 1A (×6); 2s.6d. to £1 None.

Sheets: 60 (6×10) ½d. to 1s.6d.; (10×6) 1s.9d.; 25 (5×5) 2s.6d. to £1

Quantities sold: ½d. 999,439; 1d. 1,050,124; 2d. 726,837; 3d. 635,019; 4d. 7,148,849; 5d. 4,886,016; 6d. 550,766; 9d. 954,649; 1s. 577,086; 1s.6d. 419,872; 1s.9d. 306,674; 2s.6d. 244,894; 5s. 206,629; 10s. 179,981; £1 271,194.

Withdrawn: 14.2.72 (except ½d., sold out 10.69, and £1 withdrawn 31.8.77).

Invalidated: 14.2.72 (except £1).

28 First Day Cover

Inauguration of Post Office

(Des R. Sellar. Photo Harrison)

1969 (1 Oct). Multicoloured; background colours given. Perf 14 (c).

30	**28**	4d. magenta	10	15
31		5d. new blue	20	10
32		1s.6d. red-brown	50	75
33		1s.9d. bright emerald	80	1·00
30/3 *Set of 4*			1·40	1·80
First Day Cover				4·00
Presentation Pack			2·00	

Cylinder Nos.: All values 1A (×4).

Sheets: 60 (6×10).

Quantities sold: 4d. 1,483,686; 5d. 742,820; 1s.6d. 272,155; 1s.9d. 238,856.

Withdrawn: 1.10.70.

Invalidated: 14.2.72.

29 'Lord Coutanche' (Sir James Gunn)

30 'Sir Winston Churchill' (Van Praag)

31 'Liberation' (Edmund Blampied)

32 S.S. *Vega* (unknown artist)

25th Anniversary of Liberation

(Des Rosalind Dease from paintings. Photo Courvoisier)

1970 (9 May). Granite paper. Perf 11½ (c).

34	**29**	4d. multicoloured	20	20
35	**30**	5d. multicoloured	20	20
36	**31**	1s.6d. multicoloured	90	1·00
37	**32**	1s.9d. multicoloured	90	1·00
34/7 *Set of 4*			2·00	2·00
First Day Cover				4·00
Presentation Pack			2·75	

A special Presentation Pack in gold, red and blue-green on olive was given to Jersey schoolchildren (Price £15). The normal Presentation Pack is printed in gold and blue-green.

Sheets: 50 (10×5) 4d., 5d.; (5×10) 1s.6d., 1s.9d.

Quantities sold: 4d. 1,617,751; 5d. 1,296,678; 1s.6d. 334,468; 1s.9d. 319,893.

Withdrawn: 9.5.71.

Invalidated: 14.2.72.

33 'A Tribute to Enid Blyton'

34 'Rags to Riches'

35 'Gourmet's Delight'

36 'We're the Greatest'

'Battle of Flowers' Parade

(Des Jennifer Toombs. Photo Courvoisier)

1970 (28 July). Granite paper. Perf 11½ (c).

38	**33**	4d. multicoloured	20	10
39	**34**	5d. multicoloured	20	20
40	**35**	1s.6d. multicoloured	2·50	2·20
41	**36**	1s.9d. multicoloured	2·75	2·20
38/41 *Set of 4*			5·00	4·25
First Day Cover				4·25
Presentation Pack			6·50	

Sheets: 50 (5×10).
Quantities sold: 4d. 1,905,109; 5d. 1,498,301; 1s.6d. 262,072; 1s.9d. 231,077.
Withdrawn: 27.7.71.
Invalidated: 14.2.72.

37 Martello Tower, Archirondel

Decimal Currency

(Des V. Whiteley. Photo Harrison (½ to 9p.), Courvoisier (others)).

1970–74. Designs as Type **37** etc., but with values inscribed in decimal currency and new design (6p.). Chalk-surfaced paper (4½p., 5½p., 8p.), granite paper (10p., 20p., 50p.).

42	**14**	½p. multicoloured (bgk)	10	10
		a. Booklet stamp with blank margins (b)	20	
43	**17**	1p. multicoloured (bn)	10	10
		a. Orange omitted	£425	
44	**20**	1½p. multicoloured (b)	10	10
45	**18**	2p. multicoloured (b)	10	10
		a. Booklet stamp with blank margins	60	
46	**19**	2½p. multicoloured (bk)	10	10
		a. Booklet stamp with blank margins (b)	60	
		ab. Gold (Mace) omitted	£750	
		ac. Gold (Mace) ptg double	£375	
47	**15**	3p. multicoloured (bch)	10	10
		a. Booklet stamp with blank margins (e)	60	
48	**16**	3½p. multicoloured (bh)	10	10
		a. Booklet stamp with blank margins (h)	25	
49	**21**	4p. multicoloured (bfimo)	10	10
49*a*	**19**	4½p. multicoloured (j)*	75	75
		ab. Uncoated paper	4·00	
50	**22**	5p. multicoloured (blmo)	10	10
50*a*	**20**	5½p. multicoloured (j)	75	75
51	**37**	6p. multicoloured (b)	20	10
52	**21**	7½p. multicoloured (b)	50	50
52*a*	**18**	8p. multicoloured (j)	75	75
53	**23**	9p. multicoloured (b)	70	70
54	**24**	10p. multicoloured (adh)	40	30
55	**25**	20p. multicoloured (adh)	90	80
56	**26**	50p. multicoloured (al)	1·50	1·20
42/56 *Set of 18*			4·50	4·50
First Day Covers (3) 42/56, 29				6·50
Presentation Packs (4)			6·75	

Gum: From 1974 printings appeared with dextrin added to the PVA gum giving a bluish-green tinge and mottled appearance. The ½p., 1p., 2½p., 3p., 3½p., 4p., 5p. and 8p. all exist both PVA and PVA dextrin. The 4½ and 5½p. only come with dextrin, and the 10, 20 and 50p. only with gum arabic.

The Presentation Packs for this series exist in two different sizes, 4¼ in×5½ in of the initial supply and 8½×4½ in for replacement stock.

Printings: (a) 1.10.70; (b) 15.2.71; (c) 1.8.72; (d) 15.11.72; (e) 1.12.72; (f) 1.10.73; (g) 3.12.73; (h) 1.7.74; (i) 12.8.74; (j) 31.10.74; (k) 1.11.74; (l) 28.1.75; (m) 1.4.75; (n) 21.4.75; (o) 30.10.75.
Plate Nos.: ½p., 2p., 3½p., 6p., 8p. 1A (×5); 1p. 1A (×7), 2A–1A (×6) (n); 1½p., 2½p., 4½p., 5½p., 7½p., 9p. 1A (×6); 3p. 1A (×5), 1A (×4)–2A (h); 4p. 1A (×6), 2A–1A (×5) (mo); 5p. 1A (×5), 2A–1A (×4) (mo); 10p. to 50p. None.
Sheets: 50 (5×10) ½p. to 8p.; (10×5) 9p.; 25 (5×5) 10p. to 50p.
Quantities sold: ½p. 2,247,128; 1p. 1,654,860; 1½p. 817,871; 2p. 2,305,239; 2½p. 5,096,912; 3p. 4,780,836; 3½p. 2,069,095; 4p. 3,908,727; 4½p. 349,157; 5p. 3,593,226; 5½p. 333,125; 6p. 1,072,224; 7½p. 538,810; 8p. 329,361; 9p. 458,977; 10p. 862,524; 20p. 765,524; 50p. 490,675.
Withdrawn: 31.1.77 (½p. to 9p.); 31.8.77 (others).

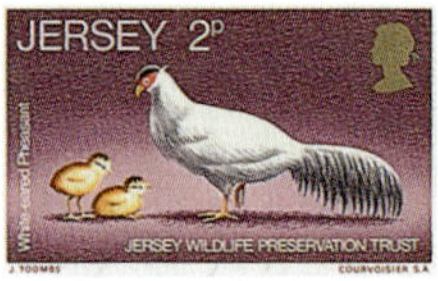

38 White-eared Pheasant

39 Thick-billed Parrot

40 Western Black and White Colobus Monkey

41 Ring-tailed Lemur

Wildlife Preservation Trust (1st series)

(Des Jennifer Toombs. Photo Courvoisier)

1971 (12 Mar). Granite paper. Perf 11½ (c).

57	**38**	2p. multicoloured	20	10
58	**39**	2½p. multicoloured	20	15
59	**40**	7½p. multicoloured	1·75	1·75
60	**41**	9p. multicoloured	2·50	2·50
57/60 *Set of 4*			4·00	4·00
First Day Cover				8·00
Presentation Pack			5·00	

See also Nos. 73/6, 217/21, 324/9, 447/51 and 824/9.
Sheets: 50 (5×10) 2p., 9p.; (10×5) others.
Quantities sold: 2p. 1,025,544; 2½p. 1,363,427; 7½p. 233,147; 9p. 220,710.
Withdrawn: 11.3.72.

42 Royal British Legion Badge

43 Poppy Emblem and Field

44 Jack Counter VC, and Victoria Cross

45 Crossed Tricolour and Union Jack

50th Anniversary of Royal British Legion

(Des G. Drummond. Litho Questa)

1971 (15 June). Perf 14 (c).

61	**42**	2p. multicoloured	20	10
62	**43**	2½p. multicoloured	20	10
63	**44**	7½p. multicoloured	1·00	1·10
64	**45**	9p. multicoloured	1·00	1·10
61/4 *Set of 4*			2·00	2·10
First Day Cover				3·50
Presentation Pack			2·50	

Plate Nos.: 2p., 2½p. 1A, 1B (each ×4); others 1A, 1B (each ×5).
Sheets: 50 (5×10).
Imprint: Right-hand corner, bottom margin.
Quantities sold: 2p. 1,381,873; 2½p. 1,529,866; 7½p. 239,477; 9p. 226,407.
Withdrawn: 14.6.72.

46 'Tante Elizabeth' (E. Blampied)

47 'English Fleet in the Channel' (P. Monamy)

48 'The Boyhood of Raleigh' (Millais)

49 'The Blind Beggar' (W. W. Ouless)

Paintings

(Des and photo Courvoisier)

1971 (5 Oct). Granite paper. Perf 11½ (c).

65	**46**	2p. multicoloured	15	10
66	**47**	2½p. multicoloured	20	10
67	**48**	7½p. multicoloured	85	95
68	**49**	9p. multicoloured	1·00	1·10
65/8 *Set of 4*			1·75	2·00
First Day Cover				4·75
Presentation Pack			2·50	

See also Nos. 115/18 and 213/16.
Sheets: 50 (5×10) 2p., 9p.; (10×5) others.
Quantities sold: 2p. 1,243,198; 2½p. 1,490,595; 7½p. 264,532; 9p. 251,770 .
Withdrawn: 4.10.72.

50 Jersey Fern

51 Jersey Thrift

52 Jersey Orchid

53 Jersey Viper's Bugloss

Wild Flowers of Jersey

(Des G. Drummond. Photo Courvoisier)

1972 (18 Jan). Granite paper. Perf 11½ (c).

69	**50**	3p. multicoloured	20	10
70	**51**	5p. multicoloured	30	20
71	**52**	7½p. multicoloured	95	95
72	**53**	9p. multicoloured	1·00	1·00
69/72 *Set of 4*			2·00	2·00
First Day Cover				3·50
Presentation Pack			2·50	

Sheets: 50 (5×10).
Quantities sold: 3p. 1,124,878; 5p. 332,764; 7½p. 202,404; 9p. 196,998.
Withdrawn: 17.1.73.

54 Cheetah

55 Rothschild's Mynah

56 Spectacled Bear

57 Tuatara

Wildlife Preservation Trust (2nd series)

(Des Jennifer Toombs. Photo Courvoisier)

1972 (17 Mar). Granite paper. Perf 11½ (c).

73	**54**	2½p. multicoloured	30	10
74	**55**	3p. multicoloured	25	20
75	**56**	7½p. multicoloured	50	70
76	**57**	9p. multicoloured	80	90
73/6 *Set of 4*			1·60	1·70
First Day Cover				4·50
Presentation Pack			2·50	

Sheets: 50 (10×5) 3p.; (5×10) others.
Quantities sold: 2½p. 1,223,916; 3p. 1,631,752; 7½p. 279,935; 9p. 235,968.
Withdrawn: 16.3.73.

58 Artillery Shako

59 Shako (2nd North Regt)

60 Shako (5th South-West Regt)

61 Helmet (3rd Jersey Light Infantry)

Royal Jersey Militia (1s.t series)

(Des and photo Courvoisier)

1972 (27 June). Granite paper. Perf 11½ (c).

77	**58**	2½p. multicoloured	10	10
78	**59**	3p. multicoloured	10	10
79	**60**	7½p. multicoloured	30	20
80	**61**	9p. multicoloured	50	60
77/80 *Set of 4*			90	90
First Day Cover				3·00
Presentation Pack			1·70	

See also Nos. 1253/7.

Sheets: 50 (10×5).

Quantities sold: 2½p. 1,240,393; 3p. 1,857,224; 7½p. 300,554; 9p. 271,832.

Withdrawn: 26.6.73.

62 Princess Anne

63 Queen Elizabeth and Prince Philip

64 Prince Charles

65 The Royal Family

Royal Silver Wedding

(Des G. Drummond from photographs by D. Groves. Photo Courvoisier)

1972 (1 Nov). Granite paper. Perf 11½ (c).

81	**62**	2½p. multicoloured	10	10
82	**63**	3p. multicoloured	10	10
83	**64**	7½p. multicoloured	35	35
84	**65**	20p. multicoloured	35	35
81/4 *Set of 4*			80	80
First Day Cover				1·50
Presentation Pack			1·10	

Sheets: 25 (5×5).

Quantities sold: 2½p. 1,743,240; 3p. 1,638,566; 7½p. 424,029; 20p. 418,824.

Sold out: by 23.1.73 (7½p., 20p.); 16.5.73 (3p.).

Withdrawn: 31.10.73 (2½p.).

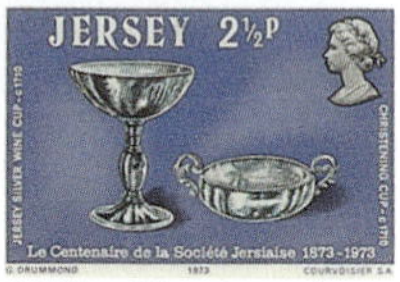

66 Silver Wine Cup and Christening Cup

67 Gold Torque

68 Royal Seal of Charles II

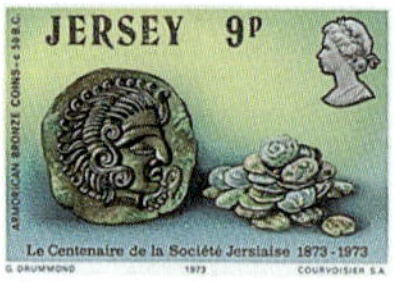

69 Armorican Bronze Coins

Centenary of La Sociètè Jersiaise

(Des G. Drummond. Photo Courvoisier)

1973 (23 Jan). Granite paper. Perf 11½ (c).

85	**66**	2½p. violet-blue, new blue and black	10	10
86	**67**	3p. bright cerise, orange-yellow and black	10	10
87	**68**	7½p. multicoloured	25	20
88	**69**	9p. multicoloured	30	30
85/8 *Set of 4*			70	60
First Day Cover				1·20
Presentation Pack			1·20	

Sheets: 50 (10×5) 3p., 7½p.; (5×10) others.

Quantities sold: 2½p. 2,008,923; 3p. 2,437,421; 7½p. 363,543; 9p. 327,917.

Sold out: by 31.10.73 (7½p.).

Withdrawn: 22.1.74. (2½p, 3p., 9p.).

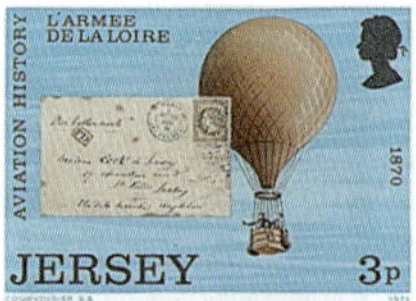

70 Balloon *L'Armee de La Loire* and Letter, Paris, 1870

71 Astra Seaplane, 1912

72 Supermarine Sea Eagle

73 De Havilland D.H.86 Dragon Express *Giffard Bay*

Jersey Aviation History

(Des and photo Courvoisier)

1973 (16 May). Granite paper. Perf 11½ (c).

89	**70**	3p. multicoloured	10	10
90	**71**	5p. multicoloured	10	10
91	**72**	7½p. multicoloured	35	35
92	**73**	9p. multicoloured	45	45
89/92 *Set of 4*			90	90

First Day Cover				1·50
Presentation Pack			1·20	

Sheets: 50 (5×10).
Quantities sold: 3p. 3,085,497; 5p. 641,583; 7½p. 368,069; 9p. 356,379.
Sold out: by 31.10.73 (7½p.).
Withdrawn: 15.5.74 (3p., 5p., 9p.).

74 *North Western*, 1870

75 *Calvados*, 1873

76 *Carteret* at Grouville Station, 1893

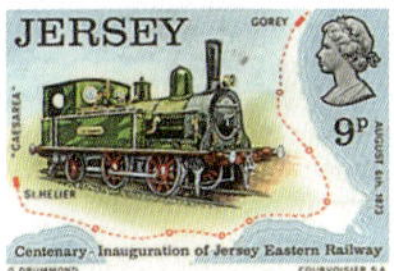

77 *Caesarea*, 1873, and Route Map

Centenary of Jersey Eastern Railway

(Des G. Drummond. Photo Courvoisier)

1973 (6 Aug). Granite paper. Perf 11½ (c).

93	**74**	2½p. multicoloured	10	10
94	**75**	3p. multicoloured	10	10
95	**76**	7½p. multicoloured	35	35
96	**77**	9p. multicoloured	45	45
93/6 *Set of 4*			90	90
First Day Cover				1·40
Presentation Pack			1·20	

Sheets: 50 (5×10).
Quantities sold: 2½p. 1,591,063; 3p. 3,051,097; 7½p. 396,919; 9p. 365,310.
Sold out: by 31.10.73 (7½p.).
Withdrawn: 5.8.74. (2½p, 3p., 9p.).

78 Princess Anne and Captain Mark Phillips

Royal Wedding

(Des and photo Courvoisier)

1973 (14 Nov). Granite paper. Perf 11½ (c).

97	**78**	3p. multicoloured	10	10
98		20p. multicoloured	50	50
97/8 *Set of 2*			60	60
First Day Cover				80
Presentation Pack			95	

Sheets: 25 (5×5).
Quantities sold: 3p. 1,988,407; 20p. 522,793.
Withdrawn: 30.11.74.

79 Spider Crab

80 Conger Eel

81 Lobster

82 Tuberculate Ormer

Marine Life

(Des Jennifer Toombs. Photo Courvoisier)

1973 (15 Nov). Granite paper. Perf 11½ (c).

99	**79**	2½p. multicoloured	10	10
100	**80**	3p. multicoloured	10	10
101	**81**	7½p. multicoloured	30	35
102	**82**	20p. multicoloured	40	45
99/102 *Set of 4*			80	90
First Day Cover				1·20
Presentation Pack			1·40	

Sheets: 50 (5×10).
Quantities sold: 2½p. 1,596,526; 3p. 1,243,541; 7½p. 501,541; 20p. 517,440.
Sold out: by 28.2.74 (7½p.).
Withdrawn: 30.11.74 (2½p., 3p., 20p.).

83 Freesias

84 Anemones

85 Carnations and Gladioli

86 Daffodils and Iris

Spring Flowers

(Des G. Drummond. Photo Courvoisier)

1974 (13 Feb). Granite paper. Perf 11½ (c).

103	**83**	3p. multicoloured	10	10
104	**84**	5½p. multicoloured	15	15
105	**85**	8p. multicoloured	25	30
106	**86**	10p. multicoloured	30	35
103/6 *Set of 4*			70	80
First Day Cover				1·20
Presentation Pack			1·20	

Sheets: 50 (10×5).
Quantities sold: 3p. 1,239,968; 5½p. 590,376; 8p. 475,665; 10p. 507,542.
Withdrawn: 28.2.75.

87 First U.K. Pillar-box and Contemporary Cover

88 Jersey Postmen, 1862 and 1969

89 Modern Pillar-box and Cover

90 Mail Transport, 1874 and 1974

Centenary of Universal Postal Union

(Des G. Drummond. Photo Courvoisier)

1974 (7 June). Granite paper. Perf 11½ (c).

107	**87**	2½p. multicoloured	10	10
108	**88**	3p. multicoloured	10	15

109	**89**	5½p. multicoloured	25	20
110	**90**	20p. multicoloured	35	40
107/10 *Set of 4*			70	75
First Day Cover				95
Presentation Pack			1·20	

Sheets: 50 (5×10).
Quantities sold: 2½p. 461,174; 3p. 1,380,018; 5½p. 421,674; 20p. 386,348.
Withdrawn: 30.6.75.

91 John Wesley

92 Sir William Hillary

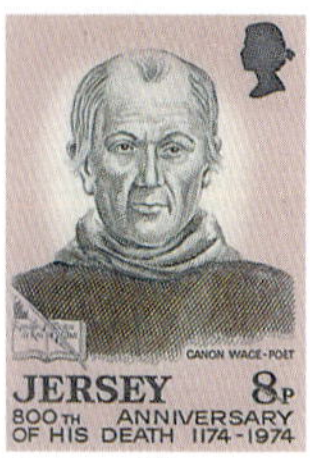

93 Canon Wace

94 Sir Winston Churchill

Anniversaries. Events described on stamps

(Des recess and litho De La Rue)

1974 (31 July). Perf 13×14 (c).

111	**91**	3p. agate and light cinnamon	10	10
112	**92**	3½p. blackish violet & light azure	10	10
113	**93**	8p. blue-black and pale rose-lilac	20	20
114	**94**	20p. black and pale buff	45	45
		a. Pale buff (background omitted)		
111/14 *Set of 4*			75	75
First Day Cover				90
Presentation Pack			1·20	

Plate Nos.: 3p. and 20p. 1A–1A, 1B–1B; 3½p. and 8p. 1A–1A, 1B–1B, 2A–1A, 2B–1B.
Sheets: 50 (10×5).
Imprint: Right-hand corner, bottom margin.
Quantities sold: 3p. 908,852; 3½p. 2,355,391; 8p. 338,397; 20p. 409,291.
Withdrawn: 31.7.75.

95 *Catherine* and *Mary* (royal yachts)

96 French Two-decker

97 Dutch Vessel

98 Battle of Cap La Hague, 1692

Marine Paintings by Peter Monamy

(Des and photo Courvoisier)

1974 (22 Nov). Granite paper. Perf 11½ (c).

115	**95**	3½p. multicoloured	10	10
116	**96**	5½p. multicoloured	15	10
117	**97**	8p. multicoloured	25	20
118	**98**	25p. multicoloured	55	55
115/18 *Set of 4*			95	90
First Day Cover				2·00
Presentation Pack			1·70	

Sheets: 50 (10×5) 8p.; (5×10) others.
Quantities sold: 3½p. 1,670,994; 5½p. 448,137; 8p. 416,296; 25p. 415,991.
Withdrawn: 30.11.75.

99 Potato Digger

100 Cider Crusher

101 Six-Horse Plough

102 Hay Cart

Nineteenth-Century Farming

(Des G. Drummond. Photo Courvoisier)

1975 (25 Feb). Granite paper. Perf 11½ (c).

119	**99**	3p. multicoloured	10	10
120	**100**	3½p. multicoloured	10	10
121	**101**	8p. multicoloured	20	20
122	**102**	10p. multicoloured	35	40
119/22 *Set of 4*			70	75
First Day Cover				85
Presentation Pack			90	

Sheets: 50 (5×10).
Quantities sold: 3p. 588,185; 3½p. 1,025,295; 8p. 432,432; 10p. 457,196.
Withdrawn: 28.2.76.

103 H.M. Queen Elizabeth, the Queen Mother (photograph by Cecil Beaton)

Royal Visit

(Des and photo Courvoisier)

1975 (30 May). Granite paper. Perf 11½ (c).

123	**103**	20p. multicoloured	50	45
First Day Cover				1·70
Presentation Pack			90	

Cylinder Nos.: A1–1–1–1–1, B1–1–1–1–1.
Sheets: 25 (5×5).
Quantity sold: 572,675.
Withdrawn: 31.5.76.

104 Nautilus Shell

105 Parasol

106 Deckchair

107 Sandcastle with flags of Jersey and the U.K.

Jersey Tourism

(Des A. Games. Photo Courvoisier)

1975 (6 June). Designs based on holiday posters. Granite paper. Perf 11½ (c).

124	**104**	5p. multicoloured	10	10
125	**105**	8p. multicoloured	10	10
126	**106**	10p. multicoloured	30	25
127	**107**	12p. multicoloured	40	35
124/7 *Set of 4*			80	70
First Day Cover				1·10
Presentation Pack			1·70	
MS128 147×69 mm. Nos. 124/7			90	1·10
First Day Cover				4·00

Cylinder Nos.: All values A1–1–1–1–1, B1–1–1–1–1.
Sheets: 50 (10×5).
Quantities sold: 5p. 1,377,519; 8p. 368,521; 10p. 467,278; 12p. 389,574; miniature sheet 298,689.
Withdrawn: 30.6.76.

108 Common Tern

109 British Storm Petrel

110 Brent Geese

111 Shag

Sea Birds

(Des Jennifer Toombs. Photo Courvoisier)

1975 (28 July). Granite paper. Perf 11½ (c).

129	**108**	4p. multicoloured	10	10
130	**109**	5p. multicoloured	15	10
131	**110**	8p. multicoloured	40	25
132	**111**	25p. multicoloured	70	50
129/32 *Set of 4*			1·00	85
First Day Cover				1·25
Presentation Pack			1·60	

Sheets: 50 (10×5).
Quantities sold: 4p. 872,260; 5p. 2,871,390; 8p. 384,550; 25p. 362,160.
Withdrawn: 31.7.76.

112 Armstrong Whitworth Siskin IIIA

113 Supermarine Southampton I Flying Boat

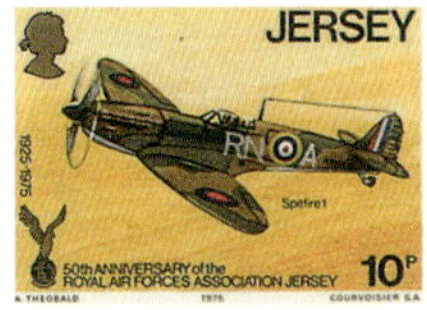

114 Supermarine Spitfire Mk I

115 Folland Fo. 144 Gnat T.1

50th Anniversary of Royal Air Forces Association, Jersey Branch

(Des A. Theobald. Photo Courvoisier)

1975 (30 Oct). Granite paper. Perf 11½ (c).

133	**112**	4p. multicoloured	10	10
134	**113**	5p. multicoloured	15	10
135	**114**	10p. multicoloured	40	25
136	**115**	25p. multicoloured	70	50
133/6 *Set of 4*			1·20	85
First Day Cover				1·60
Presentation Pack			1·50	

Cylinder Nos.: All values A1–1–1–1–1, B1–1–1–1–1.
Sheets: 50 (5×10).
Quantities sold: 4p. 1,496,640; 5p. 1,805,624; 10p. 581,627; 25p. 407,423.
Withdrawn: 30.10.76.

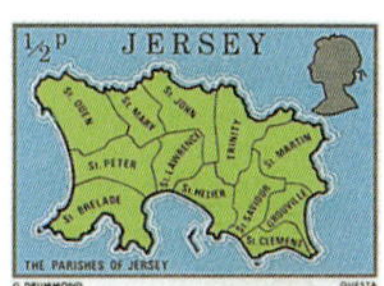

116 Map of Jersey Parishes

117 Zoological Park

118 St. Mary's Church

119 Seymour Tower

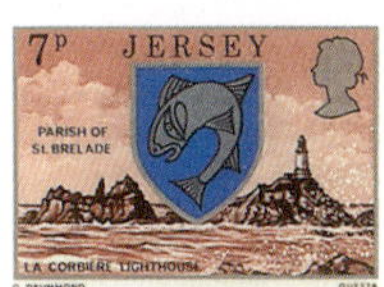

120 La Corbière Lighthouse

121 St. Saviour's Church

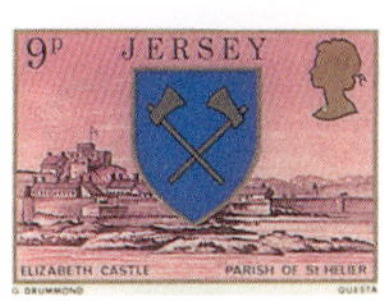

122 Elizabeth Castle

123 Gorey Harbour

124 Jersey Airport

125 Grosnez Castle

126 Bonne Nuit Harbour

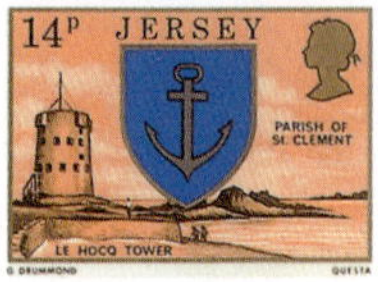

127 Le Hocq Tower

128 Morel Farm

129 Parish Arms and Island Scene

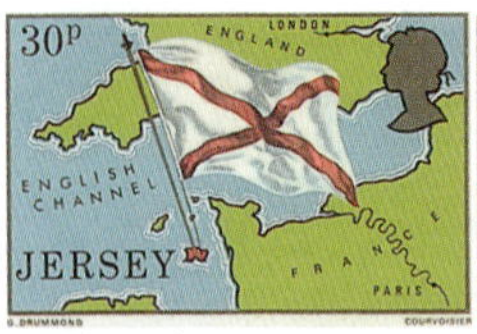

130 Flag and Map

131 Postal H.Q. and Badge

132 Parliament, Royal Court and Arms

133 Lieutenant-Governor's Flag and Government House

134 Queen Elizabeth II (photograph by Alex Wilson)

Parish Arms and Views

(Des Courvoisier (£2), G. Drummond (others). Litho Questa (½p. to 15p.). Photo Courvoisier (others))

1976–80. Granite paper (20p. to £2). Perf 14½ (½p. to 15p.) or 12 (others), all comb.

137	**116**	½p. multicoloured (af)	10	10
138	**117**	1p. multicoloured (af)	10	10
		a. Booklet pane of 4 (No. 13832 plus 2 *se-tenant* labels) (b)	70	
		b. Booklet pane. No. 138×4 (begh)	80	
139	**118**	5p. multicoloured (ad)	10	10
		a. Booklet pane of 4 (b)	40	
140	**119**	6p. multicoloured (ad)	10	10
		a. Booklet pane of 4 (eg)	40	
141	**120**	7p. multicoloured (ad)	10	10
		a. Booklet pane of 4 (bh)	40	
142	**121**	8p. multicoloured (ad)	15	10
		a. Booklet pane of 4 (eg)	80	
143	**122**	9p. multicoloured (a)	15	10
		a. Booklet pane of 4 (h)	60	
144	**123**	10p. multicoloured (af)	20	10
145	**124**	11p. multicoloured (a)	25	25
146	**125**	12p. multicoloured (a)	25	20
147	**126**	13p. multicoloured (a)	25	20
148	**127**	14p. multicoloured (a)	30	20
149	**128**	15p. multicoloured (a)	30	25
150	**129**	20p. multicoloured (c)	45	45
151	**130**	30p. multicoloured (c)	55	50
152	**131**	40p. multicoloured (c)	80	80
153	**132**	50p. multicoloured (c)	1·00	1·00
154	**133**	£1 multicoloured (c)	3·00	3·00
155	**134**	£2 multicoloured (d)	4·00	4·00
137/55 *Set of* 19			11·00	11·00
First Day Covers (4)				11·00
Presentation Packs (4)			12·00	

Printings: (a) 29.1.76; (b) 5.4.76; (c) 20.8.76; (d) 16.11.77; (e) 28.2.78; (f) 31.8.78; (g) 1.10.79; (h) 6.5.80.

Plate or cylinder Nos.: ½p. to 9p., 13p., 14p. 1A, 1B, 1C, 1D. (each ×4); 10p. 1A, 1B, 1C, 1d. (each ×4), 1B–1B–1B–2B, 2A–1A–1A–2A, 2B–1B–1B–2B, 2C–1C–1C–2C, 2D.1D.1D.2D.; 11p. 1A, 1B, 1C, 1d. (each ×5); 12p. 1A, 1B, 1C, 1D. (each ×4), 1A–1A–2A–2A, 1B–1B–2B–2B, 1C–1C–2C–2C, 1D–1D–2D–2D; 15p. 1A, 1B, 1C, 1d. (each ×4), 1A–2A–1A–1A, 1B–2B–1B–1B, 1C–2C–1C–1C, 1D–2D–2D–1D, 1A-3A-2A-1A, 1B–3B–2B–1B, 1C–3C–2C–1C, 1D–3D-–2D–1D.; 20p. A1–1–1–1–1, B1–1–1–1–1, C1–1–1–1–1, D1–1–1–1–1; 30p. £1 A1–1–1–1–1, B1–1–1–1-–1; 40p, 50p. A1–1–1–1, B1–1–1–1; £2 A1–1–1–1–1–1–1–1, B1–1–1–1–1–1–1–1, C1–1–1–1–1–1–1–1, D1–1–1–1–1–1–1–1.

Sheets: 50 (5×10) ½p. to 15p.; 25 (5×5) others.

Imprint: Right-hand corner, bottom margin (½p. to 15p.); central, bottom margin (others).

Withdrawn: 27.2.82 ½p. to 9p. (sheets); 20.4.82 1p., 5p. to 9p. (booklets); 31.7.82 10p. to 15p.; 28.2.83 20p. to £1; 31.3.92 £2.

135 Sir Walter Raleigh and Map of Virginia

136 Sir George Carteret and Map of New Jersey

137 Philippe D'Auvergne and Long Island Landing

138 John Copley and Sketch

Bicentenary of American Independence

(Des M. Orbell. Photo Courvoisier)

1976 (29 May). Granite paper. Perf 11½ (c).

160	**135**	5p. multicoloured	10	10
161	**136**	7p. multicoloured	15	10
162	**137**	11p. multicoloured	40	40
163	**138**	13p. multicoloured	50	50
160/3 *Set of 4*			1·00	1·00
First Day Cover				1·20
Presentation Pack			1·40	

Cylinder Nos.: 5p., 11p. A1–1–1–1–1, B1–1–1–1–1; others A1–1–1–1, B1–1–1–1.
Sheets: 25 (5×5).
Quantities sold: 5p. 980,029; 7p. 1,352,629; 11p. 582,706; 13p. 435,561.
Withdrawn: 31.5.77.

139 Dr. Grandin and Map of China

140 Sampan on the Yangtze

141 Overland Trek

142 Dr. Grandin at Work

Birth Centenary of Dr. Lilian Grandin (medical missionary)

(Des Jennifer Toombs. Photo Courvoisier)

1976 (25 Nov). Granite paper. Perf 11½ (c).

164	**139**	5p. multicoloured	10	10
165	**140**	7p. lt yellow, yellow-brown & blk	10	10
166	**141**	11p. multicoloured	35	25
167	**142**	13p. multicoloured	50	40
164/7 *Set of 4*			95	75
First Day Cover				1·20
Presentation Pack			1·40	

Cylinder Nos.: 7p. A1–1–1, B1–1–1; 13p. A1–1–1–1–1, B1–1–1–1–1; others A1–1–1–1, B1–1–1–1.
Sheets: 50 (5×10).
Quantities sold: 5p. 757,843; 7p. 1,043,198; 11p. 384,436; 13p. 354,096.
Withdrawn: 30.11.77.

143 Coronation, 1953 (photograph by Cecil Beaton)

144 Visit to Jersey, 1957

145 Queen Elizabeth II (photograph by Peter Grugeon)

Silver Jubilee

(Des G. Drummond. Photo Courvoisier)

1977 (7 Feb). Granite paper. Perf 11½ (c).

168	**143**	5p. multicoloured	15	10
169	**144**	7p. multicoloured	20	15
170	**145**	25p. multicoloured	40	55
168/70 *Set of 3*			70	70
First Day Cover				1·20
Presentation Pack			1·20	

Cylinder Nos.: All values A1–1–1–1–1, B1–1–1–1–1.
Sheets: 25 (5×5).
Imprint: Central, bottom margin.
Quantities sold: 5p. 1,220,986; 7p. 1,212,639; 25p. 681,241.
Withdrawn: 28.2.78.

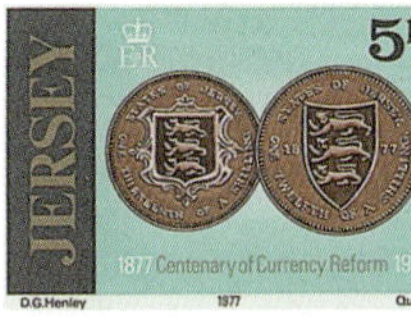

146 Coins of 1871 and 1877

147 One-twelfth Shilling, 1949

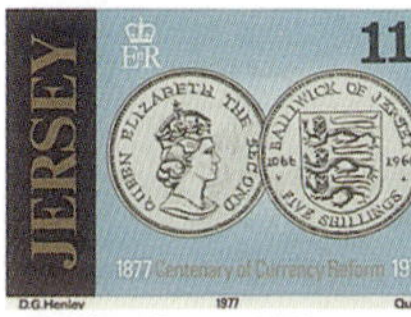

148 Silver Crown, 1966

149 £2 Piece, 1972

Centenary of Currency Reform

(Des D. Henley. Litho Questa)

1977 (25 Mar). Perf 14 (c).

171	**146**	5p. multicoloured	10	10
172	**147**	7p. multicoloured	15	10
173	**148**	11p. multicoloured	30	30
174	**149**	13p. multicoloured	35	35
171/4 *Set of 4*			80	75
First Day Cover				1·10
Presentation Pack			1·40	

Plate Nos.: 7p. 1A, 1B (each ×5), 1A–2A–1A (×3), 1B–-2B–1B (×3); others 1A, 1B (each ×5).
Sheets: 50 (5×10).
Imprint: Right-hand corner, bottom margin.
Quantities sold: 5p. 1,029,661; 7p. 923,950; 11p. 383,834; 13p. 368,249.
Withdrawn: 31.3.78.

150 Sir William Weston and *Santa Anna*, 1530

151 Sir William Drogo and Ambulance, 1877

152 Duke of Connaught and Rolls-Royce Ambulance, 1917

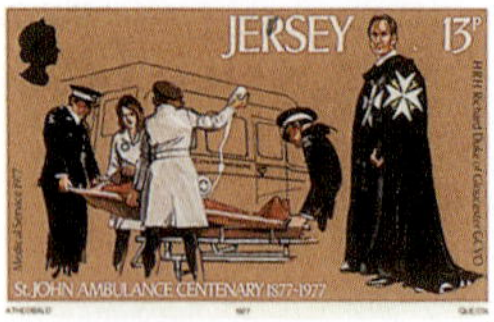

153 Duke of Gloucester and Stretcher-team, 1977

St. John Ambulance Centenary

(Des A. Theobald. Litho Questa)

1977 (24 June). Perf 14×13½ (c).

175	**150**	5p. multicoloured	10	10
176	**151**	7p. multicoloured	10	10
177	**152**	11p. multicoloured	25	20
178	**153**	13p. multicoloured	30	25
175/8 *Set of 4*			70	60
First Day Cover				1·10
Presentation Pack			1·20	

Plate Nos.: 5p. 1A, 1B, 1C (each ×5); 7p., 11p. 1A, 1B, 1C (each ×6); 13p. 1A, 1B, 1C (each ×5), 1B–2B–1B–1B–1B.
Sheets: 40 (8×5).
Imprint: Bottom corner, right-hand margin.
Quantities sold: 5p. 849,532; 7p. 1,089,526; 11p. 421,039; 13p. 370,887.
Withdrawn: 30.6.78.

154 Arrival of Queen Victoria, 1846

155 Victoria College, 1852

156 Sir Galahad Statue, 1924

157 College Hall

125th Anniversary of Victoria College

(Des R. Granger Barrett. Litho Questa)

1977 (29 Sept). Perf 14½ (c).

179	**154**	7p. multicoloured	15	10
180	**155**	10½p. multicoloured	20	15
		a. Black ptg double		
181	**156**	11p. multicoloured	25	25
182	**157**	13p. multicoloured	30	25
179/82 *Set of 4*			80	70
First Day Cover				1·10
Presentation Pack			1·40	

Plate Nos.: 7p. 1A, 1B (each ×6), 1A–1A–2A–1A–1A–1A, 1B–1B–2B–1B–1B–1B; 13p. 1A, 1B (each ×6); others 1A, 1B (each ×5).
Sheets: 50 (5×10) 7 and 10½p., (10×5) others.
Imprint: Right-hand corner, bottom margin.
Quantities sold: 7p. 1,496,997; 10½p. 906,669; 11p. 528,293; 13p. 371,251.
Withdrawn: 30.9.78.

158 Harry Vardon Satuette and Map of Royal Jersey Course

159 Harry Vardon's Grip and Swing

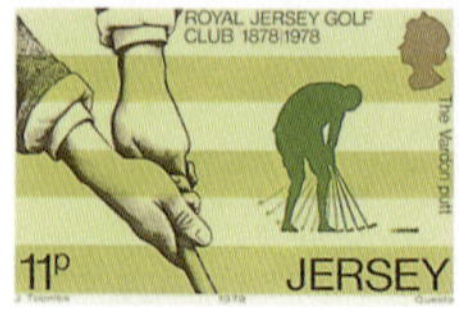

160 Harry Vardon's Putt

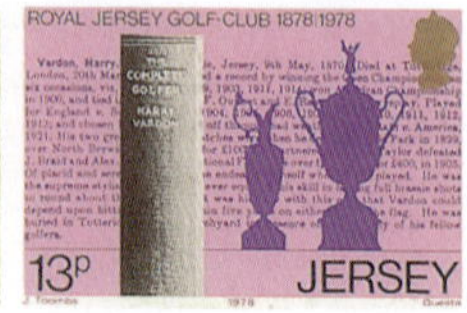

161 Golf Trophies and Book by Harry Vardon

Centenary of Royal Jersey Golf Club

(Des Jennifer Toombs. Litho Questa)

1978 (28 Feb). Perf 14 (c).

183	**158**	6p. multicoloured	10	10
184	**159**	8p. multicoloured	15	10
185	**160**	11p. multicoloured	35	25
186	**161**	13p. multicoloured	40	35
183/6 *Set of 4*			90	70
First Day Cover				1·10
Presentation Pack			1·40	

Plate Nos.: 6p. 1A, 1B (each ×5); 8p., 11p. 1A, 1B (each ×4); 13p. 1A, 1B (each ×4), 2A–1A–1A–1A, 2B–1B–1B–1B.
Sheets: 50 (5×10).
Imprint: Right-hand corner, bottom margin.
Quantities sold: 6p. 837,427; 8p. 851,904; 11p. 466,343; 13p. 368,648.
Withdrawn: 28.2.79.

162 Mont Orgueil Castle

163 St. Aubin's Fort

164 Elizabeth Castle

Europa Monuments. Castles from Paintings by Thomas Phillips

(Des from paintings by Thomas Philips. Photo Courvoisier)

1978 (1 May). Granite paper. Perf 11½ (c).

187	**162**	6p. multicoloured	10	10
188	**163**	8p. multicoloured	15	15
189	**164**	10½p. multicoloured	35	25
187/9 *Set of 3*			55	45
First Day Cover				70
Presentation Pack			80	

Cylinder Nos.: All values A1–1–1–1–1, B1–1–1–1–1, C1–1–1–1–1, D1–1–1–1–1.
Sheets: 20 (5×4).
Imprint: Central, bottom margin.
Quantities sold: 6p. 2,602,412; 8p. 2,592,722; 10½p. 2,564,535.
Withdrawn: 31.5.79.

165 'Gaspé' Basin' (P. J. Ouless)

166 Map of Gaspé Peninsula Ouless)

167 *Century* (brigantine)

168 Early Map of Jersey

169 St. Aubin's Bay, Town and Harbour

Links with Canada

(Des R. Granger Barrett. Litho Questa)

1978 (9 June). Perf 14½ (c).

190	**165**	6p. multicoloured	10	10
191	**166**	8p. multicoloured	15	10
192	**167**	10½p. multicoloured	20	15
193	**168**	11p. multicoloured	40	25
194	**169**	13p. multicoloured	45	40
190/4 *Set of 5*			1·10	90
First Day Cover				1·10
Presentation Pack			1·50	

Plate Nos.: 6p. 1A, 1B, 1C, 1D. (each ×5); others 1A, 1B, 1C, 1D (each ×6).
Sheets: 50 (5×10).
Imprint: Right-hand corner, bottom margin.
Quantities sold: 6p. 1,047,825; 8p. 1,095,489; 10½p. 999,002; 11p. 443,932; 13p. 367,472.
Withdrawn: 30.6.79.

170 Queen Elizabeth and Prince Philip

171 Hallmarks of 1953 and 1977

25th Anniversary of Coronation

(Des and photo Courvoisier)

1978 (26 June). Granite paper. Perf 11½ (c).

195	**170**	8p. silver, black and cerise	20	10
196	**171**	25p. silver, black and new blue	50	45
195/6 *Set of 2*			70	55
First Day Cover				90
Presentation Pack			95	

Cylinder Nos.: Both values A1–1–1, B1–1–1.
Sheets: 50 (10×5).
Quantities sold: 8p. 1,060,259; 25p. 459,558.
Withdrawn: 30.6.79.

172 Mail Cutter, 1778–1827

173 *Flamer*, 1831–37

174 *Diana*, 1877–90

175 *Ibex*, 1891–1925

176 *Caesarea*, 1960–75

Bicentenary of England–Jersey Government Mail Packet Service

(Des Jersey P.O. Litho Harrison)

1978 (18 Oct). Perf 14½×14 (c).

197	**172**	6p. black, yellow-brown and greenish yellow	10	10
198	**173**	8p. black, dull yellowish green and pale yellow-green	15	10
199	**174**	10½p. black, ultramarine & cobalt	30	20
200	**175**	11p. blk, purple & pale rose-lilac	35	30
201	**176**	13p. black, Venetian red and pink	40	40
197/201 *Set of 5*			1·10	1·00
First Day Cover				1·40
Presentation Pack			1·50	

Plate Nos.: All values 1A, 1B (each ×3).
Sheets: 50 (5×10).
Imprint: Right-hand corner, bottom margin.
Quantities sold: 6p. 1,157,597; 8p. 1,149,500; 10½p. 528,170; 11p. 468,589; 13p. 371,210.
Withdrawn: 31.10.79.

177 Jersey Calf

178 'Ansom Designette' (calf presented to the Queen, 27 June 1978)

9th World Jersey Cattle Bureau Conference

(Des Jersey P.O. and Questa. Litho Questa)

1979 (1 Mar). Perf 13½ (c).

202	**177**	6p. multicoloured	10	10
		a. Gold ptg double	£400	
203	**178**	25p. multicoloured	50	45
		a. Gold ptg double	£400	
202/3 *Set of 2*			60	55
First Day Cover				95
Presentation Pack			1·10	

Plate Nos.: Both values 1A, 1B, 1C, 1D., 1E, 1F (eac h×8).
Sheets: 20 (4×5).
Imprint: Right-hand corner, bottom margin.
Withdrawn: 29.2.80.

179 Jersey Pillar Box, c.1860

180 Clearing a Modern Jersey Post Box

181 Telephone Switchboard, c. 1900

182 Modern S.P.C. Telephone System

Europa. Communications

(Des Jennifer Toombs. Litho Questa)

1979 (1 Mar). Thin paper. Perf 14 (c).

204	**179**	8p. multicoloured	15	15
		a. Horiz pair. Nos. 204/5	50	50
		b. Thick paper	40	40

		ba. Horiz pair. Nos. 204b/5b	80	90
		c. Perf 14½ (thick paper)	30	30
		ca. Horiz pair. Nos. 204c/5c	60	70
		cb. Yellow omitted*		
205	**180**	8p. multicoloured	15	15
		b. Thick paper	40	40
		c. Perf 14½ (thick paper)	30	30
		cb. Pale rose-red omitted*		
206	**181**	10½p. multicoloured	15	15
		a. Horiz pair. Nos. 206/7	50	70
		b. Thick paper	70	70
		ba. Horiz pair. Nos. 206b/7b	1·40	1·50
		c. Perf 14½	70	70
		ca. Horiz pair. Nos. 206c/7c	1·40	1·50
207	**182**	10½p. multicoloured	15	15
		b. Thick paper	70	70
		c. Perf 14½	70	70
		ca. Greenish blue omitted		
204/7 Set of 4			90	90
First Day Cover (Nos. 204/5, 206c/7c)				1·10
First Day Cover (Nos. 204/7)				
Presentation Pack (either perforation)			1·10	

Although both perforations were supplied to Jersey at the same time the 8p. perforated 14½ is not known used before early April.

*Nos. 204cb and 205cb appear to have only five arcs of colour in the background instead of the usual eight. They come from the same sheet.

Plate Nos.: Both values 1A, 1B, 1C, 1D., 1E, 1F, 1G, 1H (each ×8).
Sheets: 20 (4×5) the two designs of each value were printed together, *se-tenant*, in horizontal pairs throughout
Imprint: Central, bottom margin.
Quantities sold: 8p. 5,149,852; 10½p. 3,047,039.
Withdrawn: 29.2.80.

183 Percival Mew Gull *Golden City*

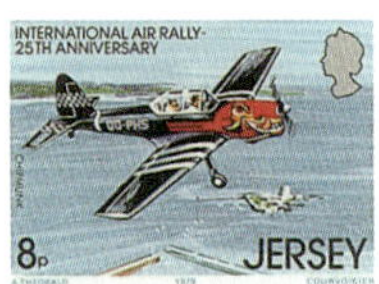

184 De Havilland D.H.C.1 Chipmunk

185 Druine D.31 Turbulent

186 De Havilland D.H.82A Tiger Moth

187 North American AT-6 Harvard

25th Anniversary of International Air Rally

(Des A. Theobald. Photo Courvoisier)

1979 (24 Apr). Granite paper. Perf 11½ (c).

208	**183**	6p. multicoloured	10	10
209	**184**	8p. multicoloured	25	15
210	**185**	10½p. multicoloured	25	20
211	**186**	11p. multicoloured	30	25
212	**187**	13p. multicoloured	40	35
208/12 Set of 5			1·10	95
First Day Cover				1·50
Presentation Pack			1·60	

Cylinder Nos.: 13p. A1–1–1–1–1, B1–1–1–1–1, C1–1–1–1–1, D1–1–1–1–1; others A1–1–1–1, B1–1–1–1, C1–1–1–1, D1–1–1–1.
Sheets 20 (5×4).
Imprint: Central, bottom margin.
Quantities sold: 6p. 1,327,279; 8p. 1,338,234; 10½p. 433,127; 11p. 457,566; 13p. 426,528.
Withdrawn: 30.4.80.

188 'My First Sermon'

189 'Orphans'

190 'The Princes in the Tower'

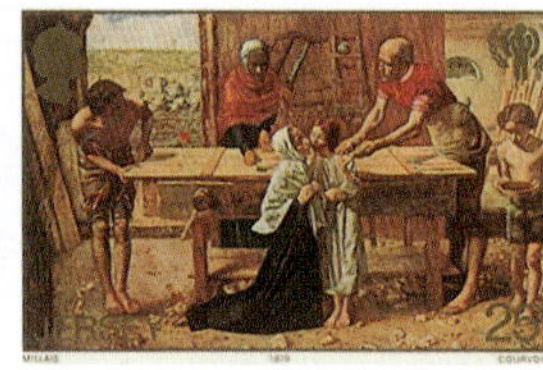

191 'Christ in the House of His Parents'

International Year of the Child and 150th Birth Anniversary of Sir John Millais (painter)

(Des Jersey P.O. and Courvoisier. Photo Courvoisier)

1979 (13 Aug). Granite paper. Perf 12×12½ (25p.) or 12×11½ (others), all comb.

213	**188**	8p. multicoloured	20	15
214	**189**	10½p. multicoloured	30	20
215	**190**	11p. multicoloured	30	30
216	**191**	25p. multicoloured	50	40
213/16 Set of 4			1·20	95
First Day Cover				1·40
Presentation Pack			1·60	

Cylinder Nos.: 25p. A1–1–1–1–1, B1–1–1–1–1; others A1–1–1–1, B1–1–1–1, C1–1–1–1, D1–1–1–1.
Sheets: 20 (4×5) 25p. or (5×4) others.
Quantities sold: 8p. 1,187,969; 10½p. 953,826; 11p. 508,316; 25p. 463,234.
Withdrawn: 30.8.80.

192 Pink Pigeon

193 Orang-utan

194 Waldrapp

195 Lowland Gorilla

196 Rodriguez Flying Fox

Wildlife Preservation Trust (3rd series)

(Des Jennifer Toombs. Photo Courvoisier)

1979 (8 Nov). Granite paper. Perf 11½ (c).

217	**192**	6p. multicoloured	10	10
218	**193**	8p. multicoloured	20	15
219	**194**	11½p. multicoloured	30	30
220	**195**	13p. multicoloured	45	35
221	**196**	15p. multicoloured	45	35
217/21 *Set of 5*			1·20	1·10
First Day Cover				1·40
Presentation Pack			1·60	

Cylinder Nos.: All values A1–1–1–1–1, B1–1–1–1–1, C1–1–1–1–1, D1–1–1–1–1.
Sheets: 20 (11½p. 4×5; others 5×4).
Imprint: Right-hand corner, bottom margin.
Quantities sold: 6p. 1,128,144; 8p. 1,080,889; 11½p. 559,534; 13p. 443,140; 15p. 433,115.
Withdrawn: 30.11.80.

197 Plan of Mont Orgueil

198 Plan of La Tour de St. Aubin

199 Plan of Elizabeth Castle

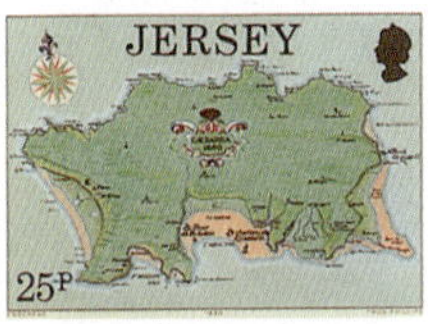

200 Map of Jersey showing Fortresses

Jersey Fortresses. Drawings by Thomas Phillips

(Litho Enschedé)

1980 (5 Feb). Perf 13×13½ (25p.) or 13½×13 (others), all comb.

222	**197**	8p. multicoloured	20	15
223	**198**	11½p. multicoloured	30	30
224	**199**	13p. multicoloured	30	30
225	**200**	25p. multicoloured	50	45
222/5 *Set of 4*			1·20	1·10
First Day Cover				1·40
Presentation Pack			1·60	

Pack Sheets: 20 (4×5).
Imprint: Right-hand corner, bottom margin.
Quantities sold: 8p. 665,647; 11½p. 363,246; 13p. 415,790; 25p. 379,743.
Withdrawn: 28.2.81.

201 Sir Walter Raleigh and Paul Ivy (engineer) **202** discussing Elizabeth Castle

203 Sir George Carteret receiving rights to Smith's Island, Virginia, from King Charles II

204 Lady Carteret, maid Jean Chevalier

Europa. Personalities. Links with Britain

(Des Jersey Post Office and Questa. Litho Questa)

1980 (6 May). Perf 14 (c).

226	**201**	9p. multicoloured	15	15
		a. Horiz pair. Nos. 226/7	40	50
227	**202**	9p. multicoloured	15	15
228	**203**	13½p. multicoloured	20	20
		a. Horiz pair. Nos. 228/9	60	70
229	**204**	13½p. multicoloured	20	20
226/9 *Set of 4*			90	80
First Day Cover				1·20
Presentation Pack			1·40	

Plate Nos.: Both values 1A, 1B, 1C, 1D., 1E, 1F (each ×4).
Sheets: 20 (4×5). The two designs of each value were printed together, *se-tenant*, in horizontal pairs throughout, forming composite designs.
Imprint: Central, left-hand margin.
Quantities sold: 9p. 4,793,980; 13½p. 2,638,136.
Withdrawn: 31.5.81.

205 Planting

206 Digging

207 Weighbridge

Centenary of Jersey Royal Potato

(Des R. Granger Barrett. Litho Questa)

1980 (6 May). Perf 14 (c).

230	**205**	7p. multicoloured	15	10
231	**206**	15p. multicoloured	30	25
232	**207**	17½p. multicoloured	30	35
230/2 *Set of 3*			65	65
First Day Cover				95
Presentation Pack			1·20	

Plate Nos.: All values 1A, 1B, 1C, 1D., 1E, 1F (each ×6).
Sheets: 20 (4×5).
Imprint: Central, left-hand margin.
Quantities sold: 7p. 1,379,048; 15p. 383,956; 17½p. 375,082.
Withdrawn: 31.5.83.

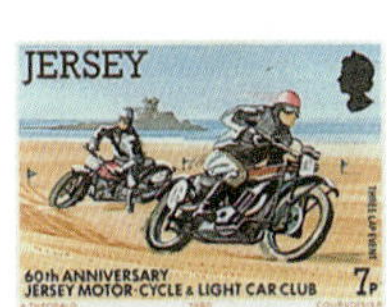

208 Three Lap Event

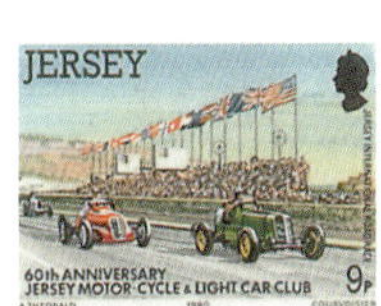

209 Jersey International Road Race

210 Motocross Scrambling

211 Sand Racing (saloon cars)

212 National Hill Climb

60th Anniversary of Jersey Motor-cycle and Light Car Club

(Des A. Theobald. Photo Courvoisier)

1980 (24 July). Granite paper. Perf 11½ (c).

233	**208**	7p. multicoloured	15	15
234	**209**	9p. multicoloured	20	15
235	**210**	13½p. multicoloured	30	25
236	**211**	15p. multicoloured	30	30
237	**212**	17½p. multicoloured	35	35
233/7 *Set of 5*			1·20	1·10
First Day Cover				1·60
Presentation Pack			1·70	

Cylinder Nos.: 7p., 15p. A1–1–1–1–1, B1–1–1–1–1, C1–1–1–1–1, D1–1–1–1–1; others A1–1–1–1, B1–1–1–1, C1–1–1–1, D1–1–1–1.
Sheets: 20 (5×4).
Imprint: Left-hand corner, bottom margin.
Quantities sold: 7p. 1,452,280; 9p. 1,426,548; 13½p. 384,861; 15p. 350,608; 17½p. 338,658.
Withdrawn: 31.7.81.

213 *Eye of the Wind*

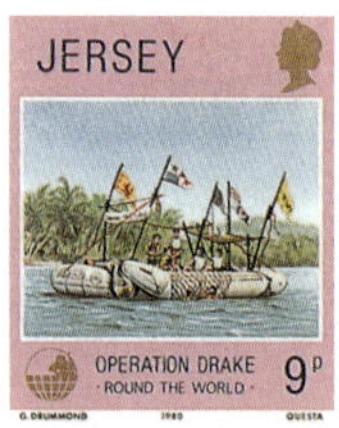

214 Diving from Inflatable Dinghy

215 Exploration of Papua New Guinea

216 Captain Scott's *Discovery*

217 Using Aerial Walkways, Conservation Project, Sulawesi

218 *Eye of the Wind*, and Goodyear Aerospace Airship *Europa*

Operation Drake and 150th Anniversary of Royal Geographical Society (14p.)

(Des G. Drummond. Litho Questa)

1980 (1 Oct). Perf 14 (c).

238	**213**	7p. multicoloured	15	15
239	**214**	9p. multicoloured	20	20
240	**215**	13½p. multicoloured	30	25
241	**216**	14p. multicoloured	30	30
242	**217**	15p. multicoloured	35	35
		a. Black (face value and inscr) ptg double		
243	**218**	17½p. multicoloured	40	40
		a. Black (face value and inscr) ptg double		
238/43 *Set of 6*			1·50	1·50
First Day Cover				1·70
Presentation Pack			2·00	

Plate Nos.: All values 1A, 1B, 1C, 1D., 1E, 1F (each×6).
Sheets: 20 (5×4).
Imprint: Upper left-hand margin.
Quantities sold: 7p. 1,631,558; 9p. 1,071,684; 13½p. 432,201; 14p. 357,109; 15p. 357,922; 17½p. 351,215.
Withdrawn: 31.10.81.

219

220

221

222

Bicentenary of Battle of Jersey. Details of painting 'The Death of Major Peirson' by J. S. Copley

(Photo Courvoisier)

1981 (6 Jan). Granite paper. Perf 12½×12 (c).

244	**219**	7p. multicoloured	15	15
245	**220**	10p. multicoloured	25	20
246	**221**	15p. multicoloured	35	30
247	**222**	17½p. multicoloured	40	35
244/7 *Set of 4*			1·00	90
First Day Cover				1·40
Presentation Pack			1·50	
MS248 144×97 mm. Nos. 244/7			1·40	1·60
First Day Cover				7·00

Stamps from No. **MS**248 are without white margins.
Cylinder Nos.: All values A1–1–1–1–1, B1–1–1–1–1.
Sheets: 20 (5×4).
Imprint: Right-hand corner, bottom margin.
Quantities sold: 7p. 997,416; 10p. 1,107,456; 15p. 367,971; 17½p. 359,794; miniature sheet 469,953.
Withdrawn: 31.1.82.

223 De Bagot

224 De Carteret

225 La Cloche

226 Dumaresq

227 Payn

228 Janvrin

229 Poingdestre

230 Pipon

231 Marett

232 Le Breton

233 Le Maistre

234 Bisson

235 Robin

236 Herault

237 Messervy

238 Fiott

239 Malet

240 Mabon

241 De St. Martin

242 Hamptonne

243 Badier

244 L'Arbalestier

245 Journeaulx

246 Lempriere

247 Auvergne

248 Remon

249 Jersey Crest and Map of Channel

250 'Queen Elizabeth II' (Norman Hepple)

Arms of Jersey Families

(Des Courvoisier (£5), G. Drummond (others). Litho Questa (½p. to £1). Photo Courvoisier (£5))

1981 (24 Feb)–**88**. Granite paper (£5). Perf 15×14 (16p., 17p., 18p., 19p., 26p., 75p.), 12½×12 (£5) or 14 (others), all comb.

249	**223**	½p. black, silver & turq-grn (a)	20	20
250	**224**	1p. multicoloured (a)	10	10
		a. Booklet pane of 6 (acf)	40	
		b. Perf 15×14 (o)	30	30
251	**225**	2p. multicoloured (a)	10	10
		a. Booklet pane of 6 (cf)	70	
		b. Perf 15×14 (io)	20	20
		ba. Booklet pane of 6 (l)	1·00	
252	**226**	3p. multicoloured (a)	10	15
		a. Booklet pane of 6 (a)	80	
		b. Perf 15×14 (ik)	15	15
		ba. Booklet pane of 6 (h)	1·00	
253	**227**	4p. black, silver and mauve (a)	15	15
		a. Perf 15×14 (k)	20	20
		ab. Booklet pane of 6 (mq)	1·00	
254	**228**	5p. multicoloured (a)	15	15
		a. Perf 15×14 (k)	30	30
255	**229**	6p. multicoloured (a)	20	20
		a. Perf 15×14 (k)	40	40
256	**230**	7p. multicoloured (a)	25	25
		a. Booklet pane of 6 (ac)	1·40	
257	**231**	8p. multicoloured (a)	30	30
		a. Booklet pane of 6 (f)	1·70	
258	**232**	9p. multicoloured (ae)	30	25
		a. Perf 15×14 (h)	40	40
		ab. Booklet pane of 6 (h)	2·50	
		ac. 'Ghost impression' from No. 261a*		
259	**233**	10p. multicoloured(a)	25	25
		a. Booklet pane of 6 (ac)	1·50	
		b. Perf 15×14 (l)	40	40
		ba. Booklet pane of 6 (l)	1·60	
260	**234**	11p. multicoloured (be)	30	30
		a. Booklet pane of 6 (f)	1·90	
		b. Perf 15×14 (m)	45	45
		ba. Booklet pane of 6 (m)	1·70	
261	**235**	12p. multicoloured (be)	35	30
		a. Perf 15×14 (hq)	50	50
		ab. Booklet pane of 6 (hq)	3·00	
262	**236**	13p. multicoloured (b)	35	35
		a. Perf 15×14 (i)	50	50
263	**237**	14p. multicoloured (b)	40	40
		a. Perf 15×14 (i)	40	40
		ab. Booklet pane of 6 (l)	2·40	
264	**238**	15p. multicoloured (b)	40	40
		a. Perf 15×14 (mo)	45	45
		ab. Booklet pane of 6 (m)	2·20	
265	**239**	16p. multicoloured (jo)	35	35
		a. Booklet pane of 6 (q)	2·20	
266	**240**	17p. multicoloured (j)	45	45
266*a*	**241**	18p. multicoloured (p)	50	50
266*b*	**242**	19p. multicoloured (p)	60	60
267	**243**	20p. black, silver and lemon (b)	50	50
		a. Perf 15×14 (k)	80	80
268	**244**	25p. black and dull blue (d)	45	45
268*a*	**223**	26p. black, silver and carmine (p)	50	50
269	**245**	30p. multicoloured (d)	50	60
		a. Perf 15×14 (k)	1·00	1·00
270	**246**	40p. multicoloured (d)	80	80
		a. Perf 15×14 (m)	1·50	1·40
271	**247**	50p. multicoloured (d)	1·00	1·00
		a. Perf 15×14 (m)	1·90	1·90
272	**248**	75p. multicoloured (n)	1·50	1·50
273	**249**	£1 multicoloured (d)	2·00	2·00
274	**250**	£5 multicoloured (g)	8·00	8·00
249/74 Set of 29			18·00	18·00
First Day Covers (7)				20·00
Presentation Packs (4)			20·00	

*Examples of No. 258ac show an impression of the blue (shield) plate from the 12p. value. The error was caused by an impression of the 12p. plate remaining on the transfer roller.

No. 258a only occurs in the £2.16 stamp booklet issued 27 April 1984, No. 259b from the £3.12 booklet of 1 April 1986, No. 260b from the £3.60 booklet of 6 April 1987 and No. 261a from the £2.16 booklet of 27 April 1984 and the £3.84 booklet of 17 May 1988.

No. 252b first occurred in the £2.16 stamp booklet of 27 April 1984, but was subsequently issued in sheets.

Printings: (a) 24.2.81; (b) 28.7.81; (c) 1.12.81; (d) 23.2.82; (e) 11.6.82; (f) 19.4.83; (g) 17.11.83; (h) 27.4.84; (i) 15.11.84; (j) 25.10.85; (k) 4.3.86; (l) 1.4.86; (m) 6.4.87; (n) 23.4.87; (o) 12.1.88; (p) 26.4.88; (q) 17.5.88.

Plate and Cylinder Nos.: ½p., 20p. 1A, 1B, 1C, 1D., 1E, 1F, 1G, 1H (each ×3); 6p., 11p., 12p., 13p., 14p., 50p., 75p. 1A, 1B, 1C, 1D., 1E, 1F, 1G, 1H (each ×5); 10p. 1A, 1B, 1C, 1D., 1F, 1G, 1H (each ×5), 2A–1A (×4), 2B–1B (×4), 2C–1C (×4), 2D–1D. (×4), 2E–1E (×4), 2F–1F (×4), 2G–1G (×4), 2H–1H (×4); 25p. 1A–1A, 1B–1B, 1C–C, 1D–1D., 1E–1E, 1F–1F, 1G–1G, 1H–1H; 26p. 1A, 1B, 1C, 1D., 1F,

1G, 1H (each ×3); £1 1A, 1B, 1C, 1D., 1E, 1F, 1G, 1H (each ×6); £5 A1–1–1–1–1, B1–1–1–1–1, C1–1–1–1–1, D1–1–1–1–1; others 1A, 1B, 1C, 1D., 1E, 1G, 1H (each ×4).
Sheets: £1 25 (5×5); £5 10 (5×2); others 50 (10×5).
Imprint: Right-hand corner, bottom margin.
Withdrawn: 31.12.85 ½p.; 30.4.87 £1; 31.3.90 1p. to 10p.; 31.1.91 11p. to 20p.; 31.3.91 25p. to 75p.; 30.4.97 £5.

251 Knight of Hambye slaying Dragon

252 Servant slaying Knight and awaiting Execution

253 St. Brelade celebrating Easter on Island

254 Island revealing itself as Huge Fish

Europa. Folklore

(Des Jennifer Toombs. Litho Questa)

1981 (7 Apr). Perf 14½ (c).

275	**251**	10p. multicoloured	25	15
		a. Horiz pair. Nos. 275/6	60	60
276	**252**	10p. multicoloured	25	15
277	**253**	18p. multicoloured	30	20
		a. Horiz pair. Nos. 277/8	1·00	1·00
278	**254**	18p. multicoloured	30	20
275/8 *Set of 4*			1·40	1·70
First Day Cover				1·50
Presentation Pack			1·75	

Legends: 10p., Slaying of the Dragon of Lawrence by the Knight of Hambye; 18p. Voyages of St. Brelade.
Plate Nos.: 10p. 1A, 1B, 1C, 1D., 1E, 1F, 1G, 1H (each ×6); 18p. 1A, 1B, 1C, 1D., 1E, 1F, 1G, 1H (each ×5).
Sheets: 20 (4×5). The two designs of each value were each printed together, *se-tenant*, in horizontal pairs throughout .
Imprint: Central, left-hand margin.
Quantities sold: 10p. 3,459,902; 18p. 2,494,444.
Withdrawn: 30.4.82.

255 The Harbour by Gaslight

256 The Quay

257 Royal Square

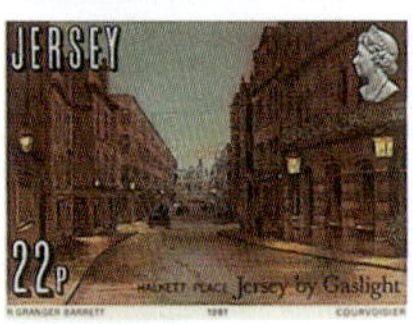

258 Halkett Place

259 Central Market

150th Anniversary of Gas Lighting in Jersey

(Des R. Granger Barrett. Photo Courvoisier)

1981 (22 May). Granite paper. Perf 11½ (c).

279	**255**	7p. multicoloured	20	15
280	**256**	10p. multicoloured	25	25
281	**257**	18p. multicoloured	40	40
282	**258**	22p. multicoloured	45	45
283	**259**	25p. multicoloured	55	55
279/83 *Set of 5*			1·60	1·60
First Day Covers				1·70
Presentation Packs			2·00	

Cylinder Nos.: All values A1–1–1–1–1, B1–1–1–1–1, C1–1–1–1–1, D1–1–1–1–1.
Sheets: 20 (5×4).
Imprint: Left-hand corner, bottom margin.
Quantities sold: 7p. 1,433,090; 10p. 1,416,051; 18p. 384,043; 22p. 417,191; 25p. 333,402.
Withdrawn: 31.5.82.

260 Prince Charles and Lady Diana Spencer

Royal Wedding

(Des Jersey P.O. and Courvoisier. Photo Courvoisier)

1981 (28 July). Granite paper. Perf 11½ (c).

284	**260**	10p. multicoloured	20	20
285		25p. multicoloured	75	90
284/5 *Set of 2*			95	1·10
First Day Covers				2·50
Presentation Packs			2·00	

Cylinder Nos.: Both values A1–1–1–1–1, B1–1–1–1–1.
Sheets: 20 (5×4).
Imprint: Left-hand corner, bottom margin.
Quantities sold: 10p. 935,571; 25p. 580,597.
Withdrawn: 31.7.82.

261 Christmas Tree in Royal Square

262 East Window, Parish Church, St. Helier

263 Boxing Day Meet of Jersey Drag Hunt

Christmas

(Des A. Copp. Litho Questa)

1981 (29 Sept). Perf 14½ (c).

286	**261**	7p. multicoloured	15	10
287	**262**	10p. multicoloured	25	25
		a. *Black* (face value, inscr and choir) printed double	£150	
288	**263**	18p. multicoloured	30	30
286/8 *Set of 3*			60	60
First Day Cover				95
Presentation Pack			1·20	
Postcards (set of 3)			1·10	2·50

Plate Nos.: All values 1A, 1B, 1C, 1D., 1E, 1F, 1G, 1H (each ×5).
Sheets: 20 (4×5).
Imprint: Central, left-hand margin.
Quantities sold: 7p. 1,437,626; 10p. 1,386,934; 18p. 422,693.
Withdrawn: 30.9.82.

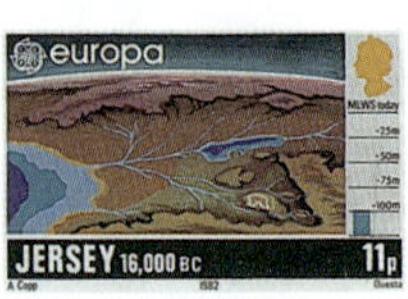

264 Jersey, 16,000 B.C.

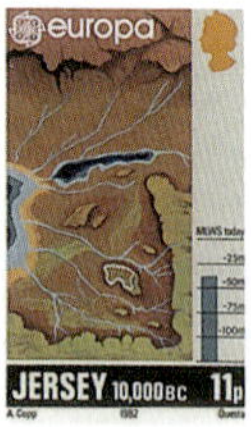

265 10,000 B.C.

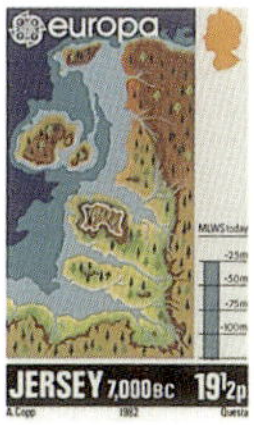

266 7,000 B.C.

267 4,000 B.C.

Europa. History. Formation of Jersey

(Des A. Copp. Litho Questa)

1982 (20 Apr). Perf 14 (c).

289	**264**	11p. multicoloured	20	20
290	**265**	11p. multicoloured	20	20
291	**266**	19½p. multicoloured	45	45
292	**267**	19½p. multicoloured	45	45
289/92		*Set of 4*	1·10	1·10
		First Day Cover		1·50
		Presentation Pack	1·50	

Plate Nos.: All values 1A, 1B, 1C, 1D., 1E, 1F (each×6).
Sheets: 20 (Nos. 289, 292, 4×5; others 5×4).
Imprint: Central, left-hand margin.
Quantities sold: 11p. (both designs) 3,414,424; 19½p. (both designs) 2,307,769.
Withdrawn: 30.4.83.

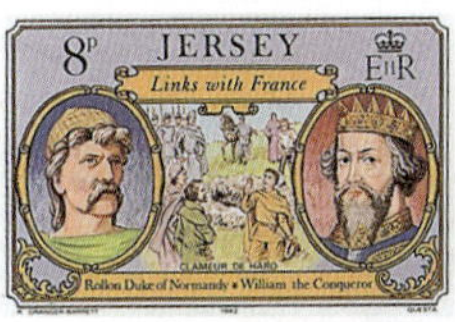

268 Rollo, Duke of Normandy, William the Conqueror and 'Clameur de Haro'

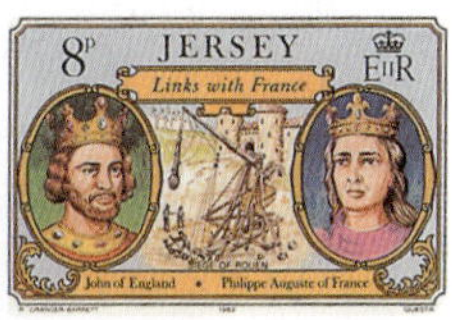

269 John of England, Philippe Auguste of France and Siege of Rouen

270 Jean Martell (brandy merchant), early Still and view of Cognac

271 Victor Hugo 'Le Rocher des Proscrits' (rock where he used to meditate) and Marine Terrace

272 Pierre Teilhard de Chardin (philosopher) and 'Maison Saint Louis' (science institute)

273 Père Charles Rey (scientist), anemotachymeter and The Observatory, St. Louis

Links with France

(Des R. Granger Barrett. Litho Questa)

1982 (11 June–7 Sept). Perf 14 (c).

293	**268**	8p. multicoloured	20	15
		a. Horiz pair. Nos. 293/4	50	50
		b. Booklet pane. Nos. 293/4 each ×2 (7.9.82)	1·00	
294	**269**	8p. multicoloured	20	15
295	**270**	11p. multicoloured	30	15
		a. Horiz pair. Nos. 295/6	60	60
		b. Booklet pane. Nos. 295/6 each ×2 (7.9.82	1·50	
296	**271**	11p. multicoloured	30	15
297	**272**	19½p. multicoloured	45	20
		a. Horiz pair. Nos. 297/8	90	90
		b. Booklet pane. Nos. 297/8 each ×2 (7.9.82)	2·20	
		c. Black (face value and inscr) printed double		
298	**273**	19½p. multicoloured	45	20
		c. Black (face value and inscr) printed double		
293/8		*Set of 6*	1·70	1·70
		First Day Cover		1·80
		Presentation Pack	2·00	

Each booklet pane has margins all round and text, in English or French, printed on the binding selvedge.

Nos. 297c and 298c come from an example of booklet pane No. 297b.

Plate Nos.: All values 1A, 1B, 1C, 1D. (each ×4).
Sheets: 20 (4×5). The two designs of each value were printed together, *se-tenant*, in horizontal pairs throughout.
Imprint: Central, left-hand margin.
Quantities sold (sheet stamps): 8p. (both designs) 2,019,854; 11p. (both designs) 1,914,536; 19½p. (both designs) 828,272.
Withdrawn: 30.6.83 (sheets).

274 Sir William Smith and Proclamation of King George V, Jersey, 1910

275 Sir William Smith and Lord Baden-Powell at Boys' Brigade Display, 1903

276 Boys' Brigade Band, Jersey Liberation Parade, 1945

277 Lord and Lady Baden-Powell in St. Helier, 1924

278 Scouts in Summer Camp, Jersey

Youth Organizations

(Des A. Theobald. Photo Courvoisier)

1982 (18 Nov). Granite paper. Perf 11½ (c).

299	**274**	8p. multicoloured	20	15
300	**275**	11p. multicoloured	20	15
301	**276**	24p. multicoloured	45	40
302	**277**	26p. multicoloured	60	50
303	**278**	29p. multicoloured	75	60
299/303		*Set of 5*	2·00	1·60
		First Day Cover		1·90
		Presentation Pack	2·20	

Nos. 299/303 were issued on the occasion of the 75th anniversary of the Boy Scout Movement, the 125th birth anniversary of Lord Baden-Powell and the centenary of the Boys' Brigade (1983).

Cylinder Nos.: All values A1–1–1–1–1, B1–1–1–1–1, C1–1–1–1–1, D1–1–1–1–1.
Sheets: 20 (11p., 26p. 5×4; others 4×5).
Imprint: Lower left-hand margin.
Quantities sold: 8p. 1,006,110; 11p. 1,006,206; 24p. 242,482; 26p. 255,359; 29p. 244,746.
Withdrawn: 30.11.83.

279 H.M.S. *Tamar* with H.M.S. *Dolphin* at Port Egmont

280 H.M.S. *Dolphin* and H.M.S. *Swallow* off Magellan Strait

281 Discovering Pitcairn Island

282 Carteret taking possession of English Cove, New Zealand

283 H.M.S. *Swallow* sinking a Pirate Ship, Macassar Strait

284 H.M.S. *Endymion* leading Convoy from West Indies

Jersey Adventurers (1s.t series). 250th Birth Anniv of Philippe de Carteret

(Des R. Granger Barrett. Litho Questa)

1983 (15 Feb). Perf 14×14½ (c).

304	**279**	8p. multicoloured	20	15
		a. Black (face value and inscr) printed double		
305	**280**	11p. multicoloured	25	15
		a. Black (face value and inscr) printed double		
306	**281**	19½p. multicoloured	40	35
307	**282**	24p. multicoloured	45	45
		a. Black (face value and inscr) printed double		
308	**283**	26p. multicoloured	50	50
		a. Black (face value and inscr) printed double		
309	**284**	29p. multicoloured	65	60
304/9 *Set of 6*			2·20	2·00
First Day Cover				2·75
Presentation Pack			3·50	

See also Nos. 417/21 and 573/8.

Plate Nos.: All values 1A, 1B, 1C, 1D., 1E, 1F (each×6).
Sheets: 20 (4×5).
Imprint: Central, left-hand margin.
Quantities sold: 8p. 983,227; 11p. 979,640; 19½p. 377,535; 24p. 264,595; 26p. 279,424; 29p. 254,023.
Withdrawn: 29.2.84.

285 1969 5s. Legislative Chamber Definitive

286 Royal Mace

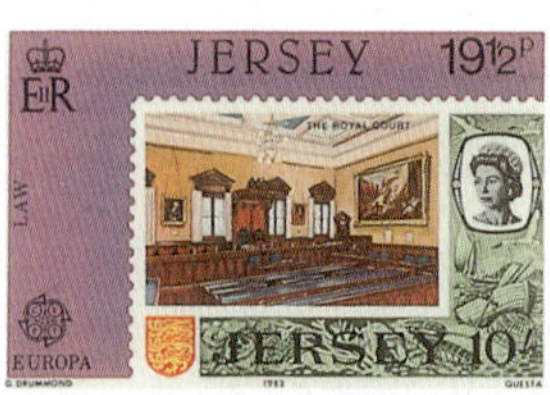

287 1969 10s. Royal Court Definitive showing Green Border Error

288 Bailiff's Seal

Europa. Great Works of Human Genius

(Des G. Drummond. Litho Questa)

1983 (19 Apr). Perf 14½ (c).

310	**285**	11p. multicoloured	25	30
		a. Horiz pair. Nos. 310/11	80	80
311	**286**	11p. multicoloured	25	30
312	**287**	19½p. multicoloured	35	35
		a. Horiz pair. Nos. 312/13	90	90
313	**288**	19½p. multicoloured	35	35
310/13 *Set of 4*			1·50	1·50
First Day Cover				2·00
Presentation Pack			2·20	

Plate Nos.: Both values 1A, 1B, 1C, 1D., 1E, 1F (each ×6).
Sheets: 20 (4×5). The two designs of each value were printed together, *se-tenant*, in horizontal pairs throughout.
Imprint: Central, left-hand margin.
Quantities sold: 11p. (both designs) 2,973,691; 19½p. (both designs) 1,301,579 .
Withdrawn: 30.4.84.

289 Charles Le Geyt and Battle of Minden (1759)

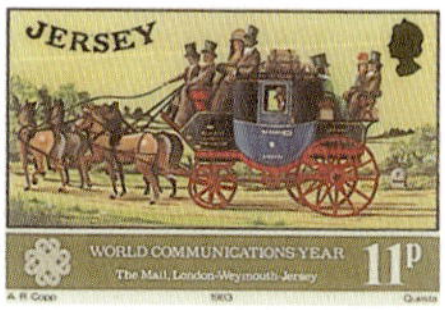

290 London to Weymouth Mail Coach

291 P.O. Mail Packet *Chesterfield* attacked by French Privateer

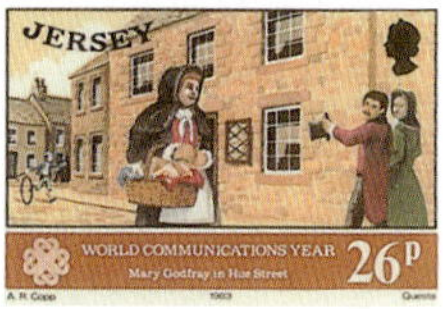

292 Mary Godfray and the Hue Street Post Office

293 Mail Steamer leaving St. Helier Harbour

World Communications Year and 250th Birth Anniversary of Charles Le Geyt (first Jersey postmaster)

(Des A. Copp. Litho Questa)

1983 (21 June). Perf 14 (c).

314	**289**	8p. multicoloured	20	20
315	**290**	11p. multicoloured	30	30
316	**291**	24p. multicoloured	55	55
317	**292**	26p. multicoloured	65	65
318	**293**	29p. multicoloured	80	80
314/18 *Set of 5*			2·20	2·20
First Day Cover				2·50
Presentation Pack			2·75	

Plate Nos.: All values 1A, 1B, 1C, 1D. (each ×5).
Sheets: 20 (4×5).
Imprint: Central, left-hand margin.
Quantities sold: 8p. 1,136,008; 11p. 961,725; 24p. 244,690; 26p. 247,654; 29p. 230,325.
Withdrawn: 30.6.84.

294 Assembly Emblem

13th General Assembly of the A.I.P.L.F. (Association Internationale des Parlementaires de Langue Francaise)

(Des A. Copp. Litho Questa)

1983 (21 June). Perf 14½ (c).

319	**294**	19½p. multicoloured	50	50
First Day Cover				95
Presentation Pack			1·20	

Plate Nos.: 1A, 1B, 1C, 1D. (each ×5).
Sheets: 20 (4×5).
Imprint: Central, left-hand margin.
Quantity sold: 312,304.
Withdrawn: 30.6.84.

295 'Cardinal Newman'

296 'Incident in the French Revolution'

297 'Thomas Hardy'

298 'David with the Head of Goliath'

50th Death Anniversary of Walter Ouless (artist)

(Des and photo Courvoisier)

1983 (20 Sept). Granite paper. Perf 11½ (c).

320	**295**	8p. multicoloured	20	20
321	**296**	11p. multicoloured	30	30
322	**297**	20½p. multicoloured	50	50
323	**298**	31p. multicoloured	80	80
320/3 *Set of 4*			1·60	1·60
First Day Cover				2·00
Presentation Pack			2·20	

Cylinder Nos.: All values 1A, 1B (each ×5).
Sheets: 20 (4×5) 31p. or (5×4) others.
Imprint: Central, left-hand margin.
Quantities sold: 8p. 1,054,200; 11p. 1,055,429; 20½p. 424,049; 31p. 216,128.
Withdrawn: 30.9.84.

299 Goldern Lion Tamarin

300 Snow Leopard

301 Jamacian Boa

302 Road Island Gecko

303 Coscoroba Swan

304 St. Lucia Amazon

Wildlife Preservation Trust (4th series)

(Des W. Oliver. Litho Questa)

1984 (17 Jan). Perf 13½×14 (c).

324	**299**	9p. multicoloured	25	10
325	**300**	12p. multicoloured	25	15
326	**301**	20½p. multicoloured	45	40
327	**302**	26p. multicoloured	75	65
328	**303**	28p. multicoloured	80	70
329	**304**	31p. multicoloured	1·00	90
324/9 *Set of 6*			3·00	2·50
First Day Cover				4·00
Presentation Pack			3·75	

Plate Nos.: 20½p., 28p. 1B, 1C, 1E, 1F (each ×4); others 1A, 1B, 1C, 1D., 1E, 1F (each ×4).
Sheets: 20 (5×4).
Imprint: Central, left-hand margin.
Quantities sold: 9p. 1,229,713; 12p. 1,365,973; 20½p. 266,444; 26p. 239,180; 28p. 255,205; 31p. 221,422.
Withdrawn: 31.1.85.

305 C.E.P.T. 25th Anniversary Logo

Europa

(Des J. Larrivière. Litho Questa)

1984 (12 Mar). Perf 14½×15 (c).

330	**305**	9p. cobalt, ultramarine & black	20	15
331		12p. light green, green and black	30	25
332		20½p. rose-lilac, dp magenta & blk	60	60
330/2 *Set of 3*			1·00	1·00
First Day Cover				1·50
Presentation Pack			1·60	

Plate Nos.: All values 1A, 1B, 1C, 1D., 1E, 1F (each×3).
Sheets: 20 (4×5).
Imprint: Central, left-hand margin.
Quantities sold: 9p. 1,352,245; 12p. 1,388,802; 20½p. 742,046.
Withdrawn: 31.3.85.

306 Map showing Commonwealth

Links with the Commonwealth

(Des A. Copp. Litho Questa)

1984 (12 Mar). Sheet 108×74 mm. Perf 15×14½ (c).

MS333	**306**	multicoloured	2·00	2·00
First Day Cover				2·50
Presentation Pack			2·75	

Quantity sold: 215,566.
Withdrawn: 31.3.85.

307 *Sarah Bloomshoft* at Demie de Pas Light, 1906

308 *Hearts of Oak* and *Maurice Georges'* 1949

309 *Elizabeth Rippon* and Hanna, 1949

310 *Elizabeth Rippon* and *Santa Maria*, 1951

311 *Elizabeth Rippon* and *Bacchus*, 1973

312 *Thomas James King* and *Cythara*, 1983

Centenary of the Jersey R.N.L.I. Lifeboat Station

(Des G. Palmer. Litho Questa)

1984 (1 June). Perf 14½ (c).

334	**307**	9p. multicoloured	25	15
335	**308**	9p. multicoloured	25	15
336	**309**	12p. multicoloured	35	30
337	**310**	12p. multicoloured	35	30
338	**311**	20½p. multicoloured	60	70
339	**312**	20½p. multicoloured	60	70
334/9 *Set of 6*			2·10	2·20
First Day Cover				3·00
Presentation Pack			3·25	
Postcard (as No. 339)			1·20	2·20

Plate Nos.: All values 1A, 1B, 1C, 1D., 1E, 1F (each ×5).
Sheets: 20 (4×5).
Imprint: Central, left-hand margin.
Quantities sold: 9p. (No. 3×4) 485,538; 9p. (No. 3×5) 435,647; 12p. (No. 336) 534,920; 12p. (No. 337) 518,807; 20½p. (No. 338) 298,935; 20½p. (No. 339) 290, 945.
Withdrawn: 30.6.85.

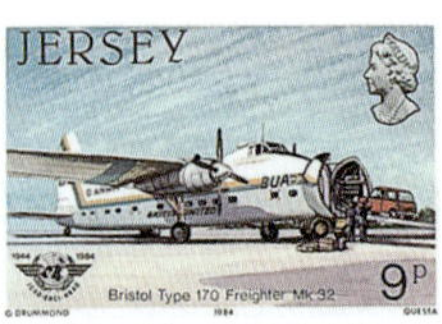

313 Bristol Type 170 Freighter Mk 32

314 Airspeed A.S. 57 Ambassador 2

315 De Havilland D.H.114 Heron 1B

316 De Havilland D.H.89A Dragon Rapide

40th Anniversary of International Civil Aviation Organization

(Des G. Drummond. Litho Questa)

1984 (24 July). Perf 14 (c).

340	**313**	9p. multicoloured	20	15
341	**314**	12p. multicoloured	35	35
342	**315**	26p. multicoloured	75	75
343	**316**	31p. multicoloured	1·00	1·00
340/3 *Set of 4*			2·10	2·00
First Day Cover				2·75
Presentation Pack			3·25	

Plate Nos.: All values 1A, 1B, 1C, 1D. (each ×4).
Sheets: 20 (4×5).
Imprint: Central, left-hand margin.
Quantities sold: 9p. 563,394; 12p. 751,072; 26p. 262,640; 31p. 193,703.
Withdrawn: 31.7.85.

317 'Robinson Crusoe leaves the Wreck'

318 'Edinburgh Castle'

319 'Maori Village'

320 'Australian Landscape'

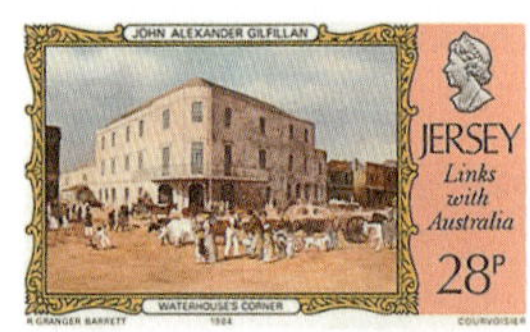

321 'Waterhouse's Corner, Adelaide'

322 'Captain Cook at Botany Bay'

Links with Australia. Paintings by John Alexander Gilfillan

(Des R. Granger Barrett. Photo Courvoisier)

1984 (21 Sept). Granite paper. Perf 11½×12 (c).

344	**317**	9p. multicoloured	25	20
345	**318**	12p. multicoloured	30	20
346	**319**	20½p. multicoloured	60	50
347	**320**	26p. multicoloured	70	60
348	**321**	28p. multicoloured	80	80
349	**322**	31p. multicoloured	80	80
344/9 *Set of 6*			3·00	2·75
First Day Cover				3·75
Presentation Pack			3·75	
Postcards (Set of 3 as Nos. 347/9)			1·70	4·50

Cylinder Nos.: All values A1, B1 (each ×6)
Sheets: 20 (4×5).
Imprint: Central, left-hand margin.

Quantities sold: 9p. 541,384; 12p. 635,192; 20½p. 210,119; 26p. 234,836; 28p. 188,052; 31p. 192,353.
Withdrawn: 30.9.85.

323 'B.L.C. St. Helier'

324 'Oda Mt Bingham'

Christmas. Jersey Orchids (1s.t series)

(Photo Courvoisier)

1984 (15 Nov). Granite paper. Perf 12×11½ (c).

350	**323**	9p. multicoloured	25	20
351	**324**	12p. multicoloured	50	50
350/1 *Set of 2*			75	70
First Day Cover				1·50
Presentation Pack			1·50	

See also Nos. 433/7, 613/17, 892/7 and 1143/**MS**1149.
Cylinder Nos.: Both values A1, B1, C1, D1 (each ×6).
Sheets: 20 (4×5).
Imprint: Central, left-hand margin.
Quantities sold: 9p. 1,197,796; 12p. 1,116,097.
Withdrawn: 30.11.85.

325 'Hebe off Corbière, 1874'

326 'The *Gaspe* engaging the *Diomede*'

327 'The Paddle-steamer *London* entering Naples, 1856'

328 'The *Rambler* entering Cape Town, 1840'

329 'St. Aubin's Bay from Mount Bingham, 1871'

Death Centenary of Philip John Ouless (artist)

(Photo Harrison)

1985 (26 Feb). Perf 14×15 (c).

352	**325**	9p. multicoloured	25	20
353	**326**	12p. multicoloured	30	30
354	**327**	22p. multicoloured	65	60
355	**328**	31p. multicoloured	1·00	90
356	**329**	34p. multicoloured	1·20	1·00
352/6 *Set of 5*			2·75	2·75
First Day Cover				3·50
Presentation Pack			4·00	

Cylinder Nos.: 31p. 1B (×5); others 1A, 1B (each ×5).
Sheets: 20 (4×5).
Imprint: Central, left-hand margin.
Quantities sold: 9p. 463,589; 12p. 405,133; 22p. 407,598; 31p. 193,772; 34p. 185,467.
Withdrawn: 28.2.86.

330 John Ireland (composer) and Faldouet Dolmen

331 Ivy St. Helier (actress) and His Majesty's Theatre, London

332 Claude Debussy (composer) and Elizabeth Castle

Europa. European Music Year

(Des Jennifer Toombs. Litho Questa)

1985 (23 Apr). Perf 14 (c).

357	**330**	10p. multicoloured	30	30
358	**331**	13p. multicoloured	45	45
359	**332**	22p. multicoloured	80	80
357/9 *Set of 3*			1·40	1·40
First Day Cover				1·90
Presentation Pack			2·00	

Nos.: 10p. 1A, 1B, 1C, 1D., 1E, 1F (each ×5); 13p. 1A, 1C, 1D., 1E, 1F (each ×5); 22p. 1A, 1B, 1D., 1E, 1F (each ×5).
Sheets: 20 (4×5).
Imprint: Central, left-hand margin.
Quantities sold: 10p. 916,040; 13p. 766,179; 22p. 620,375.
Withdrawn: 30.4.86.

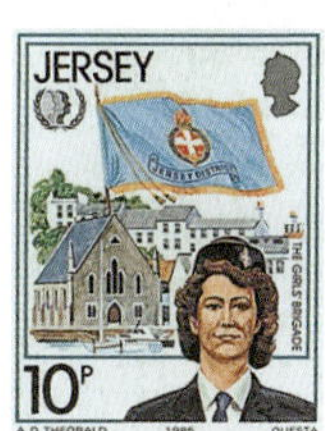

333 Girls' Brigade

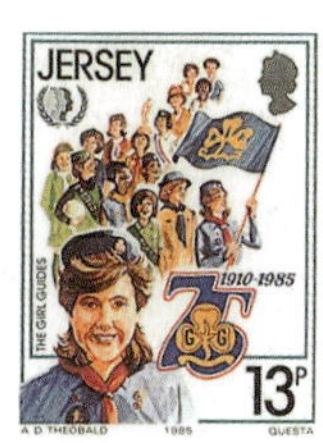

334 Girl Guides (75th anniversary)

335 Prince Charles and Jersey Youth Service Activities Base

336 Sea Cadet Corps

337 Air Training Corps

International Youth Year

(Des A. Theobald. Litho Questa)

1985 (30 May). Perf 14½×14 (c).

360	**333**	10p. multicoloured	30	30
361	**334**	13p. multicoloured	40	40
362	**335**	29p. multicoloured	70	70
363	**336**	31p. multicoloured	75	75
364	**337**	34p. multicoloured	90	90
360/4 *Set of 5*			2·75	2·75
First Day Cover				3·25
Presentation Pack			3·75	

Plate Nos.: All values 1A, 1B, 1C, 1D., 1E, 1F (each ×4).
Sheets: 20 (5×4).
Imprint: Central, left-hand margin.
Quantities sold: 10p. 943,351; 13p. 944,724; 29p. 175,365; 31p. 183,551; 34p. 175,842.
Withdrawn: 30.5.86.

338 *Duke of Normandy* at Cheapside

339 Saddletank at First Tower

340 *La Moye* at Millbrook

341 *St. Heliers* at St. Aubin

342 *St. Aubyns* at Corbiere

Jersey Western Railway

(Des G. Palmer. Photo Courvoisier)

1985 (16 July). Granite paper. Perf 11½ (c).

365	**338**	10p. multicoloured	45	45
366	**339**	13p. multicoloured	50	50
367	**340**	22p. multicoloured	90	90
368	**341**	29p. multicoloured	95	95
369	**342**	34p. multicoloured	1·00	1·00
365/9 *Set of 5*			3·50	3·50
First Day Cover				3·75
Presentation Pack			4·00	

Cylinder Nos.: 10p., 13p. A1, B1 (each ×5); others A1 (×5).
Sheets: 20 (4×5).
Imprint: Central, left-hand margin.
Quantities sold: 10p. 708,912; 13p. 706,189; 22p. 249,659; 29p. 179,849; 34p. 179,977.
Withdrawn: 31.7.86.

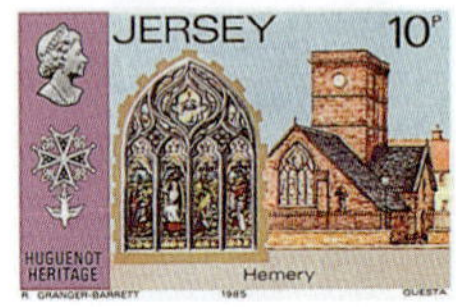

343 Memorial Window to Revd. James Hemery (former Dean) and St. Helier Parish Church

344 Judge Francis Jeune, Baron St. Helier, and Houses of Parliament

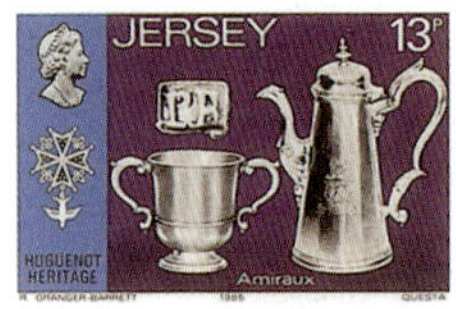

345 Silverware by Pierre Amiraux

346 Francis Voisin (merchant) and Russian Port

347 Robert Brohier, Schweppes Carbonation Plant and Bottles

348 George Ingouville, V.C., R.N., and Attack on Viborg

300th Anniversary of Huguenot Immigration

(Des R. Granger Barrett. Litho Questa)

1985 (10 Sept). Perf 14 (c).

370	**343**	10p. multicoloured	30	30
		a. Booklet pane of 4	1·20	
371	**344**	10p. multicoloured	30	30
		a. Booklet pane of 4	1·20	
372	**345**	13p. multicoloured	40	40
		a. Booklet pane of 4	1·60	
373	**346**	13p. multicoloured	40	40
		a. Booklet pane of 4	1·60	
		ab. Black (face value and inscr) printed double		
374	**347**	22p. multicoloured	55	50
		a. Booklet pane of 4	2·20	
		b. Black (inscr) printed double		
375	**348**	22p. multicoloured	55	50
		a. Booklet pane of 4	2·20	
370/5 *Set of 6*			2·20	2·10
First Day Cover				2·75
Presentation Pack			2·75	

Each booklet pane has margins all round and text printed on the binding selvedge.

Plate Nos.: 13p. (No. 372) 1A, 1B, 1C, 1D. (each ×4); 22p. (No. 375) 1A, 1C, 1D. (each ×5); others 1A, 1B, 1C, 1D. (each ×5).
Sheets: 20 (4×5).
Imprint: Central, left-hand margin.
Quantities sold (sheets): 10p. (No. 370) 308,085; 10p. (No. 371) 310,475; 13p. (No. 372) 488,224; 13p. (No. 373) 477,764; 22p. (No. 374) 259,921; 22p. (No. 375) 253,607.
Withdrawn: 30.9.86 (sheets).

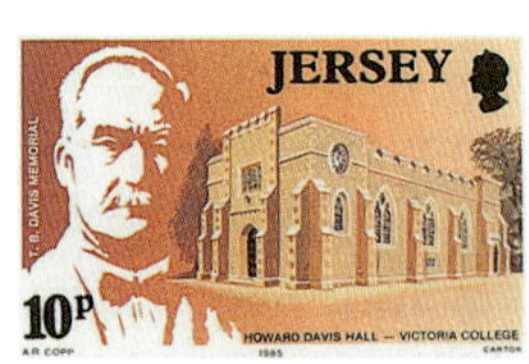

349 Howard Davis Hall, Victoria College

350 Racing Schooner *Westward*

351 Howard Davis Park, St. Helier

352 Howard Davis Experimental Farm, Trinity

Thomas Davis (philanthropist) Commemoration

(Des A. Copp. Litho Cartor)

1985 (25 Oct). Perf 13½ (c).

376	**349**	10p. multicoloured	35	35
377	**350**	13p. multicoloured	50	50
378	**351**	31p. multicoloured	70	70
379	**352**	34p. multicoloured	85	85
376/9 *Set of 4*			2·20	2·20
First Day Cover				2·75
Presentation Pack			3·00	

Plate Nos.: 10p. 1A, 1B, 1C, 1D. (each ×5); 13p. 2A, 2B, 2C, 2d. (each ×5); 31p. 3A, 3B, 3C, 3D. (each ×5); 34p. 4A, 4B, 4C, 4D. (each ×5).
Sheets: 20 (4×5).
Imprint: Central, left-hand margin.
Quantities sold: 10p. 939,104; 13p. 831,351; 31p. 170,020; 34p. 156,653.
Withdrawn: 31.10.86.

353 *Amaryllis belladonna* (Pandora Sellars)

354 'A Jersey Lily' (Lily Langtry) (Sir John Millais)

Jersey Lilies

(Des C. Abbott. Litho Questa)

1986 (28 Jan). Perf 15×14½ (c).

380	**353**	13p. multicoloured	45	45
381	**354**	34p. multicoloured	1·00	1·10
380/1 *Set of 2*			1·40	1·50
First Day Cover				2·00
Presentation Pack			2·20	
MS382 140×96 mm. Nos. 380×4 and 381			2·75	3·00
First Day Cover				6·50
Presentation Pack			4·00	

Plate Nos.: 13p. 1A, 1B, 1C, 1D., 1E, 1F, 1G, 1H (each ×6); 34p. 1A, 1B, 1C, 1D. (each ×5).
Sheets: 20 (4×5); (5×4) 34p.
Imprint: Central, left-hand margin.
Quantities sold: 13p. 444,175; 34p. 169,811; miniature sheet 157,575.
Withdrawn: 31.1.87.

355 King Harold, Wiliam of Normandy and Halley's Comet, 1066 (from Bayeux Tapestry)

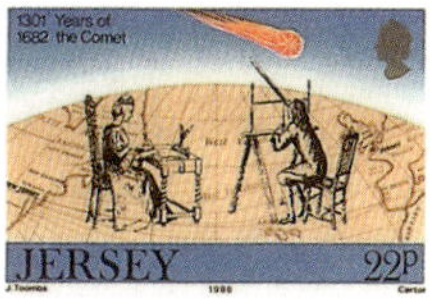

356 Lady Carteret, Edmond Halley, Map and Comet

357 Aspects of Communications in 1910 and 1986 on TV Screens

Appearance of Halleys Comet

(Des Jennifer Toombs. Litho Cartor)

1986 (4 Mar). Perf 13½×13 (c).

383	**355**	10p. multicoloured	35	35
384	**356**	22p. multicoloured	80	85
385	**357**	31p. multicoloured	1·00	1·10
383/5 *Set of 3*			1·90	2·10
First Day Cover				2·20
Presentation Pack			2·75	

Plate Nos.: All values 1A, 1B, 1C, 1D. (each ×5).
Sheets: 20 (4×5).
Imprint: Central, left-hand margin.
Quantities sold: 10p. 552,062; 22p. 245,111; 31p. 182,390.
Withdrawn: 31.3.87.

358 Dwarf Pansy

359 Sea Stock

360 Sand Crocus

Europa. Environmental Conservation

(Des Pandora Sellars. Litho Questa)

1986 (21 Apr). Perf 14½×14 (c).

386	**358**	10p. multicoloured	35	35
387	**359**	14p. multicoloured	45	45
388	**360**	22p. multicoloured	70	70
386/8 *Set of 3*			1·40	1·40
First Day Cover				1·70
Presentation Pack			2·20	

Plate Nos.: 22p. 1A, 1B, 1C, 1E, 1F (each ×5); others 1A, 1B, 1C, 1D., 1E, 1F (each ×5).
Sheets: 20 (5×4).
Imprint: Central, left-hand margin.
Quantities sold: 10p. 892,977; 14p. 892,631; 22p. 612,513.
Withdrawn: 30.4.87.

361 Queen Elizabeth II (from photo by Karsh)

367 Prince Andrew and Miss Sarah Ferguson

60th Birthday of Queen Elizabeth II

(Photo Courvoisier)

1986 (21 Apr). Granite paper. Perf 14½ (c).

389	**361**	£1 multicoloured	2·50	2·00
First Day Cover				3·25
Presentation Pack			3·00	

No. 389 was retained in use as part of the current definitive series until replaced by No. 500.

For a £2 value in this design see No. 491b.

Cylinder Nos.: 1A, 1B, 1C, 1D. (each ×6).
Sheets: 20 (4×5).
Imprint: Central, left-hand margin.
Quantity sold: 431,591.
Withdrawn: 31.5.90.

Royal Wedding

(Des A. Copp. Litho Cartor)

1986 (23 July). Perf 13½ (c).

395	**367**	14p. multicoloured	35	35
396		40p. multicoloured	1·20	1·20
395/6 *Set of 2*			1·50	1·50
First Day Cover				2·00
Presentation Pack			2·20	

Plate Nos.: Both values 1A, 1B, 1C, 1D. (each ×6).
Sheets: 20 (5×4).
Imprint: Central, left-hand margin.
Quantities sold: 14p. 991,943; 40p. 267,312.
Withdrawn: 31.7.87.

362 Le Rât Cottage

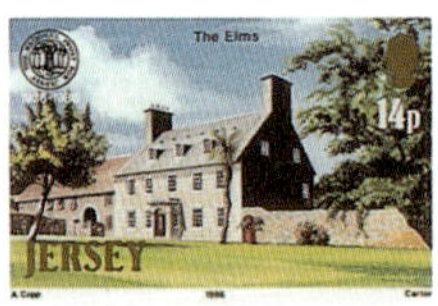

363 The Elms (Trust Headquarters)

364 Morel Farm

365 Quétivel Mill

366 La Vallette

50th Anniversary of the National Trust for Jersey

(Des A. Copp. Litho Cartor)

1986 (17 June). Perf 13½×13 (c).

390	**362**	10p. multicoloured	25	20
391	**363**	14p. multicoloured	35	30
392	**364**	22p. multicoloured	65	65
393	**365**	29p. multicoloured	70	70
394	**366**	31p. multicoloured	75	75
390/4 *Set of 5*			2·40	2·40
First Day Cover				2·75
Presentation Pack			3·75	

Plate Nos.: All values 1A, 1B, 1C, 1D. (each ×5).
Sheets: 20 (4×5).
Imprint: Central, left-hand margin.
Quantities sold: 10p. 946,735; 14p. 919,823; 22p. 427,370; 29p. 173,763; 31p. 178,353.
Withdrawn: 30.6.87.

368 'Gathering Vraic'

369 'Driving Home in the Rain'

370 'The Miller'

371 'The Joy Ride'

372 'Tante Elizabeth'

Birth Centenary of Edmund Blampied (artist)

(Des A. Copp. Litho Questa)

1986 (28 Aug). Perf 14 (c).

397	**368**	10p. multicoloured	25	25
398	**369**	14p. black, brownish grey & lt bl	40	40
399	**370**	29p. multicoloured	75	75
400	**371**	31p. black, brownish grey and pale orange	90	90
401	**372**	34p. multicoloured	95	95
397/401 *Set of 5*			3·00	3·00
First Day Cover				3·75
Presentation Pack			4·00	

Plate Nos.: 14p., 31p. 1A, 1B, 1C, 1D. (each×3); others 1A, 1B, 1C, 1D. (each ×5).
Sheets: 20 (4×5).
Imprint: Central, left-hand margin.
Quantities sold: 10p., 885,979; 14p. 675,290; 29p. 163,085; 31p. 157,559; 34p. 151,128.
Withdrawn: 31.8.87.

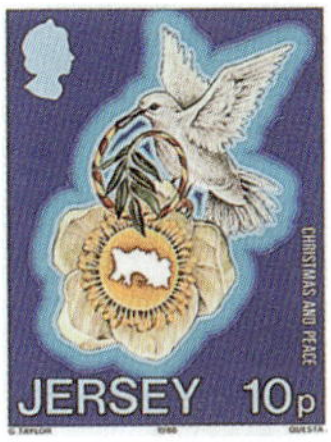

373 Island Map on Jersey Lily, and Dove holding Olive Branch

374 Mistletoe Wreath encircling European Robin and Dove

375 Christmas Cracker releasing Dove

Christmas. International Year of Peace

(Des G. Taylor. Litho Questa)

1986 (4 Nov). Perf 14½×14 (c).

402	**373**	10p. multicoloured	20	20
403	**374**	14p. multicoloured	40	40
404	**375**	34p. multicoloured	95	95
402/4 *Set of 3*			1·40	1·40
First Day Cover				2·20
Presentation Pack			2·00	

Plate Nos.: All values 1A, 1B, 1C, 1D., 1E, 1F (each ×6).
Sheets: 20 (5×4).
Imprint: Central, left-hand margin.
Quantities sold: 10p. 947,614; 14p. 940,123; 34p. 169,269.
Withdrawn: 30.11.87.

Post Office Yearbook

1986 (4 Nov). Comprises Nos. 380/404.
Yearbook .... 45·00
Withdrawn: 31.1.88.

376 *Westward* under Full Sail

377 T. B. Davis at the Helm

378 *Westward* overhauling *Britannia*

379 *Westward* fitting-out at St. Helier

Racing Schooner *Westward*

(Des A. Copp. Litho Cartor)

1987 (15 Jan). Perf 13½ (c).

405	**376**	10p. multicoloured	40	35
406	**377**	14p. multicoloured	50	55
407	**378**	31p. multicoloured	95	95
408	**379**	34p. multicoloured	95	95
405/8 *Set of 4*			2·50	2·50
First Day Cover				2·75
Presentation Pack			3·75	

Plate Nos.: All values 1A, 1B, 1C, 1D. (each ×5).
Sheets: 20 (4×5).
Imprint: Central, left-hand margin.
Quantites sold: 10p. 519,330; 14p. 370,229; 31p. 173,046; 34p. 158,754.
Withdrawn: 31.1.88.

380 De Havilland D.H.86 Dragon Express *Belcroute Bay*

381 Boeing 757 and Douglas DC-9-155

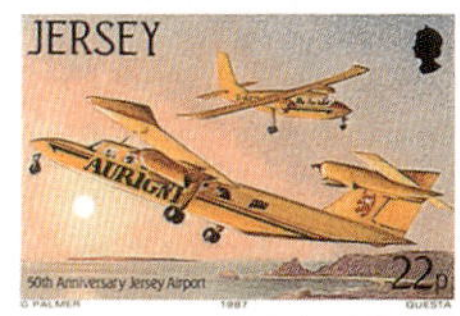

382 Britten Norman 'long nose' Trislander and Islander

383 Shorts 330 and Vickers Viscount 800

384 B.A.C. One Eleven 500 and Handley Page H.P.R.7 Dart Herald

50th Anniversary of Jersey Airport

(Des G. Palmer. Litho Questa)

1987 (3 Mar). Perf 14 (c).

409	**380**	10p. multicoloured	25	25
410	**381**	14p. multicoloured	40	45
411	**382**	22p. multicoloured	55	50
412	**383**	29p. multicoloured	90	90
413	**384**	31p. multicoloured	95	95
409/13 *Set of 5*			2·75	2·75
First Day Cover				4·00
Presentation Pack			3·75	

Plate Nos.: All values 1A, 1B, 1C, 1D. (each ×4).
Sheets: 20 (4×5).
Imprint: Central, left-hand margin.
Quantities sold: 10p. 313,733; 14p. 281,226; 22p. 368,486; 29p. 155,159; 31p. 167,709.
Withdrawn: 31.3.88.

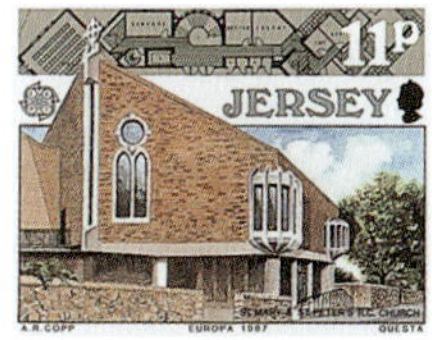

385 St. Mary and St. Peter's Roman Catholic Church

386 Villa Devereux St. Brelade

387 Fort Regent Leisure Centre, St. Helier

Europa. Modern Architecture

(Des A. Copp. Litho Questa)

1987 (23 Apr). Perf 15×14 (c).

414	**385**	11p. multicoloured	40	40
415	**386**	15p. multicoloured	50	45
416	**387**	22p. multicoloured	75	75
414/16 *Set of 3*			1·50	1·40
First Day Cover				2·00
Presentation Pack			2·20	

Plate Nos.: 11p., 15p. 1A, 1B, 1C, 1D., 1E, 1F, 1G, 1H, 1I, 1J (each ×6); 22p. 1A, 1B, 1C, 1D., 1E, 1F, 1G, 1H (each×6).
Sheets: 10 (2×5).
Imprint: Central, left-hand margin.
Quantities sold: 11p. 847,735; 15p. 883,825; 22p. 467,615.
Withdrawn: 30.4.88.

388 H.M.S. *Racehorse* and H.M.S *Carcass* (bomb-ketches) trapped in Arctic

389 H.M.S. *Alarm* on Fire, Rhode Island

390 H.M.S. *Arethusa* wrecked off Ushant

391 H.M.S. *Rattlesnake* stranded on Isle de Trinidad

392 Mont Orgueil Castle and Fishing Boats

Jersey Adventurers (2nd series). Philippe D'Auvergne

(Des R. Granger Barrett. Litho Questa)

1987 (9 July). Perf 14 (c).

417	**388**	11p. multicoloured	30	35
418	**389**	15p. multicoloured	40	45
419	**390**	29p. multicoloured	70	75
420	**391**	31p. multicoloured	80	90
421	**392**	34p. multicoloured	85	95
417/21 *Set of 5*			2·75	3·00
First Day Cover				3·25
Presentation Pack			4·25	

See also Nos. 501/6 and 539/44.
Plate Nos.: All values 1A, 1B, 1C, 1D. (each ×4).
Sheets: 20 (4×5).
Imprint: Central, left-hand margin.
Quantities sold: 11p. 694,506; 15p. 897,162; 29p. 138,711; 31p. 144,518; 34p. 140,968.
Withdrawn: 31.7.88.

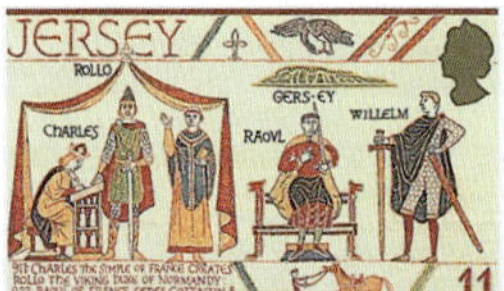

393 Grant of Lands to Normandy, 911 and 933

394 Edward the Confessor and Duke Robert I of Normandy landing on Jersey, 1030

395 King William's Coronation, 1066, and Fatal Fall, 1087

396 Death of William Rufus, 1100, and Battle of Tinchebrai, 1106

397 Civil War between Matilda and Stephen, 1135–41

398 Henry inherits Normandy, 1151: John asserts Ducal Rights in Jersey, 1213

900th Death Anniversary of William the Conqueror

(Des Jennifer Toombs, Litho Cartor)

1987 (9 Sept–16 Oct). Perf 13½ (c).

422	**393**	11p. multicoloured (a)	30	30
		a. Booklet pane of 4 (b)	1·20	
423	**394**	15p. multicoloured (a)	35	35
		a. Booklet pane of 4 (b)	1·40	
424	**395**	22p. multicoloured (a)	70	65
		a. Booklet pane of 4 (b)	2·75	
425	**396**	29p. multicoloured (a)	75	75
		a. Booklet pane of 4 (b)	3·00	
426	**397**	31p. multicoloured (a)	85	85
		a. Booklet pane of 4 (b)	3·25	
427	**398**	34p. multicoloured (a)	95	95
		a. Booklet pane of 4 (b)	3·75	
422/7 *Set of 6*			3·50	3·50
First Day Cover				3·75
Presentation Pack			4·50	

Each booklet pane has margins all round and text printed on the binding selvedge.

Printings: (a) 9.9.87; (b) 16.10.87.
Plate Nos.: All values 1A, 1B, 1C, 1D. (each×6).
Imprint: Central, left-hand margin.
Quantities sold (sheets): 11p. 869,726; 15p. 968,815; 22p. 217,160; 29p. 139,905; 31p. 147,527; 34p. 143,684.
Withdrawn: 30.9.88 (sheets).

399 'Grosnez Castle'

400 'St. Aubin's Bay'

401 'Mont Orgueil Castle'

402 'Town Fort and Harbour, St. Helier'

403 'The Hermitage'

Christmas. Paintings by John Le Capelain

(Photo Courvoisier)

1987 (3 Nov). Granite paper. Perf 11½ (c).

428	**399**	11p. multicoloured	35	30
429	**400**	15p. multicoloured	50	50
430	**401**	22p. multicoloured	65	65
431	**402**	31p. multicoloured	90	80
432	**403**	34p. multicoloured	1·00	1·00
428/32 *Set of 5*			3·00	3·00
First Day Cover				3·75
Presentation Pack			4·00	

Cylinder Nos.: 11p., 15p., 22p. 1A, 1B (each ×6); 31p., 34p. 1A (×6).
Sheets: 20 (5×4).
Imprint: Central, left-hand margin.
Quantities sold: 11p. 951,916; 15p. 874,209; 22p. 371,992; 31p. 154,824; 34p. 145,550.
Withdrawn: 30.11.88.

Post Office Yearbook

1987 (3 Nov). Comprises Nos. 272 and 405/32.

Yearbook ..... 38·00

Withdrawn: 28.2.89.

404 *Cymbidium pontac*

405 *Odontioda* Eric Young

406 *Lycaste auburn* Seaford and Ditchling

407 *Odontoglossum* St. Brelade

408 *Cymbidium mavourneen* Jester

Jersey Orchids (2nd series)

(Litho Questa)

1988 (12 Jan). Perf 14 (c).

433	**404**	11p. multicoloured	40	35
434	**405**	15p. multicoloured	45	45
435	**406**	29p. multicoloured	70	70
436	**407**	31p. multicoloured	80	80
437	**408**	34p. multicoloured	95	95
433/7 *Set of 5*			3·00	3·00
First Day Cover				3·50
Presentation Pack			3·75	

Plate Nos.: All values 1A, 1B, 1C, 1D. (each ×5).
Sheets: 20 (4×5) 11p., 29p., 34p.; (5×4) 15p., 31p.
Imprint: Central, left-hand margin.
Quantities sold: 11p. 558,185; 15p. 374,117; 29p. 143,613; 31p. 162,096; 34p. 151,193.
Withdrawn: 31.1.89.

409 Labrador Retriever

410 Wiire-haired Dachshund

411 Pekingese

412 Cavalier King Charles Spaniel

413 Dalmatian

Centenary of Jersey Dog Club

(Des P. Layton. Litho Questa)

1988 (2 Mar). Perf 14 (c).

438	**409**	11p. multicoloured	40	30
439	**410**	15p. multicoloured	60	30
440	**411**	22p. multicoloured	80	80
441	**412**	31p. multicoloured	90	95
442	**413**	34p. multicoloured	1·00	1·00
438/42 *Set of 5*			3·00	3·00
First Day Cover				3·75
Presentation Pack			4·25	

Plate Nos.: All values 1A, 1B, 1C, 1D. (each ×4).
Sheets: 20 (4×5).
Imprint: Central, left-hand margin.
Quantities sold: 11p. 371,583; 15p. 374,953; 22p. 178,132; 31p. 154,530; 34p. 146,628.
Withdrawn: 31.3.89.

414 De Havilland D.H.C. 7 Dash Seven, London Landmarks and Jersey Control Tower

415 Weather Radar and Jersey Airport Landing System

416 Hydrofoil, St. Malo, and Elizabeth Castle, St. Helier

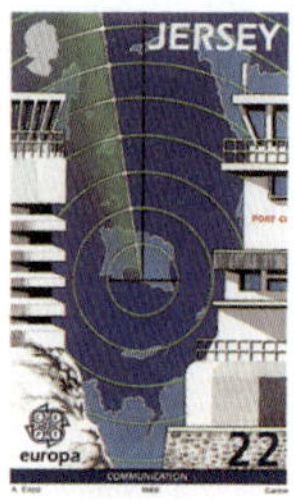

417 Port Control Tower and Jersey Radio Maritime Communication Centre, La Moye

Europa. Transport and Communications

(Des A. Copp. Litho Cartor)

1988 (26 Apr). Perf 14×13½ (horiz) or 13½×14 (vert), both comb.

443	**414**	16p. multicoloured	40	45
444	**415**	16p. multicoloured	40	45
445	**416**	22p. multicoloured	75	75
446	**417**	22p. multicoloured	75	75
443/6 *Set of 4*			2·10	2·40
First Day Cover				2·75
Presentation Pack			3·00	

Plate Nos.: Nos. 443/4, 446 1A, 1B, 1C, 1D. (each ×5); No. 445 1A, 1B, 1C, 1D. (each ×6).
Sheets: 20 (4×5) Nos. 443, 445; (5×4) Nos. 444, 446.
Imprint: Central, left-hand margin.
Quantities sold: 16p. (No. 443) 881,324; 16p. (No. 444) 865,868; 22p. (No. 445) 509,086; 22p. (No. 446) 510,104.
Withdrawn: 30.4.89.

418 Rodriguez Fody

419 Volcano Rabbit

420 White-faced Marmoset

421 Ploughshare Tortoise

422 Mauritius Kestrel

Wildlife Preservation Trust (5th series)

(Des W. Oliver. Litho Cartor)

1988 (6 July). Perf 13½×14 (vert) or 14×13½ (horiz), both comb.

447	**418**	12p. multicoloured	45	45
448	**419**	16p. multicoloured	55	50
449	**420**	29p. multicoloured	90	1·00
450	**421**	31p. multicoloured	1·10	1·10
451	**422**	34p. multicoloured	1·20	1·20
447/51 *Set of 5*			3·75	3·75
First Day Cover				4·50
Presentation Pack			4·50	

Plate Nos.: All values 1A, 1B, 1C, 1D. (each ×6).
Sheets: 20 (5×4) 12p., 29p., 34p.; (4×5) 16p., 31p.
Imprint: Central, left-hand margin.
Quantities sold: 12p. 875,722; 16p. 969,800; 29p. 146,567; 31p. 155,348; 34p. 151,723.
Withdrawn: 31.7.89.

423 Rain Forest Leaf Frog, Costa Rica

424 Archaeological Survey, Peru

425 Climbing Glacier, Chile

426 Red Cross Centre, Solomon Islands

427 Underwater Exploration, Australia

428 *Zebu* (brigantine) returning to St. Helier

Operation Raleigh

(Des V. Ambrus. Photo Courvoisier)

1988 (27 Sept). Granite paper. Perf 12 (c).

452	**423**	12p. multicoloured	35	25
453	**424**	16p. multicoloured	40	40
454	**425**	22p. multicoloured	60	60
455	**426**	29p. multicoloured	70	70
456	**427**	31p. multicoloured	80	90
457	**428**	34p. multicoloured	90	1·00
452/7 *Set of 6*			3·50	3·50
First Day Cover				3·75
Presentation Pack			4·50	

No. 455 also commemorates the 40th anniversary of the World Health Organization.

Cylinder Nos.: All values 1A (×5).
Sheets: 20 (5×4).
Imprint: Central, left-hand margin.
Quantities sold: 12p. 706,594; 16p. 507,077; 22p. 226,791; 29p. 127,647; 31p. 127,658; 34p. 128,055.
Withdrawn: 30.9.89.

429 St. Clement

430 St. Ouen

431 St. Brelade

432 St. Lawrence

Christmas. Jersey Parish Churches (1s.t series)

(Des P. Layton. Litho B.D.T.)

1988 (15 Nov). Perf 13½ (c).

458	**429**	12p. multicoloured	30	15
459	**430**	16p. multicoloured	45	30
460	**431**	31p. multicoloured	90	90
461	**432**	34p. multicoloured	85	95
458/61 *Set of 4*			2·20	2·20
First Day Cover				2·75
Presentation Pack			3·75	
Postcards (set of 4)			2·00	5·50

See also Nos. 535/8 and 597/600.

Plate Nos.: All values 1A, 1B, 1C, 1D. (each ×5).
Sheets: 20 (4×5).
Imprint: Central, left-hand margin.
Quantities sold: 12p. 964,161; 16p. 917,883; 31p. 170,477; 34p. 159,688.
Withdrawn: 30.11.89.

Post Office Yearbook

1988 (15 Nov). Comprises Nos. 266a/b, 268a and 433/61.
Yearbook .... 42·00
Withdrawn: 23.10.89.

433 Talbot Type 4 CT Tourer, 1912

434 De Dion Bouton Type 1-D, 1920

435 Austin 7 'Chummy' 1926

436 Ford 'Model T', 1926

437 Bentley 8 Litre, 1930

438 Cadillac '452A-V16 Fleetwood Sports Phaeton', 1931

Vintage Cars (1st series)

(Des A. Copp. Litho Questa)

1989 (31 Jan). Perf 14 (c).

462	**433**	12p. multicoloured	35	30
463	**434**	16p. multicoloured	50	45
464	**435**	23p. multicoloured	60	55
		a. Black (inscr etc) printed double		
465	**436**	30p. multicoloured	80	80
466	**437**	32p. multicoloured	1·00	1·00
467	**438**	35p. multicoloured	1·00	1·00
462/7 *Set of 6*			3·75	3·75
First Day Cover				4·25
Presentation Pack			4·50	

See also Nos. 591/6 and 905/10.

Plate Nos.: 12p., 30p. 1A, 1B (each ×4); 16p., 32p. 1C, 1D. (each ×4); 23p., 35p. 1A, 1B, 1C, 1D. (each ×4).
Sheets: 20 (4×5).
Imprint: Central, left-hand margin.
Quantities sold: 12p. 253,257; 16p. 230,695; 23p. 228,895; 30p. 130,974; 32p. 144,798; 35p. 148,189.
Withdrawn: 31.1.90.

439 Belcroute Bay

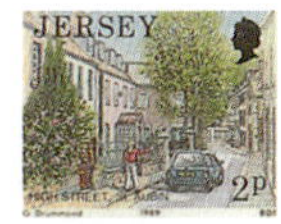

440 High Street, St. Aubin

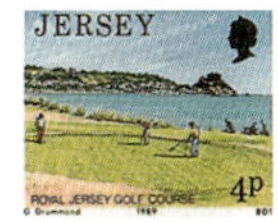

441 Royal Jersey Golf Course

442 Portelet Bay

443 Les Charrières D'Anneport

444 St. Helier Marina

445 Sand Yacht Racing, St. Ouen's Bay

446 Rozel Harbour

447 St. Aubin's Harbour

448 Jersey Airport

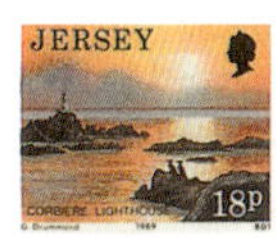

449 Corbière Lighthouse

450 Val de la Mare

451 Elizabeth Castle

452 Greve de Lecq

453 Samarès Manor

454 Bonne Nuit Harbour

455 Grosnez Castle

456 Augrès Manor

457 Central Market

458 St. Brelades Bay

459 St. Ouen's Manor

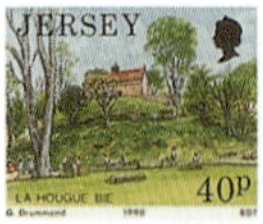

460 La Hougue Bie

461 Mont Orgueil Castle

462 Royal Square, St. Helier

463 Queen Elizabeth II (from photo by Karsh)

464 Arms of King George VI

Jersey Scenes

(Des G. Drummond (1p. to 75p.). Photo Courvoisier (£2), Litho Questa (£4), B.D.T. (others))

1989 (21 Mar)–**95**. Perf 11½×12 (£2), 15×14 (£4) or 13×13½ (others), all comb.

468	**439**	1p. multicoloured (a)	10	10
469	**440**	2p. multicoloured (a)	10	10
470	**441**	4p. multicoloured (a)	10	10
		a. Booklet pane of 6 with margins all round (d)	60	
471	**442**	5p. multicoloured (a)	10	15
		a. Booklet pane of 6 with margins all round (f)	75	
472	**443**	10p. multicoloured (a)	30	30
473	**444**	13p. multicoloured (a)	40	45
474	**445**	14p. multicoloured (ae)	40	45
		a. Booklet pane of 6 with margins all round (d)	2·00	
		b. Booklet pane of 8 with margins all round (i)	2·75	
475	**446**	15p. multicoloured (ae)	45	50
		a. Booklet pane of 6 with margins all round (f)	2·00	
476	**447**	16p. multicoloured (ah)	50	55
		a. Booklet pane of 8 with margins all round (i)	3·50	
477	**448**	17p. multicoloured (aj)	50	55
478	**449**	18p. multicoloured (akm)	55	60
		a. Booklet pane of 6 with margins all round (d)	2·50	
479	**450**	19p. multicoloured (ano)	55	60
480	**451**	20p. multicoloured (ae)	45	45
		a. Booklet pane of 6 with margins all round (f)	3·00	
481	**452**	21p. multicoloured (b)	50	55
482	**453**	22p. multicoloured (bh)	45	50
		a. Booklet pane of 8 with margins all round (i)	4·50	
483	**454**	23p. multicoloured (bjkmo)	75	55
484	**455**	24p. multicoloured (b)	60	60
485	**456**	25p. multicoloured (b)	70	75
486	**457**	26p. multicoloured (bh)	75	80
487	**458**	27p. multicoloured (b)	80	90
488	**459**	30p. multicoloured (c)	85	90
489	**460**	40p. multicoloured (c)	1·00	1·00
490	**461**	50p. multicoloured (c)	1·20	1·40
491	**462**	75p. multicoloured (c)	2·00	1·50
491*b*	**463**	£2 multicoloured (g)	4·00	3·25
491*c*	**464**	£4 multicoloured (l)	7·00	6·75
468/91*c* *Set of 26*			22·00	22·00
First Day Covers (5)				28·00
Presentation Packs (5)			27·00	

For £1 value as No. 491b see No. 389.

Printings: (a) 21.3.89; (b) 16.1.90; (c). 13.3.90; (d) 3.5.90; (e) 13.11.90; (f) 12.2.91; (g) 19.3.91; (h) 7.1.92; (i) 22.5.92; (j) 11.1.93; (k) 18.2.94; (l) 24.1.95; (m) 21.3.95; (n) 1.9.95; (o) 12.11.96.

Cylinder or Plate Nos.: £2 A1, B1, C1, D1 (each ×6); £4 1A (×5); others 1A, 1B, 1C, 1D., 1E, 1F (each ×4).

Sheets: £2 20 (4×5); £4 10 (5×2); others 50 (5×10).

Imprint: Left-hand corner, bottom margin (£4) or central, left-hand margin (others).

Withdrawn: 31.3.99 1p. to £2.

465 Agile Frog

466 *Heteropterus morpheus* (butterfly)

467 Barn Owl

468 Green Lizard

Endangered Jersey Fauna

(Des W. Oliver. Litho Cartor)

1989 (25 Apr). Perf 13½×13 (Nos. 492 and 495), 13×13½ (No. 493) or 13½×14 (No. 494), all comb.

492	**465**	13p. multicoloured	80	85
493	**466**	13p. multicoloured	80	85
494	**467**	17p. multicoloured	80	85
495	**468**	17p. multicoloured	80	85
492/5 *Set of 4*			2·75	3·00
First Day Cover				4·00
Presentation Pack			3·75	

Plate Nos.: All designs 1A, 1B, 1C, 1D. (each ×5).

Sheets: 20 (4×5) Nos. 492 and 495; (5×4) Nos. 493/4.

Imprint: Central, left-hand margin.

Quantities sold: 13p. (No. 492) 650,061; 13p. (No. 493) 589,329; 17p. (No. 494) 552,582; 17p. (No. 495) 515,262.

Withdrawn: 30.4.90.

469 Toddlers' Toys

470 Playground Games

471 Party Games

472 Teenage Sports

Europa. Children's Toys and Games

(Des from clay plaques by Clare Luke. Litho Questa)

1989 (25 Apr). Perf 14 (c).

496	**469**	17p. multicoloured	45	45
497	**470**	17p. multicoloured	45	45
498	**471**	23p. multicoloured	80	80
499	**472**	23p. multicoloured	80	80
496/9 *Set of 4*			2·20	2·20
First Day Cover				2·50
Presentation Pack			2·75	

Plate Nos.: All designs 1A, 1B, 1C, 1D., 1E, 1F (each ×4).

Sheets: 20 (4×5).

Imprint: Central, left-hand margin.

Quantities sold: 17p. (No. 496) 473,930; 17p. (No. 497) 471,124; 23p. (No. 498) 424,212; 23p. (No. 499) 424,340.

Withdrawn: 30.4.90.

473 Queen Elizabeth II and Royal Yacht *Britannia* in Elizabeth Harbour

Royal Visit

(Des A. Copp. Litho Questa)

1989 (24 May). Perf 14½ (c).

500	**473**	£1 multicoloured	2·50	2·50
First Day Cover				3·00
Presentation Pack			3·00	

No. 500 was retained in use as part of the current definitive series until replaced by No. 634.

Sheets: 20 (4×5).
Imprint: Central, left-hand margin.
Withdrawn: 30.6.94.

474 Philippe d'Auvergne presented to Louis XVI, 1786

475 Storming the Bastille, 1789

476 Marie de Boullion and Revolutionaries, 1790

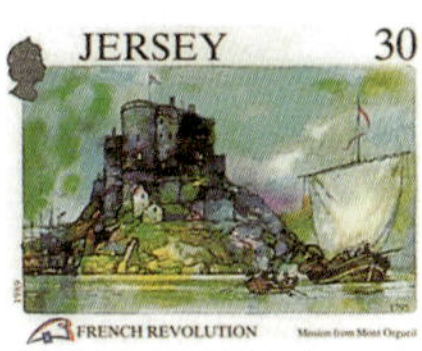

477 D'Auvergne's Headquarters at Mont Orgueil, 1795

478 Landing Arms for Chouan Rebels, 1796

479 The Last Chouan Revolt, 1799

Bicentenary of the French Revolution. Philippe D'Auvergne

(Des V. Ambrus. Litho Cartor)

1989 (7 July). Perf 13½ (c).

501	**474**	13p. multicoloured	40	30
		a. Booklet pane of 4	1·20	
502	**475**	17p. multicoloured	50	40
		a. Booklet pane of 4	2·00	
503	**476**	23p. multicoloured	60	50
		a. Booklet pane of 4	2·20	
504	**477**	30p. multicoloured	95	1·00
		a. Booklet pane of 4	3·75	
505	**478**	32p. multicoloured	1·00	1·10
		a. Booklet pane of 4	4·00	
506	**479**	35p. multicoloured	1·20	1·30
		a. Booklet pane of 4	5·00	
501/6 *Set of 6*			4·25	4·00
First Day Cover				4·25
Presentation Pack			4·50	

Each booklet pane has margins all round and text printed on the binding selvedge.

See also Nos. 539/44.

Plate Nos.: All values 1A, 1B, 1C, 1D. (each ×4).
Sheets: 20 (5×4).
Imprint: Central, left-hand margin.
Quantities sold: 13p. 637,422; 17p. 840,904; 23p. 408,967; 30p. 133,642; 32p. 148,474; 35p. 151,639.
Withdrawn: 31.7.90.

480 *St. Helier* off Elizabeth Castle

481 *Caesarea II* off Corbière Lighthouse

482 *Reindeer* in St. Helier Harbour

483 *Ibex* racing *Frederica* off Portelet

484 *Lynx* off Noirmont

Centenary of Great Western Railway Steamer Service to Channel Islands

(Des G. Palmer. Litho Questa)

1989 (5 Sept). Perf 13½×14 (c).

507	**480**	13p. multicoloured	30	30
508	**481**	17p. multicoloured	35	35
509	**482**	27p. multicoloured	80	80
510	**483**	32p. multicoloured	95	95
511	**484**	35p. multicoloured	1·10	1·10
507/11 *Set of 5*			3·00	3·00
First Day Cover				3·50
Presentation Pack			3·75	

Plate Nos.: 13p., 27p. 1A, 1B (each×4); 17p., 32p. 1C, 1D. (each ×4); 35p. 1A, 1B, 1C, 1D. (each ×4).
Sheets: 20 (4×5).
Imprint: Central, left-hand margin.
Quantities sold: 13p. 265,382; 17p. 294,992; 27p. 135,226; 32p. 128,966; 35p. 134,800.
Withdrawn: 28.9.90.

485 Gorey Harbour

486 La Corbiere

487 Grève de Lecq

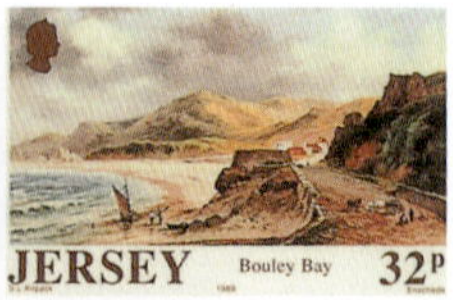

488 Bouley Bay

489 Mont Orgueil

150th Birth Anniversary of Sarah Louisa Kilpack (artist)

(Litho Enschedé)

1989 (24 Oct). Perf 13×12½ (c).

512	**485**	13p. multicoloured	25	25
513	**486**	17p. multicoloured	30	30
514	**487**	23p. multicoloured	80	75
515	**488**	32p. multicoloured	85	85
516	**489**	35p. multicoloured	90	1·00
512/16 *Set of 5*			2·75	2·75
First Day Cover				3·25
Presentation Pack			4·00	

Plate Nos.: 13p., 17p., 1A, 1B, 1C (each ×5); 23p., 32p., 35p. 1A, 1B (each ×5).
Sheets: 20 (4×5).
Imprint: Central, left-hand margin.
Quantities sold: 13p. 649,308; 17p. 571,503; 23p. 159,487; 32p. 138,562; 35p. 137,950.
Withdrawn: 31.10.90.

Post Office Yearbook

1989 (24 Oct). Comprises Nos. 462/80 and 492/516.
Yearbook .... 37·00
Sold out: 12.11.90.

490 Head Post Office, Broad Street, 1969

491 Postal Headquarters, Mont Millais, 1990

492 Hue Street Post Office, 1815

493 Head Post Office, Halkett Place, 1890

Europa. Post Office Buildings

(Des P. Layton. Litho Cartor)

1990 (13 Mar). Perf 13½×14 (vert) or 14×13½ (horiz), both comb.

517	**490**	18p. multicoloured	50	40
518	**491**	18p. multicoloured	50	50
519	**492**	24p. multicoloured	65	65
520	**493**	24p. multicoloured	65	65
517/20 *Set of 4*			2·10	2·00
First Day Cover				2·50
Presentation Pack			3·00	

Plate Nos.: All designs 1A, 1B, 1C, 1D. (each ×5).
Sheets: 20 (5×4) 18p.; (4×5) 24p.
Imprint: Central, left-hand margin.
Quantities sold: 18p. (No. 517) 596,221; 18p. (No. 518) 595,918; 24p. (No. 519) 400,441; 24p. (No. 520) 406,656.
Withdrawn: 31.3.91.

494 'Battle of Flowers' Parade

495 Sports

496 Mont Orgueil Castle and German Underground Hospital Museum

497 Salon Culinaire

Festival of Tourism

(Des A. Copp. Litho Enschedé)

1990 (3 May). Perf 14×13½ (c).

521	**494**	18p. multicoloured	55	55
522	**495**	24p. multicoloured	70	70
523	**496**	29p. multicoloured	85	85
524	**497**	32p. multicoloured	90	90
521/4 *Set of 4*			2·75	2·75
First Day Cover				3·25
Presentation Pack			4·00	
MS525 151×100 mm. Nos. 521/4			2·75	3·00
First Day Cover				6·50
Presentation Pack			4·50	

Plate Nos.: 18p. 1A, 1B, 1C, 1D., 1E (each ×5); 24p. 1A, 1B, 1C, 1D. (each ×5); 29p. 1A (×5); 32p. 1A, 1B (each ×5).
Sheets: 20 (5×4).
Imprint: Central, left-hand margin.
Quantities sold: 18p. 630,610; 24p. 252,670; 29p. 168,528; 32p. 127,334; miniature sheet 110,177.
Withdrawn: 31.5.91.

498 Early Printing Press and Jersey Newspaper Mastheads

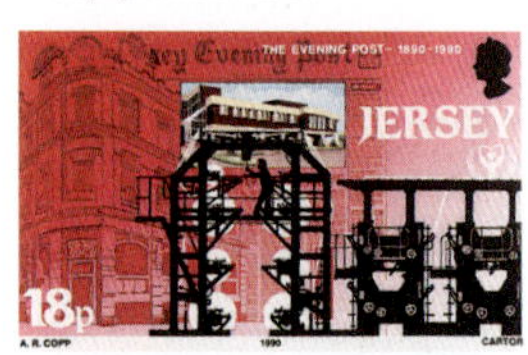

499 Modern Press, and Offices of *Jersey Evening Post* in 1890 and 1990

500 Radio Jersey Broadcaster

501 Channel Television Studio Cameraman

International Literacy Year. Jersey News Media

(Des A. Copp. Litho Cartor)

1990 (26 June). Perf 13½ (c).

526	**498**	14p. multicoloured	45	45
527	**499**	18p. multicoloured	45	45
528	**500**	34p. multicoloured	90	90
529	**501**	37p. multicoloured	95	95
526/9 *Set of 4*			2·50	2·50
First Day Cover				2·75
Presentation Pack			3·50	

Plate Nos.: All values 1A, 1B, 1C, 1D. (each ×4).
Sheets: 20 (4×5).
Imprint: Central, left-hand margin.
Quantities sold: 14p. 926,906; 18p. 795,733; 34p. 121,842; 37p. 129,468.
Withdrawn: 30.6.91.

502 British Aerospace Hawk T.1

503 Supermarine Spitfire

504 Hawker Hurricane Mk I

505 Vickers-Armstrong Wellington

506 Avro Lancaster

50th Anniversary of Battle of Britain

(Des G. Palmer. Litho Questa)

1990 (4 Sept). Perf 14 (c).

530	**502**	14p. multicoloured	40	45
531	**503**	18p. multicoloured	55	60
532	**504**	24p. multicoloured	85	85
533	**505**	34p. multicoloured	1·50	1·60
534	**506**	37p. multicoloured	1·60	1·60
530/4 *Set of 5*			4·50	4·50
First Day Cover				5·25
Presentation Pack			5·25	

Plate Nos.: 14p., 34p. 1A, 1B (each ×5); 18p., 37p. 1C, 1D. (each ×5); 24p. 1A, 1B, 1C, 1D. (each ×5).
Sheets: 20 (4×5).
Imprint: Central, left-hand margin.
Quantities sold: 14p. 495,815; 18p. 519,684; 24p. 206,541; 34p. 136,330; 37p. 134,747.
Withdrawn: 30.9.91.

507 St. Helier

508 Grouville

509 St. Saviour

510 St. John

Christmas. Jersey Parish Churches (2nd series)

(Des P. Layton. Litho B.D.T.)

1990 (13 Nov). Perf 13½ (c).

535	**507**	14p. multicoloured	45	40
536	**508**	18p. multicoloured	45	40
		a. deep blue-green (Queen's head, value and 'JERSEY') omitted	£1500	
537	**509**	34p. multicoloured	1·00	1·10
538	**510**	37p. multicoloured	1·20	1·40
535/8 *Set of 4*			3·00	3·00
First Day Cover				3·50
Presentation Pack			4·00	
Postcards (set of 4)			2·20	5·00

Plate Nos.: All values 1A, 1B, 1C, 1D. (each ×5).
Sheets: 20 (4×5).
Imprint: Central, left-hand margin.
Quantities sold: 14p. 948,076; 18p. 690,282; 34p. 141,514; 37p. 147,768.
Withdrawn: 30.11.91.

Post Office Yearbook

1990 (13 Nov). Comprises Nos. 481/91 and 517/38.

Yearbook	35·00

Withdrawn: 30.11.91.

511 Prince's Tower, La Hougue Bie

512 D'Auvergne's Arrest in Paris

513 D'Auvergne plotting against Napoleon

514 Execution of George Cadoudal

515 H.M.S. *Surly* (cutter) attacking French Convoy

516 D'Auvergne's Last Days in London

175th Death Anniversary of Philippe D'Auvergne

(Des V. Ambrus. Litho Cartor)

1991 (22 Jan). Perf 13½ (c).

539	**511**	15p. multicoloured	45	40
540	**512**	20p. multicoloured	55	55
541	**513**	26p. multicoloured	70	75
542	**514**	31p. multicoloured	90	90
543	**515**	37p. multicoloured	1·10	1·10
544	**516**	44p. multicoloured	1·20	1·20
539/44 *Set of 6*			4·50	4·50
First Day Cover				4·75
Presentation Pack			5·00	

Plate Nos.: All values 1A, 1B, 1C, 1D. (each ×4).
Sheets: 20 (4×5).
Imprint: Central, left-hand margin.

Quantities sold: 15p. 709,403; 20p. 454,921; 26p. 159,902; 31p. 140,379; 37p. 341,103; 44p. 153,157.
Withdrawn: 31.1.92.

517 'Landsat 5' and Thematic Mapper Image over Jersey

518 'ERS-1' Earth Resources Remote Sensing Satellite

519 'Meteosat' Weather Satellite

520 'Olympus' Direct Broadcasting Satellite

Europa. Europe in Space

(Des A. Copp. Litho Enschedé)

1991 (19 Mar). Perf 14½×13 (c).

545	**517**	20p. multicoloured	50	50
546	**518**	20p. multicoloured	50	50
547	**519**	26p. multicoloured	80	85
548	**520**	26p. multicoloured	80	85
545/8 *Set of 4*			2·40	2·40
First Day Cover				2·75
Presentation Pack			3·00	

Plate Nos.: All designs 1A, 1B, 1C (each ×5).
Sheets: 20 (5×4).
Imprint: Central, left-hand margin.
Quantities sold: 20p. (No. 545) 682,799; 20p. (No. 546) 690,871; 26p. (No. 547) 442,476; 26p. (No. 548) 439,415.
Withdrawn: 31.3.92.

521 1941 1d. Stamp (50th anniv of first Jersey postage stamp)

522 Steam Train (centenary of Jersey Eastern Railway extension to Gorey Pier)

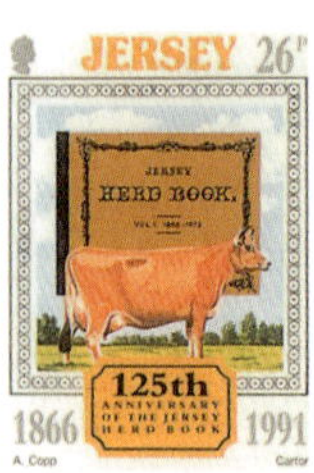

523 jersey Cow and Herd Book (125th anniv of Jersey Herd Book)

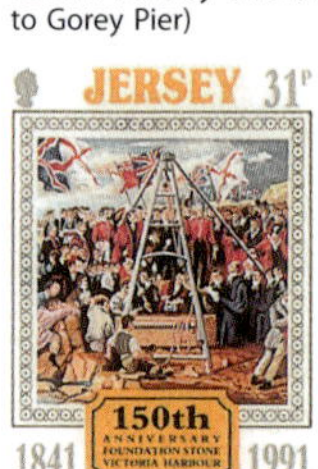

524 Stone-laying Ceremony (painting by P. Ouless) (150th anniv of Victoria Harbour)

525 Marie Bartlett and Hospital (250th anniversary of Marie Bartlett's hospital bequest)

Anniversaries

(Des A. Copp. Litho Cartor)

1991 (16 May). Perf 13½ (c).

549	**521**	15p. multicoloured	30	30
550	**522**	20p. multicoloured	50	55
551	**523**	26p. multicoloured	60	70
552	**524**	31p. multicoloured	75	80
553	**525**	53p. multicoloured	1·70	1·70
549/53 *Set of 5*			3·50	3·75
First Day Cover				4·25
Presentation Pack			4·50	

Plate Nos.: All values 1A, 1B, 1C, 1D. (each ×4).
Sheets: 20 (5×4).
Imprint: Central, left-hand margin.
Quantities sold: 15p. 618,479; 20p. 608,585; 26p. 245,772; 31p. 133,604; 53p. 135,394.
Withdrawn: 30.5.92.

526 *Melitaea cinxia*

527 *Euplagia quadripunctaria*

528 *Deilephila porcellus*

529 *Inachis io*

Butterflies and Moths

(Des W. Oliver. Litho Enschedé)

1991 (9 July). Perf 13×12½ (c).

554	**526**	15p. multicoloured	35	35
555	**527**	20p. multicoloured	45	30
556	**528**	37p. multicoloured	1·40	1·50
557	**529**	57p. multicoloured	1·70	1·90
554/7 *Set of 4*			3·50	3·75
First Day Cover				4·50
Presentation Pack			4·50	

Plate Nos.: All values 1A, 1B, 1C (each ×4).
Sheets: 20 (4×5).
Imprint: Central, left-hand margin.
Quantities sold: 15p. 489,632; 20p. 646,607; 37p. 130,494; 57p. 142,646.
Withdrawn: 31.7.92.

530 Drilling for Water, Ethiopia

531 Building Construction, Rwanda

532 Village Polytechnic, Kenya

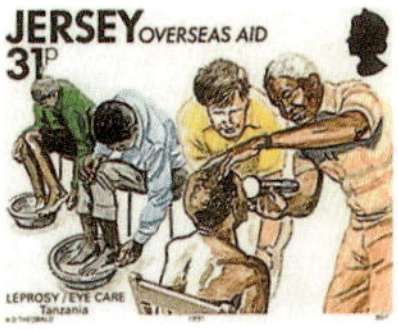

533 Treating Leprosy, Tanzania

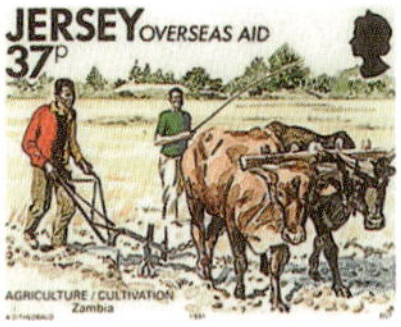

534 Ploughing, Zambia

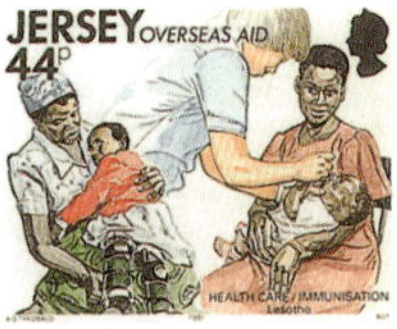

535 Immunisation Clinic, Lesotho

Overseas Aid

(Des A. Theobald. Litho B.D.T.)

1991 (3 Sept). Perf 13½×14 (c).

558	**530**	15p. multicoloured	45	40
559	**531**	20p. multicoloured	50	45
560	**532**	26p. multicoloured	70	70
561	**533**	31p. multicoloured	85	90
562	**534**	37p. multicoloured	1·10	1·10
563	**535**	44p. multicoloured	1·20	1·40
558/63 *Set of 6*			4·50	4·50
First Day Cover				5·00
Presentation Pack			5·00	

Plate Nos.: All values 1A, 1B (each ×4).
Sheets: 20 (4×5).
Imprint: Central, left-hand margin.
Quantities sold: 15p. 517,917; 20p. 644,721; 26p. 177,179; 31p. 115,769; 37p. 111,112; 44p. 142,024.
Withdrawn: 30.9.92.

536 'This is the Place for Me'

537 'The Island Come True'

538 'The Never Bird'

539 'The Great White Father'

Christmas. Illustrations by Edmund Blampied for J. M. Barrie's 'Peter Pan'

(Litho Questa)

1991 (5 Nov). Perf 14 (c).

564	**536**	15p. multicoloured	40	40
565	**537**	20p. multicoloured	65	65
566	**538**	37p. multicoloured	1·20	1·20
567	**539**	53p. multicoloured	1·60	1·60
564/7 *Set of 4*			3·50	3·50
First Day Cover				4·00
Presentation Pack			4·50	

Sheets: 20 (5×4).
Imprint: Central, left-hand margin.
Quantities sold: 15p. 917,860; 20p. 693,203; 37p. 128,585; 53p. 117,877.
Withdrawn: 30.11.92.

Post Office Yearbook

1991 (5 Nov). Comprises Nos. 491*b* and 539/67.
Yearbook .... 32·00
Sold out: By 9.93.

540 Pied Wagtail

541 Firecrest

542 Common Snipe

543 Northern Lapwing

544 Fieldfare

Winter Birds

(Des W. Oliver. Litho Cartor)

1992 (7 Jan). Perf 13½×14 (c).

568	**540**	16p. multicoloured	50	25
569	**541**	22p. multicoloured	70	55
570	**542**	28p. multicoloured	80	85
571	**543**	39p. multicoloured	1·20	1·20
572	**544**	57p. multicoloured	1·70	1·70
568/72 *Set of 5*			4·50	4·25
First Day Cover				5·25
Presentation Pack			5·50	

See also Nos. 635/9.
Plate Nos.: All values 1A, 1B, 1C, 1D. (each ×4).
Sheets: 20 (5×4).
Imprint: Central, left-hand margin.
Quantities sold: 16p. 481,678; 22p. 462,647; 28p. 268,973; 39p. 151,671; 57p. 132,065.
Withdrawn: 30.1.93.

545 Shipping at Shanghai, 1860

546 Mesny's Junk running Taiping Blockade, 1862

547 General Mesny outside River Gate, 1874

548 Mesny in Burma, 1877

549 Mesny and Governor Chang, 1882

550 Mesny in Mandarin's Sedan Chair, 1886

Jersey Adventures (3rd series). 150th Birth Anniversary of William Mesny

(Des V. Ambrus. Litho Cartor)

1992 (25 Feb). Perf 13½ (c).

573	**545**	16p. multicoloured	40	45
		a. Black printed double		
		b. Booklet pane of 4	1·50	
574	**546**	16p. multicoloured	40	45
		a. Booklet pane of 4	1·50	
575	**547**	22p. multicoloured	65	65
		a. Booklet pane of 4	2·00	
576	**548**	22p. multicoloured	65	65
		a. Booklet pane of 4	2·00	
577	**549**	33p. multicoloured	90	95
		a. Booklet pane of 4	3·00	
578	**550**	33p. multicoloured	90	95
		a. Booklet pane of 4	3·00	
573/8 *Set of 6*			3·50	3·75
First Day Cover				4·25
Presentation Pack			4·50	

Each booklet pane has margins all round and text printed on the binding selvedge.

Plate Nos.: All values 1A, 1B, 1C, 1D. (each ×4).
Sheets: 20 (4×5).
Imprint: Central, left-hand margin.
Quantities sold: 16p. (No. 573) 346,732; 16p. (No. 574) 336,655; 22p. (No. 575) 377,299; 22p. (No. 576) 360,220; 33p. (No. 577) 129,904; 33p. (No. 578) 130,637.
Withdrawn: 27.2.93 (sheets).

551 *Tickler* (brigantine)

552 *Hebe* (brig)

553 *Gemini* (barque)

554 *Percy Douglas* (full-rigged ship)

Jersey Shipbuilding

(Des A. Copp. Litho Questa)(sheets)

1992 (14 Apr). Perf 14 (c).

579	**551**	16p. multicoloured	45	40
580	**552**	22p. multicoloured	70	75
581	**553**	50p. multicoloured	1·40	1·50
582	**554**	57p. multicoloured	1·60	1·70
579/82 *Set of 4*			3·75	4·00
First Day Cover				4·50
Presentation Pack			4·50	
MS583 148×98 mm. Nos. 579/82			4·00	4·25
First Day Cover				4·50
Presentation Pack			4·50	

Plate Nos.: 16p. 1A, 1B, 1C, 1D., 1E, 1F (each ×4); 22p., 57p. 1A, 1B, 1C, 1D. (each ×4); 50p. 1A, 1B (each ×4).
Sheets: 20 (5×4).
Imprint: Central, left-hand margin.
Quantities sold: 16p. 673,830; 22p. 462,972; 50p. 138,158; 57p. 111,044; miniature sheet 126,594.
Withdrawn: 30.4.93.

555 John Bertram (ship owner) and Columbus

556 Sir George Carteret (founder of New Jersey)

557 Sir Walter Ralegh (founder of Virginia)

Europa. 500th Anniversary of Discovery of America by Columbus

(Des V. Ambrus. Litho Questa)

1992 (14 Apr). Perf 14×14½ (c).

584	**555**	22p. multicoloured	65	50
585	**556**	28p. multicoloured	75	80
586	**557**	39p. multicoloured	1·10	1·40
584/6 *Set of 3*			2·20	2·40
First Day Cover				3·00
Presentation Pack			3·25	

Plate Nos.: 22p. 1A, 1B (each ×5); 28p. 1A, 1B, 1C, 1D. (each×5); 39p. 1C, 1D. (each ×5).
Sheets: 20 (4×5).
Imprint: Central, left-hand margin.
Quantities sold: 22p. 459,817; 28p. 664,537; 39p. 298,597.
Withdrawn: 30.4.93.

558 'Snow Leopards' (Allison Griffiths)

559 'Three Elements' (Nataly Miorin)

560 'Three Men in a Tub' (Amanda Crocker)

561 'Cockatoos' (Michelle Millard)

Batik Designs

(Litho Questa)

1992 (23 June). Perf 14½ (c).

587	**558**	16p. multicoloured	45	40
588	**559**	22p. multicoloured	65	45
589	**560**	39p. multicoloured	1·10	1·20
590	**561**	57p. multicoloured	1·50	1·70
587/90 *Set of 4*			3·25	3·50
First Day Cover				4·00
Presentation Pack			4·25	

Plate Nos.: 16p., 39p. 1A, 1B (each ×4); 22p., 57p. 1C, 1D. (each ×4).
Sheets: 20 (5×4).
Imprint: Central, left-hand margin.
Quantities sold: 16p. 427,970; 22p. 472,443; 39p. 112,188; 57p. 113,465.
Withdrawn: 30.6.93.

562 Morris Cowley 'Bullnose', 1925

563 Rolls-Royce 20/25, 1932

564 Chenard and Walcker T5, 1924

565 Packard 900, series Light Eight, 1932

566 Lanchester 21, 1927

567 Buick 30 Roadster, 1913

Vintage Cars (2nd series)

(Des A. Copp. Litho Enschedè)

1992 (8 Sept). Perf 13×12½ (c).

591	**562**	16p. multicoloured	30	30
592	**563**	22p. multicoloured	45	45
593	**564**	28p. multicoloured	70	75
594	**565**	33p. multicoloured	90	95
595	**566**	39p. multicoloured	1·00	1·10
596	**567**	50p. multicoloured	1·50	1·70
591/6 *Set of 6*			4·50	4·75
First Day Cover				5·00
Presentation Pack			5·25	

Plate Nos.: All values 1A, 1B (each ×4).
Sheets: 20 (4×5).
Imprint: Central, left-hand margin.
Quantities sold: 16p. 434,984; 22p. 426,734; 28p. 290,202; 33p. 134,477; 39p. 124,759; 50p. 127,917.
Withdrawn: 30.9.93.

568 Trinity

569 St. Mary

570 St. Martin

571 St. Peter

Christmas. Jersey Parish Churches (3rd series)

(Des P. Layton. Litho B.D.T.)

1992 (3 Nov). Perf 13½ (c).

597	**568**	16p. multicoloured	40	30
598	**569**	22p. multicoloured	55	50
599	**570**	39p. multicoloured	1·10	1·10
600	**571**	57p. multicoloured	1·50	1·50
597/600 *Set of 4*			3·25	3·25
First Day Cover				3·75
Presentation Pack			4·00	
Postcards (set of 4)			2·00	5·00

Plate Nos.: All values 1A, 1B, 1C, 1D. (each ×5).
Sheets: 20 (4×5).
Imprint: Central, left-hand margin.
Quantities sold: 16p. 894,098; 22p. 729,413; 39p. 93,764; 57p. 95,936.
Withdrawn: 30.11.93.

Post Office Yearbook

1992 (3 Nov). Comprises Nos. 568/600.

Yearbook	32·00	

Sold out: By 10.95.

572 Farmhouse

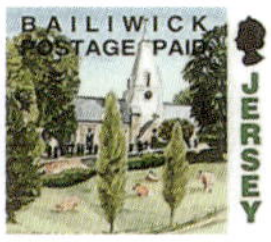

573 Trinity Church

574 Daffodils and Cows

575 Jersey Cows

576 Sunbathing

577 Windsurfing

578 Crab (Queen's head at left)

579 Crab (Queen's head at right)

580 'Singin' in the Rain' Float

581 'Dragon Dance Float

582 'Bali, Morning of the world' Float

583 'Zulu Fantasy' Float

Booklet Stamps

(Des A. Copp. Litho B.D.T.)

1993 (11 Jan). Perf 13 (c).

601	**572**	17p. multicoloured	60	70
		a. Booklet pane. Nos. 601/4, each ×2, with margins all round	5·00	
602	**573**	17p. multicoloured	60	70
603	**574**	17p. multicoloured	60	70
604	**575**	17p. multicoloured	60	70
605	**576**	23p. multicoloured	70	60
		a. Booklet pane. Nos. 605/8, each ×2, with margins all round	5·50	
606	**577**	23p. multicoloured	70	60
607	**578**	23p. multicoloured	70	60
608	**579**	23p. multicoloured	70	60
609	**580**	28p. multicoloured	85	80
		a. Booklet pane. Nos. 609/12, each ×2, with margins all round	7·00	
610	**581**	28p. multicoloured	85	80
611	**582**	28p. multicoloured	85	80
612	**583**	28p. multicoloured	85	80
601/12 *Set of 12*			7·75	7·50
First Day Cover				16·00
Presentation Pack			10·00	

The above do not show face values, but are inscribed 'BAILIWICK POSTAGE PAID' (Nos. 601/4), 'U.K. MINIMUM POSTAGE PAID' (Nos. 605/8) or 'EUROPE POSTAGE PAID' (Nos. 609/12). They were initially sold at 17p., 23p. or 28p., but Nos. 601/4 and 609/12 were increased to 18p. and 30p. on 10 January 1994 and Nos. 601/4 to 19p. on 4 July 1995. On 10 March 1997 Nos. 601/4 were increased to 20p., Nos. 605/8 to 24p. and Nos. 609/12 to 31p.
Withdrawn: 30.9.99.

584 *Phragmipedium* Eric Young 'Jersey'

585 *Odontoglossum* Augres 'Trinity'

586 *Miltonia* St. Helier 'Colomberie',

587 *Phragmipedium pearcei*

588 *Calanthe* Grouville 'Gorey'

Jersey Orchids (3rd series)

(Litho Enschedé)

1993 (26 Jan). Perf 14×13 (c).

613	**584**	17p. multicoloured	45	35
		a. Black printed double		
614	**585**	23p. multicoloured	70	65
		a. Black printed double		
615	**586**	28p. multicoloured	80	75
		a. Black printed double		
616	**587**	39p. multicoloured	1·20	1·40
617	**588**	57p. multicoloured	1·70	1·90
		a. Black printed double		
613/17 *Set of 5*			4·50	4·50
First Day Cover				5·00
Presentation Pack			5·25	

Plate Nos.: 17p., 23p. 1A, 1B, 1C (each ×5); 28p., 39p., 57p. 1A, 1B (each ×5).
Sheets: 20 (5×4).
Imprint: Central, left-hand margin.
Quantities sold: 17p. 391,802; 23p. 391,444; 28p. 188,149; 39p. 141,610; 57p. 141,463.
Withdrawn: 31.1.94.

589 Douglas Dakota

590 Wight Seaplane

591 Avro Shackleton A.E.W.2

592 Gloster Meteor Mk III and De Havilland D.H.100 Vampire FB.5

593 BAe Harrier GR.1A

594 Panavia Tornado F.3

75th Anniversary of Royal Air Force

(Des A. Theobald. Litho Questa)

1993 (1 Apr). Perf 14 (c).

618	**589**	17p. multicoloured	45	30
619	**590**	23p. multicoloured	60	65
620	**591**	28p. multicoloured	70	70
621	**592**	33p. multicoloured	80	85
622	**593**	39p. multicoloured	1·00	1·10
623	**594**	57p. multicoloured	1·50	1·60
618/23 *Set of 6*			4·50	4·75
First Day Cover				6·00
Presentation Pack			5·25	
MS624 147×98 mm. Nos. 619 and 623			4·50	4·75
First Day Cover				6·00
Presentation Pack			5·25	

Nos. 618/24 also commemorate the 50th anniversary of the Royal Air Force Association and the 40th anniversary of the first air display on Jersey.

Plate Nos.: 17p., 23p. 1A, 1B, 1C, 1D. (each ×4); 28p., 33p., 39p., 57p. 1A, 1B (each ×4).
Sheets: 20 (5×4).
Imprint: Central, left-hand margin.
Quantities sold: 17p., 578,871; 23p. 581,661; 28p. 184,066; 33p. 140,430; 39p. 144,522; 57p. 159,447; miniature sheet 113,236.
Withdrawn: 30.4.94.

595 'Jersey's Opera House' (Ian Rolls)

596 'The Ham and Tomato Bap' (Jonathan Hubbard)

597 'Vase of Flowers' (Neil Mackenzie)

Europa. Contemporary Art

(Litho Cartor)

1993 (1 Apr). Perf 13½×14 (c).

625	**595**	23p. multicoloured	60	60
626	**596**	28p. multicoloured	70	70
627	**597**	39p. multicoloured	1·10	1·10
625/7 *Set of 3*			2·20	2·20

First Day Cover				2·75
Presentation Pack			2·75	

Plate Nos.: All values 1A, 1B, 1C, 1D. (each ×4).
Sheets: 20 (5×4).
Imprint: Central, left-hand margin.
Quantities sold: 23p. 422,536; 28p. 340,206; 39p. 230,510.
Withdrawn: 30.4.94.

598 1943 Occupation ½d. Stamp

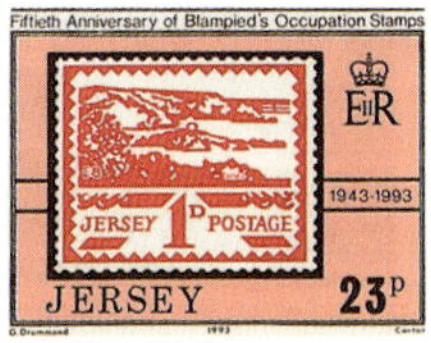

599 1943 1d. Stamp

600 1943 1½d. Stamp

601 1943 2d. Stamp

602 1943 2½d. Stamp

603 1943 3d. Stamp

50th Anniversary of Edmund Blampied's Occupation Stamps

(Des G. Drummond. Litho Cartor)

1993 (2 June). Perf 13½ (c).

628	**598**	17p. myrtle-green, pale grn & blk	35	35
629	**599**	23p. vermilion, salmon-pink & blk	50	50
630	**600**	28p. chocolate, cinnamon & black	70	70
631	**601**	33p. reddish orge, salmon & blk	85	85
632	**602**	39p. royal blue, cobalt and black	1·20	1·20
633	**603**	50p. bright magenta, pale mauve and black	1·40	1·40
628/33 *Set of 6*			4·50	4·50
First Day Cover				4·75
Presentation Pack			5·25	

Plate Nos.: All values 1A, 1B, 1C, 1D. (each×3).
Sheets: 20 (4×5).
Imprint: Central, left-hand margin.
Quantities sold: 17p. 549,708; 23p. 565,711; 28p. 174,159; 33p. 120,570; 39p. 93,502; 50p. 99,135.
Withdrawn: 30.6.94.

604 Queen Elizabeth II (from painting by Mara McGregor)

40th Anniversary of Coronation

(Litho Questa)

1993 (2 June). Perf 14½ (c).

634	**604**	£1 multicoloured (ab)	2·75	2·75
First Day Cover				3·00
Presentation Pack			3·50	

No. 634 was retained in use as part of the current definitive series until replaced by No. 804.

Printings: (a) 2.6.93; (b) 1.9.95.
Plate Nos.: 1A, 1B, 1C, 1D. (each ×4).
Sheets: 20 (5×4).
Imprint: Central, left-hand margin.
Withdrawn: 31.3.99 but used again by the Philatelic Bureau for a Millennium cover, issued 31.12.99.

605 Short-toed Treecreeper

606 Dartford Warbler

607 Northern Wheatear

608 Cirl Bunting

609 Jay

Summer Birds

(Des W. Oliver. Litho Cartor)

1993 (7 Sept). Perf 13½×14 (c).

635	**605**	17p. multicoloured	45	50
636	**606**	23p. multicoloured	70	75
637	**607**	28p. multicoloured	80	85
638	**608**	39p. multicoloured	1·20	1·20
639	**609**	57p. multicoloured	1·70	1·70
635/9 *Set of 5*			4·50	4·50
First Day Cover				5·25
Presentation Pack			5·00	

Plate Nos.: All values 1A, 1B, 1C, 1D. (each ×4).
Sheets: 20 (5×4).
Imprint: Central, left-hand margin.
Quantities sold: 17p. 495,975; 23p. 496,942; 28p. 170,135; 39p. 139,630; 57p. 138,994.
Withdrawn: 30.9.94.

610 Two Angels holding 'Hark the Herald Angels Sing' Banner

611 Two Angels playing Harps

612 Two Angels playing Violins

613 Two Angels holding 'Once in Royal David's City' Banner

Christmas. Stained Glass Windows by Henry Bosdet from St. Aubin on the Hill Church

(Des N. Mackenzie. Litho Enschedé)

1993 (2 Nov). Perf 14×13 (c).

640	**610**	17p. multicoloured	40	35
641	**611**	23p. multicoloured	60	60
642	**612**	39p. multicoloured	1·10	1·20
643	**613**	57p. multicoloured	1·70	1·90
640/3 *Set of 4*			3·50	3·75
First Day Cover				4·00
Presentation Pack			4·25	

Plate Nos.: All values 1A, 1B, 1C (each ×4).
Sheets: 20 (5×4).
Imprint: Central, left-hand margin.
Quantities sold: 17p. 877,806; 23p. 744,661; 39p. 110,131; 57p. 108,703.
Withdrawn: 30.11.94.

Post Office Yearbook

1993 (2 Nov). Comprises Nos. 601/43.

Yearbook	33·00

Sold out: By 9.97.

614 *Coprinus comatus*

615 Amanita muscaria

616 *Cantharellus cibarius*

617 *Macrolepiota procera*

618 *Clathrus ruber*

Fungi (1st series)

(Des W. Oliver. Litho Questa)

1994 (11 Jan). Perf 14½ (c).

644	**614**	18p. multicoloured	45	40
645	**615**	23p. multicoloured	65	70
646	**616**	30p. multicoloured	80	85
647	**617**	41p. multicoloured	1·20	1·20
648	**618**	60p. multicoloured	1·60	1·60
644/8 *Set of 5*			4·00	4·00
First Day Cover				4·25
Presentation Pack			4·50	

Plate Nos.: 18p. 1A (×4); 23p. 1B (×4); 30p. 1C (×4); 41p. 1D. (×4); 60p. 1E (×4).
Sheets: 20 (5×4).
Imprint: Central, left-hand margin.
Quantities sold: 18p. 735,158; 23p. 482,461; 30p. 188,095; 41p. 184,418; 60p. 137,309.
Withdrawn: 30.1.95.

619a Pekingnese (*Illustration reduced. Actual size* 110×75 *mm*)

' 'Hong Kong' 94' International Stamp Exhibition. Chinese Year of the Dog'

(Des P. Layton, adapted A. Copp. Litho Questa)

1994 (18 Feb). Sheet 110×75 mm. Perf 15×14½ (c).

MS649 **619a** multicoloured	2·50	2·75
First Day Cover		4·00
Presentation Pack	3·50	

Quantity sold: 120,029.
Withdrawn: 28.2.95.

620 Maine Coon

621 British Shorthair

622 Persian

623 Siamese

624 Non-pedigree

21st Anniversary of Jersey Cat Club

(Des P. Layton. Litho B.D.T.)

1994 (5 Apr). Perf 14 (c).

650	**620**	18p. multicoloured	40	30
651	**621**	23p. multicoloured	60	50
652	**622**	35p. multicoloured	80	80
653	**623**	41p. multicoloured	1·00	1·20
654	**624**	60p. multicoloured	1·20	1·50
650/4 *Set of 5*			3·50	3·75
First Day Cover				4·50
Presentation Pack			4·50	

Plate Nos.: 35p. 1A, 1B, 1C, 1D. (each ×4); others 1A, 1B (each ×4).
Sheets: 20 (5×4) 18p., 35p., 60p.; (4×5) 23p., 41p.
Imprint: Central, left-hand margin.
Quantities sold: 18p. 491,500; 23p. 490,820; 35p. 221,769; 41p. 185,206; 60p. 132,276.
Withdrawn: 29.4.95.

625 Mammoth Hunt, La Cotte de St. Brelade

626 Stone Age Hunters pulling Mammoth into Cave

627 Chambered Passage, La Hougue Bie

628 Transporting Stones

Europa. Archaeological Discoveries

(Des A. Copp. Litho Enschedé)

1994 (5 Apr). Perf 13½×14 (c).

655	**625**	23p. multicoloured	50	55
		a. Horiz pair. Nos. 655/6	1·00	1·10
656	**626**	23p. multicoloured	50	55
657	**627**	30p. multicoloured	75	85
		a. Horiz pair. Nos. 657/8	1·50	1·70
658	**628**	30p. multicoloured	75	85
655/8 *Set of 4*			2·20	2·50
First Day Cover				3·00
Presentation Pack			3·00	

Plate Nos.: Both values 1A, 1B (each ×4).
Sheets: 20 (4×5) the two horizontal designs for each value printed together, *se-tenant*, in horizontal pairs throughout the sheets.
Imprint: Central, left-hand margin.
Quantities sold: No. 655, 371,149; No. 656, 373,190; No. 657, 273,889; No. 658, 275,833.
Withdrawn: 29.4.95.

629 Gliders and Towing Aircraft approaching France

630 Landing Craft approaching Beaches

631 Disembarking from Landing Craft on Gold Beach

632 British Troops on Sword Beach

633 Spitfires over Beaches

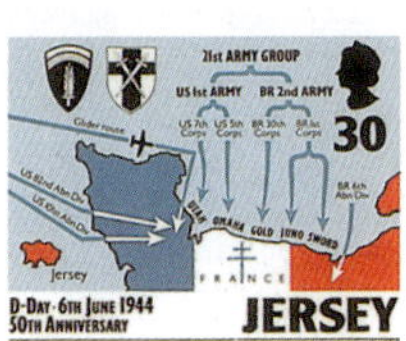

634 Invasion Map

50th Anniversary of D-Day

(Des A. Theobald. Litho B.D.T.)

1994 (6 June). Perf 13½×14 (c).

659	**629**	18p. multicoloured	55	50
		a. Booklet pane. Nos. 659/60, each ×3, with margins all round	3·00	
		b. Booklet pane. Nos. 659/64, with margins all round	4·50	
660	**630**	18p. multicoloured	55	50
661	**631**	23p. multicoloured	75	70
		a. Booklet pane. Nos. 661/2, each ×3, with margins all round	5·00	
662	**632**	23p. multicoloured	75	70
663	**633**	30p. multicoloured	80	75
		a. Booklet pane. Nos. 663/4, each ×3, with margins all round	5·00	
664	**634**	30p. multicoloured	80	75
659/64 *Set of 6*			3·75	3·50
First Day Cover				4·25
Presentation Pack			4·50	

No. 659b was also available as a loose pane (with no stitch holes) from the Philatelic Bureau.

Plate Nos.: All values 1A, 1B (each ×4).
Sheets: 20 (4×5).
Imprint: Central, left-hand margin.
Quantities sold: No. 659, 361,667; No. 660, 365,169; No. 661, 377,546; No. 662, 367,033; No. 663, 229,455; No. 664, 226,520.
Withdrawn: 30.6.95.

635 Sailing

636 Rifle Shooting

637 Hurdling

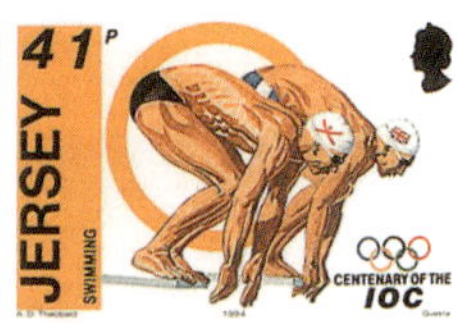

638 Swimming

639 Hockey

Centenary of International Olympic Committee

(Des A. Theobald. Litho Questa)

1994 (6 June). Perf 14 (c).

665	**635**	18p. multicoloured	40	35
666	**636**	23p. multicoloured	55	55
667	**637**	30p. multicoloured	75	75
668	**638**	41p. multicoloured	1·10	1·10
669	**639**	60p. multicoloured	1·50	1·60
665/9 *Set of 5*			4·00	4·00
First Day Cover				4·50
Presentation Pack			4·50	

Plate Nos.: All values 1A (×4).
Sheets: 20 (5×4).
Imprint: Central, left-hand margin.
Quantities sold: 18p. 279,163; 23p. 276,438; 30p. 178,234; 41p. 183,875; 60p. 133,357.
Withdrawn: 30.6.95.

640 Strawberry Anemone

641 Hermit Crab and Parasitic Anemone

642 Velvet Swimming Crab

643 Common Jellyfish

Marine Life

(Des W. Oliver. Litho Cartor)

1994 (2 Aug). Perf 13½ (c).

670	**640**	18p. multicoloured	40	45
671	**641**	23p. multicoloured	60	65
672	**642**	41p. multicoloured	1·20	1·40
673	**643**	60p. multicoloured	1·60	1·60
670/3 *Set of 4*			3·50	3·75
First Day Cover				4·25
Presentation Pack			4·50	

Plate Nos.: All values 1A, 1B, 1C, 1D. (each ×4).
Sheets: 20 (4×5).
Imprint: Central, left-hand margin.
Quantities sold: 18p. 465,890; 23p. 453,750; 41p. 171,459; 60p. 175,656.
Withdrawn: 31.8.95.

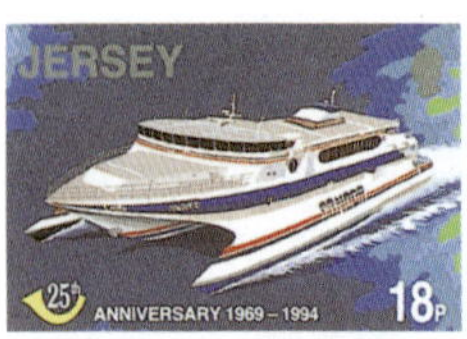

644 *Condor 10* (catamaran)

645 Map of Jersey and Pillar Box

646 Vicker's Type 953 Vanguard of B.E.A.

647 Short 360 of Aurigny Air Services

648 *Caesarea* (Sealink ferry)

25th Anniversary of Jersey Postal Administration

(Des A. Copp. Litho Questa)

1994 (1 Oct). Perf 14 (c).

674	**644**	18p. multicoloured	50	45
675	**645**	23p. multicoloured	60	50
676	**646**	35p. multicoloured	85	85
677	**647**	41p. multicoloured	1·10	1·00
678	**648**	60p. multicoloured	1·60	1·50
674/8 *Set of 5*			4·25	4·00
First Day Cover				4·50
Presentation Pack			5·00	
MS679 150×100 mm. Nos. 674/8			4·50	4·50
First Day Cover				5·25
Presentation Pack			4·75	

Plate Nos.: All values 1A (×5).
Sheets: 20 (5×4).
Imprint: Central, left-hand margin.
Quantities sold: 18p. 473,837; 23p. 472,468; 35p. 184,871; 41p. 186,653; 60p. 182,108; miniature sheet 76,623.
Withdrawn: 31.10.95.

649 'Away in a Manger'

650 'Hark! the Herald Angels Sing'

651 'While Shepherds watched'

652 'We Three Kings of Orient Are'

Christmas. Carols

(Des A. Copp. Litho Questa)

1994 (8 Nov). Perf 14 (c).

680	**649**	18p. multicoloured	40	40
681	**650**	23p. multicoloured	50	50
682	**651**	41p. multicoloured	1·20	1·20
683	**652**	60p. multicoloured	1·50	1·50
680/3 *Set of 4*			3·25	3·25
First Day Cover				4·25
Presentation Pack			4·25	

Plate Nos.: All values 1A, 1B (each ×4).
Sheets: 20 (5×4).
Imprint: Central, left-hand margin.
Quantities sold: 18p. 981,010; 23p. 883,715; 41p. 174,413; 60p. 179,888.
Withdrawn: 30.11.95.

Post Office Yearbook

1994 (8 Nov). Comprises Nos. **MS**248 and 644/83.

Yearbook .... 30·00

Sold out: By 2.2000.

653 Dog and 'GOOD LUCK'

654 Rose and 'WITH LOVE'

655 Chick and "CONGRATULATIONS'

656 Bouquet of Flowers and 'THANK YOU'

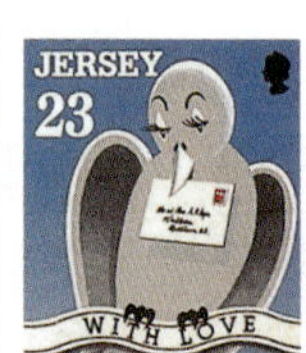

657 Dove with Letter and 'WITH LOVE'

658 Cat with 'GOOD LUCK'

659 Carnations and 'THANK YOU'

660 Parrot and 'CONGRATULATIONS'

661 'Pig and 'HAPPY NEW YEAR'

Greetings Stamps

(Des A. Copp. Litho B.D.T.)

1995 (24 Jan). Perf 13 (c).

684	**653**	18p. multicoloured	30	20
		a. Horiz strip of 4. Nos. 684/7	2·00	2·00
		b. Booklet pane of 9. Nos. 684/92	6·00	
685	**654**	18p. multicoloured	30	20
686	**655**	18p. multicoloured	30	20
687	**656**	18p. multicoloured	30	20
688	**657**	23p. multicoloured	45	25
		a. Horiz strip of 4. Nos. 688/91	2·40	2·40
689	**658**	23p. multicoloured	45	25
690	**659**	23p. multicoloured	45	25
691	**660**	23p. multicoloured	45	25
692	**661**	60p. multicoloured	45	25
684/92 *Set of 9*			5·50	5·50
First Day Cover (Nos. 684/91)				6·00
First Day Cover (Nos. 692)				2·40
Presentation Pack			5·75	

No. 684a was available as a loose pane from the Philatelic Bureau and was also included in the presentation pack.No. 692 commemorates the Chinese New Year of the Pig.

Plate Nos.: All values 1A, 1B, 1C, 1D. (each ×4).
Sheets: 60p. 10 (5×2); others 20 (4×5) the four designs for each value printed together, *se-tenant*, in horizontal strips of 4 throughout the sheets.
Imprint: Central, left-hand margin.
Quantities sold: 18p. 369,217; 23p. 338,047; 60p. 101,753.
Withdrawn: 31.1.96 (sheets).

662 'Captain Rawes'

663 'Brigadoon'

664 'Elsie Jury'

665 'Augusto L' Gouveia Pinto'

666 'Bella Romana'

Camellias

(Des and litho Questa)

1995 (21 Mar). Perf 14½ (c).

693	**662**	18p. multicoloured	55	50
694	**663**	23p. multicoloured	80	70
695	**664**	30p. multicoloured	90	85
696	**665**	35p. multicoloured	1·10	1·20
697	**666**	41p. multicoloured	1·20	1·30
693/7 *Set of 5*			4·00	4·00
First Day Cover				4·50
Presentation Pack			4·50	

Plate Nos.: All values 1A (×5).
Sheets: 20 (5×4).
Imprint: Central, left-hand margin.
Quantities sold: 18p. 398,810; 23p. 480,040; 30p. 187,651; 35p. 160,765; 41p. 133,208.
Withdrawn: 31.3.96.

667 'Liberation' (sculpture, Philip Jackson)

Europa. Peace and Freedom

(Des A. Theobald. Litho Cartor)

1995 (9 May). Perf 13½ (c).

698	**667**	23p. black and dull violet-blue	55	55
699		30p. black and rose-pink	70	95
698/9 *Set of 2*			1·20	1·50
First Day Cover				2·20
Presentation Pack			2·00	

Plate Nos.: Both values 1A, 1B, 1C (each ×4).
Sheets: 10 (5×2).
Imprint: Bottom margin.
Quantities sold: 19p. 251,352; 30p. 278,162.
Withdrawn: 31.5.96.

668 Baliff and Crown Officers in Launch

669 *Vega* (Red Cross supply ship)

670 H.M.S. *Beagle* (destroyer)

671 British Troops in Ordnance Yard, St. Helier

672 King George VI and Queen Elizabeth in Jersey

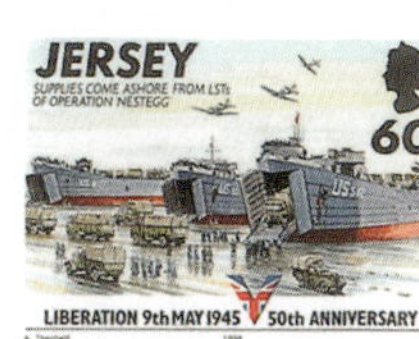

673 Unloading Supplies from Landing Craft, St. Aubin's

674a Royal Family with Winston Churchill on Buckingham Palace Balcony, V.E. Day (*Illustration reduced. Actual size 110×75 mm*)

50th Anniversary of Liberation

(Des A. Theobald. Litho B.D.T.)

1995 (9 May). Perf 15×14 (c).

700	**668**	18p. multicoloured	40	40
		a. Booklet pane. Nos. 700/1, each ×3, with margins all round	2·00	
701	**669**	18p. multicoloured	40	40
702	**670**	23p. multicoloured	60	60
		a. Booklet pane. Nos. 702/3, each ×3, with margins all round	2·75	
703	**671**	23p. multicoloured	60	60
704	**672**	60p. multicoloured	1·50	1·50
		a. Booklet pane. Nos. 704/5, each ×3, with margins all round	7·50	
705	**673**	60p. multicoloured	1·50	1·50
700/5 *Set of 6*			4·50	4·50
First Day Cover				5·25
Presentation Pack			5·50	
MS706 110×75 mm. **674a** £1 multicoloured			2·75	2·75
		a. Booklet pane. As No. **MS**706 with additional margins all round showing arms, mace and inscriptions	2·50	
First Day Cover				3·50
Presentation Pack			3·50	

Plate Nos.: All values 1A, 1B (each ×4).
Sheets: 20 (4×5).
Imprint: Central, left-hand margin.
Quantities sold: 18p. (No. 700) 207,666; 18p. (No. 701) 214,869; 23p. (No. 702) 279,930; 23p. (No. 703) 274,379; 60p. (No. 704) 131,342; 60p. (No. 705) 136,508; £1 122,855.
Withdrawn: 31.5.96 (sheets).

675 Bell Heather

676 Sea Campion

677 Spotted Rock-rose

678 Thrift

679 Sheep's-bit Scabious

680 Field Bind-weed

681 Common Bird's-foot Trefoil

682 Sea holly

683 Common Centaury

684 Dwarf Pansy

European Nature Conservation Year. Wild Flowers

(Des N. Parlett. Litho B.D.T.)

1995 (4 July). Perf 13 (c).

707	**675**	19p. multicoloured	40	20
		a. Horiz strip of 5. Nos. 707/11	3·00	3·00
708	**676**	19p. multicoloured	40	20
709	**677**	19p. multicoloured	40	20
710	**678**	19p. multicoloured	40	20
711	**679**	19p. multicoloured	40	20
712	**680**	23p. multicoloured	50	25
		a. Horiz strip of 5. Nos. 712/16	3·50	3·50
713	**681**	23p. multicoloured	50	25
714	**682**	23p. multicoloured	50	25
715	**683**	23p. multicoloured	50	25
716	**684**	23p. multicoloured	50	25
707/16 *Set of 10*			6·00	6·00
First Day Cover				6·25
Presentation Pack			6·50	

Plate Nos.: Both values 1A, 1B (each ×4).
Sheets: 20 (5×4) the five designs for each value printed together, *se-tenant*, in horizontal strips of 5 throughout the sheets, the backgrounds forming composite designs.
Imprint: Central, left-hand margin.
Quantities sold: 19p. 454,143; 23p. 554,070.
Withdrawn: 31.7.96.

685 *Precis almana*

686 *Papilio palinurus*

687 *Catopsilia scylla*

688 *Papilio rumanzovia*

689 *Troides helena*

Butterflies

(Des W. Oliver. Litho Questa)

1995 (1 Sept). Perf 14 (c).

717	**685**	19p. multicoloured	50	55
718	**686**	23p. multicoloured	55	60
719	**687**	30p. multicoloured	80	85
720	**688**	41p. multicoloured	1·00	1·10
721	**689**	60p. multicoloured	1·60	1·70
717/21 *Set of 5*			4·00	4·25
First Day Cover				4·75
Presentation Pack			4·50	
MS722 150×100 mm. Nos. 720/1			2·40	2·50
		a. 41p. value imperforate		
First Day Cover				3·25
Presentation Pack			3·25	

No. **MS**722 includes the 'Singapore '95' International Stamp Exhibition logo on the sheet margin and shows the two stamp designs without frames.

Plate Nos.: All values 1A (×4).
Sheets: 20 (5×4).
Imprint: Central, left-hand margin.
Quantities sold: 19p. 475,496; 23p. 466,880; 30p. 246,270; 41p. 117,354; 60p. 133,026; miniature sheet 76,062.
Withdrawn: 30.9.96.

690 Peace Doves and United Nations Anniversary Emblem

691 Symbolic Wheat and Anniversary Emblem

50th Anniversary of United Nations

(Des A. Copp. Litho Enschedé)

1995 (24 Oct). Perf 13×14½ (c).

723	**690**	19p. cobalt and royal blue	60	50
724	**691**	23p. turq-green & dp blue-green	70	70
725		41p. dp blue-green & turq-green	1·20	1·20
726	**690**	60p. royal blue and cobalt	1·50	1·50
723/6 *Set of 4*			3·50	3·50
First Day Cover				4·50
Presentation Pack			4·50	

Plate Nos.: 19p., 23p. 1A, 1B (each ×2); others 1A (×2).
Sheets: 20 (5×4).
Imprint: Central, left-hand margin.
Quantities sold: 19p. 152,550; 23p. 201,977; 41p. 75,032; 60p. 73,943.
Withdrawn: 31.10.96.

692 'Puss in Boots'

693 'Cinderella'

694 'Sleeping Beauty'

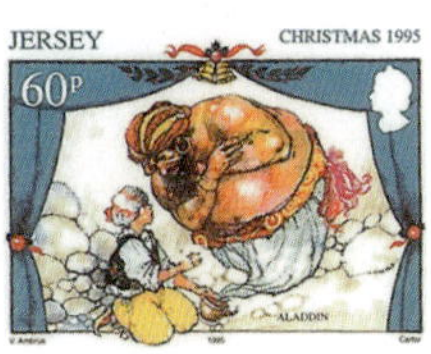

695 'Aladdin'

Christmas. Pantomimes

(Des V. Ambrus. Litho Cartor)

1995 (24 Oct). Perf 13½ (c).

727	**692**	19p. multicoloured	50	40
728	**693**	23p. multicoloured	55	45
729	**694**	41p. multicoloured	1·00	1·00
730	**695**	60p. multicoloured	1·60	1·50
727/30 *Set of 4*			3·25	3·00
First Day Cover				4·25
Presentation Pack			4·50	

Plate Nos.: All values 1A, 1B, 1C, 1D. (each ×4).
Sheets: 20 (5×4).
Imprint: Central, left-hand margin.
Quantities sold: 19p. 986,299; 23p. 716,510; 41p. 118,699; 60p. 131,497.
Withdrawn: 31.10.96.

Post Office Yearbook

1995 (24 Oct). Comprises Nos. 491c and 684/730.

Yearbook	32·00

Sold out: 12.99.

696a Rat with Top Hat (*Illustration reduced. Actual size* 110×75 *mm*)

Chinese New Year ('Year of the Rat')

(Des V. Ambrus. Litho Questa)

1996 (19 Feb). Sheet 110×75 mm. Perf 13½×14 (c).

MS731	**696a**	multicoloured	2·50	2·50
First Day Cover				3·25
Presentation Pack			3·50	

Withdrawn: 28.2.97.

697 African Child and Map

698 Children and Globe

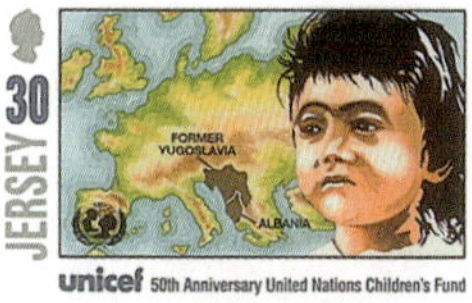

699 European Child and Map

700 South American Child and Map

701 Asian Child and Map

702 South Pacific Child and Map

50th Anniversary of U.N.I.C.E.F.

(Des A. Copp. Litho Questa)

1996 (19 Feb). Perf 14½ (c).

732	**697**	19p. multicoloured	45	40
733	**698**	23p. multicoloured	55	45
734	**699**	30p. multicoloured	70	65

735	**700**	35p. multicoloured	90	95
736	**701**	41p. multicoloured	1·00	1·10
737	**702**	60p. multicoloured	1·50	1·60
732/7 *Set of 6*			4·50	4·50
First Day Cover				5·25
Presentation Cover			5·25	

Plate Nos.: All values 1A (×4).
Sheets: 20 (4×5).
Imprint: Central, left-hand margin.
Quantities sold: 19p. 464,379; 23p. 413,906; 30p. 152,043; 35p. 84,359; 41p. 86,886; 60p. 90,074.
Withdrawn: 28.2.97.

703 Queen Elizabeth II (from photo by T. O'Neill)

70th Birthday of Queen Elizabeth II

(Litho Questa)

1996 (21 Apr). Perf 14×15 (c).

738	**703**	£5 multicoloured	10·00	10·00
First Day Cover				12·00
Presentation Pack			11·00	

After one year No. 738 was retained as a definitive.
Plate Nos.: 1A (×5).
Sheets: 10 (2×5).
Imprint: Central, left-hand margin.

704 Elizabeth Garrett (first British woman doctor)

705 Emmeline Pankhurst (suffragette)

Europa. Famous Women

(Des Jennifer Toombs. Litho B.D.T.)

1996 (25 Apr). Perf 13½×14 (c).

739	**704**	23p. multicoloured	60	60
740	**705**	30p. multicoloured	90	90
739/40 *Set of 2*			1·50	1·50
First Day Cover				2·00
Presentation Pack			2·00	

Plate Nos.: 23p. 1A, 1B, 1C (each ×4); 30p. 1A, 1B, 1C, 1D., 1E (each ×4).
Sheets: 10 (5×2).
Imprint: Bottom margin.
Quantities sold: 23p. 245,907; 30p. 432,935.
Withdrawn: 30.4.97.

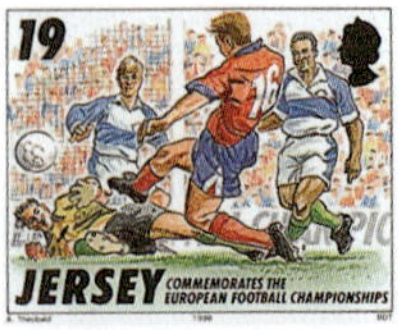

706 Player shooting at Goal

707 Two Players chasing Ball

708 Player avoiding Tackle

709 Two Players competing for Ball

710 Players heading Ball

European Football Championship, England

(Des A. Theobald. Litho B.D.T.)

1996 (25 Apr). Perf 13½×14 (c).

741	**706**	19p. multicoloured	50	40
742	**707**	23p. multicoloured	60	50
743	**708**	35p. multicoloured	95	90
744	**709**	41p. multicoloured	1·00	1·00
745	**710**	60p. multicoloured	1·60	1·60
741/5 *Set of 5*			4·25	4·00
First Day Cover				4·50
Presentation Pack			4·75	

Plate Nos.: 19p., 23p. 1A, 1B (each ×4); others 1A (×4).
Sheets: 20 (5×4).
Imprint: Central, left-hand margin.
Quantities sold: 19p. 450,588; 23p. 458,412; 35p. 105,519; 41p. 106,826; 60p. 109,092.
Withdrawn: 30.4.97.

711 Rowing

712 Judo

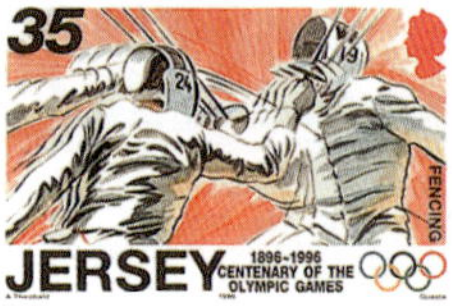

713 Fencing

714 Boxing

715 Basketball

716a Olympic Torch and Stadium (*Illustration reduced. Actual size* 150×100 *mm*)

Sporting Anniversaries

(Des A. Theobald. Litho Questa)

1996 (8 June). Perf 13½ (No. **MS**751) or 14 (others), both comb.

746	**711**	19p. multicoloured	50	40
747	**712**	23p. multicoloured	60	50
748	**713**	35p. multicoloured	95	95
749	**714**	41p. multicoloured	1·00	1·00
750	**715**	60p. multicoloured	1·60	1·60
746/50 *Set of 5*			4·25	4·25

First Day Cover		5·00
Presentation Pack	5·00	
MS751 150×100 mm. **716a** £1 mult	2·50	2·50
First Day Cover		3·50
Presentation Pack	3·50	

Anniversaries:—Nos. 746/8, 750/1, Centenary of Modern Olympic Games; No. 749, 50th anniversary of International Amateur Boxing Association.

No. **MS**751 also includes the 'CAPEX '96' International Stamp Exhibition logo.

Plate Nos.: All values 1A (×4).
Sheets: 20 (5×4).
Imprint: Central, left-hand margin.
Withdrawn: 30.6.97.

717 Bay on North Coast

718 Portelet Bay

719 Greve de Lecq Bay

720 Beauport Beach

721 Plemont Bay

722 St. Brelade's Bay

Tourism. Beaches

(Des A. Copp. Litho B.D.T.)

1996 (8 June). Perf 14 (c).

752	**717**	19p. multicoloured	50	50
		a. Booklet pane. Nos. 752/3, each ×3, with margins all round	2·50	
		b. Booklet pane. Nos. 752/7, with margins all round	4·25	
753	**718**	23p. multicoloured	60	60
754	**719**	30p. multicoloured	80	80
		a. Booklet pane. Nos. 754/5, each ×3, with margins all round	4·00	
755	**720**	35p. multicoloured	95	95
756	**721**	41p. multicoloured	1·10	1·10
		a. Booklet pane. Nos. 756/7, each ×3, with margins all round	6·00	
757	**722**	60p. multicoloured	1·60	1·60
752/7 *Set of 6*			5·00	5·00
First Day Cover				5·25
Presentation Pack			5·25	
Postcards (set of 6)			3·00	8·50

Plate Nos.: 19p., 23p. 1A, 1B (each ×4); others 1A (×4).
Sheets: 20 (5×4).
Imprint: Central, left-hand margin.
Withdrawn: 30.6.97 (sheets).

723 Drag Hunt

724 Pony and Trap

725 Training Racehorses on Beach

726 Show-jumping

727 Pony Club Event

728 Shire Mare and Foal

Horses

(Des P. Layton. Litho Enschedé)

1996 (13 Sept). Perf 13½×14 (c).

758	**723**	19p. multicoloured	50	50
759	**724**	23p. multicoloured	60	60
760	**725**	30p. multicoloured	80	80
761	**726**	35p. multicoloured	95	95
762	**727**	41p. multicoloured	1·10	1·10
763	**728**	60p. multicoloured	1·60	1·60
758/63 *Set of 6*			5·00	5·00
First Day Cover				5·25
Presentation Pack			5·25	
Postcards (set of6)			3·00	8·50

Plate Nos.: All values 1A, 1B (each ×4).
Sheets: 20 (4×5).
Imprint: Central, left-hand margin.
Withdrawn: 30.9.97.

729 The Journey to Bethlehem

730 The Shepherds

731 The Nativity

732 The Three Kings

Christmas

(Des V. Ambrus. Litho Cartor)

1996 (12 Nov). Perf 13×13½ (c).

764	**729**	19p. multicoloured	50	50
765	**730**	23p. multicoloured	60	70
766	**731**	30p. multicoloured	90	95
767	**732**	60p. multicoloured	1·40	1·50
764/7 *Set of 4*			3·00	3·25
First Day Cover				4·25
Presentation Pack			4·25	

Plate Nos.: All values 1A, 1B, 1C (each ×4).
Sheets: 20 (4×5).
Imprint: Central, left-hand margin.
Withdrawn: 28.11.97.

Post Office Yearbook

1996 (12 Nov). Comprises Nos. **MS**731/67.

Yearbook	36·00

Sold out: 12.99.

733b Jersey Cow wearing Scarf (*Illustration reduced. Actual size* 110×75 mm)

Chinese New Year ('Year of the Ox')

(Des V. Ambrus. Litho Questa)

1997 (7 Feb). Sheet 110×74 mm. Perf 14×13½ (c).

MS768 **733a** multicoloured	3·25	3·75
First Day Cover		4·50
Presentation Pack	4·50	

Withdrawn: 28.2.98.

'HONG KONG '97' International Stamp Exhibition

1997 (7 Feb). No. **MS**768 optd with exhibition emblem in black and 'JERSEY AT HONG KONG '97' in red, both on sheet margin.

MS769 **733b** multicoloured	3·75	4·00
First Day Cover		5·00
Presentation Pack	4·00	

Withdrawn: 28.2.98.

734 Lillie the Cow on the Beach

735 Lillie taking Photograph

736 Carrying Bucket and Spade

737 Eating Meal at Mont Orgueil

Tourism. 'Lillie the Cow'

(Des A. Copp. Litho B.D.T.)

1997 (12 Feb)–**99**. Self-adhesive. Perf 9½ (c).

770	**734** (23p). multicoloured (a)	80	85
	a. With copyright symbol after date (bc)	4·50	4·50
771	**735** (23p). multicoloured (a)	80	85
	a. With copyright symbol after date (bc)	4·50	4·50
772	**736** (23p). multicoloured (a)	80	85
	a. With copyright symbol after date (bc)	4·50	4·50
773	**737** (23p). multicoloured (a)	80	85
	a. With copyright symbol after date (bc)	4·50	4·50
770/3 *Set of 4*		2·75	3·00
770a/3a *Set of 4*		16·00	16·00
First Day Cover			4·50
Presentation Pack		4·00	

Nos. 770/3, which are inscribed 'UK MINIMUM POSTAGE PAID', come, *se-tenant*, in strips of 4 or rolls of 100 with the surplus self-adhesive paper around each stamp removed. Nos. 770/3 were initially sold at 23p. each; this was increased to 24p. on 10 March 1997.

Initially released with '1997' imprint dates, Nos. 770a/3a were subsequently reissued inscribed '1999' (price per set, mint or used, £18) and '2000' (price £16).

Printings: (a) 12.2.97. Inscr '1997'; (b) 16.4.99. Inscr '1999'; (c). 9.12.00. Inscr '2000'.

Sold out: By 5.2001.

738 Red-breasted Merganser

739 Sanderling

740 Northern Gannet

741 Great Crested Grebe

742 Common Tern

743 Black-headed Gull

744 Dunlin

745 Sandwich Tern

746 Ringed Plover

747 Bar-tailed Godwit

748 Atlantic Puffin

749 Brent Goose

750 Grey Plover

751 Balck Scoter

752 Lesser Black-backed Gull

753 Little Egret

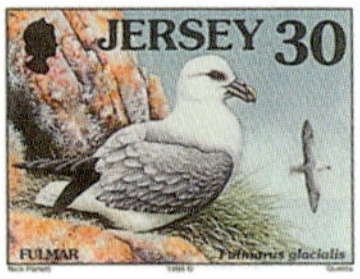

754 Fulmar

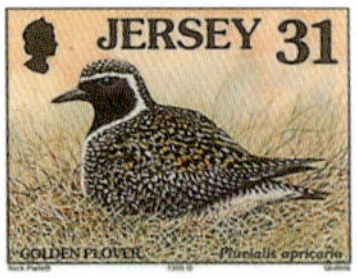

755 Golden Plover

756 Common Greenshank

757 Little Grebe

758 Great Cormorant

759 Western Curlew

760 Oystercatcher

761 Ruddy Turnstone

762 Herring Gull

763 Rock Pipit

764 Greater Black-backed Gull

765 Pied Avocet

766 Grey Heron

767 Common Redshank

768 Razorbill

769 Shag

Seabirds and Waders

(Des N. Parlett. Litho Questa)

1997 (12 Feb)–**99**. Perf 14½ (c).

774	**738**	1p. multicoloured (a)	10	10
775	**739**	2p. multicoloured (b)	10	10
776	**740**	4p. multicoloured (d)	10	10
777	**741**	5p. multicoloured (b)	10	15
778	**742**	10p. multicoloured (a)	20	25
779	**743**	15p. multicoloured (a)	30	35
780	**744**	20p. multicoloured (a)	60	45
		a. With copyright symbol after date (c)	40	45
781	**745**	21p. multicoloured (b)	40	45
782	**746**	22p. multicoloured (d)	45	50
783	**747**	23p. multicoloured (e)	45	50
784	**748**	24p. multicoloured (a)	70	50
		a. With copyright symbol after date (c)	45	50
785	**749**	25p. multicoloured (b)	50	55
786	**750**	26p. multicoloured (d)	50	55
787	**751**	27p. multicoloured (e)	55	60
788	**752**	28p. multicoloured (e)	60	65
789	**753**	29p. multicoloured (e)	60	65
790	**754**	30p. multicoloured (b)	60	65
791	**755**	31p. multicoloured (d)	60	65
792	**756**	32p. multicoloured (d)	65	70
793	**757**	33p. multicoloured (e)	65	70
794	**758**	34p. multicoloured (e)	70	75
795	**759**	35p. multicoloured (d)	70	75
796	**760**	37p. multicoloured (a)	75	80
797	**761**	40p. multicoloured (b)	80	85
798	**762**	44p. multicoloured (d)	90	95
799	**763**	45p. multicoloured (e)	90	95
800	**764**	50p. multicoloured (d)	1·00	1·10
801	**765**	60p. multicoloured (b)	1·20	1·40
802	**766**	65p. multicoloured (e)	1·20	1·40
803	**767**	75p. multicoloured (a)	2·00	2·10
804	**768**	£1 multicoloured (b)	2·50	2·50
805	**769**	£2 multicoloured (a)	5·00	5·25
774/805 *Set of 32*			24·00	26·00
First Day Covers (4)				30·00
Presentation Packs (4)			28·00	
Postcards (set of 32)			13·00	40·00

MS806 Four sheets, each 136×130 mm. (a) Nos. 774, 778/80, 784, 796, 803 and 805 (a). (b) Nos. 775, 777, 781, 785, 790, 797, 801 and 804 (b). (c). Nos. 776, 782, 786, 791/2, 795, 798 and 800 (d). (d) Nos. 783, 787/9, 793/4, 799 and 802 (e)

Set of 4 sheets	25·00	25·00
First Day Covers (4)		40·00
Souvenir Folders (4)	32·00	
Complete series Souvenir Folder	28·00	

Printings: (a) 12.2.97. Inscr '1997' without copyright symbol; (b) 28.1.98. Inscr '1998' with copyright symbol; (c) 2.4.98. Inscr '1998' with copyright symbol; (d) 11.8.98. Inscr '1998' with copyright symbol; (e) 21.8.99. Inscr '1999' with copyright symbol.

Plate Nos.: 1p., 2p., 22p., 25p., 26p., £2 1A, 1B, 1C, 1D. (each ×4); 20p., 24p. 1A, 1B, 1C, 1D. (each ×4), 2A, 2B, 2C, 2D. (each ×4) (Nos. 780a, 784a); 4p., 21p., 50p., 60p. 1A, 1B, 1C, 1d., 1E, 1F, 1G, 1H (each ×4); **MS**806 1A (×4); others 1A, 1B (each ×4).

Sheets: 20 (4×5).

Imprint: Central, left-hand margin.

Withdrawn: 31.12.2007.

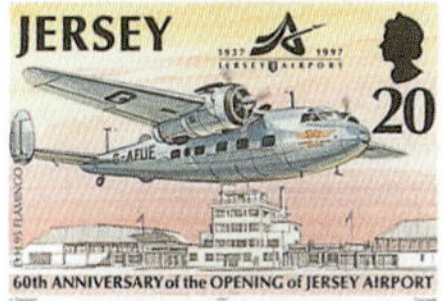

770 De Havilland D.H.95 Flamingo

771 Handley Page H.P.R.5 Marathon

772 De Havilland D.H.114 Heron

773 Boeing 737-236

774 Britten Norman Trislander

775 BAe 146-200

60th Anniversary of Jersey Airport

(Des A. Theobald. Litho Enschedé)

1997 (10 Mar). Perf 13½×14 (c).

807	**770**	20p. multicoloured	45	40
808	**771**	24p. multicoloured	55	40
809	**772**	31p. multicoloured	65	65
810	**773**	37p. multicoloured	95	95
811	**774**	43p. multicoloured	1·10	1·10
812	**775**	63p. multicoloured	1·70	1·70
807/12 *Set of* 6			5·00	5·00

First Day Cover			5·25
Presentation Pack		5·50	

Plate Nos.: All values 1A, 1B, 1C (each ×4).
Sheets: 20 (4×5).
Imprint: Central, left-hand margin.
Withdrawn: 31.3.98.

776 The Bull of St. Clement

777 The Black Horse of St. Ouen

778 The Black Dog of Bouley Bay

779 Les Fontainnes des Mittes

Europa. Tales and Legends

(Des Jennifer Toombs. Litho B.D.T.)

1997 (15 Apr). Perf 15×14 (c).

813	**776**	20p. multicoloured	65	60
814	**777**	24p. multicoloured	75	70
815	**778**	31p. multicoloured	1·00	1·10
816	**779**	63p. multicoloured	1·25	1·80
813/16		*Set of 4*	3·00	3·75
		First Day Cover		4·50
		Presentation Pack	4·50	

Nos. 814/15 include the EUROPA emblem.
Plate Nos.: All values 1A, 1B (each ×5).
Sheets: 10 (5×2).
Imprint: Bottom margin.
Withdrawn: 30.4.98.

'Pacific 97' International Stamp Exhibition, San Francisco

1997 (29 May). No. **MS**806a optd with exhibition emblem on sheet margin.

MS817 136×130 mm. Nos. 774, 778/80, 784, 796, 803 and 805	7·50	8·50
Souvenir Folder	9·50	

780 Cycling

781 Archery

782 Windsurfing

783 Gymnastics

784 Volleyball

785 Running

7th Island Games, Jersey

(Des A. Theobald. Litho B.D.T.)

1997 (28 June). Perf 13½ (c).

818	**780**	20p. multicoloured	55	55
		a. Booklet pane. Nos. 818/19, each ×3, with margins all round	2·50	
		b. Booklet pane. Nos. 818/23, with margins all round	5·25	
819	**781**	24p. multicoloured	65	65
820	**782**	31p. multicoloured	80	80
		a. Booklet pane. Nos. 820/1, each ×3, with margins all round	4·00	
821	**783**	37p. multicoloured	1·00	1·00
822	**784**	43p. multicoloured	1·10	1·10
		a. Booklet pane. Nos. 822/3, each ×3, with margins all round	6·25	
823	**785**	63p. multicoloured	1·70	1·70
818/23		*Set of 6*	5·25	5·25
		First Day Cover		5·75
		Presentation Pack	6·00	

Plate Nos.: 20p., 24p. 1A, 1B (each ×4); others 1A (×4).
Sheets: 20 (5×4).
Imprint: Central, left-hand margin.
Withdrawn: 30.6.98 (sheets).

786 Mallorcan Midwife Toad

787 Aye-Aye

788 Mauritius Parakeet

789 Pigmy Hog

790 St. Lucia Whip-tail

791 Madagascar Teal

Wildlife Preservation Trust (6th series)

(Des W. Oliver. Litho Cartor)

1997 (2 Sept). Perf 13 (c).

824	**786**	20p. multicoloured	50	45
825	**787**	24p. multicoloured	60	50
826	**788**	31p. multicoloured	90	90
827	**789**	37p. multicoloured	1·00	1·10
828	**790**	43p. multicoloured	1·10	1·20
829	**791**	63p. multicoloured	1·70	1·80
824/9		*Set of 6*	5·25	5·25
		First Day Cover		5·50
		Presentation Pack	6·00	

Plate Nos.: All values 1A, 1B (each ×4).
Sheets: 20 (5×4).
Imprint: Central, left-hand margin.
Withdrawn: 30.9.98.

792 Ash

793 Elder

794 Beech

795 Sweet Chestnut

796 Hawthorn

797 Common Oak

Trees

(Des Norah Bryan. Litho Questa)

1997 (2 Sept). Perf 14½ (c).

830	**792**	20p. multicoloured	50	45
831	**793**	24p. multicoloured	60	50
832	**794**	31p. multicoloured	90	90
833	**795**	37p. multicoloured	1·00	1·10
834	**796**	43p. multicoloured	1·10	1·20
835	**797**	63p. multicoloured	1·70	1·80
830/5		*Set of 6*	5·25	5·25
		First Day Cover		5·50
		Presentation Pack	6·00	

Plate Nos.: 20p., 24p. 1A, 1B (each ×4); others 1A (×4).
Sheets: 20 (5×4).
Imprint: Central, left-hand margin.
Withdrawn: 30.9.98.

798 Father Christmas and Reindeer outside Jersey Airport

799 Father Christmas with Presents, St. Aubin's Harbour

800 Father Christmas in Sleigh, Mont Orgueil Castle

801 Father Christmas with Children, Royal Square, St. Helier

Christmas

(Des Colleen Corlett. Litho B.D.T.)

1997 (11 Nov). Perf 14 (c).

836	**798**	20p. multicoloured	60	60
837	**799**	24p. multicoloured	70	70
838	**800**	31p. multicoloured	1·00	1·00
839	**801**	63p. multicoloured	1·90	1·90
836/9		*Set of 4*	3·75	3·75
		First Day Cover		4·50
		Presentation Pack	4·50	

Plate Nos.: 20p., 31p. 1A, 1B (each ×5); others 1A, 1B (each ×4).
Sheets: 20 (4×5).
Imprint: Central, left-hand margin.
Withdrawn: 30.11.98.

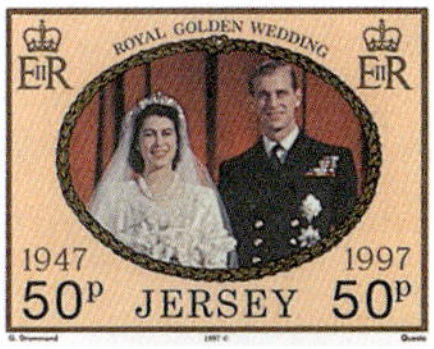

802 Wedding Photograph, 1947

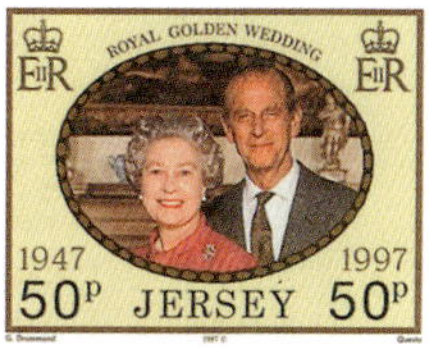

803 Queen Elizabeth and Prince Philip, 1997

804a Full-length Wedding Photograph, 1947
(*Illustration reduced, Actual size* 150×100 *mm*)

Golden Wedding of Queen Elizabeth and Prince Philip

(Des G. Drummond. Litho Questa)

1997 (20 Nov). Perf 13½ (**MS**842) or 14½ (others), both comb.

840	**802**	50p. multicoloured	1·00	60
		a. Horiz pair. Nos. 840/1	3·00	3·00
841	**803**	50p. multicoloured	1·00	60
840/1		*Set of 2*	3·00	3·00
		First Day Cover		3·75
		Presentation Pack	3·75	
MS842		150×100 mm. **804a** £1.50, multicoloured	4·50	4·50
		First Day Cover		5·00
		Presentation Pack	4·75	

Plate Nos.: 1A, 1B, 1C, 1D. (each ×5).
Sheets: 20 (4×5). The two designs were printed together, *se-tenant*, in horizontal pairs throughout the sheets.
Imprint: Central, left-hand margin.
Withdrawn: 30.11.98.
Sold out: By 7.04.

Year Pack 1997

1997 (20 Nov). Comprises Nos. **MS**768, 770/4, 778/80, 784, 796, 803, 805, 807/16 and 818/42.

Year Pack .... 45·00

Sold out: By 11.02.

Post Office Yearbook 1997

1997 (20 Nov). Comprises Nos. **MS**768, 770/4, 778/80, 784, 796, 803, 805, 807/16 and 818/42.

Yearbook .... 45·00

Sold out: By 7.04.

805a Tiger wearing Scarf (*Illustration reduced. Actual size* 110×75 *mm*)

Chinese New Year ('Year of the Tiger')

(Des V. Ambrus. Litho Questa)

1998 (28 Jan). Sheet 110×75 mm. Perf 14×13½ (c).

MS843	**805a** multicoloured	2·50	2·75
	First Day Cover		3·75
	Presentation Pack	4·25	

Withdrawn: 30.1.99.

806 J.M.T. Bristol 4 Tonner, 1923

807 Safety Coach Service Regent Double Decker, 1934

808 Slade's Dennis Lancet, *circa* 1936

809 Tantivy Leyland PLSC, Lion, 1947

810 J.B.S. Morris, circa 1958

811 J.M.T. Titan TD4 Double Decker, circa 1961

75th Anniversary of Jersey Motor Transport Company. Buses (1st series)

(Des A. Copp. Litho B.D.T.)

1998 (2 Apr). Perf 14 (c).

844	**806**	20p. multicoloured	55	50
		a. Booklet pane. Nos. 844/5, each ×3, with margins all round	2·50	
		b. Booklet pane. Nos. 844/9, with margins all round	4·50	
845	**807**	24p. multicoloured	65	50
846	**808**	31p. multicoloured	75	70
		a. Booklet pane. Nos. 846/7, each ×3, with margins all round	4·00	
847	**809**	37p. multicoloured	1·00	1·00
848	**810**	43p. multicoloured	1·10	1·10
		a. Booklet pane. Nos. 848/9, each ×3, with margins all round	6·50	
849	**811**	63p. multicoloured	1·50	1·60
844/9 *Set of 6*			5·00	5·00
First Day Cover				5·75
Presentation Pack			5·75	

Plate Nos.: 20p., 24p. 1A, 1B (each×4); others 1A (×4).
Sheets: 20 (4×5).
Imprint: Central, left-hand margin.
Withdrawn: 30.4.99 (sheets).

812 Creative Arts Festival

813 Jazz Festival

814 Good Food Festival

815 Floral Festival

Europa. National Festivals

(Des A. Copp. Litho Enschedé)

1998 (2 Apr). Perf 14×13½ (c).

850	**812**	20p. multicoloured	65	45
851	**813**	24p. multicoloured	70	55
852	**814**	31p. multicoloured	90	1·00
853	**815**	63p. multicoloured	1·70	1·90
850/3 *Set of 4*			3·50	3·50
First Day Cover				4·00
Presentation Pack			4·00	

Nos. 851/2 include the 'EUROPA' emblem.
Plate Nos.: All values 1A, 1B (each ×4).
Sheets: 10 (5×2).
Imprint: Bottom, left-hand corner margin.
Withdrawn: 30.4.99.

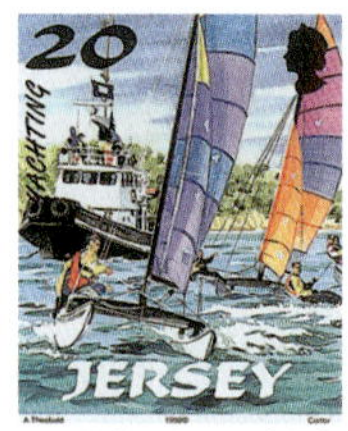

816 Hobie Cat and *Duke of Normandy* (launch)

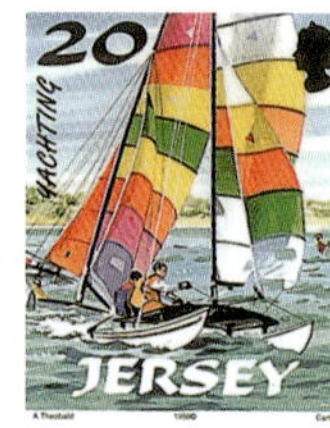

817 Hobie Cat with White, Yellow, Red and Green Sails

818 Hobie Cats with Pink, Purple and Orange Sails

819 Bow of Hobie Cat with Yellow, Blue and Purple Sails

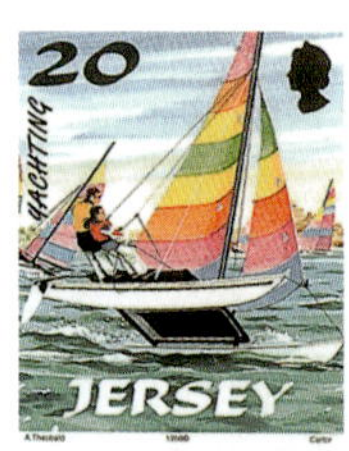

820 Hobie Cat Heeling

821 Yacht with Red, White and Blue Spinnaker

822 Yacht with Pink Spinnaker

823 Yacht with Two White Sails

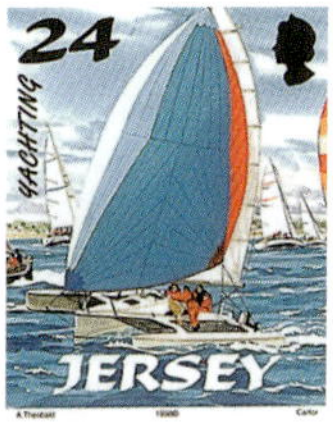

824 Trimaram

825 Yacht with Blue, White and Yellow Spinnaker in Foreground

Jersey Yachting (1s.t issue). Opening of Elizabeth Marina, St. Helier

(Des A. Theobald. Litho Cartor)

1998 (15 May). Perf 13 (c).

854	**816**	20p. multicoloured	40	20
		a. Horiz strip of 5. Nos. 854/8	2·50	2·50
855	**817**	20p. multicoloured	40	20
856	**818**	20p. multicoloured	40	20
857	**819**	20p. multicoloured	40	20
858	**820**	20p. multicoloured	40	20
859	**821**	24p. multicoloured	45	25
		a. Horiz strip of 5. Nos. 859/63	3·00	3·00
860	**822**	24p. multicoloured	45	25
861	**823**	24p. multicoloured	45	25
862	**824**	24p. multicoloured	45	25
863	**825**	24p. multicoloured	45	25
854/63 *Set of* 10			5·00	5·00
First Day Cover				6·00
Presentation Pack			6·00	

Plate Nos.: Both values 1A (×4).
Sheets: 20 (5×4), the designs were each printed together, *se-tenant*, in horizontal strips of five throughout the sheets, each strip forming a composite design.
Imprint: Central, left-hand margin.
Withdrawn: 31.5.99.

826 Bass

827 Red Gurnard

828 Skate

829 Mackerel

830 Tope

831 Cuckoo Wrasse

International year of the Ocean. Fish

(Des W. Oliver. Litho B.D.T.)

1998 (11 Aug). Perf 15×14 (c).

864	**826**	20p. multicoloured	50	50
865	**827**	24p. multicoloured	65	65
866	**828**	31p. multicoloured	80	80
867	**829**	37p. multicoloured	1·00	1·00
868	**830**	43p. multicoloured	1·10	1·10
869	**831**	63p. multicoloured	1·50	1·50
864/9 *Set of* 6			5·00	5·00
First Day Cover				6·00
Presentation Pack			6·00	

Plate Nos.: 20p., 24p. 1A, 1B (each ×4); others 1A (×4).
Sheets: 20 (4×5).
Imprint: Central, left-hand margin.
Withdrawn: 31.8.99.

832 Cider-making

833 Potato Barrels on Cart

834 Collecting Seaweed for Fertiliser

835 Milking Jersey Cows

Days Gone By

(Des A. Copp. Litho SNP Cambec, Melbourne)

1998 (11 Aug). Self-adhesive. With copyright symbol after date. Perf 11½×11 (Die-cut).

870	**832**	(20p). multicoloured (abcde)	90	90
871	**833**	(20p). multicoloured (abcde)	90	90
872	**834**	(20p). multicoloured (abcde)	90	90
873	**835**	(20p). multicoloured (abcde)	90	90
870/3 *Set of* 4			3·25	3·25
First Day Cover				3·50
Presentation Pack			3·25	

Nos. 870/3, which are inscribed 'BAILIWICK MINIMUM POSTAGE PAID' and were initially sold at 20p. each, come, *se-tenant*, in strips of 4 or rolls of 100 with the surplus self-adhesive paper around each stamp removed. Initially released with '1998' imprint dates, Nos. 870/3 were subsequently reissued inscribed '1999' (price per set, unused or used, £18), '2000' (price £16), '2001' (price £10) and 2003 (price £6).

Printings: (a) 11.8.98, Inscr '1998'; (b) 16.7.99. Inscr '1999'; (c). 3.11.2000. Inscr '2000'; (d) 19.11.2001. Inscr '2001'; (e) 4.4.2003. Inscr '2003'.

836 Irises

837 Carnations

838 Chrysanthemums

839 Pinks

840 Roses

841 Lilies

842a *Lilium* 'Star Gazer' (*Illustration reduced. Actual size* 150×100 *mm*)

Flowers

(Des Wendy Tait. Litho Questa)

1998 (23 Oct). Perf 14×13½ (No. **MS**880) or 14½ (others), both comb.

874	**836**	20p. multicoloured	50	40
875	**837**	24p. multicoloured	60	50
876	**838**	31p. multicoloured	75	70
877	**839**	37p. multicoloured	90	90
878	**840**	43p. multicoloured	1·00	1·10
879	**841**	63p. multicoloured	1·40	1·50
874/9 *Set of 6*			4·75	4·75
First Day Cover				5·50
Presentation Pack			5·50	
MS880 150×100 mm. **842a** £1.50, multicoloured			3·25	3·75
First Day Cover				4·50
Presentation Pack			4·50	

No. **MS** 880 includes the 'ITALIA' 98' stamp exhibition emblem on the margin.

Plate Nos.: 20p., 24p. 1A, 1B (each ×4); 31p., 37p. 1A (×4); 43p., 63p. 1A, 1B, 1C (each ×4).
Sheets: 20 (4×5).
Imprint: Central, left-hand margin.
Withdrawn: 30.10.99.

843 Central Market Crib

844 St. Thomas's Church Crib

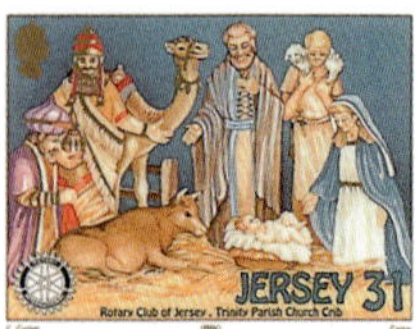

845 Trinity Parish Church Crib

846 Royal Square Crib

Christmas. Cribs

(Des Colleen Corlett. Litho Cartor)

1998 (10 Nov). Perf 13 (C).

881	**843**	20p. multicoloured	40	40
882	**844**	24p. multicoloured	50	55
883	**845**	31p. multicoloured	65	65
884	**846**	63p. multicoloured	1·60	1·60
881/4 *Set of 4*			3·00	3·00
First Day Cover				4·00
Presentation Pack			4·00	

Plate Nos.: All values 1A (×4).
Sheets: 20 (4×5).
Imprint: Central, left-hand margin.
Withdrawn: 30.11.99.

Year Pack 1998

1998 (10 Nov). Comprises Nos. 775/7, 781/2, 785/6, 790/2, 795, 797/8, 800/1, 804 and **MS**843/84.

Year Pack .... 45·00

Sold out: By 7.04.

Post Office Yearbook

1998 (10 Nov). Comprises Nos. 775/7, 781/2, 785/6, 790/2, 795, 797/8, 800/1, 804 and **MS**843/84.

Yearbook .... 45·00

Sold out: By 7.04.

847a Rabbit (*Illustration reduced. Actual size* 110×75 mm)

Chinese New Year ('Year of the Rabbit')

(Des V. Ambrus. Litho Questa)

1999 (16 Feb). Sheet 110×75 mm. Perf 14×13½ (C).

MS885	**847a**	£1 multicoloured	2·50	2·75
First Day Cover				4·00
Presentation Pack			3·75	

Withdrawn: 29.2.2000.

848 Jersey Eastern Railway Mail Train

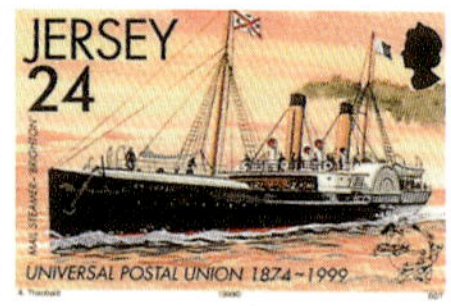

849 *Brighton* (paddle-steamer)

850 De Havilland D.H.86 Dragon Express at Jersey Airport

851 Jersey Postal Service Morris Minor Van

125th Anniversary of Universal Postal Union

(Des A. Theobald. Litho B.D.T.)

1999 (16 Feb). Perf 14 (C).

886	**848**	20p. multicoloured	55	50
887	**849**	24p. multicoloured	65	60
888	**850**	43p. multicoloured	95	1·10
889	**851**	63p. multicoloured	1·40	1·70
886/9 *Set of 4*			3·25	3·50
First Day Cover				4·50
Presentation Pack			4·50	

Plate Nos.: All values 1A (×4).
Sheets: 20 (4×5).
Imprint: Central, left-hand margin.
Withdrawn: 29.2.2000.

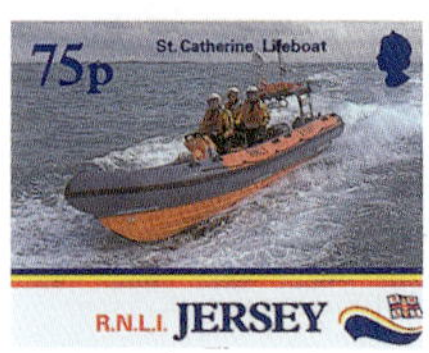

852 *Jessie Eliza*, St. Catherine

853 *Alexander Coutanche*, St. Helier

175th Anniversary of Royal National Lifeboat Institution

(Litho Questa)

1999 (16 Feb). Perf 14½ (C).

890	**852**	75p. multicoloured	2·00	80
		a. Horiz pair. Nos. 890/1	4·50	4·50
891	**853**	£1 multicoloured	2·50	1·00
890/1 *Set of 2*			4·50	4·50

First Day Cover		5·00
Presentation Pack	5·00	

Plate Nos.: 1A, 1B (each ×7).
Sheets: 20 (4×5), the two values printed together, *se-tenant*, in horizontal pairs throughout the sheet.
Imprint: Central, left-hand margin.
Withdrawn: 29.2.2000.

854 *Cymbidium Maufant* 'Jersey'

855 *Miltonia Millbrook* 'Jersey'

856 *Paphiopedilum* Transvaal

857 *Paphiopedilum* Elizabeth Castle

858 *Calanthe* Five Oaks

859 *Cymbidium* Icho Tower 'Trinity'

860a *Miltonia* Portelet (*Illustration reduced. Actual size* 150×100 mm)

Jersey Orchids (4th series)

(Litho Enschedé)

1999 (19 Mar). Perf 13½ (No. **MS**898) or 14×13, both comb.

892	**854**	21p. multicoloured	55	50
893	**855**	25p. multicoloured	55	50
894	**856**	31p. multicoloured	75	70
895	**857**	37p. multicoloured	85	80
896	**858**	43p. multicoloured	90	90
897	**859**	63p. multicoloured	2·00	2·00
892/7 *Set of 6*			5·00	5·00
First Day Cover				5·50
Presentation Pack			5·50	
MS898 150×100 mm. **860a** £1.50, mult			4·00	4·50
First Day Cover				6·00
Presentation Pack			4·50	

No. **MS**898 also includes the 'Australia '99' World Stamp Exhibition, Melbourne, emblem on the margin at top left.
Plate Nos.: 21p., 25p. 1A, 1B (each ×5); others 1A (×5).
Sheets: 20 (5×4).
Imprint: Central, left-hand margin.
Withdrawn: 31.3.2000.

861 Howard Davis Park

862 Sir Winston Churchill Memorial Park

863 Coronation Park

864 La Collette Gardens

Europa. Parks and Gardens

(Des Ariel Luke. Litho Cartor)

1999 (27 Apr). Perf 13×13½ (C).

899	**861**	21p. multicoloured	50	50
900	**862**	25p. multicoloured	70	70
901	**863**	31p. multicoloured	1·00	1·00
902	**864**	63p. multicoloured	2·00	2·00
899/902 *Set of 4*			4·00	4·00
First Day Cover				4·50
Presentation Pack			4·50	

Nos. 900/1 include the 'EUROPA' logo at top left and all four values show the 'ibra '99' International Stamp Exhibition, Nuremberg, emblem at top right.
Plate Nos.: All values 1A (×4).
Sheets: 10 (2×5).
Imprint: Central, left-hand margin.
Withdrawn: 29.4.2000.

865 Prince Edward and Miss Sophie Rhys-Jones

Royal Wedding

(Des A. Copp. Litho Questa)

1999 (19 June). Perf 14½ (C).

903	**865**	35p. mult (yellow background)	60	35
		a. Pair. Nos. 903/4	2·20	2·20
904		35p. mult (blue background)	60	35
903/4 *Set of 2*			2·20	2·20
First Day Cover				2·75
Presentation Pack			3·00	

Plate Nos.: 1A, 1B, 1C, 1D (each ×4).
Sheets: 20 (4×5) with the two designs printed together, *se-tenant*, in horizontal or vertical pairs throughout the sheet.
Imprint: Central, left-hand margin.
Withdrawn: 30.6.2000.

866 Jersey-built Benz, 1899

867 Star Tourer, 1910

868 Citroen 'Traction Avant', 1938

869 Talbot BG110 Tourer, 1937

870 Morris Cowley Six Special Coupé, 1934

871 Ford Anglia Saloon, 1946

Vintage Cars (3rd series). Centenary of Motoring in Jersey

(Des A. Copp. Litho B.D.T.)

1999 (2 July). Perf 14 (C).

905	**866**	21p. multicoloured	45	45
		a. Booklet pane. Nos. 905/6, each ×3, with margins all round	2·75	
		b. Booklet pane. Nos. 905/10, with margins all round	5·00	
906	**867**	25p. multicoloured	55	55
907	**868**	31p. multicoloured	65	65
		a. Booklet pane. Nos. 907/8, each ×3, with margins all round	5·00	
908	**869**	37p. multicoloured	1·00	1·00
909	**870**	43p. multicoloured	1·20	1·20
		a. Booklet pane. Nos. 909/10, each ×3, with margins all round	8·00	
910	**871**	63p. multicoloured	1·50	1·50
905/10 *Set of 6*			5·00	5·00
First Day Cover				5·50
Presentation Pack			5·50	

Nos. 905a/b, 907a and 909a also include the 'PhilexFrance 99' International Stamp Exhibition emblem on the margins at top right.

Plate Nos.: 21p., 25p. 1A, 1B (each ×4); others 1A (×4).
Sheets: 20 (4×5).
Imprint: Central, left-hand margin.
Withdrawn: 31.7.2000 (sheets).

872 West European Hedgehog

873 Eurasian Red Squirrel

874 Nathusius Pipistrelle

875 Jersey Bank Vole

876 Lesser White-toothed Shrew

877 Common Mole

Small Mammals

(Des W. Oliver. Litho Cartor)

1999 (21 Aug). Perf 13½×13 (C).

911	**872**	21p. multicoloured	45	45
912	**873**	25p. multicoloured	55	55
913	**874**	31p. multicoloured	65	65
914	**875**	37p. multicoloured	1·00	1·10
915	**876**	43p. multicoloured	1·00	1·10
916	**877**	63p. multicoloured	2·00	2·20
911/16 *Set of 6*			5·25	5·50
First Day Cover				6·00
Presentation Pack			6·00	

No. 913 is inscribed 'Pipestrelle' in error.

Plate Nos.: All values 1A (×4).
Sheets: 20 (4×5).
Imprint: Central, left-hand margin.
Withdrawn: 31.8.2000.

878 Gorey Pierhead Light

879 La Corbiere

880 Noirmont Point

881 Demie de Pas

882 Greve d'Azette

883 Sorel Point

150th Anniversary of First Lighthouse on Jersey (First series)

(Des A. Copp. Litho Walsall)

1999 (5 Oct). Perf 14 (C).

917	**878**	21p. multicoloured	45	45
918	**879**	25p. multicoloured	55	55
919	**880**	34p. multicoloured	75	75
920	**881**	38p. multicoloured	1·00	1·00
921	**882**	44p. multicoloured	1·20	1·20
922	**883**	64p. multicoloured	2·00	2·00
917/22 *Set of 6*			5·50	5·50

First Day Cover		6·00
Presentation Pack	6·00	

See also Nos. 1086/91.

Plate Nos.: All values 1A, 1B (each ×4).
Sheets: 20 (5×4).
Imprint: Central, left-hand margin.
Withdrawn: 31.10.2000.

884 Mistletoe

885 Holly

886 Ivy

887 Christmas Rose

Christmas. Festive Foliage

(Des Colleen Corlett. Litho B.D.T.)

1999 (9 Nov). Perf 14 (C).

923	**884**	21p. multicoloured	45	45
924	**885**	25p. multicoloured	55	55
925	**886**	34p. multicoloured	1·10	75
926	**887**	64p. multicoloured	1·60	2·00
923/6 *Set of 4*			3·50	3·50
First Day Cover				4·50
Presentation Pack			4·50	

Plate Nos.: All values 1A, 1B (each ×4).
Sheets: 20 (5×4).
Imprint: Central, left-hand margin.
Withdrawn: 30.11.2000.

Year Pack 1999

1999 (1 Dec). Comprises Nos. 783, 787/9, 793/4, 799, 802 and **MS**885/926.

Year Pack	48·00

Post Office Yearbook

1999 (1 Dec). Comprises Nos. 783, 787/9, 793/4, 799, 802 and **MS**885/926.

Yearbook	50·00

Sold out: By 11.03.

888 Jersey Crest

New Millennium

(Des A. Copp. Litho, die-stamped and embossed Cartor)

2000 (1 Jan). Perf 13½ (C).

927	**888**	£10 gold, bright red and deep carmine	20·00	20·00
First Day Cover				23·00
Presentation Pack			21·00	

The printing of No. 927 incorporates metallic die-stamping and embossing using 22 carat gold.

No. 927 was retained in use as a definitive stamp.

Plate Nos.: 1A (×3).
Sheets: 10 (5×2).
Imprint: Upper left-hand margin.

889a Dragon (*Illustration reduced. Actual size* 110×75 mm)

Chinese New Year ('Year of the Dragon')

(Des V. Ambrus. Litho Questa)

2000 (5 Feb). Sheet 110×75 mm. Perf 14½×13½ (C).

MS928 **889a** £1 multicoloured	3·00	3·00
First Day Cover		4·00
Presentation Pack	4·00	

Withdrawn: 29.2.2001.

890 'Ocean Adventure' (Gemma Carré)

891 'Solar Power' (Chantal Varley-Best)

892 'Floating City and Space Cars' (Nicola Singleton)

893 'Conservation' (Carly Logan)

'Stampin' the Future (children's stamp design competition) Winners

(Litho Questa)

2000 (9 May). Perf 14 (C).

929	**890**	22p. multicoloured	65	65
930	**891**	22p. multicoloured	65	65
931	**892**	22p. multicoloured	65	65
932	**893**	22p. multicoloured	65	65
929/32 *Set of 4*			2·40	2·40
First Day Cover				3·50
Presentation Pack			3·50	
MS933 150×100 mm. Nos. 929/32			3·00	3·50
First Day Cover				5·00
Presentation Pack			5·00	

Plate Nos.: All designs 1A (×4).
Sheets: 10 (2×5).
Imprint: Central, left-hand margin.
Withdrawn: 31.5.2001.

894 'Jersey in Europe'

895 'Building Europe'

904 19th-century Oyster Cutter

905 10th-century Ketch

Europa

(Des A. Copp (26p.), J.-P. Cousin (34p.). Litho Cartor)

2000 (9 May). Perf 13½×13 (C).

934	**894**	26p. multicoloured	2·00	2·00
935	**895**	34p. multicoloured	3·00	3·50
934/5 *Set of 2*			4·50	4·75
First Day Cover				6·00
Presentation Pack			5·50	

Plate Nos.: Both values 1A (×4).
Sheets: 10 (2×5) 26p.; (5×2) 34p.
Imprint: Central, left-hand margin (26p.); upper left-hand margin (34p.).
Withdrawn: 31.5.2001.

896 Roman Merchant Ship

897 Viking Longship

898 13th-century Warship

899 14th-15th century Merchant Ship

900 Tudor Warship

901 17th-century Warship

902 18th-century Naval Cutter

903 19th-century Barque

'The Stamp Show 2000' International Stamp Exhibition, London. Maritime Heritage

(Des A. Theobald. Litho B.D.T.)

2000 (22 May). Perf 14×13½ (C).

936	**896**	22p. multicoloured	45	25
		a. Horiz strip of 5. Nos. 936/40	3·00	3·00
		b. Booklet pane. Nos. 936/9 and 941/4	4·50	
		c. Booklet pane. Nos. 936/7, 939/41 and 943/5	4·50	
		d. Booklet pane. Nos. 936, 938/42 and 944/5	4·50	
		e. Booklet pane. Nos. 936/8, 940/3 and 945	4·50	
937	**897**	22p. multicoloured	45	25
		a. Booklet pane. Nos. 937/40 and 942/5	4·50	
938	**898**	22p. multicoloured	45	25
939	**899**	22p. multicoloured	45	25
940	**900**	22p. multicoloured	45	25
941	**901**	26p. multicoloured	50	30
		a. Horiz strip of 5. Nos. 941/5	3·25	3·25
942	**902**	26p. multicoloured	50	30
943	**903**	26p. multicoloured	50	30
944	**904**	26p. multicoloured	50	30
945	**905**	26p. multicoloured	50	30
936/45 *Set of 10*			6·00	6·00
First Day Cover				6·50
First Day Cover (set of 5 booklet panes)				31·00
Presentation Pack			6·50	
Souvenir Folder			13·00	
MS946 174×104 mm. Nos. 936/45			6·00	6·00
First Day Cover				7·00
Presentation Pack			7·00	
		a. With 'The Stamp Show 2000' logo added to top margin	6·00	6·00
First Day Cover				7·00
Presentation Pack			7·00	

Plate Nos.: Both values and miniature sheet 1A (×5).
Sheet: 10 (5×2). The five designs for each value printed together, *se-tenant*, in horizontal strips of 5 throughout the sheets, with 'The Stamp Show 2000' logo on the bottom sheet margin.
Withdrawn: 31.5.2001 (sheets).

906 Bottle-nosed Dolphins

907 Long-finned Pilot Whales

908 Common Porpoises

909 Grey Seals

910 Risso's Dolphins

911 White-beaked Dolphin

912a Common Dolphins (*Illustration reduced. Actual size* 150×100 mm)

World Environment Day. Marine Mammals

(Des W. Oliver. Litho B.D.T.)

2000 (5 June). Perf 15×14 (C).

947	**906**	22p. multicoloured	50	55
948	**907**	26p. multicoloured	55	60
949	**908**	34p. multicoloured	80	85
950	**909**	38p. multicoloured	1·00	1·10
951	**910**	44p. multicoloured	1·10	1·20
952	**911**	64p. multicoloured	1·50	1·70
947/52 *Set of 6*			5·00	5·50
First Day Cover				6·00
Presentation Pack			6·50	
MS953 150×100 mm. **912a** £1.50, multicoloured			4·00	4·50
First Day Cover				6·00
Presentation Pack			6·00	

Plate Nos.: All values 1A, 1B, 1C (each ×4).
Sheets: 10 (2×5).
Imprint: Central, left-hand margin.
Withdrawn: 30.6.2001.

913 Prince William and Alps

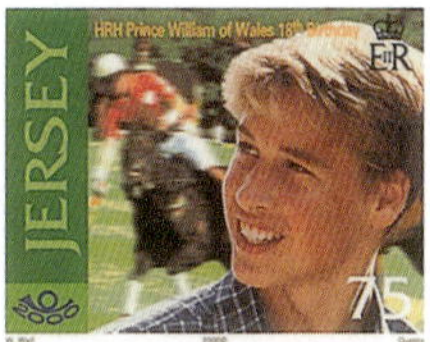

914 Prince William and Polo Player

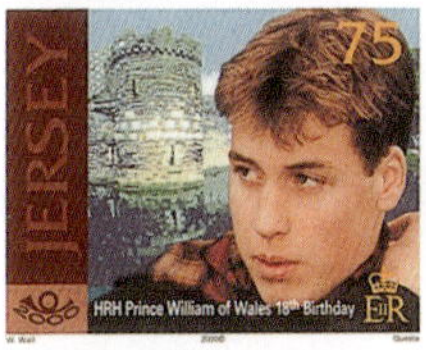

915 Prince William and Beaumaris Castle

916 Prince William and Fireworks

18th Birthday of Prince William

(Des W. Wall. Litho Questa)

2000 (21 June). Perf 14½ (C).

954	**913**	75p. multicoloured	1·50	1·50
955	**914**	75p. multicoloured	1·50	1·50
956	**915**	75p. multicoloured	1·50	1·50
957	**916**	75p. multicoloured	1·50	1·50
954/7 *Set of 4*			6·00	6·00
First Day Cover				7·00
Presentation Pack			6·75	

Plate Nos.: All designs 1A (×4).
Sheets: 10 (2×5).
Imprint: Central, left-hand margin.
Withdrawn: 30.6.2001.

'World Stamp Expo 2000', Anaheim, U.S.A.

(Litho B.D.T.)

2000 (7 July). As No. **MS**953, but with multicoloured exhibition logo added to top left corner of sheet margin. Perf 15×14 (C).

MS958 150×100 mm. **912a** £1.50, multicoloured	4·00	4·00
First Day Cover		6·00

Withdrawn: 31.7.2001.

917 Queen Elizabeth the Queen Mother with Roses

918 Queen Elizabeth the Queen Mother with Daisies

Queen Elizabeth the Queen Mother's 100th Birthday

(Des Colleen Corlett. Litho and die-stamped Questa)

2000 (4 Aug). Perf 14½ (C).

959	**917**	50p. multicoloured	1·20	1·20
960	**918**	50p. multicoloured	1·20	1·20
959/60 *Set of 2*			2·50	2·50
First Day Cover				3·25
Presentation Pack			3·25	
MS961 150×100 mm. Nos. 959/60			2·50	3·00
First Day Cover				4·50
Presentation Pack			3·50	
Souvenir Folder (containing **MS**961, *first day cover and presentation pack)*			16·00	

Plate Nos.: Both designs 1A (×6).
Sheets: 10 (5×2).
Imprint: Bottom margin.
Withdrawn: 31.8.2001.

919 Supermarine Spitfire MK Ia

920 Hawker Hurricane Mk I

921 Bristol Blenheim Mk IV

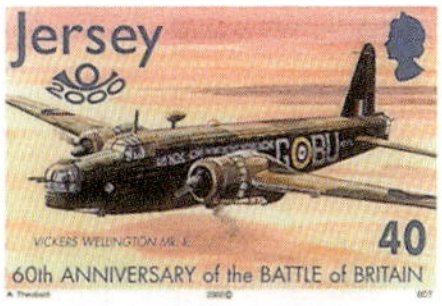

922 Vickers Wellington Mk Ic

923 Boulton Paul Defiant Mk I

924 Short Sunderland Mk I

60th Anniversary of Battle of Britain

(Des A. Theobald. Litho Questa B.D.T.)

2000 (15 Sept). Perf 14 (C).

962	**919**	22p. multicoloured	50	55
963	**920**	26p. multicoloured	60	65
964	**921**	36p. multicoloured	80	85
965	**922**	40p. multicoloured	90	95
966	**923**	45p. multicoloured	1·00	1·10
967	**924**	65p. multicoloured	1·50	1·60
962/7 *Set of 6*			4·75	5·00

First Day Cover		5·50
Presentation Pack	6·00	

Plate Nos.: All values 1A.
Sheets: 10 (2×5).
Imprint: Bottom margin.
Withdrawn: 29.9.2001.

925 Virgin Mary

926 Shepherd

927 Angel

928 Magi with Gift

Christmas. Children's Nativity Play

(Des F. Venton. Litho Cartor)

2000 (7 Nov). Perf 13 (C).

968	**925**	22p. multicoloured	55	55
969	**926**	26p. multicoloured	65	65
970	**927**	36p. multicoloured	1·00	1·00
971	**928**	65p. multicoloured	1·60	1·60
968/71 *Set of 4*			3·50	3·50
First Day Cover				4·50
Presentation Pack			4·50	

Plate Nos.: All values 1A (each ×4).
Sheets: 10 (5×2).
Imprint: Bottom margin.
Withdrawn: 30.11.2001.

Year Pack 2000

2000 (1 Dec). Comprises Nos. 927/32, 934/45, 947/57 and 959/71.

Year Pack	50·00

Sold out: By 4.05.

Post Office Yearbook

2000 (1 Dec). Comprises Nos. 927/32, 934/45, 947/57 and 959/71.

Yearbook	55·00

Sold out: By 8.05.

929a Snake (*Illustration reduced. Actual size* 110×75 mm)

Chinese New Year ('Year of the Snake')

(Des V. Ambrus. Litho Questa)

2001 (24 Jan). Sheet 110×75 mm. Perf 14×13½ (C).

MS972	**929a**	£1 multicoloured	2·75	3·00
First Day Cover				4·50
Presentation Pack			4·75	

Withdrawn: 31.1.2002.

930 *Rose* (1851–61)

931 *Comete* (1856–67)

932 *Cygne* (1894–1912)

933 *Victoria* (1896–1918)

934 *Attala* (1920–25)

935 *Brittany* (1933–62)

Maritime Links with France. Mail Packet Ships

(Des I. Boyd. Litho Cartor)

2001 (24 Jan). Perf 13×13½ (C).

973	**930**	22p. multicoloured	50	55
974	**931**	26p. multicoloured	60	65
975	**932**	36p. multicoloured	80	85
976	**933**	40p. multicoloured	90	95
977	**934**	45p. multicoloured	1·20	1·30
978	**935**	65p. multicoloured	1·70	1·80
973/8 *Set of 6*			5·25	5·50
First Day Cover				6·00
Presentation Pack			6·00	

Plate Nos.: All values 1A (×4).
Sheets: 10 (2×5).
Imprint: Central, left-hand margin.
Withdrawn: 31.1.2002.

936 H.H.S. *Jersey* (4th Rate), 1654–91

937 H.M.S. *Jersey* (6th Rate), 1694–98

938 H.M.S. *Jersey* (4th Rate), 1698–1731

939 H.M.S. *Jersey* (4th Rate), 1736–83

940 H.M.S. *Jersey* (cutter), 1860–73

941 H.M.S. *Jersey* (destroyer), 1938–41

Jersey Naval Connections (1st series). Royal Navy Ships named after Jersey

(Des A. Theobald. Litho B.D.T.)

2001 (3 Apr). Perf 14 (C).

979	**936**	23p. multicoloured	50	55
980	**937**	26p. multicoloured	60	65
981	**938**	37p. multicoloured	80	85
982	**939**	41p. multicoloured	1·00	95
983	**940**	46p. multicoloured	1·20	1·10
984	**941**	66p. multicoloured	1·50	1·60
979/84 *Set of 6*			5·00	5·00
First Day Cover				6·00
Presentation Pack			5·50	

Plate Nos.: 23p., 26p. 1A, 1B (each ×4); others 1A (×4).
Sheets: 10 (2×5).
Imprint: Bottom, left-hand corner margin.
Withdrawn: 30.4.2002.

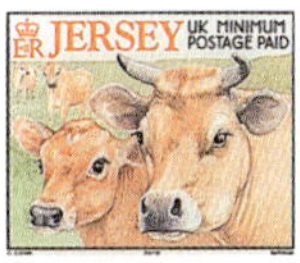

942 Jersey Cows

943 Potatoes

944 Tomatoes

945 Cauliflower and Purple-sprouting Broccoli

946 Peppers and Courgettes

Jersey Cows and Farm Produce

(Des Colleen Corlett. Litho SNP Ausprint, Melbourne)

2001 (3 Apr). Self-adhesive. Perf 11½ (C).

985	**942**	(26p.) multicoloured (abcd)	2·75	2·75
986	**943**	(26p.) multicoloured (abcd)	2·75	2·75
987	**944**	(26p.) multicoloured (abcd)	2·75	2·75
988	**945**	(26p.) multicoloured (abcd)	2·75	2·75
989	**946**	(26p.) multicoloured (abcd)	2·75	2·75
985/9 *Set of 5*			13·00	13·00
First Day Cover				10·00
Presentation Pack			14·00	

Nos. 985/9, which are inscribed 'UK MINIMUM POSTAGE PAID' and were initially sold at 26p. each, come, *se-tenant*, in strips of 5 or rolls of 100 with the surplus self-adhesive paper around each stamp removed.

Initially released with '2001' imprint dates (price per set, £10 unused, £11 used), Nos. 985/9 were subsequently reissued inscribed '2002' (price, unused or used, £9), '2003' (price, unused or used, £8) and '2005' (price £7).

Printings: (a) 3.4.2001. Inscr '2001'; (b) 4.10.2002. Inscr '2002'; (c) 4.4.2003. Inscr '2003'; (d) 21.10.2005. Inscr '2005'.

947 Queen Elizabeth II

75th Birthday of Queen Elizabeth II

(Des W. Wall. Litho Questa)

2001 (21 Apr). Perf 14×15 (C).

990	**947**	£3 multicoloured	6·00	6·50
First Day Cover				7·00
Presentation Pack			7·00	

No. 990 was retained in use as part of the current definitive series.
Plate Nos.: 1A, 1B, 1C, 1D, 1E, 1F (each ×4).
Sheets: 10 (2×5).
Imprint: Bottom margin.
Withdrawn: 30.11.2008.

948 Agile Frog

949 Trout

950 White Water-Lily

951 Common Blue Damselfly

952 Palmate Newt

953 Tufted Duck

954a Common Kingfisher (*Illustration reduced. Actual size* 150×100 mm)

Europa. Water, a Natural Treasure. Pond Life

(Des N. Parlett. Litho B.D.T.)

2001 (22 May). Perf 14 (No. **MS**997) or 14½×14 (others), both comb.

991	**948**	23p. multicoloured	60	65
992	**949**	26p. multicoloured	70	75
993	**950**	37p. multicoloured	1·00	1·10
994	**951**	41p. multicoloured	1·10	1·20
995	**952**	46p. multicoloured	1·20	1·40
996	**953**	66p. multicoloured	2·00	2·20
991/6 *Set of 6*			6·00	6·50
First Day Cover				7·00
Presentation Pack			7·00	
MS997 150×100 mm. **954a** £1.50, multicoloured			5·00	5·00
First Day Cover				5·50
Presentation Pack			5·25	

The 26p. and 37p. values include the 'EUROPA' emblem.
Plate Nos.: All values 1A, 1B (each ×4).
Sheets: 10 (2×5).
Imprint: Central, left-hand margin.
Withdrawn: 31.5.2002.

'Belgica 2001' International Stamp Exhibition, Brussels

(Litho B.D.T.)

2001 (9 June). No. **MS**997 optd 'JERSEY AT BELGICA 2001' on sheet margin. Perf 14 (C).

MS998	**954a**	£1.50 multicoloured	5·00	4·50

First Day Cover		5·50
Presentation Pack	5·50	

Withdrawn: 29.6.2002.

955 Long-eared Owl

956 Peregrine Falcon

957 Short-eared Owl

958 Western Marsh Harrier

959 Nothern Sparrow Hawk

960 Tawny Owl

961a Barn Owl (*Illustration reduced. Actual size* 110×75 mm)

Birds of Prey

(Des M. Chester. Litho Cartor)

2001 (3 July). Perf 13½×13 (C).

999	**955**	23p. multicoloured	50	55
		a. Booklet pane. Nos. 999/1004	3·75	
		b. Booklet pane. Nos. 999, 1001 and 1004, each ×2	4·25	
		c. Booklet pane. Nos. 999×2, 1000/1 and 1003 ×2	3·25	
		d. Booklet pane. Nos. 999/1001, 1002 ×2 and 1004	4·00	
1000	**956**	26p. multicoloured	60	65
1001	**957**	37p. multicoloured	80	85
1002	**958**	41p. multicoloured	1·00	95
1003	**959**	46p. multicoloured	1·20	1·10
1004	**960**	66p. multicoloured	1·50	1·60
999/1004 *Set of 6*			5·00	5·00
First Day Cover				6·00
Presentation Pack			5·75	

MS1005 110×75 mm. **961a** £1.50, multicoloured	5·00	5·00
a. Booklet pane. As No. **MS**1005, but 153×100 mm with line of roulettes at left	9·00	9·50
First Day Cover		6·50
Presentation Pack	6·50	

Nos. 999a/d each have margins all round and a bird Illustration on the tab at left.

No. **MS**1005a also differs from the normal miniature sheet by the owl on the post being centred on the stamp. No. **MS**1005 shows the '£1.5' of the face value across the post, but on the booklet pane the figures are to the right of the post.

Plate Nos.: All values 1A (×4).
Sheets: 10 (5×2).
Imprint: Bottom margin.
Withdrawn: 31.7.2002 (sheets).

962a *Jersey Clipper* (yacht) (*illustraion reduced. Actual size* 150×100 mm)

The Times Clipper 2000 Round the World Yacht Race

(Des B. Ozard. Litho Questa)

2001 (17 Sept). Sheet 150×100 mm. Perf 13½×14 (C).

MS1006 **962a** £1.50 multicoloured	4·00	5·00
First Day Cover		6·00
Presentation Pack	5·50	

Withdrawn: 30.9.2002.

963 Tilley 26 Manual Fire Engine, *circa* 1845

964 Albion Merryweather, *circa* 1935

965 Dennis Ace, *circa* 1940

966 Dennis F8 Pump Escape, *circa* 1952

967 Landrover Merry-weather, *circa* 1968

968 Dennis Carmichael, *circa* 1989

Centenary of Jersey Fire and Rescue Service. Fire Engines

(Des A. Copp. Litho Cartor)

2001 (25 Sept). Perf 13×13½ (C).

1007	**963**	23p. multicoloured	50	55
1008	**964**	26p. multicoloured	60	65
1009	**965**	37p. multicoloured	80	85
1010	**966**	41p. multicoloured	90	95
1011	**967**	46p. multicoloured	1·00	1·10
1012	**968**	66p. multicoloured	1·50	1·60
1007/12 *Set of 6*			4·75	5·00

First Day Cover		6·00
Presentation Pack	6·00	

Plate Nos.: All values 1A (×4).
Sheets: 10 (2×5).
Imprint: Central, left-hand margin.
Withdrawn: 30.9.2002.

'Hafnia 01' International Stamp Exhibition, Copenhagen

(Litho Cartor)

2001 (16 Oct). As No. **MS**1005, but with brown-red exhibition logo added to bottom left corner of sheet margin and additionally inscr 'Jersey visits Hafnia 01 Denmark'. Perf 13½×13 (C).

MS1013 **961a** £1.50, multicoloured	4·00	4·00
First Day Cover		5·00
Presentation Pack	5·50	

Withdrawn: 31.10.2002.

969 Nativity

970 Street Decorations

971 Carol Singers with Hand Bells

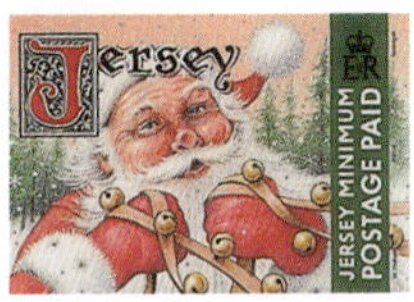

972 Father Christmas

973 Christmas Tree Decorations

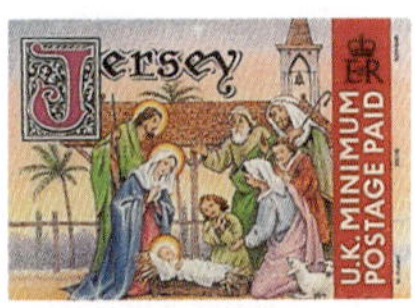

974 Adoration of the Shepherds

975 Carol Singers and Father Christmas in Sleigh

976 Paper Bell, Chains and Christmas Tree

977 Church Bells ringing

978 Christmas Cracker

Christmas. Bells

(Des M. Pollard. Litho SNP Ausprint, Melbourne)

2001 (6 Nov). Self-adhesive. Perf 11×11½ (die-cut).

1014	**969**	(23p.) multicoloured (abc)	70	70
		a. Booklet pane. Nos. 1014, 1016/18, 1019/20 and 1022/3, each ×2 (a)		9·00
1015	**970**	(23p.) multicoloured (abc)	70	70
1016	**971**	(23p.) multicoloured (abc)	70	70
1017	**972**	(23p.) multicoloured (abc)	70	70
1018	**973**	(23p.) multicoloured (abc)	70	70
1019	**974**	(26p.) multicoloured (ab)	70	70
1020	**975**	(26p.) multicoloured (ab)	70	70
1021	**976**	(26p.) multicoloured (ab)	70	70
1022	**977**	(26p.) multicoloured (ab)	70	70
1023	**978**	(26p.) multicoloured (ab)	70	70
1014/23 *Set of 10*			6·50	6·50
First Day Cover				7·00
Presentation Pack			7·50	

Nos. 1014/18 are inscribed 'JERSEY MINIMUM POSTAGE PAID' and were initially sold for 23p., and Nos. 1019/23 are inscribed 'U.K. MINIMUM POSTAGE PAID' and were initially sold for 26p. The 5 designs for each value were printed together, *se-tenant*, in strips of 5 or rolls of 100. Nos. 1014, 1016/20 and 1022/3 also come from £3.92 booklets, containing pane No. 1014a on which the surplus self-adhesive paper was retained.

Initially released with '2001' imprint dates Nos. 1014/23 were subsequently reissued inscribed '2002' and '2003' (all the same price).

Printings: (a) 6.11.2001. Inscr '2001'; (b) 23.11.2002. Inscr '2002'; (c) 10.11.2003. Inscr '2003'.
Sold out: By 6.2003 (booklets) or by end of 2005 (coils).

Post Office Yearbook

2001 (1 Dec). Comprises Nos. **MS**972/97, 999/1012 and 1014/23.

Yearbook	55·00

Sold out: By 7.1.2008.

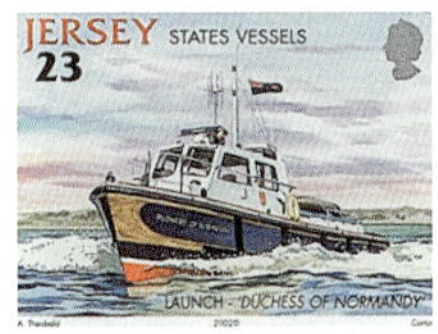

979 *Duchess of Normandy* (launch)

980 *Duke of Normandy* (tug)

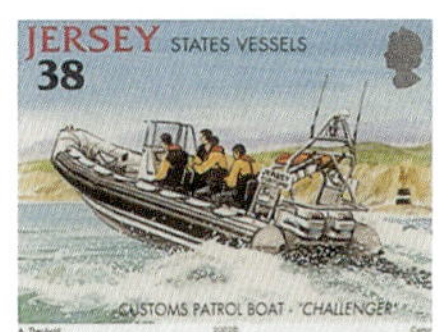

981 *Challenger* (customs patrol boat)

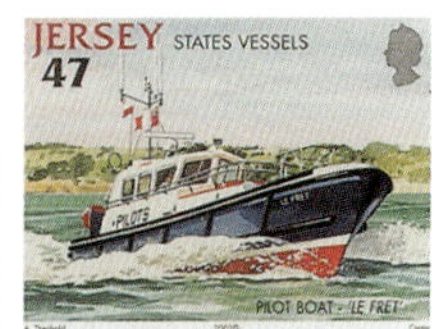

982 *Le Fret* (pilot boat)

983 *Norman le Brocq* (fisheries protection vessel)

States Vessels

(Des A. Theobald. Litho Cartor)

2002 (22 Jan). Perf 13×13½ (C).

1024	**979**	23p. multicoloured	50	55
1025	**980**	29p. multicoloured	65	70
1026	**981**	38p. multicoloured	80	85
1027	**982**	47p. multicoloured	1·20	1·30
1028	**983**	68p. multicoloured	1·70	1·90
1024/8 *Set of 5*			4·50	4·75
First Day Cover				5·75
Presentation Pack			5·75	

Plate Nos.: All values 1A (×4).
Sheets: 10 (2×5).
Imprint: Bottom, left-hand margin.
Withdrawn: 31.1.2003.

984 Queen Elizabeth in Coronation Robes (after Cecil Beaton)

Golden Jubilee

(Litho with gold and silver embossing Cartor)

2002 (6 Feb). Perf 13½ (C).

1029	**984**	£3 multicoloured	6·25	6·50
First Day Cover				7·50
Presentation Pack			6·75	

Plate Nos.: 1A (×5).
Sheets: 4 (2×2).
Imprint: Upper left-hand margin.
Withdrawn: 28.2.2003.

985a Horse (*Illustration reduced. Actual size* 110×75 mm)

Chinese New Year ('Year of the Horse')

(Des V. Ambrus. Litho Questa)

2002 (12 Feb). Sheet 110×75 mm. Perf 14×13½ (C).

MS1030	**985a**	£1 multicoloured	2·20	2·50
First Day Cover				4·50
Presentation Pack			4·50	

Withdrawn: 28.2.2003.

986 Elephant Float, Parish of St. John, 1980

987 Clown with Red Hair, Grouville, 1996

988 Clown with White Hat, Optimists, 1988

989 Performing Seal, Grouville, 1996

Europa. Circus. Carnival Floats

(Des N. Shewring. Litho B.D.T.)

2002 (12 Mar). Perf 14 (C).

1031	**986**	23p. multicoloured	50	55
1032	**987**	29p. multicoloured	65	70
1033	**988**	38p. multicoloured	1·00	1·10
1034	**989**	68p. multicoloured	1·70	2·00
1031/4 *Set of 4*			3·50	4·00
First Day Cover				4·50
Presentation Pack			4·50	

The 29p. and 38p. values include the 'EUROPA' emblem.
Plate Nos.: All values 1A, 1B (each ×4).
Sheets: 10 (5×2).
Imprint: Bottom margin, right-hand side.
Withdrawn: 31.3.2003.

990 Aubrey Boomer

991 Harry Vardon

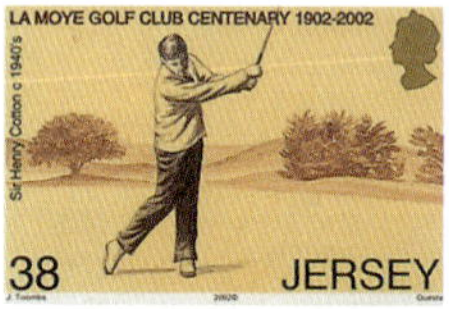

992 Sir Henry Cotton

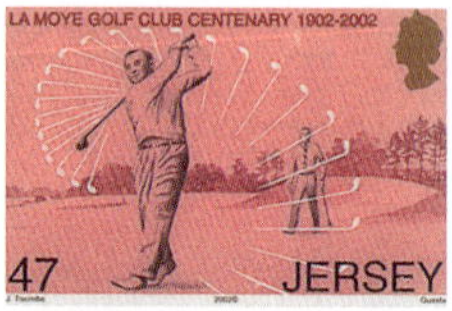

993 Diagram of Golf Swing

994 Putting

Centenary of La Moye Golf Club

(Des Jennifer Toombs. Litho Questa)

2002 (16 Apr). Perf 14 (C).

1035	**990**	23p. multicoloured	50	55
1036	**991**	29p. multicoloured	65	70
1037	**992**	38p. multicoloured	80	85
1038	**993**	47p. multicoloured	1·00	1·10
1039	**994**	68p. multicoloured	1·50	1·70
1035/9 *Set of 5*			4·00	4·50
First Day Cover				5·50
Presentation Pack			5·50	

Plate Nos.: 23p., 29p. 1A, 1B, 1C, 1D, 1E, 1F (each ×7); 38p. 1A, 1B, 1C, 1D, 1E, 1F, 1G, 1H, 1J (each ×7); 47p., 68p. 1A, 1B, 1C (each ×7).
Sheets: 10 (2×5) with enlarged illustrated right margins.
Imprint: Lower left-hand margin.
Withdrawn: 30.4.2003.

995 Vauxhall 12, 1952

996 Jaguar 2.4 MkII, 1959–60

997 Austin 1800 1972–73

998 Ford Cortina MkIV, 1978

999 Honda ST 1100 Motorcycle, 1995–2000

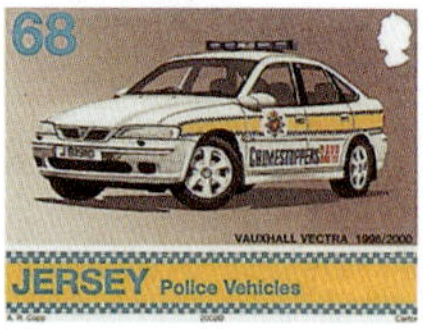

1000 Vauxhall Vectra, 1998–2000

50th Anniversary of States of Jersey Police. Patrol Vehicles

(Des A. Copp. Litho Cartor)

2002 (24 May). Perf 13 (C).

1040	**995**	23p. multicoloured	50	55
1041	**996**	29p. multicoloured	65	70
1042	**997**	38p. multicoloured	80	85
1043	**998**	40p. multicoloured	85	90
1044	**999**	47p. multicoloured	1·00	1·10
1045	**1000**	68p. multicoloured	1·50	1·70
1040/5 *Set of 6*			5·00	5·25
First Day Cover				6·25
Presentation Pack			6·00	

Plate Nos.: All values 1A (each ×4).
Sheets: 10 (2×5).
Imprint: Bottom, left-hand margin.
Withdrawn: 31.5.2003.

1001 Honey Bee

1002 Seven-spot Ladybird

1003 Great Green Bush-cricket

1004 Greater Horn-tail

1005 Emperor Dragonfly

1006 Hawthorn Shield Bug

Insects (1st series)

(Des W. Oliver. Litho B.D.T.)

2002 (18 June). Perf 15×14 (C).

1046	**1001**	23p. multicoloured	50	55
1047	**1002**	29p. multicoloured	65	70
1048	**1003**	38p. multicoloured	80	85
1049	**1004**	40p. multicoloured	85	90
1050	**1005**	47p. multicoloured	1·10	1·20
1051	**1006**	68p. multicoloured	1·50	1·70
1046/51 *Set of 6*			4·75	5·50
First Day Cover				6·50
Presentation Pack			6·00	

Plate Nos.: All values 1A, 1B (each ×4).
Sheets: 10 (2×5).
Imprint: Bottom margin, left-hand corner.
Withdrawn: 30.6.2003.

1007 Queen Elizabeth the Queen Mother in 1910, 1923 and 2002

Queen Elizabeth the Queen Mother Commemoration

(Des W. Wall. Litho Questa)

2002 (4 Aug). Perf 14×15 (C).

1052	**1007**	£2 multicoloured	4·25	4·50
First Day Cover				5·50
Presentation Pack			5·50	

Plate Nos.: 1A, 1B, 1C, 1D, 1E, 1F (each ×4).
Sheets: 10 (2×5).
Imprint: Lower left-hand margin.
Withdrawn: 30.8.2003.

1008 Hydrangeas

1009 Chrysanthemums

1010 Hare's Tails and Pampas Grasses

1011 Asters

1012 Carnations

1013 Gladioli

1014a 'Zanzibar' Float (winner of Prix d'Honneur, 1999)
(Illustration reduced. Actual size 150×100 mm)

Centenary of 'Battle of Flowers' Parade

(Des M. Pollard. Litho Cartor)

2002 (8 Aug). Perf 13 (C).

1053	**1008**	23p. multicoloured	50	55
		a. Booklet pane. Nos. 1053/8, with margins all round	5·25	
1054	**1009**	29p. multicoloured	65	70
1055	**1010**	38p. multicoloured	80	85
1056	**1011**	40p. multicoloured	85	90
1057	**1012**	47p. multicoloured	1·00	1·10
1058	**1013**	68p. multicoloured	1·50	1·70
1053/8 *Set of 6*			4·75	5·25
First Day Cover				6·00
Presentation Pack			6·00	
MS1059 150×100 mm. **1014a** £2 multicoloured			4·25	4·50
		a. Booklet pane. As No. **MS**1059, but with line of roulettes at left.	4·25	
First Day Cover				5·50
Presentation Pack			5·00	

Booklet pane No. 1053a exists in three versions which differ in the order of the stamps within the block of six.

Plate Nos.: All values 1A (×4).
Sheets: 10 (2×5).
Imprint: Central, left-hand margin.
Withdrawn: 30.8.2003 (sheets).

1015 British Dilute Tortoiseshell

1016 Cream Persian

1017 Blue Exotic Shorthair

1018 Black Smoke Devon Rex

1019 British Silver Tabby

1020 Usual Abyssinian

1021a British Cream/White Bi-colour Cross (*Illustration reduced. Actual size* 110×75 mm)

25th Anniversary of Caesarea Cat Club

(Des G. Vasarhelyi. Litho B.D.T.)

2002 (12 Oct). Perf 14 (No. **MS**1066) or 15×14 (others), both comb.

1060	**1015**	23p. multicoloured	50	55
1061	**1016**	29p. multicoloured	65	70
1062	**1017**	38p. multicoloured	80	85
1063	**1018**	40p. multicoloured	85	90
1064	**1019**	47p. multicoloured	1·00	1·10
1065	**1020**	68p. multicoloured	1·50	1·70
1060/5 *Set of 6*			4·75	5·25
First Day Cover				6·00
Presentation Pack			5·75	
MS1066 110×75 mm. **1021a** £2 multicoloured			4·25	4·50
First Day Cover				6·00
Presentation Pack			5·50	

Plate Nos.: All values 1A, 1B (each ×4).
Sheets: 10 (2×5).
Imprint: Lower left-hand margin.
Withdrawn: 31.10.2003.

1022 Victorian Pillar Box in Central Market

1023 Edward VII Wall Box, Colomberie

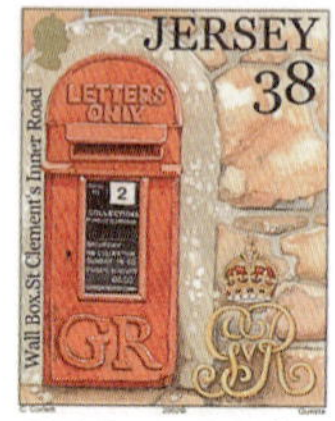

1024 George V Wall Box, St. Clement's Inner Road

1025 George V 'Boite Mobile' Ship Box

1026 Elizabeth II Pillar Box, Parade

1027 Modern Pillar Boxes, La Collette

1028a Posting Letter in First Pillar Box, David Place (*Illustration reduced. Actual size* 150×100 mm)

Jersey Postal History (1st series). 150th Anniversary of the First Pillar Box

(Des Colleen Corlett. Litho Questa)

2002 (23 Nov). Perf 14½ (No. **MS**1073) or 14½×14 (others), both comb.

1067	**1022**	23p. multicoloured	50	55
1068	**1023**	29p. multicoloured	65	70
1069	**1024**	38p. multicoloured	80	85
1070	**1025**	40p. multicoloured	85	90
1071	**1026**	47p. multicoloured	1·00	1·10
1072	**1027**	68p. multicoloured	1·50	1·60
1067/72 *Set of 6*			4·75	5·25
First Day Cover				6·00
Presentation Pack			5·75	
MS1073 150×100 mm. **1028a** £2 multicoloured			4·25	4·50
First Day Cover				7·00
Presentation Pack			5·50	

See also Nos. 1286/92.

Plate Nos.: All values 1A (×5).
Sheets: 10 (5×2).
Imprint: Bottom, right-hand corner margin.
Withdrawn: 31.10.2003.

Post Office Yearbook

2002 (2 Dec). Comprises Nos. 1024/73.

Yearbook	60·00

Sold out.

1029 Sanchez-Besa Hydroplane

1030 Supermarine S.6B Seaplane

1031 De Havilland DH84 Dragon

1032 De Havilland DH89a Rapide

1033 Vickers 701 Viscount

1034 BAC One Eleven

1035a Jacob Ellehammer's Biplane, 1906 (*Illustration reduced. Actual size* 112×76 mm)

Centenary of Powered Flight

(Des T. Theobald. Litho Cartor)

2003 (21 Jan). Perf 13½×13 (No. **MS**1080) or 13×13½ (others), both comb.

1074	**1029**	23p. multicoloured	50	55
		a. Booklet pane. Nos. 1074/9 with margins all round	4·75	
1075	**1030**	29p. multicoloured	65	70
1076	**1031**	38p. multicoloured	80	85
1077	**1032**	40p. multicoloured	85	90
1078	**1033**	47p. multicoloured	1·00	1·10
1079	**1034**	68p. multicoloured	1·50	1·60
1074/9 *Set of 6*			4·75	5·25
First Day Cover				6·75
Presentation Pack			6·75	
MS1080 112×76 mm. **1035a** £2 multicoloured			4·25	4·50
		a. Booklet pane. As No. **MS**1080, but 153×100 mm with line of roulettes at left	6·50	
First Day Cover				6·50
Presentation Pack			4·75	

No. 1074a comes with three different Illustrations on the margins.

The stamp in booklet pane No. **MS**1080a differs from that in the normal miniature sheet by having the imprint date centred, rather than ranged to the left.

Plate Nos.: All values 1A (×4).
Sheets: 10 (2×5).
Imprint: Bottom, right-hand corner margin.
Withdrawn: 31.1.2004.

1036 Ram (*Illustration reduced. Actual size* 110×75 mm)

Chinese New Year ('Year of the Ram')

(Des V. Ambrus. Litho Questa)

2003 (1 Feb). Sheet 110×75 mm. Perf 14×13½ (C).

MS1081 **1036** £1 multicoloured	2·50	2·75
First Day Cover		4·00
Presentation Pack	3·25	

Withdrawn: 28.2.2004.

1037 'Portelet' (Adrian Allinson)

1038 'Jersey' (Lander)

1039 'Channel Islands Map'

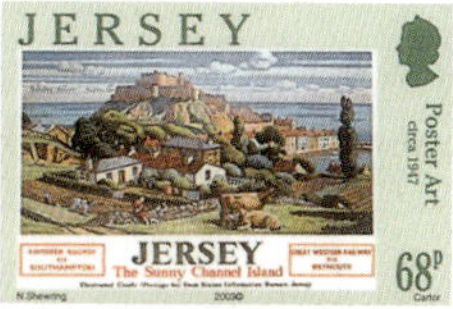

1040 'Jersey, the Sunny Channel Island' (A. Allinson)

Europa. Poster Art. Travel Posters

(Des N. Shewring. Litho Cartor)

2003 (11 Mar). Perf 13½ (C).

1082	**1037**	23p. multicoloured	50	55
1083	**1038**	29p. multicoloured	80	80
1084	**1039**	38p. multicoloured	1·25	1·50
1085	**1040**	68p. multicoloured	1·75	2·00
1082/5 *Set of 4*			4·00	4·50
First Day Cover				5·00
Presentation Pack			5·00	

The 29p. and 38p. values include the 'EUROPA' emblem.

Plate Nos.: All values 1A (×4).
Sheets: 10 (2×5) 23p., 68p.; (5×2) 29p., 38p.
Imprint: Lower left-hand margin.
Withdrawn: 31.3.2004.

1041 Violet Channel Light Buoy

1042 St. Catherine's Breakwater Light

1043 Frouquie Aubert Light Buoy

1044 Mont Ube Lighthouse

1045 Banc des Ormes Light Buoy

1046 Gronez Point Lighthouse

Jersey Lighthouses (2nd series)

(Des A. Copp. Litho B.D.T.)

2003 (15 Apr). Perf 13½ (C).

1086	**1041**	29p. multicoloured	50	30
		a. Pair. Nos. 1086/7	1·30	1·30
1087	**1042**	29p. multicoloured	50	30
1088	**1043**	30p. multicoloured	55	35
		a. Pair. Nos. 1088/9	1·30	1·30
1089	**1044**	30p. multicoloured	55	35
1090	**1045**	48p. multicoloured	85	50
		a. Pair. Nos. 1090/1	2·00	2·10
1091	**1046**	48p. multicoloured	85	50
1086/91 *Set of 6*			4·25	4·50
First Day Cover				5·50
Presentation Pack			5·50	

The two designs for each value were printed together, *se-tenant*, both horizontally and vertically in sheets of ten stamps.

Plate Nos.: All values 1A (×4).
Sheets: 10 (5×2).
Imprint: Lower left-hand margin.
Withdrawn: 30.4.2004.

1053a Loose-flowered Orchid (*Illustration reduced. Actual size* 110×75 mm)

Wild Orchids

(Des B. Ozard. Litho Cartor)

2003 (13 May). Perf 13 (C).

1092	**1047**	29p. multicoloured	60	65
1093	**1048**	30p. multicoloured	60	65
1094	**1049**	39p. multicoloured	80	85
1095	**1050**	50p. multicoloured	1·00	1·10
1096	**1051**	53p. multicoloured	1·10	1·20
1097	**1052**	69p. multicoloured	1·40	1·50
1092/7 *Set of 6*			5·25	5·75
First Day Cover				6·50
Presentation Pack			6·50	
MS1098 110×75 mm. **1053a** £2 multicoloured			4·00	4·25
First Day Cover				5·25
Presentation Pack			5·25	

Plate Nos.: All values 1A (×4).
Sheets: 10 (5×2).
Imprint: Lower left-hand margin.
Withdrawn: 31.5.2004.

1047 Southern-marsh Orchid

1048 Loose-flowered Orchid

1049 Spotted Orchid

1050 Autumn Ladies Tresses

1051 Green-winged Orchid

1052 Pyramidal Orchid

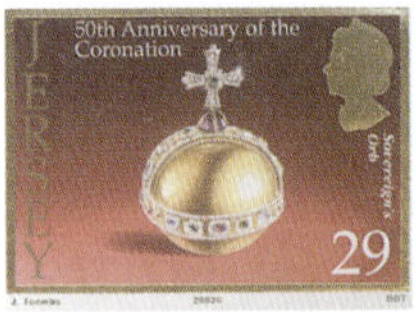

1054 Sovereign's Orb

1055 St. Edward's Crown

1056 Sceptre with Cross

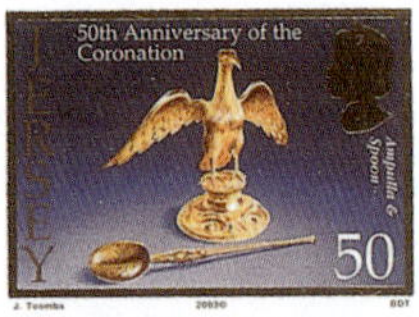

1057 Ampulla and Spoon

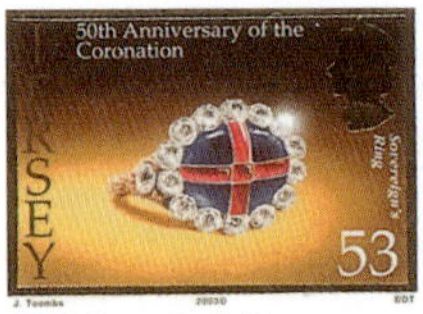

1058 Sovereign's Ring

1059 Armills

50th Anniversary of Coronation. Coronation Regalia

(Des Jennifer Toombs. Litho and die-stamped B.D.T.)

2003 (2 June). Perf 15×14 (C).

1099	**1054**	29p. multicoloured	60	65
1100	**1055**	30p. multicoloured	60	65
1101	**1056**	39p. multicoloured	80	85
1102	**1057**	50p. multicoloured	1·00	1·10
1103	**1058**	53p. multicoloured	1·00	1·10
1104	**1059**	69p. multicoloured	1·40	1·50
1099/1104 *Set of 6*			5·25	5·75
First Day Cover				6·50
Presentation Pack			6·50	
MS1105 150×100 mm. Nos. 1099/1104			5·25	5·75
First Day Cover				6·50
Presentation Pack			6·50	

Nos. 1099/1104 were each printed in sheets of 10 (2×5) with enlarged illustrated right-hand margins.
Plate Nos.: All values 1A (×6).
Sheets: 10 (2×5) with enlarged illustrated right-hand margins.
Imprint: Lower left-hand margin.
Withdrawn: 30.6.2004.

1060a Prince William, Prince Charles and Queen Elizabeth (*Illustration reduced. Actual size* 110×75 mm)

Royal Links

(Des The Partnership. Litho Questa)

2003 (21 June). Sheet 110×75 mm. Perf 14×13½ (C).

MS1106 **1060a** £2 multicoloured	4·00	4·25
First Day Cover		5·25
Presentation Pack	5·25	

Withdrawn: 30.6.2004.

1061 Rock Samphire and Paternosters

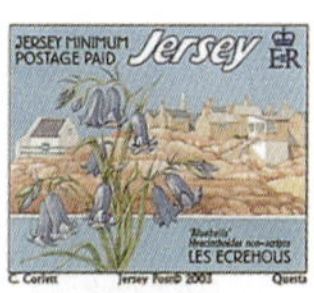

1062 Bluebells and Les Ecrehous

1063 Tree-mallow and Les Ecrehous

1064 Smooth Sow-thistle and Les Minquiers

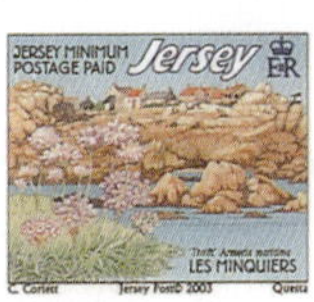

1065 Thrift and Les Minquiers

Offshore Reefs

(Des Colleen Corlett. Photo Questa)

2003 (5 Aug). Self-adhesive. Perf 11 (die-cut).

1107	**1061**	(29p.) multicoloured	1·10	1·25
1108	**1062**	(29p.) multicoloured	1·10	1·25
1109	**1063**	(29p.) multicoloured	1·10	1·25
1110	**1064**	(29p.) multicoloured	1·10	1·25
1111	**1065**	(29p.) multicoloured	1·10	1·25
1107/11 *Set of 5*			5·00	5·50
First Day Cover				5·50
Presentation Pack			5·50	

Nos. 1107/11, which are inscribed 'JERSEY MINIMUM POSTAGE PAID' and were initially sold at 29p. each, come *se-tenant* in strips of 5 or rolls of 100 with the surplus self-adhesive paper around each stamp removed.

Nos. 1107/11 are inscr '2003' with copyright symbol before date.

For designs as Nos. 1107/11 printed in lithography by Sprintpak see Nos. 1180/4.

1066 Albino Rex Rabbit

1067 Black Labrador Puppy

1068 Canary and Budgerigar

1069 Hamster

1070 Guinea Pig

1071a Border Collie (*Illustration reduced. Actual size* 150×100 mm)

Pets

(Des N. Parlett. Litho B.D.T.)

2003 (9 Sept). Perf 13×13½ (No. **MS**1117) or 13½ (others), both comb.

1112	**1066**	29p. multicoloured	95	95
1113	**1067**	30p. multicoloured	95	95
1114	**1068**	38p. multicoloured	1·20	1·20
1115	**1069**	53p. multicoloured	1·70	1·70
1116	**1070**	69p. multicoloured	2·20	2·20
1112/16 *Set of 5*			6·00	6·00
First Day Cover				7·00
Presentation Pack			7·00	
MS1117 150×100 mm. **1071a** £2 Border collie			5·50	5·50
First Day Cover				7·00
Presentation Pack			6·50	

Nos.: All values 1A (×4).
Sheets: 10 (2×5).
Imprint: Central, bottom margin.
Withdrawn: 30.9.2004.

'Bangkok 2003' International Stamp Exhibition

2003 (4 Oct). No. **MS**1098 optd with 'Jersey at Bangkok 2003' and emblem on sheet margin. Perf 13 (C).

MS1118 110×75 mm. £2 multicoloured	5·50	5·50
First Day Cover		7·00
Presentation Pack	6·50	

Withdrawn: 31.10.2004.

1072 Japanese Quince

1073 Winter Jasmine

1074 Snowdrop

1075 Winter Heath

1076 Chinese Witch-hazel

1077 Winter Daphne

Winter Flowers

(Des Wendy Tait. Litho Questa)

2003 (10 Nov). Perf 14½ (C).

1119	**1072**	29p. multicoloured	60	65
1120	**1073**	30p. multicoloured	60	65
1121	**1074**	39p. multicoloured	80	85
1122	**1075**	48p. multicoloured	95	1·00
1123	**1076**	53p. multicoloured	1·00	1·10
1124	**1077**	69p. multicoloured	1·40	1·50
1119/24 *Set of 6*			5·25	5·75
First Day Cover				6·75
Presentation Pack			6·50	

Plate Nos.: 29p. 1A, 1B, 1C, 1D; 30p. 1A, 1B, 1C, 1D, 1E, 1F; others 1A, 1B (each ×5).
Sheets: 10 (5×2).
Imprint: Right-hand side, bottom margin.
Withdrawn: 30.11.2004.

Post Office Yearbook

2003 (1 Dec). Comprises Nos. 1074/1104 and **MS**1106/17 and 1119/24.

Yearbook .... 60·00

Sold out: By 11.04.

1078 Rook

1079 Knight

1080 Bishop

1081 Pawn

1082 Queen

1083 King

Jersey Festivals (1st issue). Festival of Chess

(Des Jennifer Toombs. Litho BDT)

2004 (22 Jan). Perf 14×13½ (C).

1125	**1078**	29p. multicoloured	95	95
1126	**1079**	30p. multicoloured	1·00	1·00
1127	**1080**	39p. multicoloured	1·30	1·30
1128	**1081**	48p. multicoloured	1·60	1·60
1129	**1082**	53p. multicoloured	1·70	1·70
1130	**1083**	69p. multicoloured	2·20	2·20
1125/30 *Set of 6*			8·75	8·75
First Day Cover				10·00
Presentation Pack			9·00	

Plate Nos.: All values 1A (×5).
Sheets: 10 (5×2).
Imprint: Bottom margin.
Withdrawn: 31.1.2005.

1084a Monkey (*Illustration reduced. Actual size* 110×75 mm)

Chinese New Year ('Year of the Monkey')

(Des V. Ambrus. Litho Questa)

2004 (22 Jan). Sheet 110×75 mm. Perf 14×13½ (C).

MS1131	**1084a**	£1 multicoloured	3·25	3·25
First Day Cover				5·25
Presentation Pack			5·25	

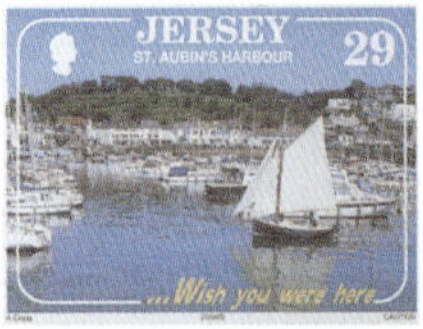

1085 St. Aubin's Harbour

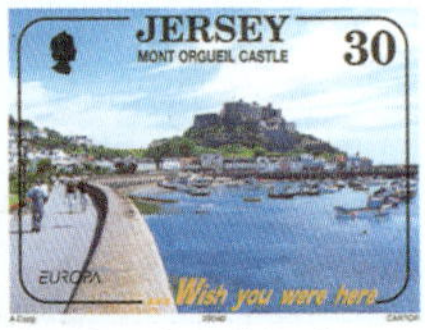

1086 Mont Orgueil Castle

1087 Corbiere Lighthouse

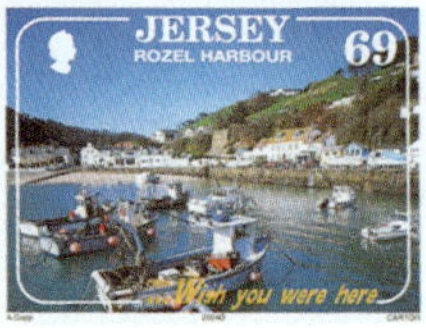

1088 Rozel Harbour

Europa. Holidays

(Des A. Copp. Litho Cartor)

2004 (9 Mar). Perf 13×13½ (C).

1132	**1085**	29p. multicoloured	95	95
1133	**1086**	30p. multicoloured	95	95
1134	**1087**	39p. multicoloured	1·30	1·30
1135	**1088**	69p. multicoloured	2·30	2·30
1132/5 *Set of 4*			5·50	5·50

First Day Cover		6·00
Presentation Pack	6·50	

The 30p. and 39p. values include the 'EUROPA' emblem.
Plate Nos.: All values 1A (×4).
Sheets: 10 (2×5).
Imprint: Upper left-hand margin.
Withdrawn: 31.3.2005.

1089 Green-winged Teal ('Eurasian Teal')

1090 Mute Swan

1091 Northern Shoveler

1092 Common Pochard

1093 Black Swan

1094 European Wigeon ('Eurasian Wigeon')

1095a Mallard (*Illustration reduced. Actual size* 150×100 mm)

Ducks and Swans

(Des N. Parlett. Litho BDT)

2004 (6 Apr). Perf 15×14 (C).

1136	**1089**	32p. multicoloured	1·00	1·00
1137	**1090**	33p. multicoloured	1·10	1·10
1138	**1091**	40p. multicoloured	1·30	1·30
1139	**1092**	49p. multicoloured	1·60	1·60
1140	**1093**	62p. multicoloured	2·00	2·00
1141	**1094**	70p. multicoloured	2·30	2·30
1136/41 *Set of 6*			9·25	9·25
First Day Cover				11·25
Presentation Pack			11·25	
MS1142 150×100 mm. **1095a** £2 multicoloured. Perf 14			6·50	6·50
First Day Cover				7·50
Presentation Pack			7·50	

Plate Nos.: All values 1A (×4).
Sheets: 10 (2×5).
Imprint: Central, left-hand margin.
Withdrawn: 30.4.2005.

1096 *Cymbidium lowianum* 'Concolor'

1097 *Phragmipedium besseae* var. *flavum*

1098 *Peristeria elata*

1099 *Cymbidium tracyanum*

1100 *Paphiopedilum* Victoria Village 'Isle of Jersey'

1101 *Paphiopedilum hirsutissimum*

1102a *Phragmipedium* 'Jason Fischer' (*Illustration reduced. Actual size* 110×75 mm)

Jersey Orchids (5th series)

(Des S. Giovinazzi. Litho Cartor)

2004 (25 May). Perf 13×13½ (C).

1143	**1096**	32p. multicoloured	1·00	1·00
		a. Booklet pane. Nos. 1143/8 with margins all round	9·50	
1144	**1097**	33p. multicoloured	1·10	1·10
1145	**1098**	40p. multicoloured	1·30	1·30
1146	**1099**	54p. multicoloured	1·80	1·80
1147	**1100**	62p. multicoloured	2·00	2·00
1148	**1101**	70p. multicoloured	2·30	2·30
1143/8 *Set of 6*			9·50	9·50
First Day Cover				11·00
Presentation Pack			11·50	
MS1149 110×75 mm. **1102a** £2 multicoloured			6·50	6·50
		a. Booklet pane. No. **MS**1149, but 151×100 mm with line of roulettes at left	6·50	
First Day Cover				7·50
Presentation Pack			7·00	

Booklet pane No. 1143a exists in three versions which differ in the order of the stamps within the block of six.
Plate Nos.: All values 1A (×5).
Sheets: 10 (2×5).
Imprint: Lower left-hand margin.
Withdrawn: 31.5.2005.

1103a Invasion Map (*Illustration reduced. Actual size 110×75 mm*)

60th Anniversary of D-Day

(Des A. Theobald. Litho Cartor)

2004 (6 June). Sheet 110×75 mm. Perf 13 (C).

MS1150	**1103a** £2 multicoloured	6·50	6·50
First Day Cover			8·75
Presentation Pack		7·50	

Withdrawn: 30.6.2005.

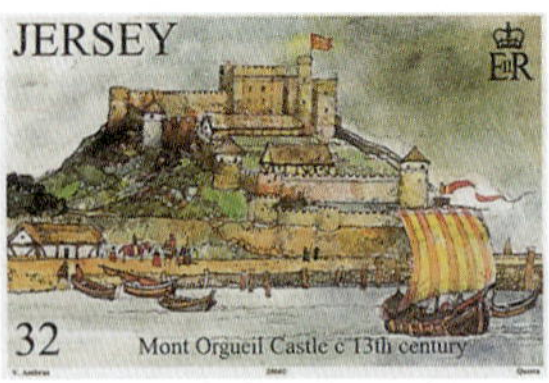

1104 Mont Orgueil Castle in 13th Century

1105 King John, *c.* 1204

1106 Mont Orgueil Castle in 17th Century

1107 King Charles II, *c.* 1684

1108 Mont Orgueil Castle, 2004

1109 Queen Elizabeth II, 2002

Jersey — 'A Peculiar of the Crown'

(Des V. Ambrus. Litho Questa)

2004 (25 June). Perf 14½×15 (C).

1151	**1104**	32p. multicoloured	60	35
		a. Horiz pair. Nos. 1151/2	2·00	2·00
1152	**1105**	32p. multicoloured	60	35
1153	**1106**	33p. multicoloured	60	35
		a. Horiz pair. Nos. 1153/4	2·00	2·00
1154	**1107**	33p. multicoloured	60	35
1155	**1108**	40p. multicoloured	80	45
		a. Horiz pair. Nos. 1155/6	2·50	2·50
1156	**1109**	40p. multicoloured	80	45
1151/6 *Set of* 6			6·50	6·50
First Day Cover				7·75
Presentation Pack			7·00	

Plate Nos.: All values 1A (×4).
Sheets: 10 (2×5). Nos. 1151/2, 1153/4 and 1155/6 were each printed together, *se-tenant*, in horizontal pairs.
Imprint: Upper left-hand margin (32p., 33p.) or central, left-hand margin (40p.).
Withdrawn: 30.6.2005.

Salon du Timbre Stamp Exhibition, Paris

2004 (26 June). As No. **MS**1149, but optd with 'Jersey at Le Salon du Timbre 2004' at top left corner of sheet margin. Perf 13×13½ (C).

MS1157 110×75 mm. **1102a** £2 multicoloured		6·50	6·50
First Day Cover			7·50
Presentation Pack		7·50	

Withdrawn: 30.6.2005.

1110 Wall Lizard

1111 Ant Lion

1112 Field Cricket

1113 Dartford Warbler

Endangered Species of Jersey

(Des W. Oliver. Litho BDT)

2004 (27 July). Perf 15×14 (C).

1158	**1110**	32p. multicoloured	1·00	1·00
1159	**1111**	33p. multicoloured	1·10	1·10
1160	**1112**	49p. multicoloured	1·60	1·60
1161	**1113**	70p. multicoloured	2·30	2·30
1158/61 *Set of* 4			6·00	6·00
First Day Cover				8·25
Presentation Pack			7·50	
MS1162 141×174 mm. Nos. 1158/61 each ×2			12·00	12·00

Plate Nos.: All values 1A (×4).
Sheets: 10 (2×5).
Imprint: Bottom margin.
Withdrawn: 30.7.2005.

1114 Dead Man's Fingers

1115 Devonshire Cup

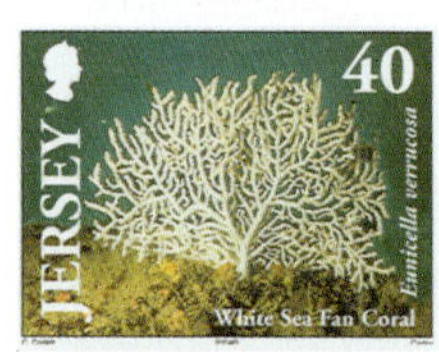

1116 White Sea Fan

1117 Pink Sea Fan

1118 Sunset Cup

1119 Red Fingers

Corals

(Des Colleen Corlett. Litho Cartor)

2004 (28 Sept). Perf 13×13½ (C).

1163	**1114**	32p. multicoloured	1·00	1·00
1164	**1115**	33p. multicoloured	1·10	1·10
1165	**1116**	40p. multicoloured	1·30	1·30
1166	**1117**	54p. multicoloured	1·80	1·80
1167	**1118**	62p. multicoloured	2·00	2·00
1168	**1119**	70p. multicoloured	2·30	2·30
1163/8 *Set of 6*			9·50	9·50
First Day Cover				11·50
Presentation Pack			10·50	
MS1169 150×100 mm. Nos. 1166/8			6·00	6·00
First Day Cover				8·25
Presentation Pack			7·00	

Plate Nos.: All values 1A (×4).
Sheets: 10 (2×5).
Imprint: Lower left-hand margin.
Withdrawn: 30.9.2005.

1120 Nativity Scene

1121 Fairy Lights over Busy Streets

1122 Santa Claus, Children and Christmas Tree

1123 Candles in Church

1124 Three Candles and Holly

1125 Mary and Jesus

1126 Stockings and Candle on Mantlepiece

1127 Five Candles

1128 Angel and Candle

1129 Candles in Window

Christmas Illuminations

(Des M. Pollard. Litho SNP Sprint)

2004 (2 Nov). Self-adhesive. Perf 11½ (die-cut).

1170	**1120**	(32p.) multicoloured (abc)	1·00	1·00
1171	**1121**	(32p.) multicoloured (abc)	1·00	1·00
1172	**1122**	(32p.) multicoloured (abc)	1·00	1·00
1173	**1123**	(32p.) multicoloured (abc)	1·00	1·00
1174	**1124**	(32p.) multicoloured (abc)	1·00	1·00
1175	**1125**	(33p.) multicoloured (abc)	1·10	1·10
1176	**1126**	(33p.) multicoloured (abc)	1·10	1·10
1177	**1127**	(33p.) multicoloured (abc)	1·10	1·10
1178	**1128**	(33p.) multicoloured (abc)	1·10	1·10
1179	**1129**	(33p.) multicoloured (abc)	1·10	1·10
1170/9 *Set of 10*			10·50	10·50
First Day Cover				12·75
Presentation Pack			12·75	

Nos. 1170/4, which are inscribed 'JERSEY MINIMUM POSTAGE PAID' and Nos. 1175/9, inscribed 'U.K. MINIMUM POSTAGE PAID' were sold at 32p. and 33p. respectively and were available in strips of 5 and rolls of 100 with the surplus self-adhesive paper around each stamp removed.

Initially released with '2004' imprint dates, Nos. 1170/9 were subsequently reissued inscribed '2005' and '2006' (all prices the same).

Printings: (a) 2.11.2004. Inscr '2004'; (b) 21.10.2005. Inscr '2005'; (c) 31.10.2006. Inscr '2006'.

(Litho SNP Sprint, Australia)

2004 (3 Nov). Designs as Nos. 1107/11 (Offshore Reefs). Self-adhesive. Perf 11½ (die-cut).

1180	**1061**	(32p.) multicoloured (ab)	1·25	1·50
1181	**1062**	(32p.) multicoloured (ab)	1·25	1·50
1182	**1063**	(32p.) multicoloured (ab)	1·25	1·50
1183	**1064**	(32p.) multicoloured (ab)	1·25	1·50
1184	**1065**	(32p.) multicoloured (ab)	1·25	1·50
1180/4 *Set of 5*			6·00	6·50

Nos. 1180/4, which are inscribed 'JERSEY MINIMUM POSTAGE PAID' and were initially sold at 32p. each, come *se-tenant* in strips of 5 or rolls of 100 with the surplus self-adhesive paper around each stamp removed.

Nos. 1180/4 are inscr '2004' or '2006' with copyright symbol after date.

Initially released with '2004' imprint dates, Nos. 1180/4 were subsequently reissued inscribed '2006' (prices the same).

Printings: (a) 3.11.2004. Inscr '2004'; (b) 16.11.2006. Inscr '2006'.

Post Office Yearbook

2004 (1 Dec). Comprises Nos. 1125/56, 1158/61, 1163/8 and 1170/9.

Yearbook .... 55·00

Sold out.

1130 C 1 Air Search Aircraft

1131 Burby Helicopter

1132 Beach Lifeguard Service

1133 Fire Rescue Inflatable

1134 RAF Sea King Helicopter

Rescue Craft

(Des A. Theobald. Litho Cartor)

2005 (18 Jan). Perf 13×13½ (C).

1185	**1130**	32p. multicoloured	65	70
1186	**1131**	33p. multicoloured	65	70
1187	**1132**	40p. multicoloured	80	85
1188	**1133**	49p. multicoloured	1·50	1·50
1189	**1134**	70p. multicoloured	1·75	1·75
1185/9 *Set of 5*			5·00	5·00
First Day Cover				6·00
Presentation Pack			5·75	

Plate Nos.: All values 1A (×4).
Sheets: 10 (2×5).
Imprint: Right-hand side, bottom margin.
Withdrawn: 31.1.2006.

1135 Rooster (*Illustration reduced. Actual size* 110×75 mm)

Chinese New Year ('Year of the Rooster')

(Des V. Ambrus. Litho BDT)

2005 (9 Feb). Sheet 110×75 mm. Perf 14½ (C).

MS1190 **1135** £1 multicoloured	2·50	2·75
First Day Cover		3·50
Presentation Pack	3·50	

Withdrawn: 28.2.2006.

1136 Conger Eel Soup

1137 Oysters

1138 Bean Crock

1139 Bourdélots with Black Butter

Europa. Gastronomy

(Des Jennifer Toombs. Litho BDT)

2005 (8 Mar). Perf 14 (C).

1191	**1136**	32p. multicoloured	65	70
1192	**1137**	33p. multicoloured	65	70
1193	**1138**	40p. multicoloured	80	85
1194	**1139**	70p. multicoloured	1·40	1·50
1191/4 *Set of 4*			3·50	3·75
First Day Cover				5·50
Presentation Pack			5·00	

The 33p. and 40p. values include the 'EUROPA' emblem.

Plate Nos.: All values 1A (×5).
Sheets: 10 (5×2).
Imprint: Right-hand side, bottom margin.
Withdrawn: 31.3.2006.

1140 *Little Red Riding Hood*

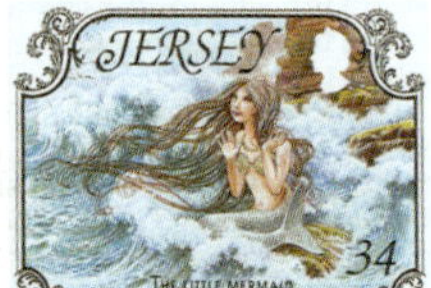

1141 *The Little Mermaid*

1142 *Beauty and the Beast*

1143 *Rumplestiltskin*

1144 *Goose that laid the Golden Egg*

1145 *The Ugly Duckling* (*Illustration reduced. Actual size* 110×75 mm)

Fairy Tales

(Des M. Pollard. Litho Cartor)

2005 (2 Apr). Perf 13×13½ (C).

1195	**1140**	33p. multicoloured	65	70
1196	**1141**	34p. multicoloured	70	75
1197	**1142**	41p. multicoloured	80	85
1198	**1143**	50p. multicoloured	1·50	1·50
1199	**1144**	73p. multicoloured	2·00	2·00
1195/9 *Set of 5*			5·50	5·50
First Day Cover				6·00
Presentation Pack			5·75	
MS1200 110×75 mm. **1145** £2 multicoloured. Perf 13½ (C)			4·50	4·75
First Day Cover				6·50
Presentation Pack			5·50	

Nos. 1195/**MS**1200 commemorate the birth bicentenary of Hans Christian Andersen.

Plate Nos.: All values 1A (×4).
Sheets: 10 (2×5).
Imprint: Lower left-hand margin.
Withdrawn: 30.4.2006.

1146 Muratti Vase Medal (*Illustration reduced. Actual size* 110×75 mm)

Centenary of Jersey Football Association and Muratti Vase

(Des A. Robinson. Litho Cartor)

2005 (27 Apr). Sheet 110×75 mm. Perf 14½ (C).

MS1201 **1146** £2 brown-ochre, black and orange-brown	4·50	4·50

First Day Cover		6·00
Presentation Pack	5·50	

Withdrawn: 29.4.2006.

1147 Peace Dove (*Illustration reduced. Actual size* 110×75 mm)

60th Anniversary of Liberation of Channel Islands. Peace and Reconciliation

(Des A. Robinson. Litho BDT)

2005 (9 May). Sheet 110×75 mm. Perf 14½ (C).

MS1202 **1147** £2 multicoloured	4·50	4·50
First Day Cover		5·50
Presentation Pack	5·00	

Withdrawn: 31.5.2006.

'Nordia 2005' Stamp Exhibition, Göteborg, Sweden

2005 (26 May). No. **MS**1200 optd 'Jersey at Nordia 2005' in blue and 'Göteborg 26–29 mai SVENSKA FRIMÄRKET 150 ÅR' in black on bottom sheet margin. Perf 13½ (C).

MS1203 110×75 mm. **1147** £2 multicoloured	4·00	4·25

Withdrawn: 31.5.2006.

1148 MGB GT

1149 Mini Cooper

1150 Citröen DS

1151 Jaguar E Type

1152 Volkswagen Beetle

1153 Aston Martin DB5

Jersey Festivals (2nd issue). Motor Festival. Classic Cars

(Des A. Copp. Litho Cartor)

2005 (6 June). Perf 13×13½ (C).

1204	**1148**	33p. multicoloured	65	70
		a. Booklet pane. Nos. 1204/9	5·75	
1205	**1149**	34p. multicoloured	70	75
1206	**1150**	41p. multicoloured	80	85
1207	**1151**	50p. multicoloured	1·00	1·10
1208	**1152**	56p. multicoloured	1·10	1·20
1209	**1153**	73p. multicoloured	1·50	1·60
1204/9 *Set of 6*			5·75	6·00
First Day Cover				7·00
Presentation Pack			7·00	

Booklet pane No. 1204a exists in three versions which differ in the order of the stamps within the block of six.

Plate Nos.: All values 1A (×4).
Sheets: 10 (2×5).
Imprint: Lower left-hand margin.
Withdrawn: 30.6.2006 (sheets).

1154 Yellow Bartsia

1155 Scarlet Pimpernel

1156 Wild Angelica

1157 Common Knapweed

1158 Marsh St. Johnswort

1159 Black Bryony

1160 Bog Pimpernel

1161 Greater Stitchwort

1162 Horseshoe Vetch

1163 Common Mallow

1164 English Stonecrop

1165 White Campion

1166 Tutsan

1167 Common Dog-violet

1168 Ox Eye Daisy

1169 Rock Sea Spurrey

1170 Herb-Robert

1171 Ragged Robin

1172 Brooklime

1173 Mouse Ear Hawkweed

1174 Cuckoo Flower

1175 Yellow Iris

1176 Three-cornered Garlic

1177 Devil's-bit Scabious

Wild Flowers

(Des N. Parlett. Litho Cartor)

2005 (19 July)–**07**. Perf 13½ (C).

1210	**1154**	1p. multicoloured (b)	10	10
1211	**1155**	2p. multicoloured (a)	10	10
1212	**1156**	3p. multicoloured (b)	10	10
1213	**1157**	4p. multicoloured (a)	10	10
1214	**1158**	5p. multicoloured (b)	10	15
1215	**1159**	10p. multicoloured (c)	30	30
1216	**1160**	15p. multicoloured (b)	30	35
1217	**1161**	20p. multicoloured (a)	40	45
1218	**1162**	25p. multicoloured (c)	75	75
1219	**1163**	30p. multicoloured (a)	60	65
1220	**1164**	35p. multicoloured (c)	1·00	1·00
1221	**1165**	40p. multicoloured (a)	80	85
1222	**1166**	45p. multicoloured (c)	1·30	1·30
1223	**1167**	50p. multicoloured (a)	1·00	1·10
1224	**1168**	55p. multicoloured (c)	1·60	1·60
1225	**1169**	60p. multicoloured (c)	1·80	1·80
1226	**1170**	65p. multicoloured (a)	1·30	1·40
1227	**1171**	70p. multicoloured (b)	1·40	1·50
1228	**1172**	75p. multicoloured (b)	1·50	1·60
1229	**1173**	80p. multicoloured (c)	2·30	2·30
1230	**1174**	85p. multicoloured (b)	1·70	1·80
1231	**1175**	90p. multicoloured (b)	1·80	1·90
1232	**1176**	£1 multicoloured (a)	2·00	2·10
1233	**1177**	£1.50 multicoloured (c)	4·50	4·50
1210/33		*Set of 24*	25·00	26·00
First Day Covers (3)				29·00
Presentation Packs (3)			29·00	

MS1234 Three sheets, each 150×100 mm. (a) Nos. 1211, 1213, 1217, 1219, 1221, 1223, 1226 and 1232 (a). (b) Nos. 1210, 1212, 1214, 1216, 1227/8 and 1230/1 (b). (c) Nos. 1215, 1218, 1220, 1222, 1224/5, 1229 and 1233 (c)

Set of 3 sheets	26·00	27·00
First Day Covers (3)		29·00
Presentation Packs (3)	29·00	

Printings: (a) 19.7.2005. Inscr '2005' with copyright symbol. (b) 26.9.2006. Inscr '2006' with copyright symbol. (c) 25.7.2007. Inscr '2007' with copyright symbol.
Plate Nos.: 1p. to 5p., 15p., 20p., 30p., 40p., 50p., 65p. to 75p., 85p. to £1 1A (×4); 10p., 25p., 35p., 45p., 55p., 60p., 80p., £1.50 1A (×5).
Sheets: 10 (5×2).
Imprint: Right-hand side, bottom margin.

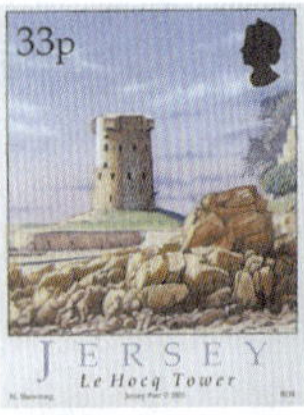

1178 Le Hocq Tower

1179 Seymour Tower

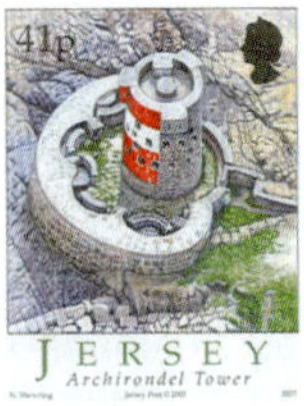

1180 Archirondel Tower

1181 Kempt Tower

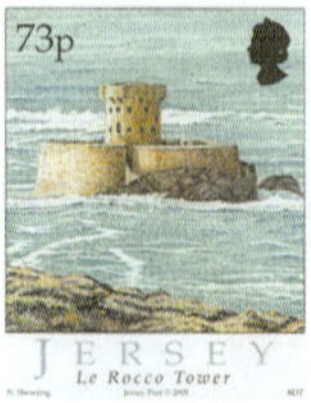

1182 Le Rocco Tower

Coastal Towers

(Des N. Shewring. Litho BDT)

2005 (9 Aug). Perf 14 (C).

1235	**1178**	33p. multicoloured	65	70
1236	**1179**	34p. multicoloured	70	75
1237	**1180**	41p. multicoloured	1·00	85
1238	**1181**	56p. multicoloured	1·50	1·75
1239	**1182**	73p. multicoloured	2·00	2·25
1235/9		*Set of 5*	5·50	5·50
First Day Cover				6·25
Presentation Pack			6·00	

Plate Nos.: All values 1A (×4).
Sheets: 10 (5×2).
Imprint: Upper left-hand margin.
Withdrawn: 31.8.2006.

1183 *Hygrocybe calyptriformis*

1184 *Boletus erythropus*

1185 *Inocybe godeyi*

1186 *Myriostoma coliforme*

1187 *Helvella crispa*

1188 *Hygrocybe coccinea*

1189 *Marasmius oreades (Illustration reduced. Actual size 150×100 mm)*

Fungi (2nd series)

(Des W. Oliver. Litho BDT)

2005 (13 Sept). Perf 14 (C).

1240	**1183**	33p. multicoloured	65	70
1241	**1184**	34p. multicoloured	70	75
1242	**1185**	41p. multicoloured	80	85
1243	**1186**	50p. multicoloured	1·00	1·10
1244	**1187**	56p. multicoloured	1·10	1·20
1245	**1188**	73p. multicoloured	1·50	1·60
1240/5 *Set of 6*			5·75	6·00
First Day Cover				7·50
Presentation Pack			5·00	
MS1246 150×100 mm. **1189** £2 *Marasmius oreades*. Perf 14½ (C)			4·50	4·75
First Day Cover				7·50
Presentation Pack			5·00	

Plate Nos.: All values 1A (×4).
Sheets: 10 (5×2).
Imprint: Upper left-hand margin.
Withdrawn: 30.9.2006.

1190 H.M.S. *Belleisle*

1191 H.M.S. *Royal Sovereign*

1192 H.M.S. *Neptune*

1193 H.M.S. *Euryalus*

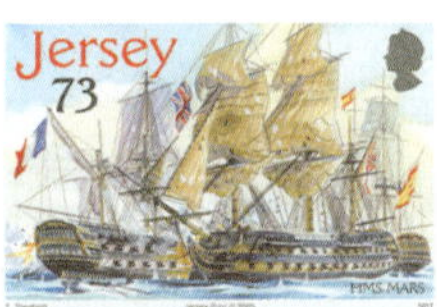

1194 H.M.S. *Mars*

1195 H.M.S. *Victory* (*Illustration reduced. Actual size 110×75 mm*)

Bicentenary of the Battle of Trafalgar

(Des A. Theobald. Litho BDT)

2005 (21 Oct). Perf 14 (C).

1247	**1190**	33p. multicoloured	65	70
1248	**1191**	34p. multicoloured	70	75
1249	**1192**	41p. multicoloured	80	95
1250	**1193**	50p. multicoloured	1·50	1·50
1251	**1194**	73p. multicoloured	2·00	2·00
1247/51 *Set of 5*			5·50	5·75
First Day Cover				6·50
Presentation Pack			6·50	
MS1252 110×75 mm. **1195** £2 multicoloured			5·00	5·00
First Day Cover				6·50
Presentation Pack			6·50	

Plate Nos.: All values 1A (×4).
Sheets: 10 (2×5).
Imprint: Lower left-hand margin.
Withdrawn: 31.10.2006.

Post Office Yearbook

2005 (1 Dec). Comprises Nos. 1185/**MS**1202, 1204/9, 1211, 1213, 1217, 1219, 1221, 1223, 1226, 1232 and 1235/52.
Yearbook .... 75·00

1196 Royal Jersey Regiment, *c.* 1830

1197 Royal Jersey Regiment, *c.* 1844

1198 Royal Jersey Artillery, *c.* 1881

1199 Royal Jersey Light Infantry, *c.* 1890

1200 Royal Engineers (modern)

Royal Jersey Militia (2nd series)

(Des A. Robinson. Litho Enschedé)

2006 (6 Jan). Perf 13½×14 (C).

1253	**1196**	33p. multicoloured	65	70
1254	**1197**	34p. multicoloured	70	75
1255	**1198**	41p. multicoloured	80	85
1256	**1199**	50p. multicoloured	1·50	1·50
1257	**1200**	73p. multicoloured	2·00	2·00
1253/7 *Set of 5*			5·50	5·50
First Day Cover				6·25
Presentation Pack			6·25	

Plate Nos.: All values 1A, 1B (each ×4).
Sheets: 10 (2×5).
Imprint: Bottom, left-hand corner margin.
Withdrawn: 31.1.2007.

1201 Victoria Cross (*Illustration reduced. Actual size 110×75 mm*)

150th Anniversary of the Victoria Cross

(Des A. Robinson. Litho Enschedé)

2006 (29 Jan). Sheet 110×75 mm. Perf 13½×14 (C).

MS1258 **1201** £2 multicoloured	5·00	5·00
First Day Cover		6·00
Presentation Pack	6·00	

Withdrawn: 31.1.2007.

1202 Dog (*Illustration reduced. Actual size* 110×75 mm)

Chinese New Year ('Year of the Dog')

(Des V. Ambrus. Litho BDT)

2006 (29 Jan). Sheet 110×75 mm. Perf 14½ (C).

MS1259 **1202** £1 multicoloured	3·50	3·75
First Day Cover		4·00
Presentation Pack	4·00	

1203 Chinese National Costumes and Mask (Elliott Grimes)

1204 Portuguese Fado Music Festival (Liam Reynolds)

1205 Polish Pisanki painted Easter Egg Design (Kelly Reynolds)

1206 Indian National Costumes (Olivia Grimes)

Europa. Winning Entries in Childrens Stamp Design Competition

(Adapted A. Copp. Litho BDT)

2006 (7 Mar). Perf 14 (C).

1260	**1203**	33p. multicoloured	65	70
1261	**1204**	34p. multicoloured	70	75
1262	**1205**	41p. multicoloured	1·75	1·50
1263	**1206**	73p. multicoloured	2·25	2·25
1260/3 *Set of 4*			5·00	5·00
First Day Cover				6·50
Presentation Pack			6·50	

Plate Nos.: All values 1A (×4).
Sheets: 10 (2×10) with enlarged illustrated margins.
Imprint: Lower left-hand margin.
Withdrawn: 31.3.2007.

1207 Flat Periwinkle

1208 Painted Top Shell

1209 Dog Cockle

1210 Variegated Scallop

1211 Blue Rayed Limpet

1212 European Cowrie

1213 Ormer Shell (*Illustration reduced. Actual size* 150×100 mm)

Sea Shells

(Des N. Parlett. Litho (with thermography (Nos. 1264/9) or embossing (**MS**1270)) Cartor)

2006 (4 Apr). Perf 13×13½ (C).

1264	**1207**	34p. multicoloured	70	75
1265	**1208**	37p. multicoloured	75	80
1266	**1209**	42p. multicoloured	85	90
1267	**1210**	51p. multicoloured	1·00	1·10
1268	**1211**	57p. multicoloured	1·10	1·20
1269	**1212**	74p. multicoloured	1·50	1·60
1264/9 *Set of 6*			6·00	6·25
First Day Cover				7·75
Presentation Pack			7·75	
MS1270 150×100 mm. **1213** £2 multicoloured. Perf 13½			4·50	4·50
First Day Cover				5·50
Presentation Pack			5·50	

Plate Nos.: All values 1A (×4).
Sheets: 10 (2×5) with enlarged illustrated margins.
Imprint: Lower left-hand margin.
Withdrawn: 30.4.2007.

1214 Wedding Photograph

First Wedding Anniversary of Prince Charles and Duchess of Cornwall

(Des A. Robinson. Litho Cartor)

2006 (9 Apr). Perf 13½ (C).

1271	**1214**	£2 multicoloured	4·00	4·50
First Day Cover				5·50
Presentation Pack			5·50	

No. 1271 was retained in use as a definitive stamp.
Plate Nos.: 1A (×5).
Sheets: 4 (2×2).
Imprint: Lower left-hand margin.

1215 Queen Elizabeth II

1216 Queen Elizabeth II (£5; New Zealand $5)
(*Illustration reduced. Actual size* 150×100 mm)

80th Birthday of Queen Elizabeth II

(Litho and embossed Cartor)

2006 (21 Apr). Perf 13½ (C).

1272	**1215**	£5 multicoloured	10·00	10·50
First Day Cover				13·00
Presentation Pack			13·50	
MS1273 150×100 mm. **1216** £5 multicoloured; New Zealand $5 multicoloured (sold at £7)			15·00	15·00
		a. Silver foil (country names, values and borders) omitted	£3250	
First Day Cover				17·00
Presentation Pack			17·00	

The background colour of the sheet stamp, No. 1272, is deep ultramarine, but both the stamps in the miniature sheet have a deep turquoise-blue background.

The miniature sheet contains a £5 Jersey stamp and a $5 New Zealand stamp. The same miniature sheet and a stamp in a similar design to No. 1272 was also issued by New Zealand.

No. 1272 was retained in use as a definitive stamp.

Plate Nos.: 1A (×6).
Sheets: 4 (2×2).
Imprint: Upper left-hand margin.

1217 Football and World Cup Trophy (*Illustration reduced. Actual size* 110×75 mm)

World Cup Football Championship, Germany

(Des N. Shewring. Litho BDT)

2006 (9 June). Sheet 110×75 mm. Perf 14½ (C).

MS1274 **1217** £2 multicoloured	4·75	5·00
First Day Cover		5·50
Presentation Pack	5·50	

Withdrawn: 30.6.2007.

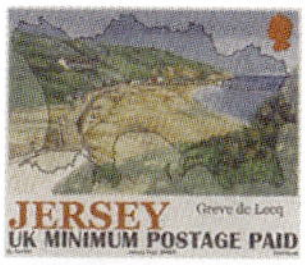

1218 Greve de Lecq

1219 La Rocque

1220 Portelet

1221 St. Brelade's Bay

Island Views

(Des Colleen Corlett. Litho SEP Sprint, Australia)

2006 (11 July). Self-adhesive. Perf 11½ (die-cut).

1275	**1218**	(37p.) multicoloured	1·50	1·50
1276	**1219**	(37p.) multicoloured	1·50	1·50
1277	**1220**	(37p.) multicoloured	1·50	1·50
1278	**1221**	(37p.) multicoloured	1·50	1·50
1275/8 *Set of 4*			5·00	5·00
First Day Cover				6·00
Presentation Pack			5·50	

Nos. 1275/8, which are inscribed 'UK MINIMUM POSTAGE PAID' and were initially sold at 37p. each, come *se-tenant* in strips of 4 or rolls of 100 with the surplus self-adhesive paper around each stamp removed.

Nos. 1275/8 were re-issued on 10 March 2009 with '2009' imprint dates.

1222 Red Underwing Moth

1223 Comma Butterfly

1224 Black Arches Moth

1225 Small Copper Butterfly

1226 Holly Blue Butterfly

1227 Orange-tip Butterfly

Butterflies and Moths

(Des W. Oliver. Litho BDT)

2006 (1 Aug). Perf 15×14 (C).

1279	**1222**	34p. multicoloured	70	75
1280	**1223**	37p. multicoloured	75	80
1281	**1224**	42p. multicoloured	85	90
1282	**1225**	51p. multicoloured	1·00	1·10
1283	**1226**	57p. multicoloured	1·10	1·20
1284	**1227**	74p. multicoloured	1·50	1·60
1279/84 *Set of 6*			5·75	6·25
First Day Cover				7·75
Presentation Pack			7·75	
MS1285 150×100 mm. Nos. 1282/4			4·50	4·50
First Day Cover				5·25
Presentation Pack			5·25	

Stamps from **MS**1285 have no white borders.

Plate Nos.: All values 1A (×4).
Sheets: 10 (2×5) with enlarged illustrated margins.
Imprint: Lower left-hand margin.
Withdrawn: 31.8.2007.

1228 LDV Luton Van, *c.* 2004

1229 Renault Kangoo, 1999–2004

1230 LDV Pilot, 1994–2004

1231 Ford Transit, Luton Body, 1988–96

1232 Morris Marina, 440/575, *c.* 1978

1233 Morris Minor, *c.* 1969

Jersey Postal History (2nd series). Postal Vehicles

(Des A. Theobald. Litho Cartor)

2006 (31 Oct). Perf 13×13½ (C).

1286	**1228**	34p. multicoloured	70	75
		a. Booklet pane. Nos. 1286/91 with margins all round	5·75	
1287	**1229**	37p. multicoloured	75	80
1288	**1230**	42p. multicoloured	85	90
1289	**1231**	51p. multicoloured	1·00	1·10
1290	**1232**	57p. multicoloured	1·10	1·20
1291	**1233**	74p. multicoloured	1·50	1·60
1286/91 *Set of 6*			5·75	6·25
First Day Cover				7·75
Presentation Pack			7·75	
MS1292 150×100 mm. Nos. 1289/91			4·50	4·75
		a. Booklet pane. No. **MS**1292, but with line of roulettes at left	4·00	
First Day Cover				5·50
Presentation Pack			5·50	

Booklet pane No. 1286a exists in three versions which differ in the order of the stamps within the block of six.

Plate Nos.: All values 1A (×4).
Sheets: 10 (2×5).
Imprint: Right-hand side, bottom margin.
Withdrawn: 31.10.2007.

Belgica '06 International Stamp Exhibition, Brussels

2006 (16 Nov). No. **MS**1270 optd with 'Jersey at' and Belgica emblem on bottom left sheet margin.

MS1293 150×100 mm. **1213** £2 multicoloured	5·00	5·50
First Day Cover		6·00
Presentation Pack	5·50	

Withdrawn: 31.10.2007.

Post Office Yearbook

2006 (1 Dec). Comprises Nos. 1210, 1212, 1214, 1216, 1227/8, 1230/1, 1253/72, **MS**1274/84 and 1286/91.

Yearbook .... 80·00

1234 Molybdenite

1235 Muscovite in Pegmatite Vein, Feldspar + Quartz

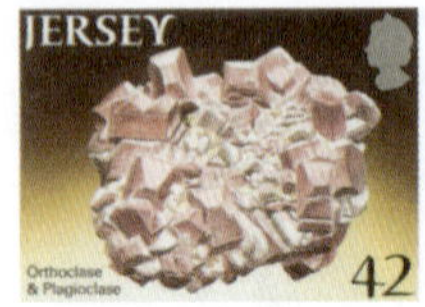

1236 Orthoclase and Plagioclase

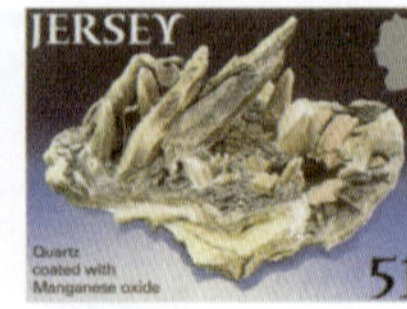

1237 Quartz coated with Manganese Oxide

1238 Smoky Quartz

Mineralogy

(Des Jennifer Toombs. Litho Cartor)

2007 (23 Jan). Perf 13×13½ (C).

1294	**1234**	34p. multicoloured	1·00	1·00
1295	**1235**	37p. multicoloured	1·10	1·10
1296	**1236**	42p. multicoloured	1·20	1·20
1297	**1237**	51p. multicoloured	1·50	1·50
1298	**1238**	74p. multicoloured	2·20	2·20
1294/8 *Set of 5*			7·00	7·00
First Day Cover				7·50
Presentation Pack			7·50	

Plate Nos.: All values 1A (×5).
Sheets: 10 (2×5) with enlarged illustrated margins.
Imprint: Lower left-hand margin.
Withdrawn: 31.1.2008.

1239 Pig (*Illustration reduced. Actual size* 110×75 mm)

Chinese New Year ('Year of the Pig')

(Des V. Ambrus. Litho BDT)

2007 (18 Feb). Sheet 110×75 mm. Perf 14½ (C).

MS1299 **1239** £1 multicoloured	3·25	3·50
First Day Cover		4·50
Presentation Pack	3·75	
Omnibus Folder (containing Nos. **MS**731, **MS**768, **MS**843, **MS**885, **MS**928, **MS**972, **MS**1030, **MS**1081, **MS**1131, **MS**1190, **MS**1259, **MS**1299	32·00	

Withdrawn: 29.2.2008.

1240 Windsurfing canoeing and land yachting ('Adventure')

1241 Scouts playing Trumpets and National Flags ('International Friendship')

1242 Climbing and go-karting ('Developing Young People')

1243 Scouts and Badges ('Changing the World for Good')

Europa. Centenary of Scouting

(Des Colleen Corlett. Litho Austrian State Ptg Wks, Vienna)

2007 (6 Mar). Perf 14 (C).

1300	**1240**	34p. multicoloured	1·00	1·00
1301	**1241**	37p. multicoloured	1·10	1·10
1302	**1242**	42p. multicoloured	1·20	1·20
1303	**1243**	74p. multicoloured	2·20	2·20
1300/3		*Set of 4*	5·50	5·50
First Day Cover				6·00
Presentation Pack			6·00	

Plate Nos.: All values 1A (×4).
Sheets: 10 (2×5) with enlarged illustrated margins.
Imprint: Lower left-hand margin.
Withdrawn: 31.3.2008.

1244 Long-tailed Field Mouse

1245 Rabbits

1246 Polecat

1247 Common Shrew

1248 Stoat

1249 Brown Rat

Countryside Animals

(Des W. Oliver. Litho BDT)

2007 (10 Apr). Perf 15×14 (C).

1304	**1244**	34p. multicoloured	1·00	1·00
1305	**1245**	37p. multicoloured	1·10	1·10
1306	**1246**	42p. multicoloured	1·30	1·30
1307	**1247**	51p. multicoloured	1·50	1·50
1308	**1248**	57p. multicoloured	1·70	1·70
1309	**1249**	74p. multicoloured	2·20	2·20
1304/9		*Set of 6*	8·75	8·75
First Day Cover				9·25
Presentation Pack			9·25	
MS1310		150×100 mm. As Nos. 1307/9	5·50	5·50
First Day Cover				6·00
Presentation Pack			6·00	

Stamps from **MS**1310 have no white borders.
Plate Nos.: All values 1A (×4).
Sheets: 10 (2×5) with enlarged illustrated margins.
Imprint: Lower left-hand margin.
Withdrawn: 30.4.2008.

1250 House Sparrow

1251 Chaffinch

1252 Blue Tit

1253 Blackbirds (pair)

1254 Magpie

1255 Great Tit

Jersey Birdlife (1st series). Garden Birds

(Des Nick Parlett. Litho Cartor)

2007 (19 June). Perf 13×13½ (C).

1311	**1250**	34p. multicoloured	1·00	1·00
1312	**1251**	37p. multicoloured	1·10	1·10
1313	**1252**	42p. multicoloured	1·30	1·30
1314	**1253**	51p. multicoloured	1·50	1·50
1315	**1254**	57p. multicoloured	1·70	1·70
1316	**1255**	74p. multicoloured	2·20	2·20
1311/16		*Set of 6*	8·75	8·75
First Day Cover				9·25
Presentation Pack			9·25	
MS1317		150×100 mm. As Nos. 1314/16	5·25	5·25
First Day Cover				5·75
Presentation Pack			5·75	
MS1318		150×100 mm. Nos. 1311/16	8·75	8·75
First Day Cover				9·25
Presentation Pack			9·25	

Stamps from **MS**1317 have no white borders.
Plate Nos.: All values 1A (×5).
Sheets: 10 (2×5) with enlarged illustrated margins.
Imprint: Lower left-hand margin.
Withdrawn: 30.6.2008 (except **MS**1318).

1256 Gorey Regatta (*Illustration reduced. Actual size* 110×75 mm)

Jersey Yachting (2nd issue). 150th Anniversary of Gorey Regatta

(Des Andrew Robinson. Litho Enschedé)

2007 (22 June). Sheet 110×75 mm. Perf 13×13½ (C).

MS1319	**1256**	£2 multicoloured	6·00	6·00
First Day Cover				6·50
Presentation Pack			6·50	

Withdrawn: 30.6.2008.

1257 Clematis 'Nelly Moser' and 'The President'

1258 Rose 'Just Joey'

1259 Honeysuckle *Lonicera × americana*

1260 Fuchsia 'Swingtime'

1261 Sweet Peas

1262 Lilac

Summer Flowers

(Des Wendy Tait. Litho Enschedé)

2007 (25 July). Perf 13½ (C).

1320	**1257**	34p. multicoloured	1·00	1·00
1321	**1258**	37p. multicoloured	1·10	1·10
1322	**1259**	42p. multicoloured	1·30	1·30
1323	**1260**	51p. multicoloured	1·50	1·50
1324	**1261**	57p. multicoloured	1·70	1·70
1325	**1262**	74p. multicoloured	2·20	2·20
1320/5 *Set of 6*			8·75	8·75
First Day Cover				9·25
Presentation Pack			9·25	

Plate Nos.: 34p., 37p. 1A, 1B; others 1A (each ×5).
Sheets: 10 (5×2).
Imprint: Bottom margin.
Withdrawn: 31.7.2008.

1263 Dornier Do 24 ATT

1264 Avro Vulcan B.2

1265 Junkers Ju 52

1266 Sukhoi Su-27 'Flanker'

1267 Boeing B-52 Stratofortress

1268 Anglo-French Concorde

1269 Red Arrows (*Illustration reduced. Actual size* 110×75 mm)

60th Anniversary of Jersey International Air Display

(Des Tony Theobald. Litho Cartor)

2007 (13 Sept). Perf 13×13½ (C).

1326	**1263**	34p. multicoloured	1·00	1·00
		a. Booklet pane. Nos. 1326/31 with margins all round	6·00	
1327	**1264**	37p. multicoloured	1·10	1·10
1328	**1265**	42p. multicoloured	1·30	1·30
1329	**1266**	51p. multicoloured	1·50	1·50
1330	**1267**	57p. multicoloured	1·70	1·70
1331	**1268**	74p. multicoloured	2·20	2·20
1326/31 *Set of 6*			8·75	8·75
First Day Cover				9·25
Presentation Pack			9·25	
MS1332 110×75 mm. **1269** £2.50 multicoloured. Perf 13½×13			7·25	7·25
		a. Booklet pane. No. **MS**1332 but 150×100 mm with line of roulettes at left	5·00	
First Day Cover				7·75
Presentation Pack			7·75	

Booklet pane No. 1326a exists in three versions which differ in the order of the stamps within the block of six.

Plate Nos.: All values 1A (×4).
Sheets: 10 (2×5) with enlarged illustrated margins.
Imprint: Lower left-hand margin.
Withdrawn: 30.9.2008 (sheets).

1270 Queen's Valley Reservoir

1271 Mont Orgueil Castle

1272 Bonne Nuit Harbour

1273 La Hougue Bie

1274 Bouley Bay

1275 La Corbiere Lighthouse

Jersey Scenery (1st series)

(Des Andrew Robinson. Litho Enschedé)

2007 (1 Oct). Perf 14×13½ (C).

1333	**1270**	34p. multicoloured	1·00	1·00
1334	**1271**	37p. multicoloured	1·10	1·10
1335	**1272**	42p. multicoloured	1·30	1·30
1336	**1273**	51p. multicoloured	1·50	1·50
1337	**1274**	57p. multicoloured	1·70	1·70
1338	**1275**	74p. multicoloured	2·20	2·20
1333/8 *Set of* 6			8·75	8·75
First Day Cover				9·25
Presentation Pack			9·25	

The 42p. value No. 1335 is inscr 'sepac' and was also available in a souvenir folder with ten other Sepac logo stamps issued by other administrations.

Plate Nos.: 34p., 37p. 1A, 1B, 1C; 42p., 74p. 1A, 1B; 51p., 57p. 1A (each ×4).
Sheets: 10 (2×5) with enlarged illustrated margins.
Imprint: Lower left-hand margin.
Withdrawn: 31.10.2008.

1276 'Minuit Chrétiens'

1277 'While Shepherds Watched'

1278 'O Come All Ye Faithful'

1279 'O Christmas Tree'

1280 'Jingle Bells'

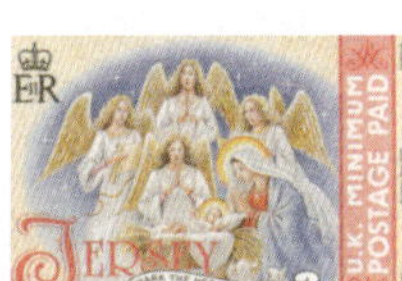

1281 'Hark the Herald Angels Sing'

1282 'We Three Kings'

1283 'Ding Dong Merrily on High'

1284 'Holly and the Ivy'

1285 'Good King Wenceslas'

Christmas Carols

(Des Michael Pollard. Litho SNP Sprint, Australia)

2007 (7 Nov). Self-adhesive. Perf 11½ (die-cut).

1339	**1276**	(35p.) multicoloured (ab)	1·00	1·00
1340	**1277**	(35p.) multicoloured (ab)	1·00	1·00
1341	**1278**	(35p.) multicoloured (ab)	1·00	1·00
1342	**1279**	(35p.) multicoloured (ab)	1·00	1·00
1343	**1280**	(35p.) multicoloured (ab)	1·00	1·00
1344	**1281**	(39p.) multicoloured (ab)	1·20	1·20
1345	**1282**	(39p.) multicoloured (ab)	1·20	1·20
1346	**1283**	(39p.) multicoloured (ab)	1·20	1·20
1347	**1284**	(39p.) multicoloured (ab)	1·20	1·20
1348	**1285**	(39p.) multicoloured (ab)	1·20	1·20
1339/48 *Set of* 10			11·00	11·00
First Day Cover				12·00
Presentation Pack			12·00	

Nos. 1339/43 which are inscribed 'JERSEY MINIMUM POSTAGE PAID' were sold for 35p., and Nos. 1344/8 which are inscribed 'U.K. MINIMUM POSTAGE PAID' were sold for 39p. Nos. 1339/43 and 1344/8 were each printed together, *se-tenant*, in strips of 5 from rolls of 100, from which the surplus self-adhesive backing paper around each stamp was removed.

Initially released with '2007' imprint dates, Nos. 1339/43 were subsequently re-issued inscribed '2008'.

Nos. 1339/48 were re-issued on 14 November 2008 with an imprint date '2008'.

Printings: (a) 7.11.2007. Inscr '2007'; (b) 14.11.2008. Inscr '2008'.

1286 Queen Elizabeth II and Duke of Edinburgh

Diamond Wedding of Queen Elizabeth II and Duke of Edinburgh

(Des Andrew Robinson. Litho Cartor)

2007 (20 Nov). Perf 13½ (C).

MS1349 **1286** multicoloured		8·75	8·75
First Day Cover			9·25
Presentation Pack		9·25	

No. 1349 was retained in use as a definitive stamp.

Plate Nos.: 1A (×5).
Sheets: 4 (2×2).
Imprint: Lower left-hand margin.

Post Office Yearbook

2007 (1 Dec). Comprises Nos. 1215, 1218, 1220, 1222, 1224/5, 1229, 1233, 1294/309, 1311/16 and **MS**1319/49.

Yearbook	82·00

1287 Sunshine

1288 Strong Wind Signals

1289 Weather Signals

1290 Temperature

1291 Tides and Wave Signals

300th Anniversary of Jersey Signal Station

(Des Nick Shewring. Litho Austrian State Ptg Wks, Vienna)

2008 (15 Jan). Perf 14 (C).

1350	**1287**	35p. multicoloured	1·00	1·00
1351	**1288**	39p. multicoloured	1·20	1·20
1352	**1289**	43p. multicoloured	1·30	1·30
1353	**1290**	58p. multicoloured	1·70	1·70
1354	**1291**	76p. multicoloured	2·30	2·30
1350/4 *Set of 5*			7·50	7·50
First Day Cover				10·00
Presentation Pack			10·00	

Plate Nos.: All values 1A (each ×4).
Sheets: 10 (2×5) with enlarged illustrated margins.
Imprint: Lower left-hand margin.
Withdrawn: 31.1.2009.

1292 Thank You Letter

1293 Love Letter

1294 Letter to Santa Claus

1295 Family Letter

Europa. The Letter

(Des Jennifer Toombs. Litho Enschedé)

2008 (14 Feb). Perf 13½×14 (C).

1355	**1292**	35p. multicoloured	1·00	1·00
1356	**1293**	39p. multicoloured	1·20	1·20
1357	**1294**	43p. multicoloured	1·30	1·30
1358	**1295**	76p. multicoloured	2·30	2·30
1355/8 *Set of 4*			5·75	5·75
First Day Cover				8·25
Presentation Pack			8·25	

The 39p. and 43p. values include the 'EUROPA' emblem.
Plate Nos.: 35p., 39p. 1A, 1B; 43p., 76p. 1A (each ×6).
Sheets: 10 (2×5) with enlarged inscribed margins.
Imprint: Lower left-hand margin.
Withdrawn: 28.2.2009.

1296 Arts and Crafts

1297 Dance and Drama

1298 Speech

1299 Films and Photography

1300 Music

Jersey Festivals (3rd issue). Centenary of Jersey Eisteddfod

(Des Jennifer Toombs. Litho Austrian State Ptg Wks, Vienna)

2008 (3 Mar). Perf 14 (C).

1359	**1296**	35p. multicoloured	1·00	1·00
1360	**1297**	39p. multicoloured	1·20	1·20
1361	**1298**	43p. multicoloured	1·30	1·30
1362	**1299**	58p. multicoloured	1·70	1·70
1363	**1300**	76p. multicoloured	2·30	2·30
1359/63 *Set of 5*			7·50	7·50
First Day Cover				10·00
Presentation Pack			10·00	

Plate Nos.: All values 1A (each ×4).
Sheets: 10 (2×5) with enlarged illustrated margins.
Imprint: Lower left-hand margin.
Withdrawn: 31.3.2009.

1301 Grey Bus Services Daimler CB, *c.* 1920

1302 SCS Ex LGOC 'K' Single Decker, *c.* 1930

1303 JMT Town Bus Service, *c.* 1941

1304 JMT Leyland Lion Charcoal Burner, *c.* 1941

1305 JBS Bedford WLB, *c.* 1956

1306 JMT Commer Commando, *c.* 1963

1307 JMT Ford Willowbrook, c. 1977 (*Illustration reduced. Actual size* 110×75 mm)

Jersey Transport. Buses (2nd series)

(Des Alan Copp. Litho Enschedé)

2008 (8 Apr). Perf 14 (C).

1364	**1301**	35p. multicoloured	85	85
1365	**1302**	39p. multicoloured	95	95
1366	**1303**	43p. multicoloured	1·00	1·00
1367	**1304**	52p. multicoloured	1·30	1·30
1368	**1305**	58p. multicoloured	1·40	1·40
1369	**1306**	76p. multicoloured	1·80	1·80
1364/9 *Set of 6*			7·25	7·25
First Day Cover				11·50
Presentation Pack			11·50	
MS1370 110×75 mm. **1307** £2.50 multicoloured. Perf 13½×14 (C)			7·25	7·25
First Day Cover				10·00
Presentation Pack			10·00	

Plate Nos.: 35p., 39p., 43p. 1A, 1B, 1C; 52p., 58p., 76p. 1A (each ×5).
Sheets: 10 (2×5) with enlarged illustrated margins.
Imprint: Lower left-hand margin.
Withdrawn: 30.4.2009.

1308 Jersey Bull 'Mermaid's Warrior Count' (*Illustration reduced. Actual size* 110×75 mm)

18th World Jersey Cattle Bureau Conference, Jersey

(Des William Oliver. Litho Cartor)

2008 (18 May). Sheet 110×75 mm. Perf 13×13½ (C).

MS1371	**1308**	£2 multicoloured	5·75	5·75
First Day Cover				8·50
Presentation Pack			8·50	

Withdrawn: 31.5.2009.

1309 *Cymbidium* Averanches 'Victoria Village'

1310 *Miltonia* 'Tesson Mill'

1311 *Anguloa* Victoire 'Trinity'

1312 *Phragmipedium* La Hougette

1313 *Phragmipedium* Havre de Pas 'Jersey'

1314 *Paphiopedilum* Rolfei 'Trinity'

1315 *Paphiopedilum* Rocco Tower (*Illustration reduced. Actual size* 110×75 mm)

Jersey Orchids (6th series)

(Des Andrew Robinson. Litho Cartor)

2008 (20 May). Perf 13×13½ (C).

1372	**1309**	35p. multicoloured	1·00	1·00
1373	**1310**	39p. multicoloured	1·20	1·20
1374	**1311**	43p. multicoloured	1·30	1·30
1375	**1312**	52p. multicoloured	1·50	1·50
1376	**1313**	58p. multicoloured	1·70	1·70
1377	**1314**	76p. multicoloured	2·30	2·30
1372/7 *Set of 6*			9·00	9·00
First Day Cover				11·50
Presentation Pack			11·50	
MS1378 110×75 mm. **1315** £2.50 multicoloured			7·25	7·25
First Day Cover				10·00
Presentation Pack			10·00	

Plate Nos.: All values 1A (each ×5).
Sheets: 10 (2×5) with enlarged illustrated margins.
Imprint: Lower left-hand margin.
Withdrawn: 31.5.2009.

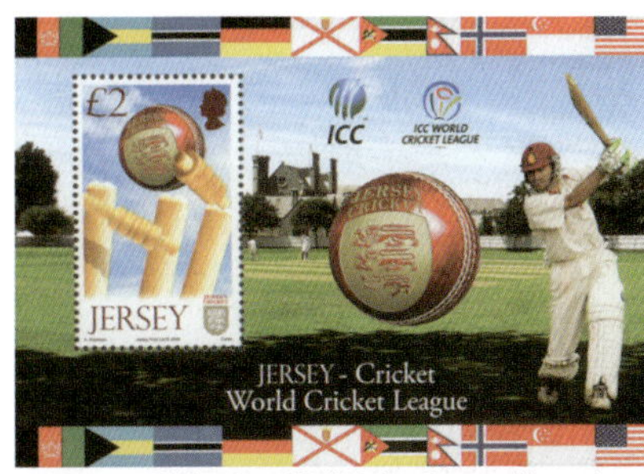

1316 Jersey Cricket Board Ball hitting Stumps (*Illustration reduced. Actual size* 110×75 mm)

World Cricket League Division 5 Tournament, Jersey

(Des Andrew Robinson. Litho Cartor)

2008 (23 May). Sheet 110×75 mm. Perf 13×13½ (C).

MS1379	**1316**	£2 multicoloured	5·75	5·75
First Day Cover				8·50
Presentation Pack			8·50	

Withdrawn: 31.5.2009.

1317 HMS *Roebuck*

1318 HMS *Monmouth*

1319 HMS *Edinburgh*

1320 HMS *Express*

1321 HMS *Severn*

1322 HMS *Cottesmore*

1323 HMY *Britannia* (*Illustration reduced. Actual size 110×75 mm*)

Jersey Naval Connections (2nd series). Visiting Naval Vessels

(Des Tony Theobald. Litho Cartor)

2008 (24 June). Perf 13×13½ (C).

1380	**1317**	35p. multicoloured	1·00	1·00
		a. Booklet pane. Nos. 1380/5 with margins all round	9·00	
1381	**1318**	39p. multicoloured	1·20	1·20
1382	**1319**	43p. multicoloured	1·30	1·30
1383	**1320**	52p. multicoloured	1·50	1·50
1384	**1321**	58p. multicoloured	1·70	1·70
1385	**1322**	76p. multicoloured	2·30	2·30
1380/5 *Set of 6*			9·00	9·00
First Day Cover				11·50
Presentation Pack			11·50	
MS1386 110×75 mm. **1323** £2.50 multicoloured. Perf 13½×13 (C)			7·25	7·25
		a. Booklet pane. No. **MS**1386, but 150×100 mm with line of roulettes at left	7·25	
First Day Cover				10·00
Presentation Pack			10·00	

Booklet pane No. 1380a exists in three versions which differ in the order of the stamps within the block of six.

Plate Nos.: All values 1A (each ×4).
Sheets: 10 (2×5) with enlarged illustrated margins.
Imprint: Lower left-hand margin.
Withdrawn: 30.6.2009.

1324 Daimler Dart (*Illustration reduced. Actual size 110×75 mm*)

Jersey Festival of Speed

(Des Alan R. Copp. Litho Cartor)

2008 (23 Aug). Sheet 110×75 mm. Perf 13×13½ (C).

MS1387	**1324**	£2.50 multicoloured	7·25	7·25
First Day Cover				10·00
Presentation Pack			10·00	

Withdrawn: 31.8.2009.

1325 Cockerel, Hen and Chicks

1326 Ewe and Lambs

1327 Sow and Piglets

1328 Geese and Goslings

1329 Jersey Cows and Calf

Farm Animals

(Des Colleen Corlett. Litho SEP Sprint, Australia)

2008 (26 Aug). Self-adhesive. Perf 11½ (die-cut).

1388	**1325**	(35p.) multicoloured	1·00	1·00
1389	**1326**	(35p.) multicoloured	1·00	1·00
1390	**1327**	(35p.) multicoloured	1·00	1·00
1391	**1328**	(35p.) multicoloured	1·00	1·00
1392	**1329**	(35p.) multicoloured	1·00	1·00
1388/92 *Set of 5*			5·00	5·00
First Day Cover				7·75
Presentation Pack			7·75	

Nos. 1388/92 are inscribed 'JERSEY MINIMUM POSTAGE PAID' and were sold for 35p. each. They were printed together, *se-tenant*, in strips of five from rolls of 100, from which the surplus self-adhesive backing paper around each stamp was removed.

Nos. 1388/92 commemorate the 175th anniversary of the Royal Jersey Agricultural and Horticultural Society.

1330 Carpenter Bee

1331 Buff-tailed Bumblebee

1332 Clown-faced Bug

1333 Large Migrant Hoverfly

1334 Ruby-tailed Wasp

1335 22-spot Ladybird

Insects (2nd series)

(Des William Oliver. Litho Cartor)

2008 (8 Sept). Perf 13×13½ (C).

1393	**1330**	35p. multicoloured	1·00	1·00
1394	**1331**	39p. multicoloured	1·20	1·20
1395	**1332**	43p. multicoloured	1·30	1·30
1396	**1333**	52p. multicoloured	1·50	1·50

1397	**1334**	58p. multicoloured	1·70	1·70
1398	**1335**	76p. multicoloured	2·30	2·30
1393/8 *Set of 6*			9·00	9·00
First Day Cover				11·50
Presentation Pack			11·50	

Plate Nos.: All values 1A (each ×4).
Sheets: 10 (2×5) with enlarged illustrated margins.
Imprint: Lower left-hand margin.
Withdrawn: 30.9.2009.

Wipa08 International Stamp Exhibition, Vienna

2008 (18 Sept). No. **MS**1370 optd 'Jersey at WIPA08' on bottom right sheet margin.

MS1399 110×75 mm. **1307** £2.50 multicoloured. Perf 13½×14 (C)	7·25	7·25

Withdrawn: 30.9.2009.

1336 Northern Wheatear

1337 Whinchat

1338 Pied Flycatcher

1339 Yellow Wagtail

1340 Ring Ouzel

1341 Common Redstart

Jersey Birdlife (2nd series). Migrating Birds

(Des Nick Parlett. Litho Cartor)

2008 (21 Oct). Perf 13×13½ (C).

1400	**1336**	35p. multicoloured	1·00	1·00
1401	**1337**	39p. multicoloured	1·20	1·20
1402	**1338**	43p. multicoloured	1·30	1·30
1403	**1339**	52p. multicoloured	1·50	1·50
1404	**1340**	58p. multicoloured	1·70	1·70
1405	**1341**	76p. multicoloured	2·30	2·30
1400/5 *Set of 6*			9·00	9·00
First Day Cover				11·50
Presentation Pack			11·50	
MS1406 150×100 mm. Nos. 1400/5			9·00	9·00
First Day Cover				11·50
Presentation Pack			11·50	
MS1407 150×100 mm. Nos. 1403/5			5·50	5·50
First Day Cover				8·00
Presentation Pack			8·00	

Stamps from **MS**1407 have no white borders.
Plate Nos.: All values 1A (each ×5).
Sheets: 10 (2×5) with enlarged illustrated margins.
Imprint: Lower left-hand margin.

1342 Prince Charles

60th Birthday of Prince Charles

(Des Andrew Robinson. Litho Cartor)

2008 (14 Nov). Perf 13½ (C).

1408 **1342** £4 multicoloured	12·00	12·00
First Day Cover		14·50
Presentation Pack	14·50	
MS1409 150×100 mm. No. 1408	12·00	12·00
First Day Cover		14·50
Presentation Pack	14·50	

After one year No. was retained as a definitive.
Plate Nos.: 1A (×5).
Sheets: 4 (2×2).
Imprint: Lower left-hand margin.

Yearbook

2008 (1 Dec).

Yearbook	95·00

1343 Douglas C-47 Dakota 3 'Pionair'

1344 Vickers Viscount 833

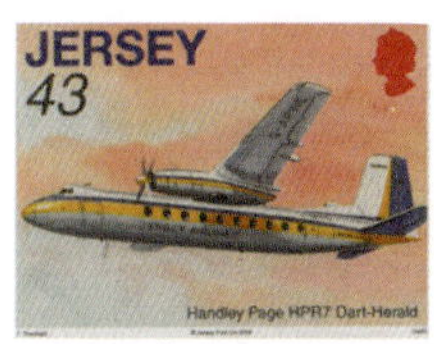

1345 Handley Page HPR7 Dart-Herald

1346 Bristol Superfreighter 32

1347 Fokker F-27 Friendship

1348 Bombardier Q400 Dash 8

1349 De Havilland D.H.84 Dragon 2 (*Illustration reduced. Actual size* 110×75 mm)

75th Anniversary of the First Flight from Jersey to Southampton

(Des Tony Theobald. Litho Austrian State Ptg Wks, Vienna)

2009 (13 Jan). Perf 14 (C).

1410	**1343**	35p. multicoloured	1·00	1·00
1411	**1344**	39p. multicoloured	1·25	1·25
1412	**1345**	43p. multicoloured	1·25	1·25
1413	**1346**	52p. multicoloured	1·50	1·50
1414	**1347**	58p. multicoloured	1·75	1·75
1415	**1348**	76p. multicoloured	2·25	2·25
1410/15 *Set of 6*			9·00	9·00
First Day Cover				10·00
Presentation Pack			10·00	
MS1416 110×75 mm. **1349** £3 multicoloured			9·00	9·00
First Day Cover				10·00
Presentation Pack			10·00	

Plate Nos.: All values 1A (each ×4).

Sheets: 10 (2×5) with enlarged illustrated margins.
Imprint: Lower left-hand margin.

1350 Io, Ursa Major and Cassiopeia

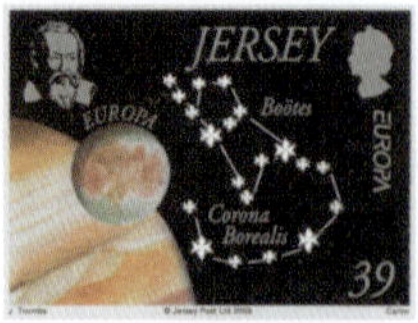

1351 Europa, Boötes and Corona Borealis

1352 Ganymede, Cygnus and Pegasus

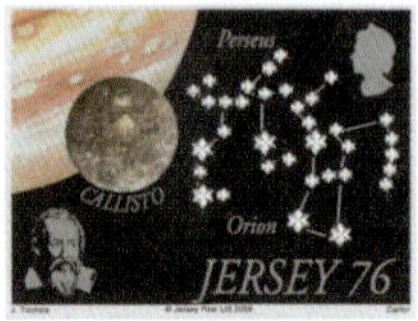

1353 Callisto, Perseus and Orion

Europa. Astronomy. Satellites of Jupiter and Constellations

(Des Jennifer Toombs. Litho and embossed in silver (stars) Cartor)

2009 (10 Feb). Perf 13 (C).

1417	**1350**	35p. multicoloured	1·00	1·00
1418	**1351**	39p. multicoloured	1·25	1·25
1419	**1352**	43p. multicoloured	1·25	1·25
1420	**1353**	76p. multicoloured	2·25	2·25
1417/20 *Set of 4*			5·75	5·75
First Day Cover				6·75
Presentation Pack			6·75	

The 39p. and 43p. values include the 'EUROPA' emblem.
Plate Nos.: All values 1A (each ×6).
Sheets: 10 (2×5) with enlarged illustrated margins.
Imprint: Lower left-hand margin.

1354 Blue Iguana (*Cyclura lewisi*)

1355 Madagascan Giant Jumping Rat (*Hypogeomys antimena*)

1356 Mountain Chicken Frog (*Leptodactylus fallax*)

1357 Livingstone's Fruit Bat (*Pteropus livingstonii*)

1358 Andean Bear (*Tremarctos ornatus*)

1359 Western Lowland Gorilla (*Gorilla g. gorilla*)

Endangered Species (1st series). 50th Anniversary of the Durrell Wildlife Conservation Trust

(Des William Oliver. Litho BDT)

2009 (10 Mar). Perf 14½×14 (C).

1421	**1354**	35p. multicoloured	1·00	1·00
1422	**1355**	39p. multicoloured	1·25	1·25
1423	**1356**	43p. multicoloured	1·25	1·25
1424	**1357**	52p. multicoloured	1·50	1·50
1425	**1358**	58p. multicoloured	1·75	1·75
1426	**1359**	76p. multicoloured	2·25	2·25
1421/6 *Set of 6*			9·00	9·00
First Day Cover				10·00
Presentation Pack			10·00	

Plate Nos.: All values 1A (each ×4).
Sheets: 10 (2×5) with enlarged illustrated margins.
Imprint: Lower left-hand margin.

1360 Crocus and Grape Hyacinths

1361 Daffodils

1362 Anemones de Caen

1363 Tulips

1364 Hyacinths

1365 Polyanthus and Primulas

Spring Flowers

(Des Wendy Tait. Litho Enschedé)

2009 (1 Apr). Perf 13 (C).

1427	**1360**	35p. multicoloured	1·00	1·00
1428	**1361**	39p. multicoloured	1·25	1·25
1429	**1362**	43p. multicoloured	1·25	1·25
1430	**1363**	52p. multicoloured	1·50	1·50
1431	**1364**	58p. multicoloured	1·75	1·75
1432	**1365**	76p. multicoloured	2·25	2·25
1427/32 Set of 6			9·00	9·00
First Day Cover				10·00
Presentation Pack			10·00	

Plate Nos.: 35p., 39p. 1A, 1B; others 1A (each ×5).
Sheets: 10 (5×2).
Imprint: Bottom margin.

1366 *Mont Orgueil*

1367 *Corbière*

1368 *Carteret*

1369 Railcar *Pioneer*

1370 *La Moye*

1371 *St. Brelades*

1372 Locomotive No. 5 *La Moye* awaits Departure from St. Aubin (*Illustration reduced. Actual size* 110×75 mm)

Jersey Railways (3rd series)

(Des Tony Theobald. Litho Cartor)

2009 (6 May). Perf 13 (C).

1433	**1366**	37p. multicoloured	1·10	1·10
		a. Booklet pane. Nos. 1433/8 with margins all round	9·25	
1434	**1367**	42p. multicoloured	1·25	1·25
1435	**1368**	45p. multicoloured	1·40	1·40
1436	**1369**	55p. multicoloured	1·60	1·60
1437	**1370**	61p. multicoloured	1·75	1·75
1438	**1371**	80p. multicoloured	2·40	2·40
1433/8 *Set of 6*			9·25	9·25
First Day Cover				10·00
Presentation Pack			10·00	
MS1439 110×75 mm. **1372** £3 multicoloured			9·00	9·00
		a. Booklet pane. No. **MS**1439, but 150×100 mm, with line of roulettes at left	9·00	
First Day Cover				10·00
Presentation Pack			10·00	

Booklet pane No. 1433a exists in three versions which differ in the order of the stamps within the block of six.

Plate Nos.: All values 1A (each ×4).

Sheets: 10 (2×5) with enlarged illustrated margins.

Imprint: Lower left-hand margin.

IBRA International Stamp Exhibition, Essen, Germany

2009 (6 May). No. **MS**1439 optd 'JERSEY AT iBRA' on upper left sheet margin.

MS1440 110×75 mm. **1372** £3 multicoloured	9·00	9·00
First Day Cover		10·00
Presentation Pack	10·00	

1373 Surfboards (*Illustration reduced. Actual size* 110×75 mm)

50th Anniversary of Jersey Surfboard Club

(Des Andrew Robinson. Litho BDT)

2009 (2 June). Sheet 110×75 mm. Perf 13 (C).

MS1441 **1373** £3 multicoloured	9·00	9·00
First Day Cover		10·00
Presentation Pack	10·00	

1374 Post Office, Broad Street, St. Helier, 1909 (*Illustration reduced. Actual size* 110×75 mm)

Jersey Postal History (3rd series). Post Office Buildings

(Des Colleen Corlett. Litho Austrian State Ptg Wks, Vienna)

2009 (21 June). Sheet 110×75 mm. Perf 14 (C).

MS1442 **1374** £3 multicoloured	9·00	9·00
First Day Cover		10·00
Presentation Pack	10·00	

No. **MS**1442 commemorates the centenary of Jersey's Head Post Office at Broad Street, St. Helier.

1375 Investiture of the Prince of Wales at Caernarfon Castle, 1969 (*Illustration reduced. Actual size* 110×75 mm)

40th Anniversary of the Investiture of Prince Charles as the Prince of Wales

(Des Andrew Robinson. Litho Cartor)

2009 (1 July). Sheet 110×75 mm. Perf 13 (C).

MS1443 **1375** £3 multicoloured	8·75	8·75
First Day Cover		9·75
Presentation Pack	9·75	

1376 *Ascophyllum nodosum* (egg wrack)

1377 *Enteromorpha* sp. (gutweed)

1378 *Dilsea carnosa* (red rags)

1379 *Ulva lactuca* (sea lettuce)

1380 *Laminaria hyperborea*

1381 *Codium tomentosum* (velvet horn)

Seaweed

(Des Nick Parlett. Litho Cartor)

2009 (7 July). Perf 13 (C).

1444	**1376**	37p. multicoloured	1·00	1·00
1445	**1377**	42p. multicoloured	1·25	1·25
1446	**1378**	45p. multicoloured	1·40	1·40
1447	**1379**	55p. multicoloured	1·50	1·50
1448	**1380**	64p. multicoloured	2·00	2·00
1449	**1381**	80p. multicoloured	2·40	2·40
1444/9 Set of 6			9·50	9·50
First Day Cover				10·50
Presentation Pack			10·50	

Plate Nos.: All values 1A (each ×5).
Sheets: 10 (2×5).
Lower left-hand margin.

1382 Dunnock

1383 Song Thrush

1384 Wren

1385 Blackcap

1386 Mistle Thrush

1387 Robin

Jersey Birdlife (3rd series). Songbirds

(Des Nick Parlett. Litho Cartor)

2009 (4 Aug). Perf 13 (C).

1450	**1382**	37p. multicoloured	1·00	1·00
1451	**1383**	42p. multicoloured	1·25	1·25
1452	**1384**	45p. multicoloured	1·40	1·40
1453	**1385**	55p. multicoloured	1·50	1·50
1454	**1386**	61p. multicoloured	2·00	2·00
1455	**1387**	80p. multicoloured	2·40	2·40
1450/5 Set of 6			9·50	9·50
First Day Cover				10·50
Presentation Pack			10·50	
MS1456 150×100 mm. Nos. 1450/5			9·50	9·50
First Day Cover				10·50
Presentation Pack			10·50	

Stamps from **MS**1457 have no white borders.
Plate Nos.: All values 1A (each ×5).
Sheets: 10 (2×5) with enlarged illustrated margins.
Imprint: Lower left-hand margin.

MS1457 150×100 mm. Nos. 1453/5	5·75	5·75
First Day Cover		6·50
Presentation Pack	6·50	

1388 Green Island

1389 Gorey Castle at Night

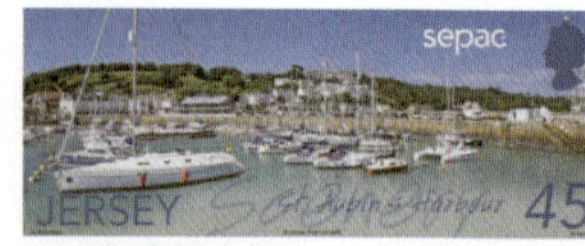

1390 St. Aubin's Harbour

1391 St. Peter's Valley

1392 La Rocque Harbour

1393 Grève de Lecq

Jersey Scenery (2nd series)

(Des Andrew Robinson. Litho Enschedé)

2009 (16 Sept). Perf 14×13 (C).

1458	**1388**	37p. multicoloured	1·00	1·00
1459	**1389**	42p. multicoloured	1·25	1·25
1460	**1390**	45p. multicoloured	1·40	1·40
1461	**1391**	55p. multicoloured	1·50	1·50
1462	**1392**	61p. multicoloured	2·00	2·00
1463	**1393**	80p. multicoloured	2·40	2·40
1458/63 *Set of 6*			9·50	9·50
First Day Cover				10·50
Presentation Pack			10·50	

The 45p. value is inscr 'sepac' and was also available in a souvenir folder with ten other sepac logo stamps issued by other postal administrations.

Plate Nos.: All values 1A (each ×4).
Sheets: 10 (2×5) with enlarged illustrated margins.
Imprint: Lower left-hand margin.

1394 Parrot Wax-cap (*Hygrocybe psittacina*)

1395 *Russula sardonia*

1396 Velvet Foot (*Flammulina velutipes*)

1397 Honey Fungus (*Armillaria mellea*)

1398 Orange Peel Fungus (*Aleuria aurantia*)

1399 Jewelled Deathcap (*Amanita gemmata*)

Fungi (3rd series)

(Des William Oliver. Litho Cartor)

2009 (15 Oct). Perf 13½×13 (C).

1464	**1394**	37p. multicoloured	1·10	1·10
1465	**1395**	42p. multicoloured	1·25	1·25
1466	**1396**	45p. multicoloured	1·25	1·25
1467	**1397**	55p. multicoloured	1·60	1·60
1468	**1398**	61p. multicoloured	1·75	1·75
1469	**1399**	80p. multicoloured	2·25	2·25
1464/9 *Set of 6*			9·00	9·00
First Day Cover				10·00
Presentation Pack			10·00	

Plate Nos.: All values 1A (each ×4).
Sheets: 10 (5×2) with enlarged illustrated margins.
Imprint: Lower left-hand margins.

1400 HMS *Garland*

1401 HMS *Eighth Lion's Whelp*

1402 HMS *Unicorn*

1403 HMS *Mary Rose*

1404 HMS *Antelope*

1405 HMS *Rainbow*

Jersey Naval Connections (3rd series). 400th Birth Anniversary of Sir George Carteret

(Des A. Theobald. Litho Cartor)

2009 (10 Nov). Perf 13 (C).

1470	**1400**	37p. multicoloured	1·10	1·10
1471	**1401**	42p. multicoloured	1·25	1·25
1472	**1402**	45p. multicoloured	1·25	1·25
1473	**1403**	55p. multicoloured	1·60	1·60
1474	**1404**	61p. multicoloured	1·75	1·75
1475	**1405**	80p. multicoloured	2·25	2·25
1470/5 Set of 6			9·00	9·00
First Day Cover				10·00
Presentation Pack			10·00	

Plate Nos.: All values 1A (each ×4).
Sheets: 10 (2×5) with enlarged illustrated margins.
Imprint: Lower left-hand margin.

1406 Gymnast and Cyclist ('Healthy Lifestyles')

1407 Broken Globe, Tap and Young Child Drinking ('global awareness')

1408 Guide Salute and Handshake ('Skills & Relationships')

1409 Guides holding Hands around Globe ('Celebrating Diversity')

1410 Guides doing Handicrafts and on Climbing Wall ('Discovery')

Centenary of the Girl Guide Association

(Des Colleen Corlett. Litho Austrian State Ptg Wks, Vienna)

2010 (12 Jan).

1476	**1406**	37p. multicoloured	1·00	1·00
1477	**1407**	42p. multicoloured	1·25	1·25
1478	**1408**	45p. multicoloured	1·25	1·25
1479	**1409**	61p. multicoloured	1·75	1·75
1480	**1410**	80p. multicoloured	2·25	2·25
1476/80 Set of 5			7·50	7·50
First Day Cover				8·50
Presentation Pack			8·50	

Plate Nos.: All values 1A (each ×4).
Sheets: 10 (2×5).
Imprint: Lower left-hand margin.

1411 A Pushmi-Pullyu (*The Story of Doctor Dolittle* by Hugh Lofting)

1412 *How the Elephant got his Trunk* (Rudyard Kipling)

1413 The Mad Hatter's Tea Party (*Alice's Adventures in Wonderland* by Lewis Carroll)

1414 *The Dong with a Luminous Nose* (Edward Lear)

Europa. Children's Books

(Des Michael Pollard. Litho Cartor)

2010 (9 Feb). Perf 13 (C).

1481	**1411**	37p. multicoloured	1·50	1·50
1482	**1412**	42p. multicoloured	1·60	1·60
1483	**1413**	45p. multicoloured	1·75	1·75
1484	**1414**	80p. multicoloured	3·25	3·25
1481/4 Set of 4			8·00	8·00

First Day Cover			9·00
Presentation Pack		9·00	

The 42p. and 45p. values are inscr 'EUROPA'.

Luminous ink has been applied to the end of the dong's long nose on No. 1484.

Plate Nos.: All values 1A (each ×4).

Sheets: 10 (2×5) with enlarged illustrated margins.

Imprint: Lower left-hand margin.

1415 Map, *c*. 1685

1416 Map, *c*. 1844

1417 Map, *c*. 1980s

1418 Map, *c*. 2000

1419 Satellite View

Maps

(Des Andrew Robinson. Litho Australia Post Sprintpak)

2010 (9 FEB). Self-adhesive. Perf 11 (die-cut).

1485	**1415**	(42p.) multicoloured	1·25	1·25
1486	**1416**	(42p.) multicoloured	1·25	1·25
1487	**1417**	(42p.) multicoloured	1·25	1·25
1488	**1418**	(42p.) multicoloured	1·25	1·25
1489	**1419**	(42p.) multicoloured	1·25	1·25
1485/9 Set of 5			6·25	6·25
First Day Cover				7·00
Presentation Pack			7·00	

Nos. 1485/9 were inscribed 'UK LETTER' and originally sold for 42p. each. They were printed together, *se-tenant*, in strips of five from rolls of 100, from which the surplus self-adhesive backing paper around each stamp was removed.

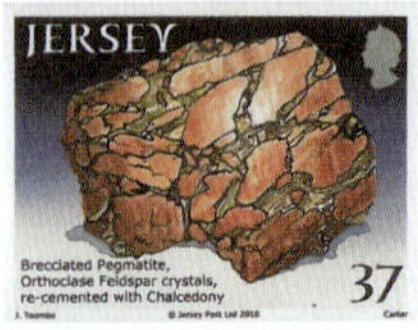

1420 Brecciated Pegmatite, Orthoclase Feldspar Crystals, re-cemented with Chalcedony

1421 Diorite with Incipient Orbicular Structure

1422 Granite

1423 Jasper in Andesite

1424 Pebbles of Granite, Andesite and Shale in Rozel Conglomerate

Petrology

(Des Jennifer Toombs. Litho Cartor)

2010 (9 Mar). Perf 13×13½ (C).

1490	**1420**	37p. multicoloured	1·10	1·10
1491	**1421**	42p. multicoloured	1·25	1·25
1492	**1422**	45p. multicoloured	1·25	1·25
1493	**1423**	61p. multicoloured	1·75	1·75
1494	**1424**	80p. multicoloured	2·40	2·40
1490/4 Set of 5			7·75	7·75
First Day Cover				8·50
Presentation Pack			8·50	

Plate Nos.: All values 1A (each ×4).

Sheets: 10 (2×5) with enlarged illustrated margins.

Imprint: Lower left-hand margin.

1425 Jay

1426 Great Spotted Woodpecker

1427 Short-toed Treecreeper

1428 Chiffchaff

1429 Long-tailed Tit

1430 Turtle Dove

Jersey Birdlife (4th series). Woodland Birds

(Des Nick Parlett. Litho Cartor)

2010 (1 Apr). P 13×13½ (C).

1495	**1425**	37p. multicoloured	1·10	1·10
1496	**1426**	42p. multicoloured	1·25	1·25
1497	**1427**	45p. multicoloured	1·40	1·40
1498	**1428**	55p. multicoloured	1·60	1·60
1499	**1429**	61p. multicoloured	1·75	1·75
1500	**1430**	80p. multicoloured	2·40	2·40
1495/500 *Set of 6*			9·50	9·50
First Day Cover				10·00
Presentation Pack			10·00	
MS1501 150×100 mm. Nos. 1495/500			9·50	9·50
First Day Cover				10·00
Presentation Pack			10·00	
MS1502 150×100 mm. As Nos. 1498/500			5·75	5·75
First Day Cover				7·00
Presentation Pack				

Stamps from **MS**1502 have no white borders.

Plate Nos.: All values 1A (each ×5).

Sheets: 10 (2×5) with enlarged illustrated margins.

Imprint: Lower left-hand margin.

1431 *Royal Charlotte*

1432 *Dispatch*

B **15** Elizabeth Castle (*Illustration reduced. Actual size* 108×63 mm)

1991 (12 Feb). Jersey Scenes. Multicoloured cover as Type B **15**.
SB43 £4.80 booklet containing Nos. 471a, 475a and 480a, each ×2 .... 11·50
Withdrawn: 30.6.96.

1992 (25 Feb). £1 Stamp Sachet. Multicoloured cover as Type B **14** showing design of 22p. stamp (No. 480). Containing 1×2p., 2×16p., 3×22p. (Nos. 467, 474 and 480).

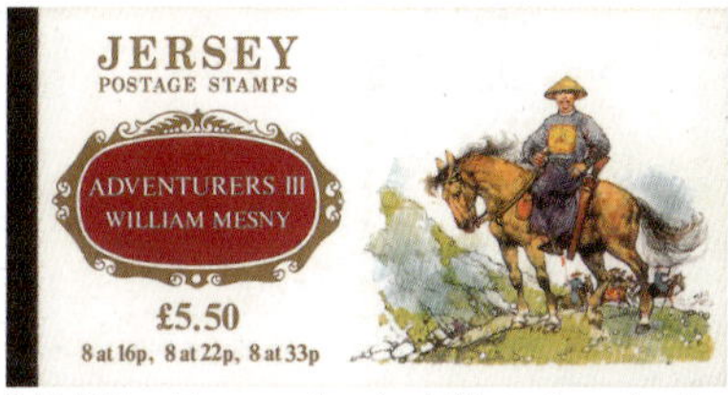

B **16** William Mesny on Horseback (*Illustration reduced. Actual size* 155×80 mm)

Jersey Adventures (3rd series). 150th Birth Anniversary of William Mesny

1992 (25 Feb). Multicoloured cover as Type B **16**. Booklet contains text on labels attached to panes and on interleaving pages.
SB44 £5.50 booklet containing Nos. 573b/8a .... 12·00
Withdrawn: 30.6.96.

B **17** Jersey Post Logo

1992 (25 May). Covers as Type B **17**. Panes attached by selvedge.
SB45 £1.12 booklet (scarlet on white cover) containing No. 474b .... 2·75
SB46 £1.28 booklet (bright yellow on scarlet cover) containing No. 476a .... 3·50
SB47 £1.76 booklet (scarlet on bright yellow cover) containing No. 482a .... 4·50
Withdrawn: 30.6.96.

1993 (26 Jan). Covers as Type B **17**. Panes attached by selvedge.
SB48 (£1.36) booklet (bright yellow on green cover) containing pane No. 601a .... 5·00
SB49 (£1.84) booklet (scarlet on flesh cover) containing pane No. 605a .... 5·50
SB50 (£2.24) booklet (white on bright new blue cover) containing pane No. 609a .... 7·00

Face values quoted for each booklet are those at which they were initially sold. The price of No. SB48 was increased to £1.44 and that of No. SB50 to £2.40 on 10 January 1994. No. SB48 was sold at £1.52 from 4 July 1995. On 10 March 1997, No. SB48 was increased to £1.60, No. SB49 to £1.92 and No. SB50 to £2.48.
Withdrawn: 30.9.99.

B **18** Invasion Map (*Illustration reduced. Actual size* 162×98 mm)

50th Anniversary of D-Day

1994 (6 June). Multicoloured cover as Type B **18**. Booklet contains text and Illustrations on panes and interleaving pages.
SB51 £5.68 booklet containing Nos. 659a/b, 661a and 663a .... 17·00
Sold out: 12.94.

B **19** 'Greetings from JERSEY' (*Illustration reduced. Actual size* 152×75 mm)

Greetings Stamps

1995 (24 Jan). Multicoloured cover as Type B **19**. Pane attached by selvedge.
SB52 £2.24 booklet containing pane No. 684b .... 6·50
Quantity sold: 65,810.
Withdrawn: 30.9.99.

B **20** Crowd Celebrating (*Illustration reduced. Actual size* 162×97 mm)

50th Anniversary of Liberation

1995 (9 May). Multicoloured cover as Type B **20**. Booklet contains text and Illustrations on panes and interleaving pages.
SB53 £7.06 booklet containing Nos. 700a, 702a, 704a and **MS**706a .... 14·00

B **21** Mont Orgueil Castle, Gorey (*Illustration reduced. Actual size* 164×97 mm)

Tourism

1996 (8 June). Multicoloured cover as Type B **21**. Booklet contains text and Illustrations on panes and interleaving pages.
SB54 £8.32 booklet containing Nos. 752a/b, 754a and 756a .... 16·00

B **22** Island Sports (*Illustration reduced. Actual size* 163×98 mm)

7th Island Games, Jersey

1997 (28 June). Multicoloured cover as Type B **22**. Booklet contains text and Illustrations on panes and interleaving pages.
SB55 £8.72 booklet containing Nos. 818a/b, 820a and 822a .... 17·00

B **23** Buses in Royal Square, St. Helier (*Illustration reduced. Actual size* 164×98 mm)

75th Anniversary of Jersey Motor Transport Company. Buses

1998 (2 Apr). Multicoloured cover as Type B **23**. Booklet contains text and Illustrations on panes and interleaving pages.
SB56 £8.72 booklet containing Nos. 844a/b, 846a and 848a .... 17·00

B **24** Four Vintage Humbers at the Weighbridge, 1905 (*Illustration reduced. Actual size* 164×98 mm)

Centenary of Motoring in Jersey

1999 (2 July). Multicoloured cover as Type B **24**. Booklet contains text and Illustrations on panes and interleaving pages.
SB57 £8.80 booklet containing Nos. 905a/b, 907a and 909a .... 19·00

B **25** Full-rigged Sailing Ship (*Illustration reduced. Actual size* 164×100 mm)

'The Stamp Show 2000' International Stamp Exhibition, London. Maritime Heritage

2000 (22 May). Multicoloured cover as Type B **25**. Booklet contains text and Illustrations on interleaving pages. Stitched.
SB58 £9.60 booklet containing Nos. 936b/e and 937a .... 19·00

B **26** Two Tawny Owls on Gate (*Illustration reduced. Actual size* 164×101 mm)

Birds of Prey

2001 (3 July). Multicoloured cover as Type B **26**. Booklet contains text and Illustrations on panes and interleaving pages. Stitched.
SB59 £10.76 booklet containing Nos. 999a/d and **MS**1005a 21·00
Sold out: By 7.2007.

B **27** Bells

Christmas

2001 (6 Nov). Multicoloured cover as Type B **27**. Self-adhesive.
SB60 £3.92 booklet containing No. 1014a .... 10·00
Sold out: By 6.2003.

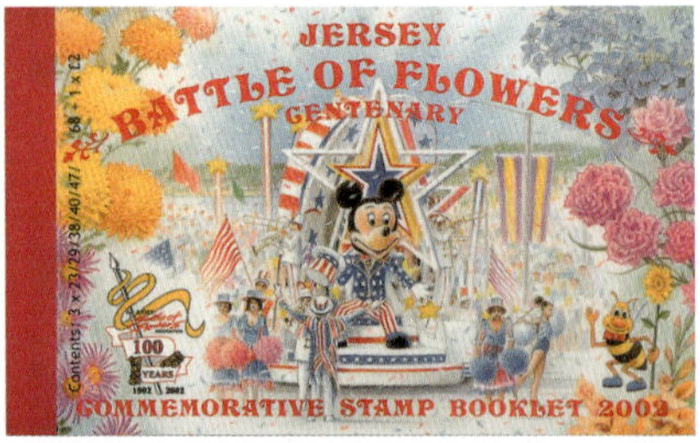

B **28** Mickey Mouse Float (*Illustration reduced. Actual size* 165×100 mm)

Centenary of 'Battle of Flowers' Parade

2002 (8 Aug). Multicoloured cover as Type B **28**. Booklet contains text and Illustrations on panes and interleaving pages. Stitched.

SB61 £9.35 booklet containing Nos. 1053ax3 and **MS**1059a .... 19·00

B **29** Ellehammer's Biplane and Space Shuttle (*Illustration reduced. Actual size* 164×100 mm)

Centenary of Powered Flight

2003 (21 Jan). Multicoloured cover as Type B **29**. Booklet contains text and Illustrations on panes and interleaving pages. Stitched.

SB62 £9.35 booklet containing No. 1074ax3, with different marginal Illustrations, and **MS**1080a .... 18·00

B **30** *Paphiopedilum chamberlainianum* (*Illustration reduced. Actual size* 165×100 mm)

Jersey Orchids (5th series)

2004 (25 May). Multicoloured cover as Type B **30**. Booklet contains text and Illustrations on panes and interleaving pages. Stitched.

SB63 £10.73 booklet containing No. 1143ax3 and **MS**1149a .... 20·00

B **31** MG (*Illustration reduced. Actual size* 165×100 mm)

Jersey Festivals (2nd issue). Motor Festival. Classic Cars

2005 (6 June). Multicoloured cover as Type B **31**. Booklet contains text and Illustrations on panes and interleaving pages. Stitched.

SB64 £8.61 booklet containing No. 1204ax3 .... 17·00

B **32** Jersey Post Vehicles (*Illustration reduced. Actual size* 164×100 mm)

Jersey Postal History (2nd series). Postal Vehicles

2006 (31 Oct). Multicoloured cover as Type B **32**. Booklet contains text and Illustrations on panes and interleaving pages. Stitched.

SB65 £10.67 booklet containing No. 1286ax3 and **MS**1292a .... 20·00

B **33** Concorde (*Illustration reduced. Actual size* 164×100 mm)

60th Anniversary of Jersey International Air Display

2007 (13 Sept). Multicoloured cover as Type B **33**. Booklet contains text and Illustrations on panes and interleaving pages. Stitched.

SB66 £11.35 booklet containing Nos. 1326ax3 and **MS**1332a .... 21·00

B **34** HMS Richmond (*Illustration reduced. Actual size* 165×100 mm)

Jersey Naval Connections (2nd series). Visiting Naval Vessels

2008 (24 June). Multicoloured cover as Type B **34**. Booklet contains text and Illustrations on panes and interleaving pages. Stitched.

SB67 £11.59 booklet containing panes Nos. 1380×3 and **MS**1386a .... 25·00

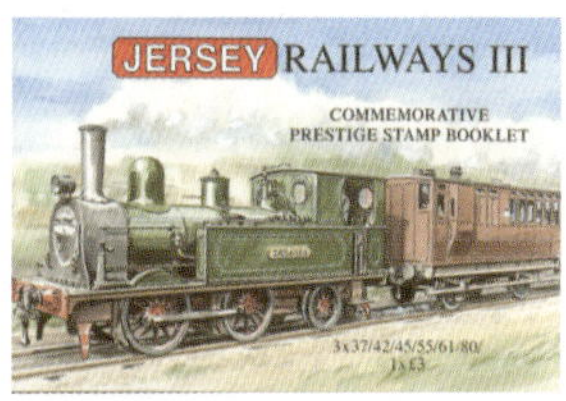

B **35** Locomotive *Caesarea* (*Illustration reduced. Actual size* 165×100 mm)

Jersey Railways (3rd issue)

2009 (6 May). Multicoloured cover as Type B **35**. Booklets contain text and Illustrations on panes and interleaving pages. Stitched.

SB68 £12.60 booklet containing panes Nos. 1433ax3 and **MS**1439*a* .... 29·00

B **36** *Royal Charlotte*

Postal History (4th series). Mail Ships

2010 (8 May). Multicoloured cover as Type B **36**. Booklet contains text and Illustrations on panes and interleaving pages. Stitched.

SB69 £13.53 booklet containing panes Nos. 1503*a*×3 and **MS**1510*a* .... 25·00

Questionnaire

Dear Catalogue User,

As a collector and Stanley Gibbons catalogue user for many years myself, I am only too aware of the need to provide you with the information you seek in an accurate, timely and easily accessible manner. Naturally, I have my own views on where changes could be made, but one thing I learned long ago is that we all have different opinions and requirements.

I would therefore be most grateful if you would complete the form below and return it to me (or send your answers on a separate sheet if you prefer not to cut the page out of your catalogue).

Very many thanks for your help.

Yours sincerely,

Hugh Jefferies,
Editor.

2010 Collect Channel Islands and Isle of Man Stamps

1. Level of detail

   Do you feel that the level of detail in this catalogue is:

   a. too specialised ○
   b. about right ○
   c. inadequate ○

2. Frequency of issue

   How often would you purchase a new edition of this catalogue?

   a. Annually ○
   b. Every two years ○
   c. Every three to five years ○
   d. Less frequently ○

3. Design and Quality

   Did you like the new layout of this catalogue?

   a. Yes ○
   b. No ○

4. How would you describe the layout and appearance of this catalogue?

   a. Excellent ○
   b. Good ○
   c. Adequate ○
   d. Poor ○

5. How important to you are the prices given in the catalogue:

   a. Important ○
   b. Quite important ○
   c. Of little interest ○
   d. Of no interest ○

6. Would you be interested in an online version of this catalogue?

   a. Yes ○
   b. No ○

7. What changes would you suggest to improve the catalogue? E.g. Which other indices would you like to see included?

   ....
   ....
   ....
   ....
   ....

8 Which other areas do you collect?

   ....
   ....
   ....
   ....

9. Would you like us to let you know when the next edition of this catalogue is due to be published?

   a. Yes ○
   b. No ○

   If so please give your contact details below.

   Name:..
   Address:...
   ....
   ....
   ....
   Email: ....
   Telephone:..

10. Which other Stanley Gibbons Catalogues are you interested in?

   a. ....
   b. ....
   c. ....

Many thanks for your comments.

Please complete and return it to: Hugh Jefferies (Catalogue Editor)
Stanley Gibbons Limited, 7 Parkside, Ringwood, Hampshire BH24 3SH, United Kingdom
or email: hjefferies@stanleygibbons.co.uk to request a soft copy

Collect Channel Islands and Isle of Man Stamps

From Stanley Gibbons, THE WORLD'S LARGEST STAMP STOCK

Priority order form – Four easy ways to order

Phone: 020 7836 8444 Overseas: +44 (0)20 7836 8444

Fax: 020 7557 4499 Overseas: +44 (0)20 7557 4499

Email: lmourne@stanleygibbons.co.uk

Post: Lesley Mourne, Stamp Mail Order Department, Stanley Gibbons Ltd, 399 Strand, London, WC2R 0LX, England

Customer Details

Account Number ....

Name ....

Address ....

....

Postcode .... Country ....

Email ....

Tel No. .... Fax No. ....

Payment details

Registered Postage & Packing £3.60

○ Please find my cheque/postal order enclosed for £..

Please make cheques payable to Stanley Gibbons Ltd.

Cheques must be in £ sterling and drawn on a UK bank

○ Please debit my credit card for £...in full payment.

○ Mastercard ○ VISA ○ Diners ○ AMEX ○ Switch

Card Number

CVC Number Issue No (Switch)

Start Date (Switch & Amex) / Expiry Date /

Signature .... Date ....

Collect Channel Islands and Isle of Man Stamps

From Stanley Gibbons, THE WORLD'S LARGEST STAMP STOCK

Condition (mint/UM/used)	Country	SG No.	Description	Price	Office use only
			POSTAGE & PACKING	£3.60	
			GRAND TOTAL		

Minimum price. The minimum catalogue price quoted in 10p. For individual stamps, prices between 10p and 95p are provided as a guide for catalogue users. The lowest price charged for individual stamps or sets purchased from Stanley Gibbons Ltd is £1.

Please complete payment, name and address details overleaf